KEYBOARD SCAN CODES

The following keyboard scan codes may be retrieved either by calling INT 16h or by calling INT 21h for keyboard input a second time (the first keyboard read returns 0). All codes are in hexadecimal:

FUNCTION KEYS

Key	Normal	With Shift	With Ctrl	With Alt
F1	3B	54	5E	68
F2	3C	55	5F	69
F3	3D	56	60	6A
F4	3E	57	61	6B
F5	3F	58	62	6C
F6	40	59	63	6D
F7	41	5A	64	6E
F8	42	5B	65	6F
F9	43	5C	66	70
F10	44	5D	67	71
F11	85			
F12	86			

Key	Alone	With Ctrl Key
Home	47	77
End	4F	75
PgUp	49	84
PgDn	51	76
PrtSc	37	72
Left arrow	4B	73
Rt arrow	4D	74
Up arrow	48	
Dn arrow	50	
Ins	52	
Del	53	
Back tab	0F	
Gray +	4E	
Gray −	4A	

Assembly Language for Intel-Based Computers

Third Edition

KIP R. IRVINE

Florida International University

Prentice-Hall, Upper Saddle River, New Jersey 07458

To Jack and Candy Irvine

Library of Congress Cataloging-in-Publication Data

CIP data available upon request

Publisher: AlanApt
Acquisition Editor: Laura Steele
Editor in Chief: Marcia Horton
Assistant Vice President of Production and Manufacturing: David W. Riccardi
Managing Editor: Eileen Clark
Editorial/Production: Ray Robinson, D&G Limited, LLC
Full Service/Manufacturing Coordinator: Donna Sullivan
Manufacturing Manager: Trudy Pisciotti
Creative Director: Jeyne Conte
Cover Designer: Bruce Kenselaar
Editorial Assistant: Kate Kaibni
Compositor: D&G Limited, LLC

Printed in the United States of America

15 14 13 12 11 10 9 8

ISBN   0-13-660390-4

Prentice-Hall International (UK) Limited, *London*
Prentice-Hall of Australia Pty. Limited, *Sydney*
Prentice-Hall Canada Inc., *Toronto*
Prentice-Hall Hispanoamericana, S.A., *Mexico*
Prentice-Hall of India Private Limited, *New Delhi*
Prentice-Hall of Japan, Inc., *Tokyo*
Simon & Schuster Asia Pte. Ltd., *Singapore*
Editora Prentice-Hall do Brasil, Ltda., *Rio de Janeiro*

Preface

Assembly language for Intel-Based Computers, Third Edition, was called *Assembly Language for the IBM-PC* in previous editions. The current edition directly addresses the needs of a college course in assembly language programming. It is completely based on the Intel 80x86 processor family, and all programs have been tested with the Microsoft Macro Assembler Version 6.13 and Borland TASM 4.0 assemblers. Prentice Hall has generously provided a full copy of the latest version of MASM for inclusion on the CD-ROM in the back of this book.

Web Site Information. Updates and corrections to this book may be found at the book's Web site, including additional programming projects for professors to assign at the ends of chapters. One or both of the following URLs should be valid:

```
www.pobox.com/~irvinek/books/asm
www.nuvisionmiami.com/books/asm
```

If for some reason you cannot access these sites, information about the book and a link to its current Web site can be found at **www.prenhall.com** by searching for the book title or for the full author name "Kip Irvine." The author's email address is **kip.irvine@pobox.com.**

The CD-ROM included with this book contains the complete professional version of Microsoft Macro Assembler 6.13, along with all the source code listings from the chapters.

Overall Goals

Each of the following goals of this book is designed to broaden the student's interest and knowledge in topics related to assembly language:

*   The Intel 80x86 Processor Family Instruction set and its basic architecture.
*   Assembly language directives, macros, operators, and program structure.
*   Programming methodology, showing how to use assembly language to create both system-level software tools and application programs.
*   Samples of computer hardware manipulation.
*   Interaction between assembly language programs, the operating system, and other application programs.

This book tries to present knowledge that is specific to Intel processors, as well as knowledge that is universal. Many of us who teach assembly language learned it first on completely different computers before the IBM-PC was invented. This knowledge was not lost—instead, it was transformed and adapted to the needs of today. The same must be true for our students who learn Intel assembly language, using whichever computer is at hand.

The book begins with simple information, the understanding of numbers and data. Then the basic architecture of the processor is introduced. Basic machine-level instructions lead us easily into writing short programs with an interactive debugger. The Macro Assembler is introduced in Chapter 3 and more fully described in Chapter 4. The middle part of the book fills out the instruction set, introduces short, useful application programs, and builds a library of procedures. The latter part of the book contains programs and techniques that take advantage of advanced programming and operating system functions.

The book is designed to accompany a college course in assembly language programming at the sophomore, junior, or senior level. Experience has shown that ten chapters can easily be covered in a 15-week semester, depending on the experience level of the students. I consider the first nine chapters to be the core of the text, with the remaining six being individually selectable topics. This book may also be used for self-study, enhanced by the CD-ROM enclosed with the book.

One of my goals is to help students approach programming problems with a machine-level mind set. It is important to think of the CPU as an interactive tool, and to learn to monitor each of its actions as directly as possible. A debugger is a programmer's best friend, not only for catching errors, but as an educational tool that teaches one about the CPU and operating system. I encourage students to look beneath the surface of high-level languages, and to realize that most programming languages are designed to be portable and, therefore, independent of their host machines.

In addition to the short examples, *Assembly Language for Intel-Based Computers* contains over 75 ready-to-run programs that demonstrate instructions or ideas as they are presented in the text. Reference materials such as guides to MS-DOS interrupts and instruction mnemonics are available at the end of the book. There is a comprehensive link library that makes the user interface much more accessible for students when they are writing their first programs. As they advance through the chapters, students learn how to write library routines themselves. A short macro library is also included, which may provide inspiration for further development by professors and students.

Required Background. The reader should already be able to program confidently in at least one other programming language, preferably Pascal, Java, C, or C++. One chapter, Chapter 13, goes into C++ interfacing in some depth, so it is very helpful to have a compiler on hand. I have used this book in the classroom with majors in computer science, management information systems, and the book has been used elsewhere in engineering schools. I used Microsoft Visual C++ 5.0 and Borland C++ 5.0 for the examples that deal with high-level language interfacing.

Features

Complete Program Listings. A companion CD-ROM contains all the source code from the examples in this book. Additional listings are available on the author's Web page. An extensive link library is supplied with the book, containing over 30 procedures that simplify user input-output, numeric processing, disk and file handling, and string handling. At the beginning stages of the course, students can use this library to enhance their programs. Later, students can create their own procedures and add them to the library. Professors adopting this book are given the complete source code for the link library, which they may optionally share with their students.

Programming Logic. Two chapters emphasize boolean logic and bit-level manipulation. A conscious attempt is made to relate high-level programming logic to the low-level details of the machine. This helps students to create more efficient implementations and to better understand how language compilers generate object code.

Hardware and Operating System Concepts. The first two chapters introduce basic hardware and data representation concepts, including binary numbers, addressing, CPU registers, status flags, and memory mapping. A survey of the computer's hardware and a historical perspective of the Intel processor family helps students to better understand their target computer system.

32-Bit Processing. Throughout the book, examples appear using 32-bit registers and advanced processor instructions. Students can still program on an 8086/8088, but those with an 80386 or higher will benefit the most

Structured Programming Approach. Beginning with Chapter 5, procedures and module decomposition are strongly emphasized. Students are given more complex programming problems that require the ability to carefully structure their code and to deal with complexity.

Disk Storage and Files. Chapters 11 and 12 demonstrate many techniques for going beyond the capabilities of high-level languages. Students gain an understanding of disk storage and hardware and are able to bypass the operating system. This usually generates a lot of excitement when one discovers new ways of programming at this level.

Creating Link Libraries. Students are free to add their own procedures to the book's link library, and they can create libraries of their own. They learn to use the toolbox approach to programming and to write code that is useful in more than one program.

Chapter on Macros and Structures. Chapter 8 is devoted to creating macros, which are important in both assembly language and high-level languages. Students learn how to use text substitution to provide extra power and flexibility. Structures are introduced in the same chapter, providing high-level organization of data.

Interfacing to High-Level Languages. A complete chapter is devoted to interfacing assembly language to C and C++. This is an important job skill for students who are likely to find jobs programming in high-level languages. They can learn to optimize their code and see actual examples of how C++ compilers optimize code.

Instructional Aids. All program listings are available on disk and on the Web. Instructors receive a comprehensive instructor manual with teaching strategies and solutions to programming exercises.

Enhancements to the Third Edition

The very need for a third edition of this book is cause for celebration, showing that the book has remained popular for quite some time. First published in 1990, it was last revised in 1993. Of course, computer hardware has changed spectacularly in the past five years. At that time, the 386 processor was king, and a 32MB hard drive was considered the norm. In addition, some pedagogic changes seemed important, based on my having used the book in the classroom for so many years. A good textbook should make the instructor's job easier by filling in the technical details and allowing the classroom instructor to focus on concepts. The following is a quick summary of changes, chapter by chapter:

Chapter 1 goes into more detail explaining the suitability of high-level and low-level languages to specific types of applications. This perspective is important because students want to know how the course they are taking is relevant to their studies.

Chapter 2 surveys the entire Intel 80x86 processor family and compares the features of each member, through the Pentium II. Also in this chapter is greater emphasis on the architecture of the 32-bit processor, current motherboard and bus architectures, and types of RAM.

Chapter 3 is more comprehensive than before, beginning with a full explanation of how to use the assembler, linker, and debugger. All programs in the chapter are designed to be assembled and linked. (In the previous edition, Debug was used the primary authoring tool in Chapter 3.)

Chapter 4 has been improved by including more detailed explanations of assembler operators and directives. The section on memory operands covers all the indirect and indexed addressing modes on both 16-bit and 32-bit processors. This chapter also introduces an extensive link library that students can use for basic input-output throughout the course.

Chapter 5 has an expanded discussion of parameter passing, which is continued in Chapter 7 with details of stack parameters. Extensions to the assembler by both Microsoft and Borland are demonstrated in separate sections. The sections in this chapter on INT 21h, INT 16h, and INT 10h have been updated and improved.

Chapter 6, covering conditional processing, introduces many bit manipulation and comparison instructions that were introduced by the 386 and 486 processors. We show how to implement a finite state machine in assembly language, applying it to simple text-processing applications.

Chapter 7, on integer arithmetic, introduces several 32-bit instructions and shows how to perform 32-bit arithmetic. There is also a new section on writing characters and attributes directly to the video display.

Chapter 8, on macros and structures, shows students how to build a useful macro library. A number of advanced macro operators are explained, with examples that generate pseudo-instructions and create data structures.

Chapter 9, on strings and arrays, introduces all the 32-bit versions of the string primitives such as SCASD and MOVSD. The scope of programming exercises has been expanded.

Chapters 11 and 12, on disk and file processing, have been updated considerably because of changes in hard disks and the retiring of obsolete floppy disk formats. Chapter 12 now contains a program that shows how to load and display a Windows bitmap.

Chapter 13, on linking to high-level languages, emphasizes C and C++ much more than Pascal. There is much more coverage of inline assembly code, and there are examples of writing subroutines in 32-bit protected mode.

ORGANIZATION AND FORMAT

Presentation Sequence

Chapters 1-8 represent the basic foundation of assembly language and are designed to be covered in sequence. A great deal of effort went into making these chapters flow smoothly:

1. **Introduction**   Applications of assembly language, basic concepts, machine language, data representation, using Debug.

2. **Hardware and Software Architecture**   Hardware fundamentals and terminology, basic architecture of the 80x86 processors, 16- and 32-bit registers, memory architecture, disks, video adapters, and system software.

3. **Assembly Language Fundamentals**   Assembling, linking and debugging, defining constants and variables, simple data transfer and arithmetic instructions, survey of operand types.

4. **Using the Assembler**   Linker and map files, operators, directives, and expressions, JMP, LOOP, indirect addressing, calling procedures from a link library.

5. **Procedures and Interrupts**   Stack, procedure declarations, calling DOS and BIOS interrupts for console, video, and keyboard I/O. Types of procedure parameters. Recursion.

6. **Conditional Processing**   Boolean and comparison instructions, conditional jumps and loops, high-level logic structures, and finite state machines.

7. **Integer Arithmetic**   Shift and rotate instructions, sample applications, multiple addition and subtraction, MUL and DIV, direct video output, ASCII decimal arithmetic.

   Chapters 9 through 15 may be covered in any order, and some may be omitted without causing any great harm. The section on separately assembled modules in Chapter 9 should be covered if the students will be adding any of their own procedures to the book's link library. The string primitive instructions in Chapter 10 (SCAS, MOVS, LODS, STOS) are part of the processor's instruction set, so we recommend that you cover at least that section of the chapter.

8. **Structures and Macros**   The chapter on macros was moved up from Chapter 10 to Chapter 8, recognizing its importance to students who want to use macros and structures in completing programming assignments in the second half of the book.

9. **Numeric Conversions and Libraries**   Character translation methods, separately assembled modules, creating a link library, binary to ASCII conversion, ASCII to binary conversion.

10. **Strings and Arrays**   String storage methods, string primitive instructions, building a library of string procedures.

11. **Disk Storage**   Disk storage fundamentals, sectors, clusters, directories, decoding the file allocation table, handling DOS error codes, drive and directory manipulation.

12. **File Processing**   File manipulation, standard DOS file services, creating and reading text files, random-access file processing.

13. **High-Level Language Interface**   Parameter passing conventions, inline assembly code, linking assembly language modules to C/C++ programs.

14. **Advanced Topics I**   Indirect jumps and calls, tables of far pointers, hardware port I/O, defining explicit segments, runtime program structure, dynamic memory allocation.

15. **Advanced Topics II**   Machine instruction encoding, interrupt service routines, terminate and stay resident procedures, real numbers, the floating-point coprocessor.

Reference Materials

In my own assembly courses, I rely heavily on instructional materials such as tutorials, review questions, workbooks, and such. In that spirit, I have tried to provide ongoing support for instructors. If you find that something important is missing, please contact me and I may be able to provide it. The following reference information is included either the book or the accompanying CD:

Assembly Language Workbook. An interactive workbook is included on the CD, covering important topics such as number conversions, addressing modes, register usage, Debug programming, and floating-point binary numbers. The content pages are HTML documents, making it easy for students and professors to add their own customized content.

Binary and Hexadecimal Number Tutorial. Appendix A contains an extensive tutorial that covers numeric conversions between binary, decimal, and hexadecimal. There is also a tutorial on binary and hexadecimal arithmetic.

Debug Tutorial. Appendix B contains an easy-to-use tutorial and refrence on Debug, the simple debugging utility supplied with MS-DOS and Windows.

CodeView and Turbo Debugger References. Appendixes C and D contain handy reference information for using Microsoft CodeView and Borland Turbo Debugger.

Link Library. Appendix E lists all programs and files on the diskette supplied with this book. The link library on this disk greatly simplifies input/output programming, and includes subroutines for the following: generating random numbers, date and time functions, disk and file manipulation, and string manipulation.

Macro Library. The macro library supplied on the companion diskette is a guide for students who want to fill out this library with additional macros. The names of the macros are also listed in Appendix E.

Reserved Word List. Appendix F lists all reserved words for the Microsoft and Borland assemblers.

DOS and BIOS Functions. Appendix G contains a listing of most BIOS and DOS interrrupts, with a special emphasis on INT 10h and INT 21h.

Instruction Set. Appendix H lists all nonpriveleged instructions for the 80x86 processor family. For each instruction, we describe its effect, show its syntax, and show which flags are affected.

PowerPoint Presentations. A number of excellent PowerPoint presentations have been created by Professor Mario Marchand, University of Ottawa, Canada.

Answers to Selected Review Questions. Answers to all the odd-numbered review questions are included on the CD. Answers to the even-numbered questions are available to instructors only.

ACKNOWLEDGEMENTS

Warm thanks are due to Laura Steele, senior computer science editor at Prentice Hall, who provided friendly, helpful guidance during the writing of the third edition.

Thanks are also due to John Griffin, who was the book's original acquisitions editor, and Ron Harris, who was its production editor at Macmillan Publishing.

I offer my special thanks and gratitude to three professors: **Gerald Cahill** from Antelope Valley College, who offered numerous excellent corrections; **Tim Downey** of Florida International University, who shared excellent explanations of computer architecture concepts; **James Brink** of Pacific Lutheran University, who created a cool 32-bit link library with flat model programs.

Microsoft generously provided its Macro Assembler software for inclusion with this book at a reasonable price.

Production Staff of the Third Edition:

Many thanks to the following people: Donna Sullivan was the project manager at Prentice Hall publishing. Ray Robinson, the project director, and Kelly Dobbs, the project manager, both from D & G Limited, LLC, provided excellent guidance in preparing the book for printing. Michael Brumitt of D & G Limited, LLC, proofread the book, catching many of my mistakes and improving my English. David Irvine did a great job creating all of the book's illustrations and many of its tables. Bill Dever, Alejandro Ferro, and Raymond Lim applied their considerable talents to proofreading the final manuscript.

Reviewers of the Third Edition:

- Kathy Blicharz (Pima Community College)
- Patricia Nettnin (Finger Lakes Community College)

Reviewers of the First and Second Editions:

- Michael J. Walton, Barry Brosch, Bruce DeSautel, and Richard White of Miami-Dade Community College.
- Richard A. Beebe of Simpson College.
- John V. Erhart, Northeast Missouri State University.
- Gonshin Liu, University of Bridgeport
- S.K. Sachdev, Eastern Michigan University
- Douglas W. Knight, University of Southern Colorado
- Don Retzlaff, University of North Texas
- Robert Galivan, a software consultant, who also wrote the Instructor's Manual.
- George Kamenz, programmer *extraordinaire*, read the manuscript for the Third Edition and offered many valuable suggestions.
- Diego Escala wrote a great bitmap viewing program, shown in Chapter 12.

    Special thanks must be given to the hundreds of students at Miami-Dade Community College between 1990 and 1999 who showed their determination to learn assembly language from this book, and who often wonderfully surpassed their teacher's expectations.

Table of Contents

1 Introduction

1.1   CONTEXT OF ASSEMBLY LANGUAGE

Assembly language unlocks the secrets of your computer's hardware and software. It teaches you about the way the computer's hardware and operating system work together and how application programs communicate with the operating system. It might be helpful here to view a computer and its software as a series of hierarchical levels such as those shown in Table 1. Most programmers work at the *high-level language* level, where individual statements are expanded into multiple machine instructions. At the assembly language and machine levels, one creates instructions directly interpreted by the computer's processor. Assembly language is a *low-level language*.

Assembly language is most often used when either communicating with the operating system or directly accessing computer hardware. Secondarily, assembly language is used to optimize certain critical areas of application programs to speed up their runtime execution. We believe that assembly language should be studied along with computer architecture and operating system concepts, to help one to better understand how assembly language programs interact with their environment.

Table 1. Software Hierarchy Levels.

Level	Description
Application Program	Software designed for a particular class of applications.
High-Level Language (HLL)	Programs are compiled into either assembly language or machine language. Each statement usually translates into multiple machine language instructions. Examples are C++, Pascal, Java, and Visual Basic.
Operating System	Contains procedures that can be called from programs written in either high-level language or assembly language. This system may also contain an application programming interface (API).
Assembly Language (ASM)	Uses instruction mnemonics that have a one-to-one correspondence with machine language.
Machine Language (ML)	Numeric instructions and operands that can be stored in memory and directly executed by the computer processor.

1.1.1 What Is Assembly Language?

Assembly language is a machine-specific programming language with a one-to-one correspondence between its statements and the computer's native machine language. There are many different types of assembly language, each specific to a processor or processor family. This is because the instructions in assembly language are designed to match a computer's machine instruction set and hardware architecture. *IBM-PC assembly language* refers to instructions recognized by a number of different microprocessors in the Intel family: 8086, 8088, 80186, 80286, 80386, 80486, and Pentium.

What Is an Assembler? An *assembler* is a program that converts source-code programs from assembly language into machine language. The assembler can optionally generate a source listing file with line numbers, memory addresses, source code statements, and a cross-reference listing of symbols and variables used in a program. A companion program, called a *linker,* combines individual files created by an assembler into a single executable program. A third program, called a *debugger,* provides a way for a programmer to trace the execution of a program and examine the contents of memory. In this book, our programs will run either under pure MS-DOS, or in an MS-DOS window under Windows 95/NT. The most popular assemblers for the Intel family are MASM (Microsoft Assembler), TASM (Borland Turbo Assembler), and ASM86.

Assembly language is called a *low-level* language because it is close to machine language in structure and function. Each assembly language instruction corresponds to one machine instruction (a one-to-one correspondence). In contrast, single statements in high-level languages such as Pascal, BASIC, C, and C++ are translated into multiple machine instructions (see Figure 1).

Why Learn Assembly Language? People learn assembly language for various reasons. You may want to learn more about the computer you work with and about the way computer

Figure 1. Machine Language Generation by ASM and HLL programs.

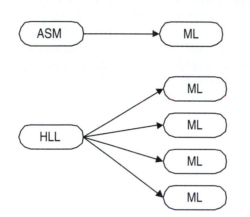

languages generate machine code. Because of assembly language's close relationship to machine language, it is closely tied to the computer's hardware and software.

You may also want to learn assembly language for its utility. Certain types of programming are difficult or impossible to do in high-level languages. For example, direct communication with the computer's operating system may be necessary. Or, a computer game application might have to directly access the video controller and sound card. A special program may be needed to interface a printer or serial device to a computer. A Visual Basic program can call a DLL procedure written in assembly language to speed up the program in critical areas of code. Assembly language is effective in a wide variety of situations because of its economical code size and blazing speed.

Assembly language programs can easily bypass restrictions imposed by high-level languages. For example, the Pascal language does not allow a character value to be assigned to an integer variable. Ordinarily, this makes good sense, unless there is a specific reason to break the rules. An experienced programmer can find a way around this restriction but, in doing so, may end up writing code that is less portable to other computer systems and is difficult to read. Assembly language, in contrast, has very few restrictions or rules; nearly everything is left to the discretion of the programmer. The price for such freedom is the need to handle many details that would otherwise be taken care of by the programming language itself.

Perhaps most important, assembly language is a tremendous tool for learning about computer architecture, operating systems, data representation, and hardware devices. Nearly every university computer science curriculum calls for a course in computer architecture, which is followed by a course in operating systems concepts. These topics give you a clear advantage when tackling unusual programming and debugging problems.

1.1.2   Assembly Language Applications

The first assembly language programs presented in this book will probably seem trivial. One cannot believe the amount of work required to perform relatively simple tasks. Assembly language requires a great deal of attention to detail. In the early days of programming, most application programs were written partially or entirely in assembly language because programs had to fit in a small area of RAM and the computers ran slowly. As computers became more powerful, programs became longer and more complex; this demanded the use of high-level languages such as C, FORTRAN, and COBOL that contained a certain amount of structuring capabilities to assist the programmer. More recently, object-oriented languages, such as C++ and Java, have made it possible to write complex programs containing millions of lines of code.

It is rare to see application programs written completely in assembly language, because they would take too much time to write and maintain. Instead, assembly language is used to optimize certain sections of application programs for speed and to access computer hardware. Assembly language is also used when writing *embedded systems* programs, which are programs stored in programmable read-only memory (PROM) chips in hardware devices. Table 2 compares the adaptability of assembly language to high-level languages in relation to various types of computer programs.

C++ has the unique quality of offering a compromise between high-level structure and low-level details. Direct hardware access is possible but completely non-portable. Most C++ compilers have the ability to generate assembly language source code, which the programmer can customize and refine before assembling into executable code.

Programmers often use a combination of C++ and assembly language for embedded systems applications such as computer cartridge games, microcontrollers in automobiles, telecommunications equipment, temperature control systems, industrial robots, security systems, and automated bank tellers just to name a few.

Assembly Language Subroutines. Programmers often write subroutines in assembly language and call them from high-level language programs. In some cases, the subroutines are called *interface subroutines* because they provide a convenient way to directly access the computer's hardware. In a computer game, for example, one might have to manipulate the hardware ports of the video display adapter and sound card in order to achieve the greatest level of performance.

Assembly language subroutines called *device drivers* are also called from the operating system, as a way of providing system services to all application programs. When a program must read a block of data from a file, for example, the operating system calls a device driver subroutine. The subroutine calling relationships are illustrated in Figure 2.

Table 2. Comparison of Assembly Language and High-Level Languages.

Type of Application	High-Level Language	Assembly Language
Business application software, written for single platform, medium to large size.	Formal structures make it easy to organize and maintain large sections of code.	No formal structure. Programmer must impose an artificial structure.
Hardware device driver.	Language may not provide for direct hardware access. Awkward coding techniques must be used, resulting in possible maintenance problems.	Hardware access is straightforward and simple. Easy to maintain when the programs are short and well documented.
Business application written for multiple platforms (different operating systems).	Usually very portable. The source code can be recompiled on each target operating system with minimal changes.	Must be recoded separately for each platform, often using an assembler with a different syntax. Difficult to maintain.
Embedded systems and computer games requiring direct hardware access.	Produces too much executable code, and may not run efficiently.	Ideal, because the executable code is small and runs quickly.

Above all, assembly language programmers must know their data, for without a detailed understanding of the physical representation of data, one makes mistakes. High-level programming languages intentionally shield programmers from implementation-specific details in the name of convenience and source-code portability. Assembly language, on the other hand, is highly machine-specific and imposes few, if any, restrictions.

Figure 2. Assembly Language Subroutines Used as Hardware Interfaces.

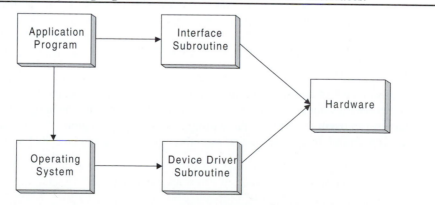

Muti-Platform Programming. A major weakness of assembly language is that a single assembly language program cannot be simply recompiled and executed on different types of computers. Each processor family has a different assembler with a different syntax. This is because the assembler has been designed around the processor's architecture. When the same source program must be compiled and run on different target machines, a high-level language such as C++ or Java may be a better tool.

1.1.3   Machine Language

A computer doesn't directly interpret assembly language, but it does understand machine language. Machine language is a language made up of numbers, which can be interpreted by a computer's processor. A processor usually has a built-in interpreter called a *microprogram* that interprets and translates machine instructions into hardware signals.

Machine language contains primitive statements that perform ordinary tasks such as data from one location to another or performing simple arithmetic. A processor's *instruction set* is the set of machine instructions that it can execute. The machine language for the Intel family of processors beginning with the 8086 shares a common subset of instructions that can be executed by all members of the family. This concept is called *downward compatibility*. For example, the 8086 and 80286 processors both understand the following instruction (shown here in assembly language):

```
push ax  ; push the AX register on the stack
```

With each upgrade to a higher-level processor, however, new instructions are introduced that cannot be understood by the lower-level ones. For example, the 80286 processor understands the following instruction, but the 8086 does not:

```
pusha    ; push all general registers on the stack
```

Machine Language Example. The following is an example of an Intel machine language instruction that moves 5 into the AL register:

```
1011000000000101
```

The first 8 bits are the *operation code* (op code), which identifies it as the instruction that moves an 8-bit number to the AL register. The second 8 bits are the *operand*. The complete instruction moves the number 5 to a register called AL. *Registers* are high-speed storage locations inside the CPU that can hold 8, 16, or 32 bits. They are identified by symbolic names such as AH, AL, AX, and EAX.

We could, of course, write entire programs in machine language simply by entering the various binary values of the machine language instructions into memory and telling the processor to begin execution at the starting address of our program. But this would be overly time-consuming. Instead, we use an assembler to convert a source code file written in assembly language into machine language. For example, instead of writing the machine instruction shown earlier, we would write the following in assembly language:

```
mov  ah,5
```

1.2   DATA REPRESENTATION

Because we are dealing with the computer at the machine level, it is necessary to examine the contents of memory and registers. Computers are constructed from digital circuits that have only two states: *on* and *off*. When data are stored in volatile memory, electrical charges are required to maintain the memory's state.

1.2.1   Binary Numbers

A computer stores instructions and data in memory as collections of electronic charges. Representing these entities with numbers requires a system geared to the concepts of *on* and *off* or *true* and *false*. *Binary numbers* are base 2 numbers in which each digit is either a 0 or 1. Typically, a 1 (*on*) indicates about 5 volts, and a 0 (*off*) indicates about 0.5 volts.

```
1       0       1       0
on      off     on      off
```

At one time, computers actually had panels filled with mechanical switches that were flipped by hand. Electromechanical relays were soon used instead, and later transistors were introduced. Eventually thousands and later millions of individual electronic switches and circuits were engraved on microprocessor chips.

Bits, Bytes, Words, and Doublewords. Each digit in a binary number is called a *bit*. Eight bits together make up a *byte*, which on the IBM, is the smallest addressable memory location. A byte can hold a single machine instruction, a character, or a number. The next largest storage type is a *word,* which on Intel processors is 16 bits (2 bytes) long:

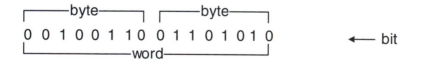

The size of a *word* is not absolute. The IBM-PC originally contained the Intel 8088 processor, which had a 16-bit operand size, so a word was identified as 16 bits. Since that time, 32-bit processors have become more common on IBM compatibles, but we still refer to a *word* as 16 bits. A *doubleword* is 32 bits (4 bytes), and a *quadword* is 64 bits (8 bytes).

Table 3 shows the number of bits and ranges of possible values for unsigned bytes, words, doublewords, and quadwords. Each range's higher value is calculated as $(2^b - 1)$, where b indicates the number of bits.

Instructions (Code) and Data. In high-level language programming, we tend to think of data and instructions as somehow being fundamentally different. Physically, however, both are constructed from identical streams of binary bits. For example, the following sequence of binary bits could be the first three letters of the alphabet stored in a string variable, or it could be a machine instruction:

01000001010000101001000011

Table 3. Storage Sizes and Ranges of Unsigned Integers.

Storage Type	Bits	Range (low - high)
Unsigned byte	8	0 to 255
Unsigned word	16	0 to 65,535
Unsigned doubleword	32	0 to 4,294,967,295
Unsigned quadword	64	0 to 18,446,744,073,709,551,615

This is why it is the programmer's responsibility to keep an assembly language's code and data separate. You probably do not want the processor to "execute" a variable, or read and write a block of code as if it were a variable.

Numbering Systems. Each numbering system has a *base*, or maximum number of values that can be assigned to a single digit. Table 4 shows the permitted digits for different numbering systems. Hexadecimal digits A through F correspond to decimal values 10 through 15. Throughout this book, we use hexadecimal numbers to represent computer memory, register values, and addresses.

When referring to binary, octal, and hexadecimal numbers, a single lowercase letter is appended to the end of each number to identify its base. For example, hexadecimal 45 is written as 45h, octal 76 is either 76o or 76q, and binary 11010011 is written as 11010011b. This is the way the assembler identifies numeric literals in assembly language source programs.

Table 4. Digits in Various Number Systems.

System	Base	Possible Digits
Binary	2	0 1
Octal	8	0 1 2 3 4 5 6 7
Decimal	10	0 1 2 3 4 5 6 7 8 9
Hexadecimal	16	0 1 2 3 4 5 6 7 8 9 A B C D E F

Terminology for Numeric Data Representation. It is important to use a precise terminology when describing the way numbers and characters are represented in memory and on the display screen. Let's use the number 65 as an example: stored in memory as a single byte, its binary bit pattern is 01000001. A debugging program would probably display the byte as "41," which is the hexadecimal notation for this bit pattern. But if the byte is moved to the video display area of memory by a running program, the letter **A** would appear onscreen. This is because 01000001 also happens to be the ASCII code for the letter A. It seems that the interpretation of numbers on a computer depends greatly on the context in which the number appears:

In this book, we use a naming method for numeric data representation that is reasonably general to avoid conflicts with terminology you might encounter from other sources:

* A *binary number* is a number stored in memory in its raw format, ready to be used in a calculation. Binary integers are stored in 8, 16, or 32 bits.

* An *ASCII digit string* is a string of ASCII characters, such as "123," or "65," which is made to look like a number. This is simply a representation of the number and can be in any of the following formats (shown for the decimal number 65):

Format	Value
ASCII binary	"01000001"
ASCII decimal	"65"
ASCII hexadecimal	"41"
ASCII octal	"101"

1.2.2 Converting Binary to Decimal

There are many occasions when you need to find the decimal equivalent of a binary number. Table 5 shows the decimal values of 2^0 through 2^{15}. Each bit position in a binary number is a power of 2.

To calculate the decimal value of a binary number, add the value of each bit position containing a 1 to the number's total value. Let's try this with the binary number 0 0 0 0 1 0 0 1, shown in Figure 3. For more explanations on how to translate numbers from one format to another, see Appendix A.

1.2.3 Hexadecimal Numbers

Large binary numbers are cumbersome to read, so hexadecimal numbers are usually used by assemblers and debuggers to represent binary data and machine instructions. Each digit in a hexadecimal number represents 4 binary bits, and two hexadecimal digits represent a byte. In

Table 5. Binary Bit Position Values.

2^n	Decimal Value	2^n	Decimal Value
2^0	1	2^8	256
2^1	2	2^9	512
2^2	4	2^{10}	1024
2^3	8	2^{11}	2048
2^4	16	2^{12}	4096
2^5	32	2^{13}	8192
2^6	64	2^{14}	16384
2^7	128	2^{15}	32768

Figure 3. Converting Binary to Decimal.

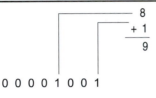

```
                          8
                        + 1
                          9

      0 0 0 0 1 0 0 1
```

the following example, we can see that the binary number 0001011000000111110010100 is represented by the hexadecimal number 160794:

```
1    6    0    7    9    4
0001 0110 0000 0111 1001 0100 = 160794h
```

A single hexadecimal digit can have a value from 0 to 15, so the letters A to F are used, as well as the digits 0-9. The letter A = 10, B = 11, C = 12, D = 13, E = 14, and F = 15. Table 6 shows how each sequence of 4 binary bits translates into a decimal or hexadecimal value.

Each hexadecimal digit position represents a power of 16. This is helpful when calculating the value of a hexadecimal number (see Table 7).

Numbers can be converted from hexadecimal to decimal by multiplying each digit by its position value. Figure 4 shows an example of converting 3BA4h. First, the highest digit, 3, is multiplied by 4096, its position value. The next digit, B, is multiplied by 256, the next digit, A, is multiplied by 16, and the last digit is multiplied by 1. The sum of these products is 15,268 decimal.

1.2.4   Signed Numbers

Binary numbers can be either signed or unsigned. An *unsigned* byte uses all 8 bits for its magnitude. For example, 11111111 = 255. Adding together the values of 8 bits, their sum (255) is the largest value that can be stored in an unsigned byte. The largest value that can be stored in an unsigned word is 65,535, the sum of the values of 16 bits. A *signed* byte uses only 7 bits for its magnitude; the highest bit is reserved for the sign, where 0 indicates positive, and 1 indicates negative. For example, the following shows the representations of both negative and positive 10:

Table 6. Binary, Decimal, and Hexadecimal Equivalents.

Binary	Decimal	Hexadecimal	Binary	Decimal	Hexadecimal
0000	0	0	1000	8	8
0001	1	1	1001	9	9
0010	2	2	1010	10	A
0011	3	3	1011	11	B
0100	4	4	1100	12	C
0101	5	5	1101	13	D
0110	6	6	1110	14	E
0111	7	7	1111	15	F

Table 7. Powers of 16, in Decimal.

16^n	Decimal Value	16^n	Decimal Value
16^0	1	16^4	65,536
16^1	16	16^5	1,048,576
16^2	256	16^6	16,777,216
16^3	4096	16^7	268,435,456

Figure 4. Converting 3BA4 Hexadecimal to Decimal.

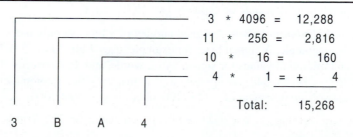

Two's Complement Notation. Rather than having separate internal logic for performing subtraction, the CPU can just add the negative value of a number (its additive inverse). The *additive inverse* of an integer *n* is the value, when added to *n*, that produces zero. For example, decimal –6 is the additive inverse of 6 because 6 + (–6) = 0. When subtracting A – B, the CPU instead performs A + (–B). For example, to simulate the subtraction of 4 from 6, the CPU adds –4 to 6:

```
6 + -4 = 2
```

When working with binary numbers, we use the term *two's complement* to refer to a number's additive inverse. The two's complement of a number *n* is formed by reversing *n*'s bits and adding 1. Using the 4-bit binary value 0001, for example, its two's complement is 1111:

```
N:         0001
Reverse N: 1110
Add 1:     1111
```

The two's complement of *n*, when added to *n*, produces zero:

```
0001 + 1111 = 0000
```

The two's complement operation is reversible. In the following example, the two's complement of –10 is +10:

```
11110110 = -10
00001001   (toggle bits)
+       1  (add 1)
----------
00001010 = +10
```

Here are additional examples of 8-bit two's complements, indicated by NEG(*n*):

```
Decimal    Binary        NEG(n)       Decimal
+2         00000010      11111110     -2
+16        00010000      11110000     -16
+127       01111111      10000001     -127
```

Reversing the bits in a number, notated as NOT(*n*), is called *forming the one's complement.* So the two's complement of *n* may be expressed as: NOT(*n*) + 1.

Maximum and Minimum Values. A signed number of *n* bits can only use *n*–1 bits to represent the number's magnitude. A signed byte, for example, uses 7 bits (0 to 127). Table 8 shows the maximum and minimum values for signed bytes, words, and doublewords. The lowest values (–128, –32768, –2147483648) are special cases in that their two's complments are invalid. For example, the two's complement of –128 (10000000) is also 10000000.

Table 8. Signed Integer Storage and Ranges.

Storage Type	Bits	Range (low - high)
Signed byte	7	-128 to +127
Signed word	15	−32,768 to +32,767
Signed doubleword	31	−2,147,483,648 to 2,147,483,647
Signed quadword	63	−9,223,372,036,854,775,808 to +9,223,372,036,854,775,807

The processor performs calculations without regard to the signs of numbers, so it is up to the programmer to remember whether certain operands are signed or unsigned. For example, using signed operands, let's add +16 and −23:

```
mov  ax,+16
add  ax,-23
```

In binary, +16 is represented as 00010000, and −23 is represented as 11101001. When the CPU adds these values, the sum is 11111001. This binary value is the representation of −7. Therefore, the signed addition is correct:

```
  00010000   (16)
+ 11101001   (-23)
----------
= 11111001    (-7)
```

Of course, 11111001 can also be interpreted as unsigned 249. The difference between signed and unsigned numbers is all in the perception of the programmer, who must know which types of values the data represent.

1.2.5   Character Storage

Computers can only store binary numbers, so how are characters such as "A" and "$" stored? The computer must use a character encoding scheme that translates numbers into letters, and vice versa. The most well-known system for microcomputers is called ASCII (pronounced "askey"), which stands for *American Standard Code for Information Interchange*. In ASCII, a unique numeric value is assigned to each character, including control characters used when printing or transmitting data between computers. Standard ASCII codes are actually only 7-bit codes, with a range of 0 to 127. Values 0-31 are control codes for printer, communications, and screen output; they do not generate visible characters. The eighth ASCII bit in each byte is optional. It is used on various computers to extend the character set. In MS-DOS, values 128-

255 represent graphics symbols and Greek characters. In Microsoft Windows, each selectable character set has different values in the 128-255 range.

A string of characters is represented in memory as a succession of bytes containing numbers. For example, the numeric codes for the string "ABC123" are 41h, 42h, 43h, 31h, 32h, and 33h. A listing of the control codes is shown on the inside front cover of this book, and a complete table of standard and extended MS-DOS ASCII codes is shown on the inside back cover of this book.

Storing Numbers. What is the most efficient way to store a number in memory? It depends on how the number will be used. Binary storage is best for numbers used in calculations, and ASCII character storage is best for numbers that will be input from the user and displayed on the console. For example, the number 123 can be stored in two different ways: as three bytes containing the ASCII codes for '1,' '2,' and '3,' or as a single byte containing binary 123:

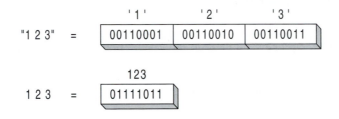

Using the ASCII Table at the Back of this Book. To find the hexadecimal ASCII code of a character, look along the top row of the table and find the column containing the character that you want to translate. The most significant digit of the hexadecimal value is in the second row at the top of the table; the least significant digit is in the second column from the left. For example, to find the ASCII code of the letter "a," find the column containing the "a," and look in the second row: The first hexadecimal digit is 6. Next look to the left along the row containing "a," and notice that the second column contains the digit 1. Therefore, the ASCII code of "a" is 61h.

Identifying Code and Data. Although we might know the binary contents of memory, the actual usage of the memory is not always clear. Suppose two bytes of memory contain the binary values 01000001 and 01000010. Are these values data, code, or text? It is impossible to know, unless the memory area has been identified. A program must keep track of its data and the type of representation used to avoid possible confusion. High-level languages impose restrictions on the way variables and instructions are manipulated, but assembly language does not. We might think of these restrictions as boundaries designed to help us avoid making fundamental errors. In assembly language, there are few restrictions, but the programmer is shouldered with the responsibility of taking care of many picky details.

1.3   INTRODUCING ASSEMBLY LANGUAGE

1.3.1   Assembly Language Instructions

Although we've already said that it is possible to program directly in machine language using numbers, assembly language makes the job easier. An assembly language *instruction* is a symbolic representation of a single machine instruction. In its simplest form, it consists of a *mnemonic,* a short alphabetic code that literally "assists the memory" in remembering a CPU instruction. The mnemonic can also be followed by a list of operands. Here are a few examples:

```
clc               ; just a mnemonic
inc ax            ; single operand
mov ax,bx         ; two operands
```

Note that each instruction can be followed by a *comment,* always beginning with a semicolon (;).

Assembly language is called a *low-level* language because it is close to machine language in structure and function—in fact, one assembly language instruction corresponds to one machine instruction (a one-to-one correspondence). In contrast, a single statement in a high-level language, such as Pascal, usually translates into several machine instructions.

An *operand* can be a register, a variable, a memory location, or an immediate value. For example:

```
10                (immediate operand)
count             (variable or memory operand)
AX                (register operand)
[0200]            (memory location)
```

Using a Debugger. In this chapter, we begin looking at short assembly language programs and show the contents of registers and memory when they run. The best way to learn about these programs and about the way the computer works is to use a debugger. A *debugger* is a program that allows you to examine registers and memory and to step through a program one statement at a time to see what is going on. This is particularly useful when testing your assembly language programs.

There are a number of excellent Debuggers to choose from: *Debug* is a simple, easy-to-use debugger supplied with MS-DOS. The *CodeView* debugger supplied with the Microsoft assembler lets you view your programs source code, memory blocks, and CPU registers. The same is true for Borland's *Turbo Debugger,* and *Debug86,* the debugger written for the Asm86 assembler. Appendix B contains a tutorial for Debug, and Appendix C contains a tutorial for CodeView, Appendix D contains a tutorial for Turbo Debugger. Additional materials can be found at the author's Web site (www.pobox.com/~irvinek/asm).

1.3.2 A Sample Debug Program

Let's write a short assembly language program that adds three numbers and stores their sum in memory. We're going to assemble and run the program using Debug, so all numbers are assumed to be in hexadecimal:

```
mov ax,5
add ax,10
add ax,20
mov [0120],ax
int 20
```

Each line in this example begins with an instruction mnemonic (MOV, ADD, or INT), followed by operands. On the right side, any text following a semicolon is treated as a comment, although you cannot type comments in Debug. A step-by-step diagram of the program is shown in Figure 5.

The MOV instruction tells the CPU to move, or copy data, from a source operand to a destination operand. Line 1 moves 5 into the AX register. Line 2 adds 10 to AX, making it equal to 15. Line 3 adds 20 to AX, making it equal to 35, and line 4 copies AX into a variable in memory at location 0120. Line 5 halts the program.

If you have access to Debug, you can assemble and test the sample program using the commands shown in Example 1. Notice that you can see the contents of the CPU registers after each instruction. Let's take a look at the Debug display after the second instruction (add ax,10) has been traced:

```
AX=0015  BX=0000  CX=0000  DX=0000  SP=FFEE  BP=0000  SI=0000  DI=0000
DS=23AD  ES=23AD  SS=23AD  CS=23AD  IP=0106    NV UP EI PL NZ NA PO NC
23AD:0106 052000          ADD     AX,0020
```

AX equals 0015, the sum of 5 and 10. The IP register (Instruction Pointer) holds the address of the next instruction about to be executed, 0106. The next instruction about to be executed is shown on the last line: ADD AX,0020.

Figure 5. Sample Program Written in Debug.

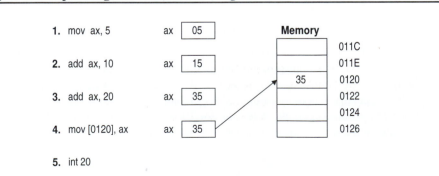

Example 1. Debug Commands to Assemble and Test the Sample Program.

Command	Description
A 100	Begin assembling statements at offset 100
mov ax, 5	First program statement: move 5 to the AX register
add ax, 10	Add 10 to the AX register
add ax, 20	Add 20 to the AX register
mov [0120], ax	Store the sum at memory location 0120
int 20	Halt the program
(press Enter)	Return to command mode
R	Display the register values before the program starts
T	Trace the first instruction
T	Trace the second instruction
T	Trace the third instruction
G	Execute the rest of the program
Q	Quit Debug

Why use an assembler at all? In fact, our sample program could have been created by entering the following sequence of binary bytes into memory. To understand this sequence of bytes, one would have to manually assemble each machine instruction:

```
B8 05 00 05 10 00 05 20 00 A3 20 01 CD 20
```

To the computer, a program is just a meaningful sequence of numbers placed in memory where it may be executed.

Running Debug from Microsoft Windows. Debug is a utility program that has always been supplied with MS-DOS. Its filename is Debug.com, and it should be in a directory on your MS-DOS path (see the autoexec.bat file). You can run Debug inside Windows by selecting **MS-DOS Prompt** from the Windows **Start** menu. When the MS-DOS prompt appears, type **Debug** and press Enter.

1.3.3 Debug Commands

The more commonly used Debug commands are described in Table 9, and a more detailed explanation is available in Appendix B.

As you assemble each line of a program, you should see a numeric address appear at the left side of the screen. These addresses show the location of each instruction as a combination of two numbers: a *segment* value and an *offset* (for the moment, we will ignore the segment value). For example,

```
-A 100
5511:0100    mov  ax,5
5511:0103    add  ax,10
```

To see the machine instructions that make up your program, type the U (Unassemble) command. We call this *disassembling* a program. For example:

Machine Instruction	Disassembled Instruction
B8 05 00	MOV AX,0005
05 10 00	ADD AX,0010
05 20 00	ADD AX,0020
A3 20 01	MOV [0120],AX
CD 20	INT 20

Table 9. Commonly Used Debug Commands.

Command	Description
A	Starts assembling a program, placing each instruction in memory. Optionally, an integer argument can be supplied, which specifies the hexadecimal location where the first instruction is to be inserted.
G	Executes the remainder of the program.
Q	Quits Debug
R	Displays the CPU registers.
T	Traces (execute) one program instruction.

In each machine instruction shown here, the first byte is the *op code* (operation code), and the next 2 bytes represent an immediate or memory operand. Of course, not all assembler instructions are 3 bytes long; their lengths vary between 1 and 6 bytes. The number [0120] in brackets is Debug's way of referring to the *contents* of memory location 0120.

The individual bytes in binary numbers are reversed when stored in memory. For example, the first instruction in the preceding table moves 0005h to AX—the machine instruction reverses the 05h and the 00h. For example, the doubleword 12345678h would be stored in memory as the following individual bytes, with the 78 stored at the lowest address:

| 78 | 56 | 34 | 12 | = 12345678h

When numbers are loaded from memory back into registers, the bytes are re-reversed to their original form.

1.4   REVIEW QUESTIONS

1. Suggest two types of programs or applications that are well suited to assembly language.

2. What type of relationship does assembly language have to machine language—one-to-one, or one-to-many?

3. What do we mean by a *one-to-many relationship* when comparing a high-level language to machine language?

4. Think of at least two applications that would be better suited to assembly language than a high-level language.

5. Why would a high-level language not be an ideal tool for writing a program that directly accesses the serial communications port?

6. Why is it important to learn about the operating system when studying assembly language?

7. Is the assembly language for the Intel 80x86 processor family the same as those of computer systems such as the DEC Alpha or the Motorola 68x00 series?

8. Will any program written for the Intel 8086 processor run on an Intel 80386 or 80486 processor?

9. Will any program written for the Intel 80386 processor run on an Intel 8086 processor?

10. How do the assembler and linker work together?

11. Is data type checking stronger in assembly language, or in Pascal?

12. Why is assembly language not used when writing large application programs?

13. Describe an example of an *embedded systems* application.

14. What is a *device driver*? Is it executed directly by application progams, or is it executed by the operating system?

15. What type of utility program allows an assembly language program written for one processor family to be translated into another type of assembly language?

16. In the following machine instruction, which byte contains the *op code*?

    05 0A 00

17. How many bytes are there in a doubleword?

18. Would each of the following values fit the range of a signed 16-bit word?

    a. -32760   b. +32,768

19. Write an example of a doubleword in both hexadecimal and binary.

20. Write the decimal representations of the following unsigned binary numbers:

    a. 10110101   b. 00010111

21. Write the decimal representation of the following signed binary numbers:

    a. 10000000   b. 01111111

22. Write the hexadecimal representation of the following unsigned 16-bit binary numbers:

    a. 1100111101010111   b. 1110110000001010

23. Write the binary representation of the following hexadecimal word values:

    a. E5B6   b. C9A4

24. Using the ASCII table on the inside back cover of this book, determine the hexadecimal and binary representations of the characters "XY."

25. Calculate the twos complement of 5 in binary.

26. What is the twos complement notation of −16 in binary?

27. Explain why the *program entry point* is important.

28. What is the smallest addressable memory location in a computer that uses the Intel 80x86 processor family?

29. Write the largest and smallest integer values that can be represented by each of the following numeric types:

    a. unsigned byte   b. unsigned word   c. unsigned doubleword
    d. signed byte   e. signed word   f. signed doubleword

30. A 1 bit in position 16 of a binary number has the decimal value of 2^{16}. What is this value in decimal?

31. What is the minimum number of binary bits needed to represent the decimal value 65?

2 Hardware and Software Architecture

2.1   16-BIT INTEL PROCESSOR ARCHITECTURE

Because the Intel processor family includes a number of diverse processors with greatly varying capabilities, we're going to examine a few basic types separately. In this first section, we will look at the Intel 8086/8088, and Intel 80286 processors because they all have a 16-bit architecture. In Section 2.2 we will do the same for the 80386, Intel486, and Pentium processors.

2.1.1   Central Processing Unit

The operation of a CPU can be reduced to three basic steps: *fetch*, *decode*, and *execute*. Each step includes intermediate steps, some of which are listed here:

```
Fetch the next instruction:
        Place it in a holding area called a queue.
        Update the program counter.
Decode the instruction:
        Perform address translation.
        Fetch operands from memory.
Execute the instruction:
        Perform the required calculation.
        Store results in memory or registers.
        Set status flags attached to the CPU.
```

Figure 1 shows a block diagram of a simple, imaginary CPU. The CPU is divided into two general parts: The *arithmetic logic unit* (ALU) and the *control unit* (CU). The former carries out arithmetic, logical, and shifting operations; the latter fetches data and instructions and decodes addresses for the ALU. The CPU's internal clock synchronizes each of the CPU and memory operations.

Figure 1. Simplified CPU Design.

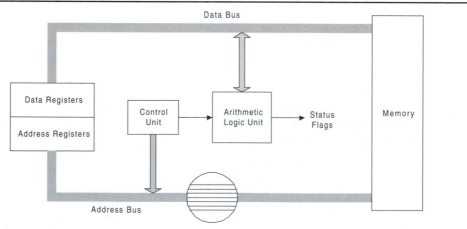

The CPU is attached to the rest of the computer via pins attached to the CPU socket in the motherboard. These pins represent an external data bus, an address bus, and various voltage and control pins that affect the CPU's operation.

Address and Data Buses. The internal data bus is a series of parallel wires that transmit data between the various parts of the CPU. When data must be read from external memory, the control unit calculates its address and places the address on the address bus. The *memory unit* (another processor on the motherboard) reads the address bus, places the requested data on the data bus, and signals to the CPU that the data is ready. The CPU transfers the data from the external data bus into its internal storage areas.

Registers. Within the CPU are high-speed storage areas called *registers*, which are directly linked to the control unit and the arithmetic logic unit. Because register access is much faster than memory access, instructions using only registers execute more quickly than do instructions having memory operands.

Clock. Each of the individual operations that take place within the CPU must be synchronized by an internal clock. The most basic unit of time for machine instructions is called the *machine cycle* or *clock cycle*, and is measured in millions of cycles per second (MHz). The clock inside most Pentium processors runs at 200 to 400MHz (million times per second).

2.1.2   Registers

Registers are 8, 16, or 32-bit high-speed storage locations directly inside the CPU, designed to be accessed at much higher speed than conventional memory (see Figure 2). The CPU has an internal data bus that is generally twice as wide as its external data bus. When a processing loop must be optimized for speed, for example, we would almost always use registers for

Figure 2. Intel 16-bit Registers.

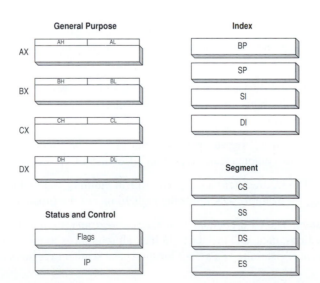

calculations and decision making inside the loop. The 8086, 8088, and 80286 processors have 16-bit registers.

Registers are categorized in this figure as general-purpose, segment, index, status and control just for the purposes of discussion. The category names may vary from one source to another. The Flags register consists of binary bits that either control the operation of the CPU or reflect the outcome of some CPU operation. They are called Overflow, Direction, Interrupt, Trap, Sign, Zero, Auxiliary Carry, Parity, and Carry.

Data Registers. The *general-purpose registers,* also called *data registers,* are used for arithmetic and data movement. Each register can be addressed as either a 16-bit or 8-bit value. For example, the AX register is a 16-bit register; its upper 8 bits are called AH, and its lower 8 bits are called AL. Bit 0 in AL corresponds to bit 0 in AX, and bit 0 in AH corresponds to bit 8 in AX:

Instructions can address either 16-bit data registers as AX, BX, CX, and DX, or 8-bit registers as AH, AL, BH, BL, CH, CL, DH, and DL. When a 16-bit register is modified, so are its corresponding 8-bit registers. Suppose that AX contained all zeros. If we moved 0001001001101111 to AX, for example, AL would immediately equal 01101111. The AH and AL registers would be pictured as follows:

Each general-purpose register has special attributes:

- **AX** (*accumulator*). AX is the *accumulator* register because it is favored by the CPU for arithmetic operations. Other operations are also slightly more efficient when performed using AX.

- **BX** (*base*). The BX register can hold the address of a procedure or variable. Three other registers with this ability are SI, DI, and BP. The BX register can also perform arithmetic and data movement.

- **CX** (*counter*). The CX register acts as a counter for repeating or looping instructions. These instructions automatically repeat and decrement CX.

- **DX** (*data*). The DX register has a special role in multiply and divide operations. When multiplying, for example, DX holds the high 16 bits of the product.

Segment Registers. The CPU contains four *segment registers,* used as base locations for program instructions, data, and the stack. In fact, all references to memory on the IBM-PC involve a segment register used as a base location. The segment registers are as follows:

- **CS** (*code segment*). The CS register holds the base location of all executable instructions (code) in a program.

- **DS** (*data segment*). The DS register is the default base location for variables. The CPU calculates their locations using the segment value in DS.

- **SS** (*stack segment*). The SS register contains the base location of the stack.

- **ES** (*extra segment*). The ES register is an additional base location for memory variables.

Index Registers. Index registers contain the offsets of data and instructions. The term *offset* refers to the distance of a variable, label, or instruction from its base segment. Index registers speed up processing of strings, arrays, and other data structures containing multiple elements. The index registers are BP, SP, SI, and DI:

- **BP** (*base pointer*). The BP register contains an assumed offset from the SS register, as does the stack pointer. The BP register is often used by a subroutine to locate variables that were passed on the stack by a calling program.

- **SP** (*stack pointer*). The SP register contains the offset of the top of the stack. The SP and SS (stack segment) registers combine to form the complete address of the top of the stack.

- **SI** (*source index*). This register takes its name from the string movement instructions, in which the source string is pointed to by the SI register.

- **DI** (*destination index*). The DI register acts as the destination for string movement instructions.

2.1.3   Status and Control Registers

- **IP** (*instruction pointer*). The IP register always contains the offset of the next instruction to be executed within the current code segment. The IP and CS (code segment) registers combine to form the complete address of the next instruction.

- The *Flags* register is a special register with individual bit positions assigned to show the status of the CPU or the results of arithmetic operations. Each relevant bit position is given a name; other positions are undefined. The following diagram shows the 8086/8088 Flags register:

```
                              Bit
                           Position
        ┌──────────────────────────────────────────┐
        │ 15  14  13  12  11  10   9   8   7   6   5   4   3   2   1   0 │
        │  x   x   x   x   O   D   I   T   S   Z   x   A   x   P   x   C │
        └──────────────────────────────────────────┘
              O = Overflow              S = Sign
              D = Direction             Z = Zero
              I = Interrupt             A = Auxiliary Carry
              T = Trap                  P = Parity
              x = undefined             C = Carry
```

Fortunately, you do not have to memorize each flag position. Instead, there are special instructions designed to test and manipulate the flags. A flag or bit is *set* when it equals 1; it is *clear* (or reset) when it equals 0. The CPU sets flags by turning on individual bits in the Flags register. There are two basic types of flags: *control flags* and *status flags.*

2.1.4   Flags

Control Flags. Individual bits can be set in the Flags register by the programmer to control the CPU's operation. These are the *Direction, Interrupt,* and *Trap* flags, abbreviated as DF, IF, and TF, respectively:

- The ***Direction*** flag (DF) affects block data transfer instructions such as MOVS, CMPS, and SCAS. The flag values are 0 = up and 1 = down. They can also be manipulated by the STD and CLD instructions.

- The ***Interrupt*** flag (IF) dictates whether or not system interrupts can occur. Interrupts are signaled by hardware devices such as the keyboard, disk drives, and the system clock timer. A program will sometimes briefly disable interrupts when performing a critical operation that cannot be interrupted. The flag values are 1 = enabled, and 0 = disabled; they are manipulated by the CLI and STI instructions.

- The ***Trap*** flag (TF) determines whether or not the CPU is halted after each instruction. When this flag is set, a debugging program can let a programmer single step (trace) through a program one instruction at a time. The flag values are 1 = on and 0 = off. The flag can be set by the INT 3 instruction.

Status Flags. The Status flags reflect the outcomes of arithmetic and logical operations performed by the CPU. They are the Overflow, Sign, Zero, Auxiliary Carry, Parity, and Carry flags. Their abbreviations are shown immediately after their names:

- The ***Carry*** flag (CF) is set when the result of an *unsigned* arithmetic operation is too large to fit into the destination. For example, if the sum of 200 and 58 were stored in the 8-bit register AL, the result would overflow the register and the Carry flag would equal 1. The flag values are 1 = carry, 0 = no carry.

- The ***Overflow*** flag (OF) is set when the result of a *signed* arithmetic operation is too wide (too many bits) to fit into the destination. For example, if the sum of –128 and –2 were placed in an 8-bit BL register, the Overflow flag would be set. The Overflow flag values are 1 = overflow and 0 = no overflow.

- The ***Sign*** flag (SF) is set when the result of an arithmetic or logical operation generates a negative result. Because a negative number always has a 1 in the highest bit position, the Sign flag is always a copy of the destination's sign bit. The flag values are 1 = negative, 0 = positive.

- The ***Zero*** flag (ZF) is set when the result of an arithmetic or logical operation generates a result of zero. The flag is used primarily by jump and *loop* instructions, to allow branching to a new location in a program based on the comparison of two values. The flag values are 1 = zero, 0 = not zero.

- The *Auxiliary Carry* flag is set when an operation causes a carry from bit 3 to bit 4 (or a borrow from bit 4 to bit 3) of an operand. Along with the Partiy flag, it is less often used than other status flags. The flag values are 1 = carry, and 0 = no carry.

- The *Parity* flag reflects the number of 1 bits in the result of an operation. If there is an even number of bits, the Parity is *even*. If there is an odd number of bits, the Parity is *odd*. This flag is used by the operating system to verify memory integrity and by communications software to verify the correct transmission of data.

2.1.5   Instruction Execution Cycle

A surprising fact is that each machine instruction must be broken down by the CPU into a sequence of individual operations before the instruction can be executed. When the CPU executes an instruction to add 1 to a memory operand, for example, it must calculate the address of the operand, place the address of the operand on the address bus, wait for memory to get the operand, and so on. There are three basic operations carried out inside the CPU: *fetch, decode,* and *execute.* Each step in the instruction cycle takes at least one tick of the system clock, called a *clock cycle:*

- *Fetch:* The control unit fetches the instruction, copying it from memory into the instruction queue, and increments the program counter.

- *Decode:* The control unit determines the type of instruction to be executed. If a memory operand is needed, the control unit initiates a read operation to retrieve the operand. It passes zero or more operands to the arithmetic logic unit (ALU) and sends signals to the ALU that indicate the type of operation to be performed.

- *Execute:* The arithmetic logic unit executes the instruction, returns its output into the destination operand, and updates status flags providing information about the output.

An important feature of today's microprocessors is their division of labor between the arithmetic logic unit and the control unit, allowing them to work in parallel. Rather than wait for the arithmetic logic unit to finish each instruction, the control unit fetches the next instruction from memory and loads it into the instruction queue.

2.1.6   Intel Microprocessor Family

The history of the Intel microprocessor family is rooted in the 8-bit Intel 8080 processor, which was able to access only 64 KBytes of memory.

The Intel 8086 processor (created in 1978) marks the beginning of the modern Intel Architecture family. The primary innovations of the 8086 over earlier processors were that it had 16-bit registers, a 16-bit data bus, and used a segmented memory model that allowed programs to address up to 1MB of RAM. This greater access to memory made it possible to write complex business applications. The IBM-PC, introduced around 1980, contained an Intel 8088 processor, which was identical to the 8086 except that it had an 8-bit data bus and was slightly less expensive to produce. Today, the Intel 8088 is primarily used in low-cost microcontrollers and costs only a few dollars.

The Intel 8087 math co-processor was introduced as a companion to the 8086/8088. It sped up floating-point calculations tremendously, which would otherwise have to be performed by complex software routines.

Binary Code Compatibility. It should be noted that each new processor introduced into the Intel family has always been binary-code compatible with earlier generations. This has made it possible for the same software to run on the newer computers without modification. Newer software eventually appeared, however, that required the features of the more advanced processors.

Intel 80286 Processor. The Intel 80286 processor appeared at the same time as the IBM-PC/ AT computer and quickly set a new standard of speed and power. The 80286 could address up to 16MB of RAM using a 24-bit address and had a clock speed between 12 and 25 MHz. One of the most important features introduced by the 80286 was its ability to run in either *real* mode (like the 8086/8088) or in *protected* mode. The latter provided a way for the operating system to protect programs from each other while running in separate memory segments. DOS runs only in real mode, but operating environments such as Microsoft Windows 3.x and certain DOS extender programs run in protected mode.

Intel 80386 Processor. In 1985, Intel introduced the 80386 processor, with 32-bit registers and a 32-bit external data path. The name *Intel386* was trademarked by Intel, a departure from the 80x86 notation used earlier. The address bus was increased to 32 bits, permitting programs to address up to 4GB of RAM. The cheaper 80386-SX had a 16-bit data bus.

The 80386 supported three modes of operation: *real mode, protected mode,* and *virtual mode*. The latter allows a single CPU to run multiple real-mode programs in separate "virtual machines." In other words, standard DOS applications can run simultaneously, each thinking it has access to a complete 1MB machine.

Using a memory addressing scheme called *virtual memory*, the total memory required by all running programs on an 80386 can exceed the computer's physical memory. The CPU automatically moves currently unused portions of programs to disk if more memory is needed by other programs. It was the 386 processor that helped Microsoft Windows 3.0 to achieve enormous popularity. The Windows operating system allowed the user to run in either protected mode or virtual mode. In particular, virtual mode made it possible to run more than one large program at the same time. This type of operation was not possible in MS-DOS.

Intel486. The Intel486 processor family includes the 486DX, 486DX2, and 486SX. The instruction set microarchitecture was reimplemented using design techniques borrowed from high-speed RISC processors. Specifically, the decoding and execution of up to five instructions could be done in parallel. This permitted many instructions to execute in only one clock cycle. The 486 was also the first Intel processor to integrate the floating-point unit directly into the CPU chip, resulting in greatly improved performance. The 486 has internal 8K high-speed *level-1 cache memory* that holds copies of instructions and data that have been most recently accessed. The cheaper 486SX is identical to the 486DX except that its floating point unit is disabled.

Intel Pentium. According to at least one important benchmark, the original 90 MHz Pentium processor was a 90% improvement in performance over the 486[1]. The Pentium is able to execute more than one instruction per clock cycle because of its *superscalar* design with two instruction pipelines. In other words, two instructions can be decoded and executed at the same time. Dual pipelining is a tried and proven technology, having been used for years in RISC processors used in engineering and graphics workstations. There are several other keys to the Pentium's success:

• It contains separate 8K internal caches for data and code (the 486 had only a single cache).

• It has faster floating-point operations than the Intel 486.

• *Branch prediction logic* allows the Pentium to analyze instructions that are about to be executed. When the instructions contain a conditional branch (in a loop or IF statement, for example), the CPU predicts where the branch is likely to go and loads the instructions at the target address.

• The first Pentium had 3.1 million transistors, in comparison to 1.3 million transistors on the 486.

• It has a 32-bit address bus and a 64-bit internal data path (in comparison to the 32-bit internal data path of the 486).

The Pentium was frequently improved, of course. Originally, its clock speed was 66MHz, but that was soon replaced by speeds ranging currently up to 400MHz.

2.2   32-BIT INTEL PROCESSOR ARCHITECTURE

2.2.1   Improved Execution Cycle

The 80386 was the first processor in the Intel family to include parallel stages in its execution cycle. The six stages and the parts of the processor that carry them out are listed here:

1. *Bus Interface Unit* (BIU): accesses memory and provides input-output.

2. *Code Prefetch Unit:* receives machine instructions from the BIU and inserts them into the instruction prefetch queue.

3. *Instruction Decode Unit:* decodes machine instructions from the prefetch queue and translates them into microcode.

4. *Execution Unit:* executes the microcode instructions produced by the instruction decode unit.

5. *Segment Unit:* translates logical addresses to linear addresses and performs protection checks.

6. *Paging Unit:* translates linear addresses into physical addresses, performs page protection checks, and keeps a list of recently accessed pages.

2.2.2   32-bit Register Set

All Intel processors from the 80386 onward have 32-bit registers (see Figure 3). This means that programs running on these processors can rapidly manipulate 32-bit quantities and can use index registers to point to a 4GB address space. New instructions were added to the CPU instruction set, along with 32-bit operand formats.

Segment registers are still 16 bits, but notice that two new registers, FS and GS, have been added. Notice that the upper halves of the 32-bit registers do not have names. To put a 16-bit value into the upper half of a 32-bit register, you must first put the number in the lower half (such as AX), and then shift the bits leftward into the upper half of the register.

Figure 3. The 32-bit Register Set.

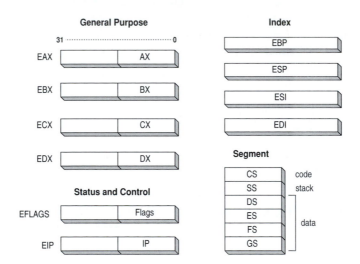

2.3   OPERATING SYSTEM AND MEMORY

2.3.1   History of PC Memory Usage

The Intel 8086 and 8088 processors can access 1,048,576 bytes of memory (1MB) using 20-bit addresses in the range 0 to FFFFF hexadecimal. The memory is divided between RAM and ROM (see Figure 4). RAM starts at location 00000 and extends to address BFFFF. ROM begins at location C0000 and extends to FFFFF.

From the time the IBM-PC was introduced, DOS has allowed only the first 640K of memory to be available for the operating system and user application programs. The remaining memory is used by system hardware such as the video display and hard disk controller, or by the ROM BIOS. One vexing problem was that application programs would often run out of memory. With the introduction of *high-memory manager* programs, the situation improved. Memory-resident software could be moved into unused portions of memory above the 640K

Figure 4. Map of the First Megabyte of PC Memory.

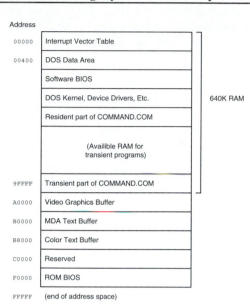

barrier. The result is that application programs have more available memory. These high memory managers were incorporated into later versions of DOS.

Software and hardware manufacturers got together and created a new way to provide more memory for programs. Lotus, Intel, and Microsoft created an expanded Memory standard called LIM that consisted of a memory expansion card and an accompanying driver program called an *expanded memory manager.* Unfortunately, expanded memory was slower than conventional memory, so other solutions were sought.

A second type of memory called *extended memory* became available when 80286-based computers were introduced. A CPU running in *protected mode* (80286 and later processors) can access up to 16MB of conventional RAM.

With the introduction of the 80386 processor and Windows 3.0, programs could address up to 4GB of RAM and could use *virtual memory* to load and run programs that used even more memory than was physically installed in the computer. It became clear, however, that swapping programs from memory to disk while they were running made the programs run very slowly. Currently, most PCs have between 32 and 128MB of RAM so there is enough physical memory to hold all running programs.

2.3.2 Memory Architecture

The lowest 1,024 bytes of memory (addresses 00000 - 003FF) contain a table of 32-bit addresses called *the interrupt vector table*. These addresses, called *interrupt vectors*, are used by the CPU when processing hardware and software interrupts.

Just above the vector table is the *software BIOS,* which includes routines for managing the keyboard, console, printer, and *time of day* clock. BIOS routines are loaded from a hidden system file on a MS-DOS boot disk called **io.sys.** The kernel is a collection of subroutines (called *services*) that are loaded from a file called **msdos.sys.** A description of the BIOS data area is shown in Table 1.

Above the MS-DOS kernel are both file buffers and installable device drivers (loaded from the config.sys) file. The resident part of the MS-DOS command processor is loaded from a file called **command.com.** The command processor interprets commands typed at the MS-DOS prompt, and loads and executes programs stored on disk.

2.3.3 System Startup Procedure

When the computer's operating system is started up (*booted*), the following happens:

Table 1. Map of the BIOS Data Area.

Offset (Segment 0400)	Description
0000 - 0007	Port addresses, COM1 – COM4
0008 – 000F	Port addresses, LPT1 – LPT4
0010 - 0011	Installed hardware list
0012	Initialization flag
0013 – 0014	Memory size, in Kbytes
0015 – 0016	Memory in I/O channel
0017 – 0018	Keyboard status flags
0019	Alternate key entry storage
001A – 001B	Keyboard buffer pointer (head)
001C – 001D	Keyboard buffer pointer (tail)
001E – 003D	Keyboard typeahead buffer
003E – 0048	Diskette data area
0049	Current video mode
004A – 004B	Number of screen columns
004C – 004D	Regen buffer length, in bytes
004E – 004F	Regen buffer starting offset
0050 – 005F	Cursor positions, video pages 1 - 8
0060	Cursor end line
0061	Cursor start line
0062	Currently displayed video page number
0063 - 0064	Active display base address
0065	CRT mode register (MDA, CGA)
0066	Register for CGA
0067 – 006B	Cassette data area
006C – 0070	Timer data area

- The CPU jumps to an initialization program in the ROM BIOS. A program called the **bootstrap loader** loads the boot record from the drive that has been designated as the startup drive. The boot record contains a program that executes as soon as it is loaded. This program in turn loads io.sys and msdos.sys. The last program loaded into memory is the MS-DOS command processor, command.com.

- The **resident** part of COMMAND.COM remains in memory all the time; it issues error messages and has routines to process Ctrl-Break and critical errors. The **initialization** part reads the autoexec.bat file; it is used only while MS-DOS is being loaded. The **transient** part is loaded into high RAM and interprets DOS commands typed at the keyboard. Finally, command.com takes over and acts as an interpreter for commands typed at the MS-DOS prompt.

Next, DOS looks for a file named config.sys. Here, for example, is a config.sys file that loads under Windows:

Line	Statement
1	DOS=HIGH
2	LASTDRIVE=G:
3	DEVICEHIGH /L:1,14016 =MTMCDAI.SYS /D:MTMIDE01
4	DEVICEHIGH /L:1,12048 =SETVER.EXE

- Line 1 indicates that DOS should load itself into the upper memory area., freeing up as much of conventional memory as possible.

- Line 2 indicates the last drive letter of the available disk drives in the system. This system can have drives A,B,C,D,E,F, and G.

- Line 3 loads the driver program for the CD-ROM drive (mtmcdai.sys) so the drive can be accessed from the DOS command line. The DEVICEHIGH statement indicates that the driver should be loaded into the high memory area.

- Line 4 loads the setver.exe program that returns an appropriate MS-DOS version number to application programs.

Autoexec.bat File. After running the commands in config.sys, the operating system loads and executes each command in a file called autoexec.bat, stored in the root directory of the boot disk. The following is a sample:

Line	Statement
1	`@ECHO OFF`
2	`PROMPT $p$g`
3	`SET TEMP=C:\TMP`
4	`SET WINTEMP=C:\TMP`
5	`PATH C:\WINDOWS;C:\WINDOWS\COMMAND`
6	`LH /L:1,36224 MSCDEX.EXE /D:MTMIDE01 /M:10`

- Line 1 turns off the echoing of commands to the screen while this file is executing.

- Line 2 configures the command prompt to show the current directory path followed the greater-than (>) symbol. For example, when in the Windows directory, the prompt appears as C:\WINDOWS>.

- Line 3 identifies a directory that is used to hold temporary files created by application programs while they are running.

- Line 4 identifies a directory that is used to hold temporary files created by the Windows operating system.

- Line 5 shows the operating system where to look for a program or command when the program cannot be found in the current directory. For example, if you are in the root directory of drive C and you type MEM, the operating system looks for a program called **mem.com** or **mem.exe** in the current directory (C:\). If the program is not found there, the operating system next looks in the C:\WINDOWS directory. If the program is still not found there, the C:\WINDOWS\COMMAND directory is searched. Upon finding the program, mem.exe is executed.

- Line 6 loads **mscdex.exe,** the Microsoft CD-ROM extensions program. This program enables the CD-ROM drive to be accessed when the computer is booted to a command prompt.

2.3.4 Video Display

The PC has what is called a *memory-mapped* video display. Rather than having to send each video character out through a hardware port to the video display, the engineers at IBM decided that it would be more efficient to give each screen position a separate memory address. When DOS writes a character to the display, it calls a subroutine in the ROM BIOS, which in turn writes the character directly to a video memory address. The video memory area is special high-speed VRAM (*video RAM*). The amount of VRAM currently varies between 1 and 8MBs, depending on the video resolution and number of simultaneous colors supported by the graphics controller.

In color text mode, the computer's video RAM is located at address B8000. In color graphics mode, the PC maps pixels to address A0000. DOS applications tend to write text and graphics directly to the video display buffer because this method is much faster than using built-in DOS subroutines. Windows applications, on the other hand, do not use direct video memory access because it corrupts the built-in redrawing of the screen by Windows itself.

2.3.5   Serial Communications Ports

The PC allows up to four serial ports to be installed in the computer, and the BIOS memory area (from 0040:0000 to 0040:0007) contains a list of the currently active port addresses. A typical system has two serial ports, so the addresses would be set up as shown in Table 2. In Windows, if you examine the system settings for the COM ports, you will notice that COM1 actually uses port addresses 03F8 through 03FF, COM2 uses addresses 02F8 through 02FF, and so on.

Table 2. Serial Port Configurations.

Serial Port	BIOS Data Location	Contents (Port I/O Addresses)
COM1	0040:0000	03F8
COM2	0040:0002	02F8
COM3	0040:0004	0000
COM4	0040:0006	0000

2.3.6   Read-Only Memory (ROM)

The *ROM BIOS* is the fundamental building block of the computer's operating system. It contains system diagnostic and configuration software, as well as low-level input-output subroutines used by DOS. The BIOS is encoded in a microprocessor chip on the system board, supplied by the manufacturer. Many systems follow a standardized BIOS specification, created by companies such as Phoenix or AMI (Award BIOS). Locations C0000h to FFFFFh are reserved for specialized ROM uses, including the hard disk controller.

Occasionally, the BIOS chip must be replaced in order to fix bugs and accommodate changes in other system hardware. Programs coded in ROM are called *firmware* because they are software stored in a hardware medium. The BIOS resides at the highest address locations that can be reached by the 8086/8088 processor (F0000 - FFFFF).

2.3.7   Absolute Address Calculation

An *address* is a number that refers to an 8-bit memory location. In any computer, logical addresses can be numbered consecutively, starting at 0, going up to the highest location in memory. Each type of computer varies, however, on how logical addresses are translated to physical address. When dealing with the Intel processor, we can interpret addresses in either of the following hexadecimal formats:

• A 32-bit *segment-offset* address, which combines a base location (segment) with an offset to represent a logical location. An example is 08F1:0100.

• A 20-bit *absolute* address, which refers to a physical memory location. An example is 09010.

In Real mode, the CPU can address up to 1,048,576 bytes of memory. The real problem is, address registers are only 16 bits wide and can only hold a maximum value of 65,535. To solve this apparent dilemma, the CPU automatically combines the segment and offset values to create an absolute address. To illustrate, let us start with a hypothetical segment-offset address of 08F1:0100 hexadecimal. The CPU converts this to a 20-bit absolute address by adding the segment and offset values. The segment has four implied zero bits appended to it. Therefore, a segment address of 08F1 actually represents an absolute address of 08F10:

```
0   8   F   1   (0)
0000 1000 1111 0001 0000 <-- 4 implied bits
```

To combine the segment and offset values into an absolute address, the CPU adds the offset to the modified segment value, yielding the 20-bit absolute address:

```
Segment value:           0 8 F 1 (0)
Add the offset:            0 1 0 0
Absolute address:        0 9 0 1 0
```

You might wonder why such a complicated method of addressing is used. Programmers using the earlier 8-bit microcomputers, for example, dealt only with a 16-bit absolute addresses. There are advantages to the segment-offset addressing method:

• First, a program can be loaded into memory at any segment address without having to recalculate the individual addresses of its variables. Each variable's location is simply a 16-bit offset value from the beginning of the program's data area. Because other programs may have already been loaded into memory, it is impossible to know in advance the segment address a program will have, so we say the program is *segment relocatable*.

• Second, a program can access large data structures by gradually modifying the segment portion of the data's address to point to new blocks of memory.

2.4 COMPONENTS OF A MICROCOMPUTER

This chapter introduces you to the architecture of PC-compatible computers from several points of view. First, the hardware (physical parts of the computer) can be viewed on the *macro* level, looking at peripherals. Then we can look at the internal details of the Intel processor, called the *central processing unit* (CPU). Finally, we look at the software architecture, which is the way the memory is organized, and how the operating system interacts with the hardware.

2.4.1 Internal Components

Motherboard. The heart of any microcomptuer is its motherboard. This is a flat board onto which are placed the computer's CPU, supporting processors, main memory, input-output connectors, power supply connectors, and expansion slots. The various components are connected to each other by a *bus*, a set of wires etched directly on the motherboard. Literally dozens of motherboards are available on the PC market that vary in expansion capabilities and speed, but they have a number of elements in common. Motherboards have some or all of the following types of connectors:

- Primary CPU socket: Different sizes, depending on the type of processor.

- Coprocessor socket: If the primary CPU does not support floating-point operations, a separate floating-point coprocessor can be added.

- External cache memory slot: For high-speed cache memory that is used by the CPU to reduce its access to slower conventional RAM.

- Slots to add main memory: Called SIMMs or DIMMs, the memory chips are on small boards that plug into available memory slots.

- ROM BIOS socket: The ROM BIOS can be upgraded as the need arises by replacing one or more chips plugged into a socket on the motherboard.

- IDE cable connectors: For internal fixed disk and CD-ROM drives.

- Sound synthesizer.

- Parallel, serial, video, keyboard, joystick, and mouse connectors.

- Network adapter.

2.4.2 Motherboard Designs

- A Slot 1 motherboard is Intel's motherboard for the Pentium II processor with its SEC (*single edge connector*) module.

- Socket 8: Intel's motherboard connector for the Pentium Pro.

- Socket 7: The industry-standard design originated by Intel that can be used for any standard Pentium 3.3-volt processor.

- Socket 4: Used only for the original 5-volt Pentium. Sockets prior to the Socket 4 were less well defined and were used on Intel486-style motherboards.

Integrated Motherboards. Some motherboard manufacturers, in order to save costs, have integrated most operations that used to be performed by external expansion boards onto a single mothereboard. For example, the Intel NX-440LX motherboard integrates nearly all video, disk, and other functions via a chip set called the 440LX AGPset. There are no expansion slots on the motherboard; instead, a single slot holds a manufacturer-designed *riser* board, which in turn contains three or four expansion slots.

Example: ATX Motherboard Specification. One of the most popular motherboards for mass-market computers is the ATX motherboard, based on the Intel ATX specification. This motherboard supports the Pentium II processor and the 440LX AGP chip set. It uses an acceleracted graphics port (AGP) for better video performance. Several variations on this motherboard are marketed by Intel:

*   The AL440LX is designed for OEMs that market custom Pentium II processor-based systems.

*   The DK440LX supports dual Pentium II processors and other advanced features for high-end workstations.

*   The LM440LX is a small NLX compliant form-factor motherboard for desktop computers.

*   The NX440LX is designed for low-profile desktop PCs.

2.4.3   Bus Architecture

The original IBM-PC used an 8-bit bus to transfer data between the computer's processor and other components. It could transfer about one million bits per second, which was adequate for the 8088 processor. As the Intel micrprocessors became more powerful, the bus architectures had to keep up.

The **PC AT** bus, introduced by IBM along with the Intel 80286 processor, supported 16-bit data transfer and 24-bit addressing. As processor speeds increased, the bus speed increased to 8 MHz.

The **ISA** bus (*Industry Standard Architecture*) bus was a standardization by a consortium of PC manufacturers of the PC AT bus. It set the bus speed at 8 MHz, for example. The ISA bus is still used today in computers having the Intel486 processor. Also, ISA-compatible slots are included in virtually every Pentium system sold today.

The **EISA** (*Extended Industry Standard Architecture*) bus, developed by Intel and Compaq, supported 32-bit data transfer and a method of sending data at high speeds called *burst* mode. The bus was expensive and its benefit was primarily for file servers, so it is little used today.

The **MCA** (*IBM Microchannel*) bus was a proprietary bus developed by IBM in 1987 to give it an edge over PC clone makers. Any expansion card used with this bus had to be licensed by IBM. Many significant improvements in bus design appeared on this bus, including an integrated video controller, independent transfer of data by expansion cards, sharing of interrupt levels by different devices, and self-configuring hardware. But it was not as fast as the EISA bus, and not compatible with existing ISA expansion cards.

The **VESA** (*Video Electronics Standards Association*) local bus was designed to complement graphics-intense environments such as Microsoft Windows. Whereas the ISA bus forced data written to the screen to be transferred over a 16-bit bus, the VESA bus design put the graphics processor on the motherboard where it could be rapidly accessed by the CPU. A few VESA slots are often included in 486 systems today for high-speed graphics cards using a 32-bit or 64-bit data path.

The **PCI** (*Peripheral Component Interconnect*) bus was developed in 1992 by Intel, primarily to provide a convenient upgrade path for increasingly fast Pentium processors. It is still the dominant bus in today's Pentium systems. The PCI specification supports both 32-bit and 64-bit motherboards. The bus can have a clock speed between 25 MHz and 100 MHz, with data transfer speeds currently at about 500MBs per second. The PCI motherboard provides a connecting bridge between the CPU's local 64-bit bus and the system's external bus. Most systems using the PCI bus also have several 16-bit ISA slots.

2.4.4 Video Adapter

The video adapter controls the display of text and graphics on IBM-compatibles. It has two components: the video controller and video display memory. The video adapter may be a separate board plugged into an expansion slot, or it may be integrated on the motherboard.

All graphics and text displayed on the monitor must be written into Video display RAM, where it is then sent to the monitor by the video controller. The video controller is itself a microprocessor, relieving the primary CPU of the job of controlling video hardware. Most video controllers use an expensive type of high-speed memory called VRAM. Video controller boards commonly have 4MBs of VRAM and are optimized for manipulating two- and three-dimensional graphics images. Most video adapters sold today support at least 256 simultaneous colors, with a resolution of 1024 horizontal pixels by 768 vertical pixels. These values, of course, are improving constantly.

Video Monitor. Video monitors use a technique called *raster scanning* to display images. A beam of electrons illuminates phosphorus dots on the screen called *pixels*. Starting at the top of the screen, the gun fires electrons from the left side to the right in a horizontal row, briefly turns off, and returns to the left side of the screen to begin a new row. *Horizontal retrace* refers to the time period when the gun is off between rows. When the last row is drawn, the gun turns off (called the *vertical retrace*) and moves to the upper left corner of the screen to start all over. An *interlaced monitor* scans every other line until it reaches the bottom of the screen. When it returns to the top, it then scans the lines that were skipped. A *non-interlaced* monitor does not skip any lines and predictably has less of a flicker than an interlaced one.

The clarity of a video display is controlled by several factors. A monitor's *dot pitch* refers to the distance between adjacent pixels. Today, a typical 17-inch video display has a dot pitch of about .26 millimeters. Also important are the horizontal and vertical frequency, that measure the speeds at which horizontal lines are drawn and the time it takes to draw all lines on the screen.

The video resolution is set by software, and is limited by the capacity of the video graphics adapter and amount of video memory. The resolution is expressed as the number of horizontal pixels followed by the number of vertical pixels. The following are typical alternatives:

640 X 480   (standard VGA)
800 X 600   (super VGA)
1024 X 768   (extended VGA)
1152 X 864
1280 X 1024

The number of simultaneous colors supported by a graphics adapter is generally between 256 and 16 million colors.

2.4.5   Memory (RAM)

Three basic types of memory are used in PCs: dynamic RAM, static RAM, and video RAM. *Dynamic RAM* must be refreshed within less than a millisecond or it loses its contents. *Static RAM* keeps its value without having to be constantly refreshed. Video RAM is used exclusively for storing data that appears on a video display. CMOS RAM stores system setup information.

Most of the memory in a PC is dynamic RAM because it is the least expensive. Some systems use ECC memory (error checking and correcting), which is memory that is able to detect multiple-bit errors and correct single-bit errors.

Dynamic RAM. Main memory, or *RAM*, is where programs and data are kept when a program is running. In general, this memory consists of dynamic RAM chips. Most PCs today have between 16 Mbytes and 128 Mbytes of dynamic RAM. Several types of dynamic RAM are available at the current time:

- **FPM RAM**, or *fast page mode RAM*, is the memory first used on early PCs. It originally was rather slow—120ns for a read/write operation. This has been trimmed to 60ns, twice the speed of the original. FPM memory operates asynchronously to the memory bus, which means that the two are not synchronized by a clock. FPM memory can only match the speed of a 30 MHz data bus, which is less than half the speed of a 66 MHz Pentium bus.

- **EDO RAM** (*enhanced data-out RAM*). EDO RAM is a faster variety of FPM RAM. When the CPU accesses memory at a certain address, EDO RAM remembers the address and provides access to subsequent memory locations as much as 40 percent faster than fast page mode RAM. Its maximum bus speed is 66 MHz, so it can only keep up with Pentium motherboards operating at 66 MHz or less.

- **BEDO RAM** (*burst enhanced data-out RAM*). When a memory address is accessed by the CPU, BEDO RAM can transmit three additional data elements in a single high-speed burst. This enables large data blocks to be sent more quickly to the CPU. At the time of this writing, BEDO RAM cannot overcome the 66-MHz bus limitation experienced by EDO RAM.

- **SDRAM** (*synchronous dynamic RAM*). SDRAM operates in a synchronized manner with the sytem clock and memory bus. Because it can handle faster bus speeds (currently up to 100 MHz) and it allows two pages of memory to be accessed at the same time, SDRAM is gradually replacing both EDO and FPM RAM on Pentium systems.

Static RAM. Static RAM is the type of RAM chip used primarily for special high-speed memory called *Level-2 cache* memory. This Level-2 cache greatly improves system performance. Two types of static RAM are used at the current time, SRAM and PBSRAM:

- **SRAM** (*static RAM*). SRAM is high-speed memory that does not require a refresh operation. It is much faster and more expensive than dynamic RAM, with speeds between 8 and 12 ns. It can be either synchonous (faster) or asynchronous (slower).

- **PBSRAM** (*pipeline burst SRAM*). PBSRAM is static RAM that has been enhanced by the use of burst technology. Multiple requests for memory can be collected together and send as a single *pipelined* request. It works with bus speeds of 75 MHz or higher, so it is ideal for high-end systems.

CMOS RAM. A small amount of CMOS RAM is used on the motherboard of a PC to store system setup information. The CMOS memory is refreshed by a small battery, so its data is retained even when the computer's power is turned off.

Connecting Memory to the Motherboard. Memory is usually placed on small expansion cards that are plugged into slots in the motherboard. The two primary types at present are called SIMM and DIMM:

- **SIMM** (*small inline memory module*). Somewhat obsolete packaging of 72-pin DRAM. Uses a 32-bit data path.

- **DIMM** (*dual inline memory module*). 168 pins, usually used in Socket 7 and Slot 1 motherboards. Uses a 64-bit data path and has replaced SIMM.

Because the CPU is so much faster than the computer's main memory, designers came up with a way to avoid a performance bottleneck when the CPU fetches data from memory. They do this by using high speed static RAM called *cache memory. Level-1 cache* is contained within the Pentium processor. *Level-2 cache* is high-speed SRAM on the motherboard that is directly attached to the microprocessor bus. A typical cache size is 512K. The cache usually contains copies of the data and code that were most recently used by the CPU. In a repeated loop, for example, the CPU is able to use the data and code in cache memory without having to waste time fetching them from slow main memory.

2.4.6 Video RAM

There are currently three types of video RAM: VRAM, WRAM, and SGRAM:

- **VRAM** (*video RAM*). Most video adapters today have either 4 or 8MBs of VRAM, which can be on a separate board or on the motherboard. It is optimized for storing color pixels. Whereas DRAM has only one access port, VRAM is dual-ported, allowing one port to continuously refresh the display while the other port writes data to the display. This results in lower eye strain than possible with DRAM.

- **WRAM** (*Windows RAM*). Similar to VRAM, WRAM is optimized for video graphics displays such as that used by Microsoft Windows. It generally outperforms VRAM, allowing the screen to be refreshed more quickly.

- **SGRAM** (*synchronous graphics RAM*). SGRAM is a single-ported RAM used on video accelerator cards. It's advantage is that two video memory pages can be opened at the same time. It is able to clear memory very quickly and is well suited to 3D applications.

2.4.7   Secondary Storage Devices

A typical PC contains a variety of secondary storage devices:

- One or more fixed disks, usually containing from 4 to 10GB of online storage.

- 1.44MB diskette drive.

- 600MB CD-ROM drive.

- A removable disk with a capacity of between 100MB and 4GB. These disks are used for both online storage and backup storage.

- A magnetic tape drive that stores data sequentially on cartridges that usually hold 100MB to 20GB of data. Tape drives can only access data sequentially, so they are used only for backing up other disks.

A fixed disk drive is also identified by its type of controller hardware. There are several types:

- **IDE** (*Intelligent Drive Electronics*): The controller is either built into the motherboard's chipset or attached to an adapter card. The EIDE (*enhanced IDE*) controller is a newer, faster version that supports data transfer speeds up to 33MBs/sec.

- **EIDE** (*Enhanced IDE*): Also called the ATA-2 specification, this interface supports more than two drives, with a big improvement in performance over the standard IDE. Drives can be up to 8GB in size, CD-ROM drives can be attached, and it supports DMA transfers

- **SCSI** controller**:** A SCSI (*Small Computer System Interface*)controller, supplied on an adapter card that can control multiple devices at the same time, typically disk drives, printers, and scanners. Specifications change constantly, but some of those currently used are SCSI-2 and SCSI-3.

Expansion Cards. Expansion cards plug into the expansion slots located either on the motherboard, or on a special *riser* board that allows the cards to use less space in the computer case. Typical uses for expansion cards are:

- Video adapter

- Sound synthesizer

- SCSI controller

- Tape drive controller

- Video capture board

- Additional serial, parallel, and joystick ports

Full-size and half-size tower systems typically contain between five and eight expansion slots and drive bays to make it easy to add new devices to the system. Desktop computers often have far fewer slots, because most of these functions are integrated directly into the motherboard in a set of processors called a *chipset*. A chipset dramatically reduces the cost of a computer and allows the computer case to be smaller.

Keyboard. The keyboard attaches to the motherboard, using one of two types of ports: one is the PS/2 keyboard port; the other is the PC/AT keyboard port, using a slightly larger plug. The keyboard contains an 8-bit Intel 8048 microcontroller chip that scans the keyboard, detects the pressing and releasing of keys, and sends numeric keycodes to another 8-bit microcontroller (the Intel 8042) on the motherboard. A clock signal generated by the keyboard controller synchronizes the serial transmission of data between the keyboard and the computer. By *serial*, we mean that binary bits are sent one at a time.

Mouse. Three types of mouse connections are currently available. The most common is the PS/2 mouse, connected directly to the motherboard in the same way as the keyboard. The mouse can also be connected to a serial port (COM1 or COM2) or to an adapter card in one of the expansion slots. The latter is called a *bus mouse*.

Support Processors. Most motherboards have a chip set consisting of two or three powerful microprocessors that include the following controllers:

- The Intel 8237 Direct Memory Access (DMA) controller transfers data between external devices and RAM, without requiring any work by the CPU.

- The Intel 8259A Interrupt Controller handles requests from the hardware to interrupt the CPU.

- The 8254 Timer Counter handles the system clock that ticks 18.2 times per second, the memory refresh timer, and the time of day clock.

- Microprocessor local bus to PCI bridge.

- System memory controller and cache controller.

- PCI bus to ISA bus bridge.

- Intel 8042 keyboard and mouse microcontroller.

ROM BIOS. Read-only memory (ROM) is memory that has had programs and data burned into it that cannot be erased or modfied. The ROM BIOS is the *firmware* (hardware with embedded programs) portion of the PC's operating system. When the computer is first turned on, the ROM BIOS contains startup code that loads the rest of the operating system from the boot disk. Most systems copy the BIOS into faster dynamic memory during the boot-up sequence.

An important feature of the ROM BIOS is its ability to detect the presence of new hardware in the computer system, and to reconfigure the operating system according to information transmitted by the devices. This is commonly referred to as *plug and play* capability.

Expansion Slots. There are anywhere from two to 10 edge connectors facing upward, into which you can plug expansion cards. Sample cards can include disk drive controllers, tape drive controllers, video controllers, network connections, input-output ports, modems, memory expansion cards, mouse controllers, FAX boards, and sound synthesizers. The possibilities are endless.

Power Supply. This unglamorous-looking but essential metal box converts the 110 alternating current from a wall outlet to direct current, which is what a computer needs. The computer voltages are 12 volts, 5 volts, and in recent Pentium processors, 3.3 volts. The capacity of a power supply is rated in terms of the number of *watts*, usually in the range of 200 to 300.

Parallel Port. Most printers connect to a computer via a *parallel port*. By "parallel" we mean that 8 data bits can travel simultaneously from the computer to the printer. Data can be transferred very quickly over short distances, usually no more than 10 feet. DOS supports up to 3 parallel ports, called LPT1, LPT2, and LPT3. Parallel ports can be *bidirectional*, allowing the computer to receive status information from a printer, for example.

Serial Port. Also called an *RS-232 interface*, a serial port can be used to connect a mouse, a modem, or any other serial device to the computer system. The chip that controls the serial ports is the 16550 UART (Universal Asynchronous Receiver Transmitter), which is located either on the motherboard or on an adapter card.

With this type of port, binary bits are sent one at a time, resulting in slower speeds than the parallel port, but with the ability to send over larger distances. DOS supports up to two serial ports, called COM1 and COM2. There are two types of serial connectors, one with 9 pins, and the other with 25 that is over double the size.

2.5   REVIEW QUESTIONS

1.   What exact type of video display is attached to the computer you use? How many horizontal and vertical pixels does it have? How much RAM? How many maximum simultaneous colors does it support?

2.   Why is the protected mode of the 80286/80386/80486 processors so useful? Think of at least two types of application programs that would benefit.

3.   Why do you think DOS does not support protected-mode programming?

4.   How does expanded memory help to alleviate some memory problems faced by large application programs?

5.   What is so useful about the XMS standard for older computers?

6.   Why does memory access take more machine cycles than register access?

7.   Name the four general-purpose data registers.

8.   Which of the general registers is called a "base register" because it may hold the address of a procedure or variable?"

9.   What is the name of the lower half of the CX register? How many bits can it hold?

10. Name the four segment registers and explain how each is used.

11. When the AH register is modified, why is AX also modified?

12. What special purpose does the CX register serve?

13. Which 16-bit register holds the high word of the product in a multiplication operation?

14. Which register acts as the base location for all executable instructions?

15. Which register acts as the base location for the stack?

16. Besides the stack pointer (SP), which other register points to variables passed on the stack by a calling program?

17. Name two index registers.

18. Which three flags are called *control flags?*

19. The status flags include the Auxiliary Carry, Parity, Carry, Overflow, and which two other flags?

20. Which flag is set when the result of an unsigned arithmetic operation is too wide to fit into the destination?

21. Which flag is set when an arithmetic or logical operation generates a negative result?

22. Which flag reflects the number of 1 bits in the result of an operation?

23. Assuming that your PC has 640K of DOS memory, what is the highest user location in which you can store a program?

24. What occupies the lowest 1,024 bytes of memory?

25. Name two examples of system data stored in the DOS and BIOS data areas.

26. If a character is written directly to the monochrome display buffer, will it also appear on the color display?

27. What is the name of the memory area containing low-level subroutines used by DOS for input-output?

28. What is name of the base location of the stack?

29. Which register holds the offset of the last value pushed on the stack?

30. The two ways of describing an address on the IBM-PC are segment-offset and
     _____.

31. True or false: Once a program has been assembled into machine language, it can be loaded into memory only at a predefined segment address coded within the program.

32. Which two registers combine to form the address of the next instruction that will be executed?

33. What does the IBMBIO.COM program do?

34. When is an AUTOEXEC.BAT file executed?

35. Convert the the following segment-offset addresses to absolute addresses:

a. 0950:0100

b. 08F1:0200

36. Assemble the following program using Debug. Use the commands shown in Appendix B to run and test the program. What are the final values in the AX and BX registers?

```
A 100
mov   ax,1234
mov   bl,al
mov   bh,ah
add   bx,03C6
```

37. Assemble the following program using Debug. What are the final values in the AX and BX registers?

```
A 100
mov   ax,6BFF
mov   [250],ax
mov   bx,[250]
inc   bx
```

2.6   PROGRAMMING EXERCISES

Use Debug for each of the following exercises. If a hardcopy printout is needed, press the Shift-PrtSc keys to take a screen snapshot. You may also wish to prepare a Debug script file, which will allow you to more easily edit the Debug commands. See Appendix B for a complete discussion of Debug commands.

1. Testing Registers

Assemble a program that moves immediate values (constants) to each of the registers. Find out which registers cannot be modified and suggest reasons why not.

2. Display the ROM BIOS Date

Use Debug to display the version date of your computer's ROM BIOS, located at FFFF:0005. (Don't be surprised if the date seems old—the version date is not always changed by computer makers.)

3. Carry Flag

Using only the ADD and SUB instructions, assemble a short program that sets the Carry flag using both unsigned addition and unsigned subtraction.

4. ROM BIOS Area

The ROM BIOS area begins at absolute address F0000; to view this, set your DS register to F000, and use the D (dump) command to look at memory at offsets 0-FF. You should be able to find the name of the BIOS manufacturer and the BIOS version number.

5.   *Dumping Memory Variables*

Use the E (Enter) command in Debug to initialize the byte at location 200 with the value 36h. Then assemble a short program that moves the byte at location 200 to the DL register. Next, move the contents of DL to memory location 201. When you are finished, use the D (Dump) command to look at locations 200 and 201, and verify that both locations contain 36h.

6.   *Overflow Flag*

Assemble and run a program that tests the Overflow flag. This flag is set when an arithmetic operation produces a signed overflow. For example, use 8-bit registers and add +1 to +127; or subtract 2 from −128. What if these values were unsigned—would an overflow have happened?

Include an ADD or SUB instruction that produces unsigned overflow, but not a signed overflow; in other words, CF = 1, and OF = 0. In Debug, these flags will display as "CY NV."

7.   *Resetting the Instruction Pointer*

The R (Register) command in Debug lets you modify registers and flags. For example, you can modify AX by typing the following:

```
R AX
```

Debug will prompt you for the new value to give the register. Assemble the following program and trace it to the last instruction. Use the R command to set the instruction pointer back to location 100 and trace the program again. The program is:

```
mov   ax,2000
mov   si,ax
mov   bx,si
mov   dx,bx
int   20
```

8.   *Evaluating the Flags*

Use Debug to assemble and trace the following program. Write down the contents of the Zero, Carry, and Sign flags after tracing each instruction. Write a short note next to each line explaining why any of the flags changed:

```
mov   al,FF
inc   al
sub   al,2
mov   dl,al
add   dx,2
int   20
```

9.   *Video Buffer Display*

Using Debug, dump (or display) your computer's video buffer in text mode. If you have a color display, the address to dump is B800:0. Use the D (Dump) command to see if you can identify characters that had just appeared on the video display. (You may have to repeat the D command several times to see any meaningful text.) Notice that in the following sample every other byte contains the number 7. This is an attribute byte that is stored along with each character:

```
B800:0260  20 07 20 07 20 07 20 07-20 07 20 07 20 07 20 07    . . . . . . . .
B800:0270  20 07 20 07 20 07 20 07-20 07 20 07 20 07 20 07    . . . . . . .
B800:0280  20 07 56 07 6F 07 6C 07-75 07 6D 07 65 07 20 07    .V.o.l.u.m.e.
B800:0290  69 07 6E 07 20 07 64 07-72 07 69 07 76 07 65 07    i.n. .d.r.i.v.e.
B800:02A0  20 07 43 07 20 07 68 07-61 07 73 07 20 07 6E 07    .C. .h.a.s. .n.
B800:02B0  6F 07 20 07 6C 07 61 07-62 07 65 07 6C 07 20 07    o. .l.a.b.e.l. .
B800:02C0  20 07 20 07 20 07 20 07-20 07 20 07 20 07 20 07    . . . . . . . .
B800:02D0  20 07 20 07 20 07 20 07-20 07 20 07 20 07 20 07    . . . . . . . .
B800:02E0  20 07 20 07 20 07 20 07-20 07 20 07 20 07 20 07    . . . . . . . .
B800:02F0  20 07 20 07 20 07 20 07-20 07 20 07 20 07 20 07    . . . . . . . .
B800:0300  20 07 20 07 20 07 20 07-20 07 20 07 20 07 20 07    . . . . . . . .
B800:0310  20 07 20 07 20 07 20 07-20 07 20 07 20 07 20 07    . . . . . . .
B800:0320  20 07 44 07 69 07 72 07-65 07 63 07 74 07 6F 07    .D.i.r.e.c.t.o.
B800:0330  72 07 79 07 20 07 6F 07-66 07 20 07 20 07 43 07    r.y. .o.f. . .C.
B800:0340  3A 07 5C 07 41 07 53 07-4D 07 5C 07 43 07 48 07    :.\.A.S.M.\.C.H.
B800:0350  32 07 20 07 20 07 20 07-20 07 20 07 20 07 20 07    2. . . . . . . .
```

10. *Filling the Video Buffer*

Use the F (Fill) command in Debug to fill the video buffer with the value 702A. Assuming that you have a color video display, the command is:

```
F B800:0 1000 2A,70
```

Provide a short explanation of why the video display looks as it does.

11. *Stack Manipulation*

Assemble a short program using Debug that performs the following tasks in order:

a. Load the data registers with the following values:
     AX = 0102, BX = 0304 , CX = 0506, DX = 0708.

b. Push each register on the stack, in the following order:
     AX, BX, CX, DX.

c. Pop each register from the stack in the following order:
     AX, BX, CX, DX.

After you have traced each instruction up through step (b), examine the stack using the D (*Dump*) command. Print a copy of the stack, using the Shift-PrtSc keys. (Remember that the stack contents always begin from the current stack pointer position.)

Next, trace the program through step (c). After the last POP instruction, explain why the register values (AX, BX, CX, and DX) have changed. Use the Shift-PrtSc keys to print out a dump of the registers. Or, if your program is running in an MS-DOS window, click on the Outline Selection tool on the toolbar and copy the register values to the Windows Clipboard.

12. Add 8-bit Values

Using Debug, assemble a program with the following list of numbers at offset 200:

```
10, 20, 30
```

At offset 100h, assemble statements that calculate the sum of the list and place it in the DL register. Run and trace the program.

13. Add 16-Bit Values

Create a program that adds three 16-bit values and stores the sum in memory (at location 0206). Use the following data declaration in Debug:

```
A 200
dw 0102,0304,0506,0
```

14. Machine Bytes

Use Debug to assemble the following program. Write down the machine language bytes displayed by the U (*unassemble*) command:

```
mov   ax,20
mov   bx,10
add   ax,bx
int   20
```

Then use the DB directive to create an array containing the same machine language bytes at offset 200. Finally, use Debug to execute the machine bytes at offset 200 with the following command:

```
G = 200
```

This should help you to see that a program can be thought of as a collection of machine language bytes.

15. Signed Numbers

Using Debug, assemble a program containing the following statements:

```
mov   ax,7FFF
```

```
inc  ax
mov  bx,8000
dec  bx
int  20
```

Before runing the program, write down what you think AX and BX will contain at the end of the program. Trace the program one instruction at a time, and dump the trace to a file for later printing. On the printout, circle the registers and flags that have changed after each instruction. Provide an explanation of how and why the Carry and Overflow flags are affected.

End Notes

[1] *Pentium Power,* by Michael Feibus and Michael Slater. *PC Magazine*, April 27, 1993.

[2] *NX440LX Motherboard Technical Product Specification*, August 1997, Intel Corp., document #674633-001. Available online at www.intel.com.

3 Assembly Language Fundamentals

From this point on in the book we will use the Microsoft assembler (called *MASM*) and Turbo assembler (called *TASM*). Although many examples in this chapter could be assembled and tested using Debug, it has limitations that make programming awkward. For example, Debug does not let you create symbolic names, or insert and delete individual source code lines. If you need to review the commands for assembling, linking, and debugging programs, refer to Section 3.3 for the specific commands applying to various assemblers.

3.1   BASIC ELEMENTS OF ASSEMBLY LANGUAGE

In this section, we elaborate on the basic elements of Intel assembly language. Compared to other computer languages, assembly language has a very simple syntax. Assembly language statements are made up of constants, literals, names, mnemonics, operands, and comments.

3.1.1   Constants and Expressions

Numeric Literal. A numeric literal is a combination of digits and other optional parts: a sign, a decimal point, and an exponent. Here are some examples:

```
5
5.5
-5.5
26.E+05
```

Integer constants can end with a radix symbol that identifies the numeric base. The bases are: h = hexadecimal, q (or o) = octal, d = decimal, b = binary. If no radix is specified, decimal is the default. Uppercase/lowercase differences are ignored. Here are examples:

```
26          decimal
1Ah         hexadecimal
1101b       binary
36q         octal
2BH         hexadecimal
42Q         octal
36D         decimal
47d         decimal
0F6h        hexadecimal
```

When a hexadecimal constant begins with a letter, it must contain a leading zero. Although the radix can be uppercase, we recommend that lowercase be used consistently for a more uniform appearance.

A *constant expression* consists of combinations of numeric literals, operators, and defined symbolic constants. The expression value must be able to be determined at assembly time, and its value cannot change at runtime. Here are some examples of expressions involving only numeric literals:

```
5
26.5
4 * 20
-3 * 4 / 6
-2.301E+04
```

A *symbolic constant* is created by assigning a constant expression to a name. For example,

```
rows = 5
columns = 10
tablePos = rows * columns
```

Although these declarations look like runtime statements written in a high-level language, it is important to realize that they can *only* be evaluated at assembly time.

Character or String Constant. A constant may also represent a string of characters enclosed in either single or double quotation marks. Embedded quotes are permitted, as the following examples show:

```
'ABC'
'X'
"This is a test"
'4096'
"This isn't a test"
'Say "hello" to Bill.'
```

Notice that the string constant containing "4096" is four bytes long, each containing the ASCII code for a single character.

3.1.2   Statements

An assembly language *statement* consists of a name, an instruction mnemonic, operands, and a comment. Statements generally fall into two classes, instructions and directives. *Instructions* are executable statements, and *directives* are statements that provide information to tell the assembler how to generate executable code. The general format of a statement is:

```
[name] [mnemonic] [operands] [;comment]
```

Statements are free-form, meaning that they can be written in any column with any number of spaces between each operand. Blank lines are permitted between statements. A statement must be written on a single line and cannot pass column 128. You can continue a line onto the next line, if the last character in the first line is \ (*backslash*):

```
longArrayDefinition dw 1000h, 1020h, 1030h  \
        1040h, 1050h, 1060h, 1070h, 1080h
```

An *instruction* is a statement that is executed by the processor at runtime. Instructions fall into general types: transfer of control, data transfer, arithmetic, logical, and input/output. Instructions are translated directly into machine code by the assembler. Here are examples of instructions, shown by category:

```
call  MySub      ; transfer of control
mov   ax,5       ; data transfer
add   ax,20      ; arithmetic
jz    next1      ; logical (jump if Zero flag was set)
in    al,20      ; input/output (reads from hardware port)
```

A *directive* is a statement that affects either the program listing or the way machine code is generated. For example, the **db** directive tells the assembler to create storage for a byte variable named **count** and initialize it to 50:

```
count  db   50
```

The following .**stack** directive tells the assembler to reserve 4096 bytes of stack space:

```
.stack 4096
```

3.1.3   Names

A *name* identifies a label, variable, symbol, or keyword. It may contain any of the following characters:

Character	Description
A . . . Z, a . . . z	Letters
0 . . . 9	Digits
?	Question mark
_	Underscore
@	@ Sign
$	Dollar sign

Names have the following restrictions:

• A maximum of 247 characters (in MASM).

• There is no distinction between uppercase and lowercase letters.

• The first character can be a letter, '@', '_', or '$'. Subsequent characters can be the same, or they can also be decimal digits. Avoid using '@' as the first character, because many predefined symbol names start with it.

• A programmer-chosen name cannot be the same as an assembler reserved word.

Variable. A *variable* is a location in a program's data area that has been assigned a name. For example:

```
count1 db 50      ; a variable (memory allocation)
```

Label. If a name appears in the code area of a program, it is called a *label*. Labels serve as place markers when a program needs to jump or loop from one location to another. A label can be on a blank line by itself, or it can share a line with an instruction. In the following example, **Label1** and **Label2** are labels identifying locations in a program:

```
Label1:  mov  ax,0
         mov  bx,0
          .
          .
Label2:
         jmp  Label1      ; jump to Label1
```

Keyword. A *keyword* always has some predefined meaning to the assembler. It can be an instruction, or it can be an assembler directive. Examples are MOV, PROC, TITLE, ADD, AX, and END. Keywords cannot be used out of context or as identifiers. In the following, the use of **add** as a label is a syntax error:

```
add:  mov  ax,10
```

3.2   SAMPLE HELLO PROGRAM

Example 1 shows a program that displays the traditional "Hello, world!" message on the screen. It contains the essential ingredients of an assembly language application. Line 1 contains the **Title** directive; all remaining characters on the line are treated as comments, as are all characters on line 3. The source code for this program was written in assembly language and must be assembled into machine language before it can run. This program is compatible with both the Microsoft and Borland assemblers.

Segments are the building blocks of programs: The *code* segment is where program instructions are stored; the *data* segment contains all variables, and the *stack* segment contains the program's runtime stack. The stack is a special area of memory that the program uses when calling and returning from subroutines.

Example 1. The Hello World Program.

```
title Hello World Program         (hello.asm)

; This program displays "Hello, world!"
.model small
.stack 100h
.data
message db "Hello, world!",0dh,0ah,'$'

.code
main proc
     mov   ax,@data
     mov   ds,ax

     mov   ah,9
     mov   dx,offset message
     int   21h

     mov   ax,4C00h
     int   21h
main endp
end main
```

Here is a brief description of the important lines in the program:

- The **.model small** directive indicates that the program uses a type of structure in which the program uses no more than 64K of memory for code, and 64K for data. The **.stack** directive sets aside 100h (256) bytes of stack space for the program. The **.data** directive marks the beginning of the data segment where variables are stored. In the declaration of **message**, the assembler allocates a block of memory to hold the string containing "Hello, world!," along with two bytes containing a *newline* character sequence (0dh,0ah). The **$** is a required string terminator character for the particular MS-DOS output subroutine being used.

- The **.code** directive marks the beginning of the code segment, where the executable instructions are located. The **PROC** directive declares the beginning of a procedure. In this program, we have a procedure called **main**.

- The first two statements in the main procedure copy the address of the data segment (@data) into the DS register. The **mov** instruction always has two operands: first the destination, then the source.

- Next in the main procedure, we write a character string on the screen. This is done by calling an MS-DOS function that displays a string whose address is in the DX register. The function number is placed in the AH register.

- The last two statements in the main procedure (mov ax,4C00h / int 21h) halt the program and return control to the operating system.

- The statement **main endp** uses the ENDP directive. ENDP marks the end of the current procedure. Procedures, by the way, are not allowed to overlap.

- The end of the program contains the **end** directive, which is the last line to be assembled. The label **main** next to it identifies the location of the program entry point, that is, the point at which the CPU starts to execute the program's instructions.

At this point you may be fondly remembering the first "Hello, world" program you wrote in C, C++, Java, or Pascal. How can the assembly language version be so complicated? Actually, if you looked at the machine code generated by a high-level language compiler, you would see a lot of extra code that was automatically added to the program. In contrast, an assembler only inserts machine code for instructions that you have written. It is interesting to compare the executable size of the same program written and compiled in C++ (8772 bytes) to that of the program in Example 1 (562 bytes). Now who's doing more work?

Table 1 contains a list of the most commonly used assembler directives.

Table 1. Standard Assembler Directives.

Directive	Description
end	End of program assembly
endp	End of procedure
page	Set a page format for the listing file
proc	Begin procedure
title	Title of the listing file
.code	Mark the beginning of the code segment
.data	Mark the beginning of the data segment
.model	Specify the program's memory model
.stack	Set the size of the stack segment

3.3   ASSEMBLING, LINKING, AND DEBUGGING

By now, we have seen that it's fairly easy to assemble and run short programs with Debug. You will soon be using the *assembler,* a utility program that converts a source program into an object file, and a *linker,* a program that converts object files into executable programs.

One major advantage to using an assembler is that source programs can be more easily modified with a text editor than with Debug. Another is that you can use symbolic names for variables, rather than hard-coded numeric addresses. The linker has one primary advantage—programs can take advantage of existing libraries full of useful subroutines; the subroutines are "attached" to our programs by the linker.

A Two-Staged Process. Figure 1 shows the stages a program goes through before it can be executed. A programmer uses a *text editor* to create the source file of ASCII text. The *assembler* program reads the source file and produces an *object file,* a machine-language translation of the program. The object file may contain calls to subroutines in an external *link library*. The linker then copies the needed subroutines from the link library into the object file, creates a special header record at the beginning of the program, and produces an *executable program*. When we are ready to run the program, we type its name on the DOS command line, and the *DOS loader* decodes the header record of the executable program and loads it into memory. The CPU begins executing the program.

Figure 1. The Assemble-Link-Execute Cycle.

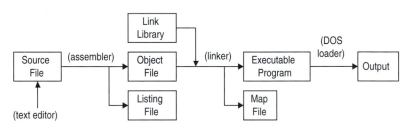

The assembler produces an optional *listing file,* which is a copy of the program's source file (suitable for printing) with line numbers and translated machine code. The linker produces an optional *map file,* which contains information about the program's code, data, and stack segments.

A *link library* is a file containing subroutines that are already compiled into machine language. Any procedures called by your program are copied into the executable program during the link step. (If you've ever programmed in Pascal or C, you have made extensive use of link libraries, perhaps without realizing it). Table 2 displays a list of filenames that would be created if we assembled and linked the Hello World program.

Table 2. Files Created by the Assembler and Linker.

Filename	Description	Step When Created
hello.asm	Source program	Edit
hello.obj	Object program	Assembly
hello.lst	Listing file	Assembly
hello.exe	Executable program	Link
hello.map	Map file	Link

3.3.1   Borland Turbo Assembler (TASM)

Once the Hello World program has been created using a text editor and saved to disk as sample.asm, it is ready to be assembled. The command to assemble **hello.asm** with the Borland assembler is:

```
C:\> tasm/l/n/z hello
```

We have shown the *MS-DOS* command prompt here as C:\> for illustrative purposes, but your command prompt may be different. This command can be typed at the command-line prompt in *MS-DOS*, or in an MS-DOS shell running under Windows. The **/l/n** options tell the assembler to produce a listing file, with no symbol table, and **/z** indicates that source lines with errors are to be displayed. The following is the screen output produced by assembling the program with the Borland assembler:

```
Turbo Assembler  Version 4.1
Copyright (c) 1988, 1996 Borland International

Assembling file:    hello.ASM
Error messages:     None
Warning messages:   None
Passes:             1
Remaining memory:   418k
```

The primary file produced by the assembly step is **hello.obj**. The assembler distinguishes between *error messages* and *warning messages*. A program with warning messages will still assemble, but the object file may have errors. In general, it is best to fix such errors before linking the program.

Syntax Errors. We were fortunate to have not made any mistakes when writing this program. But if we had, the assembler would have displayed the line with the mistake, along with an explanation. For example, **value1** was incorrectly spelled as **vlue1**:

```
mov   al,vlue1        ; load the AL register
**Error** sample.asm(13) Undefined symbol: VLUE1
```

Linking the Program. In the LINK step, the linker reads the object file, called hello.obj, as input and creates the executable file, called hello.exe. Here is the command:

```
C:\> tlink/3/m/v hello
```

The /3 option allows the use of 32-bit registers, the **/m** option tells the linker to create a *map* file, and the **/v** option includes debugging information in the executable program. Be sure to use these options when assembling and linking programs shown in this book.

Running the Program. You can run an assembly language program from the MS-DOS command prompt by just typing its name:

```
C:\> hello
```

You will probably want to use a debugger to test a newly written program. For example, we can run the sample.exe program in Borland's Turbo Debugger with the following command:

```
C:\> td hello
```

3.3.2   Microsoft Assembler (MASM)

The Microsoft Assembler package contains the ML.EXE program, which assembles and links one or more assembly language source files, producing an object file (extension .obj) and an executable file (.exe). The basic syntax is:

```
ML options filename.ASM
```

Each command-line option must be precded by at least one space. For example, the following commands assemble and link hello.asm with different options:

```
ML /Zi hello.asm              ; include debugging information
ML /Fl hello.asm              ; produce a listing file (hello.lst)
ML /Fm hello.asm              ; produce a map file (hello.map)
ML /Zm hello.asm              ; use MASM 5.12 compatibility mode
```

The following command assembles hello.asm and links hello.obj to the link library (irvine.lib) supplied with this book (you may have installed the book's sample programs in a directory other than C:\IRVINE):

```
ML /Zi /Zm /Fm /Fl hello.asm /link /co c:\irvine\irvine
```

Once hello.exe has been created, you can use the CV command to load and run it in the CodeView debugger:

```
CV hello                        ; load and run hello.exe
```

Microsoft also supplies the **MASM (masm.exe)** program to remain compatible with programs written under older versions of the assembler. The commands to assemble and link a program called sample are the following:

```
MASM /z/zi sample;
LINK /co sample;
```

You can find detailed information about the assembler, linker, and debugger by running the QH.EXE program from the C:\MASM611\BIN directory after the assembler has been installed (your exact path may vary). Our book's Web site (listed in the preface) also has detailed information to help you install and run the assembler and sample programs.

3.4   DATA ALLOCATION DIRECTIVES

A *variable* is a symbolic name for a location in memory where some data are stored. A variable's *offset* is the distance from the beginning of the segment to the variable. A variable's name is automatically associated with its offset. For example, if we declare an array containing four characters, the name **aList** identifies only the offset of the first character (A):

```
.data
aList  db "ABCD"
```

Offset	Contents
0000	'A'
0001	'B'
0002	'C'
0003	'D'

If the first letter is at offset 0, the next one is at offset 1, the next at 2, and so on. The offset of **aList** is equal to 0, the offset of the first letter.

We use *data allocation directives* to allocate storage, based on several following predefined types. (In this chapter we will discuss the DB, DW, and DD directives and leave the others for later chapters):

Mnemonic	Description	Bytes	Attribute
DB	Define byte	1	Byte
DW	Define word	2	Word
DD	Define doubleword	4	Doubleword
DF, DP	Define far pointer	6	Far pointer
DQ	Define quadword	8	Quadword
DT	Define tenbytes	10	Tenbyte

3.4.1 Define Byte (DB)

The DB (*define byte*) directive allocates storage for one or more 8-bit (byte) values. The following syntax diagram shows that *name* is optional and at least one initializer is required. If more are supplied, they must be separated by commas:

```
[name] DB initval [,initval] . . .
```

Each initializer can be a constant expression containing numeric literals, defined symbols, and quoted characters and strings. If the value is signed, it has a range of −128 to +127; if unsigned, the range is 0 to 255. A list of values can be grouped under a single label with the values separated by commas. For example:

```
char1       db 'A'                ; ASCII character
char2       db 'A'-10             ; expression
signed1     db -128               ; smallest signed value
signed2     db +127               ; largest signed value
unsigned1   db 255                ; largest unsigned value
```

A variable's initial contents may be left undefined by using a question mark for the initializer:

```
myval db ?
```

Multiple Initializers. Sometimes the name of a variable identifies the beginning of a sequence of bytes. In that case, multiple initializers can be used in the same declaration. In the following example, assume that **list** is stored at offset 0000. This means that 10 is stored at offset 0000, 20 at offset 0001, 30 at offset 0002, and 40 at offset 0003:

```
list  db  10,20,30,40
```

Characters and integers are one and the same as far as the assembler is concerned. The following variables contain exactly the same value and can be processed the same way:

```
char   db   'A'                ; a character (ASCII 41h)
hex    db   41h                ; hexadecimal
dec    db   65                 ; decimal
bin    db   01000001b          ; binary
oct    db   101q               ; octal
```

Each initializer can use a different radix when a list of items is defined, and numeric, character, and string constants can be freely mixed. When a hexadecimal number begins with a letter (A-F), a leading zero is added to prevent the assembler from interpreting it as a label. In this example, **list1** and **list2** have the same contents:

```
list1  db   10,  32,  41h,  00100010b
list2  db   0Ah, 20h, 'A',  22h
```

Representing Strings. A string can be identified by a variable, which marks the offset of the beginning of the string. There is no universal storage format for strings, although null-terminated strings used by the C language are used when calling Microsoft Windows functions. The following shows a null-terminated string called CString, and another called PString that has its length encoded in the first byte:

```
Cstring  db  "Good afternoon",0
Pstring  db  14, "Good afternoon"
```

The DB directive is ideal for allocating strings of any length. The string can continue on multiple lines without the necessity of supplying a label for each line. The following is a null-terminated string:

```
LongString  db "This is a long string, that "
            db "clearly is going to take "
            db "several lines to store",0
```

The assembler can automatically calculate the storage used by any variable by subtracting its starting offset from the next offset following the variable. The $ operator returns the current location counter, so we can use it an expression such as the following:

```
(offset)
  0000  mystring  db "This is a string"
  0010  mystring_len = ($ - mystring)
```

In this example, **mystring_len** is equal to 10h.

DUP Operator. The DUP operator only appears after a storage allocation directive, such as DB or DW. With DUP, you can repeat one or more values when allocating storage. It is especially useful when allocating space for a string or array. Notice that many of the following examples initialize storage to default values:

```
db 20 dup(0)          ; 20 bytes, all equal to zero
db 20 dup(?)          ; 20 bytes, uninitialized
db  4 dup("ABC")      ; 12 bytes: "ABCABCABCABC"
db 4096 dup(0)        ; 4096-byte buffer, all zeros
```

The DUP operator can also be nested. The first example that follows creates storage containing 000XX000XX000XX000XX. The second example creates a two-dimensional word table of 3 rows and 4 columns:

```
aTable  db  4 dup( 3 dup(0), 2 dup('X') )
aMatrix  dw  3 dup( 4 dup(0) )
```

3.4.2   Define Word (DW)

The DW (*define word*) directive creates storage for one or more 16-bit values. The syntax is:

```
[name] DW initval [,initval] . . .
```

Each initializer is equivalent to an unsigned integer between 0 and 65,535 (FFFFh). If *initval* is signed, the acceptable range is –32,768 (8000h) to +32,767 (7FFFh). A character constant can be stored in the lower half of a word. One can also leave the variable uninitialized by using the **?** operator. Here are some examples:

```
dw   0,65535                 ; smallest/largest unsigned values
dw   -32768,+32767           ; smallest/largest signed values
dw   256 * 2                 ; calculated expression (512)
dw   1000h,4096,'AB',0       ; mutiple initializers
dw   ?                       ; uninitialized
dw   5   dup(1000h)          ; 5 words, each equal to 1000h
dw   5   dup(?)              ; 5 words, uninitialized
```

Pointer. The offset of a variable or subroutine can be stored in another variable, called a *pointer.* In the next example, the assembler initializes **P** to the offset of **list**:

```
list dw 256,257,258,259      ; define 4 words
P    dw list                 ; P points to list
```

Reversed Storage Format. The assembler reverses the bytes in a word value when storing it in memory; the lowest byte occurs at the lowest address. When the variable is moved to a 16-bit register, the CPU re-reverses the bytes. For example, the value 1234h would be stored in memory as follows:

```
Offset:  00  01
 Value:  34  12
```

3.4.3   Define Doubleword (DD)

The DD (*define doubleword*) directive allocates storage for one or more 32-bit doublewords. The syntax is

```
[name] DD initval [,initval] . . .
```

Each initializer is equivalent to an integer between 0 and 0FFFFFFFFh. For example:

```
signed_val  dd  0, 0BCDA1234h, -2147483648
            dd  100h dup(?)    ; 256 doublewords (1024 bytes)
```

The bytes in a doubleword are stored in reverse order, so the least significant digits are stored at the lowest offset. For instance, the value 12345678h would be stored as:

```
Offset:  00  01  02  03
 Value:  78  56  34  12
```

A doubleword can hold the 32-bit segment-offset address of a variable or procedure. In the following example, the assembler automatically initializes **pointer1** to the address of **subroutine1**:

```
pointer1  dd  subroutine1
```

3.5   SYMBOLIC CONSTANTS

Equate directives allow constants and literals to be given symbolic names. A constant can be defined at the start of a program and, in some cases, redefined later on.

3.5.1   Equal-Sign Directive

Known as a *redefinable equate,* the equal-sign directive creates an absolute symbol by assigning the value of a numeric expression to a name. The syntax is:

```
name = expression
```

In contrast to the DB and DW directives, the equal-sign directive allocates no storage. As the program is assembled, all occurrences of *name* are replaced by *expression*. The expression must be able to be expressed by a 32-bit signed or unsigned integer (32-bit integers require that you use the .386 or higher directive). Examples are as follows:

```
prod     = 10 * 5            ; Evaluates an expression
maxInt   = 7FFFh             ; Maximum 16-bit signed value
minInt   = 8000h             ; Minimum 16-bit signed value
maxUInt  = 0FFFFh            ; Maximum 16-bit unsigned value
string   = 'XY'              ; Up to two characters allowed
count    = 500
endvalue = count + 1         ; Can use a predefined symbol

.386
maxLong  = 7FFFFFFFh         ; Maximum 32-bit signed value
minLong  = 80000000h         ; Minimum 32-bit signed value
maxULong = 0FFFFFFFFh        ; Maximum 32-bit unsigned value
```

A symbol defined with the equal-sign directive can be redefined any number of times. In Example 2, **count** changes value several times. On the right side of the example, we see how the assembler evaluates the constant:

Example 2. Using the Equal-Sign Directive.

Statement	Assembled As
count = 5	
mov al,count	mov al,5
mov dl,al	mov dl,al
count = 10	
mov cx,count	mov cx,10
mov dx,count	mov dx,10
count = 2000	
mov ax,count	mov ax,2000

3.5.2   EQU Directive

The EQU directive assigns a symbolic name to a string or numeric constant. This increases the readability of a program and makes it possible to change multiple occurrences of a constant from a single place in a program. There is an important limitation imposed on EQU: A symbol defined with EQU *cannot* be redefined later in the program.

Expressions containing integers evaluate to numeric values, but floating point values evaluate to strings. Also, string equates may be enclosed in angle brackets (< . . . >) to ensure their interpretation as string expressions. This eliminates ambiguity on the part of the assembler when assigning the correct value to a name:

Example	Type of Value
maxint equ 32767	Numeric
maxuint equ 0FFFFh	Numeric
count equ 10 * 20	Numeric
float1 equ <2.345>	String

3.5.3   TEXTEQU Directive

The TEXTEQU directive creates what is called a text macro. You can assign a sequence of characters to a symbolic name, and then use the name later in the program. The syntax is:

```
name TEXTEQU <text>
name TEXTEQU textmacro
name TEXTEQU %constExpr
```

In this syntax, *text* is any sequence of characters enclosed in angle brackets <...>, *textmacro* is a previously defined text macro, and *constExpr* is an expression that evaluates to text. Text macros can appear anywhere in a program's source code. A symbol defined with TEXTEQU can be redefined later in the program.

A symbolic name can be assigned to a string, allowing the name to be replaced by the string wherever it is found. For example, the **prompt1** variable references the **continueMsg** text macro:

```
continueMsg textequ <"Do you wish to continue (Y/N)?">
.data
prompt1 db continueMsg
```

An alias, which is a name representing another predefined symbol, can be created. For example:

```
;Symbol declarations:
move      textequ <mov>
address   textequ <offset>

;Original code:
move bx,address value1
move al,20

;Assembled as:
mov bx,offset value1
mov al,20
```

In the following example, TEXTEQU is used to define a pointer (**p1**) to a string. Later, p1 is assigned a literal containing "0":

```
.data
myString db "A string",0

.code
p1 textequ <offset myString>
mov  bx,p1        ; bx = offset myString

p1 textequ <0>
mov  si,p1        ; si = 0
```

3.6   DATA TRANSFER INSTRUCTIONS

3.6.1   MOV Instruction

The MOV (*move data*) instruction copies data from one operand to another, so it is called a *data transfer* instruction. The following basic forms of MOV can be used, where the first operand is the *target* of the move, and the second operand is the source:

```
MOV reg,reg
MOV mem,reg
MOV reg,mem
MOV mem,immed
MOV reg,immed
```

In these formats, *reg* can be any non-segment register, except that IP cannot be a target operand. The sizes of both operands must be the same. A 16-bit register must be moved to a 16-bit memory location, for example.

Where segment registers are concerned, the following types of moves are possible, with the exception that CS cannot be a target operand:

```
mov segreg,reg16
mov segreg,mem16
mov reg16,segreg
mov mem16,segreg
```

Notably missing from the MOV instruction is the ability to use two memory operands[1]. Instead, you must use a register when copying a byte, word, or doubleword from one memory location to another. The following instructions, for example, copy a word from var1 to var2:

```
mov  ax,var1
mov  var2,ax
```

Examples of MOV with all three types of operands are shown here:

```
.data
count  db  10
total  dw  4126h
bigVal dd  12345678h

.code
mov  al,bl            ; 8-bit register to register
mov  bl,count         ; 8-bit memory to register
mov  count,26         ; 8-bit immediate to memory
mov  bl,1             ; 8-bit immediate to register
```

```
mov  dx,cx                  ; 16-bit register to register
mov  bx,8FE2h               ; 16-bit immediate to register
mov  total,1000h            ; 16-bit immediate to memory
mov  eax,ebx                ; 32-bit register to register
mov  edx,bigVal             ; 32-bit memory to register
```

Type Checking. When a variable is created using DB, DW, DD, or any of the other data definition directives, the assembler gives it a default attribute (byte, word, doubleword) based on its size. This type is checked when you refer to the variable, and an error results if the types do not match. For example, the following MOV instruction is invalid because **count** has a *word* attribute and AL is a *byte:*

```
.data
count  dw  20h

.code
mov al,count    ; error: operand sizes must match
```

Type checking, while sometimes inconvenient, helps you avoid logic errors. Even when a smaller value fits into a larger one, a type mismatch error is flagged by the assembler:

```
.data
byteval  db  1

.code
mov  ax,byteval        ; error
```

If necessary, you can use the LABEL directive to create a new name with a different attribute at the same offset. The same data can now be accessed using either name:

```
.data
countB label byte       ; byte attribute
countW dw  20h          ; word attribute

.code
mov  al,countB          ; retrieve low byte of count
mov  cx,countW          ; retrieve all of count
```

3.6.2   Operands with Displacements

You can add a displacement to the name of a memory operand, using a method called *direct-offset* addressing. This lets you access memory values that do not have their own labels. For example, the following are arrays of bytes, words, and doublewords:

```
arrayB  db 10h,20h
arrayW  dw 100h,200h
arrayD  dd 10000h,20000h
```

The notation **arrayB+1** refers to the location one byte beyond the beginning of **arrayB**, and **arrayW+2** refers to the location two bytes from the beginning of **arrayW**. You can code operands in MOV instructions that use this notation to move data to and from memory. In the following example, we show the value of AL after each move has taken place:

```
mov  al,arrayB          ; AL = 10h
mov  al,arrayB+1        ; AL = 20h
```

When dealing with an array of 16-bit values, the offset of each array member is two bytes beyond the previous one:

```
mov  ax,arrayW          ; AX = 100h
mov  ax,arrayW+2        ; AX = 200h
```

The members of a doubleword array are four bytes apart:

```
mov  eax,arrayD         ; EAX = 10000h
mov  eax,arrayD+4       ; EAX = 20000h
```

3.6.3 XCHG Instruction

The XCHG (*exchange data*) instruction exchanges the contents of two registers, or the contents of a register and a variable. The syntax is:

```
XCHG reg,reg
XCHG reg,mem
XCHG mem,reg
```

XCHG is the most efficient way to exchange two operands, because you don't need a third register or variable to hold a temporary value. Particularly in sorting applications, this instruction provides a speed advantage. One or both operands can be registers, or a register can be combined with a memory operand, but two memory operands cannot be used togther. For example:

```
xchg  ax,bx       ; exchange two 16-bit registers
xchg  ah,al       ; exchange two 8-bit registers
xchg  var1,bx     ; exchange 16-bit memory operand with BX
xchg  eax,ebx     ; exchange two 32-bit registers
```

If you do want to exchange two variables, a register must be used as a temporary operand. The program in Example 3 exchanges the contents of two variables.

Example 3. Exchanging Two Variables.

```
title Exchange Two Variables         (Exchange.asm)

.model small
.stack 100h
.data
value1 db 0Ah
value2 db 14h

.code
main proc
    mov  ax,@data       ; initialize DS register
    mov  ds,ax

    mov  al,value1      ; load the AL register
    xchg value2,al      ; exchange AL and value2
    mov  value1,al      ; store AL back into value1

    mov  ax,4C00h       ; exit program
    int  21h
main endp
end main
```

3.7 ARITHMETIC INSTRUCTIONS

The original 8086 Intel instruction set contained instructions for integer arithmetic with 8- and 16-bit operands. Floating-point arithmetic was either emulated by software, or handled by a separate coprocessor chip, the 8087. The 80386 introduced 32-bit integer operands. The Intel 486 processor contained an integrated floating-point processor unit (FPU), as do all of the Pentium processor models.

In this chapter, we focus on the basics of integer addition and subtraction. (Multiplication and division are covered in Chapter 7.)

3.7.1 INC and DEC Instructions

The INC (*increment*) and DEC (*decrement*) instructions add 1 or subtract 1 from a single operand, respectively. Their syntax is

```
INC destination
DEC destination
```

Destination can be a register or memory operand. All status flags are affected except the Carry flag. Examples are shown here.

```
inc  al    ; increment 8-bit register
dec  bx    ; decrement 16-bit register
inc  eax   ; increment 32-bit register
inc  membyte              ; increment memory operand
dec  byte ptr membyte     ; increment 8-bit memory operand
dec  memword              ; decrement memory operand
inc  word ptr memword     ; increment 16-bit memory operand
```

In these examples, the BYTE PTR operator identifies an 8-bit operand, and WORD PTR identifies a 16-bit operand.

3.7.2   ADD Instruction

The ADD instruction adds a source operand to a destination operand of the same size. The syntax is:

```
ADD  destination,source
```

Source is unchanged by the operation, and *destination* is assigned the sum. The sizes of the operands must match, and no more than one operand can be a memory operand. A segment register cannot be the destination. All status flags are affected. Examples are as follows:

```
add  cl,al      ; add 8-bit register to register
add  eax,edx    ; add 32-bit registers
add  bx,1000h   ; add immediate value to 16-bit register
add  var1,ax    ; add 16-bit register to memory
add  dx,var1    ; add 16-bit memory to register
add  var1,10    ; add immediate value to memory
add  dword ptr memVal, ecx
```

The DWORD PTR operator identifies a 32-bit memory operand.

3.7.3   SUB Instruction

The SUB instruction subtracts a source operand from a destination operand. The syntax is:

```
SUB destination,source
```

The sizes of the two operands must match, and only one can be a memory operand. Inside the CPU, the source operand is first negated and then added to the destination. For example, $4 - 1$ is really $4 + (-1)$. Recall that twos complement notation is used for negative numbers, so -1 is stored as 11111111:

```
  0 0 0 0 0 1 0 0   ( 4 )
+ 1 1 1 1 1 1 1 1   (-1 )
------------------
  0 0 0 0 0 0 1 1   ( 3 )
```

Examples of SUB used with various types of operands are shown here:

```
sub  eax,12345h    ; subtract 32-bit immediate from register
sub  cl,al         ; subtract 8-bit register from register
sub  edx,eax       ; subtract 32-bit register from register
sub  bx,1000h      ; subtract immediate value from 16-bit register
sub  var1,ax       ; subtract 16-bit register from memory
sub  dx,var1       ; subtract 16-bit memory from register
sub  var1,10       ; subtract immediate value from memory
```

3.7.4   Flags Affected by ADD and SUB

If either ADD or SUB generates a result of zero, the Zero flag is set; if the result is negative, the Sign flag is set. In the following example, line 1 generates a result of zero, and line 4 generates a result of -1 (FFFFh).

```
mov  ax,10
sub  ax,10         ; AX = 0, ZF = 1
mov  bx,1
sub  bx,2          ; BX = FFFF, SF = 1
```

The *Zero flag* is set when the result of an arithmetic operation equals 0. Note that INC and DEC affect the Zero flag, but *not* the Carry flag:

```
mov  bl,4Fh
add  bl,0B1h       ; BL = 00, ZF = 1, CF = 1
mov  ax,0FFFFh
inc  ax            ; ZF = 1 (CF not affected)
```

The identification of an operand as either signed or unsigned is completely up to the programmer. The CPU updates the Carry and Overflow flags to cover both possibilities. For this reason, we need to discuss the two types of operations separately.

Unsigned Operations. When performing unsigned arithmetic, the Carry flag is useful. If the result of an addition operation is too large for the destination operand, the Carry flag is set. For example, the sum of 0FFh + 1 should equal 100h, but only the two lowest digits (00) fit into AL. The addition sets the Carry flag:

```
mov  ax,0FFh
add  al,1               ; AL = 00, CF = 1
```

This is an 8-bit operation because AL is used. If we want to get the right answer, we must add 1 to AX, making it a 16-bit operation:

```
mov  ax,0FFh
add  ax,1               ; AX = 0100, CF = 0
```

A similar situation occurs when subtracting a larger operand from a smaller one. In the next example, the Carry flag tells us the result in AL is invalid:

```
mov  al,1
sub  al,2               ; AL = FF, CF = 1
```

Signed Overflow. The *Overflow flag* is set when an arithmetic operation generates a signed value that exceeds the storage size of the destination operand. When set, the Overflow flag indicates that the value placed in the destination operand is incorrect:

```
mov  al,01111110b       ; +126
add  al,00000010b       ; 126 + 2 ==> 10000000b, OF = 1

mov  al,10000000b       ; -128
add  al,11111110b       ; -128 + (-2) ==> 01111110b, OF = 1
```

Signed overflow occurs when a positive number is added to another positive number and their sum is negative. Similarly, there is overflow when a negative number is added to a negative number and the sum is positive. Mechanically, the CPU compares the Carry flag to the bit that is carried into the sign bit of the destination operand. If they are unequal, the Overflow flag is set. For example, when adding the binary values 10000000 and 11111110, a 0 is carried from bit 6 to bit 7, and the Carry flag is set:

```
                    No carry from bit 6 to 7
                       7  6  5
      CF = 1  ←——┌─────────────────────┐
                 │ 1  0  0  0  0  0  0  0 │
              +  │ 1  1  1  1  1  1  1  0 │
                 └─────────────────────┘
              =  │ 1  0  0  0  0  0  0  0 │
                 └─────────────────────┘
```

3.8   BASIC OPERAND TYPES

There are three basic types of operands: *immediate*, *register*, and *memory*. An immediate operand is a constant. A register operand is one of the CPU registers. A memory operand is a reference to a location in memory.

The Intel instruction set provides a wide variety of ways of representing memory operands, to make it easier to handle arrays and other more complex data structures. There are six types of memory operands, shown in Table 3. We will use the first three types, *direct, direct-offset,* and *register indirect,* in the current chapter and defer the others to Chapter 4.

Some terms used in the table must be explained: A *displacement* is either a number or the offset of a variable. The *effective address* of an operand refers to the offset (distance) of the data from the beginning of its segment. Each operand type in Table 3 refers to the contents of memory at an effective address. The *addressing mode* used by an instruction refers to the type of memory operand in use. For example, the following instruction uses the *register indirect* addressing mode:

```
mov ax,[si]
```

To use a real-life analogy, each house in a neighborhood is assigned a unique address. Suppose a house is located at 121 Maple Street. **Maple Street** could be considered the house's base location, and **121** could be considered the house's *offset* from the beginning of the street. We could also use relative references to houses by using phrases such as "the second house after the house at 121 Maple Street." In a computer program, we might refer to a particular element in an array as: `intArray + 2`.

3.8.1   Register Operands

A register operand can be any register. In general, the register addressing mode is the most efficient because registers are part of the CPU and no memory access is required. Some examples using the MOV instruction with register operands are shown here:

```
mov    eax,ebx
mov    cl,20h
mov    si,offset var1
```

Table 3. Memory Operand Types.

Operand Type	Examples	Description
direct	`op1 bytelist`	EA is the offset of a variable.
direct-offset	`bytelist + 2`	EA is the sum of a variable's offset and a displacement.
register-indirect	`[si]` `[bx]`	EA is the contents of a base or index register.

indexed	`list[bx]`
	`[list + bx]`
	`list[di]`
	`[si+2]`
		EA is the sum of a base or index register and a displacement.

base-indexed	`[bx+di]`
	`[bx][di]`
	`[bp-di]`
		EA is the sum of a base register and an index register.

base-indexed with displacement	`[bx+si+2]`
	`list[bx+si]`
	`list[bx][si]`
		EA is the sum of a base register, an index register, and a displacement.

3.8.2   Immediate Operands

An immediate operand is a constant expression, such as a number, character constant, arithmetic expression, or symbolic constant. The assembler must be able to determine the value of an immediate operand at assembly time. Its value is inserted directly into the machine instruction. Examples of immediate operands are shown here:

```
mov   al,10
mov   eax,12345678h
mov   dl,'X'
mov   ax,(40 * 50)
```

3.8.3   Direct Operands

A direct operand refers to the contents of memory at a location identified by a label in the data segment. At runtime, the CPU assumes that the offset of any variable is from the beginning of the segment addressed by the DS (data segment) register. Here are examples of direct addressing using byte, word, and doubleword operands:

```
.data
count      db   20
wordList   dw   1000h,2000h
longVal    dd   0F63B948Ch
.code
mov   al,count
mov   bx,wordList + 2
mov   edx,longVal
```

OFFSET Operator. The OFFSET operator returns the 16-bit offset of a variable. The assembler automatically calculates every variable's offset as a program is being assembled. In the following example, if the variable **aWord** is located at offset 0000, the MOV statement moves 0 to BX:

```
.data
aWord dw 1234h
.code
mov   bx,offset aWord       ; BX = 0000
```

3.8.4   Direct-Offset Operands

A particularly good use of the addition and subtraction operators (+, −) is to access a list of values. The + operator adds to the offset of a variable. In the following series of instructions, the first byte of **array** is moved to AL, the second byte to BL, the third byte to CL, and the fourth byte to DL. The value of each register after a move is shown at the right:

```
.data
array db 0Ah,0Bh,0Ch,0Dh
.code
mov  al,array              ; AL = 0Ah
mov  bl,array+1            ; BL = 0Bh
mov  cl,array+2            ; CL = 0Ch
mov  dl,array+3            ; DL = 0Dh
```

You can also subtract from a label's offset. In the following example, the label **endlist** is one byte beyond the last byte in **list**. To move the last byte in **list** to AL, we write:

```
.data
list     db  1,2,3,4,5
endlist label byte
.code
mov    al,endlist-1        ; move 5 to AL
```

In a list of 16-bit numbers, add 2 to a number's offset to get the offset of the next element. This is done in the following example:

```
.data
wvals   dw  1000h,2000h,3000h,4000h
.code
mov    ax,wvals            ; AX = 1000h
mov    bx,wvals+2          ; BX = 2000h
mov    cx,wvals+4          ; CX = 3000h
mov    dx,wvals+6          ; DX = 4000h
```

3.9   REVIEW QUESTIONS

1. Show three examples of assembly language instructions: one with no operands, one with a single operand, and one with two operands.

2. Write an example of an assembly language mnemonic.

3. Explain what a *disassembler* utility does.

4. Can a comment be placed on the same line as an instruction? (y/n)

5. Name three types of objects that can be represented by operands.

6. Name at least two popular debuggers used with assemblers sold today.

7. Write a series of instructions that move the values 1, 2 and 3 to the AX, BX, and CX registers.

8. Write an instruction that adds the number in the BX register to the CX register.

9. Identify each of the following Debug commands:

    ```
    A 100
    T
    R
    G
    Q
    ```

10. Addresses are shown in Debug as a combination of two numbers, called the segment and the _____.

11. Show the storage of memory bytes for the 16-bit value 0A6Bh.

12. Show several examples of integer constants.

13. Can a symbolic constant contain an arithmetic expression? (y/n)

14. Show an example of assigning a numeric constant to a symbol, using the = operator.

15. Which radix character is used for hexadecimal constants?

16. Create several examples of string constants, including one that contains embedded quotes.

17. Name the four basic parts of assembly language statements.

18. Show how a source program statement can be divided between two lines.

19. Can multiple statements appear on the same line? (y/n)

20. In assembly language, how is a *directive* different from an *instruction*?

21. Name the six general types of memory operands.

22. Which special characters can appear in identifier names?

23. Would the following be a valid identifier name? first$try

24. Show several examples of labels.

25. How are labels used in programs?

26. What are segments in an assembly language program?

27. What is the diffference between the .stack and .code directives?

28. Write a statement that copies the location of the data segment into the DS register.

29. If any of the following MOV statements are illegal, explain why:

    ```
    a.  mov ax,bx
    b.  mov var2,al
    c.  mov ax,bl
    d.  mov bh,4A6Fh
    e.  mov dx,3
    f.  mov var1,bx
    ```

```
g.   mov  al,var3
h.   mov  cs,0
i.   mov  ip,ax
j.   mov  var1,var2
k.   mov  ds,1000h
l.   mov  ds,es


.data
var1   dw    0
var2   dw    6
var3   db    5
```

30. The three basic types of operands are *register, memory,* and _____.

31. Is the address of each operand relative to the start of the program calculated at *assembly* time or at *link* time?

32. Which directive marks the end of a procedure?

33. What is the significance of the label used with the END directive?

34. Identify the types of operands (register, immediate, direct, or indirect) used in each of the following instructions:

```
a.   mov   al,20
b.   add   cx,wordval
c.   mov   bx,offset count
d.   add   dl,[bx]
```

35. Mark and correct any syntax errors in the following listing:

```
.data
blist  db 1,2,3,4,5
wlist  dw 6,7,8,9,0Ah


.code
mov   al,blist
add   al,wlist+1
mov   bx,offset blist
mov   cx,wlist
mov   dx,cx
inc   word ptr dx
dec   ax
```

36. Write a data definition for the following string:

    "MYFILE.DTA"

37. Write a data definition statement for a list of 8-bit memory operands containing the following values:

    3, 15h, 0F6h, 11010000b

38. Write a data declaration directive for a sequence of 500 16-bit words, each containing the value 1000h.

39. An operand in an instruction can be a memory variable, a register, or

    _____ .

40. Which of the following registers cannot be used as destination operands?

    AX, CL, IP, DX, CS, BH, SS, SP, BP

41. What will be the hexadecimal value of the destination operand after each of the statements in Table 4 has executed? (If any instruction is illegal, write the word ILLEGAL as the answer.) **var1** and **var2** are 16-bit operands, and **count** is 8 bits long. All numbers are in hexadecimal.

42. Write a data definition for the variable **arrayptr** that contains the offset address of the variable **intarray**.

Table 4. Examples for Question 41.

Instruction	Before	After
a. mov ax,bx	AX = 0023, BX = 00A5	AX =
b. mov ah,3	AX = 06AF	AX =
c. mov dl,count	DX = 8F23, count = 1A	DL =
d. mov bl,ax	BX = 00A5, AX = 4000	BL =
e. mov di,100h	DI = 06E9	DI =
f. mov ds,cx	DS = 0FB2, CX = 0020	DS =
g. mov var1,bx	var1 = 0025, BX = A000	var1 =
h. mov count,ax	count = 25, AX = 4000	count =
i. mov var1,var2	var1 = 0400, var2 = 0500	var1 =

43. What will be the hexadecimal value of the destination operand after each of the statements in Table 5 has executed? You may assume that **var1** is a word variable and that **count** and **var2** are byte variables. If any instruction is illegal, write the word ILLEGAL as the answer:

44. What will AX equal after the following instructions have executed?

```
.code
    mov     ax,array1
    inc     ax
    add     ah,1
    sub     ax,array1
.data
array1  dw  10h,20h
array2  dw  30h,40h
```

45. As each of the following instructions is executed, fill in the hexadecimal value of the operand listed on the right side:

```
.code
mov     ax,array1       ; AX =
xchg    array2,ax       ; AX =
dec     ax
sub     array2,2        ; array2 =
```

Table 5. Examples for Question 43.

Instruction	Before	After
a. mov ah,bl	AX = 0023 BX = 00A5	AX =
b. add ah,3	AX = 06AF	AX =
c. sub dl,count	DX = 8F23, count = 1A	DX =
d. inc bl	BX = FFFF	BX =
e. add di,100h	DI = 06E9	DI =
f. dec cx	CX = 0000	CX =
g. add var1,bx	var1 = 0025, BX = A000	var1 =
h. xchg var2,al	AL = 41, var2 = 25	var2 =
i. sub var1,var2	var1 = 15A6, var2 = B8	var1 =
j. dec var2	var2 = 01	var2 =

```
mov     bx,array2
add     ah,bl           ; AX =

.data
array1  dw  20h,10h
array2  dw  30h,40h
```

3.10 PROGRAMMING EXERCISES

The following exercises must be completed by creating a source file and assembling it with an assembler (MASM or TASM). Be sure to trace the execution of the program with a debugger.

1. *Program Trace*

   Code a program containing the following list of instructions. Where marked, write down the anticipated values of the Carry, Sign, Zero, and Overflow flags before you actually run the program:

   ```
   mov   ax,1234h
   mov   bx,ax
   mov   cx,ax
   add   ch,al       ; CF =    , SF =    ,ZF =    , OF =
   add   bl,ah       ; CF =    , SF =    ,ZF =    , OF =
   add   ax,0FFFFh   ; CF =    , SF =    ,ZF =    , OF =
   dec   bx          ; CF =    , SF =    ,ZF =    , OF =
   inc   ax          ; CF =    , SF =    ,ZF =    , OF =
   ```

   Also, before running the program, write down what you think AX, BX, CX, and DX will contain at the end of the program. Finally, run and trace the program with a debugger. Verify the register and flag values that you wrote down before running the program.

2. *Define and Display 8-Bit Numbers*

   Write, assemble, and test a program to do the following:

   Use the DB directive to define the following list of numbers and name it **array:**

   ```
   31h, 32h, 33h, 34h
   ```

   Write instructions to load each number into DL and display it on the console. (The following instructions display the byte in DL on the console:)

   ```
   mov   ah,2
   int   21h
   ```

   Explain why the output on the screen is "1234".

3. Arithmetic Sums

Write a program that finds the sum of three 8-bit values and places the sum in another variable. Use the following data definitions. Use direct-offset addressing:

```
ThreeBytes    db   10h, 20h, 30h
TheSum        db   ?
```

4. Uppercase Conversion

Write a program that converts a string containing up to 256 lowercase characters to uppercase. (A lowercase character can be converted to uppercase by subtracting 32 from its ASCII code.)

5. Extended Registers (80386)

Write a program that moves various 32-bit memory operands to the EAX, EBX, ECX, and EDX registers. Experiment with each of the addressing modes introduced in this chapter. (This exercise requires an 80386 processor or higher.)

6. Simple Number Sequence

Write a program that generates a sequence of numbers in which each number is equal to double the previous number. The range is 1 – 1000h, shown here in hexadecimal:

```
1 2 4 8 10 20 40 80 100 200 400 800 1000
```

(This exercise, and the one following, require knowledge of the LOOP instruction from Chapter 4, as well as the Writeint procedure listed on page 118.)

7. Fibonacci Numbers

The well-known *Fibonacci* number series, reputedly discovered by Leonardo of Pisa around the year 1200, has been valued for centuries for its universal qualities by artists, mathematicians, and composers. Each number in the series after the number 1 is the sum of the two previous numbers:

```
1, 1, 2, 3, 5, 8, 13 ,21, 34, 55 . . .
```

Write a program that generates and displays the first 24 numbers in the Fibonacci series, beginning with 1 and ending with 46,368.

End Notes:

[1] There is a specialized type of memory-to-memory move instruction called MOVS, which is often used when moving large blocks of data. See Chapter 10 for details.

4 Using the Assembler

This chapter has several objectives: first, to show how to assemble and link programs; second, to introduce directives and operators interpreted directly by the assembler; third, to show how loops are created, and finally, to introduce the link library subroutines supplied with this

To get the maximum benefit from this and later chapters, take time out from reading to assemble and run the sample programs. In programming, you learn by doing.

4.1   MORE ABOUT THE ASSEMBLER AND LINKER

4.1.1   Source Listing File

A source listing file for a simple program that exchanges two integers is shown in Example 1. The listing file contains a wealth of information about the program, showing the offset of each statement, the machine code generated by the assembler, and the program source code.

Example 1. Sample Source Listing File.

```
Exchange Two Variables                            (SAMPLE.ASM)
1
2
3     0000                    .model small
4     0000                    .stack 100h
5
6     0000                     .code
7     0000                    main proc
8     0000  B8 ---- R    mov    ax,@data        ; initialize DS register
9     0003  8E D8        mov    ds,ax
10    0005                    swap:
11    0005  A0 0000 R    mov    al,value1        ; load the AL register
12    0008  86 06 0001R  xchg   al,value2        ; exchange AL, value2
13    000C  A2 0000 R    mov    value1,al        ; store new value of AL
14    000F  B8 4C00      mov    ax,4C00h         ; end program
15    0012  CD 21        int    21h
16    0014                   main endp
17
18    0014                   .data
19    0000  0A          value1  db 0Ah
20    0001  14          value2  db 14h
21
22                        end main
```

To the right of each address is a hexadecimal representation of the machine-language bytes generated by the instruction. In many cases, the hexadecimal bytes in the program listing are identical to those in the final EXE program. For example, line 9 shows the machine language bytes (8E D8) that move AX to DS. When variables are referenced, the machine instructions include references to *relocatable* addresses. For example, the instruction to move **value1** to AL is on line 11 at address 0005:

```
11   0005  A0 0000r      mov   al,value1
```

The instruction's op code is A0, the offset of **value1** is 0000, and the letter **r** indicates that the offset of **value1** is relative to the start of the data segment.

Sometimes programs make references to variables and procedures that are outside of the current module. The addresses of these *external* references cannot be determined by the assembler; instead, the linker must resolve these addresses when creating the executable program. If this were the case with the variable **value1**, the listing file would show an **e** (for *external*) next to the machine code:

```
11   0005  A0 0000e      mov   al,value1   ; external variable
```

4.1.2   Map File

Created during the LINK step, the *map* file lists information about each of the program segments (see Example 2). This file can be very helpful when debugging because it shows the starting and ending addresses and the length of each segment:

Example 2. The sample.map File.

Start	Stop	Length	Name	Class
00000H	00013H	00014H	_TEXT	CODE
00020H	00021H	00002H	_DATA	DATA
00030H	0012FH	00100H	STACK	STACK

Program entry point at 0000:0000

Look at the column labeled **Class**: the names CODE, DATA, and STACK identify the segments created by the .code, .data, and .stack directives in the source program. Suppose our program was loaded into memory at absolute address 18000. If so, the code segment would start at 18100, the data segment would start at 18120, and the stack would start at 18130. The segment registers would contain the following values:

```
ES = 1800,  CS = 1810,  DS = 1812, SS = 1813
```

From this, we see that a new area has been created between 18000 and 180FF, and the name for this area is the *Program Segment Prefix* (PSP). This 256-byte area contains valuable pointers and environment information used by DOS. Initially, both ES and DS point to this area, but programs reset DS to the beginning of the data segment. The map file does not show the PSP.

4.1.3   Assembling and Linking with MS-DOS Batch Files

Needless to say, it would be time-consuming to retype the assemble and link commands every time a program is modified. Instead, a batch file can be used to perform both steps. A useful one that generates a listing file and debugging information is shown for both the Borland and Microsoft assemblers:

asmTasm.bat	asmMasm.bat
tasm/l/z/zi %1	ml/Fl/Zi %1.asm
if errorlevel 1 goto exit	if errorlevel 1 goto exit
tlink/v %1	cv %1
if errorlevel 1 goto exit	:exit
td %1	
:exit	

Notice that **%1** appears twice in the file: This is a *replaceable parameter,* which takes on the name typed on the command line when the batch file is executed. For example, suppose we ran the **asmTasm.bat** file and passed it the name **sample** (for sample.asm):

```
asmTasm sample
```

The batch file would invoke **tasm.exe** and substitute **sample** for **%1**:

```
tasm /l /z /zi sample
if errorlevel 1 goto exit
```

If any syntax errors are generated by the assembler, it returns a non-zero value to MS-DOS, which is interpreted by the **if errorlevel** command. The latter causes a jump to the label called **:exit**.

Assuming that no errors are found, the next line in the batch file invokes the tlink.exe program and substitutes **sample** for **%1**. Again, if any errors are generated, the batch file exits:

```
tlink/v sample
if errorlevel 1 goto exit
```

You must set the MS-DOS PATH command to include the home directory of the assembler and linker. This is usually handled automatically during the assembler's installation. The batch files we have shown here can also be located in a directory on the MS-DOS path, or you can provide a shortcut to the batch file under Windows.

4.1.4   Memory Models

The .model directive selects a standard memory model for an assembly language program. A *memory model* may be thought of as a standard blueprint or configuration, which determines the way segments are used and combined. Each memory model has a different set of restrictions as to the maximum space available for code and data. But the most important thing to know about models is that they affect the way subroutines and data can be accessed by programs.

In general, choosing a memory model means making a choice between execution speed and flexibility of program size. A memory model that restricts all data to a single 64K segment, for example, assures that data addresses will be *near,* that is, 16-bit values. In this way, data can be accessed more quickly, because a 16-bit address can be loaded faster than a 32-bit segment-offset address. Similarly, a memory model that places subroutines in different segments requires both CS and IP to be loaded with a subroutine's address each time it is called.

The various memory models are defined by the number of bytes that can be used for code (instructions) and data (variables). When we limit code to 64K, for example, we indicate that all instructions must fit within a single 64K segment. Table 1 summarizes the differences between memory models. All models except the Tiny model result in the creation of EXE programs. The Tiny model creates a COM program. All models except the Flat model are available in *real* processor mode, and the Flat model is available only in *protected* processor

Table 1. Memory Models Recognized by MASM (and TASM).

Model	Description
Tiny	Code and data combined must be less than 64K.
Small	Code <= 64K, data <= 64K. One code segment, one data segment.
Medium	Data <= 64K, code any size. Multiple code segments, one data segment.
Compact	Code <= 64K, data any size. One code segment, multiple data segments.
Large	Code >64K, data > 64K. Multiple code and data segments.
Huge	Same as the Large model, except that individual variables such as arrays may be larger than 64K.
Flat	No segments. 32-bit addresses are used for both code and data. Protected mode only.

mode. Windows NT, for example, runs in protected mode. The Microsoft Visual C++ compiler can create console-based applications for Windows 95 that run under the flat memory model.

Executable Programs. Let's try to get a clear picture of what an executable program looks like after it has been loaded into memory. For example, if we assemble **hello.asm**, link **hello.obj,** and create **hello.exe,** a *map* file is produced that shows the offsets and sizes of the program segments. In the following sample map file, the code segment is 11h bytes, the data segment is 10h bytes, and the stack is 100h bytes:

```
Start      Stop      Length    Name     Class
00000      00010     00011     _TEXT    CODE
00020      0002F     00010     _DATA    DATA
00030      0012F     00100     STACK    STACK


Program entry point at 0000:0000
```

Figure 1 shows the **hello.exe** program drawn graphically as three overlapping segments. Notice that because (physical) memory segments have a range of 64K, they appear to overlap, but this is misleading. Each *program segment* (sometimes called a *logical segment*) is quite short, and there is no overlap. Physically speaking, the IP register is able to reach most of the data segment, but this would only happen if we forgot to include a program terminate instruction at the end of our code. Similarly, in *real* processor mode, if one exceeded the bounds of an

Figure 1. Overlapping Segments in the Hello program.

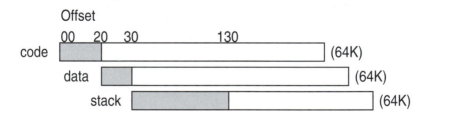

array in the data segment, one could corrupt the stack segment. In *protected* mode, on the other hand, a processor exception would occur if we tried to access memory outside a segment.

A hexadecimal dump of this program (Figure 2) shows that each segment begins on an even paragraph boundary (its address is an even multiple of 10h). The code segment, for example, is only 11h bytes long, but the next segment begins at offset 20h. The bytes at offsets 11h-1Fh are unused.

Figure 2. Hexadecimal Dump of the Hello Program.

```
(code)
2000:0000   B8 DC 23 8E D8 B4 09 BA-00 00 CD 21 B8 00 4C CD
2000:0010   21 00 00 00 00 00 00 00-00 00 00 00 00 00 00 00
```

```
(data)
2000:0020  48 65 6C 6C 6F 2C 20 77-6F 72 6C 64 21 0D 0A 24  Hello, world!..$

(stack)
2000:0030  F4 B2 56 F6 E2 8B F0 E8-34 00 A1 28 50 A9 00 04
2000:0040  74 1E F6 06 1F 49 06 74-17 F6 06 1F 49 04 74 0D
2000:0050  50 56 8A 36 22 49 33 F6-E8 13 00 5E 58 25 FF FB
2000:0060  B3 01 E8 C1 C8 8B C6 F6-F2 07 5E 5A 5B C3 32 FF
(etc.)
```

4.1.5   Target Processor Directives

The assemblers written for the Intel processor family support the entire range of processors from the 8086 through the Pentium. The Borland and Microsoft assemblers recognize *target processor directives* that specify the minimum target processor for a program. If a program contains the .8086 directive, for example, it will contain machine instructions that run on the 8086 and all subsequent processors. If a program uses the .386 directive, on the other hand, it will run only on the 80386, 80486, and Pentium. Table 2 lists the processor directives that

Table 2. Target Processor Directives.

Directive	Description
.8086	Enables assembly of 8086 and 8088 instructions. Disables assembly of instructions for the 80186 and later processors. Also enables 8087 instructions.
.186	Enables assembly of 80186 instructions and disables assembly of instructions for all later processors.
.286	Enables assembly of nonprivileged 80286 instructions and disables assembly of instructions for all later processors.
.386	Enables assembly of nonprivileged 80386 instructions and disables assembly of instructions for all later processors.
.486	Enables assembly of nonprivileged 80486 instructions and disables assembly of instructions for the Pentium.
.586	Enables assembly of nonprivileged Pentium instructions.
.287	Enables assembly of floating-point instructions for the 80287 math coprocessor.
.387	Enables assembly of floating-point instructions for the 80387 math coprocessor.

apply to Real-mode programming. If you plan to use 32-bit registers, insert the .386 directive prior to the usage of any 32-bit registers in your program. Locating it just before the .data directive, for example, works well. There is also a set of directives that enable priveleged mode instructions, which are not listed in the table. They are important for programming at the operating system level: .286P, .386P, .486P, and .586P.

4.2   OPERATORS AND EXPRESSIONS

An assembly language *expression* is a combination of operators and operands that is converted by the assembler into a single constant value. The assembler performs arithmetic and logical operations at assembly time, not at runtime. If an expression is being assigned to a register or memory operand, the size of the value must not be greater than the size of the destination operand. For example, the following assignments are legal:

```
.386
.code
mov  dl,3 * 5
mov  ax,100h + 500h
mov  eax,(1000h * 50h) + 26
```

Table 3 contains a complete listing of assembler operators recognized by most assemblers. You may, of course, find more complete descriptions of these in the reference manuals. The rich array of available operators attests to the power of these assemblers as professional programming tools.

4.2.1   Arithmetic Operators

Arithmetic operators can be used only with integers, with the exception of unary plus (+) and minus (–), which can also be used with real numbers. Examples of arithmetic expressions follow:

```
1000h * 50h        ; Value is 50000h
-4 + -2            ; Value is -6
count + 2          ; Count is a constant
31 MOD 6           ; Value is 1
6 / 4              ; Value is 1
'2'-30h            ; Value is 2
```

Character constants are compatible with integers, so an expression such as '2' - 30h subtracts 30h from from 32h, the ASCII code of the digit '2'.

Operator Precedence and Associativity. Each operator has a *precedence* level, meaning that it is evaluated before another operator of lower precedence. The set of arithmetic operators in order of precedence is shown in Table 4. Parentheses, for example, have a precedence level of 1, so any expression within parentheses is evaluated first. The order of operations is shown for each of the following examples:

Table 3. Assembler Operators.

Operator	Description
.TYPE	Returns a byte that defines the mode and scope of an expression. The result is bit mapped and is used to show whether a label or variable is program-related, data-related, undefined, or external in scope.
+, -, *, /	Addition, subtraction, multiplication, division of integers.
AND, OR, NOT	Bitwise operations on constant integers.
EQ, NE, LT, LE, GT, GE	Relational operators: Assembler returns a value of 0FFFFh when a relation is true or 0 when it is false.
HIGH	Returns the high 8 bits of a constant expession.
HIGHWORD	Returns the high 16 bits of a 32-bit operand (MASM only).
LENGTH	Returns the number of byte, word, dword, qword, or tenbyte elements in a variable. This is meaningful only if the variable is initialized with the DUP operator.
LOW	Returns the low 8 bits of a constant expression.
LOWWORD	Returns the low 16 bits of a 32-bit operand (MASM only).
MASK	Returns a bit mask for the bit positions in a field within a variable. A bit mask preserves just the important bits, setting all others equal to zero. The variable must be defined with the RECORD directive.
MOD	Modulus operator: returns the integer remainder of a division operation.
OFFSET	Returns the offset of a label or variable from the beginning of its segment.
PTR	Specifies the size of an operand, particularly when its size is not clear from the context.
SEG	Returns the segment value of an expression, whether it be a variable, a segment/group name, a label, or any other symbol.
SHORT	Sets a label's attribute to SHORT. Often used in JMP instructions, as in: `JMP SHORT Label1`.
SIZE	Returns the total number of bytes allocated for a variable. This is calculated as the LENGTH multiplied by the TYPE.
Field (.)	The name following (.) identifies a field within a predefined structure by adding the offset of the field to the offset of the variable. The format is variable.field.
THIS	Creates an operand of a specified type at the current program location. The type can be any of those used with the PTR operator or the LABEL directive.
TYPE	Returns an integer that represents either the size of a variable or its type. For example, the TYPE of a word variable is 2.
WIDTH	Returns the number of bits of a given field within a variable that has been declared with the RECORD directive.

Table 4. Operator Precedence Table.

Operator	Level	Description
( )	1	Parentheses
+, –	2	Positive and negative signs (unary)
*, /, mod	3	Multiplication, Division, Modulus
+, –	4	Addition, Subtraction

```
3 + 2 * 5                    ; multiply, add
count / 5 MOD 3              ; divide, mod
+4 * 3 - 1                   ; sign, multiply, subtract
(1000h - 30h) * 4           ; subtract, multiply
-((count MOD 5) + 2) * 4    ; mod, add, sign, multiply
```

Operators also have a property known as *associativity*, which is important when an expression involves two or more operators having the same precedence level. All of the operators shown in Table 4 associate from left to right, so in the following expressions, division is performed before multiplication, and subtraction is performed before addition:

```
count / 5 * 3
count - 2 + 3
```

4.2.2   OFFSET, SEG, PTR, LABEL, and EVEN

OFFSET Operator. The OFFSET operator returns the distance of a label or variable from the beginning of its segment. The destination operand must be a 16-bit register, as in the following example:

```
mov  bx,offset count        ; BX points to count
```

We say that BX *points* to **count** because it contains count's offset address. When a register or variable holds an address, we call it a *pointer*. As the following examples show, the offset of any element of an array can be moved to an index or base register. We assume that **bList** is located at offset 0000:

```
.data
bList  db  10h,20h,30h,40h
wList  dw  1000h,2000h,3000h

.code
```

```
mov   di,offset bList          ; DI = 0000
mov   bx,offset bList+1        ; BX = 0001
mov   si,offset wList+2        ; SI = 0006
```

SEG Operator. The SEG operator returns the segment part of a label or variable's address. It is usually used when a variable is in a segment other than the one currently pointed to by DS. In the next example, we push the current value of DS on the stack, set DS to the segment containing the variable **array,** and later restore DS to its original value:

```
push   ds                      ; save DS
mov    ax,seg array            ; set DS to segment of array
mov    ds,ax
mov    bx,offset array         ; get the array offset
.                              ; perform the array processing
.
.
pop    ds                      ; restore DS
```

PTR Operator. The PTR operator overrides the default size of an operand. Also, in instructions where the size of an operand is ambiguous, the PTR operator can explicitly state the operand's size. PTR must be used in combination with the standard assembler data types: BYTE, SBYTE, WORD, SWORD, DWORD, SDWORD, FWORD, QWORD, and TBYTE. For example:

```
mov   al,byte ptr count
mov   ax,word ptr newVal
mov   eax,dword ptr listPointer          ; (requires the .386 directive)
```

Often, the size of an operand is not clear from the context of an instruction. Consider the following instruction, which would generate an "operand must have size" error message by the assembler:

```
inc  [bx]                 ; indirect operand
```

In other words, the assembler doesn't know whether BX points to a byte or a word. The PTR operator makes the operand size crystal clear:

```
inc byte ptr [bx]
```

PTR is also useful when you need to override an operand's default size. Suppose we have a 32-bit doubleword and we want to load its high word into DX and its low word into AX. (A doubleword is stored with the least significant word at the lowest address.) The following would generate a syntax error:

```
.data
val32  dd  12345678h
.code
```

```
mov  ax, val32         ; get low word  (ERROR)
mov  dx, val32+2       ; get high word (ERROR)
```

But the following lines assemble correctly because PTR overrides the default type of **val32:**

```
mov  ax,word ptr val32         ; AX = 5678h
mov  dx,word ptr val32+2       ; DX = 1234h
```

LABEL Directive. The LABEL directive lets you insert a label and give it a size attribute, without allocating any storage. Any of the standard *size* attributes can be used with LABEL, such as BYTE, WORD, DWORD, QWORD, and so on.

One common use of LABEL is to provide an alternative name and size attribute for some existing variable in the data segment. This is a convenient way of getting around the assembler's requirement that the size attribute of a variable must match the other operand in an instruction. In the following example, we have declared a label just before **val32** called **val16** and have given it a word attribute:

```
.data
val16 label word
val32  dd  12345678h
.code
mov  ax, val16           ; AX = 5678h
mov  dx, val16+2         ; DX = 1234h
```

Notice that the two MOV instructions refer to **val16,** which is just an alias for the same storage location allocated to **val32.**

EVEN and EVENDATA Directives. The EVEN directive aligns the next instruction in the code segment to an even 16-bit offset. This can improve a program's speed by taking advantage of processors that use a 16-bit data bus. In the following code excerpt, a 1-byte NOP instruction (90h) is inserted in the program's compiled code where EVEN appears. The subsequent instruction is at 0006, an even address:

```
0000  mov ax,@data
0003  mov ds,ax
0005  EVEN                    ; byte containing 90h inserted here
0006  mov bx,offset array
```

Similarly, the EVENDATA directive in the following example inserts a null byte (0) before **array.** This causes it to begin at offset 0004 rather than 0003:

```
0000  .data
0000  str1 db 3 dup('X')
0003  EVENDATA
0004  array dw 10 dup(0FFFFh)
```

4.2.3   TYPE and SIZE Operators

SHORT Operator. The SHORT operator is most often used with a JMP instruction when we know a forward jump is less than or equal to 127 bytes from the current location. This allows the assembler to generate a 1-byte short jump instruction rather than a 2-byte near jump instruction.

TYPE Operator. The TYPE operator returns the size, in bytes, of a single element of a variable. For example, an 8-bit variable would return a type of 1, a 32-bit variable would return 4, an array of bytes would return 1, and an array of 16-bit integers would return 2. The type of a near label is FFFFh, and the type of a far label is FFFEh. Here are some examples:

```
.data
var1    db    20h
var2    dw    1000h
var3    dd    ?
var4    db    10,20,30,40,50
msg     db    'File not found',0


.code
L1:     mov   ax,type var1        ; AX = 0001
        mov   ax,type var2        ; AX = 0002
        mov   ax,type var3        ; AX = 0004
        mov   ax,type var4        ; AX = 0001
        mov   ax,type msg         ; AX = 0001
        mov   ax,type L1          ; AX = FFFF
```

LENGTH Operator. The LENGTH operator counts the number of individual elements in a variable that has been defined using DUP. If DUP is not used, LENGTH returns a value of 1. If nested DUP operators are used, only the outer one is counted by the LENGTH operator. Examples are as follows:

```
.data
val1        dw 1000h
val2        db 10,20,30
array       dw 32 dup(0)
array2      dw 5 dup(3 dup(0))
message     db 'File not found',0


.code
mov   ax,length val1        ; length = 1
mov   ax,length val2        ; length = 1
mov   ax,length array       ; length = 32
mov   ax,length array2      ; length = 5
mov   ax,length message     ; length = 1
```

SIZE Operator. The SIZE operator is equivalent to multiplying the LENGTH of a variable by its TYPE value. For example, the following array of 16-bit values has a TYPE of 2 and a LENGTH of 32. Its size is 64:

```
intArray  dw 32 dup(0)    ; SIZE = 64
```

The following string has a SIZE of 1 because its LENGTH and TYPE both equal 1:

```
message  db 'This is a message',0
```

4.2.4   Borland TASM's ENUM Directive

The Borland Turbo Assembler supports the ENUM directive. This lets you define a set of enumerated constants and automatically assign an integer value to each one. All the symbols can be defined on a single line, with the following syntax:

```
name enum [symbol1 [, symbol2,...[, symbol-n]]]
```

For example, we might define symbols for disk drive status. The name *driveStatus* is a type name for the list of enumerated constants:

```
driveStatus    enum    ready, busy, offline
```

By default, the first constant is assigned a value of zero, the second value is assigned 1, and so on. The constant called *offline*, for example, would be assigned the value 2.

You can also use multiple lines for the symbol definitions by enclosing the lines in braces. For example, a useful declaration would be for all of the possible background colors in text mode on a PC. Use comma separators between symbols occurring on the same line:

```
ColorType enum {
   black, blue
   green, cyan
   red, magenta
   brown, white }
```

The assembler selects the smallest data type that holds all the enumerated constants. ColorType, for example, is automatically given a byte attribute, so the following lines show the difference:

```
.code
mov  al,blue            ; ok
mov  ax,blue            ; error - size mismatch
```

Usage. Suppose we had defined ColorType in a program just before the .data directive. We could use the enumerated constants in both data definitions and program instructions:

```
.data
winColor db cyan
.code
mov  al,winColor    ; AL = 3
```

Furthermore, it is better programming style to use the enumerated type in place of DB when declaring winColor:

```
.data
winColor ColorType cyan
```

There is no strict type checking by the assembler, so it is up to you to use only enumerated constants when assigning values to variables declared this way. For example, the assembler allows one to assign either enumerated constants or integers to winColor:

```
mov  winColor, blue
mov  winColor, 12h
```

Explicit Values. Each enumerated constant can optionally be assigned a value between 0 and 0FFFFh. This is useful when the default values 0, 1, 2, ... are not appropriate. For example, we could use an enum declaration for one of several error status codes that we want to place in the AL register:

```
StatusVals enum  normal = 1, overheat = 5, highSpeed
.code
mov  bl, overheat              ; BL = 5
mov  al, highSpeed             ; AL = 6
```

Notice that highSpeed is automatically assigned the next sequential value (6) because its preceding value is 5.

If the explicit values assigned to enumerated constants exceed available storage for a byte, the enumerated type is assigned a word attribute:

```
StatusVals enum  {
   normal = 1000h, overheat = 2000h, highSpeed = 3000h }
.code
mov  ax, highSpeed             ; ok
mov  al, overheat              ; error - size mismatch
```

4.3   JMP AND LOOP INSTRUCTIONS

The CPU automatically loads and executes programs sequentially. As each instruction is decoded and executed, the CPU has already incremented the instruction pointer to the offset of the next instruction; it has also loaded the instruction into its internal queue. But real-life programs are not that simple. What about IF statements, gotos, and loops? They clearly require programs to transfer control to different locations within the programs.

A *transfer of control,* or *branch* is a way of altering the order in which statements are executed. All programming languages contain statements to do this. We divide such statements into two categories:

Unconditional Transfer. The program branches to a new location in all cases; a new value is loaded into the instruction pointer, causing execution to continue at the new address. The JMP instruction is a good example.

Conditional Transfer. The program branches if a certain condition is true. Intel provides a wide range of conditional transfer instructions that can be combined to make up conditional logic structures. The CPU interprets true/false conditions based on the contents of the CX and Flags registers.

4.3.1   JMP Instruction

The JMP instruction tells the CPU to continue execution at another location. The location must be identified by a label, which is translated by the assembler into an address. If the jump is to a label in the current segment, the label's offset is loaded into the IP register. If the label is in another segment, the segment's address is also loaded into CS. Assuming that *destination* is a label or 32-bit segment-offset address, there are three formats for the JMP instruction:

```
JMP SHORT destination
JMP NEAR PTR destination
JMP FAR PTR destination
```

JMP can jump to a label in the current procedure, from one procedure to another, from one segment to another, completely out of the current program, or to anywhere in RAM or ROM. Structured programming style discourages such jumps, but they are occasionally necessary in systems programming applications. Examples of various jumps are shown here:

```
jmp L1                    ; NEAR: destination in current segment
jmp near ptr L1           ; NEAR: destination in current segment
jmp short nextval         ; SHORT: within -128 to +127 bytes
jmp far ptr error_rtn     ; FAR: jump to different segment
```

The operator placed before the destination operand can be one of the following:

- SHORT: Jump to a label in the range –128 to +127 bytes from the address of the next instruction. An 8-bit signed integer (called a *displacement*) is added to IP.

- NEAR PTR: Jump to a label anywhere in the current code segment. A 16-bit displacement is moved to IP.

- FAR PTR: Jump to a label in another segment. The label's segment address is moved to CS, and its offset is moved to IP.

The SHORT operator is especially useful when coding forward jumps because the assembler doesn't know the destination address until it assembles that part of the program. For example:

```
label1:  jmp short label2          ; use SHORT here
         .
         .
label2:  jmp label1                ; automatically a SHORT jump
```

The NEAR PTR operator tells the assembler that the destination label is in the same code segment; usually this is assumed. If the jump is to a label outside the current segment, the FAR PTR operator may be required. Examples of each are shown here, using a label called **exit** as the target of the jump:

```
jmp near ptr exit
jmp far  ptr exit
```

A loop based only on JMP will never stop, as the following statements show. Fortunately, the program calls INT 21h, so you can stop the program in the debugger by pressing the Ctrl-Break keys:

```
start:  mov   ah,2           ; display a character
        mov   dl,'A'
        int   21h
        jmp   start
```

Assembling a Short Jump. You may find it interesting to know something about the way JMP instructions are assembled. The following excerpt is from a listing file generated by an assembler. At the beginning of each line is the hexadecimal offset of each instruction, followed by the object code that was generated:

```
Offset    Machine Code          Source Code
 0100     B4 02        start:   mov ah,2       ; start of loop
 0102     B2 41                 mov dl,'A'     ; display the letter A
 0104     CD 21                 int 21h        ; call DOS
 0106     EB F8                 jmp start      ; jump back to start
 0108     ...(etc.)
```

Before assembling an instruction, the assembler increments its own *location counter,* which tells it the offset of the next instruction. When assembling the instruction at 0106h, for example, the assembler has already set the location counter to 0108h. The jump at 0106h is automatically assembled as a short jump because the distance from the location counter to the label **start** is less than 128 bytes.

Two object code bytes are generated for the JMP at location 0106h: EBh and F8h. The first byte (EBh) is the *op code* for a short jump instruction. The second byte (F8h, or –8) is a *displacement* that tells the CPU how far to jump. The assembler calculates this by subtracting the location counter (0108h) from the offset of the destination (0100h). The resulting displacement (F8h) is assembled as part of the instruction:

```
op code -> EB F8  <- displacement
```

4.3.2 LOOP Instruction

The LOOP instruction is the easiest way to repeat a block of statements a specific number of times. CX is automatically used as a counter and is decremented each time the loop repeats. Its syntax is:

```
LOOP destination
```

First, the LOOP instruction subtracts 1 from CX. Then if CX is not equal to zero, control transfers to *destination*. The destination must be –128 to +127 bytes from the current location (the assembler uses its own location counter to determine this). In the following example, the loop repeats five times:

```
        mov   cx,5      ; CX is the loop counter
    start:
        .
        .
        loop start      ; jump to START
```

If CX equals zero after having been decremented, no jump takes place and control passes to the instruction(s) following the loop. The Zero flag is not affected, although CX = 0.

In the following example, we add 1 to AX each time the loop repeats. When the loop ends, AX = 5 and CX = 0:

```
        mov  ax,0              ; set AX to 0
        mov  cx,5              ; loop count
    top:
        inc  ax               ; add 1 to AX
        loop top              ; repeat until CX = 0
```

Example: Repeat the Letter A. The following program excerpt prints the letter *A* on the screen 960 times, using the LOOP instruction. The count placed in CX represents 12 rows of the screen multiplied by 80 characters per row:

```
      mov    cx,12*80            ; set count to 960
next:
      mov    ah,2                ; function: display character
      mov    dl,'A'              ; display the letter A
      int    21h                 ; call DOS
      loop   next                ; decrement CX and repeat
```

Starting with a Zero Counter. A common programming error is to inadvertently initialize CX to zero before beginning a loop. If this happens, the LOOP instruction decrements CX to FFFFh, and the loop repeats 65,535 times.

Altering the Loop Counter. Be careful not to modify the register or variable being used as a loop counter. In the following example, CX is incremented within the loop. It never reaches zero, and the loop never stops:

```
      mov   ah,2                 ; DOS function: display character
      mov   cx,10                ; loop counter
      mov   dl,'*'               ; character to be displayed

top:
      int   21h                  ; call DOS
      inc   cx                   ; add 1 to CX (!)
      loop  top                  ; loop until CX = 0
```

When using high-level languages, you should not modify a loop counter within its own loop, primarily because the internal storage of the variable is not visible to the programmer, and altering the counter can have unanticipated consequences.

4.3.3   LOOP, LOOPW, LOOPD Instructions

The LOOPD (*loop doubleword*) instruction for the 80386 processor tells the assembler to use the 32-bit ECX register as a counter. This allows a loop to execute as many as $(2^{32} - 1)$, or 4,294,967,295 times. For example:

```
     mov ecx,A0000000h
L1:  .
     .
     loopd L1                    ; use ECX as loop counter
```

If a program is assembled in 32-bit mode, the LOOP instruction automatically uses the ECX register as a loop counter. The LOOPW instruction can still be used to override the default ECX register counter and use CX.

4.4 INDIRECT ADDRESSING

4.4.1 Indirect Operands

An indirect operand is a register that contains the offset of data in memory. When the offset of a variable is placed in a register, the register becomes a pointer to the label. For variables containing a single element, this would have little value. For an array, however, a pointer can be incremented to point to each subsequent element. Among the 16-bit registers, SI, DI, BX, and BP can be used in indirect operands. If the 80386 processor is enabled by the .386, .486, or .586 directive, any one of the 32-bit general purpose registers can be used for indirect addressing. (There is one restriction on ESP, which we will show later.)

For example, if we create a string in memory at location 0200 and set BX to the offset of the string, we can process any element in the string by adding its offset to BX. The letter 'F' is at offset 5 in the following example:

```
.data
aString  db  "ABCDEFG"
.code
mov  bx,offset aString          ; BX = 0200
add  bx,5                       ; BX = 0205
mov  dl,[bx]                    ; DL = 'F'
```

Segment Defaults. The offset created by an indirect operand is assumed to be from DS, except when BP or EBP is part of the indirect operand. The latter indicate offsets from the stack segment (SS register). Assuming that the stack segment and data segment are at different locations, the second and third MOV statements would access different memory locations:

```
mov  si,bp ; SI and BP are equal
mov  dl,[si]                    ; looks in the data segment
mov  dl,[bp]                    ; looks in the stack segment
```

Overriding the Default Segment. There are occasions when it is useful to use indirect addresssing to access data in a segment other than DS. You can use a *segment override* to indicate the desired segment:

```
mov   al,cs:[si]                     ; offset from CS
mov   eax,es:[edi]                   ; offset from ES
mov   bx,fs:[edx]                    ; offset from FS
mov   dl,ss:[di]                     ; offset from SS
mov   ax,gs:[ecx]                    ; offset from GS
```

Similarly, if you want to use BP or EBP to access data pointed to by DS, CS, or ES, a segment override is needed:

```
mov   dl,ds:[bp]                     ; offset from DS
mov   al,es:[ebp]                    ; offset from ES
mov   dl,cs:[bp]                     ; offset from CS
mov   al,fs:[ebp]                    ; offset from FS
```

Example: Adding 8-bit Integers. The program fragment in Example 3 calculates the sum of three 8-bit integers, using indirect addressing. If the sum of the three integers were greater than FFh, it would overflow the AL register and produce incorrect results. The extra bits do not automatically carry into the AH register. To confirm this, assemble and trace the same code with the following three values:

```
aList db 50h,60h,70h
```

Example 3. Adding Several 8-bit Integers.

```
.data
aList db 10h,20h,30h
sum    db 0
.code
mov bx,offset aList
mov al,[bx]              ; AL = 10h
inc bx
add al,[bx]              ; AL = 30h
inc bx
add al,[bx]              ; AL = 60h
mov si,offset sum        ; get offset of sum
mov [si],al              ; store the sum
```

Another way to write this example would be to add a *displacement* to BX when accessing the second and third numbers. This would eliminate the need for separate instructions that

increment BX. We could also take advantage of the fact that sum is located at the next offset
beyond the first three numbers:

```
mov bx,offset aList
mov al,[bx]                      ; first number
add al,[bx+1]                    ; second number
add al,[bx+2]                    ; third number
mov [bx+3],al                    ; store the sum
```

Example: Adding 16-bit Integers. The program excerpt in Example 4 uses indirect addressing
to add several 16-bit integers. The important difference between this example and the 8-bit
example (Example 3) is the size of the operands. An offset of 2 must be added to access each
subsequent integer:

1000	2000	3000	(sum)
[bx]	[bx+2]	[bx+4]	[bx+6]

Example 4. Adding 16-bit Integers.

```
.data
wordList dw 1000h,2000h,3000h
sum       dw 0
.code
mov bx,offset wordList
mov ax,[bx]                      ; first number
add ax,[bx+2]                    ; second number
add ax,[bx+4]                    ; third number
mov [bx+6],ax                    ; store the sum
```

Using a Loop to Display a String. The program fragment in Example 5 combines indirect
addressing with the LOOP instruction to display a string. Each character is moved to DL and
displayed with INT 21h. The expression ($ – string) tells the assembler to calculate the length
of the string by subtracting the string's starting offset from the value of the current location
counter ($).

Example 5. Displaying a String.

```
.data
string db "This is a string."
COUNT = ($ - string)    ; calculate string length
```

```
        .code
                mov     cx,COUNT            ; loop counter
                mov     si,offset string
        L1:
                mov     ah,2                ; display the character
                mov     dl,[si]             ; get a character
                int     21h
                inc     si                  ; point to next character
                loop    L1                  ; decrement CX, repeat until 0
```

Example: Using a Loop to Sum an Integer Array. The program excerpt in Example 6 accumulates the sum of an array, using indirect addressing and the LOOP instruction. First, the accumulator (AX) is set to zero, and DI is assigned the offset of the array. CX is assigned a loop counter value equal to the number of integers. With this approach, the array could be as large as the entire data segment. Of course, the sum may be too large to fit into AX, a 16-bit accumulator.

Example 6. Summing an Integer Array.

```
        .data
        intarray dw 100h,200h,300h,400h
        COUNT = ($ - intarray) / 2

        .code
                mov     ax,0                ; zero the accumulator
                mov     di,offset intarray  ; address of intarray
                mov     cx,COUNT            ; loop counter

        L1:
                add     ax,[di]             ; add an integer
                add     di,2                ; point to next integer
                loop    L1                  ; repeat until CX = 0
```

4.4.2　Based and Indexed Operands

Based and indexed operands are essentially the same: A register (either base or index) is added to a displacement to generate an effective address. A *displacement* is a constant value—it might be the offset of a variable, for instance. The distinction between based and index is simply that BX and BP are *base* registers, and SI and DI are *index* registers. The assembler permits a variety of notational forms, shown here with 16-bit registers:

Register Added to an Offset	Register Added to a Constant
mov dx,array[bx]	mov ax,[bx + ROWVAL]
mov dx,[di + array]	mov dx,[bp+4]
mov dx,[array+si]	mov dx,2[si]

Array Example. If we create an array of byte values stored in memory at location 0200 and set BX to 5, BX will then point to the number at offset 5 into the array:

```
.data
ROWSIZE = 5
array  db 2,16,4,22,13,19,42,64,44,88
.code
mov bx,ROWSIZE
mov al,array[bx]    ; AL = 19
```

The following diagram helps to show how the array is arranged in memory:

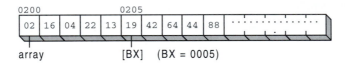

32-bit Registers. If 386 instructions are enabled (using the .386 directive shown on page 93), you can use any of the 32-bit general-purpose registers as base and index operands:

```
.386                    ; enable 32-bit registers
mov  ax,[ebx+3]         ; 16-bit operand
mov  dl,string[edx]     ; 8-bit operand
mov  ecx,6[esi]         ; 32-bit operand
mov  eax,myList[edi]    ; 32-bit operand
```

In a program running in 16-bit mode, be careful not to use a 32-bit index value that would be beyond the segment boundary (0 - FFFFh):

```
mov  esi,10000h
mov  al,[esi]           ; out of range in 16-bit mode
```

4.4.3   Base-Index Operands

A base-index operand adds the value of a base register to an index register, producing a memory offset. This type of operand is often useful when accessing a two dimensional array, where the base register contains a row offset and the index register contains a column offset. The program excerpt in Example 7 contains an array of 8-bit integers. If this array is located at offset 0150 and we set BX to the beginning of the second row and set SI to the offset of the third column, the offset represented by BX + SI is 0157:

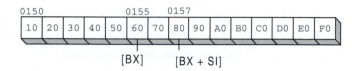

Example 7. Two-Dimensional Array Example.

```
.data
ROWSIZE = 5
array  db 10h, 20h, 30h, 40h, 50h, 60h, 70h, 80h, 90h
       db 0A0h, B0h, 0C0h, 0D0h, 0E0h, 0F0h

.code
mov  bx,offset array          ; point to the array at 0150
add  bx,ROWSIZE               ; choose second row
mov  si,2                     ; chose third column
mov  al,[bx + si]             ; get the value at 0157
```

Because BX and BP are 16-bit base registers and SI and DI are index registers, there is one important restriction. You cannot combine two base registers or two index registers:

```
mov al,[bp + bx]              ; invalid
mov al,[si + di]              ; invalid
```

32-bit Registers. The following examples are permitted by the assembler as uses of base-indexed operands. It does make a difference as to which register comes first. In the last two examples, the CPU assumes the data is in a different segment, depending on whether EBP appears first or last:

```
.386
mov  al,[ebx + esi]           ; offset from DS
mov  bx,[ecx][edx]            ; offset from DS
mov  ax,[ebp + esi]           ; offset from stack
mov  ax,[esi + ebp]           ; offset from DS
```

4.4.4   Base-Index with Displacement

An operand's effective address can be formed by combining a base register, an index register, and a displacement. The notation can have a variety of forms:

```
mov  dx,array[bx][si]
mov  ax,[bx+si+array]
add  dl,[bx+si+3]
sub  cx,array[bp+si]
```

As with base-index operands, the current type of operand is well-suited to two-dimensional tables. The name of an array can be used as the displacement portion of the operand, a base register can contain the offset of a row within the table, and an index register can contain the offset of a column within the row. In the following example, BX contains the distance (in bytes) of the second row from the beginning of the table, and SI contains the distance from the beginning of the row to the third column:

```
ROWSIZE = 5
mov  bx,ROWSIZE               ; choose second row
mov  si,2                     ; choose third column
mov  al,array[bx+si]          ; get the value at offset 0157
```

The following diagram helps to show the positions of BX and SI relative to the array:

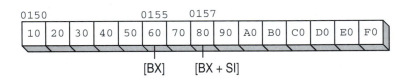

4.5   DEBUGGING WORKSHOP

Studies on programming show that we spend 20% of our time *writing* code and 80% of our time *debugging*. Clearly, two important skills need to be developed and improved in every programmer: program design and program debugging. In this section, we will concentrate on elementary assembly language debugging skills, in particular, that of avoiding syntax errors. (Of course, runtime bugs are much more difficult to catch.)

Most syntax errors result either from the incorrect use of assembler directives or from the use of invalid instruction operands. Some common types of syntax errors are:

•   Missing or misplaced .CODE, .DATA, and .STACK directives.

•   Missing or misplaced PROC and ENDP directives.

•   Missing END directive or a label missing after the END directive.

• Mismatching operand sizes.

When the assembler displays an error message, it lists the name of the source program, the line number (from the source file) in parentheses, the error number, and a description of the error. For example:

```
PROG1.ASM (7): warning A4031: Operand types must match
```

The name of the source file is PROG1.ASM, and the error occurred on line 7. The error number (A4031) refers you to a more complete explanation in the assembler manual. The message ("Operand types must match") says that a statement tried to mix operands of two different sizes. Although this is a warning message, the problem should be resolved before linking and running the program. Otherwise, the assembler can generate incorrect object code. In the sample error messages given in this chapter, we have omitted the file name, so the line number that caused the error is at the beginning of the error message.

Open Procedures. The error message "Open procedures" occurs when an ENDP directive is not found to mark the end of a procedure. The following program demonstrates this:

```
title  Error Example
.model small
.stack 100h
.code
main proc
          mov    ax,4C00h
          int    21h

                              ; <-- ENDP directive missing

end main
<< Error : Open procedures: MAIN >>
```

4.5.1   Operand Sizes and Addressing Errors

The assembler performs type checking on memory operands. Most important, it ensures that operand sizes match. Such errors are usually corrected by using the BYTE PTR or WORD PTR operators to identify the attributes of certain operands. This may seem annoying, but it helps one avoid subtle logic errors.

Mismatching Operand Sizes. In the program listed in Example 8, the 8-bit size of **value1** does not match the 16-bit size of AX, and **value2** does not match the size of AH. This is probably the most common of all syntax errors, made by beginner and expert alike.

Example 8. Program with Mismatching Operand Sizes.

```
1:    title Mismatching Operand Sizes
2:
3:    .model small
```

```
 4:     .stack 100h
 5:     .code
 6:     main proc
 7:             mov     ax,@data
 8:             mov     ds,ax
 9:             mov     ax,value1
10:             mov     ah,value2
11:             mov     ax,4C00h
12:             int     21h
13:             main endp
14:
15:     .data
16:     value1    db      0Ah
17:     value2    dw      1000h
18:     end  main


  (9): warning A4031: Operand types must match
 (10): warning A4031: Operand types must match
```

These errors can be corrected by adjusting the instruction operands to the correct sizes of the memory variables. We can rewrite lines 9 and 10 as follows:

```
mov    al,value1
mov    ax,value2
```

Miscellaneous Errors. The program shown in Example 9 contains several intentional mistakes. On line 9, the expression (**bx * cx**) is interpreted by the assembler as an immediate operand. The values of BX and CX are known only at runtime, so the assembler prints an error message. On line 10, the expression (**value1 * 2**) appears to be the product of two constants. When the assembler encounters the declaration of **value1** (as a variable) later in the program, it declares the instruction illegal. The error message for line 13 reminds us that CS cannot be used as a destination operand (nor can IP).

Example 9. Program with Miscellaneous Errors.

```
 1:     title Miscellaneous Errors Program
 2:
 3:     .model small
 4:     .stack 100h
 5:     .code
 6:     main proc
 7:             mov     ax,@data
 8:             mov     ds,ax
```

```
 9:        mov    ax,bx * cx
10:        mov    bx,value1 * 2
11:        mov    byte ptr value3, al
12:        mov    cx,ax
13:        mov    cs,ds
14:        mov    ax,4C00h
15:        int    21h
16:    main endp
17:    .data
18:    value1   db    0Ah
19:    value2   db    14h
20:    value3   dw    1000h
21:    end main
```

4.6   MORE 80386 AND 80486 INSTRUCTIONS

4.6.1   MOVZX and MOVSX Instructions

The MOVZX instruction (*move with zero-extend*) for the 80386 processor moves an 8-bit or 16-bit source operand into a larger 16-bit or 32-bit destination register. The unfilled bits in the destination register are cleared to Zero. In the following example, we move BL to AX using MOVZX; the upper bits in AX are zero-extended:

```
mov    bl,22h
movzx  ax,bl                  ; AX = 0022h
```

Or, we can move a 16-bit memory operand into EDX and zero-extend the upper 16 bits of EDX:

```
.data
var16 dw 1234h
.code
movzx  edx,var16              ; EDX = 00001234h
```

Similarly, the **MOVSX** instruction (*move with sign-extend*) for the 80386 processor moves and sign-extends the source operand into the upper half of the destination register. Notice in this example that the upper bits of CX are filled with the sign bit from FEh:

```
.data
var8 db -2                    ; FEh


.code
movsx  cx,var8                ; CX = FFFEh
```

4.6.2   XADD Instruction

The XADD (*exchange and add*) instruction for the 80486 adds the source and destination operands and stores the sum in the destination. At the same time, the original value in the destination is moved to the source operand. The Overflow, Sign, Zero, Auxiliary Carry, Parity, and Carry flags are affected. For example, we can add BX to AX, while retaining the number that was in AX:

```
.code
mov  ax,1000h
mov  bx,2000h
xadd ax,bx                    ; AX = 3000h, BX = 1000h
```

In effect, the XADD instruction in our example takes the place of the following three instructions:

```
push ax
add  ax,bx
pop  bx
```

4.7   USING A LINK LIBRARY

4.7.1   Selected Procedures in the Book's Link Library

Many of the standard input-output functions that you will need when writing your first assembly language programs can be found in a link libary supplied with this book, called **irvine.lib**. Table 5 contains a list of selected procedures from this library, and Appendix E, *Guide to the Sample Programs*, contains a complete list. Whenever input parameters are required, they are listed after the word *Input* in italics. In cases where a procedure returns a value, it is listed following the word *output*.

When the assembler finds a reference to a name that is not in the current source file, it cannot calculate the name's effective address. Use the EXTRN directive to identify names that exist outside the current source file. This tells the assembler that the name's address will be filled in by the linker. The basic format of the EXTRN directive is

```
EXTRN name:type
```

Name is the name of the procedure or label, and *type* is a size or distance attribute associated with the name. *Type* has the values shown in Table 6. The following directive identifies an external procedure named Writeint:

```
extrn Writeint:proc
```

If the program was compiled under the tiny, small or compact memory models, the procedure type will default to *near*. For other memory models, the procedure will be a *far* procedure.

The following directive identifies the declared constants named **true** and **false**. This example also shows that a single EXTRN directive can identify multiple names:

```
extrn true:abs, false:abs
```

The following identifies three variables, **bufsize**, **keystyped**, and **keybufptr**. The first has a 16-bit word attribute, the second an 8-bit byte attribute, and the third a 32-bit doubleword attribute:

```
extrn bufsize:word, keystyped:byte, keybufptr:dword
```

Table 5. Selected Procedures in the Link Library.

Procedure	Description
Clrscr	Clear the screen and locate the cursor at the upper left corner.
Crlf	Write a carriage return and line feed to standard output.
Get_time	Retrieve the current time of day. Input: DS:SI points to a TimeRecord structure. Requires the console.inc include file.
Gotoxy	Locate the cursor at a specified row and column on the screen. Input: DH = row (0-24), DL = column (0-79).
Random_range	Generate a pseudorandom integer in EAX between 0 and n−1. Input: EAX contains n.
Random32	Generate a 32-bit pseudorandom integer in the range 0 to FFFFFFFFh. Output: EAX contains the number.
Randomize	Automatically seed the random number generator with a random value, based on the current time of day.
Readint	Read a signed ASCII decimal string from standard input and store it as a 16-bit binary integer. Output: AX contains the value.
Readchar	Try to read a character from standard input without echoing the character on the screen. Output: If a character is waiting, ZF = 0 and AL contains the character. If no character is waiting, ZF = 1.
Readkey	Wait for a single key to be pressed on the keyboard. Cannot be redirected. Output: AH = key scan code, AL = ASCII code.

Table 5. Selected Procedures in the Link Library (*continued*).

Procedure	Description
Readlong	Read a signed ASCII decimal string from standard input and store it as a 32-bit binary integer. Output: EAX contains the value.
Readstring	Read a string of characters from standard input and store them in a null-terminated string. Input: DX points to the string, CX = maximum character count. Output: AX = number of characters typed.
Scroll	Scroll a window on the screen with a chosen color. Input: CH, CL = upper left corner row and column; DH, DL = lower right row and column; BH = attribute (color) of the scrolled lines.
Seconds_today	Return the number of seconds that have passed since midnight. Output: EAX contains the seconds.
Show_time	Write a given time to standard output. Input: DS:SI points to a TimeRecord structure.
Waitchar	Wait for a character to be read from standard input. Does not echo the character on the console. Output: AL contains the character.
Writechar	Write a single character to standard output. Input: AL contains the character.
Writeint	Write an unsigned 16-bit integer to standard output in ASCII binary, decimal, octal, or hexadecimal format. Input: AX = the integer to display, and BX = radix value (2, 8, 10, or 16).
Writeint_signed	Write a 16-bit integer to standard output in signed decimal ASCII format. Input: AX = the integer to display.
Writestring	Write a null-terminated string to standard output. Input: DX points to the string.

Each of the EXTRN directives should be located in a matching segment type. In other words, procedure declarations should be in the code segment, variable declarations should be in the data segment, and constant declarations can be anywhere. For example:

```
extrn true:abs
.data
extrn bufsize:word
.code
extrn Writestring:proc
```

Table 6. Data Types for the EXTRN Directive.

Type	Description
ABS	A constant defined with EQU or =
PROC	Default type for a procedure
NEAR	Name is in the same segment
FAR	Name is in a different segment
BYTE	Size is 8 bits
WORD	Size is 16 bits
DWORD	Size is 32 bits
FWORD	Size is 48 bits
QWORD	Size is 64 bits
TBYTE	Size is 10 bytes

Input Parameters. When input parameters are used, they are passed in registers. For example, before calling the Writestring procedure, move the offset of a null-terminated string into DX:

```
.data
message db "This is a message",0
.code
mov  dx,offset message
call Writestring
```

A program that demonstrates many of the link library functions is shown in Example 10. Here is the sample output produced by the program:

```
Link Library Demo Program

What is your name? Kip Irvine
Please enter a signed 16-bit integer: -1234
-1234
FB2E
1111101100101110


Press any key...
```

Example 10. Link Library Demo Program.

```
Title Link Library Demo Program           (lnkdemo.asm)

; This program calls various I/O procedures
; in the link library.

.model small
.stack 100h
WhiteOnBlue = 1Fh
GreetingLoc = 0400h

.data
greeting    db "Link Library Demo Program"
            db 0dh,0ah,0dh,0ah
            db "What is your name? ",0

numberPrompt db 0dh,0ah
            db "Please enter a 16-bit integer: ",0
userName    db 50 dup(0)
pressAnyKey  db 0dh,0ah,0dh,0ah
            db "Press any key...",0

.code
extrn Clrscr:proc, Crlf:proc, Gotoxy:proc, \
  Readint:proc, Readstring:proc, Scroll:proc, \
  Readkey:proc, Writeint:proc, Writestring:proc

main proc
   mov ax,@data
   mov ds,ax

; Clear the screen, scroll a blue window.

   call Clrscr
   mov  cx,0400h                  ; upper-left corner
   mov  dx,0B28h                  ; lower-right corner
   mov  bh,WhiteOnBlue
   call Scroll

; Display a greeting and ask for the
; user's name.
```

```
        mov   dx,GreetingLoc
        call  Gotoxy
        mov   dx,offset greeting
        call  Writestring
        mov   dx,offset userName
        call  Readstring

    ; Ask the user to enter a signed decimal integer.
    ; Redisplay the number in hexadecimal and binary.

        mov   dx,offset numberPrompt
        call  Writestring
        call  Readint              ; input an integer
        call  Crlf
        mov   bx,16                ; display in hexadecimal
        call  Writeint
        call  Crlf
        mov   bx,2                 ; display in binary
        call  Writeint

        mov   dx,offset pressAnyKey
        call  Writestring
        call  Readkey
        call  Clrscr

        mov ax,4c00h               ; end program
        int 21h
    main endp

    end main
```

4.7.2   Displaying Random Integers

The program excerpt in Example 11 displays a list of twenty 32-bit random integers between 0 and 999. We first call **Randomize** to seed the random number sequence to a random value based on the time of day, and then call **Random_range** to generate each number in EAX.

Example 11. Generating Random Integers.

```
.code
    extrn Randomize:proc, Random_range:proc, WriteInt:proc, Crlf:proc
    call Randomize
    mov  cx,20

L1: mov  eax,1000
    call Random_range        ; EAX = random integer
    mov  bx,10               ; decimal radix
    call WriteInt
    call Crlf
    Loop L1
```

4.7.3   Timing Events

You can call the **Seconds_today** procedure to get the number of seconds elapsed since midnight. This can be useful if you want to measure the time (in seconds) between two events. Call Seconds_today and store the result in a register or variable. Later, call the procedure again and compare it to the value you obtained the first time.

   In Example 12, the **Delay_seconds** procedure causes the program to pause for the number of seconds specified in the EAX register. It calls Seconds_today at the beginning of the procedure, records the time. Then in a loop, it repeatedly calls Seconds_today until the difference between the current value and the original value equals the length of the desired delay. For example, the following statements call the procedure and tell it to delay for 10 seconds:

```
mov  eax,10
call Delay_seconds
```

Example 12. The Delay_seconds Procedure.

```
extrn Seconds_today:proc

Delay_seconds proc
   pusha
   mov  ecx,eax             ; delay, in seconds
   call Seconds_today
   mov  ebx,eax             ; save start time

DLY1:
   call Seconds_today       ; get the time
```

```
        sub   eax,ebx              ; subtract from start
        cmp   eax,ecx              ; delay finished yet?
        jb    DLY1                 ; if not, continue loop


        popa
        ret
Delay_seconds endp
```

4.8   REVIEW QUESTIONS

1.   Why can't a listing file be assembled and linked?

2.   Which two files could be created by the assembler if the program PROJ1.ASM were assembled?

3.   Name two files created during the LINK step.

4.   In the following machine code from a listing file, what does the R tell us?

```
        5B 0021 R        add   bx,val1
```

5.   What is the maximum length of an assembler statement?

6.   If the program TEST.ASM has been designed as an EXE program, can the program TEST.OBJ be executed successfully?

7.   What does the MODEL directive identify?

8.   Name six different types of memory models.

9.   What does the following notation for a variable's address in a listing file indicate?

```
        0002r
```

10.   What is the meaning of the SIZE operator?

11.   Why would it be necessary for a program to make external references to variables?

12.   In a program consisting of separately compiled modules, what is the assembler's name for a reference to a label outside the current module?

The following map file will be referenced by the next three questions:

```
Start   Stop    Length  Name   Class
00000H  00023H  00024H  _TEXT  CODE
00030H  00031H  00002H  _DATA  DATA
```

```
00040H 0013FH 00100H STACK   STACK

Program entry point at 0000:0000
```

13. How many more bytes of code could be added to this program without changing the starting offset of the data segment?

14. If this program's code segment were loaded by DOS at absolute address 18400h, what would be the absolute addresses of the data and stack segments?

15. Assuming that SP is initialized to 0100, what would be the absolute address of the first word to be pushed on the stack? (Assume that the code segment is loaded at absolute address 18400h.)

16. For each of the following variables, supply its TYPE, LENGTH, and SIZE values:

```
Variable                          TYPE   LENGTH   SIZE
var1 dd 5 dup(0)
var2 dw 10 dup(0FFFFh)
var3 db 20
msg  db "Hello there",0
```

17. When the listing file displays the offset of a statement, what does the offset indicate?

18. Why is the PTR operator required in the following instruction?

```
add  word ptr [si],5
```

19. Would we need to use the PTR operator in each of the following instructions?

```
a.  mov  al,bval
b.  mov  dl,[bx]
c.  sub  [bx],2
d.  mov  cl,wval
e.  add  al,bval+1


.data
bval   db  10h,20h
wval   dw  1000h
```

20. In the following program, do you think the instruction at **L2** will be executed? Use a debugger to confirm the result:

```
L1:  mov  ax,20
     mov  ax,4C00h
     int  21h
L2:  mov  ax,10
```

21. Correct any erroneous lines in the following program, based on the error messages printed by the assembler:

```
1:      title  Find The Errors
2:
3:      .model
4:      .stack 100h
5:
6:      main proc
7:          mov    bl,val1
8:          mov    cx,val2
9:          mov    ax,4C00h
10:         int    21h
11:     main endp
12:
13:     .data
14:     val1  db  10h
15:     val2  dw  1000h
16:     end main
```

Assembler Error Messages:

```
(6):  error A2062: Missing or unreachable CS
(7):  error A2086: Data emitted with no segment
(8):  error A2086: Data emitted with no segment
(9):  error A2086: Data emitted with no segment
(10): error A2086: Data emitted with no segment
```

22. The following program contains numerous errors. Write a correction next to each erroneous statement and add any new lines you deem necessary:

```
1:      title  Find The Errors
2:
3:      .model small
4:      .stack 100h
5:      .data
6:          mov    ax,value1
7:          mov    bx,value2
8:          inc    bx,1
9:          int    21h
10:         mov    4C00h,ax
11:     main    endp
12:
13:         value1    0Ah
```

```
14:         value2   1000h
15:         end main
```

Assembler Error Messages:

```
(6):  error A2009:   Symbol not defined: VALUE1
(7):  error A2009:   Symbol not defined: VALUE2
(8):  warning A4001: Extra characters on line
(10): error A2056:   Immediate mode illegal
(11): error A2000:   Block nesting error
(13): error A2105:   Expected: instruction or directive
(14): error A2105:   Expected: instruction or directive
(15): error A2009:   Symbol not defined: MAIN
```

23. Assume that **array1** is located at offset address 0120. As each instruction is executed, fill in the value of the operand listed on the right side:

```
mov         ax,@data
mov         ds,ax
mov         ax,ptr1        ; a.  AX =
mov         bx,array1      ; b.  BX =
xchg        ax,bx          ; c.  AX =
sub         al,2           ; d.  AX =
mov         ptr2,bx        ; e.  ptr2 =


.data
array1  dw  10h,20h
ptr1    dw  array1
ptr2    dw  0
```

24. Assume that **val1** is located at offset 0120h and that **ptr1** is located at offset 0122h. As each instruction is executed, fill in the value of the operand listed on the right side:

```
.code
mov     ax,@data
mov     ds,ax
mov     ax,0
mov     al,byte ptr val1    ; a.  AX =
mov     bx,ptr1             ; b.  BX =
xchg    ax,bx               ; c.  BX =
sub     al,2                ; d.  AX =
mov     ax,offset ptr2      ; e   AX =

.data
```

```
val1    dw  3Ah
ptr1    dw  val1
ptr2    dw  ptr1
```

4.9   PROGRAMMING EXERCISES

For each of the following exercises, when an integer must be input from the user, call either the Readint or Readlong procedure from the link library. When an integer must be displayed, call the Writeint or Writelong procedure. Be sure to call the Crlf procedure to display blank lines, and call Clrscr to clear the screen at the beginning of each program.

1. *Simple Calculation Problem*

Write a program that clears the screen, locates the cursor, prompts the user for two numbers, adds the numbers, and displays their sum. Use the Clrscr, Gotoxy, Writestring, Readint, and Writeint procedures from the link library.

2. *Using the OFFSET Operator*

Define one array of 8-bit values and another of 16-bit values. Use the OFFSET operator to load the address of various numbers into BX, and write each of the numbers to standard output.

3. *Add a List of 16-Bit numbers*

Use the DW directive to define the following list of 16-bit numbers: 1000h, 2000h, 3000h. Then write instructions to add each number to the AX register, and store the sum in a variable. Move the offset of the list into BX, and use indirect addressing to access and display each of the numbers on a separate output line.

4. *Fixing an Overflow Problem*

The following program calculates the sum of a list of 8-bit values. Modify the program so the sum of the values cannot overflow the AL register:

```
.data
aList db 6Fh,0B4h,1Fh
sum    db 0

.code
mov bx,offset aList      ; get the list's offset
mov si,2                 ; prepare an index register
mov al,[bx]              ; use BX as an indirect operand
add al,[bx+1]            ; use a base-offset operand
add al,[bx+si]           ; use a base-indexed operand
mov sum,al               ; use a direct operand (sum)
```

Hint: Declare **sum** as a 16-bit value so it can hold the total of the three numbers.

5. *Sum of Values, Using Indexed Addressing*

Write a program that calculates and displays the sum of the following four 16-bit numbers: 1000h, 2000h, 7000h, 03FFh. Use indirect addressing.

6. *Generate Random Numbers*

Using the Random_range procedure from the link library, generate 20 pseudorandom numbers in the range 0-100. Store the numbers in an array variable and display the numbers.

7. *Display Random String*

Write a program that fills a null-terminated string with a random sequence of characters in the range 'A' to 'Z', using the Random_range procedure from the link library. Display the string with the Writestring procecure.

8. *Display at Random Locations*

Write a program that displays a character 500 times at various random screen locations. Use the Writechar, Random_range, and Gotoxy procedures from the link library.

9. *Using the = and EQU Directives*

Write a program to do the following: Define a variety of constants using both the = and EQU directives. Include character strings, integers, and arithmetic expressions. Be sure to use the +, −, *, /, and MOD operators. Move the constants to all 8-bit and 16-bit registers, trying to anticipate in advance which moves will generate syntax errors.

10. *Copy a String*

Write a program that copies a string from one location to another. Use indirect addressing. and display the copied string:

```
string  db  "Source string",0     ; string to be copied
dest    db  80 dup(0)              ; destination
```

11. *Copy a String Backwards*

Write a program that copies a string from one location to another, reversing it in the process. Use indirect addressing. and display the copied string:

```
string  db  "Source string",0     ; string to be copied
dest    db  80 dup(0)              ; destination
```

12. *Copy an Array*

Write a program that copies all numbers from one 16-bit array to another. Declare the arrays as follows:

```
array1  dw  1000h,2000h,3000h,4000h,5000h
array2  dw  5 dup(?)
```

13. Array Insertion

Using **array1** from the previous exercise, write a program that inserts 2500h in position 3. The program must shift all subsequent numbers two bytes higher in memory to make room for the inserted number.

14. Copy an Array

Write a program that copies the numbers in a 10-element array of long integers to another array. Display the copied array.

15. Shuffle an Array

Create a sequentially numbered array of 50 integers. Then use the Random_range procedure to shuffle the array in a random order. (Each number will only appear once in the array.) Display the shuffled array.

16. Reverse an Array

Carry out the same operation as in exercise 14, but reverse the array while copying it to a new memory location. Display the copied array.

17. Delete an Element from an Array

Write and test a procedure that deletes element *n* from an array of 16-bit integers. Pass *n* to the procedure in the AX register.

18. Pointers

Define an array of four word values; then define a 16-bit pointer variable that contains the address of the array. Write instructions to load the pointer into an index register and display the numbers:

```
anArray    dw 1000h,2000h,3000h,4000h
aPtr       dw anArray
```

5 Procedures and Interrupts

As programs become larger and more sophisticated, they have to be subdivided into *procedures*. In general terms, a procedure is a block of logically related instructions that can be called (executed) by another program or procedure. In well-designed programs, each procedure has a single purpose and does its job independently of the rest of the program.

Each procedure is like a tool; as long as it is general enough to apply to new situations, the procedure can be reused many times.

Programs of any size are hardly ever written as one continuous sequence of instructions from beginning to end. Indeed, structured design principles require programs to be divided into compact, understandable modules. This makes programs easier to write, maintain, and debug. Assembly language does not enforce structured design, but its principles can be applied to the design of assembly programs with excellent results.

Interrupt Services. The majority of this chapter deals with a special type of subroutine, called an *interrupt service routine (ISR).* Interrupt services in the BIOS and DOS offer valuable help to application programs relating to console, disk, and printer I/O, as well as to timer control and memory allocation. These routines insulate us from the lowest-level details of hardware and make it possible for the same programs to run on different IBM-compatible computers.

5.1 STACK OPERATIONS

The *stack* is a special memory buffer (outside the CPU) used as a temporary holding area for addresses and data. The stack resides in the stack segment. Each 16-bit location on the stack is pointed to by the SP register, called the *stack pointer.* The stack pointer holds the address of the last data element to be added to, or *pushed* on the stack. The last value added to a stack is also the first one to be removed, or *popped* from the stack, so we call it a *LIFO* structure (*Last In First Out*).

Let's look at a program stack containing one value, 0006, on the left side of the following illustration. The stack pointer (notated by SP) points to the most recently added value:

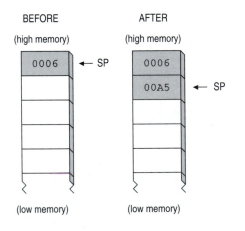

Push Operation. A *push* operation copies a value onto the stack. When we push a new value on the stack, as shown on the right side of this illustration, SP is decremented before the new value is pushed (SP always points to the last value pushed). We use the PUSH instruction to accomplish this, as shown by the following code:

```
mov  ax,0A5h
push ax
```

The PUSH instruction does not change the contents of AX; instead, it *copies* the contents of AX onto the stack.

As more values are pushed, the stack grows downward in memory. Let's assume that the BX and CX registers contain the values 0001 and 0002. The following instructions push them on the stack:

```
push bx    ; push BX on the stack
push cx    ; push CX on the stack
```

Now that 0001 and 0002 have been pushed on the stack, it appears as follows:

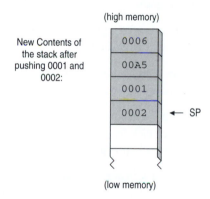

Pop Operation. A *pop* operation removes a value from the stack and places it in a register or variable. After the value is popped from the stack, the stack pointer is incremented to point to the previous value on the stack. The following diagram shows the stack before and after 0002 has been popped from the stack:

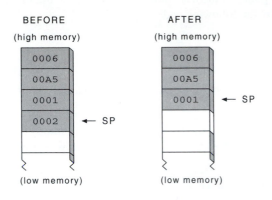

After the pop, the stack pointer has moved up and is now pointing at 0001. The area of the stack below SP is empty.

There are several important uses of stacks in programs:

- A stack makes an excellent *temporary save area* for registers. You can then use the registers as a scratch area and restore them when finished.

- When a subroutine is called, the CPU saves a *return address* on the stack, the location in the program to which the subroutine is to return.

- When calling a procedure, you can push arguments on the stack. These arguments, also called *parameters*, can be retrieved from the stack by statements inside the called procedure. This is the way high-level languages handle procedure parameters.

- High-level languages create an area on the stack inside subroutines called the *stack frame*. It is in this area that local variables are created while the subroutine is active. The variables are discarded when the subroutine returns.

5.1.1   PUSH and POP Instructions

PUSH. The PUSH instruction decrements SP and copies a 16-bit or 32-bit register or memory operand onto the stack at the location pointed to by SP. Only when using the 80286 and subsequent processors can you push an immediate value. Here are examples:

```
push   ax              ; push a 16-bit register
push   ecx             ; push a 32-bit register
push   memval          ; push a 16-bit memory operand
push   1000h           ; push immediate: 80286+ only
```

POP. The POP instruction copies the contents of the stack pointed to by the stack pointer (SP) into a register or variable, and increments SP. Two registers, CS and IP, cannot be used as operands. Examples of POP are shown here:

```
pop  cx                    ; pop stack into 16-bit register
pop  memval                ; pop stack into 16-bit memory operand
pop  edx                   ; pop stack into 32-bit register
```

Saving and Restoring Registers. There are many occasions when a register must be reused. In the following example, a call to DOS (INT 21h) displays a string on the console. DX and AX are assumed to have important values that must be restored after the message is displayed. Because the stack is a LIFO structure (*Last In First Out*), the last register to be saved is the first register to be restored:

```
.data
message  db  'This is a message.$'
.code
push  ax                    ; save AX
push  dx                    ; save DX
mov   ah,9                  ; function: display string
mov   dx,offset message     ; DX points to the string
int   21h                   ; call DOS
pop   dx                    ; restore DX
pop   ax                    ; restore AX
```

PUSHF and POPF. The PUSHF instruction pushes the Flags register on the stack, preserving it in case it is changed. At a later time, the POPF instruction can be used to restore the flags's original state. In the following example, we save the flags before calling a subroutine that can modify the flags:

```
pushf                       ; save the flags
call display_sub            ; call a subroutine
popf                        ; restore the flags
```

On the Intel 386 and later processors, the PUSHFD saves the 32-bit EFLAGS register, and POPFD restores it.

PUSHA (80286+) and PUSHAD (Intel 386+). The PUSHA instruction, introduced with the 80286 processor, pushes AX, CX, DX, BX, SP, BP, SI, and DI on the stack in the order listed. The POPA instruction pops the same registers in reverse order. The PUSHAD instruction pushes EAX, ECX, EDX, EBX, ESP, EBP, ESI, EDI, and POPAD restores them in reverse order.

5.2   PROCEDURES

Let's establish a common terminology. In high-level languages, a *function* is a subroutine that returns a result, whereas a procedure doesn't. The word *subroutine* is more language-dependent—it refers to any block of instructions that can be called from another place. To *call* a subroutine implies that a *return* must take place; this not the same as a *jump,* which does not return. In assembly language, we use the terms *subroutine* and *procedure* interchangeably. In this context, we will refer to a function simply as a procedure that returns a value.

5.2.1 PROC and ENDP Directives

In assembly language, the PROC and ENDP directives mark the beginning and ending of a procedure. Example 1 shows the **main** procedure and a procedure called **MySub**. Notice that a CALL instruction appears in main, which tells the CPU to jump to the beginning of the subroutine. At the end of the subroutine, a RET instruction forces a return to main:

Example 1. Calling a Procedure.

```
.code
main proc
    mov  ax,@data
    mov  ds,ax
    call MySub
    mov  ax,4c00h
    int  21h
main endp

MySub proc
    .

    .
    ret
MySub endp
```

It is important not to overlap procedures. In Example 2 we see a mistake that will be caught by the assembler. **Subroutine1** begins before **main** ends. To correct the mistake, we would move the **subroutine1 PROC** statement to a point beyond **main endp**:

Example 2. Overlapping Procedures.

```
main proc
   .
  call subroutine1
   .
subroutine1 proc
   .
main endp
   .
   .
```

```
        ret
subroutine1 endp
```

5.2.2   Sample Program: SUBS.ASM

This is a good time to look at a short program shown in Example 3 that calls two procedures. The **inputChar** procedure inputs a character from the keyboard and returns it in AL. The procedure contains the two instructions needed to call DOS function 1 (keyboard input). DOS automatically returns the character in AL, so the value is waiting there when inputChar returns to its caller, **main**.

The **calcSum** procedure computes the sum of an integer array containing up to 65,535 integers. To call it, main places the offset of an array in BX and a count of the number of elements in CX. Thus, in order to do its job, calcSum expects these registers to contain appropriate values. This passing of values in predetermined registers is the *calling protocol*. The calling program is forced to conform to the subroutine's wishes, but the advantage to this is that calcSum is general enough to be reused many times. In general, this is an important goal when writing subroutines: Make them as general as possible, in the hope that they can be useful in some of your other programs.

Saving and Restoring Registers. You may have noticed in the calcSum procedure that we preserve BX and CX so they will have their original values when the procedure returns. AX, on the other hand, cannot be preserved because it holds the sum of the array when returning to the caller. We save BX and CX by pushing them on the stack at the beginning of calcSum and popping them off the stack (in reverse order) before the RET instruction. No other registers are altered by the subroutine, so the calling program is not forced to save its own registers before calling calcSum.

Example 3. Demonstration of Subroutine Calls.

```
title  Subroutine Demonstration          (SUBS.ASM)


; This program calls two subroutines: one for
; keyboard input, another to add the elements
; in an array of integers.

.model small
.stack 100h
.data
char   db ?
sum    dw ?
array dw 100h,200h,300h,400h,500h
array_size = ($ − array) / 2

.code
```

```
main proc
    mov   ax,@data          ; set up the DS register
    mov   ds,ax

    call  inputChar         ; input keyboard into AL
    mov   char,AL           ; store in a variable

  ; Prepare to call the calcSum procedure.

    mov   bx,offset array   ; BX points to array
    mov   cx,array_size     ; CX = array count
    call  calcSum           ; calculate sum
    mov   sum,ax            ; store in a variable

    mov   ax,4C00h          ; return to DOS
    int   21h
main endp

inputChar proc              ; input character from keyboard
    mov   ah,1
    int   21h
    ret
inputChar endp


;----------------------------------------------------
; Calculate the sum of an array of integers. Input:
; BX points to the array and CX contains the
; array size. Returns the SUM in AX.
;----------------------------------------------------
calcSum proc
    push  bx                ; save BX, CX
    push  cx
    mov   ax,0
CS1: add  ax,[bx]
    add   bx,2              ; point to next integer
    loop  CS1              ; repeat for array size
    pop   cx               ; restore BX, CX
    pop   bx
    ret                    ; sum stored in AX
calcSum endp
end main
```

5.2.3   Nested Procedure Calls

A subroutine may itself call other subroutines, as shown in Example 4. The stack holds the list of return addresses so the CPU can find its way back to the original call. By the time **sub3** is entered, three return addresses are on the stack. The RET at the end of the procedure pops 0060 into the IP register, and execution resumes in **sub2**. When the RET in **sub2** is reached, 0050 is popped into IP and execution resumes in **sub1**. Finally 000C is popped into IP and execution resumes in the **main** procedure.

Example 4. Nested Procedure Calls.

```
        main proc
000A    call sub1
000C    mov ax,...

            .

        main endp


        sub1 proc

            .

         call sub2
0050     ret
        sub1 endp


        sub2 proc

            .

         call sub3
0060     ret
        sub2 endp


        sub3 proc

            .

            .

         ret
        sub3 endp
```

5.2.4   Near and Far Procedures

Calling a NEAR Procedure. When the CALL instruction and the subroutine it calls are in the same code segment, we term this a *near call*. Before branching to the subroutine, the CALL instruction saves the current value of IP (instruction pointer) on the stack. It then loads the subroutine's offset into IP, causing the CPU to immediately branch to the first instruction in the subroutine:

```
         Calling Program          Subroutine
         main proc                sub1 proc
0006:        call sub1      0080:     mov ax,1
0009:        inc ax                   .
             .                        .
             .                        ret
         main endp                sub1 endp
```

The CALL instruction pushes offset 0009 onto the stack and moves 0080 into IP. The RET instruction pops 0009 off the stack, copying the number into the IP register. This causes the CPU to resume execution at offset 0009. At the end of the subroutine, a RET instruction pops the old value of IP from the stack into the instruction pointer, and execution resumes right where the CALL instruction left off. Figure 1 shows a diagram of the stack both in the calling program and in the subroutine.

Calling a FAR Procedure. When the caller and the subroutine are in different code segments, we identify this as a *far call*. Before branching to the subroutine, the CALL instruction saves the current CS and IP on the stack. It then loads the subroutine's segment address into CS and its offset into IP. Execution begins immediately at the new address.

In the next example, a main procedure makes a far CALL to a subroutine in another code segment. Notice that the FAR declaration must be added after the name **subroutine1**, and the FAR PTR operator is added to the CALL instruction. Actually, there is some trickery going on here. The FAR declaration in **subroutine1** tells the assembler to generate a RETF machine instruction rather than RET, which appears in the source file. This enables the subroutine to return correctly. The execution time for a far call is greater than for a near call because of the extra time taken by the push and pop of the segment (CS) value:

```
              Calling procedure              Called procedure
              main proc                      sub1 proc far
2FC0:0006     call far ptr sub1     3AB6:0080 mov ax,1
2FC0:0009     inc ax                          .
              .                                .
              .                                ret
              main endp                       sub1 endp
```

Figure 1. Stack Usage when calling a NEAR Procedure.

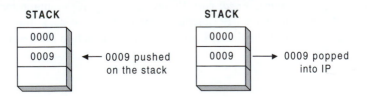

The CALL instruction pushes segment 2FC0 and offset 0009 onto the stack. It moves 3AB6 into CS and 0080 into IP. This causes the CPU to begin execution at address 3AB6:0080. The RET instruction pops 0009 into IP and then pops 2FC0 into CS. This causes the CPU to resume execution at offset 2FC0:0009. Figure 2 shows a picture of the stack.

Criteria for Using Far Calls. Why, you might ask, use far calls at all? In fact, nearly all the programs presented in this book use near calls because they are simpler and faster. There are a few times when far calls are required:

- When linking assembler subroutines to high-level languages, the calling program will dictate the type of call. For example, a *large* memory model C program requires *far* calls to assembler subroutines.

- When calling from an assembler program to library routines, the library may have been designed for only *far* calls.

- When an application program is so large that more than 64K of code is required, either the *medium* or *large* memory model must be used. There will be multiple code segments, requiring far calls.

Figure 2. Stack Usage when Calling a FAR Procedure.

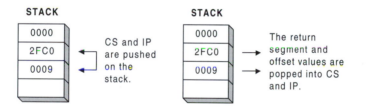

5.2.5 Using Memory Models

The **.model** directive automatically sets the default attribute for all procedures in your programs to either *near* or *far*. The tiny, small, and compact models default to near procedures. The medum, large, and huge memory models default to far procedures. The assembler automatically generates a far CALL instruction to any procedure assembled under these models. The program shown in Example 5 shows how this is done. In main, we call the Sub_far procedure. The FAR PTR operator is required by some assemblers when forward-referencing a procedure located in a different code segment:

```
call  far ptr Sub_far
```

Example 5. Large Memory Model Program.

```
title Large Memory Model Example          (largem.asm)

; You cannot mix a Large model program with a link library that
; has been assembled under the Small memory model.

.model large    ; procedures are FAR by default
.stack 100h
.data
msg2 db "In the Sub_Far procedure",0dh,0ah,0

.code
extrn Writestring:proc
main proc
    mov   ax,@data
    mov   ds,ax
    call  far ptr Sub_far
    mov   ax,4C00h
    int   21h
main endp

Sub_far proc
    mov   dx,offset msg2
    call  near ptr Writestring      ; linker error generated
    ret
Sub_far endp
end main
```

One important point, however, is that the link library supplied with this book was assembled under the Small memory model. When its procedures return, they do not pop CS from the stack. If your program executes far calls by default, you can override this behavior by using the NEAR PTR operator with the CALL instruction, but the linker will still generate a "fixup overflow" error.

A program compiled under either the Medium or Large memory model will have a separate code segment designated for each module. For example, the program in Example 5 was compiled under the Large model, and its MAP file lists the following segment names. You can see that the added code segment has the module name prepended to the default code segment name, _TEXT:

```
Start   Stop    Length  Name          Class
00000H  00015H  00016H  LARGEM_TEXT   CODE
00016H  00092H  0007DH  _TEXT         CODE
```

```
000A0H 000BBH 0001CH _DATA              DATA
000C0H 001BFH 00100H STACK              STACK
```

Optional Code Segment Name. You can optionally supply a segment name with the .code directive. This creates a new code segment, separate from the default code segment. The following directive declares a segment called MYCODE:

```
.code MYCODE
```

The modified MAP file for this program now shows the MYCODE segment:

```
Start  Stop   Length Name               Class
00000H 00000H 00000H LARGEM_TEXT        CODE
00000H 00015H 00016H MYCODE             CODE
00016H 00092H 0007DH _TEXT              CODE
000A0H 000BBH 0001CH _DATA              DATA
000C0H 001BFH 00100H STACK              STACK
```

If you create a code segment with a name that is different from the one in the book's link library, the assembler will report that a *near* call to a different segment is not permitted:

```
.code MYCODE
myProc proc
    mov  dx,offset message
    call near ptr Writestring  ; error!
```

5.3   PROCEDURE PARAMETERS

5.3.1   Passing Arguments in Registers

The most common way for assembly language programs to pass arguments to subroutines is to place the arguments in registers. This method is efficient because the called subroutine can directly use the passed values, and register access is faster for the processor than memory access. For example, the **Writeint** procedure in the book's link library requires AX to contain a 16-bit integer, and BX to contain the display radix:

```
.data
aNumber dw ?
.code
mov  ax,aNumber
mov  bx,10
call Writeint
```

Preserving Registers. Ordinarily, it is a procedure's responsibility to preserve the values of any registers it might have to modify. This ensures that the calling program will not encounter any surprises in the form of registers that have been modified. In Example 6, consider what would happen if Writeint modified CX, BX, or SI. If CX were modified, the loop would not execute correctly; if SI were modified, the pointer to the values in **aList** would be incorrect; and if BX were modified, the decimal radix would not be consistent.

Example 6. Calling Writeint in a Loop.

```
.data
DECIMAL_RADIX = 10
LIST_COUNT = 20
aList dw LIST_COUNT dup(?)

.code
    mov  cx,LIST_COUNT
    mov  bx,DECIMAL_RADIX
    mov  si,offset aList

L1: mov  ax,[si]
    call Writeint
    add  si,2
    loop L1
```

An important rule to keep in mind is this: When writing a procedure, always save and restore registers that are modified by the procedure. It is tempting to ignore this rule, in the interest of saving programming time, because it might not be necessary to preserve certain registers. If you should modify the program at a later time, however, it might become important to preserve registers that are modified by the procedure. Unwanted register modifications could cause various runtime errors.

An exception to the rule about saving registers occurs when the procedure uses one of the registers to return a value. That register should not be pushed and popped. For example, the **SumOf** procedure returns the sum of the AX, BX, and CX registers. The return value is in the AX register. If we were to push and pop AX, the procedure's return value would be lost:

```
SumOf proc
    push ax
    add  ax,bx
    add  ax,cx
    pop  ax             ; error: AX reset to original value
    ret
SumOf endp
```

5.4   SOFTWARE INTERRUPTS

The term *interrupt* is used in two different ways: A *hardware interrupt* is a signal generated by any part of the system hardware that needs immediate attention from the CPU. A *software interrupt* is a call to one of the BIOS or DOS interrupt service routines.

Hardware Interrupt. A hardware interrupt is generated by a special chip, the 8259 Interrupt Controller, which signals the CPU to suspend execution of the current program and process the interrupt.

The keyboard provides a good example: Pressing a key causes the CPU to suspend the current program and execute a BIOS-level routine that reads the character from the keyboard input port and stores it in a memory buffer. The CPU can then resume whatever it was doing before the interrupt happened.

Clearly, hardware interrupts allow important events in the background to be noticed by the CPU before essential data is lost. For example, a keyboard character waiting at the input port would be lost if not saved by the CPU, or characters received from the serial port would be lost if not for an interrupt-driven routine that stores them in a buffer.

Occasionally, programs must disable hardware interrupts when performing sensitive operations on segment registers and the stack. The CLI (*clear interrupt flag*) instruction disables interrupts and the STI (*set interrupt flag*) instruction enables interrupts.

Software Interrupt. Strictly speaking, a software interrupt is not an interrupt at all. It probably got its name because it mimics many of the actions of a hardware interrupt. A software interrupt provides a valuable tool for handling the details of everyday input-output. It would be far too time-consuming to take care of these details in application programs.

The INT instruction requests services from the operating system, usually for input-output. These services are actually small programs located in the computer's operating system.

5.4.1   INT Instruction

The INT instruction calls an operating system subroutine, identified by a number in the range 0-FFh. Before the INT instruction is executed, AH usually contains a *function number* that identifies the desired subroutine. In addition, other values can be passed to the interrupt in registers. The syntax is INT *number*

We use the INT instruction for general console input-output, file and video manipulation, and many other services.

Interrupt Vector Table. The CPU processes an interrupt instruction using the *interrupt vector table,* a table of addresses in the lowest 1,024 bytes of memory. Each entry in this table is a 32-bit segment-offset address that points to an operating system subroutine. The actual addresses in this table vary from one machine to another. Figure 3 illustrates the steps taken by the CPU when the INT instruction is invoked by a program:

1. The number following the INT mnemonic tells the CPU which entry to locate in the interrupt vector table. In the illustration, INT 10h requests a video service.

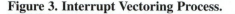

Figure 3. Interrupt Vectoring Process.

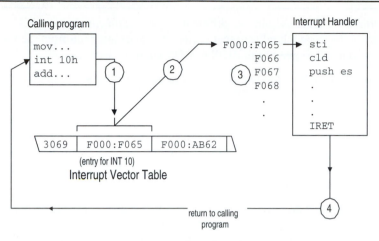

2.   The CPU jumps to the address stored in the interrupt vector table (F000:F065).

3.   The interrupt handler (DOS subroutine) at F000:F065 begins execution and finishes when the IRET instruction is reached.

4.   IRET (interrupt return) causes the program to resume execution at the next instruction in the original calling program.

This might seem a complicated way to handle a subroutine call. Fortunately, the CPU does most of the work. A program needs only to place one or more values in registers and invoke the INT instruction.

Common Software Interrupts. Software interrupts call *interrupt service routines* either in the BIOS or in DOS. Some frequently used interrupts are:

- ***INT 10h Video Services***. Video display routines that control the cursor position, scroll the screen, and display video graphics.

- ***INT 16h Keyboard Services.*** Routines that read the keyboard and check its status.

    INT 17h Printer Services. Routines that initialize, print, and return the printer status.

- ***INT 1Ah Time of Day.*** Routine that gets the number of clock ticks since the machine was turned on or sets the counter to a new value.

- ***INT 1Ch User Timer Interrupt.*** An empty routine that is executed 18.2 times per second.

- ***INT 21h DOS Services.*** DOS service routines for input-output, file handling, memory management; also known as *DOS function calls*.

5.4.2   Redirecting Input-Output

Throughout this chapter, references will be made to the *standard input device* and the *standard output device*. Both are collectively called the *console,* which involves the keyboard for input and the video display for output.

From the DOS command line, you can redirect standard input so it is read from a file or hardware port rather than the keyboard. Standard output can be redirected so it writes to a file or hardware port rather than the video display. Without this capability, programs would have to be substantially revised before their input-output could be changed. For example, an executable program named **prog1.exe** can have its I/O redirected with the following command lines:

```
prog1 > prn                    Output to printer
prog1 < infile.txt             Input from file called infile.txt
prog1 < infile.txt > prn       Input from file, output to printer
```

The name **prn** is a standard device name recognized by DOS. The complete set of device names is shown in Table 1.

Table 1. Standard DOS Device Names.

Device Name	Description
CON	Console (video display or keyboard)
LPT1 or PRN	First parallel printer
LPT2, LPT3	Parallel ports 2 and 3
COM1, COM2	Serial ports 1 and 2
NUL	Nonexistent or dummy device

5.5   MS-DOS FUNCTION CALLS

INT 21h is called an *MS-DOS function call*. There are some 90 or so different functions supported by this interrupt, identified by a *function number* placed in the AH register. We divide them into two groups, output and input. For each function, we list the necessary input parameters, indicating which registers have to be initialized before calling INT 21h. We also include short code examples that call the functions.

5.5.1   Output Functions

02h: Character Output. DOS function 2 sends a character to standard output and advances the cursor 1 position. *Input:* AH = 2, DL contains the character. *Output:* AL is modified by DOS.

```
mov  ah,2                    ; select DOS function 2
mov  dl,'*'                  ; character to be displayed
int  21h                     ; call DOS to do the job
```

05h: Printer Output. DOS function 5 sends a single character to the printer. *Input:* AH = 5, DL contains the character. DOS waits until the printer is ready to accept the character. You can terminate the wait by pressing the Ctrl-Break keys. The default output is to the printer port for LPT1. You may have to send an end of line character (0Dh) or end of page character (0Ch) to the printer to force immediate printing. Many printers keep outputs characters in a internal buffer until the buffer is full or an end of line or end of page is printed. The following statements print a dollar-sign ($) character:

```
mov  ah,5                    ; select printer output
mov  dl,'$'                  ; character to be printed
int  21h                     ; call DOS
mov  dl,0Dh                  ; print a carriage return
int  21h      ; call DOS
```

It is not necessary to reload AH with 5 before calling INT 21h the second time. This is true for INT 21h functions in general.

06h: Direct Output. Function 6 can either read from standard input or write to standard output. Here, we present only the version that displays a character. *Input:* AH = 6, and DL contains the character:

```
mov  ah,6                    ; Request DOS function 6
mov  dl,'&'                  ; DL = character to be output
int  21h                     ; Call DOS
```

09h: String Output. Function 9 writes a string to standard output. *Input:* AH = 9, and DX contains the offset of the string. The string must be terminated by the dollar-sign ($) character. Control characters such as tabs and carriage returns are recognized by DOS. In the following example, the output string includes the carriage return (0Dh) and line feed (0Ah) characters:

```
mov ah,9                     ; string output function
mov dx,offset string         ; offset address of the string
int 21h
.data
string  db 'This is a byte string.',0Dh,0Ah,'$'
```

This DOS function has one unfortunate drawback: A dollar-sign character cannot be part of the string. If a dollar sign is omitted, DOS simply outputs all subsequent characters in memory until the ASCII value for a dollar sign (24h) is found. Several hundred characters might be written before this happens.

5.5.2   Input Functions

There are a number of DOS functions for standard input:

- 01h   Filtered Input With Echo

- 06h   Direct Input Without Waiting

- 07h   Direct Input, No Ctrl-Break

- 08h   Direct Input with Ctrl-Break

- 0Ah   Buffered Input

- 0Bh   Get Input Status

- 0Ch   Clear Input Buffer, Invoke Input Function

- 3Fh   Read From File or Device

Keyboard Typeahead Buffer. The *typeahead* buffer is a 15-character circular buffer used by DOS to store keystrokes as they are pressed. This makes it possible for you to type faster than a program is able to act on the input: DOS will "remember" the keystrokes. If the buffer becomes full, the computer beeps and extra keystrokes are ignored.

Input Characteristics. The DOS functions for character input (function 1, 6, 7, and 8) display a perplexing variety of behaviors. Table 2 summarizes these characteristics for DOS functions 1, 6, 7, and 8. The following criteria are important:

- *Waits for keystroke:* Does the input function wait for a keystroke or just check the typeahead buffer for a waiting key?

- *Echoes character:* Does the input function echo the character on the screen as it is being typed? This might be a disadvantage when entering a password, for instance.

- *Ctrl-Break recognized:* Does the input function halt when the user presses Ctrl-Break? This can still be circumvented by installing one's own Ctrl-Break handler (Chapter 15). When Ctrl-Break is recognized by the DOS function, we say that *Ctrl-Break is active*.

- *Filters control characters:* Does the input function filter out ASCII control characters, such as Enter, Tab, or Backspace? If so, programmers say the input is *cooked*; otherwise, the input is *raw*. See the section entitled *ASCII Control Characters* later in this chapter for more information.

01h: Filtered Input With Echo. DOS function 1 waits for a character to be read from standard input, echoes the character to standard output, and stores the character in AL. If a character is

Table 2. DOS Console Input Functions.

DOS Function Number	1	6	7	8
Waits for keystroke?	Y	N	Y	Y
Echoes character?	Y	N	N	N
Ctrl-Break recognized?	Y	N	N	Y
Filters control characters?	Y	N	N	N

already waiting in the input buffer, the character is automatically returned in AL. Ctrl-Break is active, meaning that the user can halt the program by pressing Ctrl-Break. *Input:* AH = 1. *Output:* AL = character. In the following example, a single character is input and placed in a variable named **char**:

```
mov   ah,1          ; input function
int   21h           ; call DOS, key returned in AL
mov   char,al       ; save the character
```

06h: Direct Input Without Waiting. The primary advantage to using DOS function 6 is that it does not wait for input—instead, it retrieves the next available character (if any) from the standard input buffer. If no character is waiting, the function returns with ZF = 1. Ctrl-Break is not active, and no filtering of control characters takes place. *Input:* AH = 6, and DL = 0FFh. *Output:* AL = character.

To request input from function 6, set DL to 0FFh before invoking INT 21h. If a character is found in the input buffer, it is returned in AL and the Zero flag (ZF) = 0. If no character is found, ZF = 1:

```
mov   ah,6          ; check input buffer
mov   dl,0FFh
int   21h
```

Programs occasionally need to clear the keyboard typeahead buffer to prevent users from typing commands before the computer is ready to receive them. The following procedure combines DOS function 6 with a loop to clear the buffer:

```
clear_keyboard proc
      push   ax
      push   dx
  L1:
      mov    ah,6          ; check input buffer
      mov    dl,0FFh
      int    21h
```

```
        jnz    L1              ; jump to L1 if ZF = 0
        pop    dx
        pop    ax
        ret                    ; return to calling program
clear_keyboard endp
```

(The JNZ instruction jumps to a label if the Zero flag is clear.)

07h: Direct Input, No Ctrl-Break. Function 7 waits for an unfiltered character from standard input without echoing the character. Ctrl-Break is not active. *Input:* AH = 7. *Output:* AL contains the character:

```
mov  ah,7              ; input function
int  21h               ; call DOS
mov  char,al           ; save the character
```

08h: Direct Input with Ctrl-Break. Function 8 waits for an unfiltered character from the console without echoing the character. Ctrl-Break is active. *Input:* AH = 8. *Output:* AL contains the character:

```
mov  ah,8              ; input function
int  21h               ; call DOS
mov  char,al           ; save the character
```

0Ah: Buffered Input. Function 0Ah reads a character string of up to 255 characters from standard input and stores it in a buffer. The backspace key can be used to erase characters and back up the cursor. The user can terminate the input by pressing the Enter key. DOS filters out any non-ASCII keys, such as cursor arrows and PgDn so they will not be stored in the buffer. Ctrl-Break is active, and all characters are echoed to standard output. *Input:* AH = 0Ah, and DX contains the offset of a record containing the keyboard parameters. The format of this record is shown in Figure 4.

The byte at offset 0 contains an integer that determines the maximum number of characters the user can input, including the Enter key. If this value were 5, for example, DOS would permit only four characters plus the Enter key to be input. After INT 21h is called, DOS places

Figure 4. Keyboard Parameter Record, INT 21h Function 0Ah.

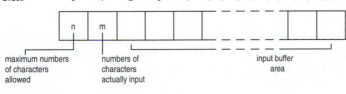

the number of keys *actually typed* in the byte at offset 1. This value does not include the Enter key. The characters themselves are placed in the buffer at offset 2. In the following example, **maxkeys** equals 32, **charsInput** is filled in by DOS after INT 21h is called, and **buffer** holds the characters typed by the user:

```
.data
keyboardArea label byte
maxkeys      db 32              ; max characters allowed
charsInput   db ?              ; characters actually input
buffer       db 32 dup(0)      ; holds the input

.code
mov  ah,0Ah                    ; select console input
mov  dx,offset keyboardArea    ; DX -> parameter area
int  21h                       ; call DOS
```

Suppose the user typed the following string of 21 characters:

```
My name is Kip Irvine
```

A dump of the buffer after calling INT 21h shows that the byte at offset 0001 contains the number of characters actually entered (15h), followed by the input characters themselves. The Enter key appears in the buffer as 0Dh, and the count does not include the Enter key:

```
max_keys   chars_input
  |          |       |
  20   15                                          buffer
                                          |                    |
  4D  79  20  6E  61  6D  65  20  69  73  20    My name is
  4B  69  70  20  49  72  76  69  6E  65  0D    Kip Irvine
                                          |
                                      Enter key
```

0Bh: Get Input Status. Function 0Bh checks the standard input buffer to see if a character is waiting. *Input:* AH = 0Bh. *Output:* if a character is waiting, AL = 0FFh; otherwise, AL = 0. For example:

```
mov  ah,0Bh                    ; check input status
int  21h                       ; call DOS
```

0Ch: Clear Input Buffer, Invoke Input Function. Function 0Ch clears the keyboard typeahead buffer and calls an INT 21h console input function. You can use this function to prevent the user of a program from typing commands ahead of displayed prompts. *Input:* AH = 0Ch, and

AL = the number of the DOS function to be called (1, 6, 7, or 8). *Output:* AL = the input character. In the following example, we clear the buffer and then call function 1 to input a character:

```
mov   ah,0Ch              ; clear buffer
mov   al,1                ; call function 1 after finished
int   21h                 ; call DOS
mov   char,al             ; store the character
```

Extended Keyboard Keys. Many keyboard keys do not have ASCII codes. They are called *extended keys,* and they include function keys, cursor arrows, PgUp, PgDown, Home, End, and so on. When an extended key is pressed, the first byte placed in the input buffer is 00h, and the second contains a numeric *keyboard scan code* for the key. A complete list of keyboard scan codes appears on the page facing the inside front cover of this book.

When INT 21h input functions are called, they return the next available byte from the keyboard typeahead buffer. Therefore, if the user presses an extended key, the value returned in AL is 0. To get the keyboard scan code, the INT 21h function must be called a second time. The following statements, for example, read and store an extended key code:

```
mov   ah,7                ; console input function
int   21h                 ; call DOS: AL = 0 for extended key
int   21h                 ; AL now contains the key's scan code
mov   scanCode,al         ; save the scan code
```

The difficulty with this approach is, of course, that if the user has pressed a standard key (having an ASCII code), the computer will wait for a second key to be pressed. In the next section, we show how to use INT 16h and avoid this problem.

3Fh: Read From File or Device. DOS Function 3Fh can be used to read a string of characters from an input file or device. *Input:* DX contains the offset of an input buffer greater than or equal to the size value passed in CX, and BX identifies the standard input device or file handle. For standard keyboard input, BX = 0. CX specifies the maximum number of characters to be read.

Function 3Fh can read input characters from standard input; it terminates when the Enter key is pressed. Set BX to 0 (the keyboard device handle), set CX to the maximum number of characters to be typed, and point DX to the input buffer. The function returns the number of input characters in AX:

```
.data
inputBuffer db 127 dup(0)
.code
mov   ah,3Fh              ; read from file/device
mov   bx,0                ; device = keyboard
mov   cx,127              ; request 127 bytes maximum
```

```
mov  dx,offset inputBuffer
int  21h                    ; AX = number of chars read
```

The backspace and left arrow keys can be used to edit the input, just as for DOS function 0Ah. When the Enter key is pressed, DOS adds both a *carriage return* (0Dh) and a line feed (0Ah) to the input buffer; DOS also adds 2 to the character count in AX. The character count placed in CX should include the CR/LF characters that DOS appends to the string.

5.5.3   Date/Time Functions

Get Date (2Ah). Function 2Ah returns the current system date, placing the year number in CX, the month number in DH, the day number in DL, and the day of the week in AL. The day number in AL uses the value of 0 for Sunday, 1 for Monday, and so on. The following statements call the function and save the values:

```
mov  ah,2Ah
int  21h
mov  year,cx
mov  month,dh
mov  day,dl
mov  dayOfWeek,al
```

Set Date (2Bh). Function 2Bh sets the current system date, using the same registers as Function 2Ah (get date). The function returns a value of 0 in AL if the change was successful, or a value of FFh if the date could not be set. For example:

```
mov  ah,2Bh
mov  cx,year
mov  dh,month
mov  dl,day
int  21h
cmp  al,0
jne  badDate
```

Get Time (2Ch). Function 2Ch returns the current system time, placing the hours in CH, the minutes in CL, the seconds in DH, and the hundredths of seconds in DL. The latter value is usually not accurate. Here is a sample call:

```
mov  ah,2Ch
int  21h
mov  hours,ch
mov  minutes,cl
mov  seconds,dh
```

Set Time (2Dh). Function 2Dh sets the current system time, using the same register values as Function 2Ch (get time). The function returns a value of 0 in AL if the change was successful, or a value of FFh if the time was invalid. For example:

```
mov  ah,2Dh
mov  ch,hours
mov  cl,minutes
mov  dh,seconds
int  21h
cmp  al,0
jne  badTime
```

5.6　 BIOS-LEVEL KEYBOARD INPUT (INT 16H)

A direct way to retrieve keyboard input is through the INT 16h keyboard services. The function code is placed in AH before calling INT 16h. One small limitation is that INT 16h keyboard input cannot be redirected on the DOS command line. Table 3 contains a listing of the more commonly-used keyboard BIOS functions.

The following example shows how to wait for a keystroke with INT 16h. Suppose the F1 key were pressed (scan code 3Bh). After calling INT 16h, AH contains the scan code and AL contains the ASCII code (0):

```
mov  ah,10h          ; request BIOS keyboard input
int  16h             ; AH = 3Bh,  AL = 0
```

Simulating Keystrokes. Sometimes it is useful for a program to push characters into the keyboard typeahead buffer to simulate the actions of a user—when playing back keyboard macros, for instance. The following statements push the letter *A* into the buffer:

```
mov  ah,5            ; BIOS function: push keystroke
mov  ch,1Eh          ; scan code for "A"
mov  cl,41h          ; ASCII code for "A"
int  16h
```

ASCII Control Characters. The ASCII character set has a number of *control characters* in the range 0-20 hex, which are interpreted by DOS but not actually displayed. They are used for screen and printer control and for asynchronous communications. The more common ones are listed in Table 4.

Characters 0Dh and 0Ah are the *carriage return* and *line feed* characters found at the end of each line in text files. When they are displayed on the screen, a carriage return moves the cursor to the left side of the screen, and a line feed moves the cursor down one line. Particularly when displaying more than one line on the screen, these characters must be present; otherwise, each new line overwrites the previous one.

Table 3. INT 16h BIOS Keyboard Functions.

AH	Description
03h	*Set Typematic Repeat Rate.* Call with AH = 3, AL = 5, BH = repeat delay, BL = repeat rate. The delay values in BH are: (0 = 250 ms; 1 = 500 ms; 2 = 750 ms; 3 = 1000ms). The repeat rate in BL varies from 0 (fastest) to 1Fh (slowest).
05h	*Push Key into Buffer.* Pushes a keyboard character and corresponding scan code into the keyboard typeahead buffer. Call with AH = 5, CH = scan code, and CL = character code. If the typeahead buffer is already full, the Carry flag will be set, and AL = 1.
10h	*Wait for Key.* If a keystroke is waiting, its scan code is returned in AH and its character code is returned in AL. If no key is waiting, the routine waits in a loop for a key to be pressed. (Function 00h duplicates this function on the older 10-function key keyboard.)
11h	*Check Keyboard Buffer.* Examines the keyboard typeahead buffer to see if a key is waiting; if one is, this function returns the scan code in AH and the character code in AL, and clears the Zero flag. Otherwise, ZF = 1. The keystroke is not removed from the buffer. (Function 01h duplicates this function on the older 10-function key keyboard.)
12h	*Get Keyboard Flags.* Shows the keyboard status byte, which is bit mapped. See Figure 5. (Function 02h duplicates this function on the older 10-function key keyboard.)

Figure 5. Keyboard Status Byte.

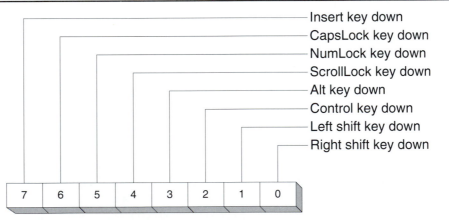

- Insert key down
- CapsLock key down
- NumLock key down
- ScrollLock key down
- Alt key down
- Control key down
- Left shift key down
- Right shift key down

| 7 | 6 | 5 | 4 | 3 | 2 | 1 | 0 |

5.7   BIOS-LEVEL VIDEO CONTROL (INT 10H)

When an application program needs to write characters on the screen, it can either write directly to video memory or issue an INT instruction to request this service from the operating system. It has a choice between three levels of access:

Table 4. Common ASCII Control Characters.

Hexadecimal	Decimal	Description
08	08	Backspace
09	09	Horizontal tab
0A	10	Line feed
0C	12	Form feed (printer only)
0D	13	Carriage return (Enter key)
1B	27	Escape

Direct video access: Characters are moved directly to the video buffer in memory. This buffer address will vary depending upon both the type of video display and (occasionally) the computer manufacturer. Features high speed and medium compatibilty. Direct video output cannot be redirected unless memory-resident software monitors access to the video buffer and reroutes it.

BIOS-level access: Characters are output using INT 10h function, known as BIOS services. Medium speed, high compatibility. Cannot be redirected unless the appropriate interrupt service routine is replaced.

DOS-level access: Any computer running DOS will work correctly, but very slowly. Screen positioning and colors are available only with the **ansi.sys** driver, which is a program file supplied with DOS. Input/output can easily be redirected to other devices such as a printer or disk.

Application programs vary in their choice of which level of access to use. Those desiring the highest performance choose direct screen access; most others choose BIOS-level access. DOS-level access is used only when there is a need to redirect the program's output.

5.7.1   Displays, Modes, and Attributes

During the early years of the IBM-PC, the monochrome display adapter (MDA) displayed text in only one color (amber, black, or green). The color graphics adapter (CGA) and enhanced graphics adapter (EGA) displayed both text and graphics, but the graphics weren't very good. Since 1991, nearly all machines have been sold with various types of VGA (video graphics array) displays, each of which displays high-resolution graphics and text. A list of common VGA display adapters and their highest graphics resolutions is shown here. The numbers are in the format h X v, where h represents the number of horzontal pixels, and v represents the vertical pixels:

        640 X 480   (standard VGA)

800 X 600   (super VGA)
1024 X 768   (extended VGA)
1152 X 864
1280 X 1024

Video Modes. There are two general types of video modes: text and graphics. When in a *text* mode, a computer can only display characters from the IBM extended character set (on the inside cover of this book). This does, however, include a number of line-drawing characters and special symbols, which can give the appearance of graphical drawings. When in a *graphics* mode, the computer can draw any combination of pixels (dots), which can be lines, circles, and various character fonts.

Why, we might ask, shouldn't computers use graphics mode all the time? As a matter of fact, that's what *graphical user interfaces* (GUIs) do. Microsoft Windows is a prime example. The CPU of the original IBM-PC was forced to perform virtually all graphics processing along with its existing work. Later, video processors were located on the video controller card, relieving the CPU of some of the processing. Regardless, given the same computer, a text-based program tends to run faster than a graphics-based program. If the IBM had been originally designed to be a graphics-based machine, it would have had a separate CPU dedicated to graphics processing. This is how the Apple Macintosh computer was designed.

Video Attributes. Each position on the screen can hold a single character, along with its own **attribute**. The attribute is stored in a separate byte, called an *attribute byte* (there is an INT 10h function call to set a character's attribute). Examples of attributes are colors, reverse video, blink, underline, and highlight.

Monochrome Text Mode. Video mode 7 displays monochrome text. The available attributes in Mode 7 are shown in Table 5. For example, normal blinking is 87h, bright blinking is 8Fh, reverse blinking is 0F0h, and so on. At the same time, a character can be made bright by setting bit 3.

Table 5. Mode 7 Attributes.

Value	Attribute
07	Normal
87	Blinking
0F	Bright (highlight)
70	Reverse (inverse)
01	Underline
09	Bright underline

5.7.2   Color Text Mode

The color video controller can use the color text mode (mode 3), which displays all characters from the standard IBM character set and allows the attributes to be colors. This mode does not support the underline attribute, but it does allow blinking and reverse video. The colors are divided into two categories: The *foreground* color is the color of text characters, and the *background* color is the color of the screen behind each letter. It is possible, therefore, to write a line of text in which every letter has a foreground and background color different from those of the previous letter. The background color is determined by bits 4, 5, and 6 of the attribute byte, and the foreground color is identified by bits 0, 1, and 2. Bit 3 is the high/low bit, which makes a color lighter when set, and bit 7 is the blink bit. Figure 6 shows how each color is controlled by attribute bits.

Figure 6. Video Attribute Byte Layout.

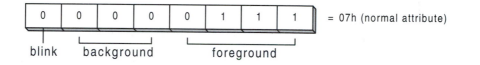

To construct a video attribute byte from two colors, use the assembler's SHL operator to shift the background color bits four positions to the left. For example, the following statements store an attribute of white text on a blue background (00010111) in the BH register:

```
BLUE = 1
WHITE = 111b
mov  bh,(BLUE shl 4) + WHITE
```

The following stores an attribute of bright white on red (01001111):

```
BRIGHT_WHITE = 1111b
RED = 100b
mov  bh,(RED shl 4) + BRIGHT_WHITE
```

The following lines produce blinking yellow letters on a brown background, a value of 11101110:

```
BLINK = 10000000b
YELLOW = 1110b
BROWN = 110b
mov  bh,(BROWN shl 4) + YELLOW + BLINK
```

A list of 3-bit background colors is shown in Table 6, and a list of 4-bit foreground colors appears in Table 7.

Video attributes can be controlled when writing individual characters or when scrolling the screen. The choice of colors and attributes is largely a matter of taste and can greatly influence the appearance of your software. In addition to the colors mentioned here, the video controller can switch to different 16-color palettes, allowing a larger overall selection.

Video Pages. All the color graphics adapters have the ability to store multiple video text screens, called *pages,* in memory. The monochrome adapter can display only a single page. On the color adapters, one can write text to one page while another is being displayed or flip back

Table 6. Background Colors (3 bits).

Binary	Hex	Color
000	00	black
001	01	blue
010	02	green
011	03	cyan
100	04	red
101	05	magenta
110	06	brown
111	07	white

Table 7. Foreground Colors (4 bits).

Binary	Hex	Color	Binary	Hex	Color
0000	00	black	1000	08	gray
0001	01	blue	1001	09	light blue
0010	02	green	1010	0A	light green
0011	03	cyan	1011	0B	light cyan
0100	04	red	1100	0C	light red
0101	05	magenta	1101	0D	light magenta
0110	06	brown	1110	0E	yellow
0111	07	white	1111	0F	bright white

and forth between multiple video pages. The pages are numbered from 0 to 7, and the number of pages available depends on the current video mode. See Table 8 for details.

5.7.3   INT 10h Video Functions

Let's summarize the functions available under INT 10h. These functions control the video display by calling ROM BIOS routines. In general, INT 10h preserves only the BX, CX, DX, and segment registers. Any other registers that you wish to preserve should be pushed on the stack prior to the INT 10h instruction.

00h: Set Video Mode. To set the display to a particular video mode, move 0 to AH and place the video mode number in AL. The screen will be cleared automatically, unless the high bit in AL is set. The following example sets the mode to 80 X 25 color text:

```
mov   ah,0              ; set video mode
mov   al,3              ; choose mode 3
int   10h              ; call the BIOS
```

To avoid clearing the screen, we could have set AL to 83h. If there are two video adapters in the system, such as, monochrome and color, the correct adapter is selected. To find out what the current video mode is, see function 0Fh, *Get Video Mode*.

The following routine sets the video mode to medium-resolution graphics, waits for a keystroke, and then sets the video mode to color text. It can be run using a CGA or EGA video adapter:

```
mov   ah,0              ; set video mode
mov   al,6              ; 640 X 200 color graphics mode
int   10h
mov   ah,1              ; get a keystroke
```

Table 8. Video Pages and Modes.

Available Pages	Mode	Video Adapter
0	07h	Mono
0-7	00h, 01h	CGA
0-3	02h, 03h	CGA, EGA, VGA
0-7	02h, 03h	CGA, EGA, VGA
0-7	0Dh	EGA, VGA
0-3	0Eh	EGA, VGA
0-1	0Fh, 10h	EGA, VGA

```
int   21h
mov   ah,0              ; set video mode
mov   al,3              ; to color text
int   10h
```

A list of the INT 10h functions discussed in this chapter appears in Table 9.

01h: Set Cursor Lines. The cursor is displayed using starting and ending scan lines, which make it possible to control its size. Application programs can do this in order to show the current status of an operation. For example, one text editor increases the cursor size when the NumLock key is toggled on; when it is pressed again, the cursor returns to its original size.

The monochrome display uses 12 lines for its cursor, while all other displays use 8 lines. We can picture the cursor as a series of horizontal lines, numbered beginning at line 0. The default color cursor starts at line 6 and ends at line 7. The default monochrome cursor starts at line 0Bh and ends at line 0Ch. Both are shown in Figure 7.

To call the set cursor lines function, set CH and CL to the top and bottom lines for the cursor and set AH to 1. The following instructions set the monochrome cursor to its maximum size, a solid block:

```
mov   ah,1              ; set cursor size
mov   ch,0              ; start line (top)
mov   cl,0Ch            ; end line (bottom)
```

It is a good idea to save the current cursor lines in a variable before changing it and then to restore the cursor on exit. Software that ignores this common courtesy is annoying, to say the least. You can retrieve the cursor size using function 3, *Get Cursor Position.* To protect yourself against those unscrupulous programs that destroy your cursor, run the following program from DOS whenever your cursor disappears. The program is written for a color display, but you can move 0B0Ch to CX to adapt it for monochrome:

Figure 7. Cursor Layout, Color and Monochrome.

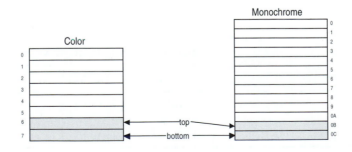

```
mov   ah,1                    ; set cursor lines
mov   cx,0607h                ; restore default CGA/EGA cursor
int   10h                     ; call BIOS
```

Table 9. Listing of INT 10h Functions.

Function Number (in AH)	Description
0	*Set Video Mode.* Set the video display to monochrome, text, graphics, or color mode.
1	*Set Cursor Lines.* Identify the starting and ending scan lines for the cursor.
2	*Set Cursor Position.* Position the cursor on the screen.
3	*Get Cursor Position.* Get the cursor's screen position and size.
4	*Read Light Pen.* Read the position and status of the light pen.
5	*Set Display Page.* Select the video page to be displayed.
6	*Scroll Window Up.* Scroll a window on the current video page upward, replacing scrolled lines with blanks.
7	*Scroll Window Down.* Scroll a window on the current video page downward, replacing scrolled lines with blanks.
8	*Read Character and Attribute.* Read the character and its attribute at the current cursor position.
9	*Write Character and Attribute.* Write a character and its attribute at the current cursor position.
0Ah	*Write Character.* Write a character only (no attribute) at the current cursor position.
0Bh	*Set Color Pallete.* Select a group of available colors for the video adapter.
0Ch	*Write Graphics Pixel.* Write a graphics pixel when in graphics mode.
0Dh	*Read Graphics Pixel.* Read the color of a single graphics pixel at a given location.
0Eh	*Write Character.* Write a character to the screen and advance the cursor.
0Fh	*Get Video Mode.* Get the current video mode.
11h	*Load Default ROM Font.* While in text mode, load one of three default ROM fonts and display on the EGA and VGA displays.

02h: Set Cursor Position. Function 2 locates the cursor at a desired row and column. Set AH to 2, set DH to the desired cursor row, set DL to the column, and set BH to the current video page number (usually page 0). The following instructions position the cursor at row 10, column 20:

```
mov   ah,2              ; set cursor position
mov   dh,10             ; row 10
mov   dl,20             ; column 20
mov   bh,0              ; video page 0
int   10h               ; call BIOS
```

It is possible to set the cursor position on a video page not currently being displayed. Indirectly, this leads to a common error—forgetting to specify the current video page. Depending on the installed BIOS version, AL can be changed during the operation. It should be saved before and restored after calling INT 10h.

03h: Get Cursor Position. Function 3 returns the row and column positions of the cursor on a specified video page, as well as the starting and ending lines that determine the cursor's size. Set AH to 3 and BH to the current video page number. The values returned are:

CH	Starting scan line
CL	Ending scan line
DH	Row location
DL	Column location

The following routine retrieves and stores the cursor information:

```
mov   ah,3                  ; get cursor position
mov   bh,0                  ; video page 0
int   10h                   ; call BIOS
mov   savecursor,cx         ; save the cursor lines
mov   current_row,dh        ; save the row
mov   current_col,dl        ; save the column
```

This function can be quite useful in programs where the user is moving the cursor around a menu. Depending on where the cursor is, you know which menu choice has been selected.

05h: Set Video Page. Function 5 is useful in text modes that support multiple pages. Text written to one page is kept intact while another page is being displayed. To call this function, set AH to 5 and AL to the desired page number:

```
mov   ah,5              ; select display page
mov   al,1              ; page 1 selected
int   10h               ; call BIOS
```

Example 7 lists PAGES.ASM, which displays text on video pages 0 and 1 and switches back and forth between the two. (This program will only work on a color display.) After assembling the program, run it several times, and you will see the text from each of the previous times you ran the program still on the page 1 screen. This happens because most programs (and DOS) write only to page 0.

Example 7. Switching Video Pages.

```
title   Video Pages Example        (PAGES.ASM)


; This program switches back and forth between
; text pages 0 and 1 on a color display.

.model small
.stack 100h
.data
page0 db 'This is video page zero.$'
page1 db 'This is video page one.$'

.code
main proc
    mov   ax,@data              ; initialize DS register
    mov   ds,ax
    mov   ah,9                  ; display a message
    mov   dx,offset page0
    int   21h
    mov   ah,1                  ; get a keystroke
    int   21h

to_page_1:
    mov   ah,5                  ; set video page
    mov   al,1                  ; to page 1
    int   10h
    mov   ah,9                  ; display a message
    mov   dx,offset page1
    int   21h
    mov   ah,1                  ; get a keystroke
    int   21h

to_page_0:
    mov   ah,5                  ; set video page
    mov   al,0                  ; to page 0
```

```
        int    10h
        mov    ax,4C00h              ; return to DOS
        int    21h
    main endp
    end main
```

06h, 07h: *Scroll Window Up or Down*. Functions 6 and 7 scroll a screen window. The term *scrolling a window* describes moving data on the video display up or down. As the display is scrolled up, for example, the bottom line is replaced by a blank line. A *window* is the area of the screen being scrolled. We define a window by using row and column coordinates for its upper left and lower right corners. Rows are numbered 0-24 from the top, and columns are numbered 0-79 from the left. Therefore, a window covering the entire screen would be from 0,0 to 24,79. Scrolling just one line or a few lines is as easy as scrolling the entire window. If all lines are scrolled, the window is cleared. Lines scrolled off the screen cannot be recovered. The input parameters for calling functions 6 and 7 are:

AH	6 to scroll up or 7 to scroll down
AL	Number of lines (0 = all)
CH, CL	Row and column of the upper left window corner
DH, DL	Row and column of the lower right window corner
BH	Video attribute given to each blank line

The following statements clear the screen by scrolling it upward with a normal attribute:

```
    mov    ah,6        ; scroll window up
    mov    al,0        ; entire window
    mov    ch,0        ; upper left row
    mov    cl,0        ; upper left column
    mov    dh,24       ; lower right row
    mov    dl,79       ; lower right column
    mov    bh,7        ; normal attribute for blank lines
    int    10h         ; call BIOS
```

08h: *Read Character and Attribute*. Function 8 returns the character and its attribute at the current cursor position on the selected video page. Call this function by placing 8 in AH and the video page number in BH. INT 10h returns the character in AL and its attribute in AH. The following statements position the cursor at row 5, column 1, and read a character:

```
    locate:
        mov    ah,2        ; set cursor position
        mov    bh,0        ; on video page 0
        mov    dx,0501h    ; at 5,1
        int    10h
    getchar:
        mov    ah,8        ; read attribute/character
```

```
mov   bh,0                    ; on video page 0
int   10h
mov   char,al                 ; save the character
mov   attrib,ah               ; save the attribute
```

09h: Write Character and Attribute. Use function 9 to write one or more characters at the current cursor position. This function can display any ASCII character, including the special graphics characters for codes 1-31. None of these are interpreted as ASCII control codes, as they would be by INT 21h DOS services. The input parameters are:

AH   Function code (9)
AL   Character to be written
BH   Video page
BL   Attribute
CX   Repetition factor

The *repetition factor* specifies how many times the character is to be repeated. (The character should not be repeated beyond the end of the current screen line.) After a character is written, you must call function 2 to move the cursor if more characters will be written.

The following statements write the graphics character identified by 0Ah on the screen 32 times, with a blinking attribute. You may recognize 0Ah as an ASCII *line feed* character, but it is interpreted here by INT 10h as a graphics character (white circle on a black background).

```
mov   ah,9                    ; write character and attribute
mov   al,0Ah                  ; ASCII character 0Ah
mov   bh,0                    ; video page 0
mov   bl,87h                  ; blinking attribute
mov   cx,32                   ; display it 32 times
int   10h
```

0Ah: Write Character. Function 0Ah writes a character to the screen at the current cursor position without changing the current screen attribute. It is identical to function 9 in every way, except that the attribute is not specified. The following statements write the letter *A* once at the current cursor position:

```
mov   ah,0Ah                  ; write character only
mov   al,'A'                  ; character 'A'
mov   bh,0                    ; video page 0
mov   cx,1                    ; display only once
int   10h
```

0Ch: Write Graphics Pixel. Function 0Ch draws a pixel on the screen, given the pixel value, video page number, row, and column:

```
mov   ah,0Ch
mov   al,pixelValue
mov   bh,videoPage
mov   cx,column              ; x coordinate
mov   dx,row                 ; y coordinate
int   10h
```

0Dh: Read Graphics Pixel. Function 0Dh reads a graphics pixel from the screen at a given row and column position, and returns the pixel value in AL:

```
mov   ah,0Dh
mov   bh,videoPage
mov   cx,column
mov   dx,row
int   10h
mov   pixelValue,al
```

0Fh: Get Video Mode. Function 0Fh returns the number of video columns in AH, the current display mode in AL, and the active display page in BH. A list of the more common video modes is given in the section of this chapter entitled "Video Modes." This function should be called before you attempt to perform any color graphics functions or color-specific operations. The following statements get the current video mode and video page:

```
mov   ah,0Fh                 ; get video mode
int   10h
mov   vmode,al               ; save the mode
mov   page,bh                ; save the page
```

11h: Load Default ROM Fonts. A rather nice enhancement provided by EGA and VGA displays is their ability to load and display different character fonts while still in text mode. Although the subject of custom user fonts is beyond our scope, we can use INT 10h to load one of three default ROM fonts: On a VGA display, the 8 x 16 font displays 25 lines of text, the 8 x 14 displays 28 lines, and the 8 x 8 font displays 50 lines.

To load a ROM font, use INT 10h function 11h, subfunctions 11h, 12h, or 14h. Set the video mode just prior to loading a font. For fun, substitute each of the three font names into the instruction that loads the subfunction into AL:

```
eightByFourteen equ  11h     ; 28 lines/screen
eightByEight    equ  12h     ; 50 lines/screen
eightBySixteen  equ  14h     ; 25 lines/screen

mov   ah,0                   ; set video mode
mov   al,3                   ; to color text
int   10h
```

```
mov   ah,11h              ; function: load ROM font
mov   al,eightByEight     ; subfunction: font type
mov   bl,0                ; block number = 0
int   10h
```

5.7.4   Writing Directly to Video Memory

The link library supplied with this book includes procedures that make it easier to write characters directly to video memory (*VRAM*). You can also change the default video segment address. Writing directly to video memory results in fast output because it bypasses the DOS and BIOS functions. The only disadvantage to using direct video is that it only works if you know the computer's video display buffer address. This used to be a problem with early PCs, but is no longer an issue. The procedures are listed in Table 10. The program excerpt in Example 8 shows how to display a string using the Writestring_direct procedure.

Example 8. Writing a String to VRAM.

```
Gray = 7
Blue = 1
BlueOnGray = (Gray SHL 4) OR Blue
.data
msg_str  db "This is written to VRAM.",0

.code
mov  si,offset msg_str
mov  dh,8
mov  dl,10
mov  ah,BlueOnGray
call Writestring_direct
```

Table 10. Direct Video Procedures in the Link Library.

Procedure	Description
Set_videoseg	Set the current video segment address. The default is B800h, which is appropriate for a color display, including all types of VGA. The alternative is B000h, the default for the older monochrome display. Input: AX contains the segment value.
Writechar_direct	Write a single character to VRAM. Input: AL = character, AH = attribute, DH/DL = row (0-24) and column (0-79) on screen.
Writestring_direct	Write a null-terminated string to VRAM, all characters in the same color. Input: DS:SI points to the string, AH = attribute, DH/DL = row (0-24) and column (0-79) on screen.

5.8   RECURSION

In Sections 5.1 throught 5.3 of this chapter we discussed procedures, the stack, and the passing of arguments to procedures. Let us now examine a related technique used by nearly all programming languages, called *recursion*. Simply put, a recursive procedure is one that calls itself. But when the procedure is called again, what prevents it from being called a third time, fourth time, and so on?

In the following example, the current value of IP is pushed on the stack each time the **Endless** procedure calls itself:

```
Endless proc
    .
    .
    call Endless            ; push IP on stack, then branch
    ret                     ; return never reached
Endless endp
```

As you might guess, Endless fills up a 128-word stack after calling itself 128 times, and the RET instruction is never reached. This helps to show that a recursive procedure must have a *terminating condition* that prevents the recursive calls from repeating forever.

Sum of Integers. Our next example is a routine that sums the numbers from 1 to some integer *n*. We use CX as a counter to control the number of times SUM calls itself, and we accumulate the sum in AX:

```
Main proc
    mov  cx,5               ; counter
    mov  ax,0               ; holds the sum
    call Sum                ; find sum of 5+4+3+2+1
L1: mov  ax,4C00h
    int  21h
Main endp


Sum proc
    or   cx,cx              ; check counter value
    jz   L2                 ; quit if zero
    add  ax,cx              ; otherwise, add to sum
    dec  cx                 ; decrement counter
    call Sum                ; recursive call
L2: ret
Sum endp
```

Table 11. Stack Frame for the Sum Program.

Pushed On Stack	CX	AX
L1	5	0
L2	4	5
L2	3	9
L2	2	12
L2	1	14
L2	0	15

The first two lines of **Sum** check the counter and skip to the label **L2** when CX = 0. This bypasses any further recursive calls. When the RET instruction is reached the first time, it backs up to the previous call to Sum, which backs up to *its* previous call, and so on. Table 11 shows the return addresses pushed on the stack by the CALL instruction, along with the concurrent values of CX (counter) and AX (sum).

From this example, we see that even the simplest recursive routine makes ample use of the stack. At the very minimum, two bytes of stack space are used up each time a procedure call takes place because the return address must be saved on the stack.

We have not yet seen any reason to use recursion. A simple loop would be a more efficient way to sum a list of numbers than our recursive version. The latter spends a lot of time executing CALL and RET instructions. But read on, because the next example recursively calculates the factorial of a number *n*.

Calculating a Factorial. The *factorial* alogrithm calculates *n!,* where *n* is an unsigned integer. The first time **factorial** is called, the parameter *n* is the starting number, as the following Pascal implementation shows:

```
function factorial(n :integer) :integer;
  begin
    if n = 1 then
      factorial := 1
    else
      factorial := n * factorial(n-1)
  end;
```

The assembler version of factorial appears in Example 9. We pass *n* on the stack to the routine, and the function result is returned in AX. IF the factorial is being stored in a 16-bit register, the largest factorial you can generate is 8! (40,320). The offset of each statement is shown at the beginning of each line.

When **factorial** is called, the offset of the next instruction after the call is pushed on the stack. From **Main**, this is offset 0007; from **Factorial**, it is 0022. In the diagram of the stack (Figure 8) shown after several recursive calls, you can see that new values for *n* and BP have been pushed on the stack.

Each procedure call in our example uses six bytes of stack space. Just before factorial recursively calls itself, *n-1* is pushed on the stack as the input argument to the called function. The function returns its own factorial value in AX, which is then multiplied by the value we pushed on the stack before the call. The result of this multiplication (in AX) is then returned as the function result. The RET instruction adds 2 to SP, discarding the argument that was pushed on the stack.

Example 9. The Factorial Procedure (Recursion).

```
      main proc
0000      mov  ax,8           ; calculate 8!
0003      push ax
0004      call Factorial
0007      mov ax,4C00h
000A      int 21h
      main endp
```

Figure 8. Stack Frame, Factorial Program.

STACK

```
┌────────┬─────────────────────────┐
│ 0008   │ n                       │
│ 0007   │ IP (return address)     │
│ 0000   │ BP                      │
├────────┼─────────────────────────┤
│ 0007   │ (n-1)                   │
│ 0022   │ IP (return address)     │
│ 00FA   │ BP                      │
├────────┼─────────────────────────┤
│ 0006   │ (n-1)                   │
│ 0022   │ IP                      │
│ 00F4   │ BP                      │
├────────┼─────────────────────────┤
│ 0005   │ (n-1)                   │
│ 0022   │ IP                      │
│ 00EE   │ BP                      │
├────────┼─────────────────────────┤
│ 0004   │ (n-1)                   │
│ (etc.) │                         │
└────────┴─────────────────────────┘
```

```
        Factorial proc
000C         push bp
000D         mov  bp,sp
000F         mov  ax,[bp+4]        ; get n
0012         cmp  ax,1             ; n <= 1?
0015         ja   L1              ; no: continue
0017         mov  ax,1            ; yes: return 1
001A         jmp  L2
001D  L1:    dec  ax
001E         push ax              ; Factorial(n-1)
001F         call Factorial
0022         mov  bx,[bp+4]        ; get n
0025         mul  bx              ; ax = ax * bx
0027  L2:    pop  bp
0028         ret  2               ; AX = result
        Factorial endp
```

5.9   REVIEW QUESTIONS

1. What is the purpose of the INT 21h instruction?

2. How is a software interrupt different from a hardware interrupt?

3. What are the largest and smallest possible interrupt numbers?

4. What are the numbers in the Interrupt Vector Table for?

5. Which advantages do interrupt routines in the BIOS have over those serviced by DOS?

6. Why don't application programs directly manipulate the computer's hardware?

7. Which interrupt (other than INT 21h) services the keyboard? Which services does it offer?

8. How are DOS function calls different from other interrupts?

9. When INT 21h displays a single character on the screen, which register holds the character to be displayed?

10. Why do DOS functions permit the redirection of device names for input and output?

11. What is the generic DOS device name for the printer?

12. What is the DOS device name for a nonexistent device?

13. Which INT 21h service routines output a single character to the console?

14. Correct any logic errors in the following code, which is supposed to display a string using INT 21h function 9:

```
message   db   'Hello, world!@'
.code
    mov    al,9                ; string output
    mov    dx,message
    int    21h
```

15. The following example uses the DOS service routine for keyboard input. Which variable holds the number of keys actually typed, and which label points to the first keystroke?

```
.data
label1   db   20
label2   db   0
label3   db   20 dup(' ')


.code
mov    ah,0Ah
mov    dx,offset label1
int    21h
```

16. Which interrupt is best when you wish to input extended keyboard characters such as function keys and cursor arrows? Provide an example.

17. If INT 21h function 9 is used to display a string, will ASCII control characters, such as tabs and line feeds, be interpreted correctly?

18. Application programs often clear the keyboard typeahead buffer before asking for more input. Which interrupt service might be best for this task?

19. What is a keyboard scan code, and how is it different from a keyboard ASCII code?

20. Which ASCII control character moves the cursor to the left side of the screen?

21. Which interrupt clears the screen, and what input value(s) should be placed in registers?

22. Name at least four video attributes that can be used with the color adapter.

23. In Table 12, fill in the bit pattern of each color video attribute. The first attribute has been created as a sample.

24. Which INT 10h function displays a character on the screen without changing any screen attributes?

25. Which INT 10h function sets the video mode?

26. Complete the following statements to set the cursor size on the color display to scan lines 3-4:

```
mov    ah,1     ; set cursor lines
mov    ch,
mov    cl,
int    10h
```

Table 12. Examples for Question 23.

Blink	Background	Foreground	Bit Pattern
Off	Brown	Yellow	0 1 1 0 1 1 1 0
Off	White	Blue	
Off	Blue	White	
On	Cyan	Gray	
Off	Black	Light magenta	
On	Black	Bright white	

27. Complete the following statements to locate the cursor at row 5, column 10 on video page 0:

```
mov   ah,2
mov   dh,
mov   dl,
mov   bh,
int   10h
```

28. Complete the following statements to scroll the entire screen upward with a reverse video attribute:

```
mov   ah,
mov   al,
mov   ch,
mov   cl,
mov   dh,
mov   dl,
mov   bh,
int   10h
```

29. Assuming that a program named **prog1.exe** uses standard input-output, write a command to run the program and tell it to receive its input from a file called **input.txt.**

30. Using the program name from the previous question, write a command to tell the program to send its output to the printer.

31. A PUSH operation adds a value to the stack, while a _____ operation removes a value from the stack.

32. When a value is pushed onto the stack, does the stack grow upward or downward in memory?

33. Why is the stack called a LIFO structure?

5.10 PROGRAMMING EXERCISES

1. *Keyboard Scan Codes*

Write a program that displays the keyboard scan code for any key pressed by the user. Let the user continue to press keyboard keys until the Esc key is pressed.

2. *Keyboard Status Indicator*

Write a procedure that displays the status of the Shift, CapsLock, and Alt keys in the lower right corner of the screen. Pass an argument to the procedure that selects the color to be used when displaying the status values.

3. *Stack Operations*

Use the PUSH and POP instructions to display a list of 16-bit integers in reverse order on the console.

4. *Window Scroll Program*

Write a short procedure to do the following:

Scroll a window from row 5, column 10 to row 20, column 70, with a reverse video attribute.

Locate the cursor at row 10, column 20.

Display a line of text, such as:

```
THIS TEXT IS IN THE WINDOW
```

5. *Enhanced Window Scroll Program*

Enhance the procedure written for Exercise 1 as follows: After the line of text is displayed, wait for a key to be pressed. Scroll a window from row 7, column 15 to row 18, column 68, with a normal attribute. Write the character A with a blinking attribute in the middle of the window. Wait for a keystroke and clear the entire screen with a normal attribute.

6. *Keyboard Echo Program*

Write a program that inputs 10 characters from standard input and echoes them to standard output (each character will appear twice). Use INT 21h functions 1 and 2. After the program has been assembled, run it in the following ways, taking advantage of DOS redirection commands:

```
a. ECHOC              (kybd input, screen output)
b. ECHOC < INFILE     (file input, screen output)
```

```
     c. ECHOC > OUTFILE              (kybd input, file output)
```

For option b, you will need to create a text file containing a string with at least 10 characters. Your program will read the file as input.

7. Compressed Type Setup

Write a procedure to initialize your printer to compressed mode, 17 characters per inch. Most printers require one or two bytes to be sent from the host program (on Epson-compatibles, the number is 15). Run your program, and then use the DOS PRINT command to print a text file. Write another program that returns the printer to its default typestyle, usually 10 characters per inch.

8. Character String Printing

Write a procedure that writes the following line of text to the printer, with only the word **compressed** in compressed mode:

```
"The word compressed is the only one that is small."
```

Use DOS function 9 to write the string. Run the program from DOS, redirecting its output to the printer. Write a carriage return and line feed at the end of the line to force the printer to empty its buffer.

9. String Input

Input a string from the console and redisplay it on the screen. Use INT 21h function 0Ah for the input and use function 9 for output.

10. Uppercase Conversion

Create a loop that inputs any number of lowercase characters from the console. As each character is input, convert it to uppercase and display it on the console. Terminate the program by typing Ctrl-Break. INT 21h, function 8 can be used for input, because it does not echo the characters, and function 2 can be used for output.

11. String with Attributes

Use INT 10h, function 9 to display a string containing the first 15 letters of the alphabet. This function does not advance the cursor position, so you still must call INT 10h function 2 after each character is displayed. Set the background color of each character to black, and give each character a different foreground color (0001 to 1111).

12. Box-Drawing Program

Use INT 10h to draw a single-line box on the screen. Refer to the extended ASCII characters on the inside cover of this book. Set the upper left corner of the box to row 5, column 10, and set the lower right corner to row 20, column 70. Do not echo the keystrokes on the screen.

13. *Multiple Boxes*

Using the box-drawing techniques from the previous exercise, draw five or more boxes on the screen of varying sizes and shapes. Use the LOOP instruction to cycle through a table containing row and column offsets. Set BX to the offset of the table, and use indirect addressing to read the row and column positions for each box. Sample box table:

```
boxes  db  5,10,20,70          ; first box
       db  12,20,18,60         ; second box
       db  1,5,3,10            ; third box
       db  5,60,24,80          ; fourth box
       db  5,25,18,75          ; fifth box
```

14. *Boxes with Colors*

Modify the program written for the previous exercise as follows: Add a color attribute byte value to the table entry for each box in the **boxes** table. When drawing each box, use the color stored in the table.

15. *Setting the Cursor Size*

Write three short procedures that set the cursor size to (1) a solid block, (2) mid-height, two scan lines thick, and (3) the "normal" cursor, which is two scan lines at the bottom.

16. *Blinking Message*

Many programs use a blinking status message to alert the user to important information. Write a program that displays a blinking message in the lower right corner of the screen, waits for a keystroke, and then erases the message.

17. *Null Attributes*

Write a program that writes a blank with an attribute value of 00 to every position on line 10 of the screen. Then write a line of text (using INT 21h, function 9) on the same line. Explain the result.

18. *Day Number of any Date*

Write a program that prompts the user for a date between 1980 and 2099. The program should then state the day of the week that corresponds to the date. Express the day as a string, such as "Sunday" or "Monday". *Hint:* In this chapter, you learned that INT 21h Function 2Ah obtains the day of the week as a number for the current date, where Sunday = 0, Monday = 1, and so on. You also know that Function 2Bh sets the current date.

6 *Conditional Processing*

6.1   BOOLEAN AND COMPARISON INSTRUCTIONS

Assembly language is happiest when working on binary data, and it absolutely shines when asked to perform *bitwise operations* (manipulate individual bits). If you have studied boolean algebra, you are already familiar with the AND, OR, NOT, and XOR logical operators. These are directly implemented as assembly language instructions, in which the logical operations take place between individual binary bits. In addition, assembly language has the NEG, TEST, and CMP instructions, which are invaluable when implementing IF statements.

Boolean instructions are based on boolean algebra operations (invented by the mathematician George Boole). These operations allow modification of individual bits in binary numbers, as summarized in Table 1.

6.1.1   The Flags Register

Each of the instructions in this section affects the Flags register. We are concerned with the way the Zero, Carry, and Sign flags show the results of boolean and comparison instructions. Four important points to remember are:

• The *Zero* flag is set when the result of an operation is zero.

• The *Carry* flag is set when the result of an unsigned addition is too large for the destination operand or when a subtraction requires a borrow.

• The *Sign* flag is set when the high bit of the destination operand is set, indicating a negative result.

Table 1. Boolean Instructions.

Operation	Description
AND	Result is 1 only when both input bits are 1.
OR	Result is 1 when either input bit is 1.
XOR	Result is 1 only when the input bits are different (called exclusive-OR).
NOT	Result is the reverse of the input bit (in other words, 1 becomes 0, and 0 becomes 1).
NEG	Convert a number to its twos complement.
TEST	Perform an implied AND operation on the destination operand, setting the flags appropriately.
BT, BTR, BTC, BTS	Copy bit n from the source operand to the Carry flag and toggle/clear/set the same bit in the source operand.
CMP	Compare two operands, setting the flags appropriately.

• The *Overflow* flag is set when a signed arithmetic operation generates a result that is out of range.

6.1.2   AND Instruction

The AND instruction performs a boolean (bitwise) AND operation between each of the bits in two operands and places the result in the first operand. The following combinations of operands are permitted:

```
AND    reg,reg
AND    reg,mem
AND    reg,immed
AND    mem,reg
AND    mem,immed
```

Reg, mem, and *immed* can be 8, 16, or 32 bits. Of course, the operands must be the same size. For each matching bit in the two operands, the following rule applies: If both bits equal 1, the result bit is 1; otherwise, it is 0. The following flags are affected: Overflow, Sign, Zero, Parity, Carry, and Auxiliary Carry. The following example shows the results of the AND operation using two 4-bit numbers:

```
                 0 0 1 1
        AND      0 1 0 1
                 -------
Result:          0 0 0 1
```

The AND instruction can clear selected bits in an operand, while carefully preserving, or *masking* the remaining bits. In the following example, the value 00001111 is called a *bit mask*:

```
mov al,00111011b
and al,00001111b                    ; AL = 00001011b
```

Application: Clear High Bits. Some word processing programs set the highest bit of ASCII characters. If we wanted to view such a file on the console, we could clear the high bit of each character as it was being displayed.

The following program excerpt inputs a stream of text from standard input, clears the high bit, and writes the revised byte to standard output. The input can be redirected from the DOS command line, making it possible to read from a file. INT 21h function 6 is used because it does not echo each input character, and DOS does not wait for input when the end of file is reached:

```
        mov    cx,10000         ; read up to 10,000 characters
L1: mov ah,6                    ; console input function
        mov    dl,0FFh          ; check for input character
        int    21h              ; call DOS
```

```
and  al,01111111b                ; strip high bit
mov  dl,al                       ; move to DL
mov  ah,2                        ; write to standard output
int  21h
loop L1                          ; repeat until CX = 0
```

An input character, for example, might be the letter *A*, but with its highest bit set. Rather than being ASCII code 01000001, the character is actually equal to 11000001. Our program performs an AND operation between the latter value and 01111111, clearing the high bit:

```
       1 1 0 0 0 0 0 1   (character A with high bit set)
(AND)  0 1 1 1 1 1 1 1   (7Fh is the bit mask)
       ---------------
       0 1 0 0 0 0 0 1   (result: 41h, the character A)
```

Clearing Status Bit Values. A similar application of AND is related to the keyboard status byte, which is located at address 0040:0017; bit 5 indicates that the *NumLock* key is on. We can turn off *NumLock* by simply clearing the bit:

```
push ds                          ; save DS
mov  ax,40h                      ; set DS to BIOS data area
mov  ds,ax
mov  bx,17h                       ; point to keyboard flag
and  byte ptr [bx],11011111b      ; turn NumLock off
pop  ds                          ; restore DS
```

Notice that we save DS on the stack before changing it, because it points to the program's own data segment. The BYTE PTR operator is required because without it, the assembler would not be able to infer the memory operand's size. For example:

```
and  [bx],11011111b              ; byte or word?
```

6.1.3   OR Instruction

The OR instruction performs a boolean OR operation between each of the bits in two operands and places the result in the first operand. The following combinations of operands are permitted:

```
OR   reg,reg
OR   reg,mem
OR   reg,immed
OR   mem,reg
OR   mem,immed
```

Reg, mem, and *immed* can be 8, 16, or 32 bits, and they must be the same size. For each matching bit in the two operands, the following applies: If both bits are 0, the result bit is 0; otherwise, it is 1. The following flags are affected: Overflow, Sign, Zero, Parity, Auxiliary Carry, and Carry. The following table shows the results of an OR operation using individual bit

```
            0 0 1 1
    OR      0 1 0 1
            -------
Result:     0 1 1 1
```

For example, let us OR 3Bh with 0Fh. The lower 4 bits of the result are set and the high 4 bits are unchanged:

```
mov al,00111011b              ; 3Bh
or  al,00001111b              ; AL = 3Fh
```

This technique can be used to convert a single decimal digit to ASCII by setting bits 4 and 5. If, for example, AL = 05h, we can convert it to the ASCII code for the digit 5 (35h): We OR the number with 30h:

```
binary value:  0 0 0 0 0 1 0 1   (05h)
boolean OR:    0 0 1 1 0 0 0 0   (30h)
               ---------------
result:        0 0 1 1 0 1 0 1   (35h)  '5'
```

The assembly language instructions to do this are:

```
mov   dl,5                    ; binary value
or    dl,30h                  ; convert to ASCII
```

Checking the Sign or Value. You can use the OR instruction to find out if an operand is less than or equal to zero. A number ORed with itself does not change, but the flags are affected:

```
or  al,al
```

If ZF = 1, then AL must be equal to 0; if SF = 1, AL is negative; if ZF = 0 and SF = 0, AL must be greater than 0.

Setting Status Bit Values. Just as the AND instruction was used earlier to clear the NumLock key in the keyboard status byte, we could turn on the CapsLock key by setting bit 6. The following could be a useful subroutine in a program that requires user input to be in uppercase letters:

```
push ds                       ; save DS
mov  ax,40h                   ; set DS to BIOS data area
mov  ds,ax
```

```
mov  bx,17h                          ; keyboard flag byte
or   byte ptr [bx],01000000b         ; turn CapsLock on
pop  ds                              ; restore DS
```

6.1.4 XOR Instruction

The XOR (*exclusive OR*) instruction performs a boolean exclusive OR operation between each of the bits in two operands. The following operand combinations are permitted:

```
XOR   reg,reg
XOR   reg,mem
XOR   reg,immed
XOR   mem,reg
XOR   mem,immed
```

Reg, mem, and *immed* can be 8, 16, or 32 bits. The first operand holds the result of the operation. Only one operand can be a memory operand. For each matching bit in the two operands, the following applies: If both bits are the same (both 0 or both 1) the result is 0; otherwise, the result is 1. The following flags are affected: Overflow, Sign, Zero, Parity, Auxiliary Carry, and Carry.

The following example shows the effect of XOR on individual bits. XOR produces a 1 only when the two input bits are different:

```
              0 0 1 1
     XOR      0 1 0 1
              -------
Result:       0 1 1 0
```

After the following instructions, AL = 00110010:

```
mov      al,10110100b
xor      al,10000110b            ; AL = 00110010b, or 32h
```

Reversing Bits. A special quality of XOR is that it reverses itself when applied twice. Suppose we have a number *x*, which is XOR'ed by a number *y*, producing *z*. Then if we XOR *z* with *y*, we end up with our starting value, *x*. For example,

```
              1 1 0 1 0 1 0 1   x
     XOR      1 1 1 1 0 0 0 0   y
              ---------------
     equals   0 0 1 0 0 1 0 1   z = x XOR y
     XOR      1 1 1 1 0 0 0 0   y
              ---------------
     equals   1 1 0 1 0 1 0 1   x = z XOR y
```

Notice that any bit XORed with 0 retains its original value, and any bit XORed with 1 is complemented.

Reversing a Status Bit. Let's apply XOR to our now-familar keyboard status flag. We toggle the *CapsLock* key by reversing bit 6 of the status flag. No other keyboard status bits are changed:

```
push ds                              ; save DS
mov  ax,40h                          ; set DS to BIOS data area
mov  ds,ax
mov  bx,17h                          ; keyboard flag byte
xor  byte ptr [bx],01000000b         ; toggle the CapsLock key
pop  ds                              ; restore DS
```

6.1.5   NOT Instruction

The NOT instruction reverses all bits in an operand, changing ones to zeros and vice versa. The result is called the *ones complement*. The following operands are permitted:

```
NOT reg
NOT mem
```

For example, the ones complement of F0h is 0Fh:

```
mov  al,11110000b
not  al                  ; AL = 00001111b
```

6.1.6   NEG Instruction

The NEG (*negate*) instruction reverses the sign of a number by converting the number to its twos complement. The following operands are permitted:

```
NEG reg
NEG mem
```

Recall that the twos complement of a number can be found by reversing all bits in the destination operand and adding 1. The following flags are affected: Overflow, Sign, Zero, Auxiliary Carry, Parity, and Carry.

After performing a NEG operation, check the Overflow flag for a possible invalid result. For example, if we move –128 to AL and negate it, the result is –128 (an invalid result) and OF = 1:

```
mov  al,-128             ; AL = 10000000b
neg  al                  ; AL = 10000000b, OF = 1
```

On the other hand, if +127 is negated, the result is valid and OF = 0:

```
mov   al,+127              ; AL = 01111111b
neg   al                   ; AL = 10000001b, OF = 0
```

6.1.7   TEST Instruction

The TEST instruction performs an implied AND operation between each of the bits in two operands and sets the flags accordingly. It is particularly valuable for finding out if individual bits in an operand are set. Neither operand is modified. The following operands are permitted:

```
TEST   reg,reg
TEST   reg,mem
TEST   reg,immed
TEST   mem,reg
TEST   mem,immed
```

If any matching bit positions are set in both operands, ZF = 0. The following flags are affected: Overflow, Sign, Zero, Carry, Auxiliary Carry, and Parity.

Example: Checking the Printer Status. INT 17h checks the status of the printer and returns a single byte in AL. If bit 5 = 1, the printer is out of paper. The following TEST checks for this and clears the Zero flag if bit 5 is set:

```
mov   ah,2                 ; function: read printer status
int   17h                  ; call BIOS
test  al,00100000b         ; ZF = 0 if out of paper
```

Example: Testing Multiple Bits. The TEST instruction can check several bits at once. Suppose we have read a byte from an I/O device, and we want to know if *either* bit 0 or bit 3 is set. From the following examples, we see that ZF = 1 only when both bits are clear:

```
0 0 1 0 0 1 0 1   ← input value
0 0 0 0 1 0 0 1   ← test value
0 0 0 0 0 0 0 1   ← result: ZF = 0

0 0 1 0 0 1 0 0   ← input value
0 0 0 0 1 0 0 1   ← test value
0 0 0 0 0 0 0 0   ← result: ZF = 1
```

6.1.8   BT, BTC, BTR, BTS Instructions

The BT, BTC, BTR, and BTS instructions belong to a group of 80386 instructions called *bit tests*, shown in Table 2. The following operand types are permitted:

Operand	reg16	reg32	mem16	mem32	immed8
op1	X	X	X	X	
n	X	X			X

The following statements, executed in sequence, show the values of the Carry flag and AX after each operation:

```
mov   ax,8AB6h
bt    ax,15            ; CF = 1, AX unchanged
btc   ax,15            ; CF = 1, AX = 0AB6h
bts   ax,0             ; CF = 0, AX = 0AB7h
btr   ax,0             ; CF = 1, AX = 0AB6h
```

Table 2. BT, BTC, BTR, and BTS Instructions.

Instruction	Description
BT op1,n	Copy bit n from the first operand to the Carry flag.
BTC op1,n	Copy bit n from the first operand to the Carry flag and complement (toggle) the bit in the first operand.
BTR op1,n	Copy bit n from the first operand to the Carry flag and reset (clears) the bit in the first operand.
BTS op1,n	Copy bit n from the first operand to the Carry flag and set the bit in the first operand.

6.1.9   BSF and BSR Instructions

The BSF (*bit scan forward*) and BSR (*bit scan reverse*) instructions for the 80386 processor scan a source operand to find the first occurence of a set bit. If a set bit is found, the Zero flag is cleared and the destination operand is assigned the bit index of the first set bit encountered. BSF scans from bit 0 towards the most significant bit, whereas BSR scans from the most significant towards bit 0. The syntax is:

```
BSF destination, source
BSR destination, source
```

The following operand types are permitted, keeping in mind that the two operands must be the same size:

Operand	reg16	reg32	mem16	mem32
source	X	X	X	X
destination	X	X		

For example, BSF and BSR move the values 1 and 4, respectively to the CX register:

```
mov  ax,00010010b
bsf  cx,ax                ; CX = 1
bsr  cx,ax                ; CX = 4
```

Or, in the next example, **dsource** is a 32-bit memory operand:

```
.data
dsource dd 80008000h
.code
bsf  ebx,dsource          ; EBX = 0Fh
bsr  ebx,dsource          ; EBX = 1Fh
```

6.1.10 CMP Instruction

The CMP (*compare*) instruction performs an implied subtraction of a source operand from a destination operand, but neither operand is modified. The result is reflected in the state of the Flags register. The following combinations of operands are permitted, where the first operand is always the destination, and the second operand is the source:

```
CMP  reg,reg
CMP  reg,mem
CMP  reg,immed
CMP  mem,reg
CMP  mem,immed
```

Segment registers cannot be used. The following flags are affected: Overflow, Sign, Zero, Carry, Auxiliary Carry, and Parity.

Flag Conditions. When *unsigned* operands are compared, the Zero and Carry flags are set by the CMP instruction:

CMP Results	CF	ZF
Destination < source	1	0
Destination = source	0	1
Destination > source	0	0

When *signed* operands are compared, the Zero, Sign, and Overflow flags are set by the CMP instruction:

CMP Results	ZF	SF, OF
Destination < source	?	SF <> OF
Destination = source	1	?
Destination > source	0	SF = OF

CMP is valuable because it provides the basis for most conditional logic structures. When you follow a CMP with a conditional jump instruction, the result is the assembly language equivalent of an *IF* statement.

Let's look at three code fragments in Example 1 that show how the flags are affected by the CMP instruction. At Label1, when we compare 10 to 5, the Carry flag is set because subtracting 10 from 5 would require what we call a "borrow". At Label2, comparing AX to 1000 sets the Zero flag because that would be the result if we subtracted 1000 from AX. At Label3, subtracting 0 from 105 would not require a borrow and the result would not be zero, so the Zero flag and Carry flag are both clear.

Example 1. Using the CMP Instruction.

```
Label1:
    mov   al,5
    cmp   al,10             ; CF = 1
Label2:
    mov   ax,1000
    mov   cx,1000
    cmp   cx,ax             ; ZF = 1

Label3:
    mov   si,105
    cmp   si,0              ; ZF = 0 and CF = 0
```

6.1.11 CMPXCHG Instruction

The CMPXCHG (*compare and exchange*) instruction for the 80486 processor compares the destination operand to the accumulator (AL, AX, or EAX). If the values are equal, the source operand is copied to the destination; otherwise, the destination is copied to the accumulator. All status flags are affected. The instruction format is:

```
CMPXCHG destination, source
```

The following operand combinations are permitted:

```
CMPXCHG  mem,reg
CMPXCHG  reg,reg
```

The instruction can be expressed in pseudocode as:

```
if dest = accum
   dest <- source
else
   accum <- dest
end if
```

For example, the value 0 is moved to **listw** because the contents of memory at **listw** are equal to the 1234h in AX:

```
.data
listw dw 1234h,3333h
.code
mov  dx,0
mov  ax,1234h
cmpxchg listw,dx           ; listw = 0
```

On the other hand, 3333h is moved to AX because the contents of memory at listw+2 are not equal to the 1234h in AX:

```
mov  dx,0
mov  ax,1234h
cmpxchg listw+2,dx         ; AX = 3333h
```

6.1.12 Boolean Assembler Operators

The AND, OR, NOT, and XOR operators perform bitwise operations on integers at assembly time. The operands can be integer constants or symbols that have already been defined as constants. For example, the following expressions are valid:

```
X = 11001101b
Y = X AND 00001111b
Z = X OR 11110000b
Q = NOT Z
W = Y XOR 0FFFFh
```

6.2   CONDITIONAL JUMPS

There are no high-level logic structures in the Intel instruction set, but you can implement any logic structure using a combination of comparisons and jumps. *A logic structure* is simply a group of conditional statements working together. The WHILE structure, for instance, has an implied IF statement at the beginning that evaluates a condition, shown in Table 3.

Two steps are involved in executing an IF statement. First, an arithmetic or comparison instruction sets one or more flags based on its result. Second, a *conditional jump* instruction can cause the CPU to jump to a new address. The instructions belong to one of two groups:

* **Group 1:** Comparison and arithmetic instructions, in which the CPU sets individual flags according to the result.

* **Group 2:** Conditional jump instructions, in which the CPU takes action based on the flags.

The instructions from the two groups work in tandem: An instruction from Group 1 is executed, affecting the flags. Then a conditional jump instruction from Group 2 executes, based on the value of one of the flags. In the following example, the JZ instruction jumps to **next** if AL = 0:

```
cmp   al,0
jz    next                  ; jump if ZF = 1
      .
      .
      .
next:
```

6.2.1   J*cond* Instruction

A conditional jump instruction transfers control to a destination address when a flag condition is true. The syntax is:

J*cond destination*

Table 3. Do-While Loop Example.

High Level	Low Level

do while (a < b)
  <statement-1>
  <statement-2>
  .
  .
enddo
	L1: if (a >= b) then
	    jump to L2
	    endif
	    statement-1
	    statement-2
	    .
	
	    jump to L1
	L2: (continue here)

Cond refers to a flag condition, identifying the state of one or more flags. For example:

```
jc                      ; jump if Carry flag set
jnc                     ; jump if Carry flag clear
jz                      ; jump if Zero flag set
jnz                     ; jump if Zero flag clear
```

The destination address must be −128 to +127 bytes from the current location, which can sometimes be a problem if a logic structure is large.

We have already seen that flags are set by arithmetic, comparison, and boolean instructions. Each conditional jump instruction checks one or more flags, returning a result of *true* or *false*. If the result is true, the jump is taken; otherwise, the program does nothing and continues to the next instruction.

Using CMP. Suppose we want to jump to location **equal** when AX and BX are equal. In the next example, CMP sets the Zero flag if AX = BX. The JE instruction jumps if ZF = 1:

```
1:          cmp   ax,bx       ; compare AX to BX
2:           je   equal
3:    not_equal:              ; continue here if AX <> BX
4:             .
5:             .
6:          jmp   exit
7:    equal:                  ; jump here if AX = BX
8:            ...
9:    exit:                   ; always end up here
```

We can best understand this program by using different test values for AX and BX. Refer to the line numbers shown in the program during the following discussion:

Case 1: AX = 5, BX = 5. The CMP instruction (line 1) sets the Zero flag because AX and BX are equal. The JE instruction (line 2) jumps to **equal** on line 7. All statements from this point on are executed in sequence.

Case 2: AX = 5, BX = 6. CMP (line 1) clears the Zero flag because AX and BX are not equal. JE (line 2) has no effect, so the program falls through to line 3, executes all instructions through the JMP on line 6, and jumps to **exit**.

Types of Conditional Jump Instructions. There are three types of conditional jump instructions: The first type are based on general comparisons, and have nothing to do with signed or unsigned numbers. The second type are based strictly on comparing unsigned operands, and the third type are based on comparing signed operands.

Table 4 shows a list of jumps based on general comparisons. The CPU bases the jump on flags such as the Zero flag, Carry flag, Parity flag, or the CX and ECX registers.

Table 4. Jumps Based on General Comparisons.

Mnemonic	Description	Flags / Registers
JZ	Jump if zero	ZF = 1
JE	Jump if equal	ZF = 1
JNZ	Jump if not zero	ZF = 0
JNE	Jump if not equal	ZF = 0
JC	Jump if carry	CF = 1
JNC	Jump if no carrry	CF = 0
JCXZ	Jump if CX = 0	CX = 0
JECXZ	Jump if ECX = 0	ECX = 0
JP	Jump if parity even	PF = 1
JNP	Jump if parity odd	PF = 0

Table 5. Jumps Based on Unsigned Comparisons.

Mnemonic	Description	Flag(s)
JA	Jump if above (if op1 > op2)	CF = 0 and ZF = 0
JNBE	Jump if not below or equal (if op1 not <= op2)	CF = 0 and ZF = 0
JAE	Jump if above or equal (if op1 >= op2)	CF = 0
JNB	Jump if not below (if op1 not < op2)	CF = 0
JB	Jump if below (if op1 < op2)	CF = 1
JNAE	Jump if not above or equal (if op1 not >= op2)	CF = 1
JBE	Jump if below or equal (if op1 <= op2)	CF = 1 or ZF = 1
JNA	Jump if not above (if op1 not > op2)	CF = 1 or ZF = 1

Unsigned Comparisons. Jumps based on comparing unsigned integers are shown in Table 5. This type of jump would be useful when comparing numbers such as 7FFFh and 8000h, where the former number would be considered smaller than the latter.

Signed Comparisons. A table of jumps based on signed comparisons is presented in Table 6. This type of comparison would be useful when comparing 80h (−128) to 7Fh (+127). The former number would be considered smaller than the latter. Note in particular how the CPU uses the Overflow flag in this type of jump.

6.2.2 Code Generation for Conditional Jumps (386+)

You can use the SHORT operator to improve code generated by the assembler for forward jumps on 386 and later processors. Consider the following simple example, in which AX is compared to itself, followed by a JNE instruction to the label L2:

```
    cmp  ax,ax
    jne  L2
    mov  bx,2
L2:
```

Table 6. Jumps Based On Signed Comparisons.

Mnemonic	Description	Flag(s)
JG	Jump if greater (if op1 > op2)	SF = OF and ZF = 0
JNLE	Jump if not less than or equal (if op1 not <= op2)	SF = OF and ZF = 0
JGE	Jump if greater than or equal (if op1 >= op2)	SF = OF
JNL	Jump if not less (if op1 not < op2)	SF = OF
JL	Jump if less (if op1 < op2)	SF <> OF
JNGE	Jump if not greater than or equal (if op1 not >= op2)	SF <> OF
JLE	Jump if less than or equal (if op1 <= op2)	ZF = 1 or SF <> OF
JNG	Jump if not greater (if op1 not > op2)	ZF = 1 or SF <> OF
JS	Jump if signed (op1 is negative)	SF = 1
JNS	Jump if not signed (op1 is positive)	SF = 0
JO	Jump if overflow	OF = 1
JNO	Jump if no overflow	OF = 0

The following machine code is produced by the assembler. Notice that because the jump is in a forward direction, two empty bytes are inserted at offset 000B because the assembler does not realize on the first pass through the source code that only a two-byte instruction (at offset 0009) is needed:

```
0007  3BC0      cmp  ax,ax
0009  7505      jne  #test#12 (0010)
000B  90        nop
000C  90        nop
000D  BB0200    mov  bx,0002
0010  (L2:)
```

To prevent the assembler from generating empty bytes in the object code for this example, we can use the SHORT operator to be specific about the range of the jump:

```
     cmp  ax,ax
     jne  short L2
     mov  bx,2
L2:
```

The following, more compact code is now generated by the assembler:

```
0007 3BC0      cmp  ax,ax
0009 7503      jne  #test#12 (000E)
000B BB0200    mov  bx,0002
000E (L2:)
```

6.2.3   Conditional Jump Examples

Extended Keyboard Keys. In Chapter 5, we showed that when the user presses an extended keyboard key, such as F1 or PgUp, the system BIOS stores two bytes in the typeahead buffer. If you want to use INT 21h function 8 to read extended keyboard keys, the interrupt must be called twice. In Example 2, the GetKey procedure handles both ASCII and extended keys.

Example 2. Reading Extended Keys with INT 21h.

```
.data
key        db  ?
extended   dw  ?       ; 1 = true, 0  false

.code
GetKey proc
   mov   extended,0  ; assume key will not be extended
   mov   ah,8        ; input a keystroke, no echo
```

```
      int   21h           ; call DOS interrupt
      cmp   al,0           ; extended key? (if so, AL = 0)
      jne   L1            ; no: AL = ASCII code
      int   21h           ; yes: get the scan code
      mov   extended,1    ; and set the <extended> switch
L1:
      mov   key,al        ; store in variable
      ret
GetKey endp
```

Testing Status Bits. Instructions such as AND, OR, NOT, CMP, and TEST can be quite useful when followed by conditional jump instructions that can use the status flag values to alter the program flow. For example, let's assume that an 8-bit memory operand called **status** contains status information about a machine connected to an interface board. The following instructions jump to a label if bit 5 is set, indicating that the machine is offline:

```
      mov   al,status
      test  al,00100000b  ; bit 5 = 1 for equipment offline
      jnz   EquipOffline
```

Or, we might want to jump to another label if either bit 0, 1, or 4 is set:

```
      mov   al,status
      test  al,00010011b  ; test bits 0,1,4
      jnz   InputDataByte
```

Finally, we might jump to a different label if bits 2, 3, and 7 are all set. This requires both the AND and CMP instructions:

```
      mov   al,status
      and   al,10001100b  ; test bits 2,3,7
      cmp   al,10001100b  ; all bits set?
      je    ResetMachine
```

Larger of Two Numbers. The following code compares the unsigned values in AX and BX and moves the larger of the two to DX:

```
      mov   dx,ax         ; assume AX is larger
      cmp   ax,bx         ; if AX is >= BX then
      jae   L1            ;    jump to L1
      mov   dx,bx         ; else move BX to DX
L1:
```

Smallest of Three Numbers. The following instructions compare the unsigned values in AL, BL, and CL and move the smallest value to a variable:

```
1:        mov   small,al        ; assume AL is the smallest
2:        cmp   small,bl        ; if small <= BL then
3:        jbe   L1              ;   jump to L1
4:        mov   small,bl        ; else move BL to small
5:  L1:   cmp   small,cl        ; if small <= CL then
6:        jbe   L2              ;   jump to L2
7:        mov   small,cl        ; else move CL to small
8:  L2:
```

We can test this program using the following register values: AL = 10, BL = 18, and CL = 10. Line 1 moves 10 to **small**. Line 3 causes a jump to L1 because small < BL. The JBE on line 6 is taken because small = CL. When line 8 is reached, small = 10, the lowest of the three register values.

File Encryption. Earlier in this chapter, we saw that the XOR instruction has a unique quality—it reverses its effects on a number when applied twice in a row. This provides a simple but convenient method of data encryption. Combined with the JMP and JZ instructions, a complete file can be input, processed, and written to standard output. The program in Example 3 takes advantage of the fact that INT 21h function 6 sets the Zero flag when there is no more input, telling us that the end of the input file has been reached. When running the program, use DOS input-output redirection. For example:

```
encrypt < plaintxt > coded
```

The encrypted file can be un-encrypted later by running the same program again, using the encrypted file as input:

```
encrypt < coded > plaintxt
```

Encrypt.exe can also be used as a DOS *filter* that processes the output data from another program. The following command line sorts a file called **in.dta,** encrypts it, and writes the result to **out.dta:**

```
sort < in.dta | encrypt > out.dta
```

The following sorts the current directory, encrypts it, and writes the result to temp.txt:

```
dir | sort | encrypt > temp.txt
```

Example 3. Single Character Encryption Using XOR.

```
Title Encryption Program                 (encrypt.asm)
```

```
.model small
.stack 100h

XORVAL = 239                   ; any value between 0-255

.code
main proc
      mov   ax,@data
      mov   ds,ax

L1:
      mov   ah,6               ; direct console input
      mov   dl,0FFh            ; don't wait for character
      int   21h               ; AL = character
      jz    L2                 ; quit if ZF = 1 (EOF)
      xor   al,XORVAL
      mov   ah,2               ; write to output
      mov   dl,al
      int   21h
      jmp   L1                 ; repeat the loop

L2:
      mov   ax,4C00h           ; return to DOS
      int   21h
main endp

end  main
```

Checking for Alphabetic Input. Programs sometimes need to verify that an input character is either within the range 'a'...'z' or 'A'...'Z'. This is made easier if we clear bit 5, forcing any lowercase letter to uppercase. In the following example, AL contains the character being evaluated:

```
      push ax                 ; save AX
      and  al,11011111b       ; convert to uppercase
      cmp  al,'A'             ; check 'A'...'Z' range
      jb   B1
      cmp  al,'Z'
      ja   B1
      test ax,0               ; set ZF = 1
B1:   pop ax                  ; restore AX
```

Example 4 shows a test program that includes the **Isalpha** procedure.

Example 4. Testing the Isalpha Procedure.

```
title Test Alphabetic Input          (ISALPHA.ASM)

; This program reads and displays characters
; until a non-alphabetic character is entered.

.model small
.stack 100h
.code
main proc
    mov  ax,@data
    mov  ds,ax

L1: mov  ah,1             ; input a character
    int  21h             ; AL = character
    call Isalpha         ; test value in AL
    jnz  exit            ; exit if not alphabetic
    jmp  L1              ; continue loop

exit:
    mov    ax,4C00h      ; return to DOS
    int    21h
main endp

; Isalpha sets ZF = 1 if the character
; in AL is alphabetic.

Isalpha proc
    push ax              ; save AX
    and  al,11011111b    ; convert to uppercase
    cmp  al,'A'          ; check 'A'...'Z' range
    jb   B1
    cmp  al,'Z'
    ja   B1
    test ax,0            ; ZF = 1
B1: pop ax               ; restore AX
    ret
Isalpha endp
end main
```

Largest and Smallest Array Values. Suppose we want to determine the largest and smallest values in an array of 16-bit signed integers. The following pseudocode shows that we initialize two variables, **smallest** and **largest,** with the first number in the array. The statements in the loop compare each subsequent integer to the to the values **smallest** and **largest:**

```
count = 0
smallest = array[count]
largest = array[count]
CX = 6
do while CX > 0
  AX = array[count]
  if (AX < smallest) then smallest = AX
  if (AX > largest) then largest = AX
  count = count + 1
  CX = CX - 1
end do
```

The program in Example 5 uses the JGE (jump greater than or equal) instruction because the array values are signed. The JAE (jump above or equal) instruction would not work correctly. For example, if we used JAE to compare –1 to 0, JAE would interpret the numbers as unsigned and consider –1 (FFFFh) to be the larger number. JGE, on the other hand, would interpret the numbers as signed and consider 0 to be greater than –1.

Example 5. Largest and Smallest Signed Array Values.

```
title Comparing Signed Numbers       (LGSMAL.ASM)

; This program displays the largest and smallest
; values in an array of signed integers.

.model small
.stack 100h

.data
largest  dw  ?
smallest dw  ?

array dw  -1,2000,-421,32767,500,0,-26,-4000
arrayCount = 8

largemsg db "Largest value:  ",0
smallmsg db "Smallest value: ",0
```

```
        .code
        extrn Clrscr:proc, Crlf:proc, Writeint_signed:proc, \
              Writestring:proc

        main proc
              mov   ax,@data            ; initialize DS
              mov   ds,ax
              mov   di,offset array
              mov   ax,[di]             ; get first element
              mov   largest,ax          ; initialize largest
              mov   smallest,ax         ; initialize smallest
              mov   cx,arrayCount       ; loop counter

        A1: mov   ax,[di]               ; get array value
            cmp   ax,smallest           ; [DI] >= smallest?
            jge   A2                    ; yes: skip
            mov   smallest,ax           ; no: move [DI] to smallest

        A2: cmp   ax,largest            ; [DI] <= largest?
            jle   A3                    ; yes: skip
            mov   largest,ax            ; no: move [DI] to largest

        A3: add   di,2                  ; point to next number
            loop A1                     ; repeat the loop until CX=0

            call ShowResults
            mov   ax,4C00h              ; return to DOS
            int   21h
        main endp


        ; Display the largest and smallest values.


        ShowResults proc
              mov   dx,offset largemsg
              call  Writestring
              mov   ax,largest
              call  Writeint_signed
              call  CrLf
              mov   dx,offset smallmsg
              call  Writestring
              mov   ax,smallest
              call  Writeint_signed
```

```
        call  CrLf
        ret
ShowResults endp
end main
```

6.2.4   The SET*condition* Instruction

The SET*condition* instruction for the 80386 processor sets a byte operand to 1 if a given condition is true, or it sets the byte to 0 if the condition is false. The syntax is:

```
SETcondition reg8
SETcondition mem8
```

Condition is a mnemonic indicating which CPU flag is to be tested. The *reg8* parameter is any 8-bit register, and the *mem8* parameter is any 8-bit memory operand. The possible values for *condition* include the suffixes of all conditional jump instructions. For example:

```
E    equal                     C    carry
A    above                     NC   no carry
B    below                     L    less
AE   above or equal            GE   greater than or equal
O    overflow                  NO   no overflow
```

Here are examples of its usage, showing alternate ways to end up with the same result:

```
setz   al                 ; set AL to 1 if ZF = 1
sete   al                 ; set AL to 1 if ZF = 1
setnc  myFlag             ; set myFlag to 1 if CF = 0
setae  myFlag             ; set myFlag to 1 if CF = 0
setge  byte ptr [si]      ; set [si] to 1 if SF = OF
setnbe byte ptr [si]      ; set [si] to 1 if SF = OF
```

For example, AL = 1 after SETB because the CMP instruction has set the Carry flag:

```
mov  bx,20h
cmp  bx,30h
setb al                   ; AL = 1
```

On the other hand, AL = 0 after SETE because the CMP instruction did not set the Zero flag:

```
mov  bx,20h
cmp  bx,30h
sete al                   ; AL = 0
```

6.3   CONDITIONAL LOOPS

6.3.1   LOOPZ and LOOPE Instructions

The LOOPZ and LOOPE (*loop if Zero, loop if Equal*) instructions let a loop continue while ZF = 1 and CX > 0. The destination of the jump must be between −128 and +127 bytes from the current location. The syntax is:

```
LOOPZ destination
LOOPE destination
```

First, CX is decremented. Then, if CX > 0 and ZF = 1, the CPU jumps to *destination*; otherwise, nothing happens and control passes to the next instruction.

Example: Scan an Array. The LOOPZ instruction makes it easy to traverse an array of integers until a nonzero value is found. As the CMP instruction compares each integer to 0, it either sets or clears the Zero flag accordingly. When a nonzero value is eventually found, LOOPZ does not jump to the label called **next:**

```
.data
intarray dw 0,0,0,0,1,20,35,-12,66,4,0
ArraySize = ($-intarray) / 2

.code
    mov    bx,offset intarray   ; point to the array
    sub    bx,2                 ; back up one position
    mov    cx,ArraySize         ; repeat ArraySize times

next:
    add    bx,2                 ; point to next entry
    cmp    word ptr [bx],0      ; compare value to zero
    loopz next                  ; loop while ZF = 1, CX > 0
```

Modifying the Flags Before the Loop Instruction. Be careful not to change the flags between a CMP instruction and a subsequent conditional loop instruction. In the following example, the ADD instruction causes the loop to terminate because it clears the Zero flag:

```
next:
    cmp    [bx],ax              ; compare array value to zero
    add    bx,2                 ; point to next entry, ZF = 0
    loopz  next                 ; error: Zero flag has changed
```

6.3.2   LOOPNZ and LOOPNE Instructions

The LOOPNZ and LOOPNE (*loop while not zero, loop while not equal*) instructions are the counterpart to LOOPZ and LOOPE. The loop continues while CX > 0 and ZF = 0. The following example scans each number in an 8-bit array until a positive number is found (when the sign bit equals zero):

```
.data
bytearray db  -3,-6,-1,-10,10,30,40,4
ArraySize  = ($-array)


.code
   mov   si,offset bytearray-1
   mov   cx,ArraySize
next:
   inc   si
   test  byte ptr [si],10000000b
   loopnz next
```

Notice that the INC instruction is before the TEST instruction to avoid altering the Zero flag between the TEST and LOOPNZ instructions.

6.4   HIGH-LEVEL LOGIC STRUCTURES

The Intel instruction set does not contain any structured IF, ELSE, or WHILE instructions. This is not a severe limitation, as several instructions can be combined to create any logical structure. In fact, you can optimize logic structures to make them execute much more efficiently than they would in a high-level language. The logic structures shown in this chapter are universal to all structured languages.

6.4.1   Simple IF Statement

An IF statement comparing two values is often followed by a list of statements to be performed when the condition is true. In the following example, **op1** and **op2** might be immediate operands, registers, or memory operands:

```
if (op1 = op2) then
  <statement1>
  <statement2>
end If
```

A high-level language compiler would translate the preceding IF statement into a *compare* followed by one or more *conditional jump* instructions. The following is a sample of what compiled code might look like:

```
        cmp  op1, op2
        je   True
        jmp  EndIf
   True:
        <statement1>
        <statement2>
   EndIf:
```

We can eliminate one of the jumps by reversing the comparison for *equal* to *not equal:*

```
        cmp  op1, op2
        jne  False
        <statement1>
        <statement2>
   False:
```

6.4.2 Compound IF Statement

Using the OR Operator. Assembly language can easily evaluate expressions that use the logical OR operator. Consider the following pseudocode, where any one of four conditions results in the execution of **statement1:**

```
if (AL > op1)
   or  (AL >= op2)
   or  (AL = op3)
   or  (AL < op4) then
   <statement1>
end if
```

This can be easily translated into assembly language if we remember that a false condition always falls through to the next statement. The following *linear nested-IF* structure chains through a series of conditions:

```
        cmp  al,op1            ; if AL > op1 then
        jg   L1               ;    jump to L1
        cmp  al,op2            ; else if AL >= op2 then
        jge  L1               ;    jump to L1
        cmp  al,op3            ; else if AL = op3 then
        je   L1               ;    jump to L1
        cmp  al,op4            ; else if AL < op4 then
        jl   L1               ;    jump to L1
        jmp  L2               ; else jump to L2.
   L1: <statement1>           ; L1: execute <statement1>
   L2:                        ; end if
```

Using the AND Operator. The logical AND operator in high-level languages ties together multiple conditions. In the following pseudocode, all four conditions must be true before **statement1** can be executed:

```
if (AL > op1)
  and (AL >= op2)
  and (AL = op3)
  and (AL < op4) then
  <statement1>
end if
```

The easiest way to translate this into assembly language is to reverse the conditions and jump to an exit label when any condition is true. The condition (**AL > op1**), for example, becomes **not (AL > op1)**. If all of the conditional tests fail, control passes to **statement1**:

```
        cmp    al,op1          ; if not (AL > op1) then
        jng    L1              ;    jump to L1
        cmp    al,op2          ; else if not (AL >= op2) then
        jnge   L1              ;    jump to L1
        cmp    al,op3          ; else if not (AL = op3) then
        jne    L1              ;    jump to L1
        cmp    al,op4          ; else if not (AL < op4) then
        jnl    L1              ;    jump to L1
                               ; else
        <statement1>           ;    <statement1>
                               ; end if
L1:  ; reached if any condition is true
```

6.4.3   WHILE Structure

The WHILE structure tests a condition first before performing a block of statements. As long as the while condition remains true, the statements are repeated:

```
do while (op1 < op2)
  <statement1>
  <statement2>
end do
```

We can reverse the condition and jump to the label **end_do** when the condition becomes true:

```
do_while:
        cmp    op1,op2         ; if not (op1 >= op2) then
        jnl    end_do          ;    jump to enddo
```

```
                                          ; else
        <statement1>                      ;    <statement1>
        <statement2>                      ;    <statement2>
        jmp do_while                      ;    jump to do_while
   end_do:
```

IF Statement Nested Inside a WHILE. High-level structured languages are particularly good at representing nested control structures. In the following example, an IF statement is nested inside a WHILE loop:

```
do while (op1 < op2)
  <statement1>
  if (op2 = op3) then
    <statement2>
    <statement3>
  else
    <statement4>
  end if
end do
```

The assembly language version of the preceding can easily be written, although the code is harder to follow because of the number of labels involved. The following rendition of the same WHILE loop follows the original pseudocode as closely as possible, shown in Example 6.

Example 6. Do-While Loop Example.

Assembly Code	Pseudocode
```while:```	
```cmp op1,op2```	```do while (op1 < op2)```
```jnl L3```	
```<statement1>```	```<statement1>```
```cmp op2,op3```	```if op2 = op3 then```
```jne L1```	
```<statement2>```	```<statement2>```
```<statement3>```	```<statement3>```
```jmp L2```	```else```
```L1: <statement4>```	```<statement4>```
```L2: jmp while```	```endif```
```L3:```	```enddo```

    Be sure to apply the principle of *one entry and one exit* when designing procedures. In this example, the label **while** is the entry point and **L3** is the exit.

6.4.4   REPEAT-UNTIL Structure

A *REPEAT-UNTIL* structure executes one or more statements within a block at least once and performs a test at the bottom of the loop. In the following example, two conditions are tested before the loop repeats:

```
repeat
  <statement1>
  <statement2>
  <statement3>
until (op1 = op2) or (op1 > op3)
```

It might be interesting to look at the assembly code generated for this loop by a high-level language compiler, shown in Example 7. In particular, the multiple condition generates a great deal of code. The result of the first test is pushed on the stack; after the second test, it is popped from the stack and ORed with the result of the second test:

Example 7. Repeat-Until Loop Generated by a Compiler.

```
repeat:
        <statement1>
        <statement2>
        <statement3>
test1: mov   ax,0          ; assume result is false
       cmp   op1,op2
       jne   test2         ; if op1 = op2 then
       mov   ax,0FFh       ;   set result to true
                           ; end if
test2: push  ax            ; save result of first test
       mov   ax,0          ; assume result is false
       cmp   op1,op3
       jng   test3         ; if op1 > op3 then
       mov   ax,0FFh       ;   set result to true
                           ; end if
test3: pop   dx            ; retrieve first result
       or    dx,ax         ; OR with the second result
       jz    endup         ; exit if neither is true
       jmp   repeat        ; otherwise, jump to repeat
endup:
```

The code generated by this compiler is not overly efficient, as it generates 13 instructions just for the *repeat* loop. It insists on evaluating both conditions even if the first returns *true* (some compilers can optimize their code generation and prevent this from happening).

If we code the same loop in assembly language, shown in Example 8, we can easily improve its performance. The best strategy is to fall through from one test to another if the first one fails. If the first test succeeds, we never reach the second test. Note that we trimmed the original 13 instructions down to only 4. Line 6 performs the first comparison: If ZF = 0, line 7 exits the loop; otherwise, we fall through to line 9 and perform the second test. If the second test fails, control passes to line 11 and the loop ends.

This is precisely the type of *hand optimization* that must be incorporated into high-performance software. You can write an entire program in a high-level language, disassemble the code, and look for sluggish sections that need to be rewritten in assembly language. Many compilers, in fact, will automatically generate an assembly language source listing of your compiled program, making the whole job easier.

Example 8. Repeat Loop Hand-Optimized in Assembly Language.

```
 1:      repeat:
 2:          <statement1>
 3:          <statement2>
 4:          <statement3>
 5:      test1:
 6:          cmp  op1,op2        ; if op1 = op2 then
 7:          je   endif          ;   exit the loop
 8:      test2:                  ; else
 9:          cmp  op1,op3        ;   if op1 <= op3 then
10:          jng  repeat         ;     repeat the loop
11:      endif:                  ;   end if
12 :                             ; end if
```

6.4.5　CASE Structure

The CASE structure allows a multiway branch by comparing a single value to a list of values. Using Pascal as an example, we can select a course of action based on the value of the variable **input**:

```
case input of
  'A'  : Process_A;
  'B'  : Process_B;
  'C'  : Process_C;
  'D'  : Process_D
end;
```

In assembly language, we can process each case with a separate comparison, followed by a jump to a label:

```
mov  al,input
```

```
cmp    al,'A'
je     Process_A
cmp    al,'B'
je     Process_B
cmp    al,'C'
je     Process_C
cmp    al,'D'
je     Process_D
```

If you would rather call a procedure when each individual case is selected, the CALL statement can be inserted, followed by a jump to the final label (**L4**) at the end of the case structure. This is shown in Example 9.

Example 9. Case Structure Using Procedure Calls.

```
        mov    al,input        ; case al of
        cmp    al,'A'          ;  'A':
        jne    L1
        call   Process_A       ;       call Process_A
        jmp    L4              ;       jump to L4
L1:     cmp    al,'B'          ;  'B':
        jne    L2
        call   Process_B       ;       call Process_B
        jmp    L4              ;       jump to L4
L2:     cmp    al,'C'          ;  'C':
        jne    L3
        call   Process_C       ;       call Process_C
        jmp    L4              ;       jump to L4
L3:     cmp    al,'D'          ;  'D':
        jne    L4
        call   Process_D       ;       call Process_D
L4:                            ; end
```

6.4.6 Table of Procedure Offsets

A more efficient way to process a CASE structure is to create an *offset table* containing the offsets of labels or procedures. The assembler can calculate a label's offset and place it in a variable. An offset table is most effective when a large number of comparisons must be made. The statements in Example 10 define a table containing the lookup values and addresses of procedures we want to call.

Example 10. Table Containing Offsets of Procedures.

```
CaseTable  db    'A'            ; lookup value
           dw    process_A      ; address of procedure
           db    'B'
           dw    process_B
           db    'C'
           dw    Process_C
           db    'D'
           dw    Process_D
```

Figure 1. Table of Procedure Offsets.

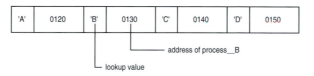

Let's assume that Process_A, Process_B, Process_C, and Process_D are located at addresses 0120h, 0130h, 0140h, and 0150h, respectively. The table would be arranged in memory as shown in Figure 1.

AL is compared to each entry in this table, using the loop shown in Example 11. The first match found in the table causes a call to the procedure offset stored immediately after the lookup value. This method involves some initial overhead, but it helps make the compiled program more efficient. A table can handle a large number of comparisons, and it can be more easily modified than a long series of compare, jump, and CALL instructions. Most important, an offset table can be modified at runtime, whereas a CASE statement is fixed at assembly time.

Example 11. Case Table Lookup Using a Loop.

```
NumberOfEntries = 4
input dw ?

.code
     mov   al,input             ; value to be found
     mov   bx,offset CaseTable  ; point BX to the table
     mov   cx,NumberOfEntries   ; loop counter

L1:  cmp   al,[bx]              ; match found?
     jne   L2                   ; no: continue
```

```
        call   word ptr [bx+1]    ; yes: call the procedure
        jmp    L3                 ; exit the search
L2: add    bx,3                   ; point to the nextentry
        loop   L1                 ; repeat until CX = 0
L3:
```

6.4.7   Finite State Machines

Programs that read input streams often must validate their input by performing a certain amount of error checking. For example, if a program's input stream contains a signed integer, the program should be able verify that the integer is in a valid format. A simple validation would permit only digits, +, and – to be entered, but that would not prevent the user from entering nonsense sequences such as "2+3–4++3." A more intelligent validation would involve *parsing,* or scanning the input and making sure the sign is only used in the leading position of the number.

One of the best design tools to use when parsing an input stream is a *finite state machine* (FSM). It is usually represented as a graph, with circles called *nodes* and lines with arrows between the circles called *arcs.* A simple example is shown in Figure 2.

Figure 2. Finite-State Machine.

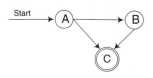

This type of diagram can also be called a more general name, a *directed graph.* Each node represents a program state, and each arc represents a transition from one state to another. One node is designated as the *start* state, shown in our diagram with an incoming arrow. The remaining states are assigned letters of the alphabet. One or more states are designated as *terminal* states, notated by a double circle.

Validating an Input String. When using an FSM to check the validity of an input string, we read the input character by character. Each input character is represented by an arc (transition) in the diagram. If no transition is available for a particular input character, the FSM fails, and the program issues an error messsage and stops checking the input. For example, let's check the validity of an input string according to the following two rules:

•   The string must begin with the letter 'x' and end with the letter 'z.'

•   Between the first and last characters, there can be zero or more letters within the range {'a'..'y'}.

The FSM in Figure 3 describes this syntax. Each transition is identified with a particular type of input. For example, the transition from state A to state B can only be accomplished if

Figure 3. FSM for String in the Form x(a..y)*z.

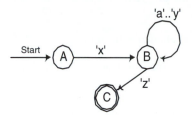

the letter "x" is read from the input stream. A transition from state B to itself is accomplished by the input of any letter of the alphabet except 'z.' A transition from state B to state C occurs when the letter "z" is read from the input stream.

If the end of the input stream is reached and the program remains in state A or B, this is considered an error condition because only state C is marked as a terminal state. Here are some input strings that would be recognized by this FSM:

```
xaabcdefgz
xz
xyyqqrrstuvz
```

The following are strings that would not be recognized by the FSM:

x	*missing trailing z*
z	*missing leading x*
xabc	*missing trailing z*
az	*missing leading x*

Signed Integer FSM Example. A finite state machine for parsing a signed integer is shown in Figure 4. Input consists of an optional leading sign, followed by a sequence of digits. There is no stated maximum number of digits implied by the diagram.

Figure 4. Signed Decimal Integer FSM.

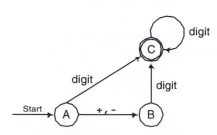

Finite state machines are very easily translated into assembly language code. Each state in the diagram (A, B, C, ...) is represented in the program by a label. The following actions are performed at each label:

- A call to an input procedure reads the next character from input.

- If the state is a terminal state, check to see if the user has pressed the Enter key to end the input.

- One or more compare instructions check for each possible transition leading away from the state. Each comparison is followed by a conditional jump instruction.

The program listing in Example 12 shows the full implementation of this Finite State Machine. But let's look at a few details. For example, at State A, the following code reads the next input character and checks for a possible transition to State B:

```
StateA:
    call Getnext            ; read next char into AL
    cmp al,'+'              ; leading + sign?
    je StateB               ; go to State B
    cmp al,'-'              ; leading - sign?
    je StateB               ; go to State C
    call Isdigit            ; ZF = 1 if AL contains a digit
    jz StateC
    call DisplayError       ; invalid input found
    jmp Exit
```

Also in state A, we call **Isdigit** to look for a possible transition to state C. Failing that, the program displays an error message and exits.

The code at state C calls Getnext and checks for a possible end of input. State C was marked as a terminal state in Figure 4. If a digit is read in this state, the program simply loops back to the StateC label and continues to read more input:

```
StateC:
    call Getnext            ; read next char into AL
    jz   Exit               ; quit if Enter pressed
    call Isdigit            ; ZF = 1 if AL contains a digit
    jz StateC
```

Isdigit. The **Isdigit** procedure compares AL to both '0' and '9,' and if AL is within their values, we set the Zero flag. Otherwise, ZF = 0 by default:

```
Isdigit proc
    cmp  al,'0'
    jb   A1
    cmp  al,'9'
```

```
    ja   A1
    test ax,0                 ; set ZF = 1
A1: ret
Isdigit endp
```

Example 12. FSM for Signed Decimal Input.

```
Title Finite State Machine              (fsm.asm)

; Chapter 6 example. Implementation of finite
; state machine that accepts an integer with an
; optional leading sign.

.model small
.stack 100h

DOS_CHAR_INPUT = 1
ENTER_KEY = 0Dh

.data
InvalidInputMessage db "Invalid input",0dh,0ah,0

.code
extrn Writestring:proc, Crlf:proc, Clrscr:proc
main proc
    mov  ax,@data
    mov  ds,ax
    call Clrscr

StateA:
    call Getnext              ; read next char into AL
    cmp al,'+'                ; leading + sign?
    je StateB                 ; go to State B
    cmp al,'-'                ; leading - sign?
    je StateB                 ; go to State C
    call Isdigit              ; ZF = 1 if AL contains a digit
    jz StateC
    call DisplayError         ; invalid input found
    jmp Exit

StateB:
    call Getnext              ; read next char into AL
```

```
        call Isdigit          ; ZF = 1 if AL contains a digit
        jz StateC
        call DisplayError      ; invalid input found
        jmp Exit

StateC:
        call Getnext           ; read next char into AL
        jz  Exit               ; quit if Enter pressed
        call Isdigit           ; ZF = 1 if AL contains a digit
        jz StateC
        call DisplayError      ; invalid input found
        jmp Exit

Exit:
        call Crlf
        mov  ax,4c00h
        int  21h
main endp

; Read char from standard input into AL,
; set ZF = 1 if Enter key was read.

Getnext proc
        mov  ah,DOS_CHAR_INPUT  ; read standard input
        int  21h                ; AL = character
        cmp  al,ENTER_KEY
        ret
Getnext endp

; Set ZF = 1 if the character in AL is a digit.

Isdigit proc
        cmp  al,'0'
        jb   A1
        cmp  al,'9'
        ja   A1
        test ax,0               ; set ZF = 1
A1: ret
Isdigit endp

; Display error message.
```

```
DisplayError proc
    push dx
    mov  dx,offset InvalidInputMessage
    call WriteString
    call Crlf
    pop  dx
    ret
DisplayError endp
end main
```

6.5 REVIEW QUESTIONS

1. Explain the difference between the JMP and JZ instructions.

2. Which CPU flags are used in unsigned comparisons?

3. Which CPU flags are used in signed comparisons?

4. Which conditional jump is based on the contents of a general-purpose register?

5. What is the difference between the JA and JNBE instructions?

6. What is the difference between the JB and JL instructions?

7. Can a conditional jump instruction jump to a label anywhere in the same segment?

8. For a JB instruction to be executed, which flag must be set?

9. Assume that a CMP instruction has just compared two operands. For each of the conditional jump instructions shown in Table 7, the contents of four flags are shown. Indicate in the last column whether or not each jump would be taken. (You may want to refer back to Table 4 and Table 6 earlier in this chapter. The first row has been completed as a sample.

10. After the following instructions are executed, what will be the values of AL and BL?

```
.data
val1   db   6Bh
val2   db   3Fh

.code
mov    al,val1
mov    bl,val2
and    ax,0B6h
cmp    al,bl
ja     label1
mov    al,bl
```

Table 7. Conditional Jumps, Flag Settings (Question 9).

	Instruction	Overflow	Sign	Zero	Carry	Jump Taken?
a.	JNZ	0	0	1	0	No
b.	JA	1	0	1	0	
c.	JNB	1	0	1	0	
d.	JBE	0	0	1	0	
e.	JGE	1	1	0	0	
f.	JNLE	0	1	0	1	
g.	JNS	0	0	1	0	
h.	JNG	1	1	0	1	
i.	JE	1	0	1	0	
j.	JNAE	1	0	1	0	

```
    jmp    exit
label1:
    mov    bl,al
exit:
```

11. After the following instructions are executed, what will be the values of AL and BL?

```
    .data
val1   db    6Bh
val2   db    3Fh

    .code
        mov    al,val2
        mov    bl,val1
        or     bl,0Fh
        sub    al,bl
        jb     label1
        mov    al,1
        jmp    exit
label1:
        mov    bl,1
exit:
```

12. After the following instructions are executed, what will be the values of AL and BL?

```
.data
val1   db    35h
val2   db    3Fh

.code
        mov    al,val2
        mov    bl,val1
        xor    bl,0FFh
        test   al,3
        jz     label1
        mov    al,1
        jmp    exit
label1:
        mov    bl,1
exit:
```

13. After the following instructions are executed, what will be the values of CX, DX, and SI?

```
.data
val1   dw    026Ah
val2   dw    3FD9h

.code
        mov    si,0
        mov    cx,val1
        mov    dx,val2
        and    cx,0FFh
        not    dx
        xchg   dx,val1
again:
        inc    si
        dec    dx
        loop   again
```

14. After the following instructions are executed, what will be the values of CX, DX, SI, and **val2**? Assume that **val1** is located at address 0006.)

```
.data
val1   dw    026Ah
val2   dw    3FD9h

.code
```

```
            mov    si,offset val1
            mov    cx,[si]
            add    si,2
            mov    dx,[si]
            xchg   dx,val1
            and    dx,0FF00h
        again:
            dec    word ptr [si]
            dec    dx
            cmp    dx,01FFh
            loopz  again
```

6.6   PROGRAMMING EXERCISES

1. *Reading Keyboard Arrow Keys*

    Write a procedure called **GetArrow** that inputs a keyboard scan code with INT 16h, checks to
    see if the key is a left arrow, right arrow, up arrow, or down arrow, and returns an integer that
    identifies the arrow. For example, { 1 = up, 2 = right, 3 = down, 4 = left, 0 = none }. Write a
    test program that calls your function and displays a message on the screen indicating which
    arrow key was pressed.

2. *Vertical Bar Menu*

    Write a program that displays a vertical menu and moves a reverse video bar up and down
    across the menu choices when the user presses an arrow key on the keyboard. You can use the
    GetArrow procedure from the previous exercise to read the keyboard.

3. *Horizontal Bar Menu*

    Create a procedure that displays a horizontal bar menu, in which the user can use the cursor
    arrow keys to move between choices. (This type of menu was first made popular by the *Lotus
    1-2-3*® spreadsheet program in the 1980s.) As the user presses arrow keys, the current menu
    choice is highlighted by displaying it in a different color from the other choices. When the user
    presses the Enter key, the selected menu item is chosen. Pass an array of strings to the proce-
    dure containing the menu choices, along with the row and column position specifying its
    location on the screen. The return value from the procedure should be an integer identifying
    which choice was selected, or whether the user pressed the Esc key to cancel the menu.

4. *Alphabetic Input*

    Write a short program to input only letters (A–Z, a–z) from the keyboard. Any other characters
    should be rejected without being echoed on the screen. Continue the input until the Enter key
    is pressed.

5. *Signed Integer Input*

Write a program that lets the user input a signed decimal integer from the console. If any invalid characters are entered, display an error message and halt the program. Use the finite-state machine diagram presented earlier in this chapter in Figure 4 to design your program.

6. *Real Number Input*

Write a program to input an unsigned real number from the keyboard. Any characters other than a digit and a single decimal point should be rejected without being echoed on the screen. Quit when the Enter key is pressed. Use the finite-state machine diagram in Figure 5 to design your program.

Figure 5. FSM for Unsigned Real.

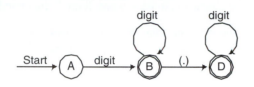

7. *Real Number Input with Leading Sign*

Expand the program from the previous exercise to include an optional leading sign. Store each character in a buffer and redisplay the buffer at the end of the program. The FSM in Figure 6 describes the syntax.

Figure 6. FSM for Signed Real.

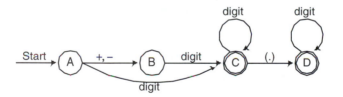

8. *Reverse an Array*

Write a program that reverses an array of 16-bit integers. The array should be reversed in place, without being copied to another array. Display the array before and after it has been reversed.

9. *Deviation of Array Values*

Given an array of 16-bit integers, write a program that calculates and displays the amount of variance between the arithmetic mean (the average) and each of the values in the array. All values should be expressed as integers.

10. *Display a String in Reverse*

Write a program that inputs a string typed by the user and redisplays the string in reverse order. Sample input/output:

Input:

```
This string was typed at the keyboard.
```
Output:

```
.draobyek eht ta depyt saw gnirts sihT
```

11. *Reverse the Words in a String*

Write a program that inputs any sentence containing several words from the console. Reverse the words in the sentence, but not the characters in each word. Sample input and output:

```
Input:     The quick brown fox jumped over the lazy dog's back.
Output:    back. dog's lazy the over jumped fox brown quick The
```

12. *Count the Words in a File*

Write a program that reads a text file from standard input and counts the numbers of words and characters entered. Use the < symbol on the DOS command line to indicate that standard input is to be read from a text file. (INT 21h Function 6 is the preferred way to read from a file, because it lets you know when the end of the input file has been reached.)

13. *Console Input Field*

Write a procedure that displays an input field on the screen, waits for user input, and returns the characters typed by the user. Let the user edit and correct input using the backspace key. The procedure's input parameters should include the following:

• field length

• row, column position on the screen

• video attribute (foreground and background)

Input ends when the user presses either the Tab key or the Enter key. Write a program that calls this procedure several times.

14. *Console Input Field with Keyboard Filter*

Using the Console Input procedure from the previous exercise, add the following feature: Pass a pointer to a null-terminated string containing the set of characters that the user will be permitted to type. For example, if only digits, backspace, and the Enter key are permitted, the string would contain the following:

```
BACKSPACE = 9
ENTERKEY = 0Dh,
validSet db "0123456789",BACKSPACE,ENTERKEY,0
```

When the procedure executes, it ignores any characters typed by the user that do not belong to *validSet*.

15. *Customer Account Program*

Write a program with separate procedures that clears the screen and displays an input form as shown in Example 13.

Position the cursor on the first input field (ACCT NUM), and let the user type an entry. When the Tab key is pressed, move the cursor to the next field (LAST NAME). As the user enters data, store each character in an input buffer for the field. When the Enter key is pressed, end the input screen. Be sure to limit the number of characters the user can enter into each field, and allocate enough buffer space for each field to hold the characters. It is useful to predefine constants for the field sizes:

```
NAME_SIZE = 30
PREVBAL_SIZE = 8
```

Use a table to describe each of the fields. Each entry should contain the row/column position of each field, the field's buffer size, a pointer to a field label, and a pointer to the field's input buffer. For example, here are possible table entries for the Last Name and Previous Balance fields:

```
fld_Name label byte
    db 5,3                      ; row, column
    db NAME_SIZE                ; field size
    dw offset buf_Name          ; input buffer
    dw offset lbl_Name          ; label next to field
fld_PrevBal label byte
    db 7, 3                     ; row, column
    db PREVBAL_SIZE             ; field size
    dw offset buf_PrevBal       ; input buffer
    dw offset lbl_PrevBal       ; label next to field
```

Example 13. Account Input Screen.

```
┌─────────────────────────────────────────────┐
│              ACCOUNT INPUT SCREEN             │
│                                               │
│           ACCT NUM: ........                  │
│          LAST NAME: ......................    │
│       PREV BALANCE: ........                  │
│           PAYMENTS: ........                  │
│            CREDITS: ........                  │
│                                               │
└─────────────────────────────────────────────┘
```

Each table entry uses exactly the same amount of storage, which makes it easy for a program to calculate the offset of any particular field's entry. Each table entry contains pointers to the corresponding field's input buffer and screen label, which are defined as separate variables. The following are buffers and labels for the Name and Previous Balance fields:

```
buf_Name db NAME_SIZE dup(0),0
lbl_Name db "LAST NAME:",0          ; label next to field

buf_PrevBal db PREVBAL_SIZE dup(0),0
lbl_PrevBal db "PREV BALANCE:",0
```

16. *Customer Account Program, Version 2*

Add the following features to the previous version of the Customer Account program: For the PREVIOUS BALANCE, PAYMENTS, and CREDITS fields, let the user type only numbers. The digits 0-9 can be typed in any position, but a plus or minus sign can be typed only in the first position. Only one decimal point can be typed. If any invalid characters are typed, reject them and sound a beep by writing ASCII character 7 to standard output. When the input screen ends, clear the screen and redisplay the contents of all fields to verify that all inputs worked correctly.

Using the suggested table from the previous Exercise, you might want to add field filtering information to each table entry:

```
MASK_ANY = 0                    ; any characters
MASK_REAL = 1                   ; sign, digits, decimal pt, exponent
MASK_INTEGER = 2                ; sign, digits
MASK_ALPHA = 3                  ; A-Z, spaces

fld_Name label byte
    db 5,3                      ; row, column
    db NAME_SIZE                ; field size
    db MASK_ANY                 ; any characters accepted
    dw offset buf_Name          ; input buffer
    dw offset lbl_Name          ; label next to field
fld_PrevBal label byte
    db 7, 3                     ; row, column
    db PREVBAL_SIZE             ; field size
    db MASK_REAL                ; real number accepted
    dw offset buf_PrevBal       ; input buffer
    dw offset lbl_PrevBal       ; label next to field
```

17. *Customer Account Program, Version 3*

Add the following features to the previous version of the Customer Account program: Display the field names in reverse video, using INT 10h. Allow the user to use the backspace key to edit field entries. (Your pointer to the input buffer must back up one position so that the buffer will accurately reflect the contents of the field on the screen.)

18. *Sorting an Array*

Write a program that fills an array with a random sequence of signed integers. Display the array, sort it, and redisplay the array.

19. *Binary Search*

Using the sorted array from the previous exercise, write a procedure that performs a binary search for a single value in an array of integers. The array must first be sorted in either ascending or descending order. Your procedure should use a loop that repeats until the search value is found, or until it discovers that the value is not in the list being searched. Write a program that demonstrates the procedure.

The Algorithm. The binary search algorithm works by repeatedly dividing the list being searched in half. (Most introductory computer science textbooks explain how to do a binary search.)

Using Indexes to Refer to List Values. The list of values being searched does not have to be in strict sequential order, but the values must be in either ascending or descending order. For example, the following list of numbers is arranged in an order conducive to a binary search:

```
Value:    1 5 6 14 15 22 23 25 27 29 45 59 64 68 88 92 99 101 113 128 144 196
Index:    0 1 2 3  4  5  6  7  8  9  10 11 12 13 14 15 16  17  18  19  20  21
```

When selecting a ranges of values to search, express the range in terms of indexes. You should begin a search by setting three variables: first, last, and mid, which point to the first item, the last item, and the midpoint of the list, respectively. The C++ code in Example 14 demonstrates the algorithm.

Example 14. Binary Search Procedure (C++).

```cpp
int BinSearch( int values[], const int searchVal, int count )
{
  int first = 0;
  int last = count - 1;
  while( first <= last )
  {
    int mid = (last + first) / 2;
    if( values[mid] < searchVal )
      first = mid + 1;
    else if( values[mid] > searchVal )
      last = mid - 1;
```

```
         else
            return mid;      // success
      }
      return -1;             // not found
   }
```

20. *File Encryption Using XOR*

This chapter introduced a program that reads a file from standard input and XORs each
character with a number. If the output is redirected to a file, the result is a simple type of data
encryption. Modify the program as follows:

Use a 128-byte string as an *encryption key*. The first 128 bytes read from the input file are
XOR'ed with their matching position of the key. The next 128 bytes from the file are again
XOR'ed by the key, and so on, until the end of the input file is reached.

This form of encryption is harder to break than the version presented earlier in the
chapter. In order to be completely secure, the encryption key should only be used once and
then discarded. Of course, unauthorized persons must not have access to the encryption
program; if it were run with an input file of binary zeros, it would display the encryption key
itself.

7 Integer Arithmetic

Bit Manipulation
Bit-Mapped Sets
Prime Numbers
Arithmetic with Large Numbers
Direct Video Output

7.1   SHIFT AND ROTATE INSTRUCTIONS

This chapter is all about performing arithmetic with integers in assembly language. Shift and rotate instructions are covered first because they are strongly related to multiplication and division. Shifts and rotates are not generally available in high level languages, so assembly language can be an absolute necessity in certain types of applications. We will cover addition, subtraction, multiplication, and division instructions. Last of all, we will briefly touch on arithmetic with ASCII numbers (one digit per byte) and packed decimal arithmetic. This chapter covers only the basic instructions and techniques in an effort to expose the reader to areas that can be of interest for later study.

Shift and rotate instructions provide a way to move bits around in an operand. They are standard in assembly language but are rarely available in high-level languages. All of these instructions affect the Overflow and Carry flags:

SHL	Shift left
SHLD	Double-precision shift left
SHR	Shift right
SHRD	Double-precision shift right
SAL	Shift arithmetic left
SAR	Shift arithmetic right
ROL	Rotate left
ROR	Rotate right
RCL	Rotate carry left
RCR	Rotate carry right

7.1.1   SHL Instruction

The SHL (shift left) instruction shifts each bit in a destination operand to the left, filling the lowest bit with 0. The highest bit is moved to the Carry flag, and the bit that was in the Carry flag is lost:

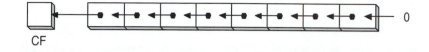

In the following formats for SHL, the first shifts a register or memory operand 1 bit to the left. The next uses a *shift count* in the CL register to determine how many times the destination operand is to be shifted. The third format, created for the 80286 processor, allows the shift count to be any 8-bit immediate value:

```
SHL  dest,1
SHL  dest,CL
SHL  dest,immed8
```

The destination operand can be 8, 16, or 32 bits. CL is not changed when used as a shift counter. These formats also apply to the SHR, SAL, SAR, ROR, ROL, RCR, and RCL instructions presented in the next few sections of this chapter. Here are some examples using both register and memory operands in the SHL instruction:

```
shl  bl,1                ; shift BL 1 bit to the left
shl  wordval,1           ; 16-bit direct memory operand
shl  byte ptr[si],1      ; 8-bit indirect memory operand
shl  al,cl               ; shift AL left, using count in CL
shl  bx,5                ; requires 80286
shl  eax,cl              ; requires 80386
shl  ebx,16
```

Setting the Carry Flag. In the following example, BL is shifted once to the left. The highest bit is copied into the Carry flag, and the lowest bit position is cleared:

```
mov  bl,8Fh              ; BL = 10001111b
shl  bl,1                ; BL = 00011110b, CF = 1
```

Fast Multiplication. One of the best uses of SHL is for performing high-speed multiplication. The standard multiplication instructions are quite slow in comparison to SHL. The multiplication must always be a power of 2, and the number of times you shift is actually the exponent. For example, shifting left one position is the same as multiplying by 2^1, shifting two positions is the same as multiplying by 2^2, and so on. The following example shows the decimal value of DL after each shift:

```
mov  dl,1                ; DL = 1
shl  dl,1                ; DL = 2
shl  dl,1                ; DL = 4
shl  dl,1                ; DL = 8
shl  dl,1                ; DL = 16
```

```
shl   dl,1                       ; DL = 32
etc...
```

Any number can be used as the starting value. If, for instance, we shift 21h left two times, the result is the same as multiplying it by 2^2 (4). It's a good idea to check the Carry flag after the shift to make sure the result is valid:

```
mov   ah,00100001b               ; AH = 21h
mov   cl,2
shl   ah,cl                      ; AH = 84h
jc    Error
```

7.1.2 SHLD/SHRD Instructions

The SHLD (*shift left double*) instruction for the 80386 processor shifts a target operand a given number of bits to the left. The bit positions opened up by the count are filled by the most significant bits of the source operand. The source operand is not affected, but the Sign, Zero, Auxiliary, Parity, and Carry flags are affected.

The SHRD (*shift right double*) instruction for the 80386 processor shifts a target operand a given number of bits to the right. The bit positions opened up by the count are filled by the least significant bits of the source operand.

The following instruction formats apply to both SHLD and SHRD. The first operand can be a register or memory operand, and the second operand must be a register. The *count* operand can be either the CL register or an 8-bit immediate operand:

```
SHLD  reg16,reg16,count8
SHLD  mem16,reg16,count8
SHLD  reg32,reg32,count8
SHLD  mem32,reg32,count8
```

For example, the following statements shift **wval** to the left 4 bits and insert the high 4 bits of AX into the low 4 bit positions of **wval:**

```
.data
wval dw 9BA6h
.code
mov   ax,0AC36h
shld  wval,ax,4                  ; wval = BA6Ah
```

In the follwing example, AX is shifted to the right 4 bits and the low 4 bits of DX are shifted into the high 4 positions of AX:

```
mov   ax,234Bh
mov   dx,7654h
shrd  ax,dx,4                    ; AX = 4234h
```

The following statements shift EBX left 1 bit and insert the high bit of **dval** in the lowest bit position of EBX:

```
.data
dval dd 8124365Ah
.code
mov  ebx,00000006h
shld ebx,dval,1              ; ebx = 0000000Dh
```

In other words, when ebx is shifted left 1 bit, its lowest byte becomes 00001100 in binary. Then the highest bit of **dval** (1) is ORed into the low byte of ebx:

```
   00001100
OR 00000001
   --------
   00001101
```

Clearly, this instruction has applications in programs that manipulate bit-mapped images, when groups of bits must be shifted left and right to reposition images on the screen. Another application would be data encryption, in which the encryption algorithm involvs the shifting of bits.

7.1.3   SHR Instruction

The SHR (shift right) instruction shifts each bit to the right, replacing the highest bit with a 0. The lowest bit is copied into the Carry flag, and the bit that was in the Carry flag is lost:

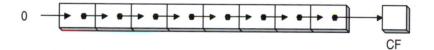

SHR uses the same instruction formats as SHL. Examples using both register and memory operands are:

```
shr   bl,1
shr   ecx,1
shr   wordval,1
shr   byte ptr[si],1
shr   al,cl
shr   edx,cl
shr   ax,5
```

In the following example, the 0 from the lowest bit in AL is copied into the Carry flag, and the highest bit in AL is cleared:

```
mov  al,0D0h              ; AL = 11010000b
shr  al,1                 ; AL = 01101000b, CF = 0
```

The SHR instruction can be used to divide an unsigned number by 2. For example, we can divide 32 by 2, yielding 16:

```
mov dl,32                 ; 00100000b
shr dl,1                  ; 00010000b     (DL = 16)
```

By coding a multiple shift, we can rapidly divide an unsigned operand by a power of 2. In the following example, 64 is divided by 8 (2^3):

```
mov  al,01000000b         ; AL = 64
shr  al,3                 ; divide by 8, AL = 00001000b
```

If you plan to perform division by shifting on signed numbers, it's best to use the SAR instruction because it preserves the number's sign bit.

7.1.4 SAL and SAR Instructions

SAL (shift arithmetic left) and SAR (shift arithmetic right) are shift instructions specifically for signed numbers. SAL is identical to SHL and is included in the instruction set only for completeness. SAR shifts each bit to the right and makes a copy of the sign bit:

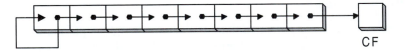

CF

SAR copies the lowest bit of the destination operand into the Carry flag, shifts the operand right 1 bit position, and duplicates the original sign bit. You can also place a shift count in CL for multiple shifts. The syntax for SAR and SHR is identical to that of SHL and SHR.

The following example shows how SAR duplicates the sign bit. AL is negative before and after it is shifted to the right:

```
mov  al,0F0h              ; AL = 11110000b (-16)
sar  al,1                 ; AL = 11111000b (-8)  CF = 0
```

In the following example, –32768 is shifted right five times, which is the same as dividing it by 2^5 (32). The result is –1024:

```
mov  dx,8000h             ; DX = 1000000000000000b
sar  dx,5                 ; DX = 1111110000000000b
```

7.1.5   ROL Instruction

The ROL (rotate left) instruction moves each bit to the left. The highest bit is copied both into the Carry flag and into the lowest bit. The instruction format is the same as for the SHL instruction:

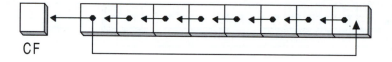

CF

In general, rotate instructions are different from shift instructions because bits are never lost. A bit that is rotated off one end of a number appears again at the other end.

In the following example, the high bit is copied into both the Carry flag and into bit position 0:

```
mov   al,40h           ; AL = 01000000b
rol   al,1             ; AL = 10000000b, CF = 0
rol   al,1             ; AL = 00000001b, CF = 1
rol   al,1             ; AL = 00000010b, CF = 0
```

You can use ROL to exchange the high and low halves of an operand. Example 1 shows how to do this with byte and word values.

Example 1. Using ROL to Exchange Values.

```
.286
.data
byteval   db   0Fh
wordval   dw   1234h

.code
byte_values:
     mov    al,26h
     rol    al,4           ; AL = 62h
     rol    byteval,4      ; byteval = F0h

word_values:
     mov    ax,0203h
     rol    ax,8           ; AX = 0302h
     rol    wordval,8      ; wordval = 3412h
```

7.1.6 ROR Instruction

The ROR (rotate right) instruction moves each bit to the right. The lowest bit is copied into the Carry flag and into the highest bit at the same time. The instruction format is the same as for SHL:

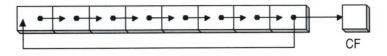

In the following example, the lowest bit is copied into the Carry flag and into the highest bit of the result:

```
mov al,01h        ; AL = 00000001b
ror al,1          ; AL = 10000000b, CF = 1
ror al,1          ; AL = 01000000b, CF = 0
```

7.1.7 RCL and RCR Instructions

The RCL (rotate carry left) instruction shifts each bit to the left and copies the highest bit into the Carry flag, which is copied into the lowest bit of the result:

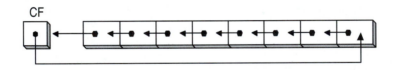

In the following example, the CLC instruction clears the Carry flag. The first RCL instruction moves the high bit of BL into the Carry flag, and shifts all other bits to the left. The second RCL instruction moves the Carry flag into the lowest bit position, and shifts all other bits to the left:

```
clc               ; CF = 0
mov   bl,88h      ; BL = 10001000b
rcl   bl,1        ; BL = 00010000b, CF = 1
rcl   bl,1        ; BL = 00100001b, CF = 0
```

Recover a Bit from the Carry Flag. RCL can recover a bit that has previously been shifted into the Carry flag. The following example checks the lowest bit of **testval** by shifting its lowest bit into the Carry flag. Then RCL restores the number to its original value:

```
.data
testval db 01101010b
.code
shr testval,1
```

```
jc    exit                   ; exit if Carry flag set
rcl   testval,1              ; else restore the number
```

RCR Instruction. The RCR (rotate carry right) instruction shifts each bit to the right and copies the lowest bit into the Carry flag. The Carry flag is copied into the highest bit of the result:

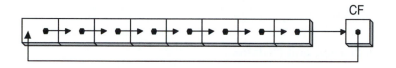

In the following example, STC sets the Carry flag before performing the rotation:

```
stc                          ; CF = 1
mov   ah,10h                 ; AH = 00010000b, CF = 1
rcr   ah,1                   ; AH = 10001000b, CF = 0
```

7.2   SAMPLE APPLICATIONS

7.2.1   Shifting Multiple Bytes on the 8086

Programs sometimes need to shift all bits within an array, as one might when moving a bit-mapped graphic image. Using three byte operands as an example, we can begin with the leftmost byte, shifting its low bit into the Carry flag. The results of a single shift to the right are as follows:

	byte1	**byte2**	**byte3**
Before:	00111011	01000110	11111111
After:	00011101	10100011	01111111

After being shifted, **byte1** equals 00011101 and CF = 1. Next, we use RCR to rotate **byte2** to the right while copying the contents of the Carry flag into the highest position of byte2. After the rotate, byte2 equals 10100011. Finally, **byte3** is rotated to the right, resulting in the value 01111111. These three steps are repeated each time we shift all bits in the three bytes. The program excerpt in Example 2 shifts the bits in all three bytes to the right four times.

Example 2. Shifting Multiple Bytes with RCR.

```
.data
byte1  db 3Bh               ; after: 03h
byte2  db 46h               ; after: B4h
```

```
byte3   db 0FFh                ; after: 6Fh

.code
    mov   cx,4                 ; repeat the shift four times
L1: shr   byte1,1             ; highest byte
    rcr   byte2,1             ; middle byte, include Carry flag
    rcr   byte3,1             ; low byte, include Carry flag
    loop  L1
```

7.2.2   Fast Multiplication and Division

As we have already seen, SHL and SHR perform multiplication and division efficiently when at least one operand is a power of 2 (for example, 2, 4, 8, 16, 32 . . .). If neither operand is a power of 2, you may still be able to factor the number into two powers of 2. To multiply the number in BX by 36, for example, we take advantage of the distributive property of multiplication and add the products of 32 and 4 together:

```
BX * 36  = BX * (32 + 4)
         = (BX * 32) + (BX * 4)
```

The following example shows how a 16-bit variable called **intval** can be multiplied by 36. The result, 360, is the sum of two products, 320 and 40:

```
.data
intval  dw  0Ah                ; result = 0168h  (360d)
product dw  ?

.code
mov   bx,intval
mov   cl,5                      ; multiply by 32
shl   bx,cl                     ; BX = 0140h  (320d)
mov   product,bx                ; save first result
mov   bx,intval                 ; get integer value again
shl   bx,1                      ; multiply by 4
shl   bx,1                      ; BX = 0028h  (40d)
add   product,bx                ; add results together
```

7.2.3   Displaying Binary Bits

A good way to apply the SHL instruction is to display a byte in ASCII binary format. We can take advantage of the fact that the highest bit is copied into the Carry flag each time the byte is shifted to the left.

The **bin.asm** program in Example 3 displays each of the bits in the AL register. The four lines at label L1 form the nucleus of the program, where each high bit is shifted into the Carry flag. If the Carry flag is set, we move the ASCII digit 1 to DL; otherwise, DL equals the digit 0. Here is a sample of the program's output:

```
Enter a decimal integer: 1379
0000010101100011
```

Example 3. The Binary Number Display Program.

```
title Display ASCII Binary              (BIN.ASM)

; This program displays a number in binary.
.model small
.stack 100h
.data
prompt db "Enter a decimal integer: ",0

.code
extrn Clrscr:proc, Crlf:proc, Readint:proc, \
    Writestring:proc

main proc
  mov  ax,@data
  mov  ds,ax

  ; Prompt for an integer:
  call Clrscr
  mov  dx,offset prompt
  call Writestring
  call Readint              ;read integer into AX
  call Crlf
  mov  cx,16                ; number of bits in AX

L1:
  shl  ax,1                 ; shift AX left into Carry flag
  mov  dl,'0'               ; choose '0' as default digit
  jnc  L2                   ; if no carry, then jump to L2
  mov  dl,'1'               ; else move '1' to DL

L2:
  push ax                   ; save AX
  mov  ah,2                 ; display DL
  int  21h
```

```
       pop   ax                    ; restore AX
       loop  L1                    ; shift another bit to left

       mov   ax,4C00h              ; exit program
       int   21h
main endp
end main
```

7.2.4   Isolating a Bit String

Often a byte or word contains more than one field, so we extract short sequences of bits, called *bit strings*. For instance, DOS function 57h returns the date stamp of a file in DX. (The date stamp shows the date on which the file was last modified.) Bits 0-4 represent a day number between 1 and 31, bits 5-8 are the month number, and bits 9-15 hold the year number. For example, let us assume that a file was last modified on March 10, 1999. The file's date stamp would appear as follows in the DX register (the year number is relative to 1980):

DH   DL

0 0 1 0 0 1 1 0 0 1 1 0 1 0 1 0

Field: Year   Month   Day
Bit numbers: 9-15   5-8   0-4

To extract a single field, shift its bits into the lowest part of DX, using the SHR instruction, and then apply AND to the irrelevant bits with zeros. To demonstrate, let's start with the day of the month. We make a copy of DL and mask off all bits not belonging to the field. AL now contains the value we want:

```
mov   al,dl                 ; make a copy of DL
and   al,00011111b          ; clear bits 5-7
mov   day,al                ; save in day
```

To extract the month number, we move bits 5-8 into the low part of AL before masking off all other bits. AL is then shifted right until the month number is in the lowest five positions:

```
mov   ax,dx                 ; make a copy of DX
mov   cl,5                  ; shift count
shr   ax,cl                 ; shift right 5 bits
and   al,00001111b          ; clear bits 4-7
mov   month,al              ; save in month
```

The year number (bits 9-15) is completely within the DH register. We move this to AL and shift it right 1 bit:

```
mov   al,dh               ; make a copy of DH
shr   al,1                ; shift right one position
mov   ah,0                ; clear AH to zeros
add   ax,1980             ; year is relative to 1980
mov   year,ax             ; save in year
```

7.2.5   RECORD Directive

The assembly language directive called RECORD is not to be confused with the conventional use of the term *record* in high-level languages. It is, rather, a description of bit groups within a byte or word operand. We use it primarily to make bit masking and bit shifting easier. First, a record must be defined with the record name and the name and width of each field. The syntax for a record definition is

```
recordname RECORD field1 [,field2] ...
```

The syntax for a *field* is

```
fieldname:width[= expression]
```

Fieldname is the name of a particular field within the record, and the first field is stored in the most signficant bits of the byte or word. *Expression* is a constant integer expression.

Let's use the RECORD directive to define the bit layout of a 16-bit date stored in the disk directory. The date is bit-mapped, with 7 bits for the year, 4 bits for the month, and 5 bits for the day of the month:

```
1 1 1 1 1 1 1 1 1 1 1 1 1 1 1 1
└───── year ─────┘ └─ month ─┘ └── day ──┘
```

A suitable use of the RECORD directive for the date is the following:

```
date_record RECORD year:7, month:4, day:5
```

Notice that each field name must be followed by its width, expressed as the number of bits. It is also possible to give default values to the fields. Let's initialize **date_record** to January 1, 1980 (a year value of 0 indicates 1980):

```
date_record RECORD year:7=0, month:4=1, day:5=1
```

If you define a record containing 8 bits or less, the record automatically refers to a byte—otherwise, it refers to a word. If all bit positions are not used, the bit fields are right-justified. For example, the following record defines only 12 bits. The assembler sets the bits to the low positions in the field and sets the unused, high 4 bits to zero:

```
bitrec RECORD field1:6=111111b, field2:6=111111b
```

The value of the entire 16 bits is

    0000111111111111

Creating a Record Variable. Once a record has been defined, it can be used to create a *record variable*. The syntax is

    [*name*] *recordname* < [*initialvalue* [,*initialvalue*]] ...>

You can assign a starting value to any of the bit fields. If the assigned value is too large, the assembler displays an error message.

    Let's create a record variable using the **date_record** defined earlier. The following declaration retains the default values (0,1,1) for January 1, 1980:

```
date_record RECORD year:7=0, month:4=1, day:5=1
    .
    .
birthDate date_record <>
```

On the other hand, we might want to initialize **birthDate** to May 30, 1999:

```
birthDate date_record <19,5,30>
```

Shifting and Masking. Last of all, the field names in a record help you to mask and shift the bit fields more easily. In Chapter 7, we saw that DOS function 57h returns the date stamp of a file. March 10, 1999 for example, is stored as

```
0  0  1  0  0  1  1   0  0  1  1   0  1  0  1  0
|_____|   |_____|   |_____|
     Year = 19         month = 3     day = 10
```

Assuming the date has been moved to AX, we can isolate the four bits making up the month number by *AND*ing AX first and then shifting it to the right:

```
and  ax,0000000111100000b  ; clear unused bits
mov  cl,5
shr  ax,cl                 ; shift right 5 bits
```

MASK Operator. Because we used the RECORD directive to define **date_record**, we can improve the preceding statements. The MASK operator creates a bit mask: All bits corresponding to the field position are set, and all other bits are cleared:

```
mov  ax,file_date     ; get the date
and  ax,MASK month    ; clear unused bits
mov  cl,month
shr  ax,cl            ; shift right 5 bits
```

When **date_record** is defined, the assembler automatically assigns a numeric value to each field, depending on its *shift value*. This can be interpreted as the field's bit offset from position 0. In the foregoing example, **month** is moved to CL, affecting the shift count. The following table shows the shift value of each field (this technique would also work for the **day** and **year** fields):

Field	Shift Value
Year	9
Month	5
Day	0

WIDTH Operator. The WIDTH operator returns the number of bits in a record field. The following example accesses the width of each field in **date_record** in various ways, as well as the width of the entire record. These values are available at assembly time (see Example 4).

Example 4. Using the WIDTH Operator.

```
date_record record   year:7=0, month:4=1, day:5=1

.data
birthDate   date_record <>
size_of_year   =  width year      ; width = 7
size_of_month  =  width month     ; width = 4

.code
mov   ax,width day                ; width = 5
if (width date_record) gt 8       ; 16-bit record?
   mov   ax,birthDate             ; move to AX
else                              ; 8-bit record?
   mov   al,birthDate             ; move to AL
endif
```

7.3   EXTENDED ADDITION AND SUBTRACTION

7.3.1   ADC Instruction

The ADC (*add with carry*) instruction permits addition of multibyte and multiword operands. Both the source operand and the Carry flag are added to the destination operand. The syntax is:

```
ADC   dest,source
```

The source and destination operands can be 8, 16, or 32-bit registers or memory operands. The source operand can also be an immediate value.

The **Multi32_Add** procedure in Example 5 adds two large integer operands and stores the result in memory. When calling it, we pass pointers to two operands, a pointer to a location where the sum will be stored, and a count of the number of doublewords to be added. The procedure assumes that each value is stored with its least significant doubleword at the lowest address. The following statements prepare the procedure arguments:

```
.386
mov   si,offset op1
mov   di,offset op2
mov   bx,offset result
mov   cx,2                  ; add 2 doublewords
call  Multi32_Add
```

Inside the procedure, before the loop starts, we clear the Carry flag to prevent a carry from being added the first time through the loop. The flags are saved by the PUSHF (push flags) instruction, to preserve the Carry flag for the next pass through the loop:

```
L1: mov   eax,[si]        ; get the first operand
    adc   eax,[di]        ; add the second operand
    pushf                 ; save the Carry flag
    (etc.)
```

The following sample values are added by the program:

```
  A2B2A406B7C62938 (op1)
+ 80108700A64938D2 (op2)
------------------
  122C32B075E0F620A (sum)
```

Example 5. The QuadWord Addition Program.

```
title QuadWord Addition                    (QWADD.ASM)
; This program adds two quadword operands.
.model small
.stack 100h
.386                              ; enable 32-bit registers
.data
op1    dq  0A2B2A406B7C62938h
op2    dq  080108700A64938D2h
result dd  3 dup(?)
```

```
        .code
        main proc
            mov   ax,@data
            mov   ds,ax
            mov   si,offset op1
            mov   di,offset op2
            mov   bx,offset result
            mov   cx,2                      ; counter
            call  Multi32_Add
            mov   ax,4C00h
            int   21h
        main endp


        ; Multi32_Add
        ;
        ; Add two integers, consisting of multiple
        ; doublewords. Input parameters: SI and DI point
        ; to the two operands, BX points to the destination
        ; operand, and CX contains the number of
        ; doublewords to be added.


        .code
        Multi32_Add proc
            pusha
            clc                    ; clear the Carry flag

        L1: mov   eax,[si]         ; get the first operand
            adc   eax,[di]         ; add the second operand
            pushf                  ; save the Carry flag
            mov   [bx],eax         ; store the result
            add   si,4             ; advance all 3 pointers
            add   di,4
            add   bx,4
            popf                   ; restore the Carry flag
            loop  L1               ; repeat count

            mov  dword ptr [bx],0
            adc  dword ptr [bx],0  ; add leftover carry
            popa
            ret
```

```
Multi32_Add endp
end main
```

7.3.2   SBB Instruction

The SBB (*subtract with borrow*) instruction is useful for multibyte or multiword subtraction. The syntax is:

```
SBB dest,source
```

The destination and source operands can be 8- or 16-bit values. First, the source operand is subtracted from the destination; then the Carry flag is subtracted from the destination.

Quadword Example. In the code shown in Example 6, one quadword (8-byte) operand is subtracted from another. The SBB instruction subtracts both the Carry flag and the contents of **op2** from AL. The DQ directive stores the bytes in memory in reverse order, so we initialize SI to the lowest address of each operand. The subtraction can be summarized as follows:

```
op1      20 40 30 04 36 20 47 A1
op2    - 05 52 10 30 4A 26 30 B2
       ----------------------------------
result   1A EE 1F D3 EB FA 16 EF
```

In this example, **op1** is larger than **op2**, so the result is positive. If the result was negative, the Carry flag would also be set after the loop had finished, and the result would be stored in twos complement form.

Still referring to Example 6, the CLC (*clear carry*) instruction clears the Carry flag. Be sure to do this before you execute an ADC or SBB instruction the first time. Otherwise, a leftover value in the flag will affect the result. The STC (*set carry*) instruction sets the Carry flag.

Example 6. Subtracting QuadWord Values.

```
.data
op1  dq  20403004362047A1h
op2  dq  055210304A2630B2h
result dq  0                  ; result = 1A EE 1F D3 EB FA 16 EF

.code
     mov cx,8            ; loop counter: 8 bytes
     mov si,0            ; set index to 0
     clc                 ; clear Carry flag
L1:  mov  al,byte ptr op1[si]
     sbb  al,byte ptr op2[si]
```

```
mov   byte ptr result[si],al
inc   si
loop  L1
```

7.4   MULTIPLICATION AND DIVISION

The Intel instruction set includes instructions that perform integer multiplication and division on 8, 16, and 32-bit integers. All operands are assumed to be binary, so if decimal or binary-coded decimal operands are involved, you must make all adjustments. Floating-point operations are handled either by a floating-point unit or by software emulation supplied in a language library.

The MUL (*multiply*) and DIV (*divide*) instructions are for unsigned binary numbers. The IMUL (*integer multiply*) and IDIV (*integer divide*) instructions are for signed binary numbers.

A Review of Signed Arithmetic. When the CPU performs arithmetic, it treats the operands as unsigned binary numbers. If you intend the values to be *signed,* the flags must be carefully watched to make sure the result does not overflow the destination. Although the CPU performs arithmetic as if the operands are unsigned, signed values are still computed correctly. Suppose, for example, that we add FFFFh to 3000h. The result is 2FFFh:

```
mov  cx,3000h            ; starting value of CX
add  cx,0FFFFh           ; CX = 2FFF, OF = 0, CF = 1
```

The *unsigned* sum of 3000h and 0FFFFh is 12FFFh, which overflows CX and sets the Carry flag. The *signed* sum of 3000h and FFFFh (–1) is 2FFFh, which is correctly calculated.

Signed Values Out of Range. The Overflow flag tells us whether or not the signed result of an arithmetic operation is out of range. For example, if AL contains 7Fh (+127) and we add 1 to AL, the signed result of 80h (–128) is clearly incorrect.

The Overflow flag is generated by a mechanical process: For an 8-bit operation, OF = ($c7$ XOR $c6$), where $c7$ is the carry out of bit 7 and $c6$ is the carry out of bit 6. In the following example, bit position 6 generates a carry, but bit 7 does not. Thus, OF = (0 XOR 1), which equals 1:

```
    0 1 1 1 1 1 1 1    (+127)
  + 0 0 0 0 0 0 0 1    (+1)
  -----------------
    1 0 0 0 0 0 0 0    (-128, OF = 1, CF = 0)
```

The same principle works for 16-bit operations, using bits 14 and 15, and for 32-bit operations, using bits 30 and 31.

7.4.1   MUL Instruction

The MUL instruction multiplies an 8, 16, or 32-bit operand by AL, AX, or EAX. The instruction formats are:

```
MUL  multiplier
IMUL multiplier
```

Multiplier can be either a register or a memory operand, but it cannot be an immediate value. The following table shows the registers that take place in each type of multiplication, depending on the size of the multiplier:

Multiplicand	Multiplier	Product
AL	*op-8*	AX
AX	*op-16*	DX:AX
EAX	*op-32*	EDX:EAX

Example 1 - Multiply AL by 10h. The following statements multiply 5 by 10h, producing 0050h in AX:

```
mov   al,5h
mov   bl,10h
mul   bl                    ; AX = 0050h
```

Example 2 - Multiply AX by 100h. The following statements multiply 2000h by 100h, producing a 32-bit product of 00200000h in DX:AX:

```
.data
val1  dw   2000h
val2  dw   0100h
.code
mov   ax,val1
mul   val2                  ; DX = 0020h, AX = 0000h
```

Example 3 - Multiply EAX by 10000h. The following example multiplies 12345678h by 10000h, producing 123456780000h in EDX:EAX:

```
mov   eax,12345678h
mov   ebx,10000h
mul   ebx                   ; EDX = 00001234h, EAX = 56780000h
```

To multiply two memory operands, move one of them to the AL, AX, or EAX register and multiply it by the other operand:

```
mov  ax,integer1
mul  integer2
```

7.4.2　IMUL Instruction

The IMUL instruction multiplies signed binary values. It sign-extends the result. An 8-bit operation sign-extends AL into AH; a 16-bit operation sign-extends AX into DX, and a 32-bit multiply sign-extends EAX into EDX.

Interpreting the Flags. For an 8-bit multiplication, IMUL sets the Carry and Overflow flags if the resulting AH is *not* a sign extension of AL. That is, the sign of AH is not the same as the sign of AL.

For both MUL and IMUL, both CF and OF are set if the high-order result contains significant digits; otherwise, CF and OF are both cleared. The following three examples help to illustrate:

Example 1: 8-bit operation: 48 x 4 = 192

```
mov  al,48
mov  bl,4
imul bl                    ; AX = 00C0h  (+192),  CF = 1,  OF = 1
```

The product in AX is 00C0h (0000000011000000). AH is not a sign extension of AL, so CF = 1 and OF = 1. The magnitude of the result is greater than 7 bits.

Example 2: 8-bit operation: –4 x 4 = –16

```
mov  al,-4
mov  bl,4
imul bl                    ; AX = FFF0h (-16),   CF = 0,  OF = 0
```

The product in AX is FFF0h (–16), and AH is a sign extension of AL (the signed result fits within AL), so CF = 0 and OF = 0.

Example 3: 16-bit operation: 48 x 4 = 192

```
mov  ax,48
mov  bx,4
imul bx      ; DX = 0000, AX = 00C0h (+192),  CF = 0,  OF = 0
```

The product in DX:AX is 000000C0h. Because the signs of DX and AX are the same (positive), the result fits in AX, CF = 0, and OF = 0.

7.4.3   DIV Instruction

The DIV instruction performs 8-bit, 16-bit, and 32-bit unsigned division. A single operand is supplied (register or memory operand), which is assumed to be the divisor. The syntax for DIV is:

```
DIV divisor
```

If the divisor is 8 bits long, AX is the dividend, AL the quotient, and AH the remainder. If the divisor is 16 bits, DX:AX is the dividend, AX the quotient, and DX the remainder:

Dividend	Divisor	Quotient	Remainder
AX	op-8	AL	AH
DX:AX	op-16	AX	DX
EDX:EAX	op-32	EAX	EDX

Example 1: 8-bit division (83h / 2 = 41h, remainder 1):

```
mov   ax,0083h          ; dividend
mov   bl,2              ; divisor
div   bl               ; AL = 41h,  AH = 01h
```

Example 2: 16-bit division (8003h / 100h = 80h, remainder 3). DX contains the high part of the dividend, so we must clear it before dividing. After the division, the quotient is in AX and the remainder is in DX:

```
mov   dx,0              ; clear dividend, high
mov   ax,8003h          ; dividend, low
mov   cx,100h           ; divisor
div   cx               ; AX = 0080h,  DX = 0003h
```

Example 3: 32-bit division using a memory operand as the divisor. The dividend is automatically stored in reversed-byte order:

```
.data
dividend   dq    0000000800300020h
divisor    dd    00000100h

.code
mov   edx,dword ptr dividend + 4 ; high doubleword
mov   eax,dword ptr dividend     ; low doubleword
div   divisor                    ; EAX = 08003000h, EDX = 00000020h
```

The status flags (Overflow, Sign, Zero, Carry) are undefined after a DIV or IDIV instruction.

7.4.4   IDIV Instruction

The IDIV instruction has the same syntax as the DIV instruction with the same operands. The difference is it performs a *signed* division, operation. For an 8-bit division the dividend is in AX, so its sign will be determined from bit 15. For example, if –48 is divided by 5, AL = –9 and AH = –3:

```
mov    ax,-48              ; AX = FFD0h
mov    bl,5
idiv   bl                  ; AX = FDF7h (quotient = -9, remainder = -3)
```

A common mistake is to prepare the dividend by moving an 8-bit dividend to AL. In the next example, IDIV incorrectly assumes the dividend is +208 (00D0h), and the quotient is wrong:

```
mov    ah,0
mov    al,-48              ; AX = 00D0h (+208)
mov    bl,5
idiv   bl                  ; AX = 0329h (quotient = 41, remainder = 3)
```

7.4.5   CBW, CWD, CDQ, and CWDE Instructions

The Intel instruction set contains four instructions that sign-extend smaller operands into larger ones. The CBW and CWD are for the 8086/8088 processor and the CWDE and CDQ are for the 80386 processor:

CBW   *Convert Byte to Word* extends AL into AX.
CWD   *Convert Word to Doubleword* extends AX into DX:AX.
CWDE   *Convert Word to Extended Double* extends AX into EAX.
CDQ   *Convert Double to Quad* extends EAX into EDX:EAX.

For example, the following statements divide –128 by 10, using an 8-bit dividend. The CBW instruction prepares the quotient, converting 80h to FF80h:

```
mov    al,-128             ; AX = ??80h
cbw                        ; AX = FF80h
mov    bl,10
idiv                       ; AL = -12,   AH = -8
```

The following statements extend AX into DX before dividing by a 16-bit operand:

```
mov    ax,-5000            ; DX:AX = ????EC78h
cwd                        ; DX:AX = FFFFEC78h
mov    bx,256
```

```
        idiv    bx                      ; AX = FFEDh, (-19)   quotient
                                        ; DX = FF78h, (-136)  remainder
```

You may recall from Chapter 4 that the MOVSX instruction for the 80386 processor both moves and sign extends its source operand. It can be used to shorten the 8-bit division example by one instruction:

```
        movsx   al,-128                 ; AX = FF80h
        mov     bl,10
        idiv                            ; AL = -12,   AH = 8
```

7.4.6 Preventing Divide Overflow

When a division operation generates too large a result, a *divide overflow* condition results, which calls system interrupt 0. This can cause the computer to freeze or the current application to terminate. An attempt to divide by 0 also produces a divide overflow.

32-bit Division Using 16-bit Operands. An easy solution to the divide overflow problem might be to simply use larger operands. For example, if you are certain that your program will be run on an 386 processor or above, you can use a 32-bit divisor, resulting in a 32-bit quotient in EAX. But if your program must run on older processors, there is still a workaround: Break up the 32-bit dividend into two separate word values and perform two separate 16-bit divisions.

For example, let's divide 08010020h by 10h in two steps. First, divide the most significant word of the dividend, (0801h / 10h). The quotient is 0080h and the remainder is 0001h:

```
        0000:0801h  /  10h  =    0080h,  remainder 1
        (DX:AX)       (CX)      (AX)       (DX)
```

The remainder in DX will be the most significant part of the new dividend. When we move with the low half of the dividend to AX, DX:AX equals 0001:0020h. When this is divided by 10h, the quotient (AX) equals 1002h and the remainder (DX) is zero. Therefore, the 32-bit quotient is 0080:1002h:

```
        0001:0020h  /  10h  =    1002h,  remainder 0000h
        (DX:AX)       (CX)      (AX)       (DX)
```

Chapter Exercises 7 and 8 on page 265 can both use this technique.

7.5   APPLICATION: DIRECT VIDEO OUTPUT

Now that we have added both shifting and multiplication instructions to your skills in assembly language, you can write useful routines for mapping output directly to video RAM (called VRAM). The color video segment is at B800h for text output, so characters can be written directly to that address. Each character requires two bytes of storage, because the character value is immediately followed by its attribute byte. For example, the string "ABC" displayed in reverse video in the upper left corner of the video display would be laid out in memory as follows:

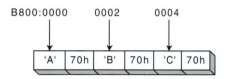

Using the standard MS-DOS font size, there are 80 characters in each row of text on the screen, and each character requires two bytes, so we map each text row to a 160-byte block of data in video RAM. Row 0 begins at offset 0000, row 1 begins at offset 00A0h, row 2 at offset 0140h, and so on. Using this information, you can write a character into video memory at any specified row and column position. For example, the offset of the character at row 2 column 3 on the screen is 0146h:

```
row = 2
column = 3
CharOffset = (row * 160) + (column * 2)
CharOffset = (2 * 160) + (3 * 2) = 326 = 0146h
```

7.5.1   Set_videoseg Procedure

The **Set_videoseg** procedure in Example 7 lets the caller modify a variable in the library that contains the video segment address.

Example 7. Setting the Video Segment Address.

```
; Set_videoseg  --------------------------------
;
; Set the current video segment address (the
; default is B800h). Input parameter: AX
; contains the address value.
;----------------------------------------------
Set_videoseg proc
      mov   videoSegment,ax
      ret
```

```
Set_videoseg endp
```

7.5.2   Writechar_direct Procedure

The **Writechar_direct** procedure (see Example 8) receives a character passed in AL, an
attribute byte in AH, and the desired row/column position in DH/DL, and writes the character
directly to video RAM. Because it tries to be as general as possible, it makes no assumptions
about the current values of ES and DI and must therefore initialize these registers before
storing the character. Although this looks like a lot of work to go through for a single character
of output, it writes to the screen much faster than the INT 10h video BIOS functions, which in
turn are much faster than the INT 21h console output functions.

Example 8. Writechar_direct Procedure.

```
;Writechar_direct ----------------------------
;
; Write a character directly to VRAM. Input
; parameters: AL = char, AH = attribute,
; DH/DL = row, column on screen (0-24, 0-79).
;----------------------------------------------
Writechar_direct proc
    push ax
    push dx
    push di
    push es

    mov  di,videoSegment
    mov  es,di

    ; multiply the row by 160
    push ax
    mov  ax,160
    mul  dh
    mov  di,ax

    ; multiply the column by 2, add to DI
    shl  dl,1
    mov  dh,0
    add  di,dx
    pop  ax

    mov  es:[di],ax          ; store char/attribute
```

```
      pop  es
      pop  di
      pop  dx
      pop  ax
      ret
Writechar_direct endp
```

7.5.3   Writestring_direct Procedure

The Writestring_direct procedure (see Example 9) writes a null-terminated string to video RAM. The calling program passes a pointer to a null-terminated string in DS:SI. Notice that we call the Writechar_direct procedure inside a loop. The caller of this procedure must also pass an attribute byte in AH, as well as the starting row and column locations in DH and DL.

Example 9. Writestring_direct Procedure.

```
; Writestring_direct ----------------------------
;
; Write a string directly to video RAM. Input
; parameters: DS:SI points to a null-terminated
; string, AH = attribute, DH/DL = row/column on
; the screen.
;------------------------------------------------
Writestring_direct proc
    push ax
    push dx
    push si

L1:
    mov  al,[si]              ; get character
    cmp  al,0                 ; check for null byte
    je   L2                   ; quit if found
    call Writechar_direct
    inc  si                   ; next character
    inc  dl                   ; next column
    jmp  L1

L2:
    pop  si
    pop  dx
    pop  ax
    ret
```

```
Writestring_direct endp
```

Optimizing Your Code. In the chapter exercises, we suggest that you rewrite the Writestring_direct procedure and optimize it for speed. For example, you could integrate the statements from Writechar_direct directly into Writestring_direct. This would eliminate extra PUSH and POP instructions, as well as the CALL and RET instructions that currently execute each time a single character is displayed. It certainly does not make sense to reset ES to the video segment address for every single character.

Another useful way to optimize code in the Writechar_direct procedure is to use a combination of shifting and addition instructions to avoid the much slower MUL instruction. Using the distributive property of multiplication, an expression such as *(row * 160)* can be factored into the expression *(row * 128) + (row * 32)*. Fortunately, 128 and 32 are powers of 2 and can be calculated by left-shifting bits with the SHL instruction.

7.6   ASCII AND PACKED DECIMAL ARITHMETIC

The integer arithmetic shown so far in this chapter has dealt only with binary values. The CPU calculates in binary, but you may need to perform arithmetic on numbers that have been input from the console or a file. Such numbers are called *ASCII digit strings*. Suppose you want to input two numbers from the console and add them together. No doubt, you have written such a program in a high-level language. The following is a sample console session:

```
Enter first number:   3402
Enter second number:  1256
The sum is:           4658
```

To calculate the sum, we add the ASCII digits themselves. Four adjustment instructions are available: the AAA (*ASCII adjust after addition*), AAS (*ASCII adjust after subtraction*), AAM (*ASCII adjust after multiplication*), and AAD (*ASCII adjust before division*).

When performing ASCII addition and subtraction, operands can be in either ASCII format or in *unpacked decimal* format. The high 4 bits of an unpacked decimal number are always zeros, whereas the high 4 bits of an ASCII number equal 0011b. The following example shows how 3,402 would be stored using both formats:

ASCII format: 33 34 30 32   Unpacked BCD: 03 04 00 02

(all values are in hexadecimal)

The unpacked decimal format is used for multiplication and division, so the high 4 bits of each byte must be cleared first. In general, ASCII arithmetic is slow because it is performed digit by digit, but it offers an advantage: the ability to process large numbers. For example, the following decimal number can be represented accurately in ASCII format, but cannot be represented by a 16-bit or 32-bit binary number:

234567800026365383456

7.6.1 AAA Instruction

The AAA (*ASCII adjust after addition*) instruction adjusts the binary result of an ADD or ADC instruction. It makes the result in AL consistent with ASCII digit representation. The following example shows how to add the ASCII digits 8 and 2 correctly, using the AAA instruction. We have to clear AH to zero before performing the addition. The last instruction converts both AH and AL to ASCII digits:

```
mov  ah,0
mov  al,'8'         ; AX = 0038h
add  al,'2'         ; AX = 006Ah
aaa                 ; AX = 0100h    (ASCII adjust result)
or   ax,3030h       ; AX = 3130h = '10' (convert to ASCII)
```

7.6.2 AAS Instruction

The AAS (*ASCII adjust after subtraction*) instruction adjusts the binary result of a SUB or SBB instruction. It makes the result in AL consistent with ASCII digit representation. Adjustment is necessary only when the subtraction generates a negative result. For example, the following statements subtract ASCII 9 from 8. After the SUB instruction, AX equals 00FFh (–1). The AAS instruction converts AX to FF09h, the tens complement of –1:

```
.data
val1 db '8'
val2 db '9'

.code
mov  ah,0
mov  al,val1        ; AX = 0038h
sub  al,val2        ; AX = 00FFh
aas                 ; AX = FF09h
pushf               ; save the Carry flag
or   al,30h         ; AX = FF39h
popf                ; restore the Carry flag
```

7.6.3 AAM Instruction

The AAM (*ASCII adjust after multiplication*) instruction adjusts the binary result of a MUL instruction. The multiplication must have been performed on unpacked decimal numbers. The multiplication also cannot be performed on ASCII numbers until the high 4 bits of each number are cleared. In the following example, we multiply 5 by 6 and adjust the result in AX. After adjusting the result, AX = 0300h, which is the unpacked decimal representation of 30:

```
.data
AscVal  db 05h, 06h

.code
mov  bl,ascVal                 ; first operand
mov  al,ascVal+1               ; second operand
mul  bl                        ; AX = 001Eh
aam                            ; AX = 0300h
```

7.6.4   AAD Instruction

The AAD (*ASCII adjust before division*) instruction adjusts the unpacked decimal dividend in AX before a division operation. The following example divides ASCII 37 by 5. First, the AAD instruction converts 0307h to 0025h. Then the DIV instruction yields a quotient of 07h in AL and a remainder of 02h in AH:

```
.data
quotient  db  ?
remainder db  ?

.code
mov  ax,0307h                  ; dividend
aad                            ; AX = 0025h
mov  bl,5                      ; divisor
div  bl                        ; AX = 0207h
mov  quotient,al
mov  remainder,ah
```

7.6.5   DAA, DAS Instructions

Packed decimal numbers store two decimal digits per byte. Each decimal digit is represented by 4 bits, as in the storage of 2,405:

```
packedBCD dd 2405h
```

Packed decimal format has at least three strengths:

• The numbers can have almost any number of significant digits. This makes it possible to perform calculations with a great deal of accuracy.

• Conversion of packed decimal numbers to ASCII (and vice versa) is relatively fast.

- An implied decimal point can be used by keeping track of its position in a separate variable.

Two instructions, DAA (*decimal adjust after addition*) and DAS (*decimal adjust after subtraction*), adjust the result of an addition or subtraction operation on packed decimal numbers. Unfortunately, no such instructions exist for multiplication and division. In those cases, the number must be unpacked, multiplied or divided, and repacked.

DAA Instruction. The DAA (*decimal adjust after addition*) instruction converts the binary result of an ADD or ADC instruction in AL to packed decimal format. For example, the following instructions add packed decimals 35 and 48. The lower digit of the result (7Dh) is greater than 9, and it is adjusted. The upper digit, which is 8 after the first adjustment, is not adjusted:

```
mov   al,35h
add   al,48h              ; AL = 7Dh
daa                       ; AL = 83h (adjusted result)
```

DAS Instruction. The DAS (*decimal adjust after subtraction*) instruction converts the binary result of a SUB or SBB instruction in AL to packed decimal format. For example, the following statements subtract packed decimal 48 from 85 and adjust the result:

```
mov   bl,48h
mov   al,85h
sub   al,bl              ; AL = 3Dh
das                      ; AL = 37h  (adjusted result)
```

7.7   REVIEW QUESTIONS

1. Discuss possible ways that decimal addition might be performed using the following two ASCII decimal numbers:

   ```
   2.1234
   300.5
   ```

2. Name at least one high-level language that contains bitwise shift operators.

3. Do you know of any high-level language that contains a rotate operator?

4. Which instruction moves each bit in an operand to the left and copies the highest bit into both the Carry flag and the lowest bit position?

5. Which instruction moves each bit to the right, copies the low bit into the Carry flag, and copies the Carry flag into the high bit position?

6. Which instruction shifts each bit to the right and replicates the sign bit?

7. Which instruction moves each bit to the left, copies the Carry flag into the low bit position, and copies the highest bit into the Carry flag?

8. Suppose there were no rotate instructions in the Intel instruction set. Show how to simulate the actions of the ROR instruction by rotating the AL register 1 bit position to the right. *Hint:* Use SHR and a conditional jump instruction.

9. What happens to the original contents of the Carry flag when the SHR instruction is executed?

10. Write a shift instruction that multiplies the contents of AX by 16.

11. Write a shift instruction that divides BX by 4.

12. Write a sequence of instructions that multiply AL by 12, using shift instructions.

13. What will be the contents of AL after each of the following instructions is executed? (Assume that AL = EAh, CL = 2, and the Carry flag is clear before each instruction is executed.)

Instruction	Contents of AL
a. shl al,1	
b. shl al,cl	
c. shr al,1	
d. sar al,1	
e. rol al,1	
f. rol al,cl	
g. ror al,1	
h. rcl al,1	
i. rcr al,1	
j. rcr al,cl	

14. Write a single rotate instruction that exchanges the high and low halves of the DL register.

15. Write an instruction that shifts the highest bit in the DL register into the lowest bit position of DH.

16. Write a series of instructions that shift the lowest bit of AX into the highest bit of BX on the 8088 processor. Perform the same operation using a single instruction on the 80486 processor.

17. Assume that the following record has been defined and State whether or not each of the following declarations is valid:

```
myrec record   field1:4,field2:3,field3:3,field4:6
```

```
a.  myrec rec1 <>
b.  db myrec <5>
c.  rec1 myrec <5,2>
d.  rec1 myrec <16,2,8>
e.  bitPattern myrec <,,,3>
```

18. Assume that the following record has been defined. Identify the mask, shift, and width values (in hexadecimal) for each of the fields. The first is done for you:

    ```
    myrec record    field1:4,field2:3,field3:3,field4:6
    ```

Field	Mask	Shift	Width
field1	F000h	0Ch	4
field2			
field3			
field4			

19. What will be the contents of DX after the following instructions are executed?

    ```
    mov   dx,5
    stc
    mov   ax,10h
    adc   dx,ax
    ```

20. The following program is supposed to subtract **val1** from **val2**. Find and correct all logic errors:

    ```
    .data
    val1   dq   20403004362047A1h
    val2   dq   055210304A2630B2h
    result dq   0
    .code
        mov cx,8              ; loop counter: 8 bytes
        mov si,val1          ; set index to start
        mov di,val2
        clc                  ; clear carry flag
    top:
        mov   al,byte ptr [si]    ; get first number
        sbb   al,byte ptr [di]    ; subtract second
        mov   byte ptr [si],al    ; store the result
        dec   si
        dec   di
        loop top
    ```

21. What will be the contents of AX after the following operation?

    ```
    mov   ax,22h
    mov   cl,2
    mul   cl
    ```

22. What will be the contents of AX and DX after the following operation?

```
mov   dx,0
mov   ax,222h
mov   cx,100h
mul   cx
```

23. What will be the contents of AX after the following operation?

```
mov   ax,63h
mov   bl,10h
div   bl
```

24. What will be the contents of AX and DX after the following operation?

```
mov   ax,1234h
mov   dx,0
mov   bx,10h
div   bx
```

25. What will be the contents of AX and DX after the following operation?

```
mov   ax,4000h
mov   dx,500h
mov   bx,10h
div   bx
```

26. Write instructions that multiply –5 by 3 and store the result in a 16-bit variable **val1.**

27. Write instructions that divide –276 by 10 and store the result in a 16-bit variable **val1.**

28. Write instructions for the 80286 processor that divide 20000000h by 10h and store the result in two 16-bit variables called **result_hi** and **result_lo.** *Hint:* be careful to avoid a divide overflow condition.

7.8 PROGRAMMING EXERCISES

7.8.1 Bit Manipulation

1. Backwards Binary Display

Write a program that displays the binary bits in any 8-bit variable *backwards*. For example, the number 84h would be displayed as 00100001.

2. Packed Decimal Conversion

Write a program to convert a packed decimal number to individual ASCII digits. Display the number on the screen. Use the following test value:

```
packedval   dt   273645193846571425
```

3. *Shifting Multiple Bytes*

The program shown earlier in this chapter in Example 2 used the RCR instruction to right-shift several bytes in memory. Also in this chapter, you learned about the SHRD instruction. Rewrite the program from Example 2 using the SHRD instruction.

4. *Room Schedule*

Assume that you have read a record from a room scheduling file. One field, called **roomstatus**, is bit-mapped, so each bit or group of bits is actually a subfield:

Bits	Usage
0-1	Type of room (0, 1, 2, 3)
2-7	Number of seats (0-63)
8-12	Department ID (0-31)
13	Overhead projector (0, 1)
14	Blackboard (0, 1)
15	P.A. system (0, 1)

Using the following data definitions, write a program that extracts each bit string from **roomstatus** and places it in its corresponding 8-bit variable:

```
roomstatus  dw  0110011101011101b
roomtype    db  ?
numseats    db  ?
deptID      db  ?
projector   db  ?
blackboard  db  ?
PAsystem    db  ?
```

7.8.2   Bit-Mapped Sets

Consider the bits in an integer to be members of a set of size n, in which each set member is identified by its bit position, 0 to $(n-1)$. For example, if bits 0, 2, 12 are each equal to 1, we say that 0, 2, and 12 are members of a set.

The exercises in this section can be implemented in several different ways. If you limit the set size to 32 members, the entire set can be contained in a single register or doubleword variable. Or, the set can span multiple doublewords, such as a 128-bit set. This is more difficult, but more flexible because the set can have virtually any size. Another decision has to do with parameter passing. For a multiword set, you can pass a pointer to the set in one of the registers, or you can pass a pointer on the stack. Your classroom instructor will probably decide how he/she wants you to implement the following programming exercises.

1. Display the Set Members

Write a procedure called *Display* that displays a list of members of the set. For example, if the set value is 8000101Bh, the output could be displayed as follows:

```
0 is a member
1 is a member
3 is a member
4 is a member
12 is a member
31 is a member
```

2. Evaluate a Subset

Create a *SubSet* procedure that returns a value of 1 if the bits in EBX are a subset of the bits in EAX. (For larger sets, EBX and EAX contain pointers to sets.)

3. Check for Set Membership

Create a procedure called *IsMember* that returns a value of 1 if the member number passed in BL is a member of the set identified by EAX; otherwise, it returns 0.

4. Count the Set Members

Create a procedure called *Count* that returns a count of the number of members in the set identified by EAX. Return the count in CX.

5. Set Union

Create a procedure called *Union*, which creates a new set that is a union of the sets identified by EBX and ECX and returns the union in a set identified by EAX.

6. Set Difference

Create a procedure called *Difference* that returns the difference between two sets. (The *difference* between sets A and B is the set of members that are in set A but not in set B.)

7. Fill Randomly

Create a procedure called *FillRandom* that creates a random sequence of bits in the set identified by the EAX register. Use the **Random_range** procedure from the book's link library.

7.8.3 Prime Numbers

1. Prime Number Program - I

Write a procedure that sets the Zero flag if the 32-bit integer passed in the EAX register is prime. (A prime number is evenly divisible by only itself and 1.) Optimize the program's loop to run as efficiently as possible. Your program should prompt the user for a number and then display a message indicating whether or not the number is prime. The program should then ask for another number from the user. Continue the loop in this fashion until the user enters a prearranged value such as −1.

2. *Prime Number Program - II*

Write a program in a high-level language such as C, C++, Java, Ada, or Pascal that satifies the requirement of the previous exercise (Prime Numbers). If you also completed the previous exercise, compare its execution time with your assembly language program.

If the high-level language's compiler you are using permits it, generate an assembly source code listing of your program. Describe the areas of the high level program that seem inefficient and discuss ways to optimize the code.

3. *Prime Number Program - III*

The *Sieve of Eratosthenes,* invented by the Greek mathematician by the same name, provides a way to find all the prime numbers within a given range. The array can be an array of bytes in which positions are "marked" by inserting 1's in the following manner: Beginning with position 2 (which is a prime number), insert a 1 in each subscript position that is a multiple of 2. Then do the same thing for 3, the next prime number. Find the next prime number after 3, which is 5, and mark all positions that are multiples of 5. Proceed in this manner until all multiples of primes have been found. The remaining positions of the array that are not marked indicate which numbers are prime. For this program, create a 65,000-element array and display all primes between 2 and 65,000.

7.8.4   Arithmetic with Large Numbers

1. *Quadword Addition Program*

Modify the QuadWord Addition program in Example 5 so that it can add two 256-bit integers.

2. *Adding 10-Digit Numbers*

Write a program that performs the following operations, in order:

* Input two 10-digit ASCII decimal numbers and store them in memory.

* Add the two numbers together and display the result.

* Prompt the user to find out if he or she wants to add another pair of numbers.

The screen display should resemble the following:

```
Addition Program

First Number  ==> 0142536475
Second Number ==> 0023466722
Result        ==> 0166003197
Action: Q)uit  R)esume
```

3. *Multidigit Packed Decimal Multiplication*

Write a program that multiplies two unpacked decimal numbers and stores the result in a variable named **product**. Run the program using a debugger and dump the contents of **product** before and after the multiplication takes place. The variables can be declared as follows:

```
factor1    dd   01020304h
factor2    dd   00000105h
product    db   8 dup(0)
```

To reserve enough space for the product, its size should be the sum of the digit positions of the two factors (4 + 2 = 6). You may want to use the same approach as in traditional longhand multiplication. After each multiply operation, AH contains the carry value, that is, the value to be added to the next product:

```
      01 02 03 04     (1,234)
    *        01 05    (    15)
      00 06 01 07 00  (product1)
  + 00 01 02 03 04 00 (product2)
    00 01 08 05 01 00 (18,510)
```

Using the lowest 2 digits of each number as an example, 4 * 5 = 20, and AX equals 0200h. The 2 in AH is added to the next product (3 * 5 = 15), giving us 17. The 7 becomes part of **product1**, and the 1 in AH is added to the next multiply operation.

4. *ASCII Multiplication Program*

Write a procedure that multiplies two 20-digit ASCII numbers together and displays the result. Test the procedure by calling it from a main program and passing the addresses of the numbers in SI and DI. Input the numbers from the console.

5. *ASCII Division Program*

Write a procedure to divide one 20-digit ASCII number by another and display the result. Test the procedure by calling it from a test program. Continue entering each pair of numbers from the console and performing the division until the user presses ENTER on a blank line to quit.

6. *Average Value Calculation*

Calculate and display the average of a list of ASCII digit strings. Be sure to place the decimal point in the correct position when displaying the result. Use the following numbers, coded in the data segment of your program:

```
ntable db "00012.30"
       db "00140.00"
       db "01000.20"
       db "00050.50"
       db "00230.10"
       db "01400.00"
       db "00300.00"
       db "00050.10"
```

Extra: Write a routine to input the numbers from the console and store them in **ntable**. Limit the number of digits that can be typed on either side of the decimal point. Also, insert a comma in the computed average and suppress any leading zeros.

7.   The DIV32 Procedure

Assuming that you are using an 80286 processor or earlier, write a 32-bit division procedure that works only with 16-bit registers.

8.   The DIV64 Procedure

Write a procedure called Divide64 that divides a 128-bit dividend by a 64-bit divisor, producing a 64-bit quotient and 64-bit remainder. Pass stack parameters to the procedure, including the offsets of the dividend, divisor, quotient, and remainder. Write a driver program that calls the procedure and displays the quotient and remainder.

7.8.5   Direct Video Output

The exercises in this section can be carried out either individually or in sequence.

1.   Testing Character Output

Write a a procedure that writes a character to every position on the screen, using the Writechar_direct procedure. Write another procedure that does the same thing, using INT 10h, function 2 to locate the cursor, and function 9 to draw a character. Write a short test program that calls both of your output procedures. Run the program and state your impression of the difference in speed between your two output procedures.

2.   Optimize the Writestring_direct Procedure

In the discussion of the Writestring_direct procedure earlier in this chapter, it was suggested that it could be optimized for speed by incorporating much of the code from the Writechar_direct procedure. This would, for example, eliminate the need to recalculate the buffer offset for each character being written, because consecutive characters in a string are stored in consecutive locations in the video buffer.

3.   Calculating the Row Offset in Writechar_direct

In the Writechar_direct procedure, the row offset in the video buffer is currently calculated using the MUL instruction. Using the MUL instruction to multiply the row number by 160 requires approximately 17 clock cycles on the 486 processor:

Instruction	Clocks
mov ax,160	1
mul dh	15 (approx)
mov di,ax	1

As an alternative, implement Writechar_direct by using the SHL instruction to perform the multiplication. Note that (row * 160) can be expressed as (row * 128) + (row * 32). The latter two operations can be accomplished by shifting left 7 bits, and 5 bits, respectively. A SHL instruction requires only 2 clocks, and all other MOV and ADD instructions require only 1 clock. You should be able to perform the complete multiplication in 10 clocks or less. Test your new implementation of Writechar_direct by displaying several hundred characters in a loop, and compare it to the original implementation. Can you detect a noticeable improvement?

4.   *Drawing a Menu*

Write a Procedure called Draw_menu that is passed a pointer to a data structure that contains all the information needed to display a menu. From Draw_menu, call Writestring_direct (in the link library). Here is a suggested data structure for the menu, where *count* is the number of menu entries, and *row1, col1, color1* are the row, column, and color of the first menu line, and so on:

```
<count>
<row1>, <col1>, <color1>, <textPtr1>
<row2>, <col2>, <color2>, <textPtr2>
<row3>, <col3>, <color3>, <textPtr3>
```

Each of the *textPtr* fields holds the offset of a null-terminated containing the text for a specific line in the menu. The text for the menu lines is stored separately, each with a label and a varying length string:

```
<text1>
<text2>
etc.
```

For example, here is one line from a sample menu:

```
BlueOnBlack = 1

db  10,15,BlueOnBlack, menuText1
.

.

menuText1  db  "1. Open the Input File",0
```

8 Structures and Macros

8.1   STRUCTURES

The STRUC directive defines a *structure* (template or pattern) that can be overlayed on an area of memory. It is comparable to a record in Pascal, or a struct in C/C++. A structure can also initialize an area within a program to default values. The individual parts of a structure are called *fields*.

A structure must be defined before it can be used. For example, we can define a structure describing fields from a student record. The following *structure definition* should be placed in the source file before the data segment:

```
STUNUMBER_SIZE = 7
LASTNAME_SIZE = 20


typStudent struc
    IdNum       db  STUNUMBER_SIZE + 1 dup(0)
    Lastname    db  LASTNAME_SIZE + 1 dup(0)
    Credits     dw  ?
    Status      db  ?
typStudent ends
```

Within the data segment we can define a structure variable:

```
.data
srec typStudent <>
```

The required angle brackets (<>) instruct the assembler to retain the default field values provided in the structure definition.

Override Default Values. When declaring a structure variable, you can override any of the default field values. The new values must be separated by commas, and each leading field can be skipped by inserting a comma. The following examples override various fields in **typStudent**:

```
; override all fields.
srec  typStudent <"1234","Jones",32,0>

; override the last two fields.
myRec typStudent <,,50,0>

; override only the second field.
yourRec typStudent <,"Gonzalez">
```

Using a Structure Variable. Once a structure variable has been created, references to individual field offsets are made by separating the variable name and the field name by a period:

```
mov   dl,srec.IdNum
mov   ax,srec.Credits
```

The assembler adds the offset of the structure variable to the offset of the field within the structure in order to generate an effective address. In the **typStudent** structure, the offset of **IdNum** is 0 because it is the first field in the structure. The offset of **LastName** is 8.

If a base or index register contains the offset of a structure object, a period separates the indirect operator from the field name. The PTR operator is required by the Microsoft assembler:

```
mov  bx,offset srec
mov  ax, (typStudent PTR [bx]).Credits
mov  dl,(typStudent PTR [bx]).Status
```

Various other addressing modes can be used when referencing structure fields:

```
mov  ax,srec[si].credits
mov  dl,[bx+si].status
```

Arrays of Structure Objects. The structure variable declaration can use the DUP operator to create an array of structure objects:

```
allStudents typStudent 100 dup(<>)
```

The following loop uses SI to point to each element of the array of student structure objects. The SIZE operator returns 32, the number of bytes in the typStudent structure:

```
        mov  si,offset allStudents
        mov  cx,STUDENT_COUNT
L1:     call InputStudent
        add  si,SIZE typStudent
        Loop L1
```

The program in Example 1 demonstrates various ways to initialize a structure, as well as a procedure that lets the user input values into each element within an array of typStudent structure objects.

Example 1. Student Structure Demonstration.

```
        title Structure Input Example        (STRUC.ASM)

        .model small
        .stack 100h
        STUNUMBER_SIZE = 7
        LASTNAME_SIZE = 20
        ACTIVE_STATUS = 1
        STUDENT_COUNT = 5
```

```
typStudent struc
   IdNum    db  STUNUMBER_SIZE + 1 dup(?)
   Lastname db  LASTNAME_SIZE + 1  dup(?)
   Credits  dw  ?
   Status   db  ?
typStudent ends

.data
progTitle db  "Student Structure Demonstration",0
srec typStudent <>   ; create a blank student

; Initialize and declare a structure variable:
rec2 typStudent <"1234","Baker",32,ACTIVE_STATUS>

; Declare an array of students:
allStudents typStudent STUDENT_COUNT dup( <> )

.code
extrn Clrscr:proc, Writestring:proc, Readstring:proc
extrn Crlf:proc, Readint:proc

main proc
    mov   ax,@data
    mov   ds,ax

    call  Clrscr
    mov   dx,offset progTitle
    call  Writestring
    call  Crlf

    mov   si,offset srec
    call  InputStudent

; Use a loop to input an array of students.

    mov   si,offset allStudents
    mov   cx,STUDENT_COUNT

L1: call  InputStudent
    add   si,SIZE typStudent
    Loop L1
```

```
        mov   ax,4C00h
        int   21h
main endp

; Input the fields for a single student from
; the console. Input parameter: SI points to the
; typStudent object.

InputStudent proc
        push ax
        push cx
        push dx

        mov   dx,si                 ; point to the structure
        add   dx,IdNum              ; point to the IdNum field
        mov   cx,STUNUMBER_SIZE
        call  Readstring            ; get the student ID
        call  Crlf

        mov   dx, si
        add   dx,LastName
        mov   cx,LASTNAME_SIZE
        call  Readstring            ; get the last name
        call  Crlf

        call  Readint               ; get the credits
        mov   (typStudent PTR [si]).Credits,ax
        call  Crlf
        mov   (typStudent PTR [si]).Status, ACTIVE_STATUS

        pop   dx
        pop   cx
        pop   ax
        ret
InputStudent endp

end main
```

8.2 INTRODUCING MACROS

A *macro* is a symbolic name given to one or more assembly language statements. Once defined, it can be invoked as many times in a program as you wish. When you *invoke* a macro, a copy of the macro's statements is inserted directly into the program. It is also customary to refer to *calling* a macro as the same as invoking a macro, although technically there is no CALL instruction involved.

A macro usually executes more quickly than a procedure, given that both contain the same statements. This is because a procedure has the extra overhead of CALL and RET instructions that tell the processor to branch to the procedure and return to the calling point. There is one disadvantage to using macros: repeated use of complex macros tends to increase a program's size because each call to a macro inserts a new copy of the macro's statements in the program.

mPutchar Example. The following instructions display a character on the console, using INT 21h:

```
mov  ah,2              ; write DL to the console
int  21h               ; call DOS interrupt
```

These statements could be hand-copied into every point in a program where we want to display a character, or we could store these instructions in a procedure and call it each time it is needed. But there would still be the added overhead of the CALL and RET instructions. A better way is to create a macro called **mPutchar**. Once the macro has been defined, it can be called from anywhere in the program. Calling a macro is not the same as calling a procedure—it means the macro's statements are inserted in the program from where it was called. The following lines define the **mPutchar** macro:

```
mPutchar  macro          ;; begin macro definition
    mov  ah,2
    int  21h
endm                     ;; end macro definition
```

In the code segment we invoke mPutchar by inserting its name in the source program (see Table 1). At each point in the program where the macro name appears, the assembler inserts the instructions from the macro definition into the program code (marked here with a '+' sign). Macro expansion is performed by the assembler during its first pass through the source file, and the expanded code appears in the source listing file generated by the assembler.

8.2.1 Macros with Parameters

One important feature of macros is their ability to include parameters. When calling the first version of mPutchar, for example, we loaded DL with the character to be displayed before calling the macro. But now, if we add a parameter to the macro called **char**, we can pass a character on the same line when calling the macro. The new version of the macro is shown in Example 2 and the following is a sample call that displays the first 20 letters of the alphabet:

```
        mov   al,'A'
        mov   cx,20
L1: mPutchar al
        inc   al
        Loop  L1
```

Example 2. The mPutchar Macro.

```
mPutchar macro char
    push  ax
    push  dx
    mov   ah,2
    mov   dl,char     ;; char is a parameter
    int   21h
    pop   dx
    pop   ax
endm
```

Calling a Macro. A macro is called by inserting its name into a program's source code, possibly followed by macro arguments. The syntax for calling a macro is:

```
macroname argument-1, argument-2, ...
```

The *macroname* must be the name of a macro defined prior to this point in the source code. Each argument is a value passed to the macro, which in return replaces a parameter in the original macro definition. The order of arguments must correspond to the parameters, but the number of arguments does not have to match the number of parameters. If too many arguments are passed, the assembler issues a warning. If too few arguments are passed to a macro, the unfilled parameters are blank. There is also a conditional assembler directive called IFB that lets you check for missing macro arguments, shown later in this chapter.

Table 1. Expanding the mPutchar Macro.

Source Code	Expanded Code
mov dl,'A' mPutchar	mov dl,'A' + mov ah,2 + int 21h
mov dl,'*' mPutchar	mov dl,'*' + mov ah,2 + int 21h

8.2.2   Defining a Macro

A macro can be defined anywhere in a program's source code, using the MACRO and ENDM directives. The syntax is:

```
macroname macro parameter-1, parameter-2...
   statement-list
endm
```

There is no set rule regarding indentation, but you should indent statements between *macroname* and **endm** to show that they belong to the macro. For consistency, you may want to use a special prefix character. In this book, we use a lowercase "m" prefix, creating recognizable macro names such as mPutchar, mDisplay, and mGotoRowCol.

The statements between the MACRO and ENDM directives are not assembled until the macro is called. *Macroname* can be any identifier, and the parameters are optional. There can be any number of parameters in the macro definition, as long as they are separated by commas and they appear on the same program line. These parameters, also called *dummy parameters,* are place-holders for values that are supplied when the macro is used. All statements before ENDM are considered part of the macro. A macro's statements are not assembled unless the macro is actually called.

Comments. You may want to use a double semicolon (;;) to mark comments inside macro definitions. This causes the macro comments to appear only when the macro is defined and not when the macro is expanded.

Required Parameters. Using the REQ qualifier, you can specify that a macro parameter is required. If the macro is called without an argument to match the required parameter, the assembler displays an error. For example:

```
mPutchar macro  char:REQ              ;; required parameter
    mov    ah,2
    mov    dl,char
    int  21h
endm
```

If a macro has multiple required parameters, each one must include the REQ qualifier. A macro called **mGotoRowCol** that positions the cursor at a specific row and column, for example, requires both parameters:

```
mGotoRowCol macro  row:REQ, column:REQ
    mov    ah,2
    mov    dh,row
    mov    dl,column
    mov    bh,0
    int  10h
endm
```

8.2.3   Example: mDisplayStr Macro

Let's create a macro called **mDisplayStr** that writes a string to standard output. There is one parameter called **string**, the name of the string to be displayed:

```
mDisplayStr macro string
    push ax
    push dx
    mov  ah,9
    mov  dx,offset string
    int  21h
    pop  dx
    pop  ax
endm
```

The parameter called **string** is replaced each time the macro is called. For example, to display three different strings, we call the macro three times, passing a different argument each time:

```
mDisplayStr msg1
mDisplayStr msg2
mDisplayStr msg3

 .
 .

msg1 db "This is message 1.",0Dh,0Ah,'$'
msg2 db "This is message 2.",0Dh,0Ah,'$'
msg3 db "This is message 3.",0Dh,0Ah,'$'
```

Names used in dummy parameters do not appear in the program listing generated by the assembler, and can be duplicates of other names without causing a conflict.

Parameters clearly make the **mDisplayStr** macro useful. We can also avoid the usual complications involved when passing arguments to procedures. Example 3 shows the code generated by the assembler. The macro calls themselves are listed ahead of the statements they generate. We do, however, pay a price in terms of increasing a program's executable code size when making extensive use of macros.

Example 3. Calling the mDisplayStr Macro.

```
mDisplayStr msg1
         push ax
         push dx
         mov  ah,9
         mov  dx,offset msg1
         int  21h
```

```
        pop   dx
        pop   ax
mDisplayStr msg2
        push  ax
        push  dx
        mov   ah,9
        mov   dx,offset msg2
        int   21h
        pop   dx
        pop   ax
mDisplayStr msg3
        push  ax
        push  dx
        mov   ah,9
        mov   dx,offset msg3
        int   21h
        pop   dx
        pop   ax
```

8.2.4   Example: mGotoRowCol Macro

The mGotoRowCol macro (see Example 4) locates the cursor at a desired row and column on the screen. mGotoRowCol can be called and passed immediate values, memory operands, or register values, as long as they are 8-bit integers:

```
mGotoRowCol   10,20          ; immediate values
mGotoRowCol   row,col        ; memory operands
mGotoRowCol   ch,cl          ; pass registers
```

Example 4. The mGotoRowCol Macro.

```
mGotoRowCol macro   row:REQ, column:REQ
        push   ax                    ;; do not pass AH, DH, DL, or BX
        push   bx
        push   dx
        mov    bx,0                   ;; choose page 0
        mov    ah,2                   ;; locate cursor
        mov    dh,row
        mov    dl,column
        int    10h                    ;; call the BIOS
        pop    dx
        pop    bx
```

```
        pop    ax
    endm
```

Check for Conflicts. Be sure that register values passed as arguments do not conflict with registers used inside the macro. If we call **mGotoRowCol** using AH and AL, for instance, the macro does not work properly. To see why, inspect the expanded code after the parameters have been substituted:

```
push   ax
push   bx
push   dx
mov    bx,0            ;; choose page 0
mov    ah,2            ;; locate cursor
mov    dh,ah           ;; too late: AH changed
mov    dl,al
int    10h             ;; call the BIOS
pop    dx
pop    bx
pop    ax
```

Assuming that AH is passed as the row value and AL is the column, line 5 replaces AH before we have a chance to copy the value in AH to DH on line 6. Therefore, the macro will incorrectly locate the cursor on screen row 2.

8.2.5   Macros That Allocate Storage

Macros can be invoked in the data segment to allocate storage for variables. In the next example, each table entry created by the **mAlloc** macro consists of four spaces and four bytes of zeros:

```
mAlloc macro varname,numbytes
  varname db numbytes dup('    ',0,0,0,0)
endm


.data
mAlloc value1,20          ; allocate 20 entries
mAlloc value2,50          ; allocate 50 entries
```

Expanded Code:

```
value1 db 20 dup('    ',0,0,0,0)
value2 db 50 dup('    ',0,0,0,0)
```

Varname and **numbytes** are parameters that take on the arguments that are passed when the macro is called. The former is assembled as the variable's name, and the latter determines the number of bytes to be allocated with the DUP operator.

8.2.6 LOCAL Directive

Macros often use labels as reference points for jump and loop instructions. A problem occurs if a macro containing a label is invoked more than once in the same program. The label name is duplicated, causing a syntax error. The solution to this problem is to use the LOCAL directive, which lets the assembler create a unique label name each time a macro is used:

```
LOCAL labelname
```

For example, the **mRepeat** macro displays any character a requested number of times. Label L1 is local to the macro:

```
mRepeat macro char, count
    local L1
    mov   cx,count
L1: mov   ah,2
    mov   dl,char
    int   21h
    loop  L1
endm
```

If we invoke mRepeat more than once, the assembler creates a unique label each time, as in Example 5. The labels are automatically numbered sequentially, starting at 0000h.

Example 5. Invoking the mRepeat Macro.

```
        mRepeat 'A',10
        mov cx,10
??0000: mov ah,2
        mov dl,'A'
        int 21h
        loop ??0000

        mRepeat '*',20
        mov cx,20
??0001: mov ah,2
        mov dl,'*'
        int 21h
        loop ??0001
```

8.3   SPECIAL MACRO TECHNIQUES

8.3.1   Nested Macros

A good way to write a complex macro is to construct it from existing macros. The enclosing macro is then called a *nested* macro. Let's create a macro called mDisplayRowCol that displays a string at a requested row and column. It calls the mGotoRowCol and mDisplayStr macros by taking its own parameters and passing them as arguments to the other two macros:

```
mDisplayRowCol macro row,col,string
  mGotoRowCol  row,col        ; call mGotoRowCol macro
  mDisplayStr string          ; call DISPLAY macro
endm
```

The following statements call mDisplayRowCol, passing it row 10, column 15, and the string called **greeting.** The corresponding statements generated by the macro appear in Example 6. The listing file automatically shows the *nesting level* of all statements generated by macros. A nesting level of 2, for example, indicates that the statements are in a macro that has been invoked by another macro.

```
.data
greeting  db "Hello from row 10, column 15.$"
.code
mDisplayRowCol 10, 15, greeting
```

Example 6. Invoking a Nested Macro.

Nesting Level	Statements
	mDisplayRowCol 10, 15, greeting
	mGotoRowCol 10, 15
2	push ax
2	push bx
2	push dx
2	mov bx,0
2	mov ah,2
2	mov dh,10
2	mov dl,15
2	int 10h
2	pop dx
2	pop bx
2	pop ax
	mDisplayStr greeting
2	push ax

```
2                    push  dx
2                    mov   ah,9
2                    mov   dx,offset greeting
2                    int   21h
2                    pop   dx
2                    pop   ax
```

8.3.2   Macros Calling Procedures

We have already mentioned the primary disadvantage to using macros. They increase the amount of code generated by the assembler because each macro call generates a *separate copy* of the macro. From the point of view of program size, procedures are more economical. On the other hand, procedure calls can be awkward when we have to pass parameters in registers. A good compromise is to use macros as a "wrapper" around procedure calls. A macro can place each procedure argument in its correct register before calling the procedure. We will use this technique to call the **Writeint** procedure, which writes an unsigned integer to standard output.

The mWriteint Macro. Let's look at a macro called **mWriteint** in Example 7 that calls the Writeint procedure. Two parameters, **value** and **radix**, are loaded into AX and BX. We save and restore the two registers before and after the procedure call to minimize its impact on the program's surrounding code. Arguments passed to the macro can be registers, variables, or constants, making it easier to call the procedure:

```
.data
wordval  dw  1000h

.code
mWriteint  2000h,10          ; immediate value in decimal
mWriteint  dx,16             ; register value in hexadecimal
mWriteint  wordval,2         ; memory operand in binary
```

Example 7. The mWriteint Macro.

```
mWriteint macro  value, radix
   push  ax                  ;; save registers
   push  bx
   mov   ax,value            ;; value to be displayed
   mov   bx,radix            ;; select radix
   call  Writeint
   pop   bx
   pop   ax
endm
```

8.3.3 Conditional-Assembly Directives

A number of different conditional-assembly directives can be used in conjunction with macros to make them more flexible. The general syntax for conditional-assembly directives is:

```
IF condition
    statements
[ELSE
    statements]
ENDIF
```

Table 2 lists the conditional assembly directives. When we say that the directive *permits assembly,* we mean that any subsequent statements will be assembled until the ENDIF directive is encountered.

Checking for Missing Arguments. A macro can have one or more optional arguments. It should check to see if any of these arguments are blank. If a blank argument value is actually used by the macro, invalid instructions can result. For example, if we invoke the **mWriteint** macro without passing the *radix* argument, the macro assembles with an invalid instruction when moving the radix to BX:

```
Macro call:  mWriteint  1000h
```

Generated Statements:

```
mWriteint 1000h
    push  ax        ;; save AX, BX
    push  bx
    mov   ax,1000h  ;; value to be displayed
    mov   bx,           ;; error: missing operand
    (etc.)
```

The IFB (*if blank*) directive returns *true* if a macro argument is blank, and IFNB (*if not blank*) returns *true* if a macro argument is not blank. For example, the following macro, called **mymac,** checks to see if a value for **parm1** was passed when the macro was called. If mymac is called with no arguments, the EXITM directive prevents any code from being generated:

```
mymac macro  parm1
    ifb <parm1>    ; no argument supplied?
      exitm        ;   then exit the macro
    endif          ;   and generate no code
    .
    .
    .code
```

```
mymac                              ; no code generated
mymac val1                         ; code is generated
```

Default Arguments. Another way you can handle the problem of missing macro arguments is to supply default values for optional arguments. For example, in the mWriteint macro, we could make the default radix equal to decimal, a value of 10. The default value must be enclosed in angle brackets (< >) in the macro's definition:

```
mWriteint macro value, radix:=<10>
```

Table 2. Conditional Assembly Directives.

IF *expr*	Permits assembly if the value of *expression* is true (nonzero). Possible relational operators are LT, GT, EQ, NE, LE, and GE.
IFE *expr*	Permits assembly if the value of *expression* is false (zero).
IF1	Permits assembly if this is currently the assembler's first pass through the source file *(Microsoft Assembler only)*.
IF2	Permits assembly if this is currently the assembler's second pass through the source file *(Microsoft Assembler only)*.
IFB *<argument>*	Permits assembly if *argument* is blank. The argument name must be enclosed in angle brackets (<>).
IFNB *<argument>*	Permits assembly if *argument* is not blank. The argument name must be enclosed in angle brackets (<>).
IFIDN *<arg1>,<arg2>*	Permits assembly if the two arguments are equal. The comparison may be made case-insensitive if the IFIDNI directive is used.
IFDIF *<arg1>,<arg2>*	Permits assembly if the two arguments are unequal. The comparison is case-insensitive if the IFDIFI directive is used.
IFDEF *name*	Permits assembly if *name* has been defined.
IFNDEF *name*	Permits assembly if *name* has not been defined.
ENDIF	Ends a block that was begun using one of the conditional-assembly directives.
ELSE	Assembles all statements up to ENDIF if the condition specified by a previous IF directive is false.

8.3.4   EXITM Directive

The EXITM (*exit macro*) directive tells the assembler to exit from the current macro expansion. This reduces the amount of code in the compiled program if unnecessary instructions are eliminated. For example, let's create a variation of the mGotoRowCol macro and call it mGotoConstXY. This version, shown in Example 8, checks the ranges of the two constant arguments. The IF condition compares **xval** to zero using LT (*less than*) and exits if the result is true. The same is done for **yval**.

A conditional directive such as IF must be followed by an expression that can be evaluated to either true or false at assembly time. This does not work for values in registers or memory variables, because they are only known at runtime. The ENDIF directive must also be used to mark the end of each IF block.

Example 8. The mGotoConstXY Macro.

```
mGotoConstXY macro   xval,yval
     if xval LT 0                ;; xval < 0?
        exitm                    ;; if so, exit
     endif
     if yval LT 0                ;; yval < 0?
        exitm                    ;; if so, exit
     endif
     mov   bx,0                  ;; choose video page 0
     mov   ah,2                  ;; locate cursor
     mov   dh,yval
     mov   dl,xval
     int   10h
  endm
```

Displaying Messages During Assembly. The **%out** directive lets you write a message to standard output during assembly. This could be used in the mGotoConstXY macro to display a message whenever an invalid argument is passed to the macro (see Example 9).

Example 9. mGotoConstXY Macro, Revised.

```
mGotoConstXY macro   xval,yval
   if xval LT 0                  ;; xval < 0?
      %out First argument (xval) passed to mGotoConstXY is invalid.
      %out (value must be >= 0)
   endif
```

```
            if yval LT 0      ;; yval < 0?
               %out Second argument (yval) passed to mGotoConstXY is invalid.
               %out (value must be >= 0)
            endif
            mov   bx,0                    ;; choose video page 0
            mov   ah,2                    ;; locate cursor
            mov   dh,yval                 ;; row
            mov   dl,xval                 ;; column
            int   10h                     ;; call the BIOS
         endm
```

If we call mGotoConstXY with the arguments –1 and –2, the following messages display during assembly:

```
First argument (-1) passed to mGotoConstXY is invalid.
(value must be >= 0)


Second argument (-2) passed to mGotoConstXY is invalid.
(value must be >= 0)
```

Clearly, range checking of constant macro arguments is a good way to improve the reliability of macros, and diagnostic messages are a great help to someone learning to use a macro.

8.3.5   Macro Operators

There are five macro operators that serve to make macros more flexible. One, the macro comment (;;) is not an operator in the usual sense—it suppresses printing of comment lines when a macro is expanded:

```
&           Substitute operator
<>          Literal-text operator
!           Literal-character operator
%           Expression operator
;;          Macro comment
```

Substitute (&) Operator. The *substitute* (&) operator lets you replace a parameter with the value that was passed as an argument. The syntax is:

```
&parameter
```

This operator is particularly useful when text passed as an argument must be inserted into a string or instruction within the macro. For example, the **mDOSmsg** macro listed here lets you create storage for the string passed as an argument:

```
mDOSmsg macro  num,string
  msg&num  db "DOS error: &string",0
endm
```

Table 3 shows sample calls to **mDOSmsg** along with the code expanded by the macro. Notice that strings passed to mDOSmsg are enclosed in angle brackets (<>). They cause the entire string to be passed as a single argument.

Expression Operator (%). The expression operator (%) permits the calculated result of an expression to be passed as a macro argument. The (%) operator tells the assembler that the value of the expression, not the expression itself, is to be passed to the macro. For example, the following macro called **mDirectVideo** writes a string directly to the video buffer:

```
mDirectVideo macro ofset,string
  mov   ax,videoseg          ;; address of video buffer
  mov   es,ax
  mov   di,ofset             ;; offset into video buffer
  (etc.)
endm
```

When calling mDirectVideo, the first argument is the offset into the video buffer for the first character that we want to display. The second argument is the name of the string. The offset can be a single value such as 320, or it can be the result of an expression involving constant symbols:

```
row = 10
col = 40
.code
mDirectVideo %((row*160)+(col*2)),string1
mDirectVideo 320,string2
```

Literal-Text Operator (<>). The literal-text operator ties together a string of characters. It prevents the assembler from interpreting members of the list as separate arguments. (This operator is also required around the operands in conditional-assembly directives such as IFB and IFIDN.) This is particularly important when the string contains special characters (",",

Table 3. Expansions of the mDOSmsg Macro.

Called As	Expanded Code
mDOSmsg 1,<Invalid function>	msg1 db "DOS error: Invalid function",0
mDOSmsg 2,<File not found>	msg2 db "DOS error: File not found",0
mDOSmsg 3,<Path not found>	msg3 db "DOS error: Path not found",0

"%", "&", and ";") that would otherwise be interpreted as macro operators. Let's create a macro named **mMessage** as an example:

```
mMessage macro text
  db "&text",0
endm
```

The following macro call

```
mMessage <Efficiency is 50%, & falling;>
```

is assembled as

```
db "Efficiency is 50%, & falling;",0
```

Literal-Character Operator (!). The literal-character operator was invented for much the same purpose as the literal-text operator: It forces the assembler to treat a special character as just a character instead of an operator. Using the mMessage macro again as an example, we might want to pass a string containing the ">" character:

```
mMessage <Efficiency is !> 50 percent>
```

This will be assembled as

```
db "Efficiency is > 50 percent"
```

8.4   A SIMPLE MACRO LIBRARY

This section introduces a few general-purpose macros that illustrate some of the special macro operators.

8.4.1   mWriteliteral (Write Literal)

The **mWriteliteral** in Example 10 writes a literal string to standard output. Notice that it contains a .data directive and a variable called string. This is necessary when using simplified segment directives because the assembler always calculates offsets of variables from the data segment. The variable created by this macro is stored in the data segment. mWriteliteral provides a convenient way to display messages on the console because the programmer doesn't have to declare a string variable. The following are sample calls:

```
mWriteliteral  <"Macro Testing Program",0dh,0ah>
mWriteliteral  "Please enter your name: "
```

If the literal string argument contains commas, surround it with bracket delimiters < >, as we have here.

Example 10. The mWriteliteral Macro.

```
mWriteliteral macro text
    local string
    push   ax
    push   dx
    mov    dx,offset string
    call   Writestring
    pop    dx
    pop    ax
.data                          ;; local data
string  db  text,0             ;; define the string
.code
endm
```

8.4.2   mCondCall (Conditional Call)

A clever use for macros is to enhance the existing Intel instruction set—this can make programs easier to write. The following mCondCall (*conditional call*) macro makes it possible to call a procedure based on the flags, using a single instruction:

```
mCondCall macro cond,procname
        local   L1,L2
        j&cond  L1
        jmp     L2
    L1: call    procname
    L2: exitm
endm
```

The mCondCall macro can be based on any flag condition. For example, we might wish to call the DOS_error procedure when the Carry flag is set. The macro allows us to write the following:

```
mCondCall  c,DOS_error
```

Or we may wish to call a procedure called Lower if value1 is less than or equal to AX:

Original	**Generated Code**
`cmp value1,ax`	`cmp  value1,ax`
`mCondCall le,lower`	`jle  ??0002`
	`jmp  ??0003`
	`??0002: call lower`
	`??0003: exitm`

We can use the same macro to call a procedure called NotEqual if AX is not equal to BX:

```
cmp       ax,bx
mCondCall  ne,NotEqual
```

After comparing two strings, we can call the Exchange procedure:

```
call      compare          ; compare source to dest
mCondCall a,Exchange        ; call Exchange if source > dest
```

8.4.3　mCompJmp (Compare and Jump)

The **mCompJmp** (*compare and jump*) macro compares two operands and jumps to a label based on the flags:

```
mCompJmp macro dest, flag, source, label
   cmp    dest,source
   j&flag label
endm
```

Sample calls:

```
mCompJmp ax,le,bx,label1    ; if AX <= BX, jump to label1
mCompJmp cx,e,count,exit    ; if CX = count, jump to exit
```

8.4.4　mMult16 (Memory Multiply/16)

As we know, the MUL instruction imposes certain limitations: AL or AX is automatically the implied destination operand, and immediate source operands are not allowed. The **mMult16** macro shown in Example 11 allows you to multiply any 16-bit operand by a register, memory operand, or immediate operand of the same size.

Example 11. The mMult16 Macro.

```
mMult16 macro  dest,source
    push  ax                ;; save registers
    push  bx
    mov   ax,dest           ;; AX = destination
    mov   bx,source         ;; BX = source
    mul   bx                ;; DX:AX = product
    mov   dest,ax
    pop   bx
    pop   ax
endm
```

The mMult16 macro multiplies **dest** by **source**, placing the low 16 bits of the result in **dest**. If the result is larger than 16 bits, the Carry flag is set, and the high part of the result is in DX. The following sample demonstrates the macro's flexibility in multiplying operands of various types:

```
.data
value1  dw 1234h, 0
value2  dw 10h


.code
mov   cx,value1
mMult16 cx,2               ; CX = 2468h
mMult16 value2,5           ; value2 = 50h
mov   value2,10h
mMult16 value1,value2      ; value1 = 2340h, CF = 1
jnc   L1
mov   value1+2,dx          ; store high word of product
```

You may have noticed a small limitation of this macro: AX cannot be used as the source operand because its value is replaced by the **dest** parameter.

8.4.5   mMOVE (Memory to Memory Move)

The Intel instruction set does not include a memory-to-memory move instruction, other than MOVS. The **mMove** macro accomplishes this—the TYPE operator determines if the operands are 8 or 16 bits, and then **source** is moved to **dest** via AL or AX (see Example 12). Here are sample statements that invoke mMove:

```
mMove word2,word1         ; 16-bit move
mMove byte2,byte1         ; 8-bit move
```

Because the TYPE operator is used in this macro, a single-pass assembler generates an error message unless the .data directive appears in the source file before the macro definition. This is because the assembler needs to locate variables before it can evaluate their type. If you encounter errors when using this Macro, just place the data segment before the code segment.

Example 12. The mMove Macro.

```
mMove macro  dest,source
   push ax
   if (type dest) EQ 1       ; 8-bit type?
     mov   al,source         ; yes: use AL
     mov   dest,al
   else
     if (type dest) EQ 2     ; 16-bit type?
```

```
        mov   ax,source              ; yes: use AX
        mov   dest,ax
      endif
    endif
    pop  ax
endm
```

8.4.6   mLongLoop (Long Loop)

The Intel instruction set limits the span of conditional jump instructions—including LOOP—to 127 bytes forward or 128 bytes backward. Particularly when your program has a number of macro calls within the area spanned by a conditional jump or loop, the jump or loop may be out of range. For example, suppose mWritestring, mReadstring, and mWriteint are macros, and we invoke them in the following loop:

```
    mov cx,10                   ; loop counter
L1: mWritestring prompt         ; display a prompt
    mReadstring buffer          ; input a string
    mWriteint 1000h,10          ; display 1000h in decimal
    loop  L1                    ; loop is out of range
```

A syntax error results because more than 127 bytes of code are generated by the macros in the loop. The target of the LOOP instruction is out of range.

The **mLongLoop** (long loop) macro allows you to loop to any label in the current segment. It does this by looping to a JMP instruction that in turn jumps to the destination. JMP, unlike LOOP, can reach any label in the current code segment:

```
mLongLoop macro dest
    local A1,A2
    loop  A1                    ;; loop to short label
    jmp   A2
A1: jmp   dest                  ;; jump to destination
A2:
endm
```

This macro uses the LOOP instruction in an unusual way: It jumps *forward* to the label **A1**. At this location, the JMP instruction takes us back to **dest**. When CX = 0, the LOOP falls through and jumps to A2, which is the location of the next instruction. A small amount of execution overhead is added, but we gain the flexibility of having a larger loop. The following shows the new macro in place of the LOOP instruction in our original example:

```
    mov cx,10                   ; loop counter
L1: mWritestring  prompt        ; display a prompt
    mReadstring  buffer         ; input a string
```

```
        mWriteint  1000h,10          ; display 1000h in decimal
        mLongLoop  L1                ; use mLongLoop macro
```

8.5 ADVANCED MACROS AND DIRECTIVES

8.5.1   REPT Directive

One or more statements can be repeated using the REPT, IRP, and IRPC directives. This makes it possible for a single macro to create a large data structure. The REPT directive repeats a block of statements based on a counter. The syntax is:

```
REPT expression
   statement-list
ENDM
```

Expression determines the number of repetitions and evaluates to a 16-bit unsigned number. Suppose one wanted to use REPT to define space for a table containing 100 student records:

```
index label byte             ; start of table
rept 100                     ; begin REPT loop
    db  7 dup(?)             ; student number
    db  20 dup(' ')          ; last name
    dw  ?                    ; status
endm
```

One could use the same technique to create a macro that shifts an operand left a specific number of times. In the following example, **count** determines the number of SHL instructions generated by the assembler:

```
mSHL macro dest,count
  rept count
    shl dest,1
  endm
endm
```

This is a nested macro definition. We can see the macro invoked two different ways here, followed by the statements generated by the assembler:

```
mshl ax,1
mshl bx,4
```

Expanded code:

```
shl ax,1
shl bx,1
```

```
shl bx,1
shl bx,1
shl bx,1
```

8.5.2   Linked List Example

It's possible to combine a structure declaration with the REPT directive to instruct the assembler to create a linked list data structure. Each node of a linked list contains a data area and a link area. In the data area, one or more variables can hold data that is unique to each node. In the link area, a pointer variable contains the address of the next node in the list.

In Example 13 we show a program that creates and displays a linked list. First, the program defines the node structure:

```
ListNode struc
  NodeData dw ?                    ; the node's data
  NextPtr  dw ?                    ; pointer to next node
ends
```

Next, a REPT loop creates multiple instances of ListNode objects. For testing purposes, the NodeData field contains an integer sequentially numbered from 1 to 50. Inside the REPT loop, we increment a counter and insert values into the ListNode fields:

```
.data
COUNT = 0
NUMBER_OF_NODES = 50

LinkedList label word
rept NUMBER_OF_NODES
  COUNT = COUNT + 1
  ListNode < COUNT, ($ + 2) >
endm
```

The expression "$ + 2" tells the assembler to add 2 to the current location counter and pass that value to the NextPtr field in the ListNode structure. The NextPtr field contains the offset of the node that follows.

Example 13. Creating a Linked List.

```
title Creating a Linked List      (list.asm)

.model small
.stack 100h
```

```
ListNode struc
  NodeData dw ?
  NextPtr  dw ?
ends

.data
COUNT = 0
NUMBER_OF_NODES = 50

LinkedList label word
rept NUMBER_OF_NODES
  COUNT = COUNT + 1
  ListNode < COUNT, ($ + 2) >
endm

.code
extrn Writeint:proc, Crlf:proc

main proc
    mov  ax,@data
    mov  ds,ax
    mov  si,offset LinkedList
    mov  cx,NUMBER_OF_NODES

L1: mov  ax,[si].NodeData
    mov  bx,10
    call Writeint              ; display node contents
    call Crlf
    mov  si,[si].NextPtr       ; pointer to next node
    Loop L1

    mov  ax,4C00h
    int  21h
main endp
end main
```

8.5.3   IRP Directive

The IRP directive creates a repeat block where each repetition contains a different value. The syntax is:

```
IRP parameter,<argument [,argument] ...>
```

```
        statements
    ENDM
```

The block is repeated once for each argument. As it repeats, the current argument value is substituted for the parameter. This directive is useful for initializing a table or block of data where some of the values are varied. Arguments can be symbol names, strings, or numeric constants. Using the following macro declaration, you can see the resulting data declarations generated by the assembler:

```
irp parm,<10,20,30,40>
  dw  parm, parm * 2, parm * 3, parm * 4
endm


; Generated:
dw  10, 10 * 2, 10 * 3, 10 * 4
dw  20, 20 * 2, 20 * 3, 20 * 4
dw  30, 30 * 2, 30 * 3, 30 * 4
dw  40, 40 * 2, 40 * 3, 40 * 4
```

IRP can initialize a table of procedure offsets. This may prove useful if you want to code a multiway branch based on the value of an index. For example:

```
mov  bx,indexvalue        ; choose the table entry
call proctable[bx]        ; indirect call
```

Four procedure names are passed as arguments in the following IRP example. Each is inserted where the **procname** appears, resulting in a table containing the procedures's offsets:

```
proctable label word
irp  procname,<movup,movdn,movlft,movrt>
   dw procname
endm
```

The following statements are generated by the assembler:

```
proctable label word
dw  movup
dw  movdn
dw  movlft
dw  movrt
```

8.5.4   Extended Jump Macro

Prior to the 80386 processor, programs that used macros invariably ran into problems with conditional jumps because of their limited range of +/– 127 bytes. As we did with the mLongLoop macro earlier in this chapter, we can also create extended jump macros that allow conditional jumps to labels outside the usual range. For example:

```
jxe macro dest
    local  L1,L2
    je L1                    ; condition true?
    jmp short L2             ; no: exit
L1: jmp dest                 ; yes: jump to destination
L2:
endm
```

This somewhat cryptic-looking code implements an extended JE (*jump equal*) instruction. With it, we can code an instruction such as the following, where **loopTop** is anywhere in the current segment:

```
jxe  loopTop
```

It would be rather tedious to code a separate macro for each of the conditional jump instructions. This is where IRP does its magic and creates conditional jump macros "on the fly:"

```
irp cond,<a,ae,b,be,e,ne,z,nz,g,ge,l,le,c,nc,o,no,p,np,s,ns>
   jx&cond macro dest
     local  L1,L2
     j&cond L1               ;; condition true?
     jmp short L2            ;; no: exit
   L1: jmp dest              ;; yes: jump to destination
   L2:
   endm
endm
```

For brevity's sake, synonyms have been left out of the list (for example, jnb = jae). The following statements invoke the **jx&*cond*** macro, generating what appear to be new assembler instructions:

```
jxa   L1             ; jump extended if above
jxae  L3             ; jump extended if above or equal
jxz   L1             ; jump extended if zero
jxne  L4             ; jump extended if not equal
jxg   L2             ; jump extended if greater
jxo   L1             ; jump extended on overflow
```

8.5.5   Generic Shift/Rotate Macro

Earlier, we used the REPT directive to form a macro called mSHL that shifted an operand left a specified number of times. If we want the same feature for all the other shift and rotate instructions, we have to create eight different macros. But there is a much better way: IRP can be combined with a macro definition to create variations on the macro. The following macro generates eight separate macros, named mSHL, mSHR, mSAL, mSAR, mROL, mROR, mRCL, and mRCR:

```
irp styp,<shl,shr,sal,sar,rol,ror,rcl,rcr>
  m&styp macro dest,count
    push cx
    mov  cl,count
    styp dest,cl
    pop  cx
  endm
endm
```

The **dest** parameter can be any 8, 16, or 32-bit register or variable, as long it is not CL, CX, or ECX. The **count** parameter can be an immediate value, register, or memory operand, as long its size is 8 bits.

The substitute operator (&) allows the substitution of an argument string in the macro definition. At the outermost level, IRP repeats the macro definition eight times, using a different value for **styp** each time. The macro **m&styp** changes its name each time the IRP loop repeats. Oddly enough, none of the eight macros appear in the program listing—we see their effects only when code is generated. Sample calls are as follows:

```
mSHL  ax,3              ; shift AX left 3 times
mROL  mem16,bl          ; rotate left, use BL as counter
mSHR  bx,mem8           ; shift BX right, using variable as counter
```

The instructions generated by the first two macro calls are shown here:

```
mSHL  ax,3
+     push cx
+     mov  cl,3
+     SHL  ax,cl
+     pop  cx
mROL  mem16,bl
+     push cx
+     mov  cl,bl
+     ROL  mem16,cl
+     pop  cx
```

Notice that incorrect output results if CX is passed as the **dest** argument:

```
mSHL  cx,3
+     push cx
+     mov  cl,3                    ; error: dest has changed
+     SHL  cx,cl
+     pop  cx
```

IRPC Directive. The IRPC directive is essentially the same as IRP, except that the number of characters in the argument string determines the number of repetitions. The syntax is:

```
IRPC parameter,string
  statements
ENDM
```

String must be enclosed in angle brackets (<>) if it contains spaces, commas, or any other special characters. The following example generates five variables (**value_A**, **value_B**, etc.) using the characters in the string ABCDE as arguments:

```
irpc  parm,ABCDE
  value_&parm db '&parm'
endm
```

Generated Statements:

```
value_A  db 'A'
value_B  db 'B'
value_C  db 'C'
value_D  db 'D'
value_E  db 'E'
```

There are many other clever ways to use the REPT, IRP, and IRPC directives, particularly when they are combined with macro operators. Macros represent the ultimate extension of the assembler instruction set—you are limited only by your imagination.

8.5.6   Additional Tips

Store Macros in an Include File. Once you collect a wide assortment of macros, it becomes inconvenient to manually copy them into each new program. Instead, create a file containing only macros and use the INCLUDE directive to copy them at assembly time. Only the macros actually used become part of your final program. If you are using a two-pass assembler, such as the Microsoft Assembler, it is a good idea to surround the INCLUDE with the IF1 and ENDIF directives, telling the assembler to include the macros only on its first pass:

```
 if1                          ; if this is the first pass,
   include macros.inc         ; include macro listings
 endif
```

If the include filename does not contain a full path, the assembler will look for it in the current directory. You can optionally specify a complete path or a relative path, such as:

```
 include ..\..\library\macros.inc
```

Example 14 lists all macros in a source code file supplied on the disk with this book. Many of these macros were already introduced in this chapter.

Example 14. The Macro Include Library.

```
 ; MACROS.INC - Macro Library for Irvine: Assembly Language for Intel-
 ; Based Computers, 3rd Edition.
 ; Use the INCLUDE directive to include this file in a source program
 ; that invokes the macros. The program must also link to IRVINE.LIB.
 ; All macros in this file, listed with their parameter names:

 ;mCondCall macro cond,procname
 ;mCompJmp macro dest,flag,source,label
 ;mDisplaystr macro string
 ;mDisplaystr_at macro row,col,string
 ;mExitdos macro ecode
 ;mGetyesno macro prompt
 ;mGotoXY macro row, column
 ;jx&cond macro dest
 ;mLongloop macro dest
 ;mMove macro dest,source
 ;mMult16 macro dest,source
 ;mPrompt_Readint macro row,col,prompt,dest
 ;mPrompt_Readstring macro row,col,prompt,dest,max
 ;mPutchar macro char
 ;mRepeatchar macro char,count
 ;mStartup macro
 ;m&styp macro dest,count (<shl,shr,sal,sar,rol,
 ;   ror,rcl,rcr>)
 ;mWriteint macro value, radix
 ;mWriteliteral macro text
 ;-----------------------------------------------
 ; Simulations of 80286 instructions:
 ;mENTER
```

```
;mLEAVE
;mPUSHA
;mPOPA
;mSET&cond
;-------------------------------------------------
extrn Crlf:proc, Readint:proc, Readstring:proc, \
     Writeint:proc, Writestring:proc

; If <cond> flag is true, call the
; procedure <procname>.

mCondCall macro cond,procname
     local L1,L2
     j&cond short L1
     jmp short L2
 L1: call procname
 L2: exitm
endm

; Compare <dest> to <source>; if <flag> is
; true, jump to <label>.

mCompJmp macro dest,flag,source,label
    cmp     dest,source
    j&flag  short label
endm

; Display a null-terminated string.

mDisplaystr macro string
    push ax
    push dx
    mov  dx,offset string
    call Writestring
    pop  dx
    pop  ax
endm

; Display a string at row,col on console

mDisplaystr_at macro row,col,string
   mGotoXY  row,col                 ;; call mGotoXY macro
```

```
      mDisplaystr string              ;; call mDisplaystr macro
endm

; Exit to DOS, return a status code

mExitdos macro ecode
    mov  ah,4Ch
    mov  al,ecode
    int  21h
endm

; Show a prompt, wait for a keystroke.
; Set the Zero flag if either "y" or "Y"
; was pressed.

mGetyesno macro prompt
    mWriteliteral prompt             ;; display a prompt
    mov  ah,1
    int  21h
    and  al,11011111b                ;; convert to uppercase
    cmp  al,'Y'                      ;; set ZF if Y pressed
endm

; Locate the cursor at <row>, <column> on
; video page 0.

mGotoXY macro  row, column
    push  ax
    push  bx
    push  dx
    mov   bx,0                       ;; choose page 0
    mov   ah,2                       ;; locate cursor
    mov   dh,row
    mov   dl,column
    int   10h                        ;; call the BIOS
    pop   dx
    pop   bx
    pop   ax
endm

; Jump eXtended (JX_): Conditionally jump
; to a NEAR label (anywhere in the segment).
```

```
irp cond,<a,na,b,nb,e,ne,z,nz,g,ng,l,nl,c,nc,o,no,p,np>
  jx&cond macro dest
    local  L1,L2
    j&cond short L1            ;; condition true?
    jmp short L2              ;; no:  exit
  L1: jmp near dest           ;; yes: jump to destination
  L2:
  endm
endm


; Loop to a near label.


mLongloop macro dest
    local A1,A2
    loop  A1                  ;; loop to short label
    jmp   short A2
A1: jmp   dest                ;; jump to destination
A2:
endm


; Move a word or byte from memory to memory.
; The TYPE operator returns 0 for registers.


mMove macro  dest,source
    push ax
    mov  bx,type dest
    if (type dest) EQ 1       ;; 8-bit type?
      mov   al,source         ;; yes: use AL
      mov   dest,al
    else
      if (type dest) EQ 2     ;; 16-bit type?
        mov   ax,source       ;; yes: use AX
        mov   dest,ax
      endif
    endif
    pop  ax
endm


; Multiply two 16-bit memory operands, returning
; the 32-bit product in DX:AX. Limitation: The
; <source> argument cannot be AX.
```

```
mMult16 macro  dest,source
    push  ax
    mov   ax,dest                  ;; AX = destination
    mov   dx,source                ;; DX = source
    mul   dx                       ;; DX:AX = product
    pop   ax
endm
```

```
; Display a literal prompt at <row>,<col>. Then
; input an integer and store it at <dest>.
```

```
mPrompt_Readint macro row,col,prompt,dest
    mGotoXY row,col
    mWriteliteral prompt
    call Readint                   ;; read integer into AX
    mov  dest,ax
endm
```

```
; Display a literal prompt at <row>,<col>. Then input a
; null-terminated string and store it at <dest>. Maximum
; characters = <max>.
```

```
mPrompt_Readstring macro row,col,prompt,dest,max
    mGotoXY row,col
    mWriteliteral prompt
    push  cx
    push  dx
    mov   dx,offset dest
    mov   cx,max
    call  Readstring
    pop   dx
    pop   cx
endm
```

```
; Output a character to the console.
```

```
mPutchar macro char
    mov   ah,2
    mov   dl,char
    int   21h
endm
```

```
; Output a character <count> times.

mRepeatchar macro char,count
    local L1
    mov  cx,count
    mov  ah,2
    mov  dl,char
L1: int  21h
    loop L1
endm


; Set DS and ES to the data segment location.

mStartup macro
    mov   ax,@data              ;; initialize DS, ES
    mov   ds,ax                 ;; to the data segment
    mov   es,ax
endm


; The following macro generates eight macros with
; the names mSHL, mSHR, mSAL, mSAR, mROL, mROR,
; mRCL, AND mRCR. The shift count may be any value
; between 0-255, as an immediate operand, register,
; or memory operand.

irp styp,<shl,shr,sal,sar,rol,ror,rcl,rcr>
  m&styp macro dest,count
    push cx
    mov  cl,count
    styp dest,cl
    pop  cx
  endm
endm


; Write an integer to standard output.

mWriteint macro  value, radix
    push  ax                    ;; save AX, BX
    push  bx
    mov   ax,value              ;; value to be displayed
    mov   bx,radix              ;; radix to be used
```

```
        call  Writeint          ;; display AX on console
        pop   bx
        pop   ax
endm


; The mWriteliteral macro writes a string literal
; to standard output. <text> is a string surrounded
; by quotes or string delimiters.

mWriteliteral macro text
    local string
    push   ax
    push   dx
    mov    dx,offset string
    call   Writestring
    pop    dx
    pop    ax
.data                              ;; local data
string  db  text,0                 ;; define the string
.code
endm


;=================================================
; MACROS THAT SIMULATE 80286 INSTRUCTIONS ON THE 8086/8088
;=================================================


; Create a stack frame for a procedure that contains
; <localBytes> bytes of stack space reserved for its
; local variables.

mENTER macro localBytes
    push  bp
    mov   bp,sp
    sub   sp,localBytes
endm


; Restore the stack pointer to the point that it
; was before the mENTER macro created space for
; local procedure variables.

mLEAVE macro
    mov   sp,bp
```

```
        pop    bp
endm

; Push the general-purpose and index registers on
; the stack. Simulates the PUSHA instruction from
; the 80286, except that SP is not saved.

mPUSHA macro
        push   ax
        push   cx
        push   dx
        push   bx
        push   bp
        push   si
        push   di
endm

; Pop the general-purpose, index, and stack registers
; from the stack. Simulates the POPA instruction from
; the 80286. (Note that POPA just discards the value
; of SP that was pushed on the stack by the PUSHA
; instruction.)

mPOPA macro
        pop    di
        pop    si
        pop    bp
        pop    bx
        pop    dx
        pop    cx
        pop    ax
endm

; The mSET&cond macro sets the byte specified in the
; operand to 1 if <cond> is true. Or, it sets the byte
; to 0 if <cond> is false. Synonyms are omitted.

irp cond,<E,NE,A,AE,B,BE,Z,NZ,G,GE,L,LE,S,NS,C,NC,O,NO,PE,PO>
  mSET&cond macro byteVal
     Local L1, L2
     j&cond short L1
     mov    byteVal,0
```

```
        jmp   short L2
    L1: mov   byteVal,1
    L2:
      endm
    endm
```

Listing Directives. Table 4 contains a list of assembler directives that control the content of source listing files. Many of them relate to macros and conditional directives. The .SALL directive is useful for suppressing macro expansions so they do not clutter up your program listings. Place the .SALL directive anywhere in the file before the macros are called. To reenable macro expansions, use .LALL:

Debugging. When you debug a program using macros in source mode, both CodeView and Turbo Debugger suppress macro expansions. To view and trace through the expanded code, change the View option to *mixed* or *assembly.*

8.6   REVIEW QUESTIONS

1. Assume that the following structure has been defined:

    ```
    rentalStruc struc
      invoiceNum                db  5 dup(' ')
      dailyPrice                dw  ?
      daysRented                dw  ?
    rentalStruc ends
    ```

    State whether or not each of the following declarations is valid:

    a. rentals rentalStruc <>
    b. rentalStruc rentals <>
    c. march rentalStruc <'12345',10,0>
    d. rentalStruc <,10,0>
    e. current rentalStruc <,15,0,0>

2. Write a macro called mPushData that pushes AX, BX, CX, and DX on the stack, and another macro called mPopData that pops the same registers off the stack.

3. Write a macro that creates a data definition for a buffer of any size up to 65,535 bytes. Pass the length of the buffer as an argument.

4. Write a macro called mReadArray that reads a variable number of 16-bit words from standard input into an array. Parameters are the name of the array and the number of bytes to read. A sample call is

    ```
    mReadArray intArray, bufSize
    ```

5. Write a macro called mDefineString that creates a data definition for a string literal. Pass the literal as an argument, and return a pointer to a null-terminated string. For example, the following macro calls

    ```
    mDefineString 'This is a literal.',SI
    ```

    creates the following data and set SI to its offset:

    ```
    db 'This is a literal',0
    ```

6. Suppose you want to write a macro called mTestJump that tests a destination operand with a source operand and jumps to a label based on the value of a flag condition. Here is a sample usage:

    ```
    mTestJump al,1,NZ,L2 ; (test AL,1 and jump if not zero to L2)
    ```

    Find and correct any errors in this proposed macro definition:

    ```
    mTestJump macro dest,source,result,label
      test source,dest
      j%result label
    endm
    ```

7. Assume the following **mRepeat** macro has been defined:

    ```
    mRepeat macro char,count
       local L1
    ```

Table 4. Assembler Listing Directives.

Directive	Action
.LIST	List all statements (default).
.XLIST	Suppress listing of statements.
.LFCOND	List false-conditional blocks.
.SFCOND	Suppress listing of false-conditional blocks (default).
.TFCOND	Toggle false-conditional listing.
.LALL	List macro expansions (default).
.SALL	Suppress listing of macro expansions.
.XALL	Exclude comments from macro listing.

```
        mov   cx,count
    L1: mov   ah,2
        mov   dl,char
        int   21h
        loop L1
    endm
```

Write the code generated by the assembler when the mRepeat macro is expanded by each of the following statements:

```
    mRepeat  'X',50
    mRepeat  AL,20
    mRepeat  byteVal,countVal
```

8. Assume the following mLocate macro definition:

```
    mLocate macro xval,yval
        if xval LT 0                  ;; xval < 0?
           exitm                      ;; if so, exit
        endif

        if yval LT 0                  ;; yval < 0?
           exitm                      ;; if so, exit
        endif

        mov    bx,0                   ;; video page 0
        mov    ah,2                   ;; locate cursor
        mov    dh,yval
        mov    dl,xval
        int    10h                    ;; call the BIOS
    endm
```

Show the source code generated by the assembler when the macro is expanded by each of the following statements:

```
    mLocate -2,20
    mLocate 10,20
    mLocate row,col
```

9. Assume the following macro definition:

```
    mMymsg macro num,string
       msg&num db  "Status: &string",0
    endm
```

Write the statement be generated by the assembler when the following declaration is made:

```
mMymsg 10,<Currently printing.>
```

10. Write the statements generated by the following repeat macro:

```
irp val,<100,20,30>
  db 0,0,0,val
endm
```

8.7   PROGRAMMING EXERCISES

1. *Assembler Operators*

Write a program that demonstrates each of the following operators: SEG, SHORT, HIGH, LOW, LENGTH, TYPE, and SIZE. Assemble the program, create a listing file, and circle the values generated by the assembler each time one of the operators is used.

2. *mPutcharAttr Macro*

Create a macro called mPutcharAttr that displays a character on the console with a selected attribute. Pass character and attribute arguments, as in the following example:

```
BlueOnBlack = 00000001b
mPutcharAttr 'X', BlueOnBlack
```

3. *mRepeatchar Macro*

Create a macro called mRepeatchar that writes the same character to standard output a specified number of times. For example, the following statement invokes the macro and displays the character X 20 times:

```
mRepeatchar 'X',20
```

4. *mReadkey Macro*

Create a macro that waits for a keystroke and returns the key that was pressed (use INT 16h). The macro should include parameters for the ASCII code and keyboard scan code. For example, the following statement waits for a key. When a key is pressed, its ASCII code is stored in DH and its scan code is stored in DL:

```
mReadkey DH,DL
```

5. *mWritestringAttr Macro*

Create a macro that writes a null-terminated string to the console with a given attribute. The macro parameters should include the string offset and video attribute. For example:

```
.data
WHITE = OFh
myString db "Here is my string",0

.code
mWritestring myString, WHITE
```

6. *mMove Macro*

Modify the mMove macro previously shown in Example 12 so that it also accepts 32-bit operands. Write a program that tests the macro with byte, word, and doubleword operands of various types.

7. *mMultAny Macro*

Create a macro called mMultAny that is an improvement of the mMult16 macro shown previously in Example 11. Your macro should 8-bit, 16-bit, or 32-bit operands. Write a program that tests the macro and displays the results of calculations.

8. *mSetE and mSetNE Macros*

Create two macros that simulate the SETE and SETNE instructions in the 80386 instruction set. The macro parameters are:

```
mSetE macro byteVal
mSetNE macro byteVal
```

The *byteVal* parameter is either an 8-bit register or 8-bit memory operand that will be set to 1 if the specified condition is true, or 0 if the condition is false. Here are examples of its usage:

```
mSetE  al                      ; set AL to 1 if ZF = 1
mSetE  bh                      ; set BH to 1 if ZF = 1
mSetNE al                      ; set AL to 1 if ZF = 0
mSetNE bh                      ; set BH to 1 if ZF = 0
```

9. *mSet&cond Macro*

Create a macro that simulates a simplified form of the SET*condition* instruction in the 80386 instruction set. The macro parameters include *condition*, which is a mnemonic indicating which CPU flag is to be tested:

```
mSet&condition macro byteVal
```

The *byteVal* parameter is either an 8-bit register or 8-bit memory operand that will be set to 1 if the specified condition is true, or 0 if the condition is false. The possible values for *condition* are the same as the suffixes of all conditional jump instructions. For example:

E	equal	C	carry
A	above	NC	no carry
B	below	L	less
AE	above or equal	GE	greater than or equal
O	overflow	NO	no overflow

Here are examples of its usage:

```
mSetE  al                    ; set AL to 1 if ZF = 1
mSetNC dh                    ; set DH to 1 if CF = 0
mSetGE bl                    ; set BL to 1 if SF = OF
```

(You may want to take a second look at the **m&styp** macro demonstrated earlier in this chapter, which automatically generated all the various shift and rotate instructions.)

10. mReadint Macro

Create a macro named mReadint that reads a 16- or 32-bit signed integer from standard input and returns the value in an argument. Use conditional operators to allow the macro to adapt to the size of the desired result. Write a program that demonstrates the macro with operands of different sizes. *Hint:* Inside the macro definition, call both the Readint and Readlong procedures from the book's link library.

11. mWriteint Macro

Modify the mWriteint macro shown earlier in Example 7 to allow it to accept either a 16- or 32-bit integer argument. Use conditional operators to allow the macro to adapt to the size of the operand. Write a program that demonstrates the macro with operands of different sizes.

12. mDoIf Macro

Create a macro called mDoIf that executes the instruction immediately following if a condition is true. Test the macro by calling it several times in a program. The following are sample uses of the macro:

```
cmp    bx,20                      ; compare two values
mDoIf E,<mov ax,bx>               ; execute if BX = 20
cmp    cx,count
mDoIf B,<call subroutine_1>       ; execute if CX < count
```

Allow the first argument, the condition being tested, to be any of the following:

```
E,NE,Z,NZ,B,A,BE,AE,C,NC,G,NG,GE,L,NL,LE
```

13. mKeyboard_Input Macro

Create a macro that reads input from the keyboard. Include the following parameters:

inputBuffer   Input buffer where the characters are stored

maxChars   Maximum number of characters to be input

actualChars   Number of characters actually input (returned by the macro)

Let the macro allocate its own storage for the input buffer, the length of which is determined by the value of maxChars. Write a program to test the macro, calling it several times.

14. mScroll Macro

Create a macro called mScroll that scrolls a window on the screen by passing the appropriate parameters to the Scroll procedure in the book's link library. Include the following parameters in the macro definition:

ULrow	Upper-left window row
ULcol	Upper-left window column
LRrow	Lower-right window row
LRcol	Lower-right window column
attrib	Attribute or color of scrolled lines (optional)

If **numLines** is blank, assume that the entire window is to be scrolled (cleared). If **direction** is blank, assume the window is to be scrolled up. If **attrib** is blank, assume an attribute of 7 (white on black).

9 Numeric Conversions and Libraries

In this chapter, we will discuss ways to translate numbers from one format to another, using assembly language. Numeric conversions are not automatic in the Intel instruction set; they must be handled completely by our software. This chapter also introduces external subroutines, showing how to link a program to separately compiled object files.

9.1   INTRODUCTION

Numeric Formats. We will refer to several standard numeric formats throughout this chapter. *Binary* format refers to the encoded binary value of a number. One byte holds a value from 0 to 255, two bytes hold a value up to 65,535, and so on. In *unpacked BCD* format, each byte holds the binary value of a single digit. In *packed BCD* format, each half-byte stores the binary value of a single decimal digit. There are several types of ASCII formats, in which each numeric digit is stored in a separate byte. A number in *ASCII decimal* format holds the ASCII code of each decimal digit. The ASCII binary format holds the ASCII code of each binary digit. The *ASCII hexadecimal* and *ASCII octal* formats are the same for hexadecimal and octal digits, respectively. The following examples demonstrate seven ways of representing the number 32:

```
db  20h                         ; binary
db  03h,02h                     ; unpacked BCD
db  32h                         ; packed BCD
db  '32'                        ; ASCII decimal
db  '00100000'                  ; ASCII binary
db  '20'                        ; ASCII hexadecimal
db  '40'                        ; ASCII octal
```

This chapter focuses on two types of conversions:

- *Binary to ASCII Decimal.* When the CPU performs arithmetic using binary numbers, the numbers must be translated to decimal ASCII format before they can be displayed or printed.

- *ASCII Decimal to Binary.* If a program inputs a number from the console as a string of ASCII digits, we usually translate it to binary before using it in calculations.

Assembly programmers often write their own conversion routines and store them in a library. A *library* is a collection of general-purpose subroutines, which have been assembled into OBJ files and are ready to be linked to programs. Table 1 lists a number of convenient numeric I/O procedures in the book's link library.

9.2   CHARACTER TRANSLATION METHODS

One task that assembly language programs handle best is character translation. There are many computer applications for this. The rapidly expanding field of data encryption is one, where data files must be securely stored and transmitted between computers while their contents are kept secret. Another application is data communications, where keyboard and screen codes must be translated in order to emulate various terminals. Often, we need to translate characters from one encoding system to another—from ASCII to EBCDIC, for example. A critical factor in each of these applications is speed, which just happens to be a feature of assembly language.

Table 1. Numeric I/O Procedures in the Link Library.

Procedure	Description
Readint	Read a signed ASCII decimal string from standard input and store it as a 16-bit binary integer. *Output*: AX contains the value.
Readlong	Read a signed ASCII decimal string from standard input and store it as a 32-bit binary integer. *Output*: EAX contains the value.
Writebcd	Write an 8-bit binary coded decimal byte to standard output. *Input*: AL contains a BCD byte.
Writeint	Write a 16-bit unsigned binary integer to standard output. *Input*: AX contains the number, BX contains the radix, or number base (2-16).
Writeint_signed	Write a signed 16-bit binary signed decimal integer to standard output. *Input*: AX contains the number.
Writelong	Write an unsigned 32-bit binary integer to standard output in binary, decimal, octal, or hexadecimal format. *Input*: EAX = the integer to display, and BX = radix value (2, 8, 10, or 16).
PackedToBin	Convert a BCD byte to a binary value. *Input*: AL contains a BCD byte. *Output*: AL contains the binary value.

9.2.1 The XLAT Instruction

The XLAT instruction adds the contents of AL to BX and uses the resulting offset to point to an entry in an 8-bit *translate table*. This table contains values that are substituted for the original value in AL. The byte in the table entry pointed to by BX + AL is moved to AL. The syntax is

```
XLAT [tablename]
```

Tablename is optional because the table is assumed to be pointed to by BX. Therefore, be sure to load BX with the offset of the translate table before invoking XLAT. The flags are not affected by this instruction. The table can have a maximum of 256 entries, the same range of values possible in the 8-bit AL register.

Example. Let's store the characters representing all 16 hexadecimal digits in a table:

```
table db '0123456789ABCDEF'
```

The table contains the ASCII code of each hexadecimal digit:

Offset:	00	01	02	03	04	05	06	07	08	09	0A	0B	0C	0D	0E	0F
Contents:	30	31	32	33	34	35	36	37	38	39	41	42	43	44	45	46

(all values are in hexidecimal)

If we place 0Ah in AL with the thought of converting it to ASCII, we need to set BX to the table offset and invoke XLAT. This instruction does the following:

• Adds BX and AL, generating an effective address that points to the eleventh entry in the table.

• Moves the contents of this table entry to AL.

In other words, XLAT sets AL to 41h because this value is located at table offset 0Ah. 41h is the ASCII code for the letter *A*. The following instructions accomplish this:

```
mov   al,0Ah              ; index value
mov   bx,offset table     ; offset of the table
xlat                      ; AL = 41h, or 'A'
```

9.2.2   Character Filtering

One of the best uses of XLAT is to filter out unwanted characters from a stream of text. Suppose we want to input a string of characters from the keyboard and echo only those with ASCII values from 32 to 127. We can set up a translate table, place a zero in each table position corresponding to an invalid character, and place 0FFh in each valid position:

```
validchars  db 32 dup(0)      ; invalid chars: 0-31
            db 96 dup(0FFh)    ; valid chars:   32-127
            db 128 dup(0)      ; invalid chars: 128-255
```

The XLAT.ASM program in Example 1 includes code that inputs a series of characters and uses them to look up values in the **validchars** table. If XLAT returns a value of zero in AL, we skip the character and jump back to the top of the loop. (When AL is ORed with itself, the Zero flag is set if AL equals 0). If the character is valid, 0FFh is returned in AL, and we use INT 21 to display the character in DL.

Example 1. Character Filtering Example.

```
title Character Filtering          (XLAT.ASM)

; This program filters input from the console
; by screening out all ASCII codes less than
; 32 or greater than 127. Uses INT 16h for
; direct keyboard input.
```

```
        .model small
        .stack 100h
        INPUT_LENGTH = 20
        .data
        validchars label byte
          db 32 dup(0)              ; invalid chars: 0-31
          db 96 dup(0FFh)           ; valid chars:   32-127
          db 128 dup(0)             ; invalid chars: 128-255

        .code
        main proc
            mov   ax,@data
            mov   ds,ax
            mov   bx,offset validchars
            mov   cx,INPUT_LENGTH

        getchar:
            mov   ah,0               ; keyboard input
            int   16h                ; char is in AL
            mov   dl,al              ; save copy in DL
            xlat  validchars         ; look up char in AL
            or    al,al              ; invalid char?
            jz    getchar            ; yes: get another
            mov   ah,2               ; no: output the char
            int   21h
            loop  getchar

            mov   ax,4C00h
            int   21h
        main endp
        end main
```

9.2.3 Character Encoding

The XLAT instruction provides a simple way to encode data so it cannot be read by unauthorized persons. When messages are transferred across telephone lines, for instance, encoding can be a way of preventing others from reading them. Imagine a table in which all the possible digits and letters have been rearranged. A program could read each character from standard input, use XLAT to look it up in a table, and write its encoded value to standard output. A sample table is as follows:

```
codetable db  48 dup(0)              ; no translation
   db  '4590821367'                  ; 0-9
   db  7 dup (0)                      ; no translation
   db  'GVHZUSOBMIKPJCADLFTYEQNWXR'  ; A-Z
   db  6 dup (0)                      ; no translation
   db  'gvhzusobmikpjcadlftyeqnwxr'  ; a-z
   db  133 dup(0)                     ; no translation
```

Certain ranges in the table are set to zeros; characters in these ranges are not translated. The $ character (ASCII 36), for example, is not translated because position 36 in the table contains the value 0.

Sample Program. The Character Encoding program shown in Example 2 encodes each character read from an input file. When running the program, one can redirect standard input from a file, using the < symbol. For example:

```
encode < infile
```

The program output appears on the screen. Output can also be redirect to a file:

```
encode < infile > outfile
```

The following example shows a line from an input file that has been encoded:

```
This is a SECRET Message       (read from input file)
Ybmt mt g TUHFUY Juttgou       (encoded output)
```

The program cannot use the keyboard as the standard input device, because it quits looking for input as soon as the keyboard buffer is empty. The user would have to type fast enough to keep the keyboard buffer full.

Given some time and effort, a simple encoding scheme like this can be broken. The easiest way to break the code is to gain access to the program itself and use it to encode a known message. But if you can prevent others from running the program, breaking the code takes more time. Another way to discourage code breaking is to constantly change the code. In World War II, for example, pilots carried a code book for translating messages, so that message encryption could be varied on a day-to-day basis.

Example 2. Character Encoding Program.

```
title Character Encoding Program            (ENCODE.ASM)


; This program reads an input file and encodes
; the output using the XLAT instruction.
; To run it, redirect input on the DOS/Windows
; command line. For example:
```

```
;
;              encode < input.txt

.model small
.stack 100h
.data
codetable label byte
  db   48 dup(0)                        ; no translation
  db   '4590821367'                     ; ASCII codes 48-57
  db   7 dup (0)                        ; no translation
  db   'GVHZUSOBMIKPJCADLFTYEQNWXR'
  db   6 dup (0)                        ; no translation
  db   'gvhzusobmikpjcadlftyeqnwxr'
  db   133 dup(0)   ; no translation

.code
main proc
    mov   ax,@data
    mov   ds,ax
    mov   bx,offset codetable

getchar:
    mov   ah,6                  ; console input, no wait
    mov   dl,0FFh               ; specify input request
    int   21h                   ; call DOS
    jz    quit                  ; quit, no input waiting
    mov   dl,al                 ; save char in DL
    xlat  codetable             ; translate the char
    cmp   al,0                  ; not translatable?
    je    putchar               ; yes: write it as is
    mov   dl,al                 ; no: move new char to DL

putchar:
    mov   ah,2                  ; write DL to output
    int   21h                   ; call DOS
    jmp   getchar               ; get another char

quit:
    mov   ax,4C00h              ; exit program
    int   21h
main endp
end main
```

9.3 STACK PARAMETERS

9.3.1 Creating a Stack Frame

One standard way of passing arguments to subroutines involves using the stack. A calling program can push each argument on the stack just before calling a subroutine. The subroutine can retrieve the same value from the stack. Inside the procedure, this value is called a *stack parameter*. This method is employed by high-level languages when calling subroutines, and it can also be used in assembly language programs.

Suppose, for example, a procedure called **AddTwo** adds two integers and stores their sum in AX. From main, we could push the two arguments and call AddTwo:

```
.286              ; 80286 supports immediate push instruction
push  5
push  6
call  AddTwo
mov   sum,ax      ; save the sum
```

The **AddTwo** procedure begins by pushing BP on the stack and setting BP to the same value as SP. The BP register is used for all references to stack parameters:

```
AddTwo proc
    push  bp
    mov   bp,sp
    (etc.)
```

After these two instructions have executed, we can look at a diagram of the stack, called the *stack frame:*

5	[BP + 6]
6	[BP + 4]
(ret addr)	[BP + 2]
BP	← BP, SP

The two arguments, 5 and 6, are located at SS:[BP+6] and SS:[BP+4], respectively. Recall that 5 was pushed before 6, and the stack always grows downward in memory. Knowing these locations, the AddTwo procedure can add their values and store the sum in AX:

```
AddTwo proc
    push  bp
    mov   bp,sp
    mov   ax,[bp+6]       ; first argument (5)
    add   ax,[bp+4]       ; second argument (6)
```

```
        pop    bp
        ret
AddTwo  endp
```

Saving Registers inside the Subroutine. Subroutines often have to push additional registers on the stack immediately after setting BP to SP, so the registers can be restored to their original values later. For example, we push DX inside the AddTwo procedure:

```
AddTwo  proc
        push   bp
        mov    bp,sp
        push   dx
```

Here is the resulting stack frame. Notice that pushing DX did not affect the offsets of the stack parameters from BP, because DX is below BP on the stack:

Removing Arguments From the Stack. There is an important detail to take care of, that of removing arguments from the stack when a subroutine returns. When AddTwo was called, for example, the two arguments that were pushed on the stack would remain on the stack. There are two problems that might occur in this situation: First, if AddTwo was called from a procedure other than main, this procedure would eventually execute a RET instruction. But the top of the stack would not contain the correct return address. Instead, it would contain the two arguments left behind after calling the AddTwo procedure. Second, if a program had a loop that called AddTwo repeatedly, the stack would fill up and the program would corrupt memory.

Clearly, procedure arguments cannot be left on the stack. One way to solve this problem is to add an immediate operand to the RET instruction that indicates a value to be added to the SP register after the procedure returns. Pascal programs, for instance, use this method of adjusting the stack pointer. The AddTwo procedure has two 16-bit parameters, so four bytes of stack space must be released by the RET instruction:

```
        pop    bp
        ret    4                        ; adjust the stack pointer
AddTwo  endp
```

Another standard way of removing arguments from the stack is to leave the job to the calling program, which usually adds a constant value to SP after the procedure returns. C and

C++ programs use this method. For example, immediately after calling **AddTwo**, we might insert an ADD instruction:

```
push  5
push  6

call  AddTwo
add   sp,4              ; adjust the stack pointer
mov   sum,ax            ; save the sum
```

(If we used this method, we would not place a constant next to the RET instruction inside the subroutine.)

Simplifying the Calling Program. Stack parameters can greatly simplify the code in a program that calls procedures, particularly when available registers are at a preminum. In Table 2, compare the following two ways of calling the **Writeint** procedure, first using register arguments, and second using stack arguments. This example was biased in favor of stack arguments, of course, because some programs will already have the procedure arguments in AX and BX before calling Writeint. But that will not always be the case. AX and BX may have other important duties at the time, requiring us to save and restore their values. In Table 3, a loop displays an array of integers. Pushing arguments on the stack results in a loop containing one more instruction than the same loop using the register passing method.

9.3.2   Passing Arguments by Reference

In the examples shown in this section so far, all arguments were passed to procedures by value. There are occasions when we need to pass the address of a variable, and this is called *passing by reference*.

ArrayFill Procedure Example. Let's write a procedure called **ArrayFill**, shown in Example 3, that fills an array with random integers. It receives two arguments: the first is the offset of an array located in the same data segment as the procedure, and the second is an integer that specifies the length of the array. The first argument is passed by reference, and the second is passed by value. Calling the procedure is easy. We just push the offset of the array on the stack, followed by the array's size:

```
.286
.data
ARRAY_COUNT = 100
array dw ARRAY_COUNT dup(0)

.code
push  offset array
push  ARRAY_COUNT
call  ArrayFill
```

Table 2. Register Versus Stack Argument Comparison 1.

Method 1: Pass arguments in registers, saving and restoring their values:	``` push ax ; save registers push bx mov ax,wordVal mov bx,10 ; decimal radix call Writeint pop bx pop ax ; restore registers ```
Method 2: Push arguments on the stack:	``` push wordVal push 10 call Writeint ```

Table 3. Register Versus Stack Argument Comparison 2.

Method 1: Pass arguments in registers:	``` mov si,offset array mov cx,ARRAY_SIZE mov bx,10 L1: mov ax,[si] call Writeint call Crlf add si,2 Loop L1 ```
Method 2: Push arguments on the stack:	``` mov si,offset array mov cx,ARRAY_SIZE L1: push word ptr [si] push 10 call Writeint call Crlf add si,2 Loop L1 ```

The stack frame is shown here, containing the offset of **array** and the value of **count**:

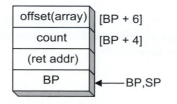

Inside the **ArrayFill** procedure, the following statement retrieves the array's offset from the stack frame. Once inside SI, the offset becomes an indirect memory operand:

```
mov  si,[bp+6]              ; offset of array
```

Example 3. ArrayFill Procedure with a Reference Parameter.

```
ArrayFill proc near
    push bp
    mov  bp,sp
    pusha
    mov  si,[bp+6]          ; offset of array
    mov  cx,[bp+4]          ; array size

AF1: mov  eax,10000h        ; get random 0 - FFFFh
     call Random_Range      ; from the link library
     mov  [si],ax
     add  si,2
     loop AF1

    popa
    pop  bp
    ret  4                  ; adjust the stack
ArrayFill endp
```

Passing a Far Pointer. There are times when a variable must be passed by reference to a procedure whose data is in a different segment from the calling program. In a large memory model program, for instance, this is likely to happen. When calling the ArrayFill procedure, we would pass the array by far reference. The segment and offset of the array would be pushed on the stack before calling the procedure. The SEG operator makes this easy to do:

```
push  seg array
push  offset array
push  ARRAY_COUNT
call  ArrayFill
```

This changes the subroutine's stack frame, of course, so the FillArray procedure must be modified. The revised version of ArrayFill, using the 32-bit pointer is shown in Example 4. The following diagram shows the new stack frame:

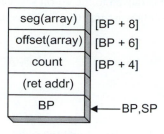

Example 4. ArrayFill Procedure with a Far Reference Parameter.

```
ArrayFill proc
    push bp
    mov  bp,sp
    pusha
    push ds

    mov  ax,[bp+8]          ; segment of array
    mov  ds,ax
    mov  si,[bp+6]          ; offset of array
    mov  cx,[bp+4]          ; array size

AF1: mov  eax,10000h        ; get rand 0 - FFFFh
    call Random_Range
    mov  [si],ax
    add  si,2
    Loop AF1

    pop  ds
    popa
    pop  bp
    ret  6                  ; adjust the stack
ArrayFill endp
```

9.3.3 LDS/LES/LFS/LGS/LSS (Load Far Pointer)

The LDS (*load far pointer*) instruction loads a 32-bit memory operand into DS and the data register specified as the instruction's first operand. The second operand must be a memory operand. The syntax is:

```
LDS reg16,mem32
```

The low-order word of the doubleword is moved to the 16-bit register, and the high-order word is moved to DS. For example, after the following instruction, DS = 02CF and AX = 0400:

```
longPtr dd 02CF0400h
    .
    .
    .
lds ax,longPtr
```

The LES instruction is identical to LDS, except that the segment value is moved to the ES register. The 80386 processor also supports the LFS, LGS, and LSS instructions, which move segment values to the FS, GS, and SS segment registers, respectively.

The *load far pointer* instructions are ideally suited to retrieving stack parameters that have been passed by far reference. When a far pointer is pushed on the stack, its segment value is pushed first, then its offset. When the called procedure begins to execute, it can use the LDS instruction to load the pointer. Similarly, the LES instruction loads a 32-bit pointer into ES and a data register.

Looking once again at the ArrayFill procedure from Example 4, we can simplify the code that loaded DS and SI to the address of the array parameter:

```
lds  si,[bp+6]              ; load array parameter into DS:SI
```

9.3.4   ENTER Instruction

The ENTER instruction (*make stack frame*) for the 80286 processor prepares a procedure to received passed parameters. It has two operands: The first is a constant specifying the number of bytes of stack space to reserve for local variables, and the second operand is a constant that specifies the procedure's nesting level. For example, if we want to declare a procedure without any local variables, the following is appropriate:

```
mySub proc
    enter 0,0
```

This is equivalent to the following instructions:

```
mySub proc
    push bp
    mov  bp,sp
```

On the other hand, we can create space for two 16-bit local variables,

```
mySub proc
    enter 4,0
```

which is equivalent to the following instructions:

```
mySub proc
    push bp
    mov  bp,sp
    sub  sp,4
```

9.3.5 LEAVE Instruction

The LEAVE instruction (*high level procedure exit*) for the 80286 processor terminates the stack frame for a procedure. It reverses the action of a previous ENTER instruction by restoring SP and BP to the values they were assigned when the procedure was called. For example, using the **mySub** procedure example again, we could write:

```
mySub proc
    enter  4,0
        .
        .
    leave
    ret
mySub endp
```

This is equivalent to the following instructions that allocate and discard the 4 bytes of space reserved for local variables:

```
mySub proc
    push bp
    mov  bp,sp
    sub  sp,4
        .
        .
    mov  sp,bp
    pop  bp
    ret
mySub endp
```

9.3.6 Passing Arguments the 'C' Language Way

Programs compiled from the C and C++ languages into assembly language use a different protocol for passing parameters than Pascal programs. For one thing, the parameters are pushed on the stack in reverse order, starting with the last parameter. If we called Writeint this way, radix would be pushed first, and then **wordVal:**

```
Writeint(wordVal, radix);
```

This translates to the following assembler instructions:

```
push  radix
push  wordVal
call  Writeint
```

A procedure using the 'C' calling protocol does not remove the passed parameters from the stack. Instead, the calling program is assigned the task:

```
push  radix
push  wordVal
call  Writeint
add   sp,4                    ; clear the stack
```

Variable Number of Arguments. A C/C++ procedure can accept a variable number of arguments if the procedure has been declared that way. This is accomplished in assembly language by pushing an extra argument on the stack that indicates the number of passed arguments. The program in Example 5 shows how this is done for a procedure called **AddSome.** The procedure is called twice, each time with a different number of integers to be summed.

Example 5. Passing a Variable Number of Arguments.

```
Title The AddSome Procedure               (addsome.asm)

; Demonstration of the 'C' calling convention,
; with a variable number of parameters.

.model small
.stack 100h
.286
.code
main proc

; Start by adding four integers:
   push 5
   push 6
   push 0Ah
   push 14h
   push 4                 ; argument count
   call AddSome           ; sum is in AX
   add  sp,10             ; clean up the stack

; Now add two integers:
   push 1200h
   push 2033h
```

```
          push 2                    ; argument count
          call AddSome              ; sum is in AX
          add  sp,6                 ; clean up the stack

          mov ax,4c00h
          int 21h
main endp


; Add a variable number of integers and return
; their sum in AX.

AddSome proc
    enter 0,0
    mov  cx,[bp+4]                  ; get the count
    mov  ax,0
    mov  si,bp                      ; point to last number
    add  si,6

L1: add  ax,[si]                    ; add a number
    add  si,2                       ; point to next
    loop L1                         ; loop until done

    leave
    ret
AddSome endp


end main
```

9.3.7   Procedure Declarations in Borland TASM

Using Borland's TASM, you can define the names and types of individual procedure parameters. The basic syntax for the PROC directive with parameters is:

```
procname PROC [language]
ARG param1 [, param2, ...]
```

Each parameter following the ARG directive is given a type, such as byte, word, or dword. If the parameter type is omitted, word is assumed. The language specifier can be C, Pascal, BASIC, or FORTRAN. If it is omitted, the default language already supplied in the program's **.model** directive is used.

For example, the **AddTwo** procedure is declared here with three parameters: two integers to be added together, followed by the offset of a variable that receives the sum of the first two numbers:

```
AddTwo proc, Pascal
ARG val1:word, val2:word, sumPtr:word
    push ax
    push si
    mov  ax,val1          ; [bp + 8]
    add  ax,val2          ; [bp + 6]
    mov  si,sumPtr        ; [bp + 4]
    mov  [si],ax
    pop  si
    pop  ax
    ret
AddTwo endp
```

Within the procedure body, the parameter names make for more readable code than the raw stack offsets they represent, such as [bp + 6]. In addition, the assembler inserts the following prologue code into the beginning of the AddTwo procedure:

```
push bp
mov  bp,sp
```

The following statements are inserted into the epilog code of the **AddTwo** procedure. The 6 next to the RET statement indicates that a value of 6 will be added to the stack pointer after the procedure returns. This removes any procedure arguments that were pushed on the stack:

```
pop bp
ret 6
```

Because this procedure uses the *Pascal* calling convention, it uses the RET instruction to restore the stack pointer to its original state when returning to the calling program.

The Call Directive. Calling the procedure is made easier with the CALL directive, which resembles an extended version of the call instruction. The following is a call to the **AddTwo** procedure:

```
.data
x1 dw 10h
x2 dw 20h
theSum dw ?

.code
call AddTwo,x1,x2,offset theSum
```

The CALL directive causes the assembler to insert PUSH instructions for each of the arguments before calling the procedure.

9.3.8   Function Procedures (TASM)

If a procedure is to return a value, the Borland assembler lets you use the RETURNS directive on the same line as ARG. The parameter following RETURNS uses the same syntax as the other procedure parameters. In Example 6, the **MaxWord** procedure compares two integer parameters and returns the larger of the two.

Example 6. The MaxWord Proc.

```
MaxWord proc
ARG v1:word,v2:word RETURNS max:word
      push ax
      mov  ax,v1
      cmp  ax,v2
      ja   @@1
      mov  ax,v2
@@1: mov  max,ax
      pop  ax
      ret
MaxWord endp
```

Before calling **MaxWord**, we push a dummy value onto the stack to create a place for the function to store its return value. After returning from the function, we pop the return value off the stack and save it in a variable:

```
.data
twoVals  dw 1000h, 1001h
theSum   dw ?


.code
push   ax
call   MaxWord, twoVals, twoVals+2
pop    theSum
```

9.3.9   Procedure Declarations in Microsoft MASM

The Microsoft Assembler also allows you to define procedure parameters in a slightly different way from Borland. The basic syntax of the PROC directive is:

procname PROC [*attributes*] [USES *reglist*] [*,paramlist*]

The *attributes* field contains four optional parts: *distance, language, visibility*, and *prolog arguments*. The distance option is NEAR or FAR; if omitted, the default procedure distance is determined by the .model attribute:

Model type	**Distance**
tiny, small, compact, flat	near
medium, large, huge	far

The *language* field determines the type of calling convention, shown in Table 4.

The *uses* field contains a list of registers used by the procedure. This permits the assembler to automatically generate appropriate push and pop instructions to save and restore the registers. Notice that only a single comma appears at the end of the list:

```
USES ax bx si,
```

The *paramlist* field is a list of procedure parameters, each given a type. For example,

```
var1:byte, count:word, bigVal:dword
```

Example: The AddTwo Procedure. The following is a definition of a procedure called AddTwo, which adds two integers and saves their sum in the address specified by the third parameter:

```
AddTwo proc Pascal val1:word, val2:word, \
    sumPtr:word
  push ax
  push si
  mov  ax,val1
  add  ax,val2
  mov  si,sumPtr
  mov  [si],ax
  pop  si
```

Table 4. Language Calling Conventions.

Language Type	Actions
BASIC, FORTRAN, PASCAL	Parameters are pushed from left to right. A RET instruction cleans up the stack. The procedure name is converted to uppercase.
C, STDCALL	Parameters are pushed from right to left. The procedure name is case-sensitive. A leading underscore is prepended to the procedure name. The caller cleans up the stack.
SYSCALL	The caller cleans up the stack when a variable number of arguments is specified. Otherwise, the RET instruction cleans up the stack. No underscore is prepended to the procedure name.

```
        pop  ax
        ret
AddTwo endp
```

You may have noticed that the same procedure was shown earlier, when using the Borland assembler. The only difference is that Microsoft does not support the ARG directive; instead, the parameters appear on the same line as PROC.

The INVOKE Directive. MASM uses the INVOKE directive to simplify the calling of procedures with stack parameters. The syntax is:

```
INVOKE procexpression [,argumentlist]
```

The *procexpression* can be either the name of a procedure or an indirect reference to a procedure. The *argumentlist* can be an expression, a register pair, or an expression preceded by ADDR.

The PROTO Directive. MASM requires the use of a procedure prototype to be included if the body of the procedure does not appear in the source code prior to the procedure call. The prototype lists the same procedure name and parameter list as its corresponding PROC directive.

The program in Example 7 uses INVOKE to call the **AddTwo** procedure and pass it three arguments. Notice that we used the ADDR directive to pass the offset of **theSum** to the procedure.

Example 7. Using the INVOKE Directive (MASM).

```
Title Using INVOKE (MASM)

.model small, Pascal
.stack 100h
.data
x1 dw 10h
x2 dw 20h
theSum dw ?

.code
AddTwo PROTO near Pascal val1:word, val2:word, \
     sumPtr:word

main proc
  mov ax,@data
  mov ds,ax
  INVOKE AddTwo, x1, x2, ADDR theSum
```

```
        mov ax,4c00h
        int 21h
main endp

AddTwo proc near Pascal val1:word, val2:word, \
      sumPtr:word
    push ax
    push si
    mov  ax,val1
    add  ax,val2
    mov  si,sumPtr
    mov  [si],ax
    pop  si
    pop  ax
    ret
AddTwo endp
end main
```

9.4 SEPARATELY ASSEMBLED MODULES

Large applications are usually constructed from multiple source code files, each of which is assembled into a separate OBJ file. Linking is much faster than assembling source code, so large programs are usually constructed from many small modules. An important structured programming principle here is *modularity*—each module can hide certain variables and procedures that it does not want to expose to the rest of the program. This approach helps to minimize the risk that modifying a variable in one module will accidentally modify a variable by the same name in another module.

When program modules are assembled separately, we define *interfaces* between them, which are the rules by which data are passed into procedures and how the procedures return values to their callers.

9.4.1 The PUBLIC Directive

The PUBLIC directive is required when a program module contains constants, variables, and procedures that will be accessed by other modules. The name of a procedure, for example, is *exported*, or *exposed* so other modules will be able to call it. The general format for PUBLIC is:

```
PUBLIC name
```

A PUBLIC directive can be placed anywhere in a program module. Multiple names can also be declared together:

```
PUBLIC name1, name2, name3 . . .
```

If a PUBLIC declaration is made for an absolute symbol, it can only represent an integer. In the following code example, ROW_COUNT and ARRAY_SIZE can be public, but **message** cannot:

```
ROW_COUNT =  25
ARRAY_SIZE EQU 100
message equ "File not found"
```

9.4.2   Creating a MultiModule Program

In this section, we show how to create a procedure called DisplayStr, place it in its own source code module, and assemble it into an OBJ file. Then we create and assemble a main program that calls DisplayStr. The two object files are linked togeter to form a single executable program.

Main Program. The main program declares DisplayStr as external and passes the offset of a string to the procedure:

```
.data
message db  'This message is displayed by the '
        db  'DisplayStr procedure.',0Dh,0Ah,'$'
.code
extrn DisplayStr:proc
main proc
    mov   ax,@data
    mov   ds,ax
    mov   dx,offset message      ; point to message
    call  DisplayStr
    mov   ax,4C00h               ; end program
    int   21h
main endp
end main
```

DisplayStr Module. The display.asm file in Example 8 contains the DisplayStr procedure. We declare DisplayStr public, making it accessible to procedures outside this module. Notice that the END directive on the last line does not include the reference to **main.** This is because an executable program can have only one entry point, and that point is already specified in the main module.

Example 8. The DisplayStr Module.

```
Title DisplayStr Procedure    (display.asm)
```

```
.model small
.code
public DisplayStr
DisplayStr proc
    push  ax                ; save AX
    mov   ah,9              ; function: display a string
    int   21h               ; call DOS
    pop   ax                ; restore AX
    ret
DisplayStr endp
end                         ; no label next to the END directive
```

Each module is assembled separately and the two object files are linked together into an executable program. The Microsoft Assembler command to assemble, link, and produce main.exe is:

```
ml main.asm display.asm
```

The comparable Borland Assembler commands are:

```
tasm main
tasm display
tlink main display
```

When you debug main.exe using Turbo Debugger or CodeView, you will have a pleasant surprise. The debugger automatically looks for the source file containing DisplayStr in the current directory and displays it when the procedure is called.

Integrated Editor. Or, if you are using the integrated assembler editor (AE.EXE) supplied on disk with this book, you put each source file in a separate editor window, assemble each from the Run/Assemble menu. Then make sure the the main.asm window is active, select the Run/ Link menu command, and type in the name of the display module in the dialog box. This links main.obj to display.obj, producing main.exe:

```
 ┌─────────────────────────────────────────┐
 │                                          │
 │   Other program module names             │
 │                                          │
 │   ┌──────────────────────────────────┐   │
 │   │ display                          │   │
 │   └──────────────────────────────────┘   │
 │                                          │
 │   ┌────────────┐    ┌────────────┐       │
 │   │    OK      │    │  Cancel    │       │
 │   └────────────┘    └────────────┘       │
 │                                          │
 └─────────────────────────────────────────┘
```

9.5 CREATING A LINK LIBRARY

Once you have created a set of useful procedures you would like to call from other programs, it is a good idea to place the procedures in a link library. From Chapter 4 onward, for example, we have used the various input-output procedures in the book's link library (irvine.lib). Rather than copy all the source code from these procedures into each program we write, it is easier to link each program to the library. In the book's link library, groups of related procedures were placed in source modules, which were in turn, assembled in to object modules (OBJ files). Using a utility program called a *library manager,* the object files are placed in a library file called irvine.lib. The Microsoft and Borland assemblers both include library manager programs in their packages.

A listing of the book's link library is shown in Example 9. Notice that procedures are placed in modules called console, disks, fileio, integer, and strings. When creating a link library, you have the option of placing related procedures in the same module. When a program calls a procedure, the linker attaches the module's object code to the executable program. For example, when we call the ClrScr procedure, 280 bytes of object code belonging to the **console** module are attached. This may seem wasteful, but if we also call GotoXY, Crlf, Scroll, Get_Time, and Show_Time, no additional bytes are attached because these procedures reside within the same module. Although the link library file might be quite large, it is important to remember that only the code from the procedure's module becomes part of the EXE program. This selective linking ability makes the use of link libraries both convenient and economical.

Example 9. Listing of the Book's Link Library.

```
Publics by module

console    size = 280
           CLRSCR                CRLF
           DELAY_SECONDS         GET_TIME
           GOTOXY                READCHAR
           READKEY               SCROLL
           SECONDS_TODAY         SET_VIDEOSEG
           SHOW_TIME             WAITCHAR
           WRITECHAR_DIRECT      WRITESTRING_DIRECT

disks      size = 218
           GET_COMMANDTAIL       GET_DEVICEPARMS
           GET_DISKFREESPACE     GET_DISKSIZE

fileio     size = 1150
           CLOSE_FILE            CREATE_FILE
           DOS_ERROR             OPEN_INFILE
```

	OPEN_OUTFILE	READ_RECORD
	SEEK_EOF	SEEK_RECORD
integer	size = 761	
	PACKEDTOBIN	RANDOM32
	RANDOMIZE	RANDOM_RANGE
	READINT	READLONG
	WRITEBCD	WRITEINT
	WRITEINT_SIGNED	WRITELONG
strings	size = 125	
	READSTRING	STR_COPY
	STR_LENGTH	STR_UCASE
	WRITESTRING	WRITE_ERRORSTR

Alternatively, each procedure can be placed in a separate module, simply by creating a separate ASM file for each procedure and adding each assembled OBJ file to the library. In this case, when you call a procedure from the library, only the object code for that procedure is attached to the executable program.

Creating Library Modules. A separate ASM source code file must be created for each module. Each file has the following basic format:

```
title procedure description (filename)
.model small
public identifier-list
constant declarations
.data
variables
.code
procedures
end
```

By default, variables, constants, or procedures declared inside the module are private to that module. This concept is called *encapsulation*. Procedures in other program modules cannot access private members of this module. This is a convenience, because it allows the same identifier to appear in more than one module, and it protects private variables from unwanted modifications by code outside their module. A module's *interface,* on the other hand, consists of all identifiers in the module that have been declared *public*.

Creating a Link Library. Both the Microsoft and Borland assemblers include a utility that lets you create a link library, add modules, remove modules, and list the contents of a library file. You can display a list of commands for either the Microsoft or Borland library utilities by typing the /help option on the command line. Example 10 shows the Microsoft LIB commands and Example 11 shows the Borland TLIB commands. For example, the following commands create a library file called **string.lib:**

```
tlib string              (Borland)
lib string;              (Microsoft)
```

Once the library file has been created, you can add individual object files (modules) to the library. For example, we can add the strwrite.obj file to the string.lib file:

```
tlib string +strwrite    (Borland)
lib string +strwrite     (Microsoft)
```

To view a listing of the library, include the library name and use CON as the listfile name. For example:

```
tlib string,con          (Borland)
lib string,con           (Microsoft)
```

Example 10. Displaying the Microsoft LIB Help.

```
C:\>lib /help
Microsoft (R) Library Manager  Version 3.20.010
Copyright (C) Microsoft Corp 1983-1992.  All rights reserved.

Usage: LIB library [options] [commands] [,listfile [,newlibrary]]
Options:
   /?                    : display LIB options
   /HELP                 : display help on LIB
   /IGNORECASE           : ignore case on names
   /NOEXTDICTIONARY      : do not build extended dictionary
   /NOIGNORECASE         : do not ignore case on names
   /NOLOGO               : do not display signon banner
   /PAGESIZE:n           : set library page size to n
Commands:
   +name                 : add object file
   -name                 : delete object file
   -+name                : replace object file
   *name                 : copy (extract) object file
   -*name                : move (delete and extract) object file
```

Example 11. Displaying the Borland TLIB Help.

```
C:\> tlib /help
```

```
Syntax: TLIB libname [/C] [/E] commands, listfile

      libname    library file pathname
      commands   sequence of operations to be performed (optional)
      listfile   filename for listing file (optional)

A command is of the form <symbol>modulename, where <symbol> is

      +                          add modulename to the library
      -                          remove modulename from the library
      *                          extract modulename without removing it
      -+ or +-                   replace modulename in library
      -* or *-                   extract modulename and remove it

      /C                         case-sensitive library
      /E                         create extended dictionary

Use @filepath to continue from file "filepath".
Use '&' at end of a line to continue onto the next line.
```

9.6   BINARY TO ASCII CONVERSION

One of the more interesting algorithms in numeric processing is that for converting a binary value to various ASCII number representations. It can easily be implemented in assembly language, and it has practical value for programs that must display numbers on the console. To convert a binary integer to decimal, for example, divide the number repeatedly by 10 until the quotient is equal to 0. The remainder from each division step becomes a digit in the ASCII digit string. The following diagram shows this process for the number 4096:

```
Dividend  /   10   =   Quotient   Remainder
  4096    /   10   =     409         6 ─────────────────────┐
   409    /   10   =      40         9 ───────────────────┐ │
    40    /   10   =       4         0 ─────────────────┐ │ │
     4    /   10   =       0         4 ───────────┐     │ │ │
                                                  │     │ │ │
                              Result:    4    0   9   6
```

Notice that the digits are generated in reverse order. As each digit is calculated, we put it in a buffer that is later written to standard output. We can express the algorithm in pseudocode:

```
repeat
  divide AX by 10
```

```
    convert remainder (DL) to ASCII
    place DL in the buffer
until AX = 0

repeat
    move digit from buffer to DL
    display the digit
    point to next digit in buffer
until all digits displayed
```

Similarly, the algorithm for displaying ASCII hexadecimal requires us to divide the number repeatedly by 16:

```
4096  / 16  =   256,   remainder 0
 256  / 16  =    16,   remainder 0
  16  / 16  =     1,   remainder 0
   1  / 16  =     0,   remainder 1

              ASCII hexadecimal:    1   0   0   0
```

9.6.1   The Writeint Procedure

Example 12 shows the source code for the Writeint procedure from the link library that we have used throughout the book. It displays the 16-bit value in AX as a string of binary, octal, decimal, or hexadecimal digits. BX contains a radix value (2-16) that determines the base of the displayed number. The source code file containing this procedure uses the .model directive to show that this procedure should be called by small model programs. This means that calling programs only execute *near* calls, and the Writeint procedure is located in the same code segment as the calling program.

Example 12. WriteInt Procedure Source Code.

```
Title The Writeint Procedure                      (writeint.asm)

public Writeint
; Writes a 16-bit unsigned binary integer to standard
; output. Input parameters: AX = value, BX = radix.

.model small
.286
.data
buffer    db  16 dup(' ')           ; buffer to hold chars
bufferEnd label byte                ; mark end of buffer
```

```
xtable    db   '0123456789ABCDEF'     ; translate table
.code
Writeint proc
     pusha
     mov   cx,0
     mov   di,offset bufferEnd

L1:  mov   dx,0                         ; clear dividend to zero
     div   bx                           ; divide AX by the radix
     xchg  ax,dx                        ; exchange quotient, remainder
     push  bx
     mov   bx,offset xtable             ; translate table
     xlat                               ; look up ASCII digit
     pop   bx
     dec   di                           ; back up in buffer
     mov   [di],al                      ; move digit into buffer
     xchg  ax,dx                        ; swap quotient into AX
     inc   cx                           ; increment digit count
     or    ax,ax                        ; quotient = 0?
     jnz   L1                           ; no: divide again

     ; Display the buffer using CX as a counter.

L2:  mov   ah,2                         ; function: display character
     mov   dl,[di]                      ; character to be displayed
     int   21h                          ; call DOS
     inc   di                           ; point to next character
     loop  L2
     popa
     ret
Writeint endp
end
```

9.7   ASCII TO BINARY CONVERSION

When a program reads a string of digits from standard input, it's useful to convert the digits to a binary integer. Particularly when the number is used in calculations, it must be saved in binary. The most widely used conversion algorithm involves repeatedly multiplying each digit by 10 and adding it to a sum. Let's use the ASCII string "4096" to demonstrate the algorithm. AX is initialized to zero. As we read each ASCII digit, we multiply AX by 10, and the digit's binary value is added to AX. After all digits have been read, AX contains the binary value of the number 4096:

AX Before				New Digit		AX After	
0	*	10	+	4	=	4	
4	*	10	+	0	=	40	
40	*	10	+	9	=	409	
409	*	10	+	6	=	4096	**final value**

9.7.1 The Readint Procedure

The Readint procedure in Example 13 reads an ASCII decimal number from standard input, converts it to binary, and stores the converted value in AX. Leading spaces are skipped, and the procedure checks for a leading sign (+ or −). The end of the number is found when the first nondigit character is read.

At labels A2 and A3, the procedure checks for a leading negative (−) or positive (+) sign. The variable called **sign** is set to −1 if a negative sign is found. If either no sign or a positive sign is found, **sign** is set to 1. At label A5, we make sure that DL contains a valid ASCII digit, and convert it to binary by clearing its high 4 bits.

The actual conversion begins with the AND instruction five lines after label A5. The current digit is converted from ASCII to binary by clearing the high 4 bits, and the result is multiplied by 10:

```
and   dx,000Fh                ; no: convert to binary
push  dx                      ; save the digit
mul   bx                      ; DX:AX = AX * BX
pop   dx                      ; restore the digit
jc    A6                      ; quit if result too large
```

These instructions detect overflow by checking the Carry flag after both the MUL and ADD instructions.

```
add   ax,dx                   ; add new digit to AX
jc    A6                      ; quit if result too large
```

You may recall that a 16-bit multiply operation sets the Carry flag when its result is larger than 16 bits. If the result is larger than 16 bits, we display the following message on the screen and exit because the value returned by Readint is no longer valid:

```
<integer overflow>
```

Example 13. The ReadInt Procedure.

```
; Readint -------------------------------------------
; Reads a signed decimal number from standard input, in
; the range -32768 to +32767. Skips leading spaces.
; Returns the 16-bit binary value of the number in AX.
; No other registers are changed.
;----------------------------------------------------
.data
sign          dw  ?
inputarea     db  10,0,10 dup(' ')    ; up to 9 digits
overflow_msg  db  0dh,0ah," <integer overflow> $"
.code
Readint proc
    push  ebx
    push  ecx
    push  edx
    push  si
    mov   dx,offset inputarea    ; input the string
    mov   ah,0Ah
    int   21h
    mov   si,offset inputarea+2
    mov   cx,0                ; scan for leading spaces
    mov   cl,inputarea+1      ; get number of chars entered
    or    cx,cx               ; any chars entered?
    jnz   A1                  ; yes: continue
    mov   ax,0                ; no: set value to zero
    jmp   A8                  ; exit procedure

A1: mov   al,[si]            ; get a character from buffer
    cmp   al,' '             ; space character found?
    jnz   A2                 ; no: check for a sign
    inc   si                 ; yes: point to next char
    loop  A1
    jcxz  A8                 ; quit if all spaces

A2: mov   sign,1            ; assume number is positive
    cmp   al,'-'             ; minus sign found?
    jnz   A3                 ; no: look for plus sign
    mov   sign,-1           ; yes: sign is negative
    inc   si                 ; point to next char
    jmp   A4
```

```
A3: cmp    al,'+'              ; plus sign found?
    jnz    A4                  ; no: must be a digit
    inc    si                  ; yes: skip over the sign

A4: mov    ax,0                ; clear accumulator
    mov    bx,10               ; BX is the multiplier

A5: mov    dl,[si]             ; get character from buffer
    cmp    dl,'0'              ; character < '0'?
    jl     A8                  ; yes: resolve sign and exit
    cmp    dl,'9'              ; character > '9'?
    jg     A8                  ; yes: resolve sign and exit
    and    dx,000Fh            ; no: convert to binary
    push   dx                  ; save the digit
    mul    bx                  ; DX:AX = AX * BX
    pop    dx                  ; restore the digit
    jo     A6                  ; quit if result too large
    add    ax,dx               ; add new digit to AX
    jo     A6                  ; quit if result too large
    inc    si                  ; point to next digit
    jmp    A5                  ; get another digit

    ; Overflow may have occurred.
A6: cmp    ax,8000h            ; If (AX <> 8000h)
    jne    A7
    cmp    sign,-1             ; or (sign <> -1),
    jne    A7                  ; show the overflow message
    jmp    A8                  ; else skip the overflow messsage

A7: mov    dx,offset overflow_msg
    mov    ah,9
    int    21h
    mov    ax,0                ; set result to zero

A8: mul    sign                ; AX = AX * sign
    pop    si
    pop    edx
    pop    ecx
    pop    ebx
    ret
Readint endp
end
```

An Interesting Bug. Often we learn more from the mistakes made while writing programs than we do when they work the first time. See if you can catch an error I made while developing the first version of Readint. I wrote the following code to multiply the number in AX by 10 and add the value of the most recent digit:

```
and   dx,000Fh          ; convert digit to binary
mul   bl                ; AX = AL * 10
jc    A6                ; quit if result too large
add   ax,dx             ; add new digit to AX
```

Before these instructions are reached, BX always contains 10. Let's say that AX = 0020h and DL = 2. AL is multiplied by BL, so AX = 0140h. DL is added to AX, yielding AX = 0142h. The routine seems to work correctly.

But let's try another example, with AX = 0200h and DL = 02. AL * BL yields AX = 0. DL is added to this, so AX = 0002h. The solution, as we now see it, is that we must multiply using BX, not BL. This means the result is stored in both DX and AX:

```
DX:AX = AX * BX
```

Of course, as soon as we do this, we destroy the digit that was being held in DL, so we have a new bug:

```
and   dx,000Fh          ; convert digit to binary
mul   bx                ; DX:AX = AX * 10
jc    A6                ; quit if result too large
add   ax,dx             ; add new digit to AX
```

This is also a hard bug to catch unless you know that a 16-bit multiply always replaces the contents of DX, no matter how small the product is. So we must push DX on the stack before the multiplication and restore it afterward:

```
and   dx,000Fh          ; convert digit to binary
push  dx                ; save the digit
mul   bx                ; DX:AX = AX * 10
pop   dx                ; restore the digit
jc    A6                ; quit if result too large
add   ax,dx             ; add new digit to AX
```

In retrospect, the error seems all too obvious, because the number in AX must always be multiplied by 10. If only such answers would seem obvious from the start.

9.8   REVIEW QUESTIONS

1.   What is the difference between an ASCII decimal number and a binary number?

2. If we stored the ASCII decimal number 4096 in four bytes of memory, what would be the hexadecimal contents of each byte?

3. Which register is used by XLAT to hold the address of a translate table?

4. Can the XLAT instruction work with a table containing 16-bit values? (y/n)

5. If the name of a table is coded as an operand, will XLAT use its address rather than the one in BX? (y/n)

6. Which flags are affected by the XLAT instruction?

7. What will AL contain after the following instructions have executed?

```
mov  bx,offset chars
mov  al,6
xlat

    .
    .

chars  db  'ABCDEFGHIJ'
```

8. What will be the hexadecimal value of AL after the following instructions have executed? Assume that **ptr1** is located at address 0106h:

```
mov  bx,ptr2
mov  al,6
xlat table

    .
    .

table  db  '1234567890'
ptr1   dw  ptr2
ptr2   dw  table
ptr3   dw  ptr1
```

9. Design a table that could be used by XLAT to translate lowercase letters into uppercase.

10. Use paper and pencil to demonstrate the algorithm used in this chapter for conversion from binary to ASCII decimal, using the number 302h.

11. Use paper and pencil to demonstrate the algorithm used in this chapter for conversion from ASCII decimal to binary, using the digit string '8196'.

12. Show how the ASCII hexadecimal digit string "3F62" is converted to binary.

13. So far, we have only been able to display 16-bit and 32-bit integers. How might we display a 64-bit integer?

14. Describe the contents of SI and DS after the following instruction is executed. Assume that the variable **long_ptr** is located at offset 0 from the beginning of the data segment:

```
lds   si,long_ptr
      .
      .
long_ptr  dd  0123ABCDh
```

15. What is the difference between the following two instructions?

```
les   si,bigval
lds   si,bigval
```

16. The following program excerpt is designed to take each character from **inputlist**, check it against **validchars**, and print the character only when the XLAT instruction returns 0FFh in AL. Correct both syntax and logic errors:

```
      mov   bx,validchars
      mov   di,offset inputlist
getchar:
      mov   al,[si]
      xlat  validchars
      or    al,al
      jz    getchar
      int   21h
      loop  getchar
      .
      .
inputlist   db 5,26,45,96,88,128
validchars  db 32 dup(0)        ; invalid chars: 0-31
            db 96 dup(0FFh)     ; valid chars:   32-127
            db 128 dup(0)       ; invalid chars: 128-255
```

17. The following excerpt is adapted from the **Writeint** procedure introduced earlier in this chapter. To test your understanding of the procedure, add explanatory comments to lines 1, 4, 6, 8, 10, and 11:

```
1.        mov   cx,0            ; _____
2..       mov   di,offset buffer+6
3.        mov   bx,10
4.   L1:  mov   dx,0            ; _____
5.        div   bx
6.        or    dl,30h          ; _____
7.        dec   di
8.        mov   [di],dl         ; _____
9.        inc   cx
10.       or    ax,ax           ; _____
```

```
11.    jnz  L1                  ; _____
       .
       .
buffer  db  6 dup(' ')
```

18. In the sample program in the previous question, if AX contained 0600h at the beginning, what would be the value of DX each time after executing line 5?

9.9 PROGRAMMING EXERCISES

1. *Display the System Date*

Write a procedure that writes the system date to standard output in either of the following formats:

```
Format 1:  8/20/89
Format 2:  20-Aug-1989
```

Use DOS function 2Ah to obtain the current date from the operating system. DOS places the year in CX, the month in DH, the day of the month in DL, and the day of the week in AL. When the procedure is called, pass it a value of 1 or 2 in AL to choose the display format. Test the procedure by calling it from a main program.

2. *Set the System Date*

Write a program that uses a date input from the keyboard to set the system date. Test your procedure by calling it from an existing program. DOS function 2Bh (set system date) requires the year number to be in CX, the month number to be in DH, and the day number to be in DL. For example:

```
mov  ah,2Bh                 ; set system date
mov  cx,1989                ; year = 1989
mov  dh,10                  ; month = October
mov  dl,18                  ; day = 18
int  21h                    s; call DOS
```

After running the program, use the DOS DATE command to verify that the program worked.

3. *Character Encoding - 1*

Modify the encode.asm program presented in Example 2 so all text can be entered from the keyboard. When the Enter key is pressed at the end of each line, redisplay the line in encoded format. Then prompt for a new input line. Continue in this manner until the ESC key is pressed. At that point, display the last encoded line and a count of the number of lines that were typed, and return to DOS.

4. *Character Decoding - 1*

Run the encode.asm program shown in Example 2 on page 318. Write a new program that decodes the file produced by encode.asm and displays the decoded text.

5. *Character Encoding - 2*

As mentioned in the discussion of the encode.asm program (Example 2, p. 318), the code used by the program could easily be broken. Improve the algorithm by using part of the current system date to control the number of bits each byte in the table is rotated. For a guide to getting the system date from DOS, see the explanation of DOS function 2Ah in Exercise 1.

Suppose DOS returns the month and day for July 1 in DX as 0701h (1,793). You can divide DX by 10 and keep the remainder (3). After using the XLAT instruction, the resulting byte can be rotated 3 bits to the left and then written to the output file. You can write the binary value of DX to the beginning of the output file before writing the encoded text, so the program that decodes the file (see Exercise 6) can also calculate the rotation value.

6. *Character Decoding - 2*

Write a program that decodes the output file created by the program in the previous exercise. It must read the 16-bit date value from the beginning of the file, calculate the bit rotation value, read each character, rotate it to the right, XLAT the character, and write the converted character to standard output. You may find it easier to debug this program if you read the entire input file into a buffer, but this will require learning how to open and close file handles, and how to read and write blocks of data from files. See pp. 448-452 for the relevant information.

7. *Window Application Program*

Write a program that does the following, using procedures from the book's link library plus procedures you write yourself:

• Clear the screen and divide it into four panels, each a different color.

• Position the cursor in the first panel (Panel 1) and prompt the user for a line of text.

• In Panel 2, display the text the user entered in Panel 1 as all uppercase letters.

• In Panel 3, have the user enter an unsigned integer. Redisplay the integer in Panel 4 in binary, octal, decimal, and hexadecimal. Label each as it is displayed—for example:

```
Binary      --> 10010101
Octal       --> 225
Decimal     --> 149
Hexadecimal --> 95
```

8. *Bin8_ToHex Procedure*

Write a general procedure named Bin8_toHex that converts an 8-bit binary number to a null-terminated string containing two hexadecimal digits. Input parameters: AL contains the binary value, and DX contains a pointer to a buffer where the hexadecimal digits are to be stored. Test the procedure by calling it from a program and passing it several different values.

9. Bin8_toAsc Procedure

Using the Bin8_toHex procedure from the previous exercise as a starting point, make the following improvement: Let the procedure's caller specify the type of ASCII digits as binary, octal, decimal, or hexadecimal. Test the procedure by calling it from a program and passing it at least ten different values.

10. Bin16_toAsc Procedure

Write a procedure called Bin16_toAsc that converts an unsigned 16-bit binary value to a null-terminated string containing decimal digits. *Input parameters:* Pass the binary value to be converted, and pass a pointer to the output string. Test the procedure by passing it several different values. Here is a sample call:

```
.data
nval    dw 1234h
buffer db 10 dup(0)          ; null-terminated string
.code
mov ax,nval                  ; binary value
mov dx,offset buffer         ; pointer to string
call Bin16_toAsc
call WriteString             ; display the string
```

Or, you may prefer to use stack parameters:

```
push nval
push offset buffer
call Bin16_toAsc
call WriteString
```

11. Asc_toBin16 Procedure

Write a procedure called Asc_toBin16 that converts a string of ASCII decimal digits into a signed 16-bit binary integer. Pass a pointer to the string when calling the procedure, and return the binary value in AX. Use the Readint procedure from this chapter as a guide.

12. Asc_toBin32 Procedure

Write a procedure called Asc_toBin32 that converts a string of ASCII decimal digits into a signed 32-bit binary integer. Pass a pointer to the string when calling the procedure, and return the binary value in EAX. Use the Readint procedure from this chapter as a guide. Here is a sample call to the procedure:

```
.data
digits    db "+123456789",0
numberVal dd ?
.code
push offset digits           ; input string
```

```
call Asc_toBin32
mov  numberVal,eax
```

13. *Improved Asc_toBin32 Procedure*

Improve the Asc_toBin32 procedure from the previous exericse by allowing the user to specify which numeric format (octal, decimal, or hexadecimal) is used in the input string. For hexadecimal strings, use "0x" as the prefix; for octal strings, prepend a leading zero to the string; for decimal strings, start with a digit between 1 and 9. (The C/C++ language uses the same rules.) For example, each of the following digit strings demonstrates a different numeric format:

```
.data
hexDigits       db "0x6A3B4F29A1",0
octalDigits     db "034526",0
decimalDigits   db "34526",0
numberVal       dd ?

.code
push offset hextDigits
call Asc_toBin32
mov  numberVal,eax
```

14. *Writeint_signed Procedure*

Implement the Writeint_signed procedure from the book's link library that was described at the beginning of this chapter, in Table 1. Write a program that tests and demonstrates the procedure with a variety of signed integers.

15. *Writelong Procedure*

Implement the Writelong procedure from the book's link library. The input to this procedure is a 32-bit unsigned binary number in EAX. Write the number to standard output.

16. *Writelong_signed Procedure*

Write a procedure called Writelong_signed that writes a 32-bit signed integer to standard output with a leading plus or minus sign. The procedure's input parameter is the binary integer that is to be displayed. Write a program that tests and demonstrates the procedure with a variety of sample integers.

17. *Display Formatted Numbers*

Using the WRITEINT procedure from Example 12 as a guide, write a new procedure that displays an ASCII decimal number in fixed-length format. In addition to passing the binary value in AX, let CX equal the desired format size. As the number is written to standard output, insert leading spaces to right-justify the number. For example, the number 4096, with a length of 8 in CX, would be displayed with four leading spaces:

"   4096"

To test the procedure, write two vertically aligned columns of numbers to standard output. For example,

```
 200              3
 -26          -5120
-3321         32767
```

18. WriteInt64 Procedure

Write a procedure called WriteInt64 that writes the 64-bit number contained in EDX:EAX to standard output.

19. Hexadecimal Memory Dump

Write a program that displays a 128-byte block of memory in ASCII hexadecimal, similar to the format used by Debug. Of course, you can use the procedures presented in this chapter and add a procedure of your own to handle conversion from 8-bit binary to ASCII hexadecimal. Display a heading showing the current value of the DS segment register, and display the offset address of the first byte in each row along the left side. Display 16 bytes in each row, as in the following sample:

```
Memory Contents at Segment 38FF:
0100  30 68 2C 20 66 75 6E 63 74 69 6F 6E 20 30 31 68
0110  2C 20 69 6E 20 6F 72 64 65 72 20 74 6F 20 0D 0A
0120  73 68 6F 77 20 77 68 69 63 68 20 6D 6F 64 65 20
0130  69 73 20 63 75 72 72 65 6E 74 6C 79 20 61 63 74
0140  69 76 65 2E 29 20 20 0D 0A 20 20 20 20 45 78 74
0150  72 61 20 23 32 3A 20 44 69 73 70 6C 61 79 20 74
0160  68 65 20 C5 20 63 68 61 72 61 63 74 65 72 20 77
0170  68 65 6E 20 6F 6E 65 20 6C 69 6E 65 20 63 72 6F
```

20. Enhanced Hexadecimal Memory Dump

Enhance the program written for the previous exercise. Prompt the operator for the starting segment and offset values to be dumped. After each block is displayed, wait for a keystroke, clear the screen, and display the next block of memory. Quit when the Esc key is pressed.

21. Hexadecimal File Dump

Read a file from standard input and dump the file in hexadecimal. Dump each 128-byte block, clear the screen, wait for a keystroke, and continue dumping the file until you reach its end. Also, display an ASCII dump of each line on the right-hand side of the hexadecimal dump. Here is a sample:

```
0100  30 68 2C 20 66 75 6E 63 74 69 6F 6E 20 30 31 68  Oh, function 01h
0110  2C 20 69 6E 20 6F 72 64 65 72 20 74 6F 20 0D 0A  , in order to ..
0120  73 68 6F 77 20 77 68 69 63 68 20 6D 6F 64 65 20  show which mode
0130  69 73 20 63 75 72 72 65 6E 74 6C 79 20 61 63 74  is currently act
0140  69 76 65 2E 29 20 20 0D 0A 20 20 20 20 45 78 74  ive.) ..    Ext
0150  72 61 20 23 32 3A 20 44 69 73 70 6C 61 79 20 74  ra #2: Display t
0160  68 65 20 C5 20 63 68 61 72 61 63 74 65 72 20 77  he E character w
0170  68 65 6E 20 6F 6E 65 20 6C 69 6E 65 20 63 72 6F  hen one line cro
```

22. *Register Snapshot Program*

Write a procedure that prints a snapshot of selected CPU registers and flags. This is a simplified version of the utility that programmers used to call "SNAP" on mainframe computers. Design the output so it is easy to read and contains only essential information. A sample register display follows:

```
08FF:0100 AX=0000 BX=0000 CX=0000 DX=0000 SI=0000 DI=0000
DS=38FF ES=38FF SS=38FF SF=1 ZF=0 CF=0 OF=0 DF=0
```

Test your SNAP procedure by calling it several times from the same program.

23. *4 x 4 Matrix Program*

Write a program that reads 16 numbers (range, 0-999) from standard input and displays them on the screen as a 4 x 4 matrix. Here is an example:

```
   0    50     2   200
  66    21    54    20
   1     3     4     6
 100   150   120    99
```

Perform the following operations:

- Compute and display the sum of row 1.

- Compute and display the sum of column 2.

- Count and display the number of values > 100.

- Wait for a key to be pressed, interchange rows 1 and 2, and redisplay the matrix.

10 *Strings And Arrays*

10.1 STRING STORAGE METHODS

10.1.1 Overview

This chapter concentrates on specific instructions designed for string processing and shows how to create a library of useful procedures. Let us broaden the usual definition of strings here, to include arrays of 8-bit or 16-bit integers.

String processing is ideally suited to assembly language because it consists of small tasks that are repeated many times. Word processing and database management programs, for example, must carry out string operations without a noticeable loss of speed. Language compilers also require a great deal of string manipulation. Highly skilled programmers are able to optimize critical string-handling routines by writing them in assembly language.

First we will look at the way strings are stored. This is more complicated than it sounds because high-level languages use different string storage formats. An assembly language program must be able to adapt to all of them. Next, we will examine the *string primitive* instructions in the Intel instruction set. These powerful, efficient instructions are optimized by the processor for searching, copying, and comparing large blocks of data. Last, we will develop a set of general-purpose string routines (procedures) and write an application program that tests them.

10.1.2 Types of Strings

Nearly all programming languages contain statements that process character strings. They differ greatly, however, in the way they store and manipulate strings. Several basic formats are used most often.

Fixed-Length Buffer. A fixed-length buffer holds the characters, and unused positions at the end are filled with spaces. This method is used by COBOL, for instance:

S	T	R	I	N	G		O	N	E										

This type of string would be declared in assembly language as

```
db "STRING ONE            "
```

Length Descriptor. A *length descriptor* byte can be stored at the beginning of a string. In Turbo Pascal, for example, this format allows a string to vary in length from 0 to the number of bytes reserved by the string's declaration. Unused positions in the string have undetermined values, marked here by a question mark:

0Ah

This string would be declared in assembly language as

```
db 0Ah,"STRING TWO",10 dup(?)
```

Null-Terminated. An *ASCIIZ string*, or *null-terminated string,* is a string of characters followed by a byte containing the value zero. The active length of the string can vary from zero to the number of bytes reserved by the string's declaration. Unused positions have an undetermined value, shown here by the question mark (?) character. This format is used by the C language, and for strings passed to DLL procedures in Microsoft Windows:

(null byte)

This would be declared in assembly language as

```
db "STRING THREE",0,6 dup(?)
```

Variable-Length. A variable-length *BASIC string* is defined by a 32-bit string descriptor, which in turn contains a pointer to the actual characters in the string. This is how a string descriptor can be simulated in assembly language:

```
stringData db "This is a string referenced by a descriptor"
strDataSize = ($ - stringData)

Descriptor struct
  length dw  strDataSize
  strPtr dw  stringData
Descriptor ends
```

The primary advantage to this format, however, is that the string can vary in size. But this requires that the program allocate additional storage for the string when it expands.

10.2   STRING PRIMITIVE INSTRUCTIONS

There are five specialized instructions for processing sequences of bytes, words, or doublewords: MOVS, CMPS, SCAS, STOS, and LODS. Intel calls these instructions *string primitives*. Now that international standards for character storage have been established for languages such as C++, strings often consist of sequences of either 8- or 16-bit characters.

Table 1 contains a summary of the string primitive instructions, showing the implied operands for each. The instructions require us to use DI and SI, which contain offsets from the DS and ES segment registers, respectively. String primitives can be automatically repeated, making them especially useful. They can also have two memory operands, a feature missing in other instructions. Programs running on the Intel 8086/088 processor enjoy a spectacular improvement in processing speed when using string primitives rather than using loops with the MOV instruction. This advantage is less pronounced in programs running on the 80286 and later processors, primarily because the efficiency of the MOV instruction and effective address calculation was greatly improved on the 80286 over earlier processors.

In these instructions, the *source* operand is a location addressed by DS:SI and the *destination* operand is addressed by ES:DI. The ES register must point to the start of the data segment before we can use a string instruction with a destination operand. ES can be initialized at the same time as DS. For example:

Table 1. String Primitive Instructions, Implied Operands.

Instruction	Description	Implied Operands
MOVS	Move String Data: Copy a memory byte, word, or doubleword from one memory location to another.	MOVS [DI],[SI]
CMPS	Compare String: Compare a memory byte, word, or doubleword to memory.	CMPS [SI],[DI]
SCAS	Scan String: Compare AL, AX, or EAX to the contents of memory, affecting the Flags register.	SCAS [DI],AL SCAS [DI],AX SCAS [DI],EAX
STOS	Store String Data: Store AL, AX, or EAX into memory.	STOS [DI],AL STOS [DI],AX STOS [DI],EAX
LODS	Load Accumulator from String: Load a byte, word, or doubleword into AL, AX, or EAX from memory.	LODS AL,[SI] LODS AX,[SI] LODS EAX,[SI]

```
mov   ax,@data        ; get address of data segment
mov   ds,ax           ; initialize DS
mov   es,ax           ; initialize ES
```

Each string primitive instruction has three possible formats. The *general* format can be used with byte, word, or doubleword operands. The formats ending with **B** (MOVSB, CMPSB, . . .) imply the use of 8-bit operands, those ending with **W** imply 16-bit operands, and those ending with **D** imply 32-bit operands, shown in Table 2. Also implied by each size suffix is the value to be used when automatically incrementing index registers. The *general* format does not specify an operand size (for example, MOVS or SCAS), so the operands must be coded explicitly:

```
MOVS   dest,source    ; copy source to destination
CMPS   dest,source    ; compare source to destination
SCAS   dest           ; scan destination string
STOS   dest           ; store accumulator into destination
LODS   source         ; load accumulator from source
```

If a specific operand size is specified, the operands need not be supplied with the instruction. In any case, SI and DI must be set to the offsets of the operands. For example:

```
mov   si,offset source    ; point SI to source
```

```
mov     di,offset dest            ; point DI to destination
movsb                             ; copy from source to destination
```

If explicit operands are used, SI and DI must still be initialized:

```
mov     si,offset source          ; point SI to source
mov     di,offset dest            ; point DI to destination
```

When explicit operands are used, a segment override (ES:) lets the assembler know that **dest** represents an offset from ES. This segment override is required if you use simplified segment directives (.CODE, .DATA, and .STACK):

```
movs    es:dest,source            ; copy from source to destination
```

Table 2. Overview of String Primitive Instructions.

General	Specific Size	Description	Increment Value for SI and DI
MOVS	MOVSB	Move (copy) byte	1
	MOVSW	Move (copy) word	2
	MOVSD	Move (copy) doubleword*	4
CMPS	CMPSB	Compare bytes	1
	CMPSW	Compare words	2
	CMPSD	Compare doublewords*	4
SCAS	SCASB	Scan byte	1
	SCASW	Scan word	2
	SCASD	Scan doubleword*	4
STOS	STOSB	Store byte	1
	STOSW	Store word	2
	STOSD	Store doubleword*	4
LODS	LODSB	Load byte	1
	LODSW	Load word	2
	LODSD	Load doubleword*	4

(* *Intel386, Intel486, and Pentium processors.*)

Using a Repeat Prefix. A string primitive instruction processes only a single byte or word at a time, but it can be preceded by a *repeat prefix*. This causes the instruction to be repeated, making it possible to process an entire string using only one instruction. The following repeat prefixes are used:

```
REP                      Repeat while CX > 0
REPZ, REPE               Repeat while the Zero flag is set and CX > 0
REPNZ, REPNE             Repeat while the Zero flag is clear and CX > 0
```

When using a repeat prefix, move a counter value to CX prior to the instruction. In the following example, MOVSB moves 10 bytes from **string1** to **string2**:

```
mov    si,offset string1          ; SI points to source
mov    di,offset string2          ; DI points to destination
mov    cx,10                      ; set counter to 10
rep    movsb                      ; move 10 bytes
```

The repeat prefix is assembled into a single byte of machine code that precedes the string instruction. An assembly of the preceding example is as follows:

```
BE 0000 R    mov    si,offset string1
BF 000A R    mov    di,offset string2
B9 000A      mov    cx,10
F3/ A4       rep    movsb
```

You may recall that the letter *R* next to the addresses for **string1** and **string2** identifies these as relocatable operands because the location of the data segment is unknown until runtime. The REP prefix generates the machine instruction F3, and MOVSB consists of just a single byte: A4.

Direction Flag. String primitive instructions use the Direction flag to determine whether SI and DI will be automatically incremented or decremented by string instructions:

Value of the Direction Flag	Effect on SI and DI	Address Sequence
0	Incremented	Low-high
1	Decremented	High-low

The Direction flag can be explicitly changed by the CLD and STD instructions:

```
CLD        ; clear Direction flag, direction = up
STD        ; set Direction flag, direction = down
```

10.2.1 MOVS (Move String Data)

The MOVS instruction moves (copies) data from a *source* location pointed to by DS:SI to a *destination* location pointed to by ES:DI. The syntax is:

```
MOVS    dest,source
MOVSB
MOVSW
MOVSD
```

MOVS requires both operands to be supplied. MOVSB moves 8-bit operands, MOVSW moves 16-bit operands, and MOVSD moves 32-bit operands. The Direction flag determines the incrementing or decrementing of SI and DI. The size of the increment or decrement is shown in the following table:

Instruction	Value to be automatically added/subtracted from SI and DI
MOVSB	1
MOVSW	2
MOVSD	4

Copy Bytes. In the following example, 10 bytes are copied from **source** to **dest**. After we copy the bytes, both fields contain the same string, and SI and DI point 1 byte beyond the end of each string:

```
cld                             ; direction = up
mov     cx,10                   ; set counter to 10
mov     si,offset source        ; DS:SI points to source
mov     di,offset dest          ; ES:DI points to destination
rep     movsb                   ; byte operands specified
    .
    .
source  db      'ABCDEFGHIJ'
dest    db      10 dup(?)
```

In this example, the REP prefix causes MOVSB to repeat until CX is decremented to 0. Unlike the LOOP instruction, the REP prefix first tests to see if CX = 0 *before* executing the MOVSB instruction. If it does, the instruction is ignored and control passes to the next line in the program. If CX > 0, it is decremented and the instruction repeats. In the following example, the MOVSB instruction is not executed because CX = 0:

```
mov     cx,0
rep     movsb
```

Copying the Video Screen to a Buffer. Example 1 shows how to copy the video display to a buffer, saving its contents. Before an MS-DOS program displays a pop-up window, for example, it can save the contents of the screen underneath the window. When the window is removed, the previous contents of the screen can then be restored. The buffer is defined as an array of 2000 words. DS:SI points to the video display area, and ES:DI points to the buffer in our program's data segment. There are 25 rows and 80 columns on the screen, which total 2000 characters. Each character position on the screen consists of 2 bytes; one holds a displayable character, and the other holds a binary number defining the character's attribute.

Example 1. Saving the Text Screen to a Buffer.

```
.data
VIDEO_SEG = 0B800h                  ; color video buffer segment
WORD_COUNT = 2000
buffer dw WORD_COUNT dup(?)


.code
mov   si,VIDEO_SEG                  ; DS:SI points to the video area
mov   ds,si
mov   si,0
mov   di,seg buffer                 ; ES:DI points to the buffer
mov   es,di
mov   di,offset buffer
cld                                 ; direction = up
mov   cx,WORD_COUNT                 ; number of words to copy
rep   movsw                         ; copy from DS:SI to ES:DI
```

10.2.2 The Need for Speed

For programs that run on the 8088 (and 8086) processor, string primitive instructions offer an enormous advantage in runtime performance over a loop containing MOV instructions. There are several reasons for this performance advantage:

• String instructions are only 1 byte long, causing them to take up less space in the 8088's 4-byte instruction prefetch queue than comparable MOV instructions.

• String instructions automatically increment index registers, avoiding the need for a separate instruction to advance a pointer to the next value in a sequence of bytes, words, or doublewords.

• Using the REP prefix, a string instruction can be repeated as many as 65,535 times, avoiding the need for time-consuming branching instructions. Branching instructions always cause the prefetch queue to be emptied and reloaded on the 8088.

For example, we might want to copy all values from an array called **source** to an array called **target.** Here are their definitions:

```
ARRAY_SIZE = 1000
source dw ARRAY_SIZE dup(?)
target dw ARRAY_SIZE dup(?)
```

First we will code a loop using MOV to copy the array:

```
        mov   ax,@data
        mov   ds,ax
        mov   si,0
        mov   cx,ARRAY_SIZE

L1: mov   ax,source[si]
        mov   target[si],ax
        add   si,2
        loop L1
```

Now let's use MOVSW to do the same thing:

```
        mov   ax,@data
        mov   ds,ax
        mov   es,ax
        mov   si,offset source
        mov   di,offset target
        mov   cx,ARRAY_SIZE          ; repetition count
        cld                          ; direction = UP
        rep movsw
```

10.2.3 CMPS (Compare Strings)

The CMPS instruction compares a source operand pointed to by DS:SI to a destination operand pointed to by ES:DI. The syntax is

```
CMPS    dest,source
CMPSB
CMPSW
CMPSD
```

The comparison is in the reverse order of the CMP instruction. If you use CMPS, both operands must be supplied. CMPSB compares 8-bit operands, CMPSW compares 16-bit operands, and CMPSD compares 32-bit operands. The Direction flag determines the incrementing or decrementing of SI and DI. The following repeat prefixes can be used:

```
REP                    Repeat while CX > 0
REPE, REPZ             Repeat while source = destination
REPNE, REPNZ           Repeat while source ≠ destination
```

If the source string is less than the destination, CF = 1. If the strings are equal, ZF = 1. If the source is greater than the destination, ZF = 0 and CF = 0. The conditional jumps following CMPS are summarized in Table 3:

Table 3. Unsigned and Signed Jumps.

Condition	Unsigned	Signed
source < dest	JB	JL
source <= dest	JBE	JLE
source ≠ dest	JNE (JNZ)	JNE (JNZ)
source = dest	JE (JZ)	JE (JZ)
source >= dest	JAE	JGE
source > dest	JA	JG

Implied Order of Operands. Be careful when following the CMPS instruction with a conditional jump. The order of operands is not the same as it is for CMP, which compares the destination operand to the source operand. In the following example, CMP implies subtraction of the source from the destination. CMPS, however, implies subraction of the destination from the source:

```
mov     ax,10
cmp     ax,5              ; implies (AX − 5)
cmps    es:dest,source    ; implies (source − dest)
```

In the next example, the conditional jump to **source_smaller** is taken because the seventh character in **source** is smaller than the corresponding character in **dest**:

```
.data
source    db    'MARTIN  '
dest      db    'MARTINEZ'

.code
    cld                        ; direction = up
    mov   si,offset source     ; point to source
    mov   di,offset dest       ; point to destination
```

```
        mov    cx,8                    ; length of strings
        repe   cmpsb                   ; compare source to destination
        jb     source_smaller          ; jump if source < destination
        .
source_smaller:
```

We might picture the two strings as follows before and after the comparison:

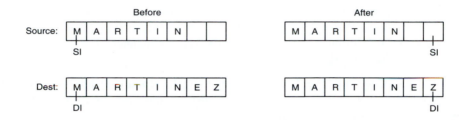

(If the strings had been equal, SI and DI would both have been left pointing one byte beyond the ends of the strings.)

We start by setting SI and DI to the offsets of the two strings. Both registers are incremented until a difference between the strings in position 7 is found. After the CMPSB finishes, SI and DI are left pointing one byte beyond the characters that were different.

Comparing Signed Integers. The CMPSW instruction can compare two lists of signed integers. In the following example, each number in **array1** is compared to **array2**. **Array1** is found to be smaller because its third number is −4, while the corresponding number in **array2** is 3:

```
.data
array1  DW   -1,2,-4,20
array2  DW   -1,2,3,20
.code
cld                             ; direction = up
mov    si,offset array1         ; source
mov    di,offset array2         ; destination
mov    cx,4                     ; counter
repe   cmpsw                    ; compare source to dest
jl     array1_smaller           ; jump if array1 < array2
```

10.2.4 SCAS (Scan String)

The SCAS instruction compares a value in AL/AX/EAX to a memory byte, word, or doubleword addressed by ES:DI. The syntax is:

```
SCAS    dest
```

```
SCASB
SCASW
SCASD
```

ES:DI holds the address of the destination operand. If SCAS is used, the name of the destination operand must be supplied. If SCASB is used, 8-bit operands are assumed; if SCASW is used, 16-bit operands are assumed; SCASD uses 32-bit operands. The Direction flag determines the incrementing or decrementing of SI and DI.

This instruction is particularly useful when looking for a single character in a long string. Combined with the REPE (or REP) prefix, the string is scanned only while the value in AL/AX matches each value in memory. The REPNE prefix scans until either AL/AX/EAX matches a value in memory or CX = 0.

Scan for a Matching Character. In the following example, **alpha** is scanned until the letter *F* is found. When the letter *F* is found, DI points 1byte beyond the matching character and is usually decremented so it points to the *F.*

```
.data
alpha   db    'ABCDEFGH',0

.code
mov     di,seg alpha
mov     ds,di
mov     di,offset alpha        ; ES:DI points to the string
mov     al,'F'                 ; search for the letter 'F'
mov     cx,8                   ; set the search count
cld                            ; direction = up
repne   scasb                  ; repeat while not equal
jnz     exit                   ; quit if letter is not found
dec     di                     ; found: back up DI one character
```

Right after the SCASB executes, DI is left pointing to the character *after* the one that was found:

Using a Conditional Jump Instruction. When a CMPSB ends, you don't know if it stopped because CX = 0, or because a matching character was found in the string. In fact, the two may have happened at the same time. In the case of REPNZ, use a JNZ instruction to jump when the character is found. You might think of it this way: If the Zero flag is clear, the character was not found. If the Zero flag is set, the character was found:

```
        repnz   cmpsb
        jnz     not_found
or:

        repnz   cmpsb
        jz      found
```

Don't make the mistake of using the JCXZ instruction to find out whether the character was found. The character might have been found in the last position scanned, and CX would still equal zero after the last comparison. The following would be incorrect:

```
    repnz   scasb
    jcxz    exit
```

Removing Trailing Blanks. The SCASB instruction can be used to remove all trailing blanks from an ASCIIZ string. In the following example, ES:DI points to the last byte in the string, CX equals the string length, AL = 20h (space character), and DF = 1. We use the REPE prefix in order to repeat the loop while AL matches each character in memory:

```
    .data
    dest    db   "DESTINATION STRING        ",0
    destlen = $ – dest – 1          ; calculate length

    .code
        mov   di,seg dest
        mov   es,di
        mov   di,offset dest        ; get string offset
        add   di,destlen – 1        ; point to last byte
        mov   cx,destlen            ; set up counter
        mov   al,20h                ; look for spaces
        std                         ; direction = backward
        repe  scasb                 ; scan the string
        jnz   exit                  ; no more blanks found
        dec   di                    ; adjust DI if CX = 0
    exit:
        mov     byte ptr es:[di+2],0  ; insert new null byte
```

After finding the first nonblank character, we insert a null byte just after it. This sets the string to its correct length. The following instruction is correct:

```
    mov byte ptr [di+2],0
```

SCASB leaves DI pointing at the character just before the first nonblank character. To refer to the position following the character, we add 2 to DI.

10.2.5 STOS (Store in String)

The STOS instruction stores the contents of AL/AX/EAX in memory at ES:DI. The different forms are:

```
STOS   dest
STOSB
STOSW
STOSD
```

ES:DI holds the address of the destination operand. STOS requires the name of the destination operand to be supplied. STOSB assumes that 8-bit operands are being used, STOSW uses 16-bit operands, and STOSD uses 32-bit operands. The Direction flag determines the incrementing or decrementing of SI and DI.

You can use STOS to initialize a block of memory to a single value. The following example initializes each byte in **string1** to 0FFh.

```
.data
string1   db   100 dup(?)

.code
mov    di,seg string1
mov    es,di
mov    al,0FFh                  ; value to be stored
mov    di,offset string1        ; ES:DI points to destination
mov    cx,100                   ; character count
cld                             ; direction = up
rep    stosb                    ; fill with contents of AL
```

10.2.6 LODS (Load String)

The LODS instruction loads a byte or word from memory at DS:SI into AL/ AX/EAX. The different forms are:

```
LODS   source
LODSB
LODSW
LODSD
```

DS:SI holds the address of the source operand. LODS requires the name of the source operand to be supplied. LODSB assumes that 8-bit operands are used, LODSW uses 16-bit operands, and LODSD uses 32-bit operands. The Direction flag determines whether SI and DI are incremented or decremented.

Repeat prefixes are rarely used with LODS because each new value loaded into AL or AX destroys its previous contents. As a single instruction, however, LODSB would substitute for the following two instructions:

```
mov  al,[si]              ; move byte at DS:SI to AL
inc  si                   ; point to next byte
```

The next example scans through **buffer**, clears the high bit from each byte, and stores it in **output**:

```
.data
buffer   db  0C8h,0FBh,0F5h,0CAh,41h,42h,43h,64h,87h,8Ch
output   db  10 dup(?)


.code
    cld                       ; direction = up
    mov  si,offset buffer     ; source buffer
    mov  di,offset output     ; destination buffer
    mov  cx,10                ; buffer length

L1: lodsb                     ; copy DS:[SI] into AL
    and  al,7Fh               ; clear high bit
    stosb                     ; store AL at ES:[DI]
    loop  L1
```

This example generates the following values in the output string. Each byte is the same as in the original, except that its highest bit has been cleared:

```
48 7B 75 4A 41 42 43 64 07 0C
```

10.3 A LIBRARY OF STRING PROCEDURES

In this section, we will create several string-handling procedures that can be called from your assembly language programs. (The procedures are already stored in the **irvine.lib** file that you received with this book.) Tasks performed by these procedures are probably familiar to you from your experience with high-level languages. Some languages contain built-in string instructions, while others are supplemented by a separate library of string-handling routines. We will borrow a few ideas from these libraries and invent some new routines. These will be collected into a library that can be linked to assembly language programs. String routines written in assembly language can mirror those available in high-level languages and, at the same time, be more compact and efficient.

The procedures (see Table 4) shown in this chapter assume the use of null-terminated strings of 8-bit characters. All procedures are assembled for the small memory model. We also assume that an 80386 or later processor is used, allowing the use of the PUSHA and POPA instructions to save and restore registers. Source code for the procedures is shown in this chapter.

Whenever one of our procedures refers to DS:SI or ES:DI, we assume that both DS and ES have already been initialized to the address of the data segment in your program. For example, if ES:DI is to point to video memory, the following statements should be executed:

```
COLOR_VIDEO_SEG = 0B800H
    .
    .
    .
push ds                       ; save current DS value
mov   ax,COLOR_VIDEO_SEG       ; set DS to the video segement
mov   ds,ax
<call the procedure>
pop   ds                      ; restore DS to the data segment
```

You can also use the SEG operator to obtain the segment address of a variable without having to know the segment's actual name:

```
mov   di,seg myArray
mov   es,di
mov   di,offset myArray
<call the procedure>
```

Table 4. String-Handling Procedures.

Procedure	Description
Str_compare	Compare two strings according to their collating sequence. CF = 1 if the first string is lesser, ZF = 1 if both strings are equal, and (CF = 0, ZF = 0) if the first string is greater.
Str_copy	Copy a source string to a destination string.
Str_length	Find the length of a string.
Str_getline	Read a null-terminated string from a file or device.
Str_read	Read a string from a file or device.
Str_ucase	Convert a string to uppercase.
Str_write	Write a string to a file or device.

If the segment name should ever change, this code will not have to be modified.

10.3.1 Str_compare Procedure

The Str_compare procedure compares a string (called *first*) pointed to by DS:SI to a string pointed to by ES:DI (called *second*). The comparison is case-sensitive, and the Flags register is affected as shown in Table 5.

Table 5. Flag Usage by the Str_compare Procedure.

Relation Between Strings	Carry Flag	Zero Flag	Related Jump Instruction
first < second	1	0	JB
first = second	0	1	JE
first > second	0	0	JA

These are exactly the flag conditions that apply to the JB (*jump below*), JE (*jump equal*), and JA (*jump above*) instructions. Example 2 shows the implementation of the Str_compare procedure. Very little code is necessary because the values of DS:SI and ES:DI are required for the CMPSB instruction. The following code calls the Str_compare procedure and implements jumps based on the result:

```
mov  si,offset stringOne
mov  di,offset stringTwo
call Str_compare                ; compare strings, set flags
jb   StringOneLess              ; jump to appropriate labels
je   StringsAreEqual
ja   StringOneGreater
```

Example 2. Str_compare Implementation.

```
.code
public Str_compare

Str_compare proc
    push  ax
    push  dx
    push  si
    push  di
```

```
L1: mov  al,[si]
    mov  dl,[di]
    cmp  al,0                        ; end of string1?
    jne  L2                          ; no
    cmp  dl,0                        ; yes: end of string2?
    jne  L2                          ; no
    jmp  L5                          ; yes, exit with ZF = 1

L2: inc  si                          ; point to next
    inc  di
    cmp  al,dl                       ; chars equal?
    je   L1                          ; yes: continue loop
                                     ; no: exit with flags set
L5: pop  di
    pop  si
    pop  dx
    pop  ax
    ret
Str_compare endp
```

10.3.2 Str_copy Procedure

The Str_copy procedure copies a null-terminated string from a source location to a destination location. Before calling this procedure, be sure the destination operand is large enough to hold the copied string. The required input parameters are the following:

Register	Description
DS:SI	The offset of the source string.
ES:DI	The offset of the destination location.

No values are returned by the procedure. Example 3 contains the implementation of the Str_copy procedure. This procedure could be made more efficient by copying 16 bits at a time, if the source and destination are aligned on 16-bit boundaries. This is left to the Chapter exercises. The following demonstrates a call to Str_copy. Notice that we use the SEG operator to initialize DS and ES to the segments containing the source and destination strings:

```
mov  si,seg source
mov  ds,si
mov  si,offset source
mov  di,seg destination
mov  es,di
mov  di,offset destination
call Str_copy
```

Example 3. Str_copy Implementation.

```
Str_copy proc
    pusha
    push    es                  ; save ES:DI
    push    di
    mov     ax,ds               ; get length of source
    mov     es,ax
    mov     di,si
    call    Str_length          ; AX = length
    pop     di                  ; restore ES:DI
    pop     es
    inc     ax                  ; add 1 for null byte
    mov     cx,ax               ; set CX to length
    cld                         ; clear direction to up
    rep     movsb               ; copy the string
    popa
    ret
Str_copy endp
```

10.3.3   Str_length Procedure

The Str_length procedure returns the length of a string in the AX register. The only required input parameter is the string's address in ES:DI. Because AX holds the return value, the string length cannot be greater than 65,535. The Str_length procedure implementation is shown in Example 4, and the following is a sample call to Str_length:

```
.data
myString db 128 dup(?)
myStringLen dw ?

.code
mov  di,set myString
mov  es,di
mov  di,offset myString
call Str_length
mov  myStringLen,ax
```

Example 4. Str_length Implementation.

```
Str_length proc
    push    cx
```

```
          push    di                  ; save pointer to string
          mov     cx,0FFFFh           ; set CX to maximum word value
          mov     al,0                ; scan for null byte
          cld                         ; direction = up
          repnz   scasb               ; compare AL to ES:[DI]
          dec     di                  ; back up one position
          mov     ax,di               ; get ending pointer
          pop     di                  ; retrieve starting pointer
          sub     ax,di               ; subtract start from end
          pop     cx
          ret                         ; AX = string length
    Str_length endp
```

10.3.4 Str_getline Procedure

The Str_getline procedure reads a sequence of characters from a file or device, stopping when the carriage return/linefeed characters (0Dh, 0Ah) are read. The delimiter is removed from the input stream. The required input parameters are shown here:

Register	Description
DS:DX	Points to the input buffer.
BX	A currently opened file or device handle. For standard input, BX = 0. Otherwise, the handle must refer to a file that is open for input.
CX	The maximum number of bytes to read.

The procedure returns the number of characters that were actually read in the AX register. If the data cannot be read, the procedure returns with CF = 1. Example 5 demonstrates a call to Str_getline.

Example 5. Calling the Str_getline Procedure.

```
.data
STDIN_HANDLE = 0
BUFFER_SIZE  = 80
inbuffer     db BUFFER_SIZE dup(0)
string_size dw ?

.code
mov  dx,offset inbuffer
mov  bx,STDIN_HANDLE
mov  cx,BUFFER_SIZE
```

```
call   Str_getline
jc     ErrorMessage                ; display an error message...
mov    string_size,ax              ; number of bytes actually read
```

If the end of the input line is not found, excess characters remain in the input stream until the next time we try to read from the same file or device. Example 6 shows the Str_getline procedure's implementation. We read one byte at a time so we can stop when a delimiter character is found.

Example 6. Str_getline Implementation.

```
Str_getline proc
    LOCAL count:word
    DOS_READ_HANDLE = 3Fh
    pusha
    mov   count,0
L1:
    mov   ah,DOS_READ_HANDLE
    push  cx                        ; save loop count
    mov   cx,1                      ; read one byte
    int   21h                       ; from file/device
    pop   cx                        ; restore loop count
    jc    L2
    mov   si,dx                     ; points to buffer
    mov   al,[si]                   ; get current byte
    cmp   al,0Dh                    ; carriage return found?
    jne   L2                        ; no: continue reading
    mov   ah,DOS_READ_HANDLE        ; yes: read a byte
    int   21h                       ; and discard linefeed
    mov   byte ptr [si],0           ; insert null byte
    jmp   L3                        ; and exit

L2: inc   count                     ; add to counter
    inc   dx                        ; next buffer address
    loop  L1                        ; continue until CX = 0

L3: popa
    mov   ax,count                  ; character count
    ret
Str_getline endp
```

10.3.5   Readstring Procedure

The Readstring procedure reads a sequence of characters from standard input until an end of line character (0Dh) is found. The characters are stored in a null-terminated string. Input parameters: DS:DX points to the input buffer, and CX contains a count of the maximum number of characters that can be read. Output: AX contains the size of the input string. The implementation is in Example 7.

Example 7. Readstring Procedure Implementation.

```
Readstring proc
    push  cx                    ; save registers
    push  si

    push  cx                    ; save digit count again
    mov   si,dx                 ; point to input buffer
A1:
    mov   ah,1                  ; function: keyboard input
    int   21h                   ; DOS returns char in AL
    cmp   al,0Dh                ; end of line?
    je    A2                    ; yes: exit
    mov   [si],al               ; no: store the character
    inc   si                    ; increment buffer pointer
    loop  A1                    ; loop until CX=0

A2: mov   byte ptr [si],0       ; end with a null byte
    pop   ax                    ; original digit count
    sub   ax,cx                 ; AX = size of input string

    pop   si                    ; restore registers
    pop   cx
    ret
Readstring endp
```

10.3.6   Str_ucase Procedure

The Str_ucase procedure converts a string pointed to by DS:SI to all uppercase characters. No value is returned by the procedure. The procedure implementation is shown in Example 8. The following demonstrates a call to Str_ucase:

```
sampleString db  'this is a sample string',0
    .
    .
```

```
mov  dx,offset sampleString
call Str_ucase
```

Example 8. Str_ucase Procedure Implementation.

```
Str_ucase proc
    push ax
    push si
    mov  si,dx

L1: mov  al,[si]
    cmp  al,0
    je   L2
    and  al,11011111b
    inc  si
    jmp  L1

L2: pop  si
    pop  ax
    ret
Str_ucase endp
```

10.3.7   Writestring Procedure

The Writestring procedure writes a null-terminated string to standard output, which is usually the console. When calling it, pass a pointer to the string in DS:DX. Example 9 shows the procedure's implementation.

Example 9. Writestring Implementation.

```
Writestring proc
    pusha
    push    ds                  ; set ES to DS
    pop     es
    mov     di,dx               ; let ES:DI point to the string
    call    Str_length          ; get length of string in AX
    mov     cx,ax               ; CX = number of bytes to write
    mov     ah,40h              ; write to file or device
    mov     bx,1                ; choose standard output
    int     21h                 ; call DOS
    popa
    ret
Writestring endp
```

10.3.8 The Str_write Procedure

Example 10 shows the source code for the module containing the Str_write procedure. Notice that only the procedure name is declared public. The Str_length procedure is declared external because it is called from Str_write. It is important to provide comments in each module that explain the procedure's purpose and list its input and output parameters.

Example 10. Source code for the Str_write Module.

```
title Str_write library module          (strwrite.asm)

; The Str_write procedure writes a string to a file or
; output device. Input: DX points to the string, and
; BX contains a file or device handle (BX = 1 for the
; standard output device).

.model small
.code
public Str_write
extrn Str_length:proc

Str_write proc
    push    ax
    push    cx
    call    Str_length          ; get length of string
    mov     cx,ax               ; CX = length
    inc     cx                  ; include the null byte
    mov     ah,40h              ; write to file or device
    int     21h                 ; call DOS
    pop     cx
    pop     ax
    ret
Str_write endp
end
```

10.4 STRING LIBRARY TEST PROGRAM

Let's write a short program (see Example 11) that demonstrates the string manipulation procedures from this chapter. The program prompts the user for a list of peoples' last names and stores the names in an array of strings. It then scans the array, locates the name with the lowest alphabetical value, and displays the name. It calls the following procedures:

Str_compare, Str_copy, Str_getline, Str_length, Str_write, Str_ucase, and Crlf (from the link library).

The following constants are declared at the beginning of the program to make the code more readable. The user can input a maximum of ten names, each of which can be as long as 30 bytes, including the null terminator. The DOS handle for console input is zero, and the handle for console output is 1:

```
MAXNAMES = 10
NAMESIZE = 30
CONSOLE_INPUT = 0
CONSOLE_OUTPUT = 1
```

In the Input_All_Names procedure, the program inputs a single name from the user. The offset in SI points to a row in the array of strings. The Str_getline procedure expects the input pointer to be in DS:DX, BX to contain the file or device handle, and CX the number of bytes to read:

```
mov    dx,si
mov    bx,CONSOLE_INPUT
mov    cx,NAMESIZE
call   Str_getline
```

After the user has entered a name, we get the name's length and exit if the length is zero. Otherwise, we move SI ahead to the start of the next array row and continue:

```
mov    di,si                ; get the name's length
call   Str_length           ; (AX = length)
or     ax,ax                ; if the length is zero then
jz     L2                   ;    exit the loop
add    si,NAMESIZE          ; else point to next row
mov    cx,loopCount         ;    restore loop counter
loop   L1                   ;    and get another name
```

In the **Find_Lowest_Name** procedure, the program compares each name to the one already chosen as the lowest. If a lower name is found, it is copied to the location pointed to by DI (the variable **lowest**).

```
L3:    call  Str_compare     ; SI (current string) < DI (smallest)?
       jae   L4              ; no: skip next instruction
       call  Str_copy        ; yes: copy current to smallest
L4:    add   si,NAMESIZE     ; point to next row
       Loop  L3              ; repeat for the other strings
```

Finally, we display the lowest name in all uppercase letters:

```
        mov   dx,offset smallest
        call  Str_ucase              ; convert to uppercase
        call  Str_write              ; display on console
```

Example 11. String Library Test Program.

```
        title String Library Test Program            (strtest.asm)

        ; This program inputs a list of words from the user
        ; and displays the word that is first in the list
        ; alphabetically.

        .model small
        .stack 100h
        .data
        MAXWORDS = 10
        WORDSIZE = 30
        CONSOLE_INPUT = 0
        CONSOLE_OUTPUT = 1

        WordCount dw ?
        loopCount dw ?
        smallest  dw WORDSIZE dup(0), 0
        WordList  db MAXWORDS dup( WORDSIZE dup(0), 0 )
        prompt1   db "Enter a word (blank to quit): ",0
        firstMsg  db "The first word (alphabetically) is ",0

        .code
        extrn Str_compare:proc, Str_copy:proc, Str_getline:proc
        extrn Str_length:proc, Str_write:proc, Str_ucase:proc
        extrn Crlf:proc

        main proc
             mov  ax,@data
             mov  ds,ax
             mov  es,ax
             call Input_All_Words
             call Find_Lowest_Word
             mov  ax,4C00h                  ; end program
             int  21h
        main endp
```

```
Input_All_Words proc
; Input a list of words and store them in an array.

        mov     si,offset wordList
        mov     cx,MAXWORDS             ; loop counter

L1:     mov     loopCount,cx            ; save loop counter
        mov     dx,offset prompt1       ; ask for a word
        mov     bx,CONSOLE_OUTPUT
        call    Str_write

        mov     dx,si                   ; input a word
        mov     bx,CONSOLE_INPUT
        mov     cx,WORDSIZE
        call    Str_getline
        call    Crlf

        mov     di,si                   ; get the word's length
        call    Str_length              ; (AX = length)
        or      ax,ax                   ; if the length is zero then
        jz      L2                      ;    exit the loop
        add     si,WORDSIZE             ; else point to next row
        mov     cx,loopCount            ;    restore loop counter
        loop    L1                      ;    and get another word

L2:     mov     wordCount,MAXWORDS      ; calc number of words
        mov     cx,loopCount
        sub     wordCount,cx
        ret
Input_All_Words endp


Find_Lowest_Word proc
; Determine which word is lowest alphabetically
; and display it.

        mov     si,offset wordList      ; copy first word to smallest
        mov     di,offset smallest
        call    Str_copy
        mov     cx,wordCount            ; initialize the loop counter

L3:     call    Str_compare             ; SI (current string) < DI (smallest)?
        jae     L4                      ; no, skip next instruction
```

```
        call  Str_copy          ; yes, copy current to smallest
L4:     add   si,WORDSIZE        ; point to next row
        Loop  L3                 ; repeat for the other strings

; Display the lowest word in uppercase letters.
        call  Crlf
        mov   dx,offset firstMsg
        mov   bx,CONSOLE_OUTPUT
        call  Str_write
        mov   dx,offset smallest
        call  Str_ucase          ; convert to uppercase
        call  Str_write          ; display on console
        call  Crlf
        ret
Find_Lowest_Word endp
end main
```

10.5   REVIEW QUESTIONS

1. Name at least three string operations performed by a text editor that might be easily implemented in assembly language.

2. If a program stores a string as a fixed-length alphabetic or alphanumeric field, what happens when a longer string is copied to a shorter string?

3. What happens to a Pascal-type string when the length descriptor byte is set to zero?

4. In the following excerpt, a list of 16-bit integers is copied from **sourcew** to **destw**. Which repeat prefix should be used: REP, REPZ, or REPNZ?

```
cld
mov     cx,count
mov     si,offset sourcew
mov     di,offset destw
movsw
```

5. Assemble and trace the following two examples using a debugger. How many bytes are loaded into AL by each?

```
Example_1:
    mov   cx,0
    mov   si,offset source
```

```
        lodsb

Example_2:
        mov    cx,0
        mov    si,offset source
        rep    lodsb
```

6. What is the value of DI at the end of the following excerpt? (Assume that **dest** begins at location 0006h.)

```
    .data
    dest    db    'XXXXAXXXX'

    .code
    cld
    mov    al,'A'
    mov    di,offset dest
    mov    cx,9
    repnz  scasb
```

7. In the following example, we want to compare two integer arrays. At the point where the two arrays differ, we want to move the lowest array element into AX. Identify and correct all logic errors:

```
    .data
    list01  DW  -1,2,-4,20
    list02  DW  -1,2,3,20

    .code
            cld
            lea   si,list01
            lea   di,list02
            mov   cx,4
            repe  cmpsw
            jl    L1
            dec   si
            mov   ax,[si]          ; move list01 to AX
            jmp   L2
    L1:     sub   di,2
            mov   ax,[di]          ; move list02 to AX
    L2:     ret
```

8. The following example scans a string backward, looking for the @ character. Identify and correct all logical errors:

```
.data
bigstring   db  'JOISD6H37DN398CX@98DF876743'
biglen      dw  $-bigstring

.code
lookforit:
    std                         ; direction = down
    mov    dl,'@'               ; DL = byte to be found
    mov    di,bigstring
    repz   scasb
    dec    di                   ; adjust DI when found
```

10.6 PROGRAMMING EXERCISES

Each of the following procedures assumes the use of null-terminated strings. Be sure to write a short driver program that tests each procedure. If you compile the procedures under the small memory model, pass 16-bit pointers as your input parameters. If you use the large memory model, pass 32-bit pointers. Table 6 lists the string-related procedures that will be requested in the Chapter exercises.

For each of the procedures listed in the following programming exercises, write a short test program that demonstrates their usage.

1. Improved Str_copy Procedure

The Str_copy procedure shown in this chapter does not check to see if the destination string area is large enough to hold the source string. Create a new version of this procedue that requires an input parameter in the CX register that is a maximal length count. Use this count to limit the number of characters that can be copied.

2. SaveScreen Procedure (16-bit version)

Example 1, shown earlier in this chapter, showed how to save the video text screen to a buffer inside a program, so the screen could be restored whenever necessary. Using the code from this example, create a procedure called SaveScreen and add it to your own link library. This procedure should work on a 16-bit processor. *Input parameter:* a 16-bit pointer to the buffer where the screen data will be saved. The following shows how the procedure might be called, if you pass the buffer pointer on the stack using the *Pascal* calling convention:

```
ROWS = 25
COLUMNS = 80
screenBuf dw (ROWS * COLUMNS) dup(?)
    .
    .
push offset screenBuf
call SaveScreen
```

Table 6. String Handling Procedures in the Chapter Exercises.

Procedure	Description
Restorescreen	Restores the video display from a buffer.
Savescreen	Saves the current contents of the video text display.
Str_concat	Concatenates one string to the end of another.
Str_copy	Copies a string, check for destination overflow.
Str_countChar	Returns a frequency count of a given character in a string.
Str_find	Finds a string within another string.
Str_int16tostr	Given a signed 16-bit binary integer, creates an equivalent decimal ASCII integer string.
Str_nextword	Scans a string for a delimiter character passed in AL and replace the delimiter with a null byte.
Str_read	Reads a string from a file or device.
Str_remove	Removes n characters from a string.
Str_rtrim	Removes all trailing spaces from a string.
Str_scan	Scans a string for the first occurrence of a particular character.
Str_set	Sets all characters in a string to the same value.
Str_setn	Sets n characters in a string to the same value.
Str_str16tobin	Given a signed ASCII integer string, calculates its binary value.
Str_transform	Translates the characters in string string2 using the characters in string string1. For each character in string2, if it is found in string1, changes the character to the corresponding character in string3.
Str_write	Writes a string to a file or device.

3.   RestoreScreen Procedure (16-bit version)

Write a procedure called RestoreScreen to accompany the SaveScreen procedure from the previous exercise. The procedure copies data from the program's buffer to video memory. *Input parameter:* a pointer to the buffer containing the screen data. The following shows how the procedure might be called:

```
ROWS = 25
COLUMNS = 80
screenBuf dw (ROWS * COLUMNS) dup(?)
 .
 .
push offset screenBuf
call RestoreScreen
```

4.   SaveScreen and RestoreScreen (32-bit versions)

Using the procedures from the previous two exercises as a starting point, write versions of the SaveScreen and RestoreScreen procedures that use 32-bit instructions. The screen buffer can be defined with a doubleword attribute. You may also want to pass a 32-bit pointer as the buffer parameter:

```
SCREENBUFSIZE = 1000
screenBuf dd SCREENBUFSIZE dup(?)
```

5.   Str_concat Procedure

Write a procedure called Str_concat that concatenates a source string to the end of a target string. Sufficient space must be available in the target string before this procedure is called. *Input parameters:* Pass pointers to the source and target strings. Here is a sample call:

```
targetStr db "ABCDE",10 dup(0)
sourceStr db "FGH",0
 .
 .
push offset targetStr
push offset sourceStr
call Str_concat                         ; targetStr = "ABCDEFGH"
```

6.   Str_countChar Procedure

Write a procedure called Str_countChar that returns an integer specifying the number of times a given character occurs in a string. The procedure will be case-sensitive. Input parameters: ES:DI points to the string, and AL contains the character. *Return value*: The frequency count will be returned in AX.

7. *Str_remove Procedure*

Write a procedure called Str_delete that removes *n* characters from a string. *Input parameters:* ES:DI points to the target string, and CX = the number of characters to delete. This procedure can remove characters from any position in a string if you increment DI before calling this procedure. The following code, for example, shows how to remove "xxxx" from targetString:

```
targetStr db "abcxxxxdefghijklmop",0
  .
  .
  .
mov di,offset targetStr + 3        ; start at offset 3
mov cx,4                           ; delete 4 characters
call Str_remove
```

8. *Str_find Procedure*

Write a procedure called Str_find that searches for the first matching occurrence of a source string inside a target string, and returns the matching position. *Input parameters:* DS:SI points to the source string, and ES:DI points to the target string. *Return values:* If a match is found, ZF = 1 and ES:DI points to the matching position in the target string. Otherwise, ZF = 0. The following code, for example, searches for "ABC" and returns with DI pointing to the fourth letter in the target string:

```
targetStr db "123ABC342432",0
sourceStr db "ABC",0
  .
  .
  .
mov si,offset sourceStr
mov di,offset targetStr
call Str_find    ; SI-> "ABC342432" in targetStr
```

9. *Str_str16toint Procedure*

Convert a string containing the ASCII representation of a signed decimal integer, calculate, and return its binary value. *Input parameters:* DS:SI points to the string. *Output:* AX contains the integer. For example,

```
numberStr db "12345",0;
value     dw  ?
  .
mov  si,offset numberStr
call Str_str16toint                ; now AX = the number
mov  value,ax
```

10. *Str_int16tostr Procedure*

Given a binary integer, create a string containing a signed ASCII decimal representation of the integer. *Input parameters:* AX contains the integer, and DS:SI points to a string buffer that holds the string generated by the procedure. For example:

```
numberStr db 30 wup(0),0;
value     dw  ?
    .
mov  si,offset numberStr
call Str_str16toint
```

11. *Str_rtrim Procedure*

Trim off all trailing spaces from a string. *Input parameter*: ES:DI points to the string.

12. *Str_nextword Procedure*

Write a procedure called Str_nextword that scans a string for the first occurrence of a certain delimiter character and replaces the delimiter with a null byte. After the call, if the delimiter is found, SI contains the offset of the next character beyond the delimiter; otherwise, SI = 0. *Input parameters:* ES:DI points to the string, and AL contains the delimiter. For example, suppose the chosen delimiter was a comma, and string contained two names:

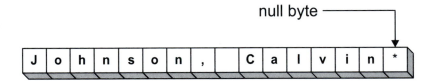

After calling Str_nextword, the string contains the following, and SI points to the space following the null byte:

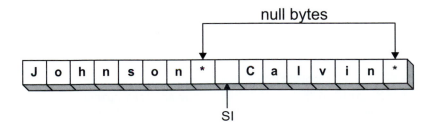

13. Str_scan Procedure

Scan a string for the first occurrence of a particular character. *Input parameters:* ES:DI points to the string, and AL contains the character to find. *Return values:* If the character is found, ZF = 1 and AX contains the character position (0..*n*) of the match. Otherwise, ZF = 0 and AX equals –1. Write a test program that scans a large string (500 bytes or more) and counts the number of occurrences of a particular character. For example:

```
targetStr db 1000 dup(?)
    .
    .
    mov  di,offset targetStr
    mov  cx,0                    ; initialize the match count

L1: mov  al,'X'                  ; look for first 'X' in target
    call Str_scan                ; if ZF = 1, AX = position of match
    jnz  NotFound                ; quit if not found
    inc  cx                      ; increment the match count
    add  di,ax                   ; move beyond the matching position
    jmp  L1                      ; and continue scanning
```

14. Constructing a Frequency Table

Write a procedure called Get_frequencies that constructs a byte frequency table. Write a test program that reads a file, calls Get_frequencies, and displays the resulting table. For each character in the buffer passed to the procedure, your table will indicate how many times that byte value was found.

Frequency tables are useful in data compression and other applications involving character processing. One of the most famous is the *Huffman* encoding algorithm, which uses a frequency table that lists each byte value in a block of data being compressed. Byte values occurring more frequently are assigned shorter bit strings, while less common characters are assigned longer bit strings. The Huffman code is explained in many different sources, including Tanenbaum, Sedgewick, and others.[1] For example, here are sample bit strings for the characters A, B, C, D, and E. The assumption is that A and E occur more frequently in the data being compressed than D, and D occurs more frequently than B and C:

```
A = 00,  B = 0101,  C = 0111,  D = 110,  E = 10
```

15. Str_set Procedure

Write a procedure called Str_set that sets all characters in a string to the character passed in AL. The length of the string should not change. *Input parameters*: AL = character to use, and ES:DI points to the string.

16. Str_setn Procedure

Write a procedure called Str_set that sets a predetermined number of characters in a string to a single character value. The length of the string should not change. *Input parameters*: AL equals the character to use, CX equals the number of characters to modify, and ES:DI points to the string.

17. Str_transform Procedure

A simple form of character encryption involves the substitution of characters in a *plaintext* message for new characters, resulting in an encrypted message. For this projecect, write a procedure called Str_transform that performs this substitution operation. For every character in the plaintext, if the character exists in *string1*, change it to its corresponding character in *string2* and insert the new character in the current position of the plaintext. *Input parameters:* Pass 32-bit pointers to all three strings on the stack when calling the procedure.

To test your program, let the user enter a string from the console, and have your program display the encrypted equivalent. Suppose the following data declarations were used:

```
plaintext db 80 dup(?
string1   db "A.BCDEFGHIJKLMNOPQRSTUVWXYZ ",0
string2   db "M$NGHACBDFE ORQWVUTSZYXJIKLP",0
```

Sample input/output:

```
User input: ORIGINAL MESSAGE
Encrypted:  WTFBFQMOPRASSMBA
```

18. Str_read Procedure

Create and test a procedure called Str_read that reads characters from a file or device and stores them in a null-terminated string. Input ends when an end of line character is read (0Dh). *Input parameters:* Pass a pointer to the input buffer, an integer that identifies an open device or file handle (for standard input, the handle is 0), and an integer that specifies a maximum input character count. *Output parameter:* Return a count of the number of characters that were read.

19. Str_write Procedure

Create and test a procedure called Str_write that writes a null-terminated string to a file or device handle. *Input parameters:* Pass a pointer to the string, an integer that specifes an open device or file handle (for standard output, the handle is 1).

20. Enhanced WRITESINT Procedure

As written, the Writeint_signed procedure from the book's link library prints a 16-bit integer with an optional leading sign. Modify the procedure so that you can pass it a pointer to a format string containing some or all of the following formatting characters:

Format Character	Usage
9	Print a digit.

B	Print a space.
–	Print a minus sign only if the number is negative.
+	Print a plus sign only if the number is positive; otherwise, print a minus sign.
$	Print a dollar sign.
,	Print a comma.

For example, suppose the value passed in AX is 4096. The following table shows how it would be written, depending on the contents of the format string:

Format String	Output
9999	4096
+9999	+4096
99999	04096
99,999	04,096
$9,999	$4,096
$B9,999	$ 4,096

21. *Clrscr_mem Procedure*

Create a procedure called Clrscr_mem that clears the screen buffer with the STOSW instruction rather than INT 10h. This method is fast because it accesses video memory directly rather than going through the BIOS. Note: The color text segment begins at B800h. To clear the screen with a normal attribute, move the value 0720h to each of the 2000 16-bit locations: 0000, 0002, 0004, 0006, and so on. The bytes are reversed in memory, so a dump of screen memory would appear as a sequence of characters alternating with attribute bytes:

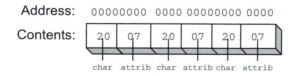

22. *Str_getpath Procedure: Get the DOS Path*

Write a procedure called Str_getpath that copies the current DOS path to a string pointed to by DS:DX. The *path* is a list of directories that you want DOS to search when trying to locate and run a program that is not in the current directory. The PATH belongs to a set of strings called the *DOS environment block*. A program can access this block via a 16-bit segment value stored at offset 002Ch in the program segment prefix (the environment block begins at offset zero from this segment). The COMSPEC is the first null-terminated string in the environment block. The PATH is another string occurring elsewhere in the block. For example:

```
COMSPEC=C:\COMMAND.COM<0>PATH=C:\DOS;C:\UTIL;C:\ASM<0><0>
```

The environment block is terminated by two consecutive null bytes.

23. mStr_compare Macro

(This exercise requires knowledge of Macros from Chapter 8.) Write a macro that calls the Str_compare procedure from the book's link library. Test the macro thoroughly with a short program. (The Str_compare procedure performs a case-sensitive comparison of a string pointed to by DS:SI to a string pointed to by ES:DI.) Assume that DS and ES both point to the same data segment. In the following sample call to the macro, the jump to **Label1** would be taken because **str1** has a lower collating order than **str2**:

```
.data
str1  db  'ABCDAFG',0
str2  db  'ABCDDAB',0

.code
mStr_compare str1,str2
jc  Label1                    ; jump if str1 < str2
```

24. mStr_length Macro

(This exercise requires knowledge of Macros from Chapter 8.) Write a macro that calls the Str_length procedure in the book's link libary. Write a program that tests your macro in a variety of ways. The Str_length procedure requires ES:DI to point to the string, and the procedure returns the string length in the AX register.

[1] Tanenbaum, Andrew W. *Structured Computer Organization*, Third Edition. Sedgewick, Robert. *Algorithms*.

11 *Disk Storage*

Assembly language rises above all other languages when it comes to tackling the details of disk handling. Disk storage exists on two levels: the hardware/BIOS level and the software/DOS level. The first level deals with the way data are physically and logically stored on disks. The second level is governed by the powerful DOS services that are called with INT 21h.

Using assembly language, you can bypass the operating system completely when accessing data. This is not always a good idea; operating systems were designed to help programmers avoid picky low-level programming and to make software portable across groups of machines. If we bypass the operating system, we run the risk of having to adapt programs to individual differences in hardware. At the same time, learning to do low-level file access is wonderful learning experience, which prepares you for situations in which conventional software solutions will not work. At some time in the future, you might have to store and retrieve data stored in an unconventional format, to recover lost data, or to perform diagnostics on disk hardware.

The first half of this chapter concentrates on the storage of data on disks and on ways to access disk data directly. The second half covers the high-level DOS functions used for drive and directory manipulation.

11.1   DISK STORAGE FUNDAMENTALS

All disks function essentially the same way: They have physical partitioning of data, they allow direct access to data, and they have a way of mapping filenames to physical storage.

11.1.1   Physical and Logical Characteristics

At the hardware level of a disk storage system are tracks, cylinders, and sectors, all of which describe the physical layout of a disk. At the software level are clusters and files, which DOS uses to locate data.

The surface of a disk is divided into invisible circular *tracks,* on which data are stored magnetically. Tracks are recorded on a disk when it is formatted. A disk's *density* refers to its number of tracks per inch. A *sector* is a 512-byte segment of a track (the sectors are numbered). In addition, each sector on a disk is assigned a separate *logical sector number.* In this chapter, we will use only logical sector numbers. On hard disks, a cylinder refers to all tracks available on multiple disk surfaces from a single position of the read/write heads.

A single physical hard drive is divided into one or more logical units named *partitions.* Each partition is represented by a separate drive letter such as C, D, or E, and it can be formatted using one of several file systems. The systems recognized by DOS and Windows are FAT16, FAT32, and NTFS. FAT16 is supported by DOS, Windows 95/98 and Windows NT 4.0. FAT32 is supported by Windows 95/98 and Windows NT 5.0. The last, NTFS, is supported by both NT 4.0 and NT 5.0.

A file system keeps track of the locations, sizes, and characteristics of files. Under Windows and DOS, files are divided into *clusters,* which are logical groups of adjacent sectors. A cluster is the smallest amount of disk space that may be used by a file. The number of bytes per cluster depends on both the type of file system in use and the size of its disk partition. FAT16 and FAT32 refer to the use of a table called a *file allocation table* (FAT) to keep track of the clusters used by each file. The starting cluster number of each file is also kept in the disk directory along with the filename and other reference information.

Standard cluster sizes and file system types for hard drives are shown in Table 1. In general, when a disk contains many small files, the use of small clusters results in more efficient use of disk space than the use of large clusters. The FAT32 file system uses much smaller clusters than FAT16 drive partitions below 2GB. Also, FAT32 supports larger hard drives than FAT16. For these reasons, FAT32 is increasingly preferred over FAT16, being supported by both Windows 98 and NT 5.0 (*Windows 2000*). Clearly, the table shows that FAT32 partitions use space most efficiently when they are smaller than 8GB.

Table 1. Comparing Hard Drive Partitions.

Partition Size	File System	Cluster Size (KB)
512MB - 1023MB	FAT16/FAT32	16/4
1GB - 1.99GB	FAT16/FAT32	32/4
2GB - 7.9GB	FAT32	4KB
8GB - 15.9GB	FAT32	8KB
16GB - 31.9GB	FAT32	16KB
32GB+	FAT32	32KB

For very large drive partitions, an excellent alternative is NTFS (*new technology file system*), used by Windows NT. NTFS is efficient because it lets you choose an optimal cluster size. It is less susceptible to data corruption than FAT32, and it includes advanced security features not found in FAT32 that allow files and directories to be assigned individual user and group permissions. (To avoid complicating matters, however, we will limit the detailed disk information in this chapter to the FAT16 and FAT32 file systems.)

Primary Disk Areas. Each disk has special areas reserved for the boot record, file allocation table, and root directory. The size of each of these is determined by DOS when the disk is formatted. For example, a 3.5-inch, 1.44MB floppy disk is divided into the following areas:

Sector	Contents
0	Boot record
1-18	FAT
19-32	Root directory
33-2879	Data area

The *boot record* in sector 0 contains a table containing diskette specifications (see Table 2), and a short boot program that loads DOS into memory. The boot program checks for the existence of certain operating system files and loads them into memory.

Table 2. Boot Record Layout.

Offset	Length	Description
00	3	Jump to boot code (JMP instruction)
03	8	Manufacturer name, version number
0B	2	Bytes per sector
0D	1	Sectors per cluster (power of 2)
0E	2	Number of reserved sectors (preceding FAT #1)
10	1	Number of copies of FAT
11	2	Maximum number of root directory entries
13	2	Number of disk sectors for drives under 32MB
15	1	Media descriptor byte
16	2	Size of FAT, in sectors
18	2	Sectors per track
1A	2	Number of drive heads
1C	4	Number of hidden sectors
20	4	Number of disk sectors for drives over 32MB
24	1	Drive number (modified by DOS)
25	1	Reserved
26	1	Extended boot signature (always 29h)
27	4	Volume ID number (binary)
2B	11	Volume label
36	8	File-system type (ASCII)
3E	--	Start of boot program and data

The *root directory* is the primary disk directory. Each entry in the root directory contains information about a file, including its name, size, attribute, and starting cluster number. The *data area* of the disk is where files are stored. The data area can contain data files, programs, or subdirectories (or *folders*).

Partitions. Each physical hard drive can have as many as four main partitions, one of which can be an *extended partition,* and the rest *primary partitions.* The extended partition can be subdivided into an unlimited number of *logical partitions.* Each logical partition appears as a separate drive letter, and may have a different file system than other partitions. Suppose for example, that a 16GB hard drive were assigned a primary 2GB partition (drive C) formatted with NTFS. Its extended partition would be 14GB. If the extended partition were then divided into two logical partitions of 6GB and 8GB, they could be individually formatted with NTFS, FAT16, or FAT32. Assuming that no other hard drives were installed, the two logical partitions would likely be assigned drive letters D and E.

It is possible to create multiple primary partitions, each bootable, each containing a different operating system. The fdisk.exe program supplied by MS-DOS and Windows creates and removes partitions. There are commercial partitioning programs (such as *PartitionMagic* by PowerQuest) that permit resizing and moving partitions without destroying existing data.

Logical partitions are primarily intended for data, and it is often possible for different operating systems to share data in the same logical partition. For example, MS-DOS, Windows 3.1, Windows 95, Windows 98, Windows NT, and OS/2 all can read the same type of file allocation table. A computer could be booted from any one of these operating systems and read the same data files in a shared logical partition.

How a Disk Boots. When you start up a computer, a program in the ROM BIOS called the *boot routine* reads the master boot record (MBR) from Sector 0 of the first physical hard disk. The MBR contains a boot program and a partition table that describes the partitions on the drive and indicates which primary partition is currently active.

Each primary partition on the disk must have its own boot record in the first sector of the partition. The boot record starts up the appropriate operating system. A boot record is created either by formatting the disk partition or by running a utility such as sys.com that transfers the operating system to a disk that is already formatted.

11.1.2   Types of Disks

Various disk formats are compared in Table 3. A *double-density* 3.5-inch diskette holds 737,280 bytes (720K), has 80 tracks per side, and has 9 sectors per track. A *high-density* 3.5-inch diskette holds 1,474,560 bytes (1.44MB), and has 80 tracks per side, and has 18 sectors per track. Most PC compatibles today support both high-density and double-density diskettes.

Fixed Disk. A fixed disk (or *hard disk*) always has multiple platters. Many disks have six platters with ten sides (each with its own read/write head). The heads move together, so at any given time they point to the same track on each side. The number of tracks on each side is far greater than that of a floppy disk because of the higher quality recording surface.

A 1.44MB floppy disk, for instance, stores 1,474,560 data bytes and has an additional 16,896 bytes set aside for the boot record, two copies of the FAT, and the root directory. When locating the FAT and disk directory, for example, you must take into account differences between disks. Several are shown in Table 4.

11.1.3   Disk Directory

Every disk has a *root directory,* which is the primary list of files on the disk. The root directory may also contain the names of other directories, called *subdirectories*. A subdirectory may be

Table 3. Comparison of Disk Formats.

Disk Size/Type	Clusters	Bytes per Cluster	Hex Sector Numbers
720K	720	1,024	0 - 59F
1.44MB	2,880	512	0 - B3F
100MB ZIP®	49,039	2,048	0 - 2FE3B
2.0GB SCSI	65,505	32,768	0 - 3FF83F

Table 4. FAT and Directory Sectors of Representative Disks.

Disk Size/Type	Maximum Files, Root Directory	FAT Sectors	Root Directory Sectors	First Data Sector
720K	112	1-6	7-13	14
1.44MB	224	1-18	19-32	33
100MB ZIP®	512	1-383	384-415	416
2.0GB SCSI	512	1-511	513-544	545

thought of as a directory whose name appears in some other directory—the latter is known as the *parent directory*. Each subdirectory can contain filenames and additional directory names. The result is a treelike structure with the root directory at the top, branching out to other directories at lower levels. For example:

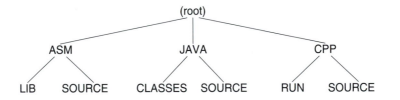

Each directory name and each file within a directory is qualified by the names of the directories above it, called the *path*. For example, the path for the file PROG1.ASM in the SOURCE directory below ASM is

```
C:\ASM\SOURCE\PROG1.ASM
```

Generally, the drive letter can be omitted from the path when an input-output operation is carried out on the current disk drive. A complete list of the directory names in our sample directory tree follows:

```
C:\
\ASM
\ASM\LIB
\ASM\SOURCE
\JAVA
\JAVA\CLASSES
\JAVA\SOURCE
\CPP
```

```
\CPP\RUN
\CPP\SOURCE
```

Thus, a *file specification* can take the form of an individual filename or a directory path followed by a filename. It can also be preceded by a drive specification.

11.1.4 Directory Structure

Each DOS directory entry is 32 bytes long and contains the fields shown in Table 5. The *filename* field holds the name of a file, a subdirectory, or the disk volume label. The first byte may indicate the file's status. Any nonstatus character in the first byte is the first character of an actual filename. The possible status values are shown in Table 6. The 16-bit *starting cluster number* field refers to the number of the first cluster allocated to the file, as well as its starting entry in the file allocation table (FAT). The *file size* field is a 32-bit number that shows the file size, in bytes.

The *attribute* field identifies the type of file. The field is bit-mapped and usually contains a combination of one of the following values shown in Figure 1. The two *reserved* bits should always be 0. The *archive* bit is set when a file is modified. The *subdirectory* bit is set if the entry contains the name of a subdirectory. The *volume label* identifies the entry as the name of a disk volume, created if the disk was formatted using the /V option. The *system file* bit indicates that the file is part of the operating system. The *hidden file* bit makes the file hidden; it can't be found by normal DOS searches, and its name doesn't appear in the directory. The *read-only* bit prevents the file from being deleted or modified in any way. Finally, an attribute value of 0Fh indicates that the current directory entry is for an extended filename.

Table 5. Disk Directory Format.

Hexadecimal Offset	Field Name	Format
00-07	Filename	ASCII
08-0A	Extension	ASCII
0B	Attribute	8-bit binary
0C-15	Reserved by DOS	
16-17	Time stamp	16-bit binary
18-19	Date stamp	16-bit binary
1A-1B	Starting cluster number	16-bit binary
1C-1F	File size	32-bit binary

Figure 1. Directory Entry, Attribute Byte.

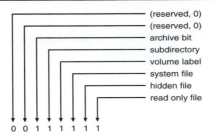

Date and Time. The *date stamp* field indicates the date when the file was created or last changed, expressed as a bit-mapped value:

1 1 1 1 1 1 1 1 1 1 1 1 1 1 1 1
└────year────┘ └month┘ └──day──┘

The years may be 0-119 (for example, 1980-2099), the months may be 1-12, and the days may be 1-31.

The *time stamp* field indicates the time when the file was created or last changed, expressed as a bit-mapped value. The hours may be 0-23, the minutes 0-59, and the seconds 0-59, stored in 2-second increments. For example, a value of 10100 equals 40 seconds. The following indicates a time of 14:02:40:

0 1 1 1 0 0 0 0 0 1 0 1 0 1 0 0
└─hours─┘ └──minutes──┘ └─seconds─┘

Table 6. Filename Status Byte.

00h	The directory entry has never been used.
05h	The first character of the filename is actually E5h (rare).
2Eh	If the following byte also contains 2Eh, the entry is an alias for the parent directory, and this entry contains the starting cluster number of the parent directory. If the following byte contains some other value, this entry is an alias for the current directory.
E5h	The file indicated by this entry has been deleted.

11.1.5 Sample Disk Directory

Let's look at an example of a 1.44MB floppy disk containing several different types of files. The root directory entry is displayed in a DOS window under Windows 95:

```
Volume in drive A is MYDISK
 Volume Serial Number is 17D4-0E59
 Directory of A:\

SECTORS  EXE       13,949   04-30-98   4:30p SECTORS.EXE
FOLDER       <DIR>           05-05-98   4:06p Folder
INSTALL  BAT          505   02-06-98  11:15a install.bat
MAIN     CPP        1,262   03-26-98   9:45a main.cpp
MASM     BAT           56   02-05-98  10:31p masm.bat
         4 file(s)        15,772 bytes
         1 dir(s)      1,440,256 bytes free
```

Let's look at a dump of the directory shown in Figure 2. The following commands tell Debug to load sectors 19 and 20 from disk drive 0 (A) into memory at location DS:0100 and dump memory from DS:0100 to 02BF (the starting sector varies depending on the disk type):

```
-L 100 0 13 2     (load sectors 19 and 20 from Drive A)
-D 100 2BF
```

At offset 0100, the beginning of the directory, is MYDISK, the volume label, identified by an attribute value of 28h. The "2" in 28 is only the archive bit, so an attribute of 08h would also be a volume label.

Figure 2. Dump of a Sample Disk Directory.

```
0100   4D 59 44 49 53 4B 20 20-20 20 20 28 00 00 00 00   MYDISK     (....
0110   00 00 00 00 00 00 C9 80-A5 24 00 00 00 00 00 00   .........$......
0120   53 45 43 54 4F 52 53 20-45 58 45 20 00 16 E7 80   SECTORS EXE ....
0130   A5 24 A5 24 00 00 D3 83-9E 24 03 00 7D 36 00 00   .$.$.....$..}6..
0140   E5 45 57 46 4F 4C 7E 31-20 20 20 10 00 53 D9 80   .EWFOL~1   ..S..
0150   A5 24 A5 24 00 00 DA 80-A5 24 02 00 00 00 00 00   .$.$.....$......
0160   41 46 00 6F 00 6C 00 64-00 65 00 0F 00 B1 72 00   AF.o.l.d.e....r.
0170   00 00 FF FF FF FF FF FF-FF FF 00 00 FF FF FF FF   ................
0180   46 4F 4C 44 45 52 20 20-20 20 20 10 00 53 D9 80   FOLDER     ..S..
0190   A5 24 A5 24 00 00 DA 80-A5 24 02 00 00 00 00 00   .$.$.....$......
01A0   41 69 00 6E 00 73 00 74-00 61 00 0F 00 1A 6C 00   Ai.n.s.t.a....l.
01B0   6C 00 2E 00 62 00 61 00-74 00 00 00 00 00 FF FF   l...b.a.t.......
01C0   49 4E 53 54 41 4C 4C 20-42 41 54 20 00 98 E7 80   INSTALL BAT ....
01D0   A5 24 A5 24 00 00 F8 59-46 24 1F 00 F9 01 00 00   .$.$...YF$......
```

```
01E0   41 6D 00 61 00 69 00 6E-00 2E 00 0F 00 89 63 00     Am.a.i.n......c.
01F0   70 00 70 00 00 00 FF FF-FF FF 00 00 FF FF FF FF     p.p.............
0200   4D 41 49 4E 20 20 20 20-43 50 50 20 00 22 E8 80     MAIN    CPP ."..
0210   A5 24 A5 24 00 00 BD 4D-7A 24 20 00 EE 04 00 00     .$.$...Mz$ .....
0220   41 6D 00 61 00 73 00 6D-00 2E 00 0F 00 6D 62 00     Am.a.s.m.....mb.
0230   61 00 74 00 00 00 FF FF-FF FF 00 00 FF FF FF FF     a.t.............
0240   4D 41 53 4D 20 20 20 20-42 41 54 20 00 75 E8 80     MASM    BAT .u..
0250   A5 24 A5 24 00 00 E8 B3-45 24 23 00 38 00 00 00     .$.$....E$#.8...
0260   E5 41 00 65 00 2E 00 63-00 66 00 0F 00 14 67 00     .A.e...c.f....g.
0270   00 00 FF FF FF FF FF FF-FF FF 00 00 FF FF FF FF     ................
0280   E5 45 20 20 20 20 20 20-43 46 47 20 00 C6 E8 80     .E      CFG ....
0290   A5 24 A5 24 00 00 B6 B6-45 24 24 00 69 00 00 00     .$.$....E$$.i...
02A0   00 00 00 00 00 00 00 00-00 00 00 00 00 00 00 00     ................
02B0   00 00 00 00 00 00 00 00-00 00 00 00 00 00 00 00     ................
```

At offset 0140 is a deleted subdirectory called NEWFOL~1, marked by indicated by the value E5h in the first byte of the filename field.

Offset 0160 marks the beginning of the extended filename "Folder," marked by 41h in the first byte and an attribute of 0Fh. Notice that extended filenames are case-sensitive, whereas DOS filenames are not. (See this book's Web site in the FAQ section for an article that more fully explains details about extended filenames.)

At offset 0180 is the DOS filename entry for FOLDER, which has an attribute of 10h, making it a subdirectory.

Let's examine the entry for MAIN.CPP more closely. This file has a normal attribute (20h), its starting cluster number is 20h, and its size is 4EEh bytes:

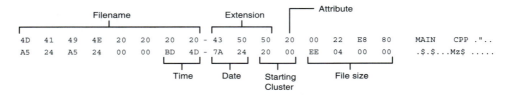

Of course, most of this information is already displayed by the DIR command in DOS. There are times, however, when it is useful to be able for programs to directly decode the root directory entry. Next, to better understand disk storage, we explore the area least understood by programmers—the file allocation table.

11.1.6   File Allocation Table (FAT)

The *file allocation table* (or FAT) is a map of all clusters on the disk, showing their ownership by specific files. Each entry corresponds to a cluster number, and each cluster is associated with one or more sectors. In other words, the 10th FAT entry identifies the 10th cluster on the disk, the 11th entry identifies the 11th cluster, and so on. On a disk that holds 10MB or less, each FAT entry is 12 bits long; on all other disks, each entry is 16 bits long.

The first entry is called the *disk ID byte;* it is useless because it does not uniquely identify the type of disk (most programs use INT 13h, the BIOS disk interrupt, to determine this information).

Let's look at a sample 12-bit FAT, starting with entry number 2, the first one that would be allocated by a file. Each entry in this table corresponds to a disk cluster containing data. A cluster, you may recall, is a group of one or more logical disk sectors. A value of FFF identifies the last cluster allocated to a file, a value of 000 shows that a cluster is unused and available, and a value of FF7 identifies a bad cluster:

```
Entry:      2     3     4     5     6     7     8     9
Value:    <FFF> <004> <005> <009> <FF7> <000> <000> <FFF>
```

Each FAT entry contains a value that points to the next cluster in a file, making the FAT a collection of linked lists. The FAT shown here indicates that there is a file that begins and ends in cluster 2. Another file begins at cluster 3 and contains clusters 4, 5, and 9. Cluster 6 is a bad cluster, and clusters 7 and 8 are available. Notice that the clusters belonging to a file do not have to be contiguous; in fact, files often become fragmented as they are modified and saved repeatedly. If enough of the files on a disk are fragmented, the disk's performance is degraded, and it is important to run a utility such as *Scandisk* to rebuild the FAT and unfragment the files. (Scandisk is a utility supplied with DOS and Windows.)

Wasted Disk Space. Coming back to the file contained in clusters 3, 4, 5, and 9 for a moment, if each cluster on a 1.44MB diskette is 512 bytes, we now know that the size of the file in question is between 1537 and 2048 bytes. The last cluster, 9, is probably only partially used, so as much as 511 bytes could be unused. This is how disk space is wasted, because the last cluster used by a file is almost never completely used. Contrast this to a hard drive with 32K clusters, where as many as 32,767 bytes could be wasted by every file on the disk. Suppose that a cache directory for an Internet browser contained 400 files, with an average size of 5,000 bytes. This would result in an average waste of 27K per file, for a total of 11MB.

11.1.7 Reading and Writing Disk Sectors

There are two ways you can read disk sectors: logically and physically. To read physical sectors, you must use INT 13h, and specify the track, sector, and the disk side number. To read a logical sector, call INT 25h (*absolute disk read*). It requires the drive number and the logical sector number. The disk drives are numbered sequentially starting at 0: A=0, B=1, C=2, and so on.

INT 25h has an unusual characteristic: It doesn't pop the Flags register off the stack when it returns, so you have to clear the stack yourself. All registers except segment registers are destroyed when the interrupt is called. If the disk size is less than 32MB, we can read the disk as shown in Example 1, where we read sector 0 from drive A into **buffer**. If DOS is unable to read the requested sector, it sets the Carry flag and places an 8-bit error code in AH. The most common errors are 0Fh (*invalid drive designation*), 15h (*drive not ready*), and 17h (*data error*).

Example 1. Reading a Sector with INT 25h.

```
DRIVE_A = 0
SECTOR_SIZE = 512
.data
buffer db SECTOR_SIZE dup(?)
sectorNum   dw 0
sectorCount dw 1

.code
read_sector:
    mov   al,DRIVE_A
    mov   cx,sectorCount
    mov   dx,sectorNum
    mov   bx,offset buffer
    int   25h
    add   sp,2              ; remove old flags
    jc    error_routine     ; CF = 1 if error occurred
```

Larger Disks. For disks larger than 32MB, INT 25h is called with DS:BX pointing to a *parameter block* and CX set to FFFFh. A parameter block and a call to INT 25h are shown in Example 2, where we read sector 0 from drive C. Notice that the sector number is a 32-bit doubleword. The fields in the parameter block must be both in the right order and of the right size.

Example 2. Disk Parameter Block, INT 25h.

```
DRIVE_C = 2

.data
parmBlock label byte
sectorNumber dd   0
sectorCount  dw   1          ; number of sectors to read
bufferOfs    dw   buffer      ; sector buffer offset
bufferSeg    dw   @data       ; sector buffer segment

.code
mov   al,DRIVE_C
mov   bx,offset parmBlock     ; point to parameter block
mov   cx,0FFFFh               ; indicates a large disk
```

```
int   25h                           ; read sector
add   sp,2                          ; restore stack pointer
```

Writing Sectors. You can write a sector to disk using INT 26h (*absolute disk write*). The same input registers are used for INT 25h, specifying the drive number, buffer, number of sectors, and so forth. As in the case of INT 25h, you must pop the flags off the stack after calling the interrupt, and the Carry flag is set when an error occurs. For disks over 32MB, DS:BX points to the same parameter block that was used for INT 25h. The sample code in Example 3 shows how to write a sector to a 1.44MB diskette in drive A. ***Caution: Use this interrupt carefully, because it has the ability to overwrite any sector on a disk.***

Example 3. Writing a Disk Sector.

```
DRIVE_A = 0
SECTOR_SIZE = 512
.data
buffer db SECTOR_SIZE dup(0FFh)
sectorNum   dw 63Fh                 ; last sector on 1.44MB disk
sectorCount dw 1

.code
write_sector:
    mov   al,DRIVE_A
    mov   cx,sectorCount
    mov   dx,sectorNum
    mov   bx,offset buffer
    int   26h
    add   sp,2                      ; remove old flags
    jc    error_routine             ; CF = 1 if error occurred
```

11.2   SECTOR DISPLAY PROGRAM

Let's put what we've learned about sectors to good use by writing a program that displays individual disk sectors in ASCII format. The Sector Display program in Example 4 reads and displays each sector on the default drive. The pseudocode is listed here:

```
sector number = 0
do while (keystroke <> ESC)
  Display heading
  Read one sector
  If DOS error then exit
  Display one sector
```

```
    Wait for a keystroke
    Increment the sector number
end do
```

In the **main** procedure, we increment the sector number, wait for a keystroke, and repeat the loop until ESC is pressed. If an error occurs while trying to read a sector, the program displays an error message and exits.

The core of the program is the ReadSector procedure, which reads each sector from the disk using INT 25h. The sector data are placed in a buffer, and the buffer is displayed by DisplaySector.

This program uses DOS function 19h (get default disk drive), which returns a number in AL identifying a drive (A = 0, B = 1, C = 2, etc.). In the GetDriveType procedure, we call Get_DiskSize from the link library to get the size of the drive in DX:AX. A 32MB drive returns a value of 01E92600h, so we compare DX to 01E9h to find out if the drive is > 32MB; if it is, **driveSize** is set to 1.

Using INT 10h. Most sectors contain binary data, and if we used INT 21h to display them, ASCII control characters would be filtered. Tab and Newline characters, for example, would cause the display to become disjointed. Instead, we use INT 10h function 9, which displays ASCII codes 0-31 as graphics characters. Of course, that means we have to advance the cursor manually after each character is displayed. The Setcursor macro was added to this program to simplify the calling of Gotoxy from the link library.

Applications. There are many interesting applications that could be derived from this example. For example, you could prompt the user for a range of sector numbers to be displayed. Each sector could also be displayed in hexadecimal. The ReadSector procedure could be more generalized, so it would be useful in other programs. Another useful variation on this program would be to indicate onscreen which part of the disk was being displayed: the boot record, the FAT, the root directory, or the data area. Depending on the type of sector being displayed, the format of the display could change. Finally, you could let the user scroll forward and backward through the sectors using the PageUp and PageDown keys. Naturally, these improvements have all been suggested in the Chapter exercises.

Example 4. Sector Display Program.

```
title Sector Display Program              (SECTOR.ASM)

; This program reads and displays disk sectors on the
; default drive, starting at sector 0.

.model small
.stack 100h
.386
extrn Clrscr:proc, Get_Disksize:proc, GotoXY:proc, \
```

```
            Readkey:proc, Writelong:proc, Writestring:proc

Setcursor macro row,col
   push dx
   mov  dh, row
   mov  dl, col
   call Gotoxy
   pop  dx
endm

CRLF equ <0dh,0ah>
ESC_KEY = 1Bh
DATA_ROW = 5
DATA_COL = 0
SECTOR_SIZE = 512

.data
driveSize db  0                  ; = 1 if drive > 32 MB
row       db  ?
col       db  ?
currDrive db  ?
line      db  CRLF,79 dup(0C4h),CRLF,0

;- Parameter block for disks over 32MB ---
parmBlock label byte
sectorNum    dd   0
sectorCount  dw   1
bufferOfs    dw   buffer
bufferSeg    dw   @data
;-----------------------------------------

buffer  db  SECTOR_SIZE dup(0),0

heading db "Sector Display Program (sector.exe)"
   db CRLF,"Press Esc to quit, or any key to continue..."
   db CRLF,"Reading sector: ",0

error_message db CRLF,"DOS error occurred while trying "
   db "to read the sector.", CRLF, "Returning to DOS.",0

.code
main  proc
```

```
        mov    ax,@data
        mov    ds,ax
        call   GetDriveType

A1:     call   Clrscr
        mov    dx,offset heading        ; display screen heading
        call   Writestring
        call   ReadSector
        jc     A2                       ; quit if DOS error
        call   DisplaySector
        call   Readkey
        cmp    al,ESC_KEY               ; Esc pressed?
        je     A3                       ; yes: quit
        inc    sectorNum                ; next sector
        jmp    A1                       ; repeat the loop

A2:     mov    dx,offset error_message  ; "DOS error ..."
        call   Writestring
        call   ReadKey

A3:     call   Clrscr
        mov    ax,4C00h                 ; return to DOS
        int    21h
main endp

ReadSector proc
        mov    al,currDrive             ; current drive number
        cmp    driveSize,1              ; drive size <= 32 MB?
        jb     B1                       ; yes: skip
        mov    bx,offset parmBlock      ; no, point to parms
        mov    cx,-1                    ; CX must be -1
        int    25h                      ; read the sector
        jmp    B2                       ; exit

B1:     mov    cx,1                     ; read 1 floppy sector
        mov    bx,offset buffer
        mov    dx,word ptr sectorNum
        int    25h                      ; read disk sector

B2:     add    sp,2                     ; remove old flags from stack
        ret
ReadSector endp
```

```
; Display all of the sector data.

DisplaySector proc
        mov   eax,sectorNum        ; display sector number
        mov   bx,10                ; with decimal radix
        call  WriteLong
        mov   dx,offset line       ; display horizontal line
        call  WriteString
        mov   si,offset buffer     ; point to buffer
        mov   row,DATA_ROW
        mov   col,DATA_COL
        SetCursor row,col

    ; Display the buffer with INT 10h rather than
    ; INT 21h, to avoid filtering ASCII control codes.

        mov   cx,SECTOR_SIZE       ; loop counter
        mov   bh,0                 ; video page 0

C1: push  cx                       ; save loop counter
        mov   ah,0Ah               ; display character
        mov   al,[si]              ; get byte from buffer
        mov   cx,1                 ; display it
        int   10h
        call  MoveCursor
        inc   si                   ; point to next byte
        pop   cx                   ; restore loop counter
        loop  C1                   ; repeat the loop
        ret
DisplaySector endp

; Advance the cursor to the next column,
; check for possible wraparound onscreen.

MoveCursor proc
        cmp   col,79               ; last column?
        jae   D1                   ; yes: go to next row
        inc   col                  ; no: increment column
        jmp   D2

D1: mov   col,0                    ; next row
```

```
        inc   row

D2:  Setcursor row,col
     ret
MoveCursor endp


; Get the drive size and set a flag if
; the drive is over 32MB.

GetDriveType proc
        mov   ah,19h              ; get default drive
        int   21h                ; AL = drive number
        mov   currDrive,al
        call  Get_Disksize       ; result in DX:AX
        cmp   dx,01F4h           ; less than 32MB?
        jbe   E1                 ; yes: exit
        mov   driveSize,1        ; no: set flag
E1:  ret
GetDriveType endp

     end main
```

11.3   DECODING THE FILE ALLOCATION TABLE

Using what we have learned about FATs and directories, it should be possible to write a program that displays a list of clusters allocated to each disk file. A program such as this is actually easier to write in assembly language than in a high-level language because the details of the disk directory are readily accessible. Let's look at part of a sample 12-bit FAT in raw form (shown by Debug) so we can learn to decode its structure:

```
F0 FF FF FF 4F 00 05 60-00 07 80 00 09 A0 00 0B
C0 00 0D E0 00 0F 00 01-11 20 01 13 40 01 15 60
```

A decoded form of entries 2 through 9 is shown here:

```
Entry:      2     3     4     5     6     7     8     9   . . .
Value:    <FFF> <004> <005> <006> <007> <008> <009> <00A> . . .
```

We can track down all clusters allocated to a particular file by following what is called a *cluster chain*. Let's follow the cluster chain starting with cluster 3. Here is how we find its matching entry in the FAT:

1. Divide the cluster number by 2, resulting in an integer quotient. Add the same cluster number to this quotient, producing the *offset* of the cluster's entry in the FAT. Using cluster 3 as a sample, this results in Int(3 /2) + 3 = 4, so we look at offset 4 in the FAT.

2. The 16-bit word at offset 4 contains 004Fh (0000 0000 0100 1111). We need to examine this entry to determine the next cluster number allocated to the file.

3. If the current cluster number is even, keep the lowest 12 bits of the 16-bit word. If the current cluster number is odd, keep the highest 12 bits of the 16-bit word. For example, our cluster number (3) is odd, so we keep the highest 12 bits (0000 0000 0100), and this indicates that cluster 4 is the next cluster.

We return to step 1 and calculate the offset of cluster 4 in the FAT table: The current cluster number is 4, so we calculate Int(4 /2) + 4 = 6. The word at offset 6 is 6005h (0110 0000 0000 0101). The value 6 is even, so we take the lowest 12 bits of 6005h, producing a new cluster number of 5. Therefore, FAT entry 4 contains the number 5.

Fortunately, a 16-bit FAT is easier to decode, because entries do not cross byte boundaries. In a 16-bit FAT, cluster *n* is represented by the entry at offset *n * 2* in the table.

Finding the Starting Sector. Given a cluster number, we need to know how to calculate its starting sector number:

1. Subtract 2 from the cluster number and multiply the result by the disk's sectors per cluster. A 1.44MB disk has one sector per cluster, so we multiply by 1.

2. Add the starting sector number of the data area. On a 1.44MB disk, this is sector 33.

For example, cluster number 3 is located at sector 34:

```
((3 - 2) * 1) + 33 = 34
```

11.3.1 Cluster Display Program

In this section, we will demonstrate a program that reads a 1.44MB diskette in drive A, loads its file allocation table and root directory into a buffer, and displays each filename along with a list of all clusters allocated to the file. The program is listed in Example 5.

The MAIN procedure displays a greeting, loads the directory and FAT into memory, and loops through each directory entry. The most important task here is to check the first character of each directory entry to see if it refers to a filename. If it does, we check the file's attribute byte at offset 0Bh to make sure the entry is not a volume label or directory name. We screen out directory entries with attributes of 00h, E5h, 2Eh, and 18h.

Regarding the attribute byte: Bit 3 is set if the entry is a volume name, and bit 4 is set if it is a directory name. The TEST instruction used here sets the Zero flag only if both bits are clear.

LoadFATandDir loads the disk directory into **dirbuf,** and it loads the FAT into **fattable**. DisplayClusters contains a loop that displays all cluster numbers allocated to a single file. The disk directory has already been read into **dirbuf**, and we assume that SI points to the current directory entry.

Next_FAT_Entry uses the current cluster number (passed in AX) to calculate the *next* cluster number, which it returns in AX. The SHR instruction in this procedure checks to see if the cluster number is even by shifting its lowest bit into the Carry flag. If it is, we retain the low 12 bits of DX; otherwise, we keep the high 12 bits. The new cluster number is returned in AX.

If you want to customize the Cluster program to work with different types of disks, take note of the three constants declared at the beginning of the program, which are specific to 1.44MB diskettes:

```
FATSectors = 9                  ; num sectors, first copy of FAT
DIRSectors = 14                 ; num sectors, root directory
DIR_START = 19                  ; starting directory sector num
```

If you want to read a hard drive, you can get the necessary information from the disk's boot record. For example, the size of the root directory can be deduced from the number at offset 11h. The starting sector of the directory can be calculated once you know the size of the FAT:

```
0D    1      Sectors per cluster
10    1      Number of copies of FAT
11    2      Maximum number of root directory entries
16    2      Size of FAT, in sectors
22    4      Number of sectors for drives > 32 MB
```

Example 5. Cluster Display Program.
──

```
title  Cluster Display Program            (CLUSTER.ASM)

; This program reads the directory of drive A, decodes
; the file allocation table, and displays the list of
; clusters allocated to each file.
; Last update: 5/5/98

; The following attributes are specific to
; 1.44MB diskettes:
;-------------------------------------------------------------
FATSectors = 9                  ; num sectors, first copy of FAT
DIRSectors = 14                 ; num sectors, root directory
DIR_START = 19                  ; starting directory sector num
;-------------------------------------------------------------
```

```
Directory struc
  fileName              db 8 dup(?)
  extension             db 3 dup(?)
  attribute             db ?
  reserved              db 10 dup(?)
  time                  dw ?
  date                  dw ?
  startingCluster       dw ?
  fileSize              dd ?
Directory ends

.model small
.stack 100h
.286
SECTOR_SIZE = 512
DRIVE_A = 0
FAT_START = 1                        ; starting sector of FAT
EOLN equ <0dh,0ah>
ENTRIES_PER_SECTOR = SECTOR_SIZE / (size Directory)

.data
heading  label byte
  db   'Cluster Display Program          (CLUSTER.EXE)'
  db    EOLN,EOLN,'The following clusters are allocated '
  db   'to each file:',EOLN,EOLN,0

fattable dw ((FATSectors * SECTOR_SIZE) / 2) dup(?)
dirbuf Directory (DIRSectors * ENTRIES_PER_SECTOR) dup(<>)
driveNumber db ?

.code
extrn Clrscr:proc, Crlf:proc, Writestring:proc, \
      Writeint:proc

main proc
      call  Initialize
      mov   ax,offset dirbuf
      mov   ax,offset driveNumber
      call  LoadFATandDir
      jc    A3                       ; quit if we failed
      mov   si,offset dirbuf         ; point to the directory
```

```
A1:    cmp    [si].filename,0         ; entry never used?
       je     A3                      ; yes: must be the end
       cmp    [si].filename,0E5h      ; entry deleted?
       je     A2                      ; yes: skip to next entry
       cmp    [si].filename,2Eh       ; parent directory?
       je     A2                      ; yes: skip to next entry
       cmp    [si].attribute, 0Fh     ; extended filename?
       je     A2
       test   [si].attribute,18h      ; vol or directory name?
       jnz    A2                      ; yes: skip to next entry
       call   displayClusters         ; must be a valid entry

A2:    add    si,32                   ; point to next entry
       jmp    A1
A3:    mov    ax,4C00h                ; return to DOS
       int    21h
main endp


LoadFATandDir proc                    ; load FAT and root directory
       pusha
    ; Load the FAT
       mov    al,DRIVE_A
       mov    cx,FATsectors
       mov    dx,FAT_START
       mov    bx,offset fattable
       int    25h                     ; read sectors
       add    sp,2                    ; pop old flags off stack


    ; Load the Directory
       mov    cx,DIRsectors
       mov    dx,DIR_START
       mov    bx,offset dirbuf
       int    25h
       add    sp,2
       popa
       ret
LoadFATandDir endp


DisplayClusters proc                  ; SI points to directory
       push   ax
       call   displayFilename          ; display the filename
       mov    ax,[si+1Ah]             ; get first cluster
```

```
C1:  cmp   ax,0FFFh            ; last cluster?
     je    C2                  ; yes: quit
     mov   bx,10               ; choose decimal radix
     call  WriteInt            ; display the number
     call  writeSpace          ; display a space
     call  next_FAT_entry      ; returns cluster # in AX
     jmp   C1                  ; find next cluster
C2:  call  crlf
     pop   ax
     ret
DisplayClusters endp


WriteSpace proc
     push  ax
     mov   ah,2                ; function: display character
     mov   dl,20h              ; 20h = space
     int   21h
     pop   ax
     ret
WriteSpace endp


; Find next cluster in the FAT
; Input: AX = current cluster number
; Output: AX = new cluster number


Next_FAT_entry proc
     push  bx                  ; save regs
     push  cx
     mov   bx,ax               ; copy the number
     shr   bx,1                ; divide by 2
     add   bx,ax               ; new cluster offset
     mov   dx,fattable[bx]     ; DX = new cluster value
     shr   ax,1                ; old cluster even?
     jc    E1                  ; no: keep high 12 bits
     and   dx,0FFFh            ; yes: keep low 12 bits
     jmp   E2
E1:  shr   dx,4                ; shift 4 bits to the right
E2:  mov   ax,dx               ; return new cluster number
     pop   cx                  ; restore regs
     pop   bx
     ret
Next_FAT_entry endp
```

```
DisplayFilename proc
        mov    byte ptr [si+11],0        ; SI points to filename
        mov    dx,si

        mov    ah,2                      ; display a space
        mov    dl,20h
        int    21h
        ret
DisplayFilename endp


Initialize proc
        mov    ax,@data                  ; initialize DS, ES
        mov    ds,ax
        mov    es,ax
        call   ClrScr
        mov    dx,offset heading         ; display program heading
        call   Writestring
        ret
Initialize endp
end main
```

Sample Output. The following output appeared on the screen when the program was run with the sample 1.44MB disk shown earlier in this chapter:

```
Cluster Display Program              (CLUSTER.EXE)

The following clusters are allocated to each file:

SECTORS EXE 3 4 5 6 7 8 9 10 11 12 13 14 15 16 17 18 19 20 21 22 23 24 25 26
27 28 29 30
INSTALL BAT 31
MAIN    CPP 32 33 34
MASM    BAT 35
```

11.4   SYSTEM-LEVEL FILE FUNCTIONS

Programming applications occasionally need to manipulate directories and files at the operating system level. It is possible to load and execute a temporary DOS shell from an application program and execute commands as if they were typed at the DOS command prompt. But this is somewhat wasteful of processing time and memory. Instead, it is more efficient to directly invoke DOS services by calling INT 21h.

INT 21h provides many functions that create and change directories, change file attributes, find matching files, and so forth. These functions tend to be less available in high-level languages and are usually specific extensions to the language at that. A list of useful DOS file services is shown in Table 7. When calling any of these services, the function number is placed in the AH. Other registers contain additional values passed to DOS.

11.4.1 DOS Error Codes

When a DOS function is called, a hardware or software error may occur. For example, the disk may be full, a file may not be found, there may be a duplicate filename, and so forth. If this happens, DOS sets the Carry flag and places a 16-bit *error code* in AX. A list of the DOS error codes 01h-1Fh and their corresponding descriptions is shown in Table 8. Only a few of these errors are relevant to each DOS function. Additional codes, not shown here, have been introduced to cover networks. You can place a table of DOS error messages in your own library so that when an error occurs, the number returned by DOS can be used to locate and display an appropriate message. Function call 59h provides additional information about DOS errors:

```
        call OpenFile            ; try to open a file
        jnc  L1                  ; successful? skip next lines
        mov  ah,59h              ; Get extended error information
        mov  bx,0
        int  21h                 ; AX = error code, BH = error class,
                                 ; BL = recommended action, CH = error locus
        .
        .
    L1:
```

The types of error codes are described here:

*   The *extended error code* (AX) is one of 90 specific error messages that cover problems relating to files, memory, hardware errors, networks, and printing.

*   The *error class* (BH) indicates the type of error that has occurred (such as, hardware, software, temporary situation).

*   The *recommended action* (BL) indicates what recommended action the program should take. You may wish to retry the action, delay and then retry, ask the user to reenter input, abort, and so on.

*   The *error locus* (CH) helps to locate the area of the computer system involved in the failure, such as a block device (usually the disk), a network, a serial device, or memory.

Table 7. Selected INT 21h Disk Services.

Function Number	Function Name
0Eh	Set default disk drive
19h	Get default disk drive
36h	Get disk free space
39h	Create subdirectory
3Ah	Remove subdirectory
3Bh	Set current directory
41h	Delete file
43h	Get/set file attribute
47h	Get current directory path
4Eh	Find first matching file
4Fh	Find next matching file
56h	Rename file
57h	Get/set file date and time
59h	Get extended error information

11.4.2 Displaying Error Messages

Several examples of DOS function calls will be given in this chapter. Each includes a JC (jump carry) instruction that jumps to a label called **display_error**. At this label, we will assume that the **DOS_error** procedure displays an error message based on the error code returned by DOS. For example, we might be trying to get the current directory path for drive D. If drive D is an invalid drive specification, DOS will set the Carry flag and return 0Fh in AX:

```
        mov     ah,47h              ; get current directory
        mov     dl,DRIVE_D          ; for drive D
        mov     si,offset pathname  ; point to a buffer
        int     21h
        jc      L1                  ; Carry set? Display message
        .
        .
L1:
```

The DOS_error Procedure. The first step in creating a procedure to display error messages is to define a table containing standard error messages as shown in Example 6. The **DOS_error** procedure shown in Example 7 uses an error number passed in AX to look up the appropriate message in **MessageTable** and write it to the console. The error messages are written to device handle 2 (standard error output), and cannot be redirected. An advantage to using this handle is that we can still redirect other program output to the printer or a file without affecting the error messages.

Table 8. DOS Extended Error Codes 01h-1Fh.

Error Code	Error Description
01	Invalid function number
02	File not found
03	Path not found
04	Too many open files (no handles left)
05	Access denied
06	Invalid handle
07	Memory control blocks destroyed
08	Insufficient memory
09	Invalid memory block address
0A	Invalid environment
0B	Invalid format
0C	Invalid access code
0D	Invalid data
0E	Reserved
0F	Invalid drive was specified
10	Attempt to remove the current directory
11	Not same device
12	No more files
13	Diskette write protected
14	Unknown unit
15	Drive not ready
16	Unknown command
17	Data error (CRC)
18	Bad request structure length
19	Seek error
1A	Unknown media type
1B	Sector not found
1C	Printer out of paper
1D	Write fault
1E	Read fault
1F	General failure

Example 6. Error Message Table.

```
MessageTable label byte
    db 'Invalid function number      '
msglen = ($ - MessageTable)
    db 'File not found               '
    db 'Path not found               '
    db 'Too many open files          '
    db 'Access denied                '
```

```
        db   'Invalid handle                '
        db   'Memory control blocks destroyed '
        db   'Insufficient memory           '
        db   'Invalid memory block address   '
        db   'Invalid environment           '
        db   'Invalid format                '
        db   'Invalid access code           '
        db   'Invalid data                  '
        db   'Reserved                      '
        db   'Invalid drive was specified   '
        db   'Attempt to remove current dir '
        db   'Not same device               '
        db   'No more files                 '
        db   'Diskette write protected      '
        db   'Unknown unit                  '
        db   'Drive not ready               '
        db   'Unknown command               '
        db   'Data error (CRC)              '
        db   'Bad request structure length  '
        db   'Seek error                    '
        db   'Unknown media type            '
        db   'Sector not found              '
        db   'Printer out of paper          '
        db   'Write fault                   '
        db   'Read fault                    '
        db   'General failure               '
num_entries = ($ - MessageTable ) / msglen
```

Example 7. The DOS_error Procedure

```
DOS_error proc
    pusha
    pushf                           ; save all flags

    mov    dx,offset message        ; "DOS error: "
    call   Write_errorstr
    cmp    ax,0                      ; error code = 0?
    je     L1                        ; unknown error
    cmp    ax,num_entries            ; out of range?
    ja     L1                        ; unknown error
    dec    ax                        ; calculate position in table
```

```
        mov   bx,msglen                 ; (errorcode - 1) * msglen
        mul   bl
        mov   dx,offset MessageTable
        add   dx,ax                      ; point to message
        call  Write_errorstr
        call  Write_errorstr             ; display error message
        jmp   L2                         ; and exit

    L1: mov   dx,offset notKnown
        call  Write_errorstr

    L2: mov   dx,offset crlf
        call  Write_errorstr
        popf
        popa
        ret
    DOS_error endp
```

11.4.3 File Specifications

Many DOS functions require you to pass a pointer (usually in DX) to a *file specification*. This is always a null-terminated string containing part or all of the following: a drive, path, filename, and extension, followed by a binary zero terminator byte. Only the filename is required. All of the following are valid examples:

```
db   'B:FILE1.ASM',0
db   'C:\FILE1.DOC',0
db   'C:\PROGS\PROG2.ASM',0
db   '*.TXT',0
db   'PROG2.*',0
```

The second example refers to a file in the *root* directory of drive C. The third example refers to a file in a subdirectory on drive C named PROGS. Some of the DOS functions used in this chapter allow the use of wildcard characters (* and ?). DOS expands wildcard characters to match all available filenames in the specified directory. For example:

```
    *.TXT    All files with extensions of .TXT
FILE?.DOC    FILE1.DOC, FILE2.DOC, FILE3.DOC, etc.
```

11.4.4   Reading the DOS Command Tail

In the programs that follow, we will often pass information to programs on the command line. Suppose we needed to pass the name file1.doc to a program named attr.exe. The DOS command line would be

```
attr file1.doc
```

When a program is run, any text typed after the program name is automatically stored in the 128-byte *DOS command tail* area, at offset 80h in the Program Segment Prefix (PSP) just ahead of the program. The first byte contains a count of the number of characters typed on the command line. Using our example of the attr.exe program, the hexadecimal contents of the command tail are as follows:

Offset:	80	81	82	83	84	85	86	87	88	89	8A	8B
Contents:	0A	20	46	49	4C	45	31	2E	44	4F	43	0D
			F	I	L	E	1	.	D	O	C	

You can see this using a debugger if you load the program and pass it a command line. The following example runs attr.exe in the Turbo Debugger and passes file1.doc as a command-line parameter:

```
td attr file1.doc
```

There is one exception to the rule that DOS stores all characters after the command or program name: It doesn't keep the file and device names used when redirecting input-output. For example, DOS does not save any text in the command tail when the following command is typed because both INFILE and PRN are used for redirection:

```
prog1 < infile > prn
```

Finding the PSP. When DOS loads an EXE program, both DS and ES point to the PSP. We usually reset both registers to the data segment at the beginning of the program. But once we do this, we lose the segment address of the PSP. We need to make a copy of the DOS command tail and store it in a null-terminated string for later use. The **Get_Commandtail** procedure does this (see Example 8). The following statements show how to call this procedure:

```
mov    bx,ds                    ; get copy of PSP segment
mov    ax,@data                 ; initialize DS, ES
mov    ds,ax
mov    es,ax
mov    dx,offset buffer         ; point to buffer
call   Get_Commandtail          ; get copy of command tail
```

When calling this procedure, place the PSP segment address in BX, and point DS:DX to the buffer where the command tail will be copied. The input buffer should be initialized to binary zeros.This procedure is intended to be called only once at the beginning of a program, so AX, CX, SI, and DI are not preserved. We skip over leading spaces with SCASB and set the Carry flag if the command tail is empty. This makes it easy for the calling program to execute a JC (*jump carry*) instruction if nothing is typed on the command line. This procedure can be found in the book's link library.

Example 8. The Get_Commandtail Procedure.

```
Get_Commandtail proc                ; DS:DX points to input buffer
        push  es
        pusha
        mov   es,bx                 ; BX = PSP segment
        mov   si,dx                 ; DX points to buffer
        mov   di,81h                ; point to command tail
        mov   cx,0
        mov   cl,es:[di-1]          ; CX = length of tail
        cmp   cx,0                  ; quit if length = 0
        je    L2
        mov   al,20h                ; compare using a space
        repz  scasb                 ; find first nonspace
        jz    L2                    ; quit if all spaces
        dec   di                    ; back up one position
        inc   cx                    ; adjust count

L1:     mov   al,es:[di]            ; copy rest of tail
        mov   [si],al
        inc   si
        inc   di
        loop  L1
        clc                         ; CF=0 means tail found
        jmp   L3

L2:     stc                         ; set carry: no command tail
L3:     popa                        ; restore registers
        pop   es
        ret
Get_Commandtail endp
```

11.5   DRIVE AND DIRECTORY MANIPULATION

The functions presented here manipulate drives and directories. They are based on commands that could be typed at the DOS prompt. But imagine, for example, being able to change directories or create a new subdirectory without having to leave your program. The DOS file functions shown here will allow you to get and set the default drive, get the disk free space, get or set the current directory, and to create or remove a subdirectory.

11.5.1   Set Default Drive (0Eh)

To set the default disk drive, call function 0Eh and pass it a number in DL corresponding to a disk drive (0 = A, 1 = B, 2 = C, etc.). If the number in DL is too large, DOS ignores the request but does not set the Carry flag. The following instructions set the default drive to A:

```
mov    ah,0Eh                  ; set default drive
mov    dl,0                    ; select drive A
int    21h
mov    numberOfDrives,al
```

The number of logical disk drives is returned by DOS in AL. This count includes all types of block devices, including RAM disks and separate DOS fixed disk partitions.

11.5.2   Get Default Drive (19h)

To find out which drive is currently the default drive, call function 19h. DOS returns the number of the logged drive in AL (0 = A, 1 = B, etc.). For example:

```
mov    ah,19h                  ; get default drive
int    21h
mov    current_drive,al
```

11.5.3   Get Disk Free Space (36h)

To find out how much free space is available on a disk, call this function and pass it the disk drive number in DL. The following values are returned by DOS:

AX = sectors per cluster
BX = number of available clusters
CX = bytes per sector
DX = clusters per drive

Drive 0 is the current drive, 1 = A, 2 = B, and so on. If the drive number passed in DL is invalid, DOS returns FFFFh in AX and the other registers are undefined. DOS functions 1Bh (allocation table information for the default drive) and 1Ch (allocation table information for a specific device) return the same basic information. But functions 1Bh and 1Ch do not return the amount of free space, and function 1Bh applies only to the default drive.

The following statements obtain both the amount of free space and total space on a hard drive:

```
mov   ah,36h                ; get disk space
mov   dl,3                  ; select drive C
int   21h
;  Return values: AX = sectors per cluster
;                 BX = available clusters
;                 CX = bytes per sector
;                 DX = clusters per drive
;   (Calculate disk free space)
push  dx                    ; clusters per drive
mul   cx                    ; AX = AX * CX = bytes per cluster
push  ax                    ; AX = cluster size (bytes)
mul   bx                    ; DX:AX = available bytes
;   (Get total disk capacity)
pop   ax                    ; cluster size
pop   dx                    ; clusters per drive
mul   dx                    ; DX:AX = total disk capacity
```

11.5.4 Get Current Directory (47h)

To get the current directory, call function 47h, pass it a drive code in DL (0 = default, 1 = A, 2 = B, etc.), and point DS:SI to a 64-byte buffer. In this buffer, DOS places a null-terminated string with the full pathname from the root directory to the current directory (the drive letter and leading backslash are omitted). If the Carry flag is set by DOS, the only error return code is 0Fh (invalid drive specification).

In the following example, DOS returns the current directory path on the default drive. Assuming that the current directory is C:\ASM\PROGS, the string returned by DOS is "ASM\PROGS":

```
.data
pathname  db 64 dup(0)            ; path stored here by DOS

.code
mov   ah,47h                      ; get current directory path
mov   dl,0                        ; on default drive
mov   si,offset pathname
int   21h
jc    display_error
```

11.5.5 Set Current Directory (3Bh)

Function 3Bh sets the current directory by supplying DOS with a pointer in DS:DX to a null-terminated string with the desired drive and path. The following example sets the current directory to C:\ASM\PROGS:

```
.data
pathname   db   'C:\ASM\PROGS',0


.code
mov    ah,3Bh                        ; set current directory
mov    dx,offset pathname
int    21h
jc     display_error
```

11.5.6 Create Subdirectory (39h)

To create a new subdirectory, call function 39h, with DS:DX pointing to a null-terminated string containing a path specification. The following example shows how to create a new subdirectory called ASM off the root directory of the default drive:

```
.data
pathname   db   '\ASM',0


.code
mov    ah,39h                        ; create subdirectory
mov    dx,offset pathname
int    21h
jc     display_error
```

If the Carry flag is set by DOS, the possible error return codes are 3 and 5. Error 3 (*path not found*) means that some part of the pathname does not exist. Suppose we have asked DOS to create the directory ASM\PROG\NEW, but the path ASM\PROG does not exist. This would generate the error 3. Error 5 (*access denied*) indicates that the proposed subdirectory already exists or the first directory in the path is the root directory and it is already full. For example, \CPP specifies the root directory as the parent directory.

11.5.7 Remove Subdirectory (3Ah)

To remove an existing subdirectory, pass a pointer to the desired drive and path in DS:DX. If the drive name is left out, the default drive is assumed. The following example removes the \ASM directory from drive C:

```
.data
pathname   db   'C:\ASM',0
```

```
.code
mov  ah,3Ah                    ; remove subdirectory
mov  dx,offset pathname
int  21h
jc   display_error
```

The Carry flag is set if the function fails, and the possible error codes are 3 (*path not found*), 5 (*access denied: the directory contains files*), and 16 (*attempt to remove the current directory*).

11.5.8　Get Device Parameters (44h)

INT 21h, function 44h, provides a way to directly manipulate a block device, usually a disk drive. The available functions are:

- Get or Set device parameters

- Write track or read track

- Format and verify track

- Get or Set access flag

A *device driver* is a system-level program that provides an interface between a hardware device and DOS. By having device drivers for disk drives, DOS is able to work with a wide variety of drive sizes and types. A device driver is loaded into memory and initialized by the operating system when DOS is loaded. Once in memory, a device driver can tell us a great deal about the capabilities of the device. For a disk drive, we might wish to know details about the arrangement of tracks, sectors, and clusters on the disk.

INT 21h, function 44h, subfunction 60h, is called *Get Device Parameters*. You must specify the drive and identify a buffer in your program that will receive a parameter block containing device information. The entries have been placed in a structure, shown in Example 9.

Example 9. MS-DOS Device Parameter Block.

```
ParameterStruc struc
  specialFunctions  db ?
  deviceType        db ?
  deviceAttributes  dw ?
  numberCylinders   dw ?
  mediaType         db ?
  bytesPerSector    dw ?
  sectorsPerCluster db ?
  reservedSectors   dw ?
  numberOfFATs      db ?
  maxRootDirEntries dw ?
```

```
numberOfSectors     dw ?
mediaDescriptor     db ?
sectorsPerFAT       dw ?
sectorsPerTrack     dw ?
numberOfHeads       dw ?
numHiddenSectors    dd ?
numberSectorsLong   dd ?
reservedBytes       db 6 dup(?)
trackLayout         dw 40 dup(0)
ParameterStruc ends
```
(The trackLayout field contains specific track data, which we will not use here.)

A procedure in the link library called **Get_Deviceparms** calls this DOS function and returns a pointer to a local variable of type **ParameterStruc**. When calling the routine, shown in Example 10, you can specify the drive to be evaluated in the BL register. Notice that an INCLUDE directive loads a file containing the **ParameterStruc** definition at assembly time. The disks.inc file is a text file that must also be included by programs that call Get_Deviceparms. The file is included on the sample disk with this book, along with the link library.

Example 10. The Get_Deviceparms Procedure.

```
; Get_Deviceparms -----------------------------------------
; This procedure gets the Device BPB table for a disk drive,
; found in its device driver. Input: BL = drive number
; (0 = default drive, 1 = A, 2 = B, etc.). Output: AX
; points to a ParameterStruc (structure) where DOS has
; stored the device information.
;----------------------------------------------------------
include disks.inc               ; ParameterStruc definition
.data
parms ParameterStruc <>
.code
Get_Deviceparms proc near
    push cx
    push dx
    mov  ah,44h                 ; major function: IOCTLDevice
    mov  al,0Dh                 ; subfunction: Generic IO Control
    mov  ch,8                   ; category: disk
    mov  cl,60h                 ; option: Get Device Parameters
    mov  dx,offset parms ; device parameter table
    int  21h                    ; call DOS
```

```
        mov  ax,dx              ; AX = pointer to parms table
        pop  dx                 ; restore all changed registers
        pop  cx
        ret
Get_Deviceparms endp
```

Calling Get_Deviceparms. A program that calls Get_Deviceparms is shown in Example 11. To reduce the amount of coding required for displaying descriptions and values of the various device parameters, we have created a macro called **mShow** that uses the TYPE operator to check the parameter called **value** and moves it to either AL, AX, or EAX as appropriate.

Example 11. Testing the Get_Deviceparms Procedure.

```
Title Test the Get_Deviceparms procedure  (device.asm)

.model small
.stack 100h
.386


; Define the mShow macro, which simplifies
; the repeated display of disk information.
;---------------------------------------------
mShow macro prompt, value
local aPrompt
.data
aPrompt db prompt,0
.code
    mov  dx,offset aPrompt
    call Writestring
    xor  eax,eax
    if   (type value) eq 1   ;; byte?
       mov al,[si].&value
    elseif (type value) eq 2 ;; word?
       mov ax,[si].&value
    else                     ;; dword?
       mov eax,[si].&value
    endif
    mov  bx,10
    call Writelong
    call Crlf
endm
;----------------------------------
```

```
      include disks.inc                ; disk parameter structure
      .code
      extrn Writelong:proc, Crlf:proc, WriteString:proc, \
            Get_Deviceparms:proc
      main proc
            mov    ax,@data
            mov    ds,ax
            mov    bl,0                 ; default drive
            call   Get_Deviceparms
            mov    si,ax
            call   Crlf
            mShow "Device type:          ", deviceType
            mShow "Device attributes:    ", deviceAttributes
            mShow "Sectors per cluster:  ", sectorsPerCluster
            mShow "Number of FATs:       ", numberOfFATs
            mShow "Max Root Dir Entries: ", maxRootDirEntries
            mShow "Reserved Sectors:     ", reservedSectors
            mShow "Sectors per FAT:      ", sectorsPerFAT
            mShow "Sectors per track:    ", sectorsPerTrack
            mShow "Number of drive heads: ", numberOfHeads
            mShow "Number of hidden sectors: ", numHiddenSectors

        ; Check for a large disk, using 32-bit sector count.
            cmp    [si].numberOfSectors, 0
            je     L1
            mShow "Total Number of Sectors:  ", numberOfSectors
            jmp    L2
      L1: mShow "Total Number of Sectors:  ", numberSectorsLong

      L2: mov ax,4c00h                  ; end program
            int 21h
      main endp
      end main
```

Here is sample output from the program, when run on a 1.44MB diskette:

```
Device type:           7
Device attributes:     2
Sectors per cluster:   1
Number of FATs:        2
Max Root Dir Entries:  224
Reserved Sectors:      1
```

```
Sectors per FAT:        9
Sectors per track:      18
Number of drive heads:  2
Number of hidden sectors: 0
Total Number of Sectors: 2880
```

The following was produced when running the program on a 100MB ZIP® disk:

```
Device type:            5
Device attributes:      2
Sectors per cluster:    4
Number of FATs:         2
Max Root Dir Entries:   512
Reserved Sectors:       1
Sectors per FAT:        192
Sectors per track:      32
Number of drive heads:  64
Number of hidden sectors: 32
Total Number of Sectors: 196576
```

The following was produced when running the program on a 2.1GB SCSI drive:

```
Device type:            5
Device attributes:      1
Sectors per cluster:    64
Number of FATs:         2
Max Root Dir Entries:   512
Reserved Sectors:       1
Sectors per FAT:        256
Sectors per track:      63
Number of drive heads:  255
Number of hidden sectors: 63
Total Number of Sectors: 4192902
```

11.6 REVIEW QUESTIONS

1. For each of the following terms, write a single-sentence definition:

    a. track   h. date stamp
    b. sector   i. attribute byte
    c. cluster   j. boot record
    d. cylinder   k. parent directory
    e. FAT   l. file specification

  f. subdirectory   m. directory path
  g. command tail   n. media descriptor byte

2. For each of the following DOS error codes returned when INT 21h is called, write a single-sentence explanation of what probably caused the error:

Error Number	Function Called
0Fh	0Eh (Set Default Drive)
15h	36h (Get Disk Free Space)
0Fh	47h (Get Current Directory)
03h	3Bh (Set Current directory)
05h	39h (Create Subdirectory)
10h	3Ah (Remove Subdirectory)

3. If a two-sided disk has 40 tracks per side and each track contains eight 512-byte sectors, what is the total disk capacity?

4. Which sector is the first data sector on a 1.44MB floppy disk?

5. Within each entry in a disk directory, what is the offset of the file size?

6. If a file is only 2 bytes long, how much space will it take up on a 1.44MB floppy disk?

7. Which area of a disk includes information about its cluster size, number of tracks per side, and number of sectors per rack?

8. What does the notation E5h in the first byte of the name field in a directory entry identify?

9. If a directory entry has an attribute of 10h, what kind of entry is it?

10. What date is indicated by the following file date stamp?

  0000011011100011

11. Calculate the starting sector number for the following file: It begins in cluster 2, the disk has 4 sectors per cluster, and the disk data area begins at sector 155.

12. What does it mean when the first byte of a filename in a directory entry contains 2Eh?

13. If an entry in a directory has an attribute of 10h, will its name be displayed by the DIR command?

14. In the following dump of a directory entry, what is the file size and starting cluster number?

```
46 49 4C 45 31 20 20 20-41 53 4D 20 00 00 00 00   FILE1   ASM ....
00 00 00 00 00 00 A2 A6-86 0F 04 00 20 00 00 00   ......"&....`...
```

15. How many bits long is each entry in the file allocation table of a 1GB hard disk?

16. Assuming that **buffer** is a 512-byte memory buffer, what is wrong with the following subroutine that reads a single sector from drive A?

```
read_sector proc
    mov    al,0
    mov    cx,1
    mov    dx,12
    mov    bx,offset buffer
    int    25h
    ret
read_sector endp
```

17. Is there any way to tell INT 25h to read a sector from the current default drive? If so, how?

18. In the Cluster Display program in Example 5, the following instruction is executed after SI is set to the offset of a directory entry. What is its purpose?

```
test [si].attribute,18h
```

19. In the Cluster Display program in Example 5, what changes would you have to make if you wanted to display the disk's volume label?

20. Assume that you are decoding the file allocation table of a 1.44MB diskette. AX contains the previous cluster number, and DX contains the current offset into the FAT. Write a series of assembly language statements that will calculate the new cluster number and place it in AX.

21. At what location is the DOS command tail?

11.7 PROGRAMMING EXERCISES

Many of the programs suggested here will alter your disk or directory. Be sure to make a backup copy of any disk affected by these programs, or create a temporary scratch disk to be used while testing them. *Under no circumstances should you run the programs on a fixed disk until you have debugged them carefully!*

1. Set Default Disk Drive

Write a procedure that prompts the user for a disk drive letter (*A, B, C,* or *D*), and then sets the default drive to the user's choice.

2. Disk Space

Implement the Get_DiskSize procedure from the book's link library, which returns the amount of total data space on a selected disk drive. *Input:* AL = drive number (0 = A, 1 = B, 2 = C, ...). *Output:* DX:AX = data space, in bytes.

3. *Disk Free Space*

    Implement the Get_DiskFreespace procedure from the book's link library, which returns the amount of free space on a selected disk drive. *Input:* AL = drive number (0 = A, 1 = B, 2 = C, ...). *Output:* DX:AX = free space, in bytes.

4. *Cluster Size*

    Write a procedure that returns the cluster size, in bytes for a selected drive. *Input:* AL = drive number. *Output:* CX = cluster size.

5. *Create a Hidden Directory*

    Write a routine that creates a hidden directory named \temp. Use the DIR command to verify its hidden status. Try copying files to the new directory.

6. *Disk Information (Boot Record)*

    Write a program that reads the boot record from the current drive and displays the following information: Manufacturer name, bytes per sector, sectors per cluster, and number of disk sectors.

7. *Get the Boot Record*

    Create a structure that matches the Boot sector data shown in Table 1 at the beginning of this chapter. Write a procedure called Get_Bootrecord that reads the boot record and fills an instance of the structure. (Structures were explained in Chapter 8.)

8. *Display the Boot Record*

    Using the Get_Bootrecord procedure from the previous exercise, write a procedure called Display_BootRecord that displays all information from the boot record on the screen.

9. *Save the Boot Record*

    A number of computer viruses are able to corrupt the boot record of a system's hard drive. As a way of protecting against them, write a program that makes a backup copy of boot record from drive C and saves it on a floppy disk as an ordinary file, perhaps named **saveboot.dat**.

10. *Decode a 16-Bit FAT Entry*

    Write a procedure that decodes a 16-bit file allocation table. Replace the Next_FAT_Entry procedure in the Cluster program (in Example 5) with your routine. Make any other adjustments to the program that you deem necessary, and run the program on a fixed disk. *Caution:* To avoid losing any data on your fixed disk, be sure you are *reading* sectors, not writing to them.

11. *Modified Cluster Display Program*

    Modify the Cluster Display program shown in Example 5 so it displays the *sector numbers* allocated to each file, rather than the clusters. Use the following algorithm to convert a cluster number to a sector number: Subtract 2 from the cluster number and multiply the result by the number of sectors per cluster. Add the starting sector number of the data area. On a 1.44MB diskette, for example, there is 1 sector per cluster and the data area begins at sector 33. For cluster number c, the sector number s would be:

$$s = (c - 2) + 33$$

12. Disk Free Space, in Clusters

Write a program that displays the following information on the screen (with labels) for the default drive (the numbers shown are only a sample):

```
Default drive              :A
Sectors per cluster        :2
Data Clusters per disk     :2847
Clusters Available         :1236
```

Use DOS function call 36h. The program must produce the correct values for any standard disk type.

13. Disk Free Space, in Bytes

Modify the program written for the previous exercise so it displays the following information about the default drive (the numbers shown are only a sample):

```
Default drive              :A
Total data bytes on disk   :1457664
Available data bytes       :632832
```

11.7.1 Sector Display Exercises

The following group of exercises are all variations on the Sector Display program presented earlier in this chapter in Example 4. Most of these exercises can be done either individually or in clusters of exercises.

1. Selecting Sector Numbers

Improve the Sector Display program by letting the user input the starting and ending sector numbers in hexadecimal.

```
Starting sector: 0C
Ending sector : 2F
```

2. Displaying the Sector Number

In the Sector Display program, add a message at the top of the screen that indicates which sector is being displayed. Show it as a 32-bit hexadecimal number with leading zeros:

```
Drive A, Sector 0000000C
```

3. **Hexadecimal Sector Display**

In the Sector Display program, let the user press F2 to display the current sector in hexadecimal, with 24 bytes on each line. The offset of the first byte in each line should be displayed at the beginning of the line. The display will be 22 lines high with a partial line at the end. Here is a sample of the first two lines:

```
0000 17311625 25425B75 279A4909 200D0655 D7303825 4B6F9234
0018 273A4655 25324B55 273A4959 293D4655 A732298C FF2323DB
(etc.)
```

4. **Displaying the Sector Type**

In the Sector Display program, obtain enough information from the boot record to let the program know whether the current sector is part of the boot record, the first or second copy of the FAT, the root directory, or the data area. On the screen heading, indicate this information.

5. **Displaying a Sector in Directory Format**

In the Sector Display program, let the user press a command key to display the current sector in directory format. That is, each filename, date, time, size, and set of attributes should appear. You may want to draw upon code shown the Cluster Display program earlier in this chapter.

6. **Displaying a Sector as a 12-bit FAT**

In the Sector Display program, let the user press a comand key to display the current sector in FAT format. To make this easier, limit your program to a 1.44MB disk, which has a 12-bit FAT. The following is a sample of part of a FAT display, where the first entry (entry 0) is the disk ID byte. It contains a link to entry 2. Entry 4 is the end of a chain, so it contains 0FFh, which we display as <EOF>:

```
<FD> <EOF> <3> <4> <EOF> <6> <7> <20> <9> <10> <EOF> ...
```

7. **Displaying a Sector as a 12/16 FAT**

Enhance the previous exercise by letting the program display either a 12-bit or 16-bit FAT, depending on the type of disk being read.

8. **Copying a File to Sectors**

Write a program that copies a file from one disk to another. On the target disk, store the file in consecutive sectors, starting with sector 0. In other words, do not use the FAT or directory to keep track of the file. Use the Sector Display program (refer to Example 4) to verify that your data was stored correctly.

9. **Copying a File to Sectors, Encrypted**

Continue the program from the previous exercise by encrypting the data as you write it to the target disk. Modify the Sector Display program so that it reverses the encryption and displays the original data.

12 *File Processing*

12.1 FILE MANIPULATION

12.1.1 Introduction

Having developed a good understanding of disk file organization, let's now examine the multitude of function calls relating to files. DOS uses the technique, borrowed from the UNIX operating system, of using handles to access files and devices. In most cases, there is no distinction between files and devices such as keyboards and video monitors. A *handle* is a 16-bit number used to identify an open file or device. There are five standard device handles recognized by DOS. Each of these supports redirection at the command prompt except the error output device:

0	Keyboard (standard input)
1	Console (standard output)
2	Error output
3	Auxiliary device (asynchronous)
4	Printer

These handles are predefined and do not have to be opened before being used. For example, one can write to the console using handle 1 without any advance preparation. Each function has a common characteristic: if it fails, the Carry flag is set and an error code is returned in AX. You can use this error code to display an appropriate message to the program's user.

Basic File Functions. Let's start by looking at a list of the most commonly used file functions, defined by a *function number* placed in AH. All the following functions are available in high-level languages (see Table 1).

The next set of file manipulation routines allows powerful control of files, often beyond that allowed at the command prompt. For example, we can hide or unhide a file, change a normal file to read-only, or change the time and date stamp on a file. We can also search for all files matching a file specifier with a wildcard character such as *.ASM.

12.1.2 Get/Set File Attribute (43h)

Function 43h can be used to either retrieve or change the attribute of a file. We set a flag in AL to decide which action to perform. The following input registers are used:

AH	43h
AL	(0 = get attribute, 1 = set attribute)
CX	New attribute (if AL = 1)
DS:DX	Points to an ASCIIZ string with a file specification

The Carry flag is set if the function fails, and the error return codes are 1 (function code invalid), 2 (file not found), 3 (path not found), and 5 (access denied). If AL = 0 (get attribute function), the file attribute is returned in CX. The attribute may also indicate a volume label (08h) or a subdirectory (10h). The following instructions set a file's attributes to hidden and read-only:

```
.data
filename  db  "TEST.DOC",0
.code
mov   ah,43h
mov   al,1                    ; set file attribute
mov   cx,3                    ; hidden, read-only
mov   dx,offset filename
```

```
int    21h
jc     display_error
```

You may want to refer to the discussion of file attributes earlier in Section 11.1.4. Sample values are shown in the following table. In addition, the archive bit (5) may have been set:

Attribute	Value
Normal file	00
Read-only file	01
Hidden file	02
Hidden, read-only file	03
System file	04
Hidden, system, read-only file	07

Table 1. Basic File Functions.

Function	Description
1Ah	Set disk transfer address.
3Ch	Create file. Create a new file or set the length of an existing file to 0 bytes.
3Dh	Open file. Open an existing file for input, output, or input-output.
3Eh	Close file handle.
3Fh	Read from file or device. Read a predetermined number of bytes from a file into an input buffer.
40h	Write to file or device. Write a predetermined number of bytes from memory to a file.
41h	Delete file.
42h	Move file pointer. Position the file pointer before reading or writing to a file.
43h	Get/Set file attribute.
4Eh	Find first matching file.
4Fh	Find next matching file.
56h	Rename file.
57h	Get/set file date and time.

One reason this function is important is that it allows you to hide a file so it won't appear when the DIR, DEL, and COPY commands are used. You can also give a file a read-only attribute to prevent it from being changed. In fact, the only way to delete or update a read-only file at the DOS command prompt is to *first* change its attribute to normal.

12.1.3   Delete File (41h)

To delete a file, set DS:DX to the address of an ASCIIZ string containing a file specification. The specification can contain a drive and path name, but wildcard characters are not allowed. For example, the following code deletes SAMPLE.OBJ from drive B:

```
.data
filespec  db  "B:SAMPLE.OBJ",0

.code
mov   ah,41h                    ; delete file
mov   dx,offset filespec
int   21h
jc    display_error
```

If DOS fails and the Carry flag is set, the possible error codes are 2 (*file not found*), 3 (*path not found*), and 5 (*access denied because the file has a read-only attribute*). To delete a file that has a read-only attribute, you must first call Function 43h (*change file mode*) to change its attribute.

12.1.4   Rename File (56h)

Function 56h renames a file if you pass a pointer to the current name in DS:DX and a pointer to the new name in ES:DI. Both names must be ASCIIZ strings, without any wildcard characters. This function can also be used to move a file from one directory to another because you can specify a different path for each filename. Moving a file is different from copying it; the file no longer exists in its original place. If the Carry flag is set, the possible error codes are 2 (*file not found*), 3 (*path not found*), 5 (*access denied*), and 11h (*not same device*). Error 11h occurs when one refers to filenames on different disk drives. The following routine renames prog1.asm to prog2.asm:

```
.data
oldname  db  "prog1.asm",0
newname  db  "prog2.asm",0

.code
mov   ah,56h                    ; rename file
mov   dx,offset oldname
mov   di,offset newname
int   21h
jc    display_error
```

The following statements move prog1.asm from the current directory to the \asm\progs directory:

```
.data
oldname  db   "prog1.asm",0
newname  db   "\asm\progs\prog1.asm",0

.code
mov   ah,56h                      ; rename file
mov   dx,offset oldname
mov   di,offset newname
int   21h
jc    display_error
```

12.1.5 Get/Set File Date/Time (57h)

Function 57h can be used to read or modify the date and time stamps of a file. Both are automatically updated when a file is modified, but there may be occasions when you wish to set them to some other value.

The file must already be open before calling this function. If you wish to read the file's date and time, set AL to 0 and set BX to the file handle. To set the date and time, set AL to 1, BX to the file handle, CX to the time, and DX to the date. The time and date values are bit-mapped exactly as they are in the directory. Here, we show the date:

```
                  DH                 DL
              ┌──────────┐      ┌──────────────┐
              0 0 1 0 0 1 1 0   0 1 1 0 1 0 1 0
              └────────┘ └──────┘ └────────────┘
Field:           Year        Month      Day
Bit numbers:     9-15         5-8       0-4
```

The seconds are stored in increments of 2. A time of 10:02:02, for example, would be mapped as

```
0101000001000001
```

The year value is assumed to be added to 1980, so the date April 16, 1992 (920416) would be stored as

```
0001100010010000
```

If you simply want to get a file's date and time, Function 4Eh (*find first matching file*) is easier to use because it does not require the file to be open.

12.1.6 Find First Matching File (4Eh)

To search for a file in a particular directory, call Function 4Eh (*find first matching file*). Pass a pointer to an ASCIIZ file specification in DS:DX and set CX to the attribute of the files you wish to find. The file specification can include wildcard characters (* and ?), making this function particularly well suited to searches for multiple files. For example, to look for all files with an extension of ASM in the C:\ASM\PROGS directory, we would use the following:

```
.data
filespec  db  "C:\ASM\PROGS\*.ASM",0

.code
mov   ah,4Eh                  ; find first matching file
mov   cx,0                    ; find normal files only
mov   dx,filespec
int   21h
jc    display_error
```

If a matching file is found, a 43-byte file description is created in memory at the current *disk transfer address* (DTA). The location defaults to offset 80h from the PSP, but we usually reset it to a location within the data segment, using Function 1Ah (*set disk transfer address*). The following is a description of the DTA when a matching file has been found:

Offset	File Information
0-20	Reserved by DOS
21	Attribute
22-23	Time stamp
24-25	Date stamp
26-29	Size (doubleword)
30-42	File name (null-terminated string)

This function provides a convenient way to get the time and date stamp of a file without having to open it. If the search fails, the Carry flag is set and AX equals either 2 (*invalid path*) or 18 (*no more files*). The latter means that no matching files were found.

12.1.7 Find Next Matching File (4Fh)

Once Function 4Eh has found the first matching file, all subsequent matches can be found using Function 4Fh (*find next matching file*). This presumes that a file specification with a wildcard character is being used, such as PROG?.EXE or *.ASM. Function 4Fh uses the same disk transfer address as Function 4Eh and updates it with information about each new file that is found. When Function 4Fh finally fails to find another matching file, the Carry flag is set. For a list of the file information in the DTA, see the explanation of Function 4Eh (*find first matching file*). To call Function 4Fh, you need only place the function number in AH:

```
mov    ah,4Fh              ; find next matching file
int    21h
jc     no_more_files
```

12.1.8 Set Disk Transfer Address (1Ah)

The *disk transfer address* (DTA) is an area set aside for the transfer of file data to memory. Originally, it was used by early DOS file functions, where file control blocks were used to access disk files. Later, its primary use was to provide a buffer for functions 4Eh (*find first matching file*) and 4Fh (*find next matching file*).

Function 1Ah can be used to set the disk transfer address to a location in the data segment. Otherwise, the DTA defaults to offset 80h from the start of the PSP. Most of the time, we reset the DTA to a buffer inside our program because the default location in the PSP is used for other purposes (such as the program's command line parameters). The following statements, for example, set the DTA to a buffer called **myDTA**:

```
mov    ah,1Ah              ; set DTA
mov    dx,offset myDTA     ; to buffer in data segment
int    21h
```

12.2 APPLICATION: DISPLAY FILENAMES AND DATES

Using what we have learned about finding matching files and file date/time formats, we can apply these to a program called **Date Stamp** (Example 1) that looks for a file or group of files and displays each name and date. This should provide some insight on how the DIR command works in DOS. We would also like to be able to enter a file specification on the program's command line that includes wildcard characters. The Date Stamp program does the following:

- It retrieves the filename typed on the command line. If no name is found, a message is displayed showing the program syntax.

- It finds the first matching file. If none is found, an appropriate message is displayed before returning to DOS.

- It decodes the date stamp and stores the day, month, and year in variables.

- It displays the filename and date.

- It finds the next matching file. The last three steps are repeated until no more files are found.

Example 1. The Date Stamp Program.

```
title Date Stamp Program              (DAT.ASM)

; This program displays the name and date stamp for
; each file matching a file specification entered
; on the DOS command line. Uses macros and a
; structure.

.model small
.stack 100h
.286
EOLN EQU <0dh,0ah>

FileControlBlock struc
          db 22 dup(?)              ; header info - not used
    fileTime dw ?                   ; time stamp of file
    fileDate dw ?                   ; date stamp of file
    fileSize dd ?                   ; size of file: not used
    fileName db 13 dup(0)           ; name of file found by DOS
FileControlBlock ends

mWriteint macro value, radix:=<10>
    push  ax
    push  bx
    mov   ax,value
    mov   bx,radix
    call  Writeint
    pop   bx
    pop   ax
endm

mWritestring macro aString
    push  dx
    mov   dx,offset aString
    call  Writestring
```

```
      pop   dx
endm
;----------------------------------------------------
.data
heading   db  "Date Stamp Program           (DAT.EXE)"
          db  EOLN,EOLN,0
helpMsg   db  "The correct syntax is:   "
          db  "DAT [d:][path]filename[.ext]",EOLN,0
filespec  db  40 dup(0)      ; DOS command line
DTA       FileControlBlock <>
;----------------------------------------------------
.code
extrn DOS_error:proc, Get_Commandtail:proc,   \
      Str_length:proc, Writeint:proc, Writestring:proc, \
      Crlf:proc

main proc
      mov   bx,ds
      mov   ax,@data              ; initialize DS, ES
      mov   ds,ax
      mov   es,ax
      mov   dx,offset filespec    ; get filespec from
      call  Get_Commandtail       ; the command line
      jc    A2                    ; quit if none found
      mWritestring heading
      call  findFirst             ; find first matching file
      jc    A3                    ; quit if none found

A1:   call  decodeDate            ; separate the date stamp
      call  display_filename
      mov   ah,4Fh                ; find next matching file
      int   21h
      jnc   A1                    ; continue searching
      jmp   A3                    ; until no more matches

A2:   mWritestring helpMsg        ; display help

A3:   mov   ax,4C00h              ; exit program
      int   21h
main endp


; Find first file that matches the file
```

```
; specification entered on command line.

findFirst proc
    mov   ah,1Ah                ; set transfer address
    mov   dx,offset DTA
    int   21h
    mov   ah,4Eh                ; find first matching file
    mov   cx,0                  ; normal attributes only
    mov   dx,offset filespec
    int   21h
    jnc   B1                    ; if DOS error occurred,
    call  DOS_error             ; display a message
B1: ret
findFirst endp

; Translate the encoded bit format of a file's
;   date stamp.

.data
month   dw  ?                   ; temporary storage for
day     dw  ?                   ; month, day, year
year    dw  ?
.code
decodeDate proc
    mov   bx,offset DTA.fileDate
    mov   dx,[bx]               ; get the day
    mov   ax,dx
    and   ax,001Fh              ; clear bits 5-15
    mov   day,ax
    mov   ax,dx                 ; get the month
    shr   ax,5                  ; shift right 5 bits
    and   ax,000Fh              ; clear bits 4-15
    mov   month,ax
    mov   ax,dx                 ; get the year
    shr   ax,9                  ; shift right 9 bits
    add   ax,80                 ; year is relative to 1980
    mov   year,ax
    ret
decodeDate endp

; Write both filename and date stamp to console.
```

```
        display_filename proc
            mWritestring DTA.fileName
            call  fill_with_spaces
            mWriteint month
            call  write_dash              ; display a "-"
            mWriteint day
            call  write_dash              ; display a "-"
            mWriteint year
            call  Crlf
            ret
        display_filename endp


        ; Pad right side of the filename with spaces.

        fill_with_spaces proc
            mov   cx,15                   ; max file size plus 3 spaces
            mov   di,offset DTA.fileName  ; get length
            call  Str_length              ; AX = length of filename
            sub   cx,ax
            mov   ah,2                    ; display character
            mov   dl,20h                  ; space
        E1: int   21h                     ; write spaces
            loop  E1                      ; until CX = 0
            ret
        fill_with_spaces endp


        write_dash proc                   ; write a hyphen
            push  ax
            push  dx
            mov   ah,2
            mov   dl,'-'
            int   21h
            pop   dx
            pop   ax
            ret
        write_dash endp
        end main
```

Main Procedure. The **main** procedure calls routines to retrieve the command tail and find the first matching file. From that point on, it is essentially a loop that decodes and displays the date and looks for other matching files.

FindFirst Procedure. The **FindFirst** procedure calls Function 1Ah to set the disk transfer address, where file information is stored when matching files are found. We call Function 4Eh to find the first matching file and return to main. The Carry flag is set if no matching files are found.

DecodeDate Procedure. The **DecodeDate** procedure is the most complex one because each field (day, month, year) must be masked and shifted to the right. As each value is isolated, it is stored in a variable. The day of the week occupies bits 0-4, so we clear bits 5-15 and move the result to **day**. The month number is stored in bits 5-8, so AX is shifted 5 bits to the right. We clear all other bits and store the result in **month**. The year number is stored in bits 9-15, so we shift AX 9 bits to the right. We add 80 because the date is always relative to 1980.

12.3   FILE I/O SERVICES

12.3.1   Create File (3Ch)

To create a new file or to truncate an existing file to 0 bytes, Function 3Ch should be used. The file is automatically opened for both reading and writing, but that can be changed by calling Function 43h (change file mode) after the file is open. DS:DX must point to an ASCIIZ string with the name of the file, and CX should contain one or more of the following attribute values:

00h   Normal file

01h   Read-only file

02h   Hidden file

04h   System file (rarely used)

   A sample routine that creates a file with a normal attribute is shown here. The file is created on the default drive in the current directory. We would pass the offset of the filename to the procedure in DX:

```
CreateFile proc                 ; Input: DX points to filename
      push  cx
      push  dx
      mov   ah,3Ch               ; function: create file
      mov   cx,0                 ; normal attribute
      int   21h                  ; call DOS
      pop   dx
      pop   cx
      ret
CreateFile endp
```

The following statements show how CreateFile might be called:

```
.data
newfile db  "NEWFILE.DOC",0
handle  dw  ?

.code
mov   dx,offset newfile        ; pass the filename offset
call  CreateFile               ; create the file
jc    display_error            ; error? display a message
mov   handle,ax                ; no error: save the handle
```

If the file is opened successfully, a 16-bit file handle is returned in AX. The value is 5 if this is the first file opened, but it is larger when other files are already open.

Protecting Existing Files. One disadvantage of using Function 3Ch (*create file*) is that one might inadvertently destroy an existing file with the same name. There are a couple of solutions to this problem. You can attempt to open the file for input, using Function 3Dh (*open file*). If the Carry flag is set and AX = 2 (*file not found*), you can safely use the *create file* function.

Another solution is to use Function 5Bh (*create new file*). It aborts and returns error 50h if the file already exists. For example:

```
.data
filename  db  "FILE1.DOC",0

.code
mov   ah,5Bh           ; create new file
mov   cx,0             ; normal attribute
mov   dx,offset filename
int   21h
jc    error_routine
```

Error Codes. If DOS sets the Carry flag, the error number it returns should be 3, 4, or 5. Error 3 (*path not found*) means the file specifier pointed to by DX probably contains a nonexistent directory name. For example, you may have specified the following, when in fact the subdirectory name is ASM, not ASMS:

```
file1  db 'C:\ASMS\FILE1.ASM',0
```

Error 4 (*too many open files*) occurs when you have exceeded the maximum number of open files set by DOS. By default, DOS allows only eight open files. Since the first five of these are in use by DOS (for standard file handles), that leaves only three files for use by application programs. You can change this number with the FILES command in the CONFIG.SYS file (activated when you boot the system). For example,

```
files=32
```

After deducting the five handles used by DOS, there would be 27 handles available for programs to use. But DOS still allows each *program* to have a maximum of 20 open files. It is possible to change this maximum value by calling INT 21h, Function 67h: BX should contain the number of desired handles (1 to 65,534). The following statements set the maximum to 30 files per program:

```
mov  ah,67h
mov  bx,30
int  21h
```

Error 5 (*access denied*) indicates that you may be trying to create a file that already exists and has a read-only attribute. You may be trying to create a file with the same name as a subdirectory, or you may also be trying to add a new entry to a root directory that is already full.

In some versions of DOS, Error 2 (*file not found*) is generated if you leave a carriage return at the end of a filename.

12.3.2   Open File (3Dh)

Function 3Dh opens an existing file in one of three modes: input, output, or input-output. AL contains the file mode to be used, and DS:DX points to a filename. Normal and hidden files can be opened. If the open is successful, a valid file handle is returned in AX:

```
.data
filename        db  'A:\FILE1.DOC',0
infilehandle  dw  ?

.code
mov  ah,3Dh                ; function: open file
mov  al,0                  ; choose the input mode
mov  dx,offset filename
int  21h                   ; call DOS
jc   display_error         ; error? display a message
mov  infilehandle,ax       ; no error: save the handle
```

File Mode. The file mode placed in AL can have one of three values:

AL	Mode
0	Input (read only)
1	Output (write only)
2	Input-output

To open a file in output mode for sequential writing, Function 3Ch (*create file*) is probably best. On the other hand, to read and write data to a file, Function 3Dh (*open file*) is best. Random-access file I/O requires Function 3Dh.

Error Codes. If CF = 1, AX contains one of the following error codes: Error 1 (*invalid function number*) means you are trying to share a file without having loaded the SHARE program. Error 2 (*file not found*) indicates that DOS was not able to find the requested file. Error 3 (*path not found*) means you specified an incorrect directory name in the filename's path. Error 4 (*too many open files*) indicates that too many files are currently open. Error 5 (*access denied*) means the file may be set to read-only, or it may be a subdirectory or volume name.

12.3.3   Close File (3Eh)

To close a file, call Function 3Eh and place the file's handle in BX. This function flushes DOS's internal file buffer by writing any remaining data to disk and makes the file handle available to other files. If the file has been written to, it is saved with a new file size, time stamp, and date stamp. The following instructions close the file identified by **infilehandle**:

```
.data
infile  db   'B:\FILE1.DOC',0
infilehandle   dw  ?


.code
mov   ah,3Eh                    ; close file handle
mov   bx,infilehandle
int   21h
jc    display_error
```

The only possible error code is 6 (*invalid handle*), which means the file handle in BX does not refer to an open file.

12.3.4   Read From File or Device (3Fh)

In Chapter 5 we showed how to use Function 3Fh to read from standard input, which ordinarily is the keyboard. This function is very flexible because it can easily read from a disk file. First, you have to call Function 3Dh to open the file for input; then, using the file handle obtained by this call, you can call Function 3Fh and read from the open file.

After calling this function, if the Carry flag is set, the error code is either 5 or 6. Error 5 (*access denied*) probably means the file was open in the output mode, and error 6 (*invalid handle*) indicates that the file handle passed in BX does not refer to an open file. If the Carry flag is clear after the operation, AX contains the number of bytes read.

The information returned by Function 3Fh is useful when checking for end of file. If there is no more data in the file, the value in AX is less than the number of bytes that were requested (in CX). In the following code example, we jump to a label called **Exit** if the end of the file has been reached:

```
        .data
        bufferSize = 512
        filehandle dw ?
        buffer  db bufferSize dup(0)

        .code
        mov   ah,3Fh                ; read from file or device
        mov   bx,filehandle         ; BX = file handle
        mov   cx,bufferize          ; number of bytes to read
        mov   dx,offset buffer      ; point to buffer
        int   21h                   ; read the data
        jc    Display_error         ; error if CF = 1
        cmp   ax,cx                 ; compare to bytes requested
        jb    Exit                  ; yes: quit reading
```

12.3.5 Write to File or Device (40h)

Function 40h is used when writing to a device or a file. Place a valid file handle in BX, place the number of bytes to write in CX, and point DS:DX to the buffer where the data are stored. DOS automatically updates the file pointer after writing to the file, so the next call to Function 40h will write beyond the current position. In the following example, we write the contents of **buffer** to the file identified by **handle**:

```
        .data
        buffer    db  100h dup(?)    ; output buffer
        handle    dw  ?              ; file handle

        .code
        write_to_file:
            mov   ah,40h             ; write to file/device
            mov   bx,handle          ; file handle returned by OPEN
            mov   cx,100h            ; number of bytes to write
            mov   dx,offset buffer   ; DX points to the buffer
            int   21h                ; call DOS
            jc    display_error      ; error? display message.
            cmp   ax,100h            ; all bytes written?
            jne   close_file         ; no: disk is full
```

If the Carry flag is set, AX contains error code 5 or 6. Error 5 (*access denied*) means the file is open in the input mode, or the file has a read-only attribute. Error 6 (*invalid handle*) means the number in BX does not refer to a currently open file handle. If the Carry flag is clear but AX contains a number that is less than the requested number of bytes, an input-output error may have occurred. For example, the disk could be full.

12.4   RANDOM FILE ACCESS

Random file processing is surprisingly simple in assembly language. Only one new function needs to be added to what we already know—Function 42h (*move file pointer*), which makes it possible to locate any record in a file. Each high-level language tends to have a specific syntax for random file processing. DOS, on the other hand, makes very little distinction between sequential and random files.

Random access is possible only when the records in a file have a *fixed length*. This is because the record length is used to calculate each record's offset from the beginning of the file. A text file usually has *variable-length* records, each delimited by an end-of-line marker (0Dh, 0Ah). There is no practical way to locate individual variable-length records because their offsets are not determined by their lengths.

In the following illustration, **File1** has fixed-length records, so we calculate the beginning of each record by multiplying the record number minus 1 by 20. **File2** stores the same data in a comma-delimited text file. There are comma delimiters between fields, and end-of-line markers (*0Dh,0Ah*) at the end of each record. The position of any one record cannot be calculated because each record has a different length. Record 2 begins at offset 000F, record 3 at offset 0022, and so on:

File1: Record offsets (hexadecimal): 0000,0014,0028,003C:

```
            1               2               3               4
0123456789ABCDEF0123456789ABCDEF0123456789ABCDEF0123456789ABCDEF0123456789ABCDEF0
1000AU          00300H1003BAKER    02000B2001DAVIDSON  40000H3000GONZALEZ  50000A
```

File2: Record offsets (hexadecimal): 0000,000F,0022,0039:

```
            1               2               3               4
0123456789ABCDEF0123456789ABCDEF0123456789ABCDEF0123456789ABCDEF0123456789ABCDEF0
1000,AU,300,H..1003,BAKER,2000,B..2001,DAVIDSON,40000,H..3000,GONZALEZ,50000,A..
```

12.4.1   Move File Pointer (42h)

Function 42h moves the file pointer to a new location (the file must already be open). The input registers are

        AH   42h

        AL   Method code (type of offset)

        BX   File handle

        CX   Offset, high

        DX   Offset, low

The *offset* can be relative to the beginning of the file, the end of the file, or the current file position. When the function is called, AL contains a *method code* that identifies how the pointer will be set, and CX:DX contains a 32-bit offset:

AL	Contents of CX:DX
0	Offset from the beginning of the file
1	Offset from the current location
2	Offset from the end of the file

Result Values. If the Carry flag is set after the function is called, DOS returns either Error 1 (*invalid function number*) or Error 6 (*invalid handle*). If the operation is successful, the Carry flag is cleared and DX:AX returns the new location of the file pointer relative to the start of the file (regardless of which method code was used).

Example: Locating a Record. Suppose we are processing a random file with 80-byte records, and we want to find a specific record. The LSEEK procedure shown in Example 2 moves the file pointer to the position implied by the record number passed in AX. Assuming that records are numbered beginning at 0, we multiply the record number by the record length to find its offset in the file:

Example 2. Locating a Record with the Lseek Procedure.

```
Lseek proc                      ; AX = record number
      push  bx
      push  cx
      mov   bx,80               ; DX:AX = (AX * 80)
      mul   bx
      mov   cx,dx               ; upper half of offset in CX
      mov   dx,ax               ; lower half of offset in DX
      mov   ah,42h
      mov   al,0                ; method: offset from beginning
      mov   bx,handle
      int   21h                 ; locate the file pointer
      pop   cx
      pop   bx
      ret
Lseek endp
```

For example, record 9 would be located at offset 720 and record 0 would be located at offset 0:

```
Offset =  9 * 80 = 720
Offset =  0 * 80 = 0
```

The ReadRecord procedure in Example 3 uses Function 3Fh to read 80 bytes from the file. To read a record, we simply place the desired record number in AX and call both Lseek and ReadRecord:

```
mov    ax,record_number
call   Lseek
call   ReadRecord
```

Example 3. The ReadRecord Procedure.

```
ReadRecord proc
    pusha
    mov    ah,3Fh          ; read from file or device
    mov    bx,handle       ; file/device handle
    mov    cx,80           ; number of bytes to read
    mov    dx,offset buffer
    int    21h
    popa
    ret
ReadRecord endp
```

Example: Append to a File. Function 42h is also used to append to a file. The file may be either a text file with variable-length records or a file with fixed-length records. The trick is to use method code 2, to position the file pointer at the end of the file before writing any new records. The SeekEOF procedure in Example 4 does this.

Example 4. The SeekEOF Procedure.

```
SeekEOF proc
    pusha
    mov    ah,42h          ; position file pointer
    mov    al,2            ; relative to end of file
    mov    bx,handle
    mov    cx,0            ; offset, high
    mov    dx,0            ; offset, low
    int    21h
    popa
    ret
SeekEOF endp
```

Using a Negative Offset. If the method code in AL is either 1 or 2, the offset value can be either positive or negative, presenting some interesting possibilities. For example, one could back up the file pointer from the current position (using method 1) and reread a record. This would even work for a text file with variable-length records:

```
mov    ah,42h                  ; function: move pointer
mov    al,1                    ; method: relative to current position
mov    bx,handle
mov    cx,0
mov    dx,-10                  ; back up 10 bytes
int    21h
jc     error_routine          ; exit if there is an error
mov    ah,3Fh                 ; function: read file
mov    cx,10                  ; read 10 bytes
mov    dx,offset inbuf
int    21h
```

12.5   READING A BITMAP FILE

In this section we present a procedure called ShowBMP that loads a Windows-style bitmap from a file and displays it on the screen. The bitmap can have a resolution up to 320x200, with 256 colors. See the program in Example 5.

When the ShowBMP procedure is called, DS:DX must point to a null-terminated filename. Inside the procedure, we call the OpenInputFile procedure from the link library and quit if the procedure cannot open the file. Next, the ShowBMP procedure reads the bitmap file's *header* record. The ReadHeader procedure reads 54 bytes into a buffer and calls the CheckValid procedure to make sure the bitmap header is recognized.

The CheckValid procedure looks for the string "BM" at the start of the file, and if it finds it, returns. The program calls GetBMPInfo to read the bitmap header record. For example, the header contains the offset of the beginning of the graphic image, the number of colors in the bitmap, and the bitmap's horizontal and vertical resoltuion

The ReadPal procedure reads the graphic pallete into memory. The procedure reads a count of the number of colors and loads the complete palette into a variable. The InitVid procedure inializes the video display into graphcis mode, and the LoadBMP procedure load sand displays the bitmap file. The LoadBMP procedure takes into account that BMP files store graphics images upside-down. The file is read one graphics line at a time, which tends to slow the program down.

This program is just a quick demonstration of the technque of loading bitmaps, but with some experimentation, you should be able to load and display a bitmap anywhere on the screen.

Example 5. Reading and Displaying a Bitmap File.

```
; Bitmap Display Procedure                    (bitmap.asm)

; The ShowBMP procedure loads a Windows type BMP file
; and display it on the screen. Input parameters:
; DS:DX points to an ASCIIZ string containing the
; BMP file path. The maximum resolution is 320x200, with
; 256 colors.
.model  small
.186
.code
extrn   OpenInputFile:proc, CloseFile:proc
PUBLIC  ShowBMP

ShowBMP proc
        pusha                       ; Save registers
        call    OpenInputFile       ; Open file pointed to by DS:DX
        jc      FileErr             ; Error? Display error message and quit
        mov     bx,ax               ; Put the file handle in BX
        call    ReadHeader          ; Read 54-byte header containing file info
        jc      InvalidBMP          ; Not a valid BMP file? Show error and quit
        call    ReadPal             ; Read the BMP's palette and put it in a buffer
        push    es
        call    InitVid             ; Set up the display for 320x200 VGA graphics
        call    SendPal             ; Send the palette to the video registers
        call    LoadBMP             ; Load the graphic and display it
        call    CloseFile           ; Close the file
        pop     es
        jmp     ProcDone

FileErr:
        mov     ah,9
        mov     dx,offset msgFileErr
        int     21h
        jmp     ProcDone

InvalidBMP:
        mov     ah,9
        mov     dx,offset msgInvBMP
        int     21h
```

```
ProcDone:
    popa                            ; Restore registers
    ret
ShowBMP endp


; Check the first two bytes of the file. If they do not
; match the standard beginning of a BMP header ("BM"),
; the carry flag is set.


CheckValid proc
    clc
    mov  si,offset Header
    mov  di,offset BMPStart
    mov  cx,2                       ; BMP ID is 2 bytes long.
CVloop:
    mov  al,[si]                    ; Get a byte from the header.
    mov  dl,[di]
    cmp  al,dl                      ; Is it what it should be?
    jne  NotValid                   ; If not, set the carry flag.
    inc  si
    inc  di
    loop CVloop

    jmp     CVdone

NotValid:
    stc

CVdone:
    ret
CheckValid  endp


GetBMPInfo  proc

; This procedure pulls some important BMP info from the header
; and puts it in the appropriate variables.

mov     ax,header[0Ah]      ; AX = Offset of the beginning of the graphic
sub     ax,54               ; Subtract the length of the header
shr     ax,2                ; and divide by 4
mov     PalSize,ax          ; to get the number of colors in the BMP
                            ; (Each palette entry is 4 bytes long).
```

```
        mov      ax,header[12h]              ; AX = Horizontal resolution of BMP.
        mov      BMPWidth,ax                 ; Store it.
        mov      ax,header[16h]              ; AX = Vertical resolution of BMP.
        mov      BMPHeight,ax                ; Store it.
        ret
GetBMPInfo      endp


InitVid proc
; This procedure initializes the video mode and makes ES point to
; video memory.

        mov     ax,13h
        int     10h                         ; Set video mode to 320x200x256.
        push    0A000h
        pop     es                          ; ES = A000h (video segment).
        ret
InitVid endp


LoadBMP proc
; BMP graphics are saved upside down. This procedure reads the graphic
; line by line, displaying the lines from bottom to top. The line at
; which it starts depends on the vertical resolution, so the upper left
; corner of the graphic will always be at the upper left corner of the screen.

; Video memory is a two-dimensional array of memory bytes which
; can be addressed and modified individually. Each byte represents
; a pixel on the screen, and each byte contains the color of the
; pixel at that location.

        mov     cx,BMPHeight        ; Will display that many lines
ShowLoop:
        push    cx
        mov     di,cx               ; Make a copy of CX
        shl     cx,6                ; Multiply CX by 64
        shl     di,8                ; Multiply DI by 256
        add     di,cx               ; DI = CX * 320, and points to the first
                                    ; pixel on the desired screen line.

        mov     ah,3fh
        mov     cx,BMPWidth
        mov     dx,offset ScrLine
```

```
        int    21h                      ; Read one line into the buffer.

        cld                             ; Clear direction flag, for movsb.
        mov    cx,BMPWidth
        mov    si,offset ScrLine
        rep    movsb                    ; Copy line in buffer to screen.

        pop    cx
        loop   ShowLoop
        ret
LoadBMP endp


; This procedure checks to make sure the file is a valid BMP,
; and gets some information about the graphic.

ReadHeader proc
        mov    ah,3fh
        mov    cx,54
        mov    dx,offset Header
        int    21h                      ; Read file header into buffer.

        call   CheckValid               ; Is it a valid BMP file?
        jc     RHdone                   ; No? Quit.
        call   GetBMPInfo               ; Otherwise, process the header.

RHdone:
        ret
ReadHeader endp


; Read the video palette.

ReadPal proc
        mov    ah,3fh
        mov    cx,PalSize               ; CX = Number of colors in palette.
        shl    cx,2                     ; CX = Multiply by 4 to get size (in bytes)
                                        ; of palette.
        mov    dx,offset palBuff
        int    21h                      ; Put the palette into the buffer.
        ret
ReadPal endp
```

```
SendPal proc
; This procedure goes through the palette buffer, sending information about
; the palette to the video registers. One byte is sent out
; port 3C8h, containing the number of the first color in the palette that
; will be sent (0=the first color). Then, RGB information about the colors
; (any number of colors) is sent out port 3C9h.


        mov    si,offset palBuff
; Point to buffer containing palette.
        mov    cx,PalSize              ; CX = Number of colors to send.
        mov    dx,3c8h
        mov    al,0                    ; We will start at 0.
        out    dx,al
        inc    dx                      ; DX = 3C9h.
sndLoop:
; Note: Colors in a BMP file are saved as BGR values rather than RGB.

        mov    al,[si+2]               ; Get red value.
        shr    al,2                    ; Max. is 255, but video only allows
                                       ; values of up to 63. Dividing by 4
                                       ; gives a good value.
        out    dx,al                   ; Send it.
        mov    al,[si+1]               ; Get green value.
        shr    al,2
        out    dx,al                   ; Send it.
        mov    al,[si]                 ; Get blue value.
        shr    al,2
        out    dx,al                   ; Send it.

        add    si,4                    ; Point to next color.
                                       ; (There is a null chr.after every color.)
        loop   sndLoop
        ret
SendPal endp


.data
Header    label word
HeadBuff  db 54 dup('H')
palBuff   db 1024 dup('P')
ScrLine   db 320 dup(0)
```

```
BMPStart      db 'BM'
PalSize       dw ?
BMPHeight     dw ?
BMPWidth      dw ?

msgInvBMP     db "Not a valid BMP file.",7,0Dh,0Ah,'$'
msgFileErr    db "Error opening file.",7,0Dh,0Ah,'$'
end
```

12.6   REVIEW QUESTIONS

1. If a file currently does not exist, what will happen if function 3Dh opens the file in the output mode?

2. If a file is created using function 3Ch, can it be both written to and read from before it is closed? What if it was created with a read-only attribute?

3. If you want to create a new file but do not want to accidentally erase an existing file with the same name, what steps would your program take?

4. For each of the following error codes returned when INT 21h is called, write a single-sentence explanation of what probably caused the error:

Error Number	Function Being Called
03h	56h (Rename file)
05h	41h (Delete file)
06h	57h (Set date/time)
10h	3Ah (Remove directory)
11h	56h (Rename file)
12h	4Eh (Find first matching file)

5. What do the following instructions imply?

```
.data
filename  db  'FIRST.RND',0

.code
mov   ah,3Dh
mov   al,2
mov   dx,offset filename
int   21h
```

6. When a file is closed, do you need to point DX to its filename?

7. What do you think the effect of the following instructions would be?

    ```
    mov   ah,3Eh
    mov   bx,0
    int   21h
    ```

8. When function 3Eh (read from file or device) is called, what does it mean when the Carry flag is set and AX = 6?

9. When function 3Eh is called (with CX = 80h), what does it mean when DOS clears the Carry flag and returns a value of 20h in AX?

10. When function 3Eh is used to read from the keyboard and CX = 0Ah, what will be the contents of the input buffer when the following string is input?

    ```
    1234567890
    ```

11. When function 40h writes a string to the console, must the string be terminated by a zero byte?

12. When using function 40h to write to an output file, does DOS automatically update the file pointer?

13. If you have just read a record from a random file and you want to rewrite it back to the same position in the file, what steps must you take?

14. Is it possible to move the file pointer within a text file?

15. Write the necessary instructions to locate the file pointer 20 bytes beyond the end of the file identified by **filehandle**.

16. What is the offset of the 20th record in a file that contains 50-byte fixed-length records?

17. What is the purpose of buffering input records?

18. Assuming that bits 0-4 hold a department number and bits 5-7 hold a store number within the following bit-mapped field, what are the values shown here?

    ```
    11000101    store =      department =
    00101001    store =      department =
    01010101    store =      department =
    ```

19. The following WRITE_BUFFER procedure is supposed to write the contents of **buffer** to the file identified by **filehandle**. The variable **buflen** contains the current length of the buffer. If the disk is full, the procedure should print an appropriate message. What is wrong with the procedure's logic?

    ```
    .data
    filehandle  dw  ?
    buflen      dw  ?
    buffer  db    80 dup(?)
    message db  'Disk is full.$'
    ```

```
.code
write_buffer proc
        mov    ah,40h
        mov    bx,filehandle
        mov    cx,buflen
        mov    dx,offset buffer
        int    21h
        jnc    L1
        mov    dx,offset message
        call   display
L1:     ret
write_buffer endp
```

12.7 PROGRAMMING EXERCISES

1. ***The "Touch" Utility***

   For a long time, programmers have used a tool called *touch* that reads a file specifier on the command line, including wildcards, and changes the date/time stamp of all matching files to the current date and time. Write this program in assembly language. If, for example, the user types the following command line, all files in the current directory with an extension of ASM will be updated:

   ```
   touch *.asm
   ```

   One way this program might be useful is, when distributing a set of files to customers for the release of a product, you could assign the same date and time to all files.

2. ***Text Matching Program***

   Write a program that opens a text file containing up to 60K bytes and performs a case-insensitive search for a string. The string and the filename are typed on the command line. Display each line from the file on which the string appears and prefix each line with a line number. For example:

   ```
   > search line file1.txt

    2: This is line 2.
   10: On line 10, we have even more text.
   11: This is a single text line that is even longer.
   ```

3. ***Enhanced Text Matching Program***

   Improve the *text matching* program from the previous exercise as follows:

- Allow wildcard characters in the file specification, so multiple files may be scanned for the same string.

- Include a command-line option to display filenames only. The command should be **+/–**, the same one used by the **grep** utility supplied with Turbo Assembler. A sample command line that displays the names of all ASM files containing the string "xlat" is

```
search -l+ xlat *.asm
```

4. *File Listing Program*

Write a program that reads a text file into a buffer and displays the first 24 lines of text. Write the text directly to video memory for the best performance. Provide the following keyboard command functions:

Key	Function
PgUp	Scroll up 24 lines
PgDn	Scroll down 24 lines
UpArrow	Scroll up 1 line
DnArrow	Scroll down 1 line
Esc	Exit to DOS

5. *Random File Creation Program*

Write a program that creates a random file containing student academic information, using data entered from the console. Each record is 27 bytes long, and there should be at least 20 records. The record format is shown here:

Field	Column
Student number	1
Last name	6
Course taken	19
Number of credits	27
Grade	28

Here is some sample data, to which you should add at least 12 more records:

```
10024ADAMS       ENG 11003A
10123BEAZLIE     CIS 23014B
10200BOOKER      MAC 11325A
10201BOZEK       BUS 30023B
10330CHARLES     MUS 23003C
```

```
10405DANIELS       ART 10022A
10524GONZALEZ      CHM 40004A
10645HART          ENG 11003B
```

6. **Student File Maintenance Program**

Using the file created in the previous exercise, write a random file update program that displays the following menu:

```
          STUDENT FILE MAINTENANCE

    S   Show a single record
    A   Add a new record
    C   Change (edit) a record
    D   Delete a record
    E   Exit program
```

The user may select records by record number. After each of the menu functions is carried out, return to the menu. Test the program with multiple additions, deletions, and changes to records.

7. **Enhanced Sector Display Program**

Using the Sector Display program from the Chapter 11 Exercises as a starting point, add the following enhancement: As a sector is displayed, let the operator press [F3] to write the sector to an output file. Prompt for the filename, and if it already exists, append the current sector to the end of the file. This helps to make the program a useful tool for recovering lost sectors on a disk, as the sectors can be reconverted into files.

12.7.1 Manipulating Disk Directories

1. **Search for Subdirectories**

Write a procedure that searches for all entries in a disk's root directory with an attribute of 10h (subdirectory name). Display the names.

2. **Display a Subdirectory**

Write a procedure that finds the first subdirectory entry in the root directory, moves to the subdirectory, and displays a list of all its files.

3. **Recursive Subdirectory Display**

(Requires knowledge of tree searching methods.) Write a recursive procedure called **ShowTree** that locates and displays the name of each subdirectory in the current directory. For each subdirectory, locate and display all its subdirectories. Use a depth-first search method. For example, print out the directory tree in the following manner:

```
A1
     A1B1
          A1B1C1
          A1B1C2
     A1B2
     A1B3
          A1B3C1
          A1B3C2
  A2
     A2B1
     A2B2
  A3
     A3B1
```

According to this listing, the root directory contains A1, A2, and A3, and A1 contains A1B1, A1B2, and A1B3. Directory A1B1 contains A1B1C1 and A1B1C2, and so on.

4. *Showing File Times and Sizes*

Enhance the Date Stamp program from Example 1 earlier in this chapter so that it also displays each file's time and size.

5. *Sorting by Filename*

Enhance the Date Stamp program from Example 1 earlier in this chapter by reading the directory into an array, sorting the array by filename, and displaying the array.

6. *Sort by Date and Time*

Enhance the Date Stamp program from Example 1 earlier in this chapter by reading the directory into an array, sorting the array by date and time, and displaying the array.

7. *Purge Multiple Files*

Write a program that takes a file specification from the command line, displays the name of each matching file, and asks if the file is to be deleted. When the user enters Y next to any filename, delete the file.

8. *Search for Files by Date*

Write a program that searches for all files in the current directory that have a date stamp that is earlier than the current system date. Displays the names of the matching files. To obtain the system date, call INT 21h function 2Ah. The year is returned in CX, the month in DH, and the day in DL. For example, October 12, 1990, would be returned as:

```
CX = 07C6h, DH = 0Ah, DL = 0Ch
```

9.   *File Hide and Unhide*

Write two programs: hide.exe, which hides all files matching a file specifier, and unhide.exe, which unhides all matching files. Only files in the current directory are affected. Output from each program should be a listing of the files that have been hidden or unhidden.

These programs, which have been available as shareware utilities for many years, are tremendously useful. A major feature of HIDE is that you can protect important files from being deleted by the DOS DEL command. Another is that the average computer user does not know how to view the contents of these files. One good application has to do with deleting all files in a directory *except* a particular file. First, hide the chosen file; next, delete all remaining files in the directory; and finally, unhide the original file.

Both programs should read a file specifier from the command line, which might be a single filename, a complete path, or a wildcard filename, such as *.ZIP.

13 *High-Level Language Interface*

13.1   INTRODUCTION

Most programmers do not write large-scale applications in assembly language, simply because it takes too long. High-level languages are designed to relieve the programmer of details that would otherwise slow down a project's development. But assembly language is still used widely to configure hardware devices and optimize both the speed and code size of programs.

In this chapter, we focus on the *interface,* or connection, between assembly language and high-level programming languages. First, we take a look at inline assembly code in C++, and then at linking separate assembly language modules to C++ programs both in Windows and MS-DOS.

13.1.1   General Conventions

A number of general considerations that need to be addressed when calling assembly language subroutines from high-level languages:

The *naming convention* used by a language refers to the way segments and modules are named, as well as rules or characteristics regarding the naming of variables and procedures.

For example, we have to answer an important question: Does the assembler or compiler alter the names of identifiers placed in object files, and if so, how?

The *memory model* used by a program, tiny, small, compact, medium, large, or huge, determines whether calls and references will be *near* (within the same segment) or *far* (between different segments).

The *calling convention* refers to the low-level details about how subroutines are called:

• Which registers must be preserved by subroutines.

• The method used to pass arguments: in registers, on the stack, in shared memory, or by some other method.

• The order in which arguments are passed by calling programs to subroutines.

• Whether arguments are passed by value or by reference.

• How the stack pointer is restored after a subroutine call.

• How functions return values to calling programs.

External Identifiers. When calling an assembly language subroutine from another language, any identifiers that are *shared* between the two languages must be compatible with both. These shared identifiers may also be called *external identifiers*. The linker resolves references to external identifiers, but can only do so if the naming conventions being used are consistent. BASIC, assembly language, and Pascal translate external identifiers to uppercase. C/C++ compilers do not change the case of names, and they are case-sensitive. C/C++ compilers also append a leading underscore to external identifiers.

Languages and compilers vary in the number of significant characters they use for identifiers. Although assembly language recognizes the first 31 characters of an identifier, any high-level language (with a shorter identifier limit) that calls the assembly routine dictates the identifier limit.

Segment Names. When linking an assembly routine to a high-level language, you must use segment names that are compatible with the calling program. This is particularly important when arguments are passed to subroutines. For example, in Borland C++, a *small* model C program expects the code segment to be called **_TEXT**, the data segment to be called **_DATA**, and an uninitialized data segment to be called **_BSS**. In assembly language subroutines shown in this chapter, we consistently use simplified segment directives such as, .MODEL, .CODE, and .DATA to make sure that our segment names are compatible with calling programs.

Memory Models. Borland and Microsoft languages support standard memory models. *Large* and *medium* memory model programs require far calls to external subroutines—the current CS and IP are both pushed on the stack. *Tiny, small,* and *compact* memory model programs require near calls to external subroutines, so only IP is pushed on the stack. Whenever possible, use a .MODEL directive in your assembly subroutine that matches the default model for the calling program. Specify a language type of C, Pascal, FORTRAN, or BASIC in the .model statement:

```
.model modelname, language
```

The *flat* memory model is used for 32-bit applications running in protected mode. Such programs have to run in a 32-bit operating system such as Windows 95, 98, or Windows NT. There are no separate segments, so all code and data are located in the same segment. All code and data offsets are 32 bits, and all are labeled *near*. The processor runs efficiently in flat mode because it doesn't have to translate segment-offset addresses to absolute addresses. By default, Microsoft Visual C++ *Win32 Console* applications use the flat memory model.

Calling Conventions. A language's calling convention refers to the way it implements a subroutine call. This is often referred to as a *low-level protocol*. It is often difficult for the same subroutine to be called by different languages. A subroutine called by Pascal, for instance, expects its parameters to be in a different order from a subroutine called by C.

One principle seems to be universal: When a high-level language calls a subroutine, it pushes its arguments on the stack before executing a CALL instruction. But beyond this basic principle, languages vary.

An important exception to the standard parameter passing protocol is what Microsoft calls the *__fastcall* calling convention, where the compiler passes function arguments in registers instead of on the stack.

The writer of a subroutine uses the calling convention to determine how to receive parameters. It also needs to know whether it must restore the stack pointer before returning, or if the calling program does this. If a function subroutine is called, both the calling program and the subroutine need to know how the function result is returned.

Passing Arguments. There are three standard ways of passing arguments to subroutines, which we have already demonstrated in Chapter 5:

*   *Pass by Value.* A copy of the argument is pushed on the stack. The subroutine can work with the copy, but any changes it makes to the copy on the stack will not affect the variable that was originally pushed by the calling program.

*   *Pass by Near Reference.* The offset of an argument is pushed on the stack, which gives the subroutine access to the argument variable in the calling program. Both the calling program and the subroutine are assumed to share the same data segment.

*   *Pass by Far Reference.* The segment-offset address of an argument is pushed on the stack, giving the subroutine access to the argument variable in the calling program. The calling program and subroutine are assumed to be using different data segments. The segment is pushed before the offset by both Microsoft and Borland compilers. This allows subroutines to use the LDS and LES instructions to load addresses from the stack.

13.2   WRITING INLINE ASSEMBLY CODE

13.2.1   Microsoft Visual C++

Inline assembly code is assembly language source code that is inserted directly into high-level language programs. Most C/C++ compilers support this feature, as do Borland C++, Pascal, and Delphi. Other languages, such as Microsoft Visual Basic, do not.

In this section, we demonstrate how to write *inline* assembly code for Microsoft Visual C++ running in 32-bit protected mode with the *flat* memory model. Other high-level language compilers support inline assembly code, but the exact syntax varies.

Inline assembly code is a straightforward alternative to writing assembly code in external modules. The primary advantage to writing inline code is simplicity, because there are no external linking issues, naming problems, and parameter passing protocols to worry about.

The primary disadvantage to using inline assembly code is its lack of portability, in cases where a high-level language program must be compiled for different target platforms. Inline assembly code that runs on an Intel Pentium processor will not run on a RISC processor, for example. To some extent, the problem can be solved by inserting conditional definitions in the program's source code to enable different versions of subroutines for different target systems. But it is easy to see that maintenance is still a problem. A link library of external assembly language subroutines, on the other hand, could easily be replaced by a similar link library designed for a different target machine.

The __asm Directive. In Visual C++, the **__asm** directive can be placed at the beginning of a single statement, or it can mark the beginning of a block of assembly language statements. The syntax is:

```
__asm   statement

__asm {
  statement-1
  statement-2
  ...
  statement-n
}
```

(There are *two* underline characters before "asm.")

Comments. Comments can be placed after any statements in the asm block, using either assembly language syntax or C/C++ syntax. The Visual C++ manual suggests that you avoid assembler-style comments because they might interfere with C macros, which expand on a single logical line. Here are examples of permissible comments:

```
mov  esi,buf   ; initialize index register
mov  esi,buf   // initialize index register
mov  esi,buf   /* initialize index register */
```

Features. Here is what you *can* do when writing inline assembly code:

• Use any instruction from the Intel 80x86 instruction set.

• Use register names as operands.

• Reference code labels and variables that were declared outside the *asm* block. (This is important, because local function variables must be declared outside the __asm block.)

• Use numeric literals that incorporate either assembler-style or C-style radix notation. For example, 0A26h and 0xA26 are equivalent and can both be used.

• Use the PTR operator in statement such as the following: inc byte ptr [esi]

• Use the EVEN and ALIGN directives.

Limitations. You *cannot* do the following when writing inline assembly code:

• Use data definition directives such as DB and DW.

• Use most assembler operators, including OFFSET and SHR.

• Use STRUC, RECORD, WIDTH, and MASK.

• Use macro directives, including MACRO, REPT, IRC, IRP, and ENDM, or macro operators (<>, !, &, %, and .TYPE).

• Reference segments by name. (You can, however, use segment register names as operands.)

Register Values. You cannot make any assumptions about register values at the beginning of an __asm block. The registers may have been modified by code that executed just before the __asm block. If a procedure is compiled using Microsoft's *__fastcall* calling convention, function parameters are not pushed on the stack—they are located in registers. Your code in an __asm block might inadvertently modify one or more function parameters. Because of this, you should not use __fastcall for functions that contain inline assembly code. (The Visual C++ documentation shows how to disable __fastcall for individual functions, by the way.)

In general, you can modify EAX, EBX, ECX, and EDX in your inline code, because the compiler does not expect these values to be preserved between statements. If you modify too many registers, however, you may make it impossible for the compiler to fully optimize the C++ code in the same area of the procedure, because optimization requires the use of registers.

Although you cannot use the OFFSET operator, you can still retrieve the offset of a variable using the LEA instruction. With Microsoft Visual C++, if the program is compiled under the *flat* memory model, the offset of a variable is 32 bits. The following LEA instruction moves the 32-bit offset of **buffer** to SI:

```
lea esi,buffer
```

In 32-bit mode, a near pointer is 32 bits and a far pointer is 48 bits. In the *flat* memory model, all pointers are near.

Length, Type, and Size. You can use LENGTH, SIZE, and TYPE. The LENGTH operator returns the number of elements in an array, and it returns the value 1 for non-array variables. The TYPE operator returns the size of a C or C++ type or variable, the number of bytes in a structure, or, for arrays, the size of a single array element. The SIZE operator returns the size of a C or C++ variable (length * type). The program excerpt in Example 1 demonstrates the values returned by the inline assembler for various C++ types.

Example 1. Using the LENGTH, TYPE, and SIZE Operators.

```
struct Package {
  long originZip;        // 4
  long destinationZip;   // 4
  float shippingPrice;   // 4
};

char myChar;
bool myBool;
short myShort;
int  myInt;
long myLong;
float myFloat;
double myDouble;
Package myPackage;
long double myLongDouble;
long myLongArray[10];

__asm {

  mov  eax,length myInt;       // 1
  mov  eax,length myLongArray; // 10

  mov  eax,type myChar;        // 1
  mov  eax,type myBool;        // 1
  mov  eax,type myShort;       // 2
  mov  eax,type myInt;         // 4
  mov  eax,type myLong;        // 4
```

```
    mov   eax,type myFloat;      // 4
    mov   eax,type myDouble;     // 8
    mov   eax,type myLongDouble; // 8
    mov   eax,type myPackage;    // 12
    mov   eax,type myLongArray;  // 4

    mov   eax,size myLong;       // 4
    mov   eax,size myPackage;    // 12
    mov   eax,size myLongArray;  // 40
}
```

13.2.2 File Encryption Example

Let's write a short program that reads a file, encrypts it, and writes the output to another file. The **TranslateBuffer** function in Example 2 uses an **__asm** block to define statements that loop through a character array and XOR each character with a predefined value. The inline statements can refer to function parameters, local variables, and code labels. Because this example was compiled under Microsoft Visual C++ as a *Win32 Console* application, the unsigned integer data type is 32 bits.

Example 2. TranslateBuffer Function (inline ASM).

```
void TranslateBuffer( char * buf,
    unsigned count, unsigned char encryptChar )
{
  __asm {
    mov esi,buf
    mov ecx,count
    mov al,encryptChar
  L1:
    xor [esi],al
    inc  esi
    Loop L1
  } // asm
}
```

In our calling C++ program shown in Example 3, TranslateBuffer is called from a loop that reads blocks of data from a file, encrypts it, and writes the translated buffer to a new file.

Example 3. C++ Program Calling the TranslateBuffer Procedure.

```
// ENCODE.CPP - Copy and encrypt a file.
```

```cpp
#include <iostream>
#include <fstream>
#include "translat.h"
using namespace std;

int main()
{
  const int BUFSIZE = 200;
  char buffer[BUFSIZE];
  unsigned int count;

  unsigned short encryptCode;
  cout << "Encryption code [0-255]? ";
  cin >> encryptCode;

  ifstream infile( "infile.txt", ios::binary );
  ofstream outfile( "outfile.txt", ios::binary );

  while (!infile.eof() )
   {
    infile.read(buffer, BUFSIZE );
    count = infile.gcount();
    TranslateBuffer(buffer, count, encryptCode);
    outfile.write(buffer, count);
   }
  return 0;
}
```

The Overhead of Calling a Procedure. If you view the *Disassembly* window while debugging this program, it is interesting to see exactly how much overhead is involved in calling and returning from a procedure. The following statements push the arguments on the stack and call **TranslateBuffer:**

```asm
        push    0F1h
        mov     ecx,dword ptr [count]
        push    ecx
        push    offset buffer
        call    TranslateBuffer
        add     esp,0Ch
```

The following is the assembly language code for TranslateBuffer. Notice that a number of statements were automatically inserted by the compiler, to set up EBP and save a standard set of registers that are always preserved whether or not they are actually modified by the procedure:

```
        push  ebp
        mov   ebp,esp
        push  ebx
        push  esi
        push  edi
        mov   esi,buf        ; inline code starts here
        mov   ecx,count
        mov   al,eChar
    L1:
        xor   [esi],al
        inc   esi
        Loop  L1             ; inline code ends here
        pop   edi
        pop   esi
        pop   ebx
        pop   ebp
        ret
```

All in all, our original 6 inline instructions required a total of 22 instructions to execute. If this procedure were called thousands of times, the overhead from the extra code would be noticeable. To avoid this, we can insert the inline code directly in the loop that called TranslateBuffer, creating a much more efficient program:

```
encryptChar = unsigned char (encryptCode);
while (!infile.eof() )
{
  infile.read(buffer, BUFSIZE );
  count = infile.gcount();
  __asm {
      lea esi,buffer
      mov ecx,count
      mov al,encryptChar
  L1:
      xor [esi],al
      inc esi
      Loop L1
  } // asm
  outfile.write(buffer, count);
}
```

Notice that we had to cast encryptCode from an unsigned integer into an *unsigned char* and store it in encryptChar. This is because integers are 4 bytes and characters are 1 byte.

13.3   LINKING TO C++ PROGRAMS

In this part of the chapter, we want to show how to write external subroutines in assembly language that can be called from C and C++ programs. Such programs consist of at least two modules: the first, written in assembly language, contains the external subroutine; the second module contains the C/C++ code that starts and ends the program. There are a few specific requirements and features of C/C++ that affect the way we write assembly code.

Arguments. Arguments are passed by C/C++ programs from right to left, as they appear in the argument list. After the subroutine returns, the calling program is responsible for cleaning up the stack. This can be done by either adding a value to the stack pointer equal to the size of the arguments, or popping an adequate number of values from the stack.

External Names.. C/C++ automatically appends an underscore (_) to the beginning of each external identifier. For example, if we call a procedure named **ReadSector** from a C/C++ program, the procedure name must begin with an underscore in the ASM module:

```
public _ReadSector        Public declaration
_ReadSector proc          Procedure name
```

When assembling a module containing an external subroutine, you must use a command line option that preserves case-sensitive names. Otherwise, a name such as _ReadSector would be automatically converted to _READSECTOR by the assembler. Then, when linking this module to a C/C++ program, the linker would not be able to match up the procedure name being called by the C++ program. To assure case sensitivity for public names, the following assemblers use the stated command line options:

/Cx	Microsoft 6.1x Assembler (ML.EXE)
/mx	Microsoft 5.12 Assembler (MASM.EXE)
/mx	Borland 4.0 Assembler (TASM.EXE)

Declaring the Function. In a C language program, use the **extern** qualifier when declaring an external assembly language function. For example, this is how we declare **ReadSector**:

```
extern ReadSector( char buffer[], long startSector,
        int driveNum, int numSectors );
```

If the function is called from a C++ program, you must also add a "C" qualifier that prevents name decoration:

```
extern "C" ReadSector( char buffer[], long startSector,
          int driveNum, int numSectors );
```

Name decoration is a standard C++ compiler technique that involves modifying a function name with extra characters that indicate the exact type of each function parameter. (The Visual C++ documentation calls this technique *decoration of external symbols*.) The problem with name decoration is that the C++ compiler tells the linker to look for the decorated name rather than the original one when producing the executable file.

13.3.1 Linking to Borland C++

In this section of the chapter we will use the 16-bit version of Borland C++ 5.01 and select MS-DOS as the target operating system with a small memory model. We use Borland TASM 4.0 as the assembler for these examples, because most users of Borland C++ are likely to use Turbo Assembler rather than MASM. We will also create 16-bit real mode applications using Borland C++ 5.01, and demonstrate both small and large memory models programs, showing how to call both near and far subroutines.

Function Results. In Borland C++, functions return 16-bit values in AX and 32-bit values in DX:AX. Larger data structures (structure values, arrays, etc.) are stored in a static data location, and a pointer to the data is returned in AX. (In medium, large, and huge memory model programs, a 32-bit pointer is returned in DX:AX.)

How to Set Up a Project. In the Borland C++ integrated development environment (IDE), create a new project. Create a source code module (CPP file) and enter the code for the main C++ program. Create the ASM file containing the subroutine you plan to call. Use TASM to assemble the program into an object module, either from the DOS command line or from the Borland C++ IDE, using its *transfer* capability.

If you have assembled the ASM module separately, add the object file created by the assembler to the C++ project. Invoke the MAKE or BUILD command from the menu. It compiles the CPP file, and if there are no errors, it links the two object modules to produce an executable program. *Suggestion:* limit the name of the CPP source file to 8 characters, or the Turbo Debugger for DOS will not be able to find it when you debug the program.

Debugging. The Borland C++ compiler does not allow the DOS debugger to be run from the IDE. Instead, you need to run Turbo Debugger for DOS either from the DOS prompt or from the Windows desktop. Using the debugger's File/Open menu command, select the executable file created by the C++ linker. The C++ source code file should immediately display, and you can begin tracing and running the program.

Saving Registers. Assembly subroutines called by Borland C++ must preserve the values of BP, DS, SS, SI, DI, and the Direction flag.

Storage Sizes. A 16-bit Borland C++ program uses specific storage sizes for all its data types. These are unique to this particular implementation and must be adjusted for every C++ compiler. Refer to Table 1.

Table 1. Borland C++ Data Types in 16-bit Applications.

Data Type	Storage Bytes	ASM Type
char, unsigned char	1	byte
int, unsigned int, short int	2	word
enum	2	word
long, unsigned long	4	dword
float	4	dword
double	8	qword
long double	10	tbyte
near pointer	2	word
far pointer	4	dword

13.3.2 ReadSector Example

Let's begin with a Borland C++ program that calls an external assembly language procedure called ReadSector. C++ compilers generally do not include library functions for reading disk sectors, because such details are too hardware-dependent, and it would be impractical to implement libraries for all possible computers. As we found in Chapter 11, assembly language programs can easily read disk sectors by calling INT 25h. Our present task, then, is to create the interface between assembly language and C++ that combines the strengths of both languages.

Program Execution. First, we will demonstrate the program's execution. When the C++ program starts up, the user selects the drive number, starting sector, and number of sectors to read. For example, this user wants to read sectors 0–19 from drive A:

```
Sector display program.

Enter drive number [1=A, 2=B, 3=C, 4=D, 5=E,...]: 1
Starting sector number to read: 0
Number of sectors to read: 20
```

This information is passed to the assembly language procedure, which reads the sectors into a buffer. The C++ program begins to display the buffer, one sector at a time. As each sector is displayed, non-ASCII characters are replaced by dots. For example, this is the program's display of sector 0 from drive A:

```
Reading sectors 0 - 20 from Drive 1


Sector 0 ---------------------------------------------------------
.<.(P3j2IHC........@..................)Y...MYDISK   FAT12   .3.
....{...x..v..V.U."..~..N..........|.E...F..E.8N$}"....w.r...:f..
|f;..W.u....V....s.3..F...f..F..V..F....v.`.F..V.. ....^...H...F
..N.a....#.r98-t.`....}..at9Nt... ;.r.....}.......t.<.t..........
..}....}.....^.f......}.}..E..N....F..V......r....p..B.-`fj.RP.Sj
.j...t...3..v...v.B...v..............V$...d.ar.@u.B.^.Iuw....'..I
nvalid system disk...Disk I/O error...Replace the disk, and then
press any key....IOSYSMSDOS   SYS...A....~...@...U.
```

Sectors continue to be displayed, one by one, until the entire buffer has been displayed.

Program Listing. The complete C++ program that calls the ReadSector procedure is shown in Example 4. At the top of the listing, we find the declaration, or prototype, of the ReadSector function. The first parameter, *buffer*, is a character array that holds the sector data after it has been read from the disk. *startSector* is the starting sector number to read, *driveNum* is the disk drive number, and *numSectors* specifies the number of sectors to read. The first parameter is a pointer, and all other parameters are passed by value:

```
extern "C" ReadSector( char buffer[], long startSector,
        int driveNum, int numSectors );
```


Example 4. Main C++ Program That Calls ReadSector.

```cpp
// main.cpp - Calls the ReadSector Procedure

#include <iostream.h>
#include <conio.h>
#include <stdlib.h>
const int SECTOR_SIZE = 512;

extern "C" ReadSector( char * buffer, long startSector,
        int driveNum, int numSectors );

void DisplayBuffer( const char * buffer, long startSector,
    int numSectors )
{
  int n = 0;
  long last = startSector + numSectors;
```

```cpp
      for(long sNum = startSector; sNum < last; sNum++)
      {
        cout << "\nSector " << sNum
             << " --------------------------"
             << "---------------------------\n";
        for(int i = 0; i < SECTOR_SIZE; i++)
        {
          char ch = buffer[n++];
          if( unsigned(ch) < 32 || unsigned(ch) > 127)
            cout << '.';
          else
            cout << ch;
        }
        cout << endl;
        getch();
      }
}

int main()
{
  char * buffer;
  long startSector;
  int driveNum;
  int numSectors;

  system("CLS");
  cout << "Sector display program.\n\n"
  << "Enter drive number [1=A, 2=B, 3=C, 4=D, 5=E,...]: ";
  cin >> driveNum;
  cout << "Starting sector number to read: ";
  cin >> startSector;
  cout << "Number of sectors to read: ";
  cin >> numSectors;
  buffer = new char[numSectors * SECTOR_SIZE];

  cout << "\n\nReading sectors " << startSector << " - "
       << (startSector + numSectors) << " from Drive "
       << driveNum << endl;

  ReadSector( buffer, startSector, driveNum, numSectors );
  DisplayBuffer( buffer, startSector, numSectors );
  system("CLS");
```

```
    return 0;
}
```

In **main**, the user is prompted for the drive number, starting sector, and number of sectors. The program also dynamically allocates storage for the buffer that holds the sector data:

```
cout << "Sector display program.\n\n"
    << "Enter drive number [1=A, 2=B, 3=C, 4=D, 5=E,...]: ";
cin >> driveNum;
cout << "Starting sector number to read: ";
cin >> startSector;
cout << "Number of sectors to read: ";
cin >> numSectors;
buffer = new char[numSectors * SECTOR_SIZE];
```

This information is passed to the external **ReadSector** procedure, which fills the buffer with sectors from the disk:

```
ReadSector( buffer, startSector, driveNum, numSectors );
```

The buffer is passed to **DisplayBuffer**, a procedure in the C++ program that displays each sector in ASCII text format:

```
DisplayBuffer( buffer, startSector, numSectors );
```

Assembly Language Module. The assembly language module containing the ReadSector procedure is shown in Example 5. Most of the code in this module is simply an adaptation of the ReadSector program from Chapter 11. Because we are using Borland TASM for this example, we use the Borland ARG keyword to specify the procedure arguments. Notice that the ARG directive allows us to specify the arguments in the same order as the corresponding C++ function declaration:

ASM:	`_ReadSector proc near C`
	`ARG bufferPtr:word, startSector:dword, \`
	`      driveNumber:word, numSectors:word`

C++:	`extern "C" ReadSector( char buffer[], long  startSector,` `             int driveNum, int numSectors );`

If we examine the code produced by ARG, we find that the arguments are pushed on the stack in reverse order, which is the standard C calling convention. Farthest away from BP is numSectors, the first parameter pushed on the stack, as shown by the following stack frame:

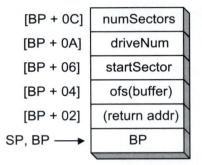

Note that **startSector** is a 32-bit doubleword and occupies locations [bp+6] through [bp+09] on the stack. This program was compiled for the small memory model, so **buffer** is passed as a 16-bit near pointer.

Notice that although this application runs in 16-bit mode, we use 32-bit registers within the ReadSector procedure. This presents no problem, just as we have used 32-bit registers in most of the stand-alone assembly language applications in earlier chapters.

Example 5. ASM Module Containing the ReadSector Procedure.

```
; Read Disk Sectors                    (readsec.asm)

; The ReadSector procedure is called from a 16-bit
; DOS application written in Borland C++ 5.01.

Public _ReadSector
.model small
.386
LARGE_DISK = 1
SMALL_DISK = 0
.data
;--- Parameter block required for disk > 32MB
parmBlock label byte
sectorNumber dd   ?
sectorCount  dw   ?
bufferOfs    dw   ?
bufferSeg    dw   @data
;-------------------------
```

```
        driveType dw ?
        .code
        ; ReadSector ----------------------------------------
        ;
        ; Read n sectors from a disk drive.
        ; We currently number drives as: A=1, B=2, etc.,
        ; ---------------------------------------------------
        _ReadSector proc near C
         ARG bufferPtr:word, startSector:dword, \
            driveNumber:word, numSectors:word
            enter 0,0
            mov    eax,startSector
            mov    sectorNumber,eax
            mov    ax,numSectors
            mov    sectorCount,ax

            mov    ax,driveNumber
            call   GetDriveType          ; set driveType to 1 or 0
            cmp    driveType,LARGE_DISK
            jb     RS1                    ; yes: skip to RS1

            ; Reading a disk > 32MB.
            dec    al                     ; Drive A=0, B=1,...
            mov    bx,offset parmBlock
            mov    cx,-1
            push   bufferPtr
            pop    bufferOfs
            int    25h                    ; read the sector(s)
            jmp    RS2                    ; exit

        RS1: ; Reading a disk <= 32MB.
            dec    al                     ; Drive A=0, B=1,...
            mov    cx,numSectors
            mov    bx,bufferPtr
            mov    dx,word ptr sectorNumber
            int    25h
        RS2: add    sp,2
            leave
            ret
        _ReadSector endp

        ; GetDriveType ---------------------------------
```

```
;
; Input: AL = drive number, where A = 1, B = 2,...
; Output: driveType = 1 or 0.
;------------------------------------------------

GetDriveType proc
    pusha
    mov   driveType,SMALL_DISK
    mov   dl,al              ; drive number (A=1, B=2)
    mov   ah,36h             ; Get Disk Free Space
    int   21h
    push  dx                 ; save clusters/drive
    mul   cx                 ; AX = bytes/cluster
    pop   dx
    mul   dx                 ; DX:AX = bytes/drive
    cmp   dx,01F4h           ; less than 32 MB?
    jbe   E1                 ; yes: exit
    mov   driveType,LARGE_DISK
E1: popa
    ret
GetDriveType endp
end
```

13.3.3 Large Random Number Example

To show a useful example of calling an external function from Borland C++, we can call **LongRand**, an assembly language function that returns a pseudorandom unsigned 32-bit integer. This is useful because the standard rand() function in the Borland C++ library only returns an integer between 0 and RAND_MAX (32,767). Our procedure returns an integer between 0 and 4,294,967,295.

This program is compiled in the large memory model, allowing the data to be larger than 64K, and requiring that 32-bit values be used for the return address and data pointer values.

The external function declaration in C++ is:

```
extern "C" unsigned long LongRandom();
```

The listing of the main program is shown in Example 6. The program allocates storage for an array called **rArray**. It uses a loop to call **LongRandom**, inserts each number in the array, and writes the number to standard output.

Example 6. C++ Program that Calls LongRandom.

```
// main.cpp
```

```
// Calls the external LongRandom function, written in
// assembly language, that returns an unsigned 32-bit
// random integer. Compile in the Large memory model.

#include <iostream.h>
extern "C" unsigned long LongRandom();
const int ARRAY_SIZE = 500;

int main()
{
  // Allocate array storage, fill with 32-bit
  // unsigned random integers, and display:

  unsigned long * rArray = new unsigned long[ARRAY_SIZE];

  for(unsigned i = 0; i < ARRAY_SIZE; i++)
  {
    rArray[i] = LongRandom();
    cout << rArray[i] << ',';
  }
  cout << endl;
  return 0;
}
```

The assembly language module containing the LongRandom function is shown in Example 7. It is a simple adaptation of the Random32 procedure from the link library supplied with this book. Borland C++ expects the 32-bit function return value to be in the DX:AX registers, so we copy the high 16-bits from EAX into DX with the SHLD instruction, which seems conveniently designed for this task:

```
shld edx,eax,16
```

Example 7. The LongRandom Function.

```
; LongRandom procedure module              (longrand.asm)

.model large
.386
Public _LongRandom
.data
seed  dd 12345678h


; Return an unsigned pseudo-random 32-bit integer
```

```
; in DX:AX,in the range 0 - FFFFFFFFh.
.code
_LongRandom  proc far, C
      mov    eax, 343FDh
      mul    seed
      xor    edx,edx
      add    eax, 269EC3h
      mov    seed, eax         ; save the seed for the next call
      shld   edx,eax,16        ; copy high 16 bits of EAX to DX
      ret
_LongRandom  endp
end
```

13.3.4 Linking to Visual C++ in Protected Mode

In this section, we will exclusively use the Microsoft Visual C++ compiler to compile the calling program, and Microsoft MASM to write assembly language subroutines. Visual C++ generates 32-bit applications that run in protected mode. We choose *Win32 Console* as the target application type for the examples shown here, although there is no reason why the same subroutines would not work in ordinary MS-Windows applications.

One of the ways you can use assembly language to optimize programs written in other languages is to look for speed bottlenecks. Loops are good candidates for this, because any extra statements in a loop may be repeated enough times to have a noticeable effect on your program's performance. Most C/C++ compilers have a command-line option that automatically generates an assembly language listing of the C/C++ program.

The listing file can contain any combination of C++ source code, assembly code, and machine code, shown by the options in Table 2. Perhaps the most useful is /FAs, which shows how C++ statements are translated into assembly language.

The following C++ procedure called FindArray searches for a single value in an array of long integers. The function returns true if the search is successful, or false if it is not.:

```
#include "findarr.h"

bool FindArray( long searchVal, long array[], long count )
{
  for(int i = 0; i < count; i++)
    if( searchVal == array[i] )
      return true;
  return false;
}
```

Table 2. Microsoft Visual C++ Command-Line Options for ASM Generation.

Command Line	Contents of Listing File
/FA	Assembly-Only Listing
/FAc	Assembly With Machine Code
/FAs	Assembly With Source Code
/FAcs	Assembly, Machine Code, and Source

The header file findarr.h contains the function prototype for FindArray. This identifies it as an external procedure that is called in the manner of a C language subroutine, without any name mangling:

```
extern "C" {
   bool FindArray( long searchVal, long array[], long count );
}
```

Example 8 shows assembly language source code generated by the C++ compiler for the FindArray function, alongside the function's C++ source code. This procedure was compiled to a *Win32 Debug* target, which automatically turns off the compiler's code optimization feature. The .386P directive enables the assembly of 80386 priveleged instructions. The *flat* memory model is selected, in which 32-bit addresses can address the entire memory space of the computer.

Three 32-bit arguments were pushed on the stack in the following order: **count, array,** and **searchVal**. Of these three, **array** is the only one passed by reference, because in C/C++, an array name is an implicit pointer to the array's first element. The procedure saves EBP on the stack and creates space for the local variable **i** by pushing an extra doubleword on the stack:

[EBP + 16]	count
[EBP + 12]	[array]
[EBP + 08]	searchVal
[EBP + 04]	ret addr
ESP, EBP →	EBP
[EBP - 04]	i

Inside the procedure, the compiler reserves local stack space for the variable i by pushing ECX (line 29). The same storage is released at the end when EBP is copied back into ESP (line 35).

Example 8. FindArray Code Generated by C++ Compiler.

```
TITLE findArr.cpp
.386P
.model FLAT
PUBLIC  _FindArray
_TEXT      SEGMENT

_searchVal$ = 8
_array$ = 12
_count$ = 16
_i$ = -4

_FindArray PROC NEAR
; 29    : {
    push    ebp
    mov     ebp, esp
    push    ecx                ; create local variable i

; 30    :    for(int i = 0; i < count; i++)
    mov     DWORD PTR _i$[ebp], 0
    jmp     SHORT $L174

$L175:
    mov     eax, DWORD PTR _i$[ebp]
    add     eax, 1
    mov     DWORD PTR _i$[ebp], eax

$L174:
    mov     ecx, DWORD PTR _i$[ebp]
    cmp     ecx, DWORD PTR _count$[ebp]
    jge     SHORT $L176

; 31    :        if( searchVal == array[i] )
    mov     edx, DWORD PTR _i$[ebp]
    mov     eax, DWORD PTR _array$[ebp]
    mov     ecx, DWORD PTR _searchVal$[ebp]
    cmp     ecx, DWORD PTR [eax+edx*4]
    jne     SHORT $L177

; 32    :            return true;
    mov     al, 1
```

```
        jmp       SHORT $L172

$L177:
; 33   :
; 34   :   return false;
        jmp       SHORT $L175

$L176:
        xor       al, al

$L172:
; 35   : }
        mov       esp, ebp
        pop       ebp
        ret       0
_FindArray ENDP
_TEXT       ENDS
END
```

Notice that there are 14 assembly code statements between the labels $L175 and $L176, which constitute the main body of the loop. We can easily write an assembly language subroutine that is more efficient than the code shown here.

Example 9 shows a hand-coded version of FindArray. A few basic principles have been applied to the optimization of this procedure:

*   Move as much processing out of the repeated loop as possible.

*   Move stack parameters and local variables to registers.

*   Take advantage of specialized instructions (in this case, SCASD).

Our code is slightly more readable than the code generated by the C++ compiler because we can use meaningful label names and define constants that simplify the use of stack parameters. An improvement would have been to use the MASM extended syntax for procedures, but experimentation showed that the following declaration prevented the C++ linker from locating the FindArray procedure:

```
_FindArray PROC NEAR C uses esi,
      srchVal:dword, array:dword, count:dword
```

In addition, it was found that adding a language name parameter to the .model directive, such as .model flat,C also results in a linker error saying that it can't locate _FindArray.

Example 9. Hand-Optimized FindArray Procedure.

```
title The FindArray Procedure        (scasd.asm)

; This version uses hand-optimized assembly
; language code, with the SCASD instruction.

.386P
.model flat
public _FindArray
true = 1
false = 0

; Stack parameters:
srchVal   equ [ebp+08]
arrayPtr  equ [ebp+12]
count     equ [ebp+16]

.code
_FindArray proc near
    push  ebp
    mov   ebp,esp
    push  edi

    mov   eax, srchVal        ; search value
    mov   ecx, count          ; number of items
    mov   edi, arrayPtr       ; pointer to array

    repne scasd               ; do the search
    jz    returnTrue          ; ZF = 1 if found

returnFalse:
    mov   al, false
    jmp   short exit

returnTrue:
    mov   al, true

exit:
    pop   edi
    pop   ebp
    ret
```

```
_FindArray endp
end
```

Code Optimization by the C++ Compiler. Before we develop an overblown sense of superiority over the C++ compiler, let's ask the compiler to try again, this time optimizing its code for speed. The new version of FindArray is shown in Example 10. The improvement over the nonoptimized version is striking, to say the least. Variables have been moved to registers, and the loop portion has been reduced from twelve instructions to six. In fact, the timed execution of this new version is roughly the same as the hand-optimized code in Example 9.

Dangers of Leaving out EBP. You may have noticed that the C++ compiler eliminated all references to EBP, shaving off a few more clock cycles. It took advantage of the fact that the 80386 processor allows ESP to be used as an indirect operand, so stack parameters can be accessed without the need of EBP. **Count**, for example, located at stack offset ESP + 12, is assigned to EDX. The stack offset is calculated in a roundabout sort of way as **_count$ + (ESP – 4)**, where **_count$** is equal to 16:

```
mov  edx, DWORD PTR _count$[esp-4]
```

Here is a picture of the revised stack frame used by the program in Example 10:

Before you get the idea that all stack parameters should be handled this way, think again. For instance, without EBP, the subroutine cannot push any registers on the stack without adjusting the offsets between ESP and the stack parameters. Suppose we had the following statements at the beginning of FindArray:

```
arrayPtr equ [esp+10]

_FindArray proc near
    push  esi
    mov   esi, arrayPtr ; esi = arrayPtr
```

This code doesn't work, of course, because as soon as ESI is pushed, the predefined stack offset of **arrayPtr** changes. And yet, if we don't push ESI before modifying it, we violate the Microsoft rule that says ESI must be preserved in high-level language subroutines. The C++ compiler compensates for this by adjusting the stack offsets after any PUSH instructions have taken place. This is fine for a compiler, but not easy for humans to do accurately.

Example 10. Optimized C++ Version of FindArray.

```
_searchVal$ = 8
_array$ = 12
_count$ = 16


_FindArray PROC NEAR
    mov     edx, DWORD PTR _count$[esp-4]
    xor     eax, eax
    push    esi
    test    edx, edx
    jle     SHORT $L176
    mov     ecx, DWORD PTR _array$[esp]
    mov     esi, DWORD PTR _searchVal$[esp]

$L174:
    cmp     esi, DWORD PTR [ecx]
    je      SHORT $L182
    inc     eax
    add     ecx, 4
    cmp     eax, edx
    jl      SHORT $L174
    xor     al, al
    pop     esi
    ret     0
$L182:
    mov     al, 1
    pop     esi
    ret     0
$L176:
    xor     al, al
    pop     esi
    ret     0
_FindArray ENDP
```

Pointers Versus Subscripts. It's not unusual for C/C++ programmers to assert that processing arrays with pointers is more efficient than using subscripts. For example, the following version of FindArray uses this approach:

```
bool FindArray( long searchVal, long array[], long count )
{
  long * p = array;
  for(i = 0; i < count; i++, p++)
```

```
      if( n == *p )
         return true;
      return false;
   }
```

Running this version of FindArray through the C++ compiler produced virtually the same assembly language code as the earlier version using subscripts. At least in this instance, using a pointer variable was no more efficient than using a subscript. Here is the loop from the FindArray target code that was produced by the C++ compiler:

```
$L176:
   cmp   esi, DWORD PTR [ecx]
   je    SHORT $L184
   inc   eax
   add   ecx, 4
   cmp   eax, edx
   jl    SHORT $L176
```

In closing this section, we can say that many high-level language compilers do an effective job of code optimization. Your time would be well spent studying the output produced by a C++ compiler, to learn about optimization techniques, parameter passing, and object code implementation. In fact, many computer science students take a compiler-writing course that includes such topics. It is also important to realize that compilers always take the general case, as they have no specific knowledge about individual applications or hardware. Hand-coded assembly language can go a step further, taking advantage of specific hardware features on the target machine, for example.

13.4 REVIEW QUESTIONS

1. How does the memory model of a calling program affect the way a subroutine accesses its parameters? Be specific in regard to the small and large memory models.

2. What special naming convention is used by a C or C++ program when it refers to an external identifier?

3. How does an assembly language programer deal with the fact that C programs recognize differences between uppercase and lowercase letters in identifiers?

4. What type of function call (near or far) is the default for a C or C++ function compiled under the *small* memory model?

5. When a subroutine written in assembly language is called by a high-level language program, why must the program and the subroutine use the same memory model?

6. Does a language's calling convention include the preserving of certain registers by subroutines?

7. Which method involves passing a variable's address? (1) passing by value, or (2) passing by reference?

8. When using the C calling convention, how is the stack restored to its original state after a subroutine call?

9. When the following C language function is called, will the argument x be pushed on the stack first or last?

```
void MySub( x, y, z );
```

10. Why is case-sensitivity important when calling assembly language subroutines from C?

11. What is the purpose of the "C" specifier in the *extern* declaration in subroutines called from C++?

12. Which memory models require *near* calls to external procedures?

13. Which memory models require *far* calls to external procedures?

14. Which memory model is used by Visual C++ when calling a 32-bit program in protected mode?

15. How are the starting locations of the segments calculated when running a Visual C++ Win32 console application?

16. Show a sample stack frame for a procedure that has one parameter passed by far reference. Assume that the large memory model is used.

17. Show a sample stack frame for a procedure that has one parameter passed by near reference. Assume that the small memory model is used.

18. What is the *__fastcall* calling method?

19. How are the LES and LDS instructions useful in procedures having parameters passed by far reference?

20. How is inline assembly code different from an inline C++ procedure?

21. What advantage does inline assembly code offer over the use of external assembly language procedures?

22. According to the author, what is the primary disadvantage to using inline assembly code in a high-level language program, as opposed to using external assembly language procedures?

The following group of questions specifically refer to inline assembly code syntax for Microsoft Visual C++ 5.0:

23. Show at least two ways of placing comments in inline assembly code.

24. Can an inline statement refer to code labels outside the __asm block? (y/n)

25. Show two ways to code the same hexadecimal constant.

26. Can both the EVEN and ALIGN directives be used?

27. Can the OFFSET operator be used?

28. Can variables be defined with both DW and the DUP operator?

29. Is it possible to define a macro inside an __asm block?

30. Is it possible to directly access the DS and ES segment registers?

31. When using the __fastcall calling convention, what might happen if your inline assembly code modifies the EAX register?

32. When not using the __fastcall calling convention, are you free to use EBX and EDX in your inline statements without interfering with the C++ compiler's built-in code optimization?

33. Rather than using the OFFSET operator, is there another way to move a variable's offset into an index register?

34. What value is returned by the LENGTH operator when applied to an array of long integers?

35. What value is returned by the SIZE operator when applied to an array of long integers?

The following questions refer to linking C++ programs to external assembly language procedures:

36. Why is name mangling important when calling external assembly language procedures from C++?

37. Which registers and flags must be preserved by assembly language subroutines called from Borland C++?

38. In Borland C++, how many bytes are used by the following types? 1) int, 2) enum, 3) float, 4) double.

39. In the C++ program that calls ReadSector in Example 4, are there any limits to the number of sectors the user can choose to display?

40. In the ReadSector module in Example 5, if the ARG directive were not used, how would you code the following statement?

```
mov eax,startSector
```

41. In the LongRandom Function in Example 7, if the SHLD instruction were not available, which sequence of instructions could be used instead?

42. In this chapter, when an optimizing C++ compiler was used, what differences in code generation occured between the loop coded with array subscripts and the loop coded with pointer variables?

13.5 PROGRAMMING EXERCISES

1. ***ReadSector, Large Model***

   Convert the ReadSector procedure in Example 5 to the large memory model, and call it from the same C++ program. Remember that the buffer parameter will now be passed as a 32-bit pointer, containing a segment and offset. Compile the C++ program under the large memory model.

2. ***ReadSector, Hexadecimal Display***

   Add a new procedure to the C++ program in Example 4 that calls the ReadSector procedure. This new procedure should display each sector in hexadecimal. Be sure to use the setfillchar manipulator from the istream class to pad each byte with a leading zero.

3. ***LongRandom Function, 16-bit***

   Rewrite the LongRandom function in Example 7 for an 80286 processor. Let it generate random integers between 0 and 65,535. Call it from a high-level language program.

4. ***LongRandomArray Procedure***

   Using the LongRandom procedure in Example 7 as a starting point, create a procedure called LongRandomArrray that fills an array with 32-bit unsigned random integers. Pass an array pointer from a C or C++ program, along with a count indicating the number of array elements to be filled:

   ```
   extern "C" void LongRandomArray( unsigned long * buffer,
       unsigned count );
   ```

5. ***External TranslateBuffer Procedure***

   Write an external procedure in assembly language that performs the same type of encryption shown in the TranslateBuffer inline procedure that appeared in Example 2 earlier in this chapter. Run the compiled program in the debugger, and judge whether this version runs any faster than the Encode program from Example 3.

6. ***Console Input Field***

   In the exercises at the end of Chapter 6, the Console Input Field exercise asked to you write a procedure that would allow the user to enter data into a field in the console. Reimplement that procedure so it can be called from a high-level language program. Test it by calling it several times from a main program. Create two versions, one for a small memory model, and the other for a large memory model.

7. ***Console Input Field with Keyboard Filter***

   In the exercises at the end of Chapter 6, you are asked to create a console input field with a keyboard filter. That is, the procedure is supposed to limit the range of characters that the user can enter. Reimplement that procedure so it can be called from a high-level language program.

Test it by calling it several times from a main program. Create two versions, one for a small memory model, and the other for a large memory model.

8. *Horizontal Bar Menu*

In the exercises for Chapter 6, we asked you to create a procedure that displays a horizontal bar menu, in which the user can use the cursor arrow keys to move between choices. In this chapter, reimplement the procedure so it is callable from C++. Pass the array of strings containing the menu choices, along with the row and column position specifying its location on the screen. The return value from the procedure should be an integer identifying which choice was selected, or whether the user pressed the Esc key to cancel the menu. Test the procedure by displaying at least three different menus.

9. *Prime Number Program*

In the exercises for Chapter 7, we asked you to write a procedure that sets the Zero flag if the 32-bit integer passed in the EAX register is prime. Call this procedure from a high-level language program. Let the user input some very large numbers, and have your program display a message for each one indicating whether or not it is prime.

10. *FindBitString Procedure*

Write a procedure called FindBitString that searches for a bit string inside an array of long integers. Assume that the bit string is always aligned on even *doubleword* boundaries. To test this procedure, generate a random array of long integers, and call your procedure from a high-level language program. When a long integer containing a matching bit string is found, display a message to the user. You may want to use the FindArray procedure from Example 9 as a guide when writing this procedure.

11. *FindBitString Procedure, Byte-Aligned*

Use the FindBitString procedure from the previous exercise as a starting point. In the current implementation, the matching bit string is still 32 bits long, but it may begin at any *byte* position within the array.

14 *Advanced Topics I*

14.1 POINTERS AND INDIRECTION

14.1.1 LEA (Load Effective Address)

The LEA (*load effective address*) instruction loads a register with the offset of a data label. Of course, the same thing can be accomplished by MOV...OFFSET. The following two instructions yield the same result:

```
mov  si,offset array
lea  si,array
```

There is an important difference, however, between LEA and MOV..OFFSET: The former calculates the label's offset at runtime, whereas the latter moves an immediate value that is already known at assembly time. In particular, we use LEA when the effective address of an operand *must* be calculated at runtime.

For example, suppose that a variable called **array** is located at offset 01B0. The following LEA instruction returns the calculated offset of the word located two bytes beyond **array.** The value moved to SI is 01B2h, and the value moved to AX is 5678h:

```
.data
array dw 1234h,5678h


.code
mov    bx,2
lea    si,array[bx]          ; SI = 01B2h
mov    ax,[si]               ; AX = 5678h
```

Near and Far Pointers. A *pointer* is a variable that contains the address of some other data. There are two types of pointer variables: A *near* pointer is a 16-bit offset that points to data within the current segment. A *far* pointer is a 32-bit segment-offset address that is able to point to data outside the current segment. In assembly language, we extend the concept of pointers to include base and index registers (BX, BP, SI, and DI). In the following declarations, arrayPtr is a near pointer that contains the offset of array1:

```
.data
array1   db   200 dup(?)
arrayPtr dw   array1
```

Suppose a variable called **array2** is located in a segment called **farseg**. You may recall from Chapter 4 that the SEG operator returns the 16-bit address of the segment containing a label. We can initialize a variable at assembly time to the segment/offset address of array2:

```
dseg segment
   farptr  dd   array2            ; far pointer
dseg ends


farseg segment
   array2  dw   100 dup(0)        ; target data
farseg ends
```

Or, at runtime, we can set the DS:BX to the segment/offset address of **array2** using the following statements:

```
mov    ax,seg array2          ; get segment address
mov    ds,ax                  ; move to DS
lea    bx,array2              ; place offset in BX
```

14.1.2 Indirect Jumps and Calls

An indirect jump or call lets you transfer control to an address stored in a variable. Because the contents of the variable can change at runtime, this technique is called *late binding* or *dynamic binding*. To do this, first set a base or index register to the offset of a pointer variable; then invoke a JMP or CALL instruction. The following program excerpt demonstrates calls to both near and far procedures, and a jump to a near code label (the procedures themselves are omitted from the listing to save space):

```
.data
ptr_16    dw nearSub          ; address of near procedure
ptr_32    dd farSub           ; address of far procedure
ptr_16a   dw CodeLabel        ; code label in main

.code
main proc
      mov   ax,@data
      mov   ds,ax
      lea   bx,ptr_16
      call  near ptr[bx]      ; call nearSub procedure
      lea   si,ptr_32
      call  far ptr [si]      ; call farSub procedure
      lea   di,ptr_16a        ; point to a near code label
      jmp   near ptr[di]      ; make an indirect jump
      ;...
CodeLabel LABEL word          ; LABEL required here
      ; (etc.)
```

Note a few restrictions. NEAR PTR and FAR PTR are required, as is the use of the LABEL directive when declaring **CodeLabel**. If you define it the usual way (*i.e.* **CodeLabel:**), the **ptr_16a** variable in the data segment generates an assembly error. There is one other consideration: because CodeLabel was defined using the LABEL directive, any direct jumps to it must be qualified by the NEAR PTR operator. Although the second instruction assembles, it does not work as expected:

```
jmp   near ptr CodeLabel    ; do this
jmp   CodeLabel             ; not this!
```

Using Direct Memory Operands. It is quite easy to place the address of a label or function in a variable and use it as a direct operand in a JMP or CALL instruction. The trick is to stick with one or two consistent forms of notation, and not be misled by the assembler's willingness to assemble and execute incorrect jumps and calls. The following is a straightforward example:

```
.data
ptr_16 dw nearSub
ptr_32 dd farSub
```

```
.code
main proc
        mov    ax,@data
        mov    ds,ax
        call   [ptr_16]
        call   [ptr_32]
```

There are, of course, several alternate forms of notation, which you can find in the sample program supplied on this book's CDROM, but the brackets around the variable seem the easiest to understand.

Pointer Table. Suppose that **pointer_array** is actually an array of pointers; that is, each word in the array contains a near pointer to some data. We can place an index value in SI and load the address of an individual array element:

```
mov   si,index                      ; start with index value
lea   bx,pointer_array[si]          ; get address from table
mov   si,[bx]                       ; SI contains pointer from table
```

Each array entry contains an address that points to data elsewhere in memory. If SI contained 0002h, for example, the effective address in BX would be **pointer_array + 2**:

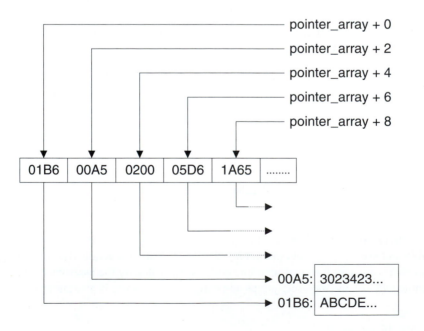

The number stored in memory at **pointer_array + 2** is 00A5h, which is the address of a string of numbers: 3023423h. This is an example of two *levels of indirection,* used here to get the address of an operand that is known only at runtime.

14.1.3 32-Bit Pointer Table

A useful task is to initialize a table of 32-bit pointers at assembly time. In the following example, **ptrTable** contains far pointers to four different buffers located in **farseg.**

```
dseg segment
ptrTable  dd  buffer1           ; far pointer to BUFFER1
          dd  buffer2           ; far pointer to BUFFER2
          dd  buffer3           ; far pointer to BUFFER3
          dd  buffer4           ; far pointer to BUFFER4
dseg ends

farseg segment
   buffer1  db  1024 dup(0)
   buffer2  db  1024 dup(0)
   buffer3  db  1024 dup(0)
   buffer4  db  1024 dup(0)
farseg ends
```

The LES instruction combines the offset of **ptrTable** with an index value in BX to produce an effective address. We use this address to copy an entry from the table into ES:DI:

```
mov   bx,index              ; index into the table
les   di,ptrTable[bx]       ; get pointer from the table
mov   al,byte ptr es:[di]   ; get a byte from the buffer
```

Suppose **index** was equal to 8. This would cause LES to move the segment-offset address of **buffer3** to ES:BX. The subsequent MOV statement would move the first character of the buffer into AL.

14.2 PROCESSOR CONTROL AND I/O

14.2.1 ESC, HLT, LOCK, and WAIT

ESC Instruction. The ESC instruction passes an instruction and/or operand to the floating-point coprocessor. Also called the *access memory location* instruction, it places the contents of a memory operand on the data bus. This makes it possible for floating-point instructions to take advantage of 80x86 addressing modes. The ESC instruction is automatically inserted by the assembler before each floating-point instruction.

HLT Instruction. The HLT instruction halts a program until a hardware interrupt occurs. Be sure hardware interrupts have been enabled before executing the HLT instruction, or the system will simply lock up.

LOCK Instruction. The LOCK instruction locks out other processors from the system bus until the immediately following instruction finishes. LOCK is an instruction prefix that prevents the math coprocessor from carrying out any operation prematurely. In the following example, LOCK affects only the MOV (not the MUL) instruction:

```
lock                            ; lock bus for next instruction
mov   ax,var1
mul   bx                        ; bus is no longer locked
```

WAIT Instruction. The WAIT instruction tells the CPU to stop processing until it receives a signal from a coprocessor that has finished a task. For example, the CPU may ask the math coprocessor to do a calculation. It then waits for the result before going on.

WAIT can be temporarily suspended if interrupts are enabled (IF = 0) and an external interrupt occurs. After the interrupt is serviced, the CPU returns to the WAIT instruction.

14.2.2 Input-Output Ports

Ports are connections, or gateways, between the CPU and other devices connected to the computer. Each port has a specific address: the CPU is capable of addressing up to 65,536 ports. I/O ports are used when controlling the speaker, for example, by turning the sound on and off. You can communicate directly with the asynchronous adapter through a serial port by setting the port parameters (baud rate, parity, and so on) and by sending data through the port.

The keyboard port is a good example of an input-output port. When a key is pressed, the keyboard controller chip sends an 8-bit scan code to port 60h. The keystroke triggers a hardware interrupt, which prompts the CPU to call INT 9 in the ROM BIOS. INT 9 inputs the scan code from the port, looks up the key's ASCII code, and stores both values in the keyboard input buffer. In fact, it would be possible to bypass the operating system completely and read characters directly from port 60h.

Most devices have one or more *status* ports. In the case of the keyboard, you might use this port check to see if a character is ready. There is also usually a *data* port, through which input-output data are transferred.

IN and OUT Instructions. The IN instruction inputs a byte or word from a port. Conversely, the OUT instruction outputs a byte or word to a port. The syntax for both instructions are:

```
IN    accumulator,port
OUT   port,accumulator
```

Port may be a constant in the range 0-FFh, or it may be a value in DX between 0 and FFFFh. *Accumulator* must be AL for 8-bit transfers, AX for 16-bit transfers, and EAX for 32-bit transfers. Examples are:

```
in   al,3Ch                   ; input byte from port 3Ch
out  3ch,al                   ; output byte to port 3Ch
mov  dx, portNumber           ; DX can contain a port number
in   ax,dx                    ; input word from port named in DX
out  dx,ax                    ; output word to the same port
in   eax,dx                   ; input doubleword from port
out  dx,eax                   ; output doubleword to same port
```

Controlling the Speaker. We can write a program that uses the IN and OUT instructions to generate sound. The speaker control port (number 61h) turns the speaker on and off by manipulating the Intel 8255 *Programmable Peripheral Interface* chip. To turn the speaker on, input the current value in port 61h, set the lowest 2 bits, and output the byte back through the port. To turn off the speaker, clear bits 0 and 1 and output the status again.

The Intel 8253 *Timer* chip controls the frequency (pitch) of the sound being generated. To use it, we send a value between 0 and 255 to port 42h. The Speaker Demo program in Example 1 shows how to generate sound by playing a series of ascending notes.

Example 1. Speaker Demo Program.

```
 1:    title Speaker Demo Program        (SPKR.ASM)
 2:
 3:    ;-------------------------------------------------
 4:    ; This program plays a series of ascending notes on
 5:    ; an IBM-PC or compatible computer.
 6:    ;-------------------------------------------------
 7:
 8:    .model small
 9:    .stack 100h
10:    speaker  equ  61h          ; address of speaker port
11:    timer    equ  42h          ; address of timer port
12:    delay    equ  0D000h       ; delay between notes
13:
14:    .code
15:    main  proc
16:    in    al,speaker           ; get speaker status byte
17:    push  ax                   ; save status on stack
18:    or    al,00000011b         ; set lowest 2 bits
19:    out   speaker,al           ; turn speaker on
20:    mov   al,60                ; starting pitch
21:
22:    L2:out   timer,al          ; timer port: pulses speaker
23:    ; Create a delay loop so we can hear the changing pitches.
```

```
24:        mov     cx,500          ; repeat outer loop 500 times
25:  L3:   push    cx
26:        mov     cx,delay
27:  L4:   loop    L4
28:        pop     cx
29:        loop    L3              ; continue the outer loop
30:        sub     al,1            ; raise the pitch
31:        jnz     L2              ; play another note
32:
33:        pop     ax              ; get original status byte
34:        and     al,11111100b    ; clear two lowest bits
35:        out     speaker,al      ; turn speaker off
36:
37:        mov     ax,4C00h        ; return to DOS
38:        int     21h
39:  main  endp
40:  end main
```

Lines 18-19 turn the speaker on using port 61h, by setting the lowest 2 bits in the speaker status byte. Line 20 sets the pitch by sending 60 to the timer chip. A delay loop makes the program pause before changing the pitch again (lines 24-29). After the delay, line 30 subtracts 1 from the frequency value, which raises the pitch. The new frequency is output to the timer on line 22. This continues until the frequency counter in AL equals 0. Lines 33-34 pop the original status byte from the speaker port and turn the speaker off by clearing the lowest two bits.

14.2.3 Flag Manipulation Instructions

Several instructions save and restore the entire Flags register. In previous chapters, instructions have been shown that manipulate specific flags:

STC	Set Carry flag
CLC	Clear Carry flag
CMC	Complement Carry flag
STD	Set Direction flag
CLD	Clear Direction flag

LAHF Instruction. The LAHF (*load AH from flags*) instruction copies the lower half of the Flags register into AH. The following flags are copied: Sign, Zero, Auxiliary Carry, Parity, and Carry. Using this instruction, you can save a copy of the flags in a memory variable or test several flags at once:

```
lahf                            ; load flags into AH
mov   saveflags,ah              ; save them in a variable
test  ah,10000001b              ; check for Sign or Carry flag
jnz   flags_set                 ; jump if either is set
```

SAHF Instruction. The SAHF (*store AH to flags*) instruction copies AH into the Flags register. This instruction is often used to transfer flag settings from the math coprocessor to the 80x86 Flags register.

PUSHF Instruction. The PUSHF (*push flags*) instruction pushes the entire 16-bit flags register on the stack. This is the best way to save the current flags in case they are about to be changed. They can later be restored by the POPF instruction.

POPF Instruction. The POPF (*pop flags*) instruction pops the top of the stack into the flags register.

14.3 DEFINING SEGMENTS

The great majority of assembly language programs can use simplified segment directives. We have used them in this book for two reasons. First, they are compatible with Microsoft C, Pascal, QuickBASIC, and FORTRAN. Second, they are convenient to use and relatively bulletproof. At the same time, what we gain in convenience we sometimes lose in flexibility.

There are a few occasions when you may prefer to code explicit segment definitions. You may want to define multiple data segments with extra memory buffers, for instance. Or, you may be linking your program to an object library that uses its own proprietary segment names. Finally, you may be writing a subroutine to be called from a high-level language that does not use Microsoft's segment names.

The SEGMENT and ENDS directives define the beginning and end of a segment. A program may contain almost any number of segments, each with a unique name. Segments can also be grouped together. In short, we can do everything simplified directives do and more.

Each segment can be up to 65,536 bytes long (0000-FFFFh). Each begins on a 16-byte boundary, so it may be addressed by one of the segment registers. You may recall that a segment address includes 4 additional implied zero bits. Thus, a segment address of 1B65h really represents an absolute address of 1B650h, shown here in binary:

```
        0001 1011 0110 0101 0000
          1    B    6    5    (4 implied bits)
```

This is why a segment can begin only on a 16-byte boundary: The 4 implied bits of its absolute address are always zeros.

A program with explicit segment definitions has two tasks to perform: First, a segment register (DS, ES, or SS) must be set to the location of each segment before it may be used. Second, the assembler must be told how to calculate the offsets of labels within the correct segments.

14.3.1 Explicit Segment Definitions

The SEGMENT and ENDS directives explicitly define the beginning and end of a segment. For example, you might want to create a data segment to hold a 60K buffer. Or, you might

want to place subroutines in a code segment that is different from the segment created by the
.code directive. Virtually any number of segments may appear in a single program. For
example, this is how a segment called ExtraData would be defined:

```
ExtraData segment
  var1   db  1000 dup(0)
  var2   dw  500 dup(?)
ExtraData ends
```

The program excerpt in Example 2 contains two programmer-defined segments. There
are several things to notice about this program: First, you must set DS or ES to the appropriate
segment value before trying to access a variable. This can be done either by explicitly naming
the segment, or by using the SEG operator:

```
mov ax,seg value1              ; use the SEG operator
mov ds,ax                      ; to obtain segment address

mov ax,data2                   ; use explicit segment name
mov es,ax
```

Example 2. User-Defined Segments.

```
Title User-Defined Segments              (segs.asm)
.model small
.stack 100h

data1 segment 'DATA'
  value1 db  1
data1 ends

data2 segment 'DATA'
  value2 db  2
data2 ends

.code
main proc
    mov   ax,seg value1        ; use the SEG operator
    mov   ds,ax                ; to obtain segment address

    mov   al,ds:value1         ; explicit segment override

    assume ds:data1            ; use ASSUME
    mov   al,value1            ; result: AL = 1
```

```
        mov   ax,data2                ; use the segment name
        mov   es,ax

        assume es:data2               ; this is required
        mov   al,value2               ; result: AL = 2
```

Obtaining a Variable's Offset. Once the segment register has been initialized, there are two ways to obtain a variable's offset inside its enclosing segment:

- Use a segment override that names the segment register the CPU will use to access the variable's segment. For example,

```
    mov al,ds:value1                  ; explicit segment override
```

- Place the ASSUME directive in the program listing prior to any references to variables. This directive alters the assembler that all subsequent data references will use the segment register named by ASSUME:

```
    assume ds:data1
    mov al,value1
```

The map file shown in Example 3 was created by the linker for this program, showing that the DATA1 and DATA2 segments were placed right after the _DATA segment.

Example 3. MAP File Showing User-Defined Segments.

```
Start   Stop    Length  Name    Class
00000H  00018H  00019H  _TEXT   CODE
0001AH  0001AH  00000H  _DATA   DATA
00020H  00020H  00001H  DATA1   DATA
00030H  00030H  00001H  DATA2   DATA
00040H  0013FH  00100H  STACK   STACK


Origin   Group
0001:0   DGROUP
Program entry point at 0000:0000
```

14.3.2 Segment Definition Syntax

The SEGMENT directive begins a segment, and the ENDS directive ends it. Their syntax is

```
name SEGMENT [align] [combine] ['class']
statements
name ENDS
```

```
Align types: BYTE, WORD, DWORD, PARA, PAGE

Combine types: PUBLIC, STACK, COMMON, MEMORY, AT address
```

The segment name may be a unique name or the name of another segment.

Align Type. When the segment being defined is to be combined with another segment, its *align type* tells the linker how many bytes to skip. Sometimes called *slack bytes,* these bytes are inserted between segments to make the CPU more efficient. Again, this only affects segments that are combined—the beginning of the first segment in a group must still begin on a paragraph boundary. This is because segment addresses always contain four implied low-order bits.

The BYTE align type causes a segment to begin immediately after the previous segment. The WORD align type causes the segment to start on the next 16-bit boundary, and DWORD starts at the next 32-bit boundary. The align type of PARA (the default) starts the segment at the next available 16-byte paragraph boundary. The PAGE align type starts at the next 256-byte boundary.

If a program will likely be run on an 8086 or 80286 processor, a WORD align type is best for data segments. This is because both CPUs have a 16-bit data bus. A variable on an even boundary requires only one memory fetch, while a variable on an odd boundary requires two. Virtually all programs written for the IBM-PC today must run on the PC/AT (which uses the 80286) so the WORD align type should be used. If a program will be run on an 80386 or higher processor, the DWORD align type is most efficient for some operations.

The EVEN directive may also be used within a segment to force the next instruction or variable to an even boundary. In the following example, **var3** would have been located at an odd-numbered address if not for the EVEN directive. Instead, the assembler inserts a byte containing 90h (a NOP, or *no operation* instruction) before **var3** to set it to an even address:

```
dseg segment word
    var1  dw  1000h
    var2  db  ?
    even
    var3  dw  2000h
dseg ends
```

The purpose of inserting a NOP is clearer when the EVEN directive is used within the code segment: A NOP instruction is ignored by the CPU.

Combine Type. The combine type tells the linker how to combine segments having the same name. The default type is *private,* meaning that such a segment will not be combined with any other segment.

The PUBLIC and MEMORY combine types cause a segment to be combined with all other public or memory segments by the same name; in effect, they become a single segment. The offsets of all labels are adjusted so they are relative to the start of the same segment.

The STACK combine type resembles the PUBLIC type, in that all stack segments will be combined with it. DOS automatically initializes SS to the start of the first segment that it finds with a combine type of STACK; DOS sets SP to the segment's length when the program is loaded. In an EXE program, there should be at least one segment with a STACK combine type; otherwise, the linker displays a warning message.

The COMMON combine type makes a segment begin at the same address as any other COMMON segments with the same name. In effect, the segments overlay each other. All offsets are calculated from the same starting address, and variables can overlap.

The AT *address* combine type lets you create a segment at an absolute address. No variables or data may be initialized, but you can create variable names that refer to specific offsets. This makes access to the variable more natural. For example:

```
BIOS segment at 40h
  org 17h
  keyboard_flag  db  ?        ; DOS keyboard flag
BIOS ends


.code
mov  ax,BIOS                  ; point to BIOS segment
mov  ds,ax
and  ds:keyboard_flag,7Fh  ; clear high bit
```

In this example, a segment override (DS:) was required because **keyboard_flag** is not in the standard data segment. We will talk about segment overrides later in this section.

Class Type. A segment's class type provides another way of combining segments, in particular, those with different names. The class type is simply a string (case-insensitive) enclosed in single quotes. Segments with the same class type are loaded together, although they may be in a different order in the original program. One standard type, 'CODE', is recognized by the linker and should be used for segments containing instructions. You must include this type label if you plan to use a debugger.

14.3.3 The ASSUME Directive

The ASSUME directive makes it possible for the assembler to calculate the offsets of labels and variables at assembly time. It is usually placed directly after the SEGMENT directive in the code segment, but you can have as many additional ASSUMEs as you like. If a new one is encountered, the assembler modifies the way it calculates addresses.

ASSUME does not actually change the value of a segment register. One still must set segment registers at runtime to the addresses of the desired segments.

Sample Program. A program containing multiple data segments is shown in Example 5. The following directive tells the assembler to use DS as the default register for the **data1** segment:

```
assume ds:data1
```

Example 4. Program with Multiple Segments.

```
title Multiple Segment Example              (seg1.asm)

cseg  segment 'CODE'
    assume cs:cseg, ds:data1, ss:mystack

main proc
    mov   ax,data1          ; point DS to data1 segment
    mov   ds,ax
    mov   ax,seg val2       ; point ES to data2 segment
    mov   es,ax

    mov   ax,val1           ; requires ASSUME for DS
    mov   bx,es:val2        ; ASSUME not required
    cmp   ax,bx
    jb    L1                ; requires ASSUME for CS
    mov   ax,0
L1:
    mov   ax,4C00h          ; exit program
    int   21h
main endp
cseg  ends

data1 segment 'DATA'        ; specify class type
   val1  dw  1001h
data1 ends

data2 segment 'DATA'
   val2  dw  1002h
data2 ends

mystack segment para STACK 'STACK'   ; combine & class type
   db  100h dup('S')
mystack ends
end main
```

CS is identified as the default segment register for CSEG, and SS is associated with **mystack** by the following statements:

```
assume cs:cseg
assume ss:mystack
```

14.3.4 Segment Overrides

A segment override instruction inserts a byte into the code stream before the op code that causes the processor to use a different segment register from the default segment when calculating the effective address. It can be used, for example, to access a variable in a segment other than the one currently referenced by DS:

```
mov  al,cs:var1          ; segment pointed to by CS
mov  al,es:var2          ; segment pointed to by ES
```

The following instruction obtains the offset of a variable in a segment not currently ASSUME'd by DS or ES:

```
mov  bx,offset AltSeg:var2
```

Multiple references to variables should be handled by inserting an ASSUME to change the default segment references:

```
assume ds:AltSeg         ; use AltSeg for a while
mov    ax,AltSeg
mov    ds,ax
mov    al,var1
         .
         .
assume ds:data           ; use the default data segment
mov    ax,data
mov    ds,ax
```

14.3.5 Combining Segments

Multiple segments may be combined by giving them the same name and specifying a PUBLIC combine type. This happens even if the segments are in separate program modules. If you use a BYTE align type, each segment will immediately follow the previous one. If a WORD align type is used, the segments will follow at the next even word boundary. The align type defaults to PARA, in which each segment follows at the next paragraph boundary.

Examples 5 and 6 show two program modules with two code segments, two data segments, and one stack segment, which combine to form only three segments (CSEG, DSEG, and SSEG). The main module contains all three segments, and both CSEG and DSEG are given a PUBLIC combine type. A BYTE align type is used for CSEG to avoid creating a gap between the two CSEG segments when they are combined.

Example 5. Main Module. Segment Example.

```
title  Combining Segments, Main           (SEG2.ASM)


extrn var2:word, subroutine_1:proc

cseg  segment byte public 'CODE'
assume cs:cseg,ds:dseg, ss:sseg

main proc
   mov   ax,dseg                ; initialize DS
   mov   ds,ax

   mov   ax,var1                ; local variable
   mov   bx,var2                ; external variable
   call  subroutine_1           ; external procedure

   mov   ax,4C00h
   int   21h
main endp
cseg  ends

dseg segment word public 'DATA'    ; local data segment
   var1  dw  1000h
dseg ends

sseg segment stack              ; stack segment
   db  100h dup('S')
sseg ends
end main
```

Example 6. Submodule, Segment Example.

```
title  Combining Segments, Sub            (SEG2A.ASM)


public subroutine_1, var2

cseg  segment byte public 'CODE'
assume cs:cseg, ds:dseg
```

```
subroutine_1 proc                   ; called from MAIN
    mov   ah,9
    mov   dx,offset msg
    int   21h
    ret
subroutine_1 endp
cseg ends

dseg segment word public 'DATA'
var2 dw  2000h                       ; accessed by MAIN
msg  db  'Now in Subroutine_1'
     db  0Dh,0Ah,'$'
dseg ends
end
```

14.4 DYNAMIC MEMORY ALLOCATION

Whenever a program needs to load a file or initialize a table, memory needs to be set aside for the data. The variables we have been using in previous chapters are called *static variables,* because their offsets and sizes are determined at assembly time. But this presents a problem: It may be difficult to know at assembly time how much memory will be needed for certain variables. High-level languages introduced the technique of *dynamic memory allocation* (variables created at runtime) quite some time ago. In Pascal, for instance, pointer variables contain addresses of data that are dynamically allocated on the *heap,* a special data storage area. In C, the *malloc()* function creates space for a variable at runtime. A most important part of dynamic allocation is that variables may be discarded (*deallocated*) when no longer needed, so that new variables may use the same memory space.

DOS has several functions for allocating memory, which form the basis for dynamic variables: Function 4Ah (*modify memory blocks)* finds out how much memory is available above the current program's code, data, and stack. Function 48h allocates a specific block of memory, and function 49h releases a memory block.

14.4.1 Modify Memory Blocks

When a program is loaded, it can call DOS function 4Ah to release all memory it does not need for its code, data, and stack. In order to find out how much memory is needed by a program, you can look at the statistics printed by the assembler at the end of the program's listing file (extension .LST). The following table from a listing file shows a program that requires 540h bytes:

Segments and Groups:

```
              N a m e         Length
_DATA  . . . . . . . . . . . 0313   (data segment)
 STACK . . . . . . . . . . . 0100   (stack segment)
_TEXT  . . . . . . . . . . . 012D   (code segment)
(total)                      0540
```

DOS allocates memory in 16-byte blocks called *paragraphs*. To find out how many paragraphs are needed, add 10h for the PSP and divide the sum by 10h; drop the lowest digit, rounding upward if necessary:

```
550h = 55h paragraphs
552h = 56h paragraphs
```

For example, at the beginning of a program, we can call function 4Ah and pass the PSP segment location in ES and the number of requested paragraphs in BX:

```
main proc
      mov   ah,4Ah          ; modify memory blocks
      mov   bx,55h          ; keep 550h bytes
      int   21h
      mov   ax,@data        ; initialize DS, ES
      mov   ds,ax
      mov   es,ax
```

14.4.2 Allocate Memory

When additional memory is needed, call DOS function 48h (allocate memory). BX must contain the number of requested paragraph blocks. If CF = 0, DOS returns the initial segment of the allocated block in AX. If CF = 1, there probably was not enough memory available, and BX contains the size of the largest available block (in paragraphs). The following example requests a 16K block of memory:

```
mov   ah,48h           ; allocate memory
mov   bx,400h          ; request 400h paragraphs (16K)
int   21h
jc    not_enough_memory
mov   buffer_seg,ax    ; segment address of new block
```

A problem one might face when loading a file into a buffer, for example, is how to decide the amount of memory to allocate for the buffer. One solution is to use DOS function 4Eh (find first matching file) to get the size of the file. This value can be divided by 16 to give us the number of paragraphs we need to allocate. After the memory is allocated, the file can be loaded into memory.

14.4.3 Release Allocated Memory

If a program has allocated a block of memory with function 48h, the block can be released when it is no longer needed. This is done by calling function 49h with the block's starting segment in ES:

```
mov   ah,49h              ; release allocated memory
mov   es,buffer_seg       ; segment of allocated block
int   21h
```

DOS sets the Carry flag if a program tries to release a memory block that either does not belong to it or was not previously allocated by function 48h. With any of the three memory allocation functions (48h, 49h, 4Ah), DOS fails if its own memory control blocks have been destroyed. This happens only when a program has accidentally corrupted a part of memory reserved by DOS.

14.5 RUNTIME PROGRAM STRUCTURE

An effective assembly language programmer needs to know a lot about DOS. This section describes COMMAND.COM, the Program Segment Prefix, and the structure of COM and EXE programs.

The COMMAND.COM program supplied with DOS and Windows is called the *command processor*. It interprets each command typed at a prompt. The following sequence takes place when you type a command:

1. DOS checks to see if the command is internal, such as DIR, REN, or ERASE. If it is, the command is immediately executed by a memory-resident DOS routine.

2. It looks for a matching file with an extension of COM. If the file is in the current directory, it is executed.

3. It looks for a matching file with an extension of EXE. If the file is in the current directory, it is executed.

4. It looks for a matching file with an extension of BAT. If the file is in the current directory, it is executed. A file with an extension of BAT is called a *batch file,* which is a text file containing DOS commands to be executed as if the commands had been typed at the console.

5. If DOS is unable to find a matching COM, EXE, or BAT file in the current directory, it searches the first directory in the current *path*. If it fails to find a match there, it proceeds to the next directory in the path and continues this process until either a matching file is found or the path search is exhausted.

Application programs with extensions of COM and EXE are called *transient programs*. They are loaded into memory long enough to be executed, and then the memory they occupied is released when they finish.

Program Segment Prefix. DOS creates a special 256-byte block at the beginning of a program as it is loaded into memory, called the *program segment prefix.* The structure of the Program Segment Prefix (PSP) is shown in Table 1.

Table 1. The Program Segment Prefix (PSP).

Offset	Comments
00-15	DOS pointers and vector addresses
16-2B	Reserved by DOS
2C-2D	Segment address of the current environment string
2E-5B	Reserved by DOS
5C-7F	File control blocks 1 and 2, used mainly by pre-DOS 2.0 programs
80-FF	Default disk transfer area and a copy of the current DOS command tail

14.5.1 COM Programs

There are two types of transient programs, depending on the extension used: COM and EXE. You may recall that we used debug to create and save short COM programs.

A *COM* program is an unmodified binary image of a machine-language program. It is loaded into memory by DOS at the lowest available segment address, and a PSP is created at offset 0. The code, data, and stack are all stored in the same physical (and logical) segment. The program may be as large as 64K, minus the size of the PSP and two reserved bytes at the end of the stack. All segment registers are set to the base address of the PSP. The code area begins at offset 100h, and the data area immediately follows the code. The stack area is at the end of the segment because DOS initializes SP to FFFEh:

Let's look at the HELLO.ASM program from Chapter 3, rewritten in COM format (see Example 7). A new directive (ORG 100h) is required. It sets the location counter to offset 100h before generating any instructions. This leaves room for the PSP, which occupies locations 0 through 0FFh.

Example 7. COM Format Program.

```
title HELLO Program in COM format   (HELLOCOM.ASM)

.model tiny
.code
org 100h       ; must be before main proc
main proc
    mov  ah,9
    mov  dx,offset hello_message
    int  21h
    mov  ax,4C00h
    int  21h
main endp

hello_message  db  'Hello, world!',0dh,0ah,'$'
end main
```

This program can be assembled by either MASM or TASM. The Borland linker (tlink.exe) requires the /t parameter to tell it to create a COM file rather than an EXE file. The same option for the Microsoft linker is /T.

COM programs are always smaller than their EXE counterparts—HELLO.COM, for example, is only 17 bytes long.

14.5.2 EXE Programs

An EXE program is stored on disk with a *EXE header* followed by a *load module* containing the program itself. The program header is not actually loaded into memory; instead, it contains information used by DOS to load and execute the program.

When DOS loads an EXE program, a program segment prefix (PSP) is created at the first available address, and the program is placed in memory just above it. As DOS decodes the program header, it sets DS and ES to the program's load address. CS and IP are set to the entry point of the program code, from where the program begins executing. SS is set to the beginning of the stack segment, and SP is set to the stack size. As a reminder, here is a diagram showing overlapping code, data, and stack segments from Chapter 3:

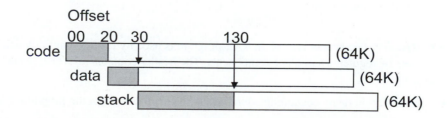

In this particular program, the code area is 20h bytes, the data area is 10h bytes, and the stack area is 100h bytes.

An EXE program may contain up to 65,535 segments, although it would be unusual to have that many. If a program has multiple data segments, the programmer usually has to manually set DS or ES to each new segment.

Memory Usage. The amount of memory an EXE program uses is determined by its program header—in particular, the values for the minimum and maximum number of paragraphs needed above the program. By default, the linker sets the maximum value to 65,535, which is more memory than could be available under DOS. When the program is loaded, therefore, DOS automatically allocates whatever memory is available.

The maximum allocation may be set when a program is linked, using the /CP option. This is shown here for a program named PROG1.OBJ. The number 1024 refers to the number of 16-byte paragraphs, expressed in decimal:

```
link/cp:1024 prog1;
```

These values can also be modified after an EXE program is compiled, using the EXEMOD program supplied with the Microsoft assembler. For example, the command to set the maximum allocation to 400h paragraphs (16,384 bytes) for a program named prog1.exe is

```
exemod prog1/max 400
```

The EXEMOD program can also display important statistics about a program. Sample output is shown here describing the prog1.exe program after it was linked with the maximum allocation set at 1,024 paragraphs:

```
PROG1                          (Hex)        (Dec)
EXE size (bytes)                876          2166
Minimum load size (bytes)       786          1926
Overlay number                    0             0
Initial CS:IP              0000:0010            16
Initial SS:SP              0068:0100           256
Minimum allocation (para)        11            17
Maximum allocation (para)       400          1024
Header size (para)               20            32
Relocation table offset          1E            30
Relocation entries                1             1
```

EXE Header. The header area of an EXE program is used by DOS to correctly calculate the addresses of segments and other components. The header contains information such as the following:

• A relocation table, containing addresses to be calculated when the program is loaded.

- The file size of the EXE program, measured in 512-byte units.

- Minimum allocation: minimum number of paragraphs needed above the program

- Maximum allocation: maximum number of paragraphs needed above the program.

- Starting values to be given to the IP and SP registers.

- *Displacement* (measured in 16-byte paragraphs) of the stack and code segments from the beginning of the load module.

- A *checksum* of all words in the file, used in catching data errors when loading the program into memory.

14.6 REVIEW QUESTIONS

1. Name two common sizes of pointer variables.

2. How is a pointer variable usually used?

3. Are there any reasons why you would want to locate all variables in the same segment?

4. Describe the difference between the following two instructions from the points of program efficiency and the resulting value(s) in SI:

   ```
   mov  si,offset count
   lea  si,count
   ```

5. Describe the difference between the following two instructions:

   ```
   mov  si,offset [bx+2]
   lea  si,[bx+2]
   ```

6. When is it important to clear the Interrupt flag?

7. Why is it important to set the Interrupt flag soon after clearing it?

8. Explain the difference between the HLT and WAIT instructions.

9. Which register must hold an 8-bit byte that is being output to a port?

10. What is wrong with each of the following instructions?

    ```
    a.  out  3BDFh,0
    b.  out  26,DL
    c.  in   DX,BL
    d.  in   3BDFh,AX
    ```

11. Explain the difference between LAHF and SAHF instructions. Which flags are not affected by LAHF and SAHF?

12. When using simplified segment directives, is there any reason why variables should not be placed in the .CODE segment?

13. What does the ASSUME directive do, and what happens if it is omitted from a program that uses explicit segment definitions?

14. What is the purpose of the ESC instruction?

15. What is the difference between the *combine type* and the *class* of a segment?

16. How does the assembler know which segment to set SS to when loading an EXE program?

17. Where do DS and ES point when an EXE program is loaded?

18. How does the starting value of CS differ between COM and EXE programs?

19. Where is the stack located in a COM program?

20. What determines the amount of memory allocated to an EXE program when it is loaded by DOS?

21. What absolute address is implied by the segment address 2CDAh?

22. Assume that **segment_A** ends at absolute location 0F102h and is immediately followed by **segment_B**. If the latter has an align type of PARA, what will be its starting address?

23. In the following example, assume that **segA** begins at address 1A060h. What will be the starting address of the *third* segment, also called **segA**?

```
segA segment common
  var1  dw  ?
  var2  db  ?
segA ends

stack segment stack
  db 100h dup(0)
stack ends

segA segment common
  var3  dw  3000h
  var4  db  40h
segA ends
```

24. Describe the difference between a near call and a far call. Explain why a far call takes longer to execute.

25. If a subroutine is called from a different program module than the one containing the subroutine, must it always be accessed via a far call? Explain your answer.

26. The following program contains three erroneous statements relating to segments. Write any corrected statements on the right-hand side of the program:

```
title   Segment Example

cseg segment
assume ds:dseg, ss:stack
main proc
      mov   ax,dseg
      mov   ds,ax
      mov   bx,value1+2
      jmp   L1
      push ax
      pop   ax
L1:   mov   ax,4C00h
      int   21h
main endp
cseg ends

dseg segment
    value1 dw   1000h,2000h
ends

sseg segment
    db   100h dup('S')
sseg ends
end main
```

27. A major feature of the 80286 processor makes it possible for programs to share memory without disturbing each other. This is called _____ mode.

28. Why is a *transient program* given its name?

29. What is the name of the 256-byte area at the beginning of a transient program?

30. Where in a transient program is the *command tail* (characters typed on the command line) saved?

31. How many program segments can a COM program contain?

32. Why does a COM program make inefficient use of memory?

33. When stored on disk, the two main parts of an EXE program are the *header* and the _____ module.

14.7   PROGRAMMING EXERCISES

1.   *Procedure Address Table*

Create a table containing ten 16-bit procedure offsets. Write a program that displays a menu with the subroutine names and inputs a number between 1 and 10 from the console. Use the number to locate the address of the corresponding procedure in the table. Call the procedure, using indirect addressing. Return to the menu and continue the cycle until the Escape key is pressed.

2.   *Linked Name List*

Write a program that creates a linked list containing names of people. Each node in the list consists of a 20-byte string, followed by a 16-bit pointer to the next entry. As the user inputs each name from the keyboard, insert it in the list. Create space for 20 nodes at assembly time by using the REPT directive. The expression **$+2** tells the assembler to add 2 to the location counter and initialize the memory operand to this value:

```
name_list label byte
rept 20
    db  20 dup(' ')        ; store a person's name
    dw  offset $+2         ; pointer to next entry
endm
```

Be sure to inspect the listing file generated by this REPT macro in order to verify that the pointers have been initialized correctly. Once all the names have been input, display them on the screen and write them to an output file as fixed-length records.

3.   *Linked Name List, Enhanced*

Enhance the Linked Name List program from Exercise 2 in the following ways:

- Make the list doubly linked so each node has a pointer to the previous and next nodes.

- Read the names from a text file rather than the keyboard.

- Display the list in reverse order on the screen.

- Prompt the user for a name; then search the list (from the beginning) for the name. Print out a number, showing its relative position in the list. For example:

```
Name to find: JONES
JONES found in position 5.
Find another (Y/n)? y
```

4.   *Segment Combine Types*

Write a short program that contains the following segments:

```
CSEG (code)
```

```
DSEG (data)
SSEG (stack)
DSEG (another data segment)
```

Choose *class and combine typse* for SSEG so that the assembler sets SS to the segment's starting address. Choose a combine type for DSEG that causes both segments with the same name to be combined. Code an ASSUME directive to identify the segment register tied to each segment. Place several variables in the two data segments, and code instructions to access the data. Run and test the program using a debugger.

5.   *Executing Far Calls*

Write a short program that contains the following three segments: CODE1, DATA, and STACK. Write another program module containing a single segment: CODE2. Write a statement in the main procedure that calls a procedure in the CODE2 segment. Assemble each module separately, link the two modules, and trace the final program with a debugger to make sure a far call was executed.

6.   *Loading File Buffers*

Write a program that loads a text file into two 64K buffers, each in its own data segment. As the first buffer fills up, switch to the second. Make sure DS points to the correct segment as the file is loading. To maximize efficiency, use a single read for each buffer. Use explicit segment definitions.

15 *Advanced Topics II*

15.1 SYSTEM HARDWARE

The system board components introduced in Chapter 2 were just a small part of the overall hardware on the IBM-PC. In this chapter, we will introduce additional devices that are in the domain of the systems programmer:

- The Floating-Point Unit (FPU) handles floating-point and extended integer calculations.

- The 8284/82C284 *Clock Generator*, known simply as the *clock*, oscillates at a speed ranging from 4.77MHz on the original IBM-PC to 400MHz on current Pentium-based computers. The clock generator synchronizes the CPU and the rest of the computer.

- The 8259 *Programmable Interrupt Controller* (PIC) handles external interrupts from hardware devices such as the keyboard, system clock, and disk drives. These devices literally "interrupt" the CPU and make it process their requests immediately.

- The 8253 *Programmable Interval Timer/Counter* interrupts the system 18.2 times per second, updates the system date and clock, and controls the speaker. It is also responsible for constantly refreshing memory, as RAM memory chips can remember their data for only a few milliseconds.

15.1.1 Real-Time Clock

On all machines using the 80286 and later processors, there is a real-time clock that keeps track of the date and time when the system is shut off. DOS reads the clock when the system is booted; it then keeps track of the date and time on its own without referencing the real-time clock. If your computer is left running for a long time, the DOS date and time may get out of synchronization with the real-time clock.

Example 1 shows a program containing the **RealClockTime** procedure, which retrieves the time from the system's real-time clock and displays it in the format HH:MM:SS. The call to Int 1Ah returns the hours in CH, minutes in CL, seconds in DH, and a Daylight Savings Time flag in DL. All values are in binary-coded decimal. The **Writebcd** procedure is from the book's link library.

Example 1. Reading the Real-Time Clock.

```
Title Reading the Real-Time Clock          (clock.asm)

.model small
.stack 100h
.code
extrn Crlf:proc, Writebcd:proc

main proc
    mov ax,@data
    mov ds,ax
    call RealClockTime
    mov ax,4C00h
    int 21h
main endp

RealClockTime proc near
    mov   ah,2
```

```
        int    1Ah                ; CH=hrs, CL=min, DH=sec, DL=dst flag
        mov    al,ch
        call   Writebcd           ; write the hours
        mov    dl,':'
        call   outChar
        mov    al,cl
        call   Writebcd           ; write the minutes
        mov    dl,':'
        call   outChar
        mov    al,dh
        call   Writebcd           ; write the seconds
        call   crlf
        ret
RealClockTime endp

outChar proc                      ; display char in DL
    push   ax
    mov    ah,2
    int    21h
    pop    ax
    ret
outChar endp
end main
```

15.1.2 CPU

In Chapter 2, we looked at the various parts of the CPU. To briefly review, they were:

* Data registers

* Flags registers

* Address registers

* Data bus

* Address bus

* Clock

* Arithmetic logic unit (ALU)

* Control unit (CU)

Instruction Cycle. When the CPU executes an instruction, it goes through an instruction cycle containing three basic steps: *fetch, decode,* and *execute:*

Fetch: The CU fetches the instruction, copying it from memory into the CPU.

Decode: The CU increments the program counter and decodes the instruction. If other operands are specified by the instruction, the CU decodes their addresses and fetches the operands. It passes the instruction and operands to the ALU via the *prefetch queue,* which acts as a waiting area for the ALU.

Execute: The ALU executes the operation and passes the result operands to the CU, where they are returned to registers and memory.

Each step in the instruction cycle takes at least one tick of the system clock, called a *clock cycle*.

One of the most important developments in microprocessors is their division of labor between the ALU and the CU, allowing them to work in parallel. Instead of waiting for the ALU to finish each instruction, the CU fetches the next instruction from memory and loads it into the instruction prefetch queue.

15.1.3 Calculating Instruction Timings

Some applications in data communications, engineering, and real-time processing require you to choose the most efficient way to code a group of instructions. By calculating the relative amount of time different instructions take to execute, you can write better programs. In order to estimate the time taken for a particular instruction, one must know the following:

- The CPU type (8088, 8086, 80286, etc.)

- The clock speed of the CPU

- The instruction mnemonic

- The addressing mode

Because of the great variety of CPUs available for the IBM-PC family, we won't deal with the possible variations on CPUs and clock speeds. For illustrative purposes, we will select the original IBM-PC, whose clock speed is 4.77 MHz, with the understanding that the same principles apply to other IBM-compatible computers. You can find a list of instruction times for each of the CPUs in Intel's reference manuals.

Clock Cycles. We measure the speed of an instruction primarily by two factors: the number of clock cycles required to execute it, and the speed of the CPU's internal clock. To help show the differences in execution speed between different Intel processors, Table 1 shows the number of clock cycles required to execute a 16-bit increment instruction (INC).

Table 1. INC Instruction Timings in Clock Cycles.

Operand Type	88/86	286	386	486
reg16	3	2	2	1
mem16	23+EA	7	6	3

The notation *EA* in the table refers to the time it takes for the processor to calculate various addressing modes. From the 80286 onward, effective address calculation is not a factor. Theoretically, if a 386 processor requires two clock cycles to increment a 16-bit register, and its internal clock runs at 33MHz, it can execute the instruction in ((1/33000000) * 2), or .00000006 seconds. (In terms of real performance, however, this instruction might appear to execute more quickly because the processor is able to execute instructions in parallel.)

15.1.4 Reading From Memory

Memory access is an important factor when understanding the speed of a program. The CPU might be capable of running at 200MHz, for example, but ordinary RAM might be able to respond at a speed of 66MHz. This could force the CPU to wait until operands have been fetched from memory before an instruction can execute. For this reason, most Pentium systems have between 512K and 1MB of high-speed level-2 cache memory that can hold the most recently used instructions and data. Whenever possible, the CPU will read from the level-2 cache, giving programs a noticeable boost in performance. In general, a computer system is designed as a compromise between the abilities of each of its components.

To us, the process of reading instructions or data from memory may seem automatic, but the process actually takes several steps, controlled by CPU clock cycles. Let's look at a diagram of the CPU instruction cycle in Figure 1: The top line shows the clock rising and falling in a repetitive pattern. Notice that there is always a leading or trailing edge as the clock changes state. This reflects the time taken by the transition between states.

The following is a simplified description of what happens during each clock cycle as memory is being read:

Cycle 1:   The address of the memory operand is placed on the address bus; the CPU does this by setting each address pin high (1) or low (0).

Cycle 2:   The Read Line (RD) is set low (0) to notify memory that a value is to be read.

Figure 1. CPU Instruction Cycle, Clock Timings.

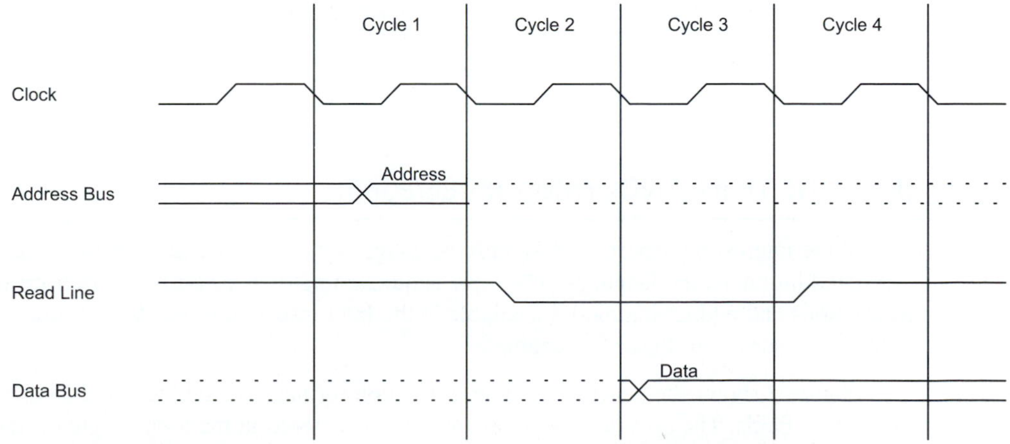

Cycle 3:   The CPU delays to give memory to respond. Memory places the operand on the data bus.

Cycle 4:   The Read Line (RD) goes to 1, signaling that the CPU can now read the values on the data bus.

Effective Address. Calculating the addresses of a memory operand may require extra work by the CPU. If the addressing mode involves arithmetic, the CPU first calculates the effective address, and then the CPU fetches the operand from memory. On the 8088/8086, the calculation of the effective address takes extra time. The Intel 80286 and later processors, on the other hand, calculate effective addresses at the hardware level, so there is no difference in execution speed between a direct operand, for example, and a base-indexed operand.

The Prefetch Queue. One factor regarding instruction timings published by Intel is important: They assume a constantly full prefetch queue. You may recall that the CU fetches instructions and places them in the prefetch queue. There they are held until the ALU can execute them. Whenever the ALU is busy executing an instruction, the CU is busy refilling the queue. (As might be expected, later processors have larger prefetch queues.)

It takes the 8088, for example, four clock cycles to fetch an instruction from memory and load it into the queue. As long as the ALU is executing an instruction that takes at least four clocks, the CU keeps up quite well. But the prefetch queue is depleted when instructions of less than four clocks are executed. The following instructions each take two clocks to execute and are two bytes long:

```
shl    al,1
shl    al,1
shl    al,1
```

Let's assume that the prefetch queue was full when we started. After six clocks have passed, the four bytes in the queue have been depleted and the CU has not had enough time to fetch the fourth instruction. This means the ALU will have to wait for the queue to be filled before going on. Therefore, it is more efficient to write the following than to code five individual shift instructions:[1]

```
mov    cl,5
shl    al,cl
```

15.2 INSTRUCTION ENCODING (8086/8088)

One of the interesting aspects of assembly language is the way assembly instructions are translated into machine language. The topic is quite complex because of the rich variety of instructions and addressing modes available in the Intel instruction set. We will use the 8086/8088 processor as an illustrative example.

Figure 2 shows the general machine instruction format, and Tables 2 and 3 describe the instruction fields. The *opcode* (operation code) field is stored in the lowest byte (at the lowest address). All remaining bytes are optional: the *ModR/M* field identifies the addressing mode and operands; the *immed-low* and *immed-high* fields are for immediate operands (constants); the *disp-low* and *disp-high* fields are for displacements added to base and index registers in the more complex addressing modes (e.g. [BX+SI+2]). Few instructions contain all of these fields; on average, most instructions are only 2-3 bytes long. (Throughout our discussions of instruction encoding, all numbers are assumed to be in hexadecimal.)

Figure 2. Intel Instruction Format (8086/8088).

	Mod R/M						
opcode	mod	reg	r/m	immed-low	immed-high	disp-low	disp-high
7 0	7 6	5 4 3	2 1 0	7 -- 0	7 -- 0	7 -- 0	7 -- 0

(The opcode indicates whether or not the immediate value field is present, as well as its size.)

Table 2. Mod Field Values.

Mod	Displacement
00	DISP = 0, disp-low and disp-high are absent (unless r/m = 110).
01	DISP = disp-low sign-extended to 16 bits; disp-high is absent.
10	DISP = disp-high and disp-low are used.
11	r/m field contains a register number.

Table 3. r/m Field Values.

r/m	Operand
000	[BX + SI] + DISP
001	[BX + DI] + DISP
010	[BP + SI] + DISP
011	[BP + DI] + DISP
100	[SI] + DISP
101	[DI] + DISP
110	[BP] + DISP DISP-16 (for mod = 00 only)
111	[BX] + DISP

(DISP may be 8-bit, 16-bit, or nonexistent.)

Opcode. The *opcode* field identifies the general instruction type (MOV, ADD, SUB, and so on) and contains a general description of the operands. For example, a **MOV AL,BL** instruction has a different opcode from **MOV AX,BX**:

```
mov  al,bl                     ; opcode = 88h
mov  ax,bx                     ; opcode = 89h
```

Many instructions have a second byte, called the *modR/M* byte, which identifies the type of addressing mode being used. Using our sample register move instructions again, the ModR/M byte is the same for both moves because they use equivalent registers:

```
mov  al,bl                     ; mod R/M = D8
mov  ax,bx                     ; mod R/M = D8
```

15.2.1 Single-Byte Instructions

The simplest type of instruction is one with either no operand or an implied operand, such as AAA, AAS, CBW, LODSB, or XLAT. These instructions require only the opcode field, the value of which is predetermined by the processor's instruction set:

Instruction	Opcode
AAA	37
AAS	3F
CBW	98
LODSB	AC
XLAT	D7
INC DX	42

It might appear that the INC DX instruction slipped into this table by mistake, but the designers of the Intel instruction set decided to supply unique opcodes for certain commonly used instructions. Because of this, incrementing a register is optimized for both code size and execution speed.

15.2.2 Immediate Operands

Many instructions contain an immediate (constant) operand. For example, the machine code for **MOV AX,1** is **B8 01 00** (hexadecimal). How would the assembler build the machine language for this? First, in the Intel documentation, the encoding of the MOV instruction that moves an immediate word into a register is

```
B8 +rw  dw
```

where +*rw* indicates that a register code (0-7) is to be added to B8, and *dw* indicates that an immediate word operand follows (low byte first). The register code for AX is 0, so (rw = 0) is added to B8; the immediate value is 0001, so the bytes are inserted in reversed order. This is how the assembler generates **B8 01 00**.

What about the instruction **MOV BX,1234h**? BX is register number 3, so we add 3 to B8; we then reverse the bytes in 1234h. The machine code is generated as **BB 34 12**. Try hand-assembling a few such MOV instructions to get the hang of it, and then check your results with a debugger. The register numbers are as follows: AX/AL = 0, CX/CL = 1, DX/DL = 2, BX/BL = 3, SP/AH = 4, BP/CH = 5, SI/DH = 6, and DI/BH = 7.

15.2.3 Register-Mode Instructions

If you write an instruction that uses only the register addressing mode, the ModR/M byte identifies the register name(s). Table 4 identifies register numbers in the r/m field. The choice of 8-bit or 16-bit register depends upon bit 0 of the opcode field; it equals 1 for a 16-bit register and 0 for an 8-bit register.

Table 4. Identifying Registers in the Mod R/M Field.

R/M	Register	R/M	Register
000	AX or AL	100	SP or AH
001	CX or CL	101	BP or CH
010	DX or DL	110	SI or DH
011	BX or BL	111	DI or BH

For example, let's assemble the instruction **PUSH CX**. The Intel encoding of a 16-bit register push is

    50 +rw

where +rw means a register number (0-7) is added to 50h. Because CX is register number 1, the machine language would be **51**. But other register-based instructions are more compli-cated, particularly those with two operands. For example, the machine language for **MOV AX,DX** is **89 D8**. The Intel encoding of a 16-bit MOV from a register to any other operand is

    89 /r

where /r indicates that a ModR/M byte follows the opcode. The *ModR/M* byte is made up of three fields. D8, for example, contains the following bit fields:

mod	reg	r/m
11	011	000

- Bits 6-7 are the *mod* field, which tells us the addressing mode. The current operands are registers, so this field equals 11.

- Bits 3-5 are the *reg* field, which indicates the source operand. In our example, DX is register number 011.

- Bits 0-2 are the *r/m* field, which indicates the destination operand. In our example, AX is register number 000.

15.2.4 Memory-Mode Instructions

The real purpose of having the ModR/M byte is for addressing memory. Because of the rich variety of addressing modes, the ModR/M byte is a model of economy: Exactly 256 different combinations of operands may be specified by this byte. The rules for generating the bit patterns in the ModR/M byte are a trifle complex, so the Intel manuals conveniently supply a table (refer to Table 5) that makes it easy to look up the values.

For example, let's encode the instruction **MOV [SI],AX.** Earlier, it was shown that the encoding format for a move from a 16-bit register was **89 /r**. All we have to do is look along the top of Table 5 for the AX register, and then along the right side for the effective address **[SI].** The ModR/M byte found at the intersection of these two values in the table is **04.** Therefore, the machine instruction is **89 04**.

Let's try to figure out why that ModR/M value was chosen. Looking back at the diagram of the Intel instruction format in Figure 2, the *mod* field assignments are listed in a table: For memory operands having no displacement, the *mod* field is 00. This is true in the instruction **MOV [SI],AX.** In the same figure, the instruction format diagram shows that bits 3-5 in the ModR/M byte are the *reg* field (register number). AX is register 000. Finally, the r/m field value for either [SI] or [SI] + DISP is **100.** Let's put all of this together, creating a ModR/M byte value of **04**:

```
mod      n       r/m
00       000     100  =  04  (ModR/M byte value)
```

What about the instruction **MOV [SI],AL**? The opcode for a move from an 8-bit register is **88**. The ModR/M byte, on the other hand, would be exactly the same, because AL also happens to be register number 000. The machine instruction would be **88 04**.

MOV Examples. If you were to write your own assembler, you would need to refer to instruction set references such as the *Intel iAPX 286 Programmmers Reference Manual,* which can be purchased directly from Intel. For example, Table 6 lists all opcodes for the MOV instruction, with a detailed description of the operand types. Table 7 and Table 8 both provide supplemental information about abbreviations used in Table 6. Use these tables as references when hand-assembling your own MOV instructions.

Table 9 contains a few additional examples of MOV instructions that you can assemble by hand and compare to the resulting machine code shown in the table.

Table 5. ModR/M Byte Values (16-Bit Segments).

Byte: Word:		AL AX 0	CL CX 1	DL DX 2	BL BX 3	AH SP 4	CH BP 5	DH SI 6	BH DI 7	
Mod	**R/M**				**ModR/M Value**					**Effective Address**
00	000 001 010 011 100 101 110 111	00 01 02 03 04 05 06 07	08 09 0A 0B 0C 0D 0E 0F	10 11 12 13 14 15 16 17	18 19 1A 1B 1C 1D 1E 1F	20 21 22 23 24 25 26 27	28 29 2A 2B 2C 2D 2E 2F	30 31 32 33 34 35 36 37	38 39 3A 3B 3C 3D 3E 3F	[BX + SI] [BX + DI] [BP + SI] [BP + DI] [SI] [DI] D16 [BX]
01	000 001 010 011 100 101 110 111	40 41 42 43 44 45 46 47	48 49 4A 4B 4C 4D 4E 4F	50 51 52 53 54 55 56 57	58 59 5A 5B 5C 5D 5E 5F	60 61 62 63 64 65 66 67	68 69 6A 6B 6C 6D 6E 6F	70 71 72 73 74 75 76 77	78 79 7A 7B 7C 7D 7E 7F	[BX + SI] + D8 [BX + DI] + D8 [BP + SI] + D8 [BP + DI] + D8 [SI] + D8 [DI] + D8 [BP] + D8 [BX] + D8
10	000 001 010 011 100 101 110 111	80 81 82 83 84 85 86 87	88 89 8A 8B 8C 8D 8E 8F	90 91 92 93 94 95 96 97	98 99 9A 9B 9C 9D 9E 9F	A0 A1 A2 A3 A4 A5 A6 A7	A8 A9 AA AB AC AD AE AF	B0 B1 B2 B3 B4 B5 B6 B7	B8 B9 BA BB BC BD BE BF	[BX + SI] + D16 [BX + DI] + D16 [BP + SI] + D16 [BP + DI] + D16 [SI] + D16 [DI] + D16 [BP] + D16 [BX] + D16
11	000 001 010 011 100 101 110 111	C0 C1 C2 C3 C4 C5 C6 C7	C8 C9 CA CB CC CD CE CF	D0 D1 D2 D3 D4 D5 D6 D7	D8 D9 DA DB DC DD DE DF	E0 E1 E2 E3 E4 E5 E6 E7	E8 E9 EA EB EC ED EE EF	F0 F1 F2 F3 F4 F5 F6 F7	F8 F9 FA FB FC FD FE FF	w = AX, b = AL w = CX, b = CL w = DX, b = DL w = BX, b = BL w = SP, b = AH w = BP, b = CH w = SI, b = DH w = DI, b = BH

Notes: (1) D8 is an 8-bit displacement following the ModR/M byte that is sign-extended and added to the

15.3 INTERRUPT HANDLING

In this section, we discuss ways to customize the BIOS and DOS by installing *interrupt handlers* (or *interrupt service routines*). As we have seen in earlier chapters, the BIOS and DOS contain procedures that simplify input ouput as well as basic system tasks. We have seen many of these so far—the INT 10h routines for video manipulation, the INT 16h keyboard routines, the INT 21h disk services, and so on. But an equally important part of the operating

Table 6. MOV Instruction Opcodes.

Opcode	Instruction	Description
88 /r	MOV eb,rb	Move byte register into EA byte
89 /r	MOV ew,rw	Move word register into EA word
8A /r	MOV rb,eb	Move EA byte into byte register
8B /r	MOV rw,ew	Move EA word into word register
8C /0	MOV ew,ES	Move ES into EA word
8C /1	MOV ew,CS	Move CS into EA word
8C /2	MOV ew,SS	Move SS into EA word
8C /3	MOV DS,ew	Move DS into EA word
8E /0	MOV ES,mw	Move memory word into ES
8E /0	MOV ES,rw	Move word register into ES
8E /2	MOV SS,mw	Move memory word into SS
8E /2	MOV SS,rw	Move register word into SS
8E /3	MOV DS,mw	Move memory word into DS
8E /3	MOV DS,rw	Move word register into DS
A0 dw	MOV AL,xb	Move byte variable (offset dw) into AL
A1 dw	MOV AX,xw	Move word variable (offset dw) into AX
A2 dw	MOV xb,AL	Move AL into byte variable (offset dw)
A3 dw	MOV xw,AX	Move AX into word register (offset dw)
B0 +rb db	MOV rb,db	Move immediate byte into byte register
B8 +rw dw	MOV rw,dw	Move immediate word into word register
C6 /0 db	MOV eb,db	Move immediate byte into EA byte
C7 /0 dw	MOV ew,dw	Move immediate word into EA word

Table 7. Key to Instruction Opcodes.

/n:	A ModR/M byte follows the opcode, possibly followed by immediate and displacement fields. The digit n (0-7) is the value of the reg field of the ModR/M byte.
/r:	A ModR/M byte follows the opcode, possibly followed by immediate and displacement fields.
db:	An immediate byte operand follows the opcode and ModR/M bytes.
dw:	An immediate word operand follows the opcode and ModR/M bytes.
+rb:	A register code (0-7) for an 8-bit register, which is added to the preceding hexadecimal byte to form an 8-bit opcode.
+rw:	A register code (0-7) for a 16-bit register, which is added to the preceding hexadecimal byte to form an 8-bit opcode.

system is its set of interrupt service routines that respond to hardware interrupts. DOS allows you to replace any of these service routines with one of your own.

An interrupt handler might be written for a variety of reasons. You might want your own program to activate when a "hot" key is pressed, even when the user is running another application. Borland's *SideKick*, for example, was one of the first programs that was able to pop up a notepad or calculator whenever a special combination of hot keys was pressed.

Table 8. Key to Instruction Operands.

db	A signed value between −128 and +127. If combined with a word operand, this value is sign-extended.
dw	An immediate word value that is an operand of the instruction.
eb	A byte-sized operand, either register or memory.
ew	A word-sized operand, either register or memory.
rb	An 8-bit register identified by the value (0-7).
rw	A 16-bit register identified by the value (0-7).
xb	A simple byte memory variable without a base or index register.
xw	A simple word memory variable without a base or index register.

Table 9. Sample MOV Instructions, with Machine Code.

Instruction	Machine Code	Addressing Mode
mov ax,[0120]	A1 20 01	direct (optimized for AX)
mov [0120],bx	89 1E 20 01	direct
mov ax,bx	89 D8	register
mov [di],bx	89 1D	indexed
mov [bx+2],ax	89 47 02	base-disp
mov [bx+si],ax	89 00	base-indxed
mov word ptr [bx+di+2],1234	C7 41 02 34 12	base-indexed-disp

You can also replace one of DOS's default interrupt handlers in order to provide more complete services. For example, the *divide by zero* interrupt activates when the CPU tries to divide a number by zero, but there is no standard way for a program to recover.

You can replace the DOS *critical error handler* or the Ctrl-Break handler with one of your own. DOS's default critical error handler causes a program to abort and return to DOS. Your own handler could recover from an error and let the user continue to run the current application program.

A user-written interrupt service routine can handle hardware interrupts more effectively than DOS. For example, the IBM-PC's asynchronous communication handler (INT 14h) performs no input/output buffering. This means that an input character is lost if it is not copied from the port before another character arrives. A memory-resident program can wait for an incoming character to generate a hardware interrupt, input the character from the port, and store it in a circular buffer. This frees an application program from having to take valuable time away from other tasks to repeatedly check the serial port.

Interrupt Vector Table. The key to DOS's flexibility lies in the *interrupt vector table* located in the first 1024 bytes of RAM (locations 0:0 through 0:03FF). Table 10 contains a short sample of vector table entries. Each entry in the table (called an interrupt vector) is a 32-bit segment-offset address that points to one of the existing service routines.

On your computer, the vector values will probably be different from these, because the locations of interrupt handlers vary from one computer to another. Each interrupt vector corresponds to an interrupt number. In the preceding table, the address of the INT 0 handler (*divide by zero*) is 02C1:5186h. The offset of any interrupt vector may be found by multiplying its interrupt number by 4. Thus, the offset of the vector for INT 9h is 9 * 4, or 0024 hexadecimal.

Executing Interrupt Handlers. An interrupt handler may be executed in one of two ways: An application program containing an INT instruction could cause a call to the routine, which is called a *software interrupt*. Another way for an interrupt routine to be executed is via a

Table 10. Interrupt Vector Table Example.

Interrupt Number	Offset	Interrupt Vectors
00-03	0000	02C1:5186 0070:0C67 0DAD:2C1B 0070:0C67
04-07	0010	0070:0C67 F000:FF54 F000:837B F000:837B
08-0B	0020	0D70:022C 0DAD:2BAD 0070:0325 0070:039F
0C-0F	0030	0070:0419 0070:0493 0070:050D 0070:0C67
10-13	0040	C000:0CD7 F000:F84D F000:F841 0070:237D

hardware interrupt, when a hardware device (asynchronous port, keyboard, timer, and so on) sends a signal to the Intel 8259 Programmable Interrupt Controller (PIC) chip.

15.3.1 Hardware Interrupts

A *hardware interrupt* is a signal received by the CPU that tells it to interrupt its current sequence of instructions and branch to a new location. The CPU supports 256 different interrupts, numbered 0 through FF hexadecimal.

IRQ Levels. Interrupts can be triggered by a number of different devices on a PC, including those listed in Table 11. Each device has a priority, based on its *interrupt level,* or *IRQ.* Level 0 has the highest priority, and level 15 has the lowest. A lower-level interrupt cannot interrupt a

Table 11. IRQ Assignments (ISA bus)[2].

IRQ	Interrupt Number	Description
0	8	System timer (18.2 times/second)
1	9	Keyboard
2	0Ah	Programmable Interrupt Controller
3	0Bh	COM2 (serial port 2)
4	0Ch	COM1 (serial port 1)
5	0Dh	LPT2 (parallel port 2)
6	0Eh	Floppy disk controller
7	0Fh	LPT1 (parallel port 1)
8	70h	CMOS real-time clock
9	71h	(redirected to INT 0Ah)
10	72h	(available) Sound card
11	73h	(available) SCSI card
12	74h	PS/2 mouse
13[z]	75h	Math coprocessor
14	76h	Hard disk controller
15	77h	(available)

higher-level one still in progress. For instance, if communications port 1 (COM1) tried to interrupt the keyboard interrupt handler, it would have to wait until the latter was finished. Also, two or more simultaneous interrupt requests are processed according to their priority levels. The scheduling of interrupts is handled by the 8259 *peripheral interrupt controller* chip, nicknamed the *8259 PIC*.

Let's use the keyboard as an example: When a key is pressed, the 8259 sends an INTR signal to the CPU, passing it the interrupt number; if external interrupts are not currently disabled, the CPU does the following:

• Pushes the Flags register on the stack.

• Clears the Interrupt flag, preventing any other hardware interrupts.

• Pushes the current CS and IP on the stack.

• Locates the interrupt vector table entry for INT 9 and places this address in CS and IP.

Now the BIOS routine for INT 9 executes: First, it reenables hardware interrupts with the STI instruction, so the system timer is not affected. Next, the INT 9 routine inputs a character from the keyboard port and stores it in the *keyboard buffer,* a 32-byte circular buffer in the BIOS data area. The routine ends with an IRET (*interrupt return*) instruction, which pops IP, CS, and the Flags register off the stack. Control returns to the program that was executing when the interrupt occurred.

Sample BIOS Routine. Let's look at an exerpt from a disassembly of INT 16h, Function 01h in an early version of the ROM BIOS. This routine examines the keyboard buffer in low memory, checking to see if a character is waiting. When a hardware interrupt occurs, the 8259 automatically disables any subsequent hardware interrupts and immediately branches to the interrupt handler procedure. It is important for this procedure not to wait too long before reenabling interrupts, or else the system clock and other devices are adversely affected. The STI instruction enables hardware interrupts:

```
          push    ds               ; interrupts are currently disabled
          push    si
          xor     si,si
          mov     ds,si
          mov     si,041Ah         ; locate keyboard buffer head pointer
          dec     ah
          jnz     L1
          mov     ax,[si]          ; get buffer head
          mov     si,0400h         ; point to DOS data area
          add     si,ax
   ; ZF = return value: ZF=1 if buffer is empty, or ZF=0 if char is waiting.
          cmp     ax,[041C]        ; buffer tail = buffer head?
          mov     ax,[si]          ; move char/scan code into AX
   L1:    sti                      ; interrupts are enabled
          pop     si
```

```
        pop     ds
        retf    0002            ; return, pop flags from the stack
```

15.3.2 Interrupt Control Instructions

The CPU has a flag called the *Interrupt flag* (IF), that controls the way the CPU responds to external (hardware) interrupts. If the Interrupt flag is set (IF = 1), we say that interrupts are *enabled;* if the flag is clear (IF = 0), then interrupts are *disabled.*

STI Instruction. The STI instruction enables external interrupts. For example, the system responds to keyboard input by suspending a program in process and doing the following: It calls INT 9, which stores the keystroke in a buffer and then returns to the current program. Normally, the interrupt flag is enabled. Otherwise, the system timer would not calculate the time and date properly, and input keystrokes would be lost.

CLI Instruction. The CLI instruction disables external interrupts. It should be used sparingly—only when a critical operation is about to be performed, one that cannot be interrupted. When an interrupt occurs, the current values of the flags, CS, and IP are pushed on the stack. The interrupt processing program executes, and then the old values of the flags, CS, and IP are restored.

When changing the value of SS and SP on the 8086/8088, for example, it is advisable to disable interrupts by clearing the Interrupt flag. Otherwise, the correct values of SS and SP could be lost if a hardware interrupt should occur between transfers:

```
cli                             ; disable interrupts
mov     ax,mystack              ; reset SS
mov     ss,ax
mov     sp,100h                 ; reset SP
sti                             ; reenable interrupts
```

Interrupts should never be disabled for more than a few milliseconds at a time, or you may lose keystrokes or slow down the system timer. When the CPU acknowledges either a software or a hardware interrupt, other interrupts are disabled. One of the first things the DOS and BIOS interrupt service routines do is to reenable interrupts.

15.3.3 Writing an Interrupt Handler Procedure

One might ask why the interrupt vector table exists at all. We could, of course, call specific subroutines in ROM to process interrrupts. The designers of the IBM-PC wanted to be able to make modifications and corrections to the BIOS routines without having to replace the ROM chips. By having an interrupt vector table, it was possible to replace addresses in the interrupt vector table so they would point to procedures in RAM.

When you modify the address in an interrupt vector, making it point to your own procedure, your procedure is called an *interrupt handler*, or *interrupt service routine* (ISR). For example, you could write a keyboard interrupt handler that replaces the default handler. There would have to be a compelling reason to do this, of course. A more likely alternative would be for your interrupt handler to directly call the default INT 9 keyboard to read a keystroke from the keyboard port. Once the key was placed in the keyboard typeahead buffer, you could manipulate its contents.

DOS has two INT 21h functions that help you install an interrupt handler: Function 35h (*get interrupt vector*) returns the segment-offset address of an interrupt vector. Call the function with the desired interrupt number in AL. The 32-bit vector is returned by DOS in ES:BX. The following statements would retrieve the INT 9 vector, for example:

```
.data
int9Save   label word
dd   ?                         ; store old INT 9 address here

.code
mov    ah,35h                  ; get interrupt vector
mov    al,9                    ; for INT 9
int    21h                     ; call DOS
mov    int9Save,BX             ; store the offset
mov    int9Save+2,ES           ; store the segment
```

DOS function 25h (*set interrupt vector*) lets you replace an interrupt handler with your own. Call it with the interrupt number in AL and the segment-offset address of your own interrupt handler in DS:DX. For example:

```
        mov    ax,seg kybd_rtn
        mov    ds,ax
        mov    ah,25h               ; set Interrupt vector
        mov    al,9h                ; for INT 9h
        mov    dx,offset kybd_rtn
        int    21h
        .
        .
kybd_rtn proc                        ; (new INT 9 interrupt handler begins here)
```

Ctrl-Break Handler Example. If Ctrl-Break is pressed by the user when a DOS program is waiting for input, control passes to the default INT 23h interrupt handler procedure. The default Ctrl-Break handler terminates the currently running program. It is possible, however, to change this behavior by writing a new handler, also called an *interrupt service routine* (ISR), that gains control when Ctrl-Break is pressed.

Example 2 shows a simple Ctrl-Break handler. The main program initializes the interrupt vector for INT 23h. Notice here that DS must be set to the segment address of new Ctrl-Break handler before calling INT 21h, function 25h, Set Interrupt Vector:

```
push   ds           ; save DS
mov    ax,@code      ; initialize DS
mov    ds,ax
mov    ah,25h        ; set interrupt vector
mov    al,23h        ; for interrupt 23h
mov    dx,offset break_handler
int    21h
pop    ds            ; restore DS
```

Example 2. Ctrl-Break Handler Example.

```
title   Control-Break Handler                 (CTRLBK.ASM)

.model small
.stack 100h
.data
breakMsg db "BREAK",0
msg label byte
  db 'Ctrl-Break demonstration. (CTRLBK.EXE).',0dh,0ah
  db 'This program disables Ctrl-Break. Press any'
  db 0dh,0ah
  db 'keys on the keyboard, and press ESC to return to DOS.'
  db 0dh,0ah,0

.code
extrn Writestring:proc

main  proc
    mov    ax,@data
    mov    ds,ax
    mov    dx,offset msg  ; display greeting message
    call   Writestring

install_handler:
    push   ds           ; save DS
    mov    ax,@code      ; initialize DS
    mov    ds,ax
    mov    ah,25h        ; set interrupt vector
    mov    al,23h        ; for interrupt 23h
    mov    dx,offset break_handler
    int    21h
    pop    ds            ; restore DS
```

```
L1:
    mov    ah,1         ; wait for a key, echo it
    int    21h
    cmp    al,1Bh       ; ESC pressed?
    jnz    L1           ; no: continue

    mov    ax,4C00h     ; yes: exit program
    int    21h
main  endp

; The following procedure executes when
; Ctrl-Break is pressed.

break_handler proc
    push   ax
    push   dx
    mov    dx,offset breakMsg
    call   Writestring
    pop    dx
    pop    ax
    iret
break_handler endp
end main
```

The main program loop simply inputs and echoes keystrokes until the Esc key is pressed. The **break_handler** procedure runs whenever Ctrl-Break is pressed and immediately returns to the calling program. Notice the required IRET instruction (*return from interrupt*) at the end of this procedure.

We don't have to worry about restoring the INT 23h vector when the program ends because DOS automatically does this when we use function 4Ch (INT 21h) to terminate a program. The original vector is stored by DOS at offset 000Eh in the program segment prefix (PSP).

15.3.4 Memory-Resident Programs (TSR)

A memory-resident program, also known as a *terminate and stay resident* (TSR) program, is one that is installed in memory and stays there either until it is removed by software or the computer is rebooted. Such a program can remain hidden and then be activated by some event such as pressing a key.

In the early days of TSRs, compatibility problems would arise when two or more programs replaced the same interrupt vectors. Older programs would make the vector point to their own program and provide no forward chain to other programs using the same vector. Later, to remedy this problem, TSR authors would save the existing vector for the interrupt they were replacing, and would forward-chain to the original interrupt handler after their own procedure was finished dealing with the interrupt. This, of course, was an improvement over the old method, but it meant that the last TSR to be installed automatically had top priority in handling the interrupt. It meant that users sometimes had to be careful to load TSR programs in a particular order. There are now commercial programming tools you can use to manage multiple memory-resident programs.

Keyboard Example. Suppose we have an interrupt service routine in memory at location 10B2:0020 that can inspect each character typed at the keyboard. To install the ISR, we fetch the current INT 9 vector from the interrupt vector table, save it, and replace the table entry with the address of our ISR.

When a keyboard key is pressed, a single byte is transferred by the keyboard controller to the computer's keyboard port, and a hardware interrupt is triggered. The 8259 Interrupt Controller passes the interrupt number to the CPU, and the latter jumps to the INT 9 address in the interrupt vector table, the address of our ISR. Our procedure gets an opportunity to inspect the keyboard byte. When our keyboard handler exits, it executes a jump to the original BIOS keyboard handler procedure.

This chaining process is shown in Figure 3. The addresses are hypothetical. When the BIOS INT 9h routine finishes, the IRET instruction pops the Flags register from the stack and returns control to the program that was executing when the character was pressed.

15.3.5 Application: The No_Reset program

To show that the foregoing scenario is indeed possible, we will write a memory-resident program that prevents the system from being rebooted by the Ctrl-Alt-Delete keys. Once our program is installed in memory, the system may only be rebooted by pressing a special combination of keys: Ctrl-Alt-RightShift-Del. (The only other way to deactivate the program is to turn off and restart the computer.) This program only works if you boot the computer in DOS. Microsoft Windows prevents the TSR from intercepting keyboard keys.

The DOS Keyboard Status Flag. One bit of information we need before we start is the location of the keyboard status flag kept by DOS in low memory, shown in Figure 4. Our

Figure 3. Vectoring an Interrupt.

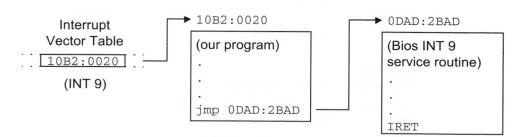

Figure 4. Keyboard Status Flag Byte.

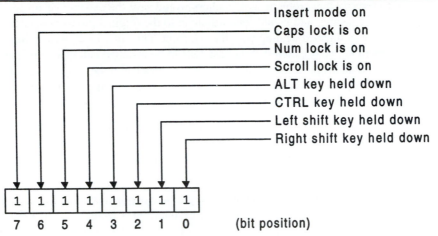

program will inspect this flag to see if the Ctrl, Alt, Del, and RightShift keys are held down. The keyboard status flag is stored in RAM at location 0040:0017h. The label on the right side of the diagram shows what each bit means when it equals 1:

An additional keyboard status byte is located at 0040:0018 that duplicates the preceding flags, except bit 3 shows when Ctrl-NumLock is currently active.

Installing the Program. Our memory-resident routine must be installed in memory before it will work. From that point on, all keyboard input filtered through the program. If routine has any bugs, the keyboard will probably lock up and require us to cold-start the machine. Keyboard interrupt handlers are particularly hard to debug because we use the keyboard constantly when debugging programs. Professionals who regularly write TSR programs usually invest in hardware-assisted debuggers that maintain a trace buffer in protected memory. Often the most elusive bugs appear only when a program is running in real time, not when you are single-stepping through it. *Note: you must boot the computer in DOS mode before installing this program.*

Program Listing. In Example 3, the installation code is located at the end because it will not remain resident in memory. The resident portion, beginning with the label **int9_handler**, is left in memory and pointed to by the INT 9h vector.

Example 3. The Reset-Disabling Program.

```
title  Reset-Disabling program          (NO_RESET.ASM)


.model tiny
; This program disables the usual DOS reset command
; (Ctrl-Alt-Del), by intercepting the INT 9 keyboard
; hardware interrupt. It checks the shift status bits
```

```
; MS-DOS keyboard flag, and changes any Ctrl-Alt-Del to Alt-Del.
; The computer can only be rebooted by typing
; Ctrl+Alt+Right-shift+Del. Assemble, link, and convert to a
; COM program by including the /t command on the TLINK command line.
; This program must be run from DOS.

rt_shift    equ   01h        ; Right shift key: bit 0
ctrl_key    equ   04h        ; Ctrl key: bit 2
alt_key     equ   08h        ; Alt key: bit 3
del_key     equ   53h        ; scan code for Del key
kybd_port   equ   60h        ; keyboard input port


.286        ; use 80286+ processor
.code
org 100h    ; COM program code must start at 100h


start:
    jmp    setup                ; jump to TSR installation routine


;   Memory-resident code begins here

int9_handler proc far
    sti                         ; re-enable hardware interrupts
    pushf                       ; save regs & flags
    push  es
    push  ax
    push  di


;   Point ES:DI to the DOS keyboard flag byte:

L1: mov    ax,40h               ; DOS data segment is at 40h
    mov    es,ax
    mov    di,17h               ; location of keyboard flag
    mov    ah,es:[di]           ; copy keyboard flag into AH


;   Test for the CTRL and ALT keys:

L2: test   ah,ctrl_key          ; Ctrl key held down?
    jz     L5                   ; no: exit
    test   ah,alt_key           ; Alt key held down?
    jz     L5                   ; no: exit
```

```
;   Test for the Del and Right-shift keys:

L3: in    al,kybd_port           ; read keyboard port
    cmp   al,del_key             ; Del key pressed?
    jne   L5                     ; no: exit
    test  ah,rt_shift            ; right shift key pressed?
    jnz   L5                     ; yes: allow system reset

L4: and   ah,not ctrl_key        ; no: turn off bit for Ctrl
    mov   es:[di],ah             ; store keyboard_flag

L5: pop   di                     ; restore regs & flags
    pop   ax
    pop   es
    popf
    jmp   cs:[old_interrupt9]    ; jump to INT 9 routine


old_interrupt9    dd ?


int9_handler endp
end_ISR label byte


; -------------- (end of TSR program) ----------------


; Save a copy of the original INT 9 vector, and set up
; the address of our program as the new vector. Terminate
; and leave the int9_handler procedure in memory.

setup:
    mov   ax,3509h                   ; get current INT 9 vector
    int   21h
    mov   word ptr old_interrupt9,bx   ; save INT 9 vector
    mov   word ptr old_interrupt9+2,es
    mov   ax,2509h                   ; set interrupt vector, INT 9
    mov   dx,offset int9_handler
    int   21h
    mov   ax,3100h                   ; terminate and stay resident
    mov   dx,offset end_ISR          ; point to end of resident code
    shr   dx,4                       ; convert bytes to paragraphs
    inc   dx                         ; and round upward
    int   21h                        ; call the DOS interrupt
end   start
```

First let's look at the instructions that install the program. At the label called **setup**, we call DOS function 35h to get the current INT 9h vector, which is then stored in **old_interrupt9**. This is done so the program will be able to forward-chain to the existing keyboard handler procedure. In the same part of the program, MSDOS function 25h sets interrupt vector 9h to the address of the resident portion of this program. At the end of the program, the call to INT 21function 31h exits to DOS, leaving the resident program in memory. MSDOS automatically saves everything from the beginning of the PSP to the offset placed in DX.

The Resident Program. The memory-resident interrupt handler begins at the label called int9_handler. It is executed every time a keyboard key is pressed. Notice that we reenable interrupts as soon as the handler gets control, because the 8259 controller chip has automatically disabled interrupts:

```
int9_handler proc far
    sti                          ; re-enable hardware interrupts
    pushf                        ; save regs & flags
    (etc...)
```

We must keep in mind that a keyboard interrupt often occurs while another program is executing. If we modified the registers or flags here, we would cause unpredictable results in an application program.

The following statements locate the keyboard flag byte stored at address 0040:0017 and copy it into AH. The byte must be tested to see which keys are currently being held down:

```
L1: mov   ax,40h               ; DOS data segment is at 40h
    mov   es,ax
    mov   di,17h                ; location of keyboard flag
    mov   ah,es:[di]            ; copy keyboard flag into AH
```

The following statements check for both the Ctrl and Alt keys. If both are not currently held down, we exit:

```
L2: test  ah,ctrl_key          ; CTRL key held down?
    jz    L5                    ; no: exit
    test  ah,alt_key           ; ALT key held down?
    jz    L5                    ; no: exit
```

If the Ctrl and Alt keys are both held down, someone may be trying to boot the computer. To find out which character was pressed, we input the character from the keyboard port and compare it to the Del key:

```
L3: in    al,kybd_port         ; read keyboard port
    cmp   al,del_key           ; Del key pressed?
```

```
        jne   L5              ; no: exit
        test  ah,rt_shift     ; Right-Shift key pressed?
        jnz   L5              ; yes: allow system reset
```

If it's not the Del key, we simply exit and let INT 9h process the keystroke. If it is the Del key, we check for the Right-Shift key: If the latter is also being held down, we exit and allow the computer to be booted. Otherwise, the Ctrl key bit in the keyboard flag byte is cleared, effectively disabling the user's attempt to reboot the computer.

Finally, we execute a far jump to the original BIOS INT 9h routine, stored in the variable called **old_interrupt9**. This allows all normal keystrokes to be processed, which is vital to the program's success:

```
        jmp   cs:[old_interrupt9]    ; jump to INT 9 routine
```

Other Possibilities. This program opens up a whole world of possibilities. By being able to examine keyboard input before it reaches the BIOS or DOS, one may remove keys from the keyboard buffer, add new keystrokes, or force certain keys to be ignored, as we have. One may rearrange all the keyboard scan codes by using a translate table: As each key is read from the input port, you can change its scan code and DOS will never suspect a thing.

It should be said in passing that there is another side to this picture: The more hardware-specific your programs are, the greater chance there is that they will not run on all PC-compatible computers. When possible, use existing DOS resources to accomplish your goal. If none are available, write your own interrupt handler in a way that will make it as universal as possible.

15.4 DEFINING REAL NUMBERS

In this section we will use assembler directives to define real numbers. The assembler can translate a number in decimal representation in a source program into an encoded real format recognized by the math coprocessor.

A *decimal real* number consists of a mantissa and an optional exponent. The *mantissa* contains the sign, integer portion, and fractional portion. In the number 234.56E+02, for example, the mantissa is 234.56 and the exponent is +02. Other examples of reals are

```
        2.5
        +0.4646
        1.024E+04     ; (1.024 X 10⁴)
        -80000.21
```

Although we will not go into the details of bit mapping all the various real-number formats, the following diagram shows the 4-byte IEEE real number format. The sign occupies the most significant bit, the exponent fills 8 bits, and the mantissa fills the least significant 23 bits:

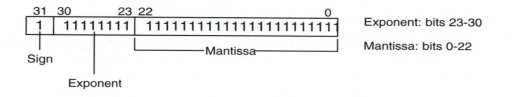

15.4.1 Define Doubleword (DD)

The DD directive tells the assembler to create storage for a 4-byte number. A real number stored as a doubleword is called a *short real*. The number may be declared using either hexadecimal or decimal digits. The latter is called a *decimal real* and may have up to 8 digits of precision. Examples of *short reals* are shown here:

```
dd    12345.678          ; digits, decimal point
dd    +1.5E+02           ; value is 1,500
dd    2.56E+38           ; largest positive exponent
dd    3.3455E-39         ; largest negative exponent
```

An *encoded real* is a real number that is expressed as a string of hexadecimal digits. The hexadecimal digits reflect the number's exact binary contents, with the mantissa, exponent, and sign already included. The assembler requires an uppercase or lowercase *R* to be appended to the number. For example, the number +1.0 would be represented as the following encoded real:

```
dd    3F800000r          ; encoded real, equal to +1.0
```

Encoded reals have limited usefulness because you have to manually encode the bit patterns for the mantissa, sign, and exponent, which is no easy matter.

15.4.2 Define Quadword (DQ)

The DQ directive creates storage for an 8-byte (quadword) variable. *Initialvalue* may be an 8-byte encoded real, a decimal real, a decimal integer, or a binary integer. DQ can be used to create a *long real* number (called a *double* in C, C++ and Visual Basic), either as a decimal real or an encoded real:

```
float1    dq    +1.5E+10              ; decimal real
float2    dq    2.56E+307             ; largest exponent
float3    dq    3F00000000000000r     ; encoded real
```

A quadword may also store either a decimal integer up to 20 digits long or a 64-bit binary integer:

```
long_int    DQ    10030768458923589123    ; decimal integer
```

```
        big_binary DQ  0FFFFFFFFFFFFFFFFFFFFh      ; binary integer
```

15.4.3 Define Tenbyte (DT)

The DT directive creates storage for a 10-byte variable. The contents may be an encoded real, a decimal real, a packed decimal number, or a binary integer. The bytes are stored in memory in low-byte order. Decimal digits are assumed to be stored in packed BCD format (2 digits per byte). The most significant byte is reserved for the sign, which contains 0 for positive numbers and 80h for negative numbers. The number itself may be up to 18 digits long, positive or negative, as the following examples show:

```
        packed_1  dt  123456789012345678
        packed_2  dt  -004600238646485678
```

The assembler assumes the radix of a number declared with DT is hexadecimal; therefore, the decimal (d) radix indicator must be used if you wish to declare a decimal value:

```
        bin_integer  DT  12345678901234567890012345d
```

Temporary Real. The DT directive creates a 10-byte real number conforming to the IEEE *temporary real* format (this format is also used by the coprocessor). A real number may be specified in either decimal or hexadecimal format. A hexadecimal encoded real must be 20 digits long:

```
        float1  dt 1.5                        ; decimal real
        float2  dt 3F000000000000000000r      ; encoded real
```

15.5 FLOATING-POINT INSTRUCTIONS

15.5.1 Floating-Point Coprocessors

A *coprocessor* is a second CPU that works in parallel with a primary CPU. This boosts a computer's power tremendously, as certain tasks can be offloaded onto a coprocessor, giving the main CPU more time for the remaining work. Coprocessors are used in various computer systems for the processing of video graphics, data communications, sound synthesis, floating-point arithmetic, and disk I/O.

The 8087 math coprocessor was originally an optional feature on the original IBM-PC, itself based on the 8088 processor. The 8087 was plugged into an empty socket on the system board near the main CPU. The same was true for 80286- and 80386-base systems, which could use the 80287 and 80387. The latter can execute all 80x87 instructions and have a number of new instructions.

Floating-Point Unit (FPU). On the Intel486DX processor, floating point instructions are executed by the *floating-point unit* (FPU) located on the same chip as the CPU. The less expensive Intel486SX processor has a disabled FPU. All Pentium processors contain an FPU.

From this point on we will use the term *coprocessor* to refer to both the earlier floating-point coprocessor and the subsequent floating-point unit. The instruction set shown in this chapter applies to the original 8087 instruction set, which is compatible with all other Intel math coprocessors.

The coprocessor performs integer and floating-point calculations automatically because the logic is designed into the chip. This makes doing calculations with the coprocessor many times faster than with an integer-based CPU because the latter must emulate floating-point operations through software. Many high-level language compilers can either generate instructions directly for the coprocessor or call subroutines from a floating-point emulation library.

Internal Architecture. The coprocessor has eight individually addressable 80-bit registers. They are arranged in the form of a stack and given the names ST(0), ST(1), ST(2), ST(3), ST(4), ST(5), ST(6), and ST(7). Register ST(0), usually referred to as ST, is located at the top of the stack. Numbers are held in registers while being used in calculations, in 10-byte temporary real format. When the coprocessor stores the result of an arithmetic operation in memory, it automatically translates the number from temporary real format to one of the following formats: integer, long integer, short real, or long real.

Numbers are transferred to and from the main CPU via memory, so one always stores an operand in memory before invoking the coprocessor. The latter loads the number from memory into its register stack, performs an arithmetic operation, stores the result in memory, and signals the CPU that it has finished.

Control Registers. The coprocessor has five control registers. The first three are each 16 bits: *control word, status word,* and *tag word;* the last two are 32 bits: *instruction pointer*, and *operand pointer*.

15.5.2 Instruction Formats

Coprocessor instructions always begin with the letter *F* to distinguish them from CPU instructions. The second letter of an instruction (often *B* or *I*) indicates how a memory operand is to be interpreted: *B* indicates a binary-coded decimal (BCD) operand, and *I* indicates a binary integer operand. If neither is specified, the memory operand is assumed to be in real-number format. For example, FBLD operates on BCD numbers, FILD operates on integers, and FMUL operates on real numbers.

Operands. A coprocessor instruction can have up to two operands, as long as one of them is a coprocessor register. Immediate operands are not allowed, except for the FSTSW (store status word) instruction. CPU registers such as AX and BX are not allowed as operands. Memory-to-memory operations are not allowed.

Instructions. There are six basic instruction formats, shown in Table 12. In the operands *n* refers to a register number (0-7), *memReal* refers to a single or double precision real memory operand, *memInt* refers to a 16-bit integer, and *op* refers to an arithmetic operation. Operands surrounded by braces {...} are implied operands and are not explicitly coded. Implied operands are not coded but are understood to be part of the operation. *Op* (operation) may be one of the following:

Table 12. Basic Arithmetic Instructions and Operands.

Instruction Form	Mnemonic Form	Operands (Dest, Source)	Example
Classical Stack	Fop	{ST(1),ST}	FADD
Classical Stack, extra pop	FopP	{ST(1),ST}	FSUBP
Register	Fop	ST(n),ST ST, ST(n)	FMUL ST(1),ST FDIV ST,ST(3)
Register, pop	FopP	ST(n),ST	FADDP ST(2),ST
Real Memory	Fop	{ST},memReal	FDIVR
Integer Memory	FIop	{ST},memInt	FSUBR hours

(Based on information from the Intel486 Programmers Reference Manual.)

ADD	Add source to destination
SUB	Subtract source from destination
SUBR	Subtract destination from source
MUL	Multiply source by destination
DIV	Divide destination by source
DIVR	Divide source by destination

A *memReal* operand can be one of the following: a 4-byte short real, an 8-byte long real, a 10-byte packed BCD, a 10-byte temporary real, A memInt operand can be a 2-byte word integer, a 4-byte short integer, or an 8-byte long integer.

Classical Stack. A *classical stack* instruction operates on the registers at the top of the stack. No explicit operands are needed. By default, ST is the source operand and ST(1) is the destination. The result is temporarily stored in ST(1). ST is then popped from the stack, leaving the result on the top of the stack. The FADD instruction, for example, adds ST to ST(1) and leaves the result at the top of the stack:

```
FADD        ; ST(1) = ST(1) + ST, pop ST(1) into ST.
```

Real Memory and Integer Memory. The *real memory* and *integer memory* instructions have an implied first operand, ST. The second operand, which is explicit, is an integer or real memory operand. Here are a few examples involving real memory operands:

```
FADD mySingle              ; ST = ST + mySingle
FSUB mySingle              ; ST = ST — mySingle
FSUBR mySingle             ; ST = mySingle — ST
```

And here are the same instructions modified for integer operands:

```
FIADD myInteger            ; ST = ST + myInteger
FISUB myInteger            ; ST = ST — myInteger
FISUBR myInteger           ; ST = myInteger — ST
```

Register. A *register* instruction uses coprocessor registers as ordinary operands. One of the operands must be ST. Here are a few examples:

```
FADD    st,st(1)           ; ST = ST + ST(1)
FDIVR   st,st(3)           ; ST = ST(3) / ST
FMUL    st(2),st           ; ST(2) = ST(2) * ST
```

Register Pop. A *register pop* instruction is identical to a Register instruction, except that when it finishes, it pops ST off the stack. For example, the following FADDP instruction adds ST to ST(1) and places the result in ST(1). Then when ST is popped from the stack, the contents of ST(1) slide up into ST. We can visualize three separate steps:

```
FADDP  st(1),st
```

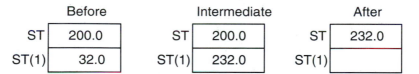

15.5.3 Example: Evaluating an Expression

Register pop instructions are well-suited to evaluating *postfix* arithmetic expressions. For example, to evaluate the following expression, we would multiply 6 by 2 and add 5 to the product:

```
6 2 * 5 +  <-- 60
```

Some well-known calculators use reverse polish notation, in which operands are keyed in before their operators. The algorithm for evaluating a postfix expressions is as follows:

•   When reading an operand from input, push it on the stack.

- When reading an operator from input, pop the two operands located at the top of the stack, perform the selected operation on the operands, and push the result back on the stack.

To implement this algorithm, we will write a short program, shown in Example 4, that pushes each operand on the coprocessor's internal stack and executes instructions that calculate the expression's value.

Example 4. Expression Evaluation Program.

```
title Expression Evaluation                    (expr.asm)

; Evaluate a reverse-polish expression:
;  6, 2 * 5 -

.model small
.8087                           ; enable 8087 instructions
.stack 100h
.data
op1    dd  6.0
op2    dd  2.0
op3    dd  5.0
result dd  ?

.code
main proc
    mov   ax,@data
    mov   ds,ax
    finit                       ; initialize coprocessor
    fld   op1                   ; push op1 onto the stack
    fld   op2                   ; push op2 onto the stack
    fmul                        ; ST(1) = ST(1) * ST; pop ST from stack
    fld   op3                   ; push op3 onto the stack
    fsub                        ; ST(1) = ST(1) - ST; pop ST from stack
    fwait                       ; wait until previous instruction finished
    fstp  result                ; pop stack into memory operand
    mov   ax,4C00h
    int   21h
main endp
end main
```

The FINIT instruction initializes the coprocessor and clears its internal stack. The FLD instruction pushes a floating-point number onto the top of the stack, causing any existing stack values to be pushed down. The FMUL instruction multiplies two stack operands, and FSUB subtracts one stack operand from another. FWAIT tells the main CPU to wait for the coprocessor to finish the previous instruction before the program continues to the next instruction. The FSTP instruction pops the top of the coprocessor stack into a memory operand. Table 13 shows the state of the register stack after each instruction has exectued.

Table 13. Register Stack Example.

Instruction	Register Stack
fld op1	ST = 6.0
fld op2	ST = 2.0 ST(1) = 6.0
fmul	ST = 12.0
fld op3	ST = 5.0 ST(1) = 12.0
fsub	ST = 7.0

15.5.4 Application: Payroll Calculation Program

The Payroll Calculation program in Example 5 shows how the 80x87 may be used to perform a simple payroll calculation. Input values used by the program are:

*   Overtime pay rate

*   Regular pay rate

*   Number of full-time hours (constant)

*   Totals hours worked by an employee

*   The program calculates the following values:

*   Regular hours worked

*   Overtime hours worked

*   Pay rate for each category

*   Total gross pay for the employee

A detailed description of individual instructions from the first part of the Payroll program appears in Table 14.

Table 14. Descriptions of Instructions, Payroll Program.

Instruction	Description	Coprocessor Stack
`finit`	Initalize the coprocessor.	
`fld regRate`	Push the regular pay rate into the ST register.	`ST = 5.0`
`fld regConst`	Push regConst into ST. This represents the standard 40 hours worked by an employee in one week.	`ST   = 40.0 (regConst)` `ST(1) = 5.0  (regRate)`

`fld totalHours`	Push the total hours worked by the employee into ST.	`ST   = 46 (totalHours)`
		`ST(1) = 40 (regConst)`
		`ST(2) = 5  (regRate)`

`fsub st,st(1)`	Subtract ST(1) from ST, and place the result in ST. (Subtract 40 from totalHours to see if there were any overtime hours.)	`ST   = 6   (otHours)`
		`ST(1) = 40 (regConst)`
		`ST(2) = 5  (regRate)`

`ftst`	Compare the overtime hours on ST to 0.	
`fstsw status`	Store the coprocessor status word in a memory variable named status.	
`fwait`	Tell the main processor to wait until the coprocessor has completed the last instruction. This prevents the 80x86 from accessing status too soon.	
`mov ax,status`	Load status into AX (coprocessor flags).	
`sahf`	Store AH into the CPU flags.	
`jle calcRegular`	If ZF = 1 or CF = 1, the overtime hours were <= 0, and overtime pay should not be calculated.	

Example 5. Payroll Calculation Program.

```
title Payroll Calculation Program        (payroll.asm)
.model small
.8087                         ; enable 8087 instructions
.stack 100h
.code
main proc
    mov   ax, @data           ; initialize DS
```

```
        mov     ds, ax
        finit                       ; initalize the 8087 coprocessor
        fld     regRate             ; push regRate into ST
        fld     regConst            ; push regConst into ST
        fld     totalHours          ; push totalHours into ST
        fsub    st,st(1)            ; subtract ST(1) from ST:
                                    ;  overtime hours = regConst - regRate
        ftst                        ; compare ST to zero
        fstsw   status              ; store coprocessor status word in
                                    ;   the memory variable status
        fwait                       ; tell main CPU to wait until
                                    ;   8087 has completed the FSTSW
        mov     ax, status          ; load status into AX
        sahf                        ; store AH into the 8088 flags
        jle     calcRegular         ; no overtime if hours <= zero

calcOvertime:                       ; overtime hours > zero
        fst     otHours             ; store ST to otHours
        fld     otRate              ; push otRate into ST
        fmul    st,st(3)            ; ST = ST * ST(3)(otRate * regRate)
        fmul                        ; multiply St by ST(1),
                                    ;   pop result into ST
        fst     grossPay            ; store ST in grossPay
        fstp    otpay               ; pop ST into otPay
        fldz                        ; push zero into ST

calcRegular:                        ; If this is reached following an overtime
                                    ;   pay calculation, then ST = 0.
        fadd                        ; ST = ST + ST(1)
        fst     reghours            ; store ST in regHours
        fmul                        ; ST =  ST * ST(1)
        fadd    grossPay            ; add grossPay to ST
        fstp    grossPay            ; pop ST into grossPay, final result
        mov     ax,4C00h            ; return to DOS
        int     21h
main endp

.data
status          dw  ?              ; holds 8087 status word
otRate          dd  1.5            ; input values:
regRate         dd  5.0
regConst        dd  40.0
```

```
totalHours dd  46.0
regHours   dd  0.0                 ; calculation results
otHours    dd  0.0
otPay      dd  0.0
grossPay   dd  0.0
netPay     dd  0.0
end main
```

15.6 REVIEW QUESTIONS

1. What is the percentage difference between the duration of a single clock tick in a 4.77MHz 8088 processor and a 300MHz Pentium?

2. Which processor interrupts the system 18.2 times per second? What are some of its practical uses?

3. The CPU contains two buses that transfer data and other information to memory, registers, and input-output ports: the data bus and the _____ bus.

4. Which part of the CPU fetches data from memory and decodes the addresses in instructions?

5. In the typical CPU *instruction cycle,* what happens after the instruction and its operands have been fetched from memory?

6. Which part of the CPU carries out arithmetic, logical, and shifting operations?

7. The three basic steps in the instruction cycle of a microcomputer CPU are fetch, _____, and execute.

8. Which part of the CPU calculates the addresses of memory operands?

9. When the CU locates an instruction in memory, it passes the instruction to the ALU in the *instruction queue*. What advantage is gained by doing this?

10. Using the DD, DQ, and DT directives, give examples of each of the following declarations:

    a. decimal short real

    b. encoded short real

    c. decimal long real

    d. encoded long real

    e. 10-byte real in BCD format

    f. 8-byte decimal integer

11. Explain the difference between an interrupt handler and a memory-resident program.

12. When a key is pressed on the keyboard, which hardware interrupt is executed?

13. When an interrupt handler finishes, how does the CPU resume execution wherever it was before the interrupt was triggered?

14. If your program is in the process of creating a disk file and you press a key on the keyboard, when do you think the key will be placed in the keyboard buffer—before or after the file has been created?

15. What do you imagine would happen if a system timer interrupt occurred between the second and third instructions shown here, running on an 8088 processor?

```
mov    ax,mystack
mov    ss,ax
mov    sp,100h
```

16. At which address is the interrupt vector for INT 10h stored?

17. The following statements are designed to modify the interrupt vector for INT 23h, the DOS Ctrl-Break handler. Write in any corrections that are needed:

```
push   ds                          ; save DS
mov    ax,@code                    ; init DS to code segment
mov    ds,ax
mov    ah,25h                      ; function: set interrupt vector
mov    ax,offset break_handler     ; DS:DX points to routine
int    21h
pop    ds                          ; restore DS
```

18. What is wrong with the following coprocessor instruction?

```
FIMUL AX
```

15.7 PROGRAMMING EXERCISES

1. Ctrl-Break Handler

Write your own Ctrl-Break handler program, modeled after the one presented in this chapter. Add the handler to one of your exercise solution programs from an earlier chapter. When the user presses Ctrl-Break, display a small window on the screen asking the user if they really want to halt the program.

2. Keyboard Redefinition

Write a memory-resident program that redefines your computer's keyboard. Your interrupt handler should begin by pushing the flags on the stack and calling the default INT 9 keyboard to read a keystroke from the keyboard port into the keyboard typeahead buffer. Then write assembly code that modifies each character placed in the buffer. For example, you could look up each keyboard scan code in a translate table and change it to another value.

3.   *Assembling MOV Instructions (I)*

Assemble the following MOV instructions by hand, using Table 6 to obtain the opcode. We have restricted these to immediate, register, and direct operands. Write the machine language for each instruction:

```
.data
val1  db  5
val2  dw  256
.code
mov  al,val1
mov  cx,val2
mov  dx,offset val1
mov  dl,2
mov  bx,1000h
```

When you are finished, type these instructions into an ASM source file, assemble it with TASM or MASM, and run it with a debugger. Check your machine code values with those generated by the assembler.

4.   *Assembling MOV Instructions (II)*

Assemble the following MOV instructions by hand, using Table 6 to obtain the opcode. The instructions contain ModR/M values. Write the machine language for each instruction:

```
mov   ax,bx
mov   al,[si]
mov   ds,ax
mov   [bx+si],ax
mov   dl,[bx+di+2]
mov   word ptr [bx],1000h
```

As in the previous exercise, compare your machine code to that generated by an assembler.

5.   *Machine Code Dissassembly*

Write a program that disassembles MOV instructions. Table 6 presented a list of opcode formats for the MOV instruction.

Step 1: Assemble a short program with Debug that contains a variety of MOV instructions with different addressing modes and registers. For example:

```
mov   dl,al
mov   ax,bx
mov   al,[si]
mov   bx,[0150]
mov   dx,[bx+si]
mov   [0152],dl
```

```
mov   dl,2
mov   ax,1234
```

Step 2: Write a program that reads the COM file and interprets each machine instruction. Display a listing similar to the following on the console:

```
1: opcode format: MOV  eb,rb
   source:        AL
   destination:   DL
2: opcode format: MOV  ew,rw
   source:        BX
   destination:   AX
3: opcode format: MOV  rb,eb
   source:        [SI]
   destination:   AL
   .
   .
(etc.)
```

You may want to store all the opcode formats in a table, along with their corresponding opcodes. As a new instruction is read from the input file, look its opcode up in the table. Then branch to the appropriate routine that decodes either a ModR/M byte or an immediate value.

6. *Update the DOS Time*

At the beginning of this chapter, the program in Example 1 contains a procedure that retrieves the time of day from the system's real-time clock. Write a program that does this and also updates the DOS time using INT 21h, function 2Dh.

7. *Timing Program Execution*

When evaluating the relative efficiency of a program, it is important to be able to time the execution of certain sections. Write routines that start and stop as many as five separate timers. When a timer is stopped, write the timer number and elapsed time to a disk file. When calling the routines, pass the timer number on the stack. For example:

```
mov   ax,1              ; start timer #1
push  ax
call  startTimer
   .
   .
mov   ax,1              ; stop timer #1
push  ax               ; write elapsed time to disk
call  stopTimer
```

8. *Dynamic Memory Allocation*

Write a program that calls the INT 21h function 48h to allocate a memory block. Create a large input buffer and read a file into the buffer. Check the file's size before allocating the memory block, and try to make the block as large as the input file.

9. *Expression Evaluation*

Rewrite and test the Expression Evaluation program from Example 4 with integer memory operands.

10. *Quadratic Equation Calculation*

Create a table containing the following doubleword real numbers, representing the values of *a*, *b*, *c*, and *x:*

```
dd  1.0, 2.0, 3.0, 4.0        ; a, b, c, x
dd  4.0, 3.0, 2.0, 1.5        ; a, b, c, x
```

Plug these values into the following quadratic equation and calculate the result:

$$ax^2 + bx + c$$

11. *Synthetic Division*

Write a program that carries out a single step of the synthetic division of a polynomial. Use a debugger to trace the program, and print a dump of the coefficients of the quotient at the end of the program. The program should be able to handle up to a sixth-degree polynomial. See Figure 5 for an explanation of synthetic division.

12. *Division (II)*

Enhance the Synthetic Division program written for Exercise 6 by carrying out the synthetic division until the polynomial is expressed as the product of linear factors, such as

```
(x - 2)² (x + 1) (3x - 5)
```

End Notes

[1] Credit for this example goes to Michael Abrash, "Bit Rotation Speeds," *PC Tech Journal,* Vol. 4, No. 5, May 1986.

[2] *From* Mazidi & Mazidi, *The 80x86 IBM PC & Compatible Computers*, 1995, Prentice-Hall, p. 387.

Figure 5. Synthetic Division Explanation.

Synthetic division provides an easy way to factor a polynomial by successively dividing it by the quantity $(x - a)$, where a is a constant. Let's perform the following division using 2 as a possible value for a:

$$\frac{3x^4 + 2x^3 - 16x^2 + 10x - 20}{(x - 2)}$$

(divisor)

```
 2 │  3   + 2   - 16  + 10   -  20   (coefficients of dividend)
   │      + 6   + 16  +  0   +  20   (divisor * previous coefficient)
   ─
      3   + 8   +  0  + 10   +   0   (coefficients of quotient)
```

The remainder is 0, so we know $(x - 2)$ is a factor, and the polynomial may now be expressed as follows:

$$(x - 2)\,(3x^3 + 8x^2 + 10)$$

Appendix A: Binary and Hexadecimal Tutorial

A.1 BINARY NUMBERS

Binary numbers are called *base 2* numbers because each digit can only be a 0 or 1. Computers store instructions and data as a series of binary digits, called bits. The binary digits are organized into groups of eight called bytes. Two bytes together make a word, although this number will vary, depending on the size of the computer.

Counting and Addition. If a carry results when two binary digits are added together, the carried digit is moved to the next highest position:

$$1 + 1 = 10$$

The following shows what happens if we add 1 to 10b and continue the process:

$$10 + 1 = 11$$
$$11 + 1 = 100$$
$$100 + 1 = 101$$

101 + 1 = 110

A.1.1   Addition Examples

When several digits are involved, the arithmetic always begins with the rightmost digits, carrying into the next highest position when necessary:

Add Binary 0011 and 0101:

```
              1      <-- Step 1: 1 + 1 = 0, carry generated
      0  0  1  1
    + 0  1  0  1
    ----------------
                 0
```

```
            1  1    <-- Step 2: 1 + 1 + 0 = 0, carry generated
      0  0  1  1
    + 0  1  0  1
    ----------------
              0  0
```

```
          1  1  1    <-- Step 3: 1 + 0 + 1 = 0, carry generated
      0  0  1  1
    + 0  1  0  1
    ----------------
            0  0  0
```

```
          1  1  1    <-- Step 4: 1 + 0 + 0 = 1, no carry generated
      0  0  1  1
    + 0  1  0  1
    ----------------
      1  0  0  0   (result)
```

Add Binary 0011 and 0011:

```
              1    <-- Step 1:  1 + 1 = 0, carry generated
      0  0  1  1
    + 0  0  1  1
    ----------------
                 0
```

```
            1  1     <-- Step 2:  1 + 1 + 1 = 1, carry generated
         0  0  1  1
     +   0  0  1  1
     ----------------
               1  0


            1  1     <-- Step 3:  1 + 0 + 0 = 1, no carry
         0  0  1  1
     +   0  0  1  1
     ----------------
            1  0  0


            1  1     <-- Step 4:  0 + 0 = 0, no carry
         0  0  1  1
     +   0  0  1  1
     ----------------
         0  1  1  0     (result)
```

A.1.2   Binary to Decimal Conversion

To convert a binary number to its decimal equivalent, evaluate each digit position as a power of 2. The decimal value of 2^0 is 1, 2^1 is 2, 2^2 is 4, and so on. For example, the binary number 1111 is equal to 15 decimal:

```
binary: 1 1 1 1

1 * 2³     8
1 * 2²   + 4
1 * 2¹   + 2
1 * 2⁰   + 1
Sum:     = 15
```

Decimal Value of Binary 1010. In the binary number 1010, bits 1 and 3 are set, so we sum 8 and 2 to produce 10 decimal:

```
binary: 1 0 1 0

1 * 2³     8
0 * 2²   + 0
1 * 2¹   + 2
0 * 2⁰   + 0
Sum:     = 10
```

Table 1. Powers of 2 as Decimal Values.

2^n	Decimal Value	2^n	Decimal Value
2^0	1	2^8	256
2^1	2	2^9	512
2^2	4	2^{10}	1024
2^3	8	2^{11}	2048
2^4	16	2^{12}	4096
2^5	32	2^{13}	8,192
2^6	64	2^{14}	16,384
2^7	128	2^{15}	32,768

At first glance, it would seem that only small numbers could be represented in binary. When you include 16 bits in a number, the values increase quickly. If you add the values for all bit positions in Table 1, the total is 65,535.

Decimal Value of Binary 11001010. We can refer to Table 1 to find the decimal value of an 8-bit binary number. The following bit positions are added together (the lowest digit in a binary number is bit 0): bits 7, 6, 3, and 1:

$$2^7 + 2^6 + 2^3 + 2^1 = 128 + 64 + 8 + 2 = 202$$

Decimal Value of Binary 11111111. Binary 11111111 turns out to be the sum of all digit positions between 0 and 7, or $2^7 + 2^6 + 2^5 ... + 2^0$. The decimal value is 255, the largest number that can be stored in a single byte.

Decimal Value of Binary 1000000010000000. Bit 15 is set (2^{15}), and bit 7 is set (2^7). The sum of 32,768 and 128 is 32,896.

Decimal Value of Binary 1111111111111111. This is the largest possible unsigned 16-bit number. One way to find its decimal value is to add up all the bit positions using the Powers of 2 table:

$$2^{15} + 2^{14} + 2^{13} + 2^{12} ... + 2^0 = 65,535 \qquad (32,767 + 16,384 + 8,192 + 4,092 ... + 1)$$

An easier way to determine this value is to take the value of 2^{16} and subtract 1: $2^{16} - 1 = 65,535$

A.1.3   Decimal to Binary Conversion

When debugging or testing assembly language programs, you often need to convert decimal values into binary and compare them to the actual contents of memory and registers.

Method 1: Divide by Decreasing Powers of 2. You can convert from decimal to binary by dividing the decimal value by powers of 2. Suppose you would like to find the binary equivalent of 76. The largest power of 2 that fits into 76 is 64 (2^6); therefore, bit 6 in the binary value is set:

```
0 1 0 0 0 0 0 0  =  64
```

If we subtract 64 from 76, the difference is 12. The largest power of 2 that fits into 12 is 8 (2^3); therefore, bit 3 is also set:

```
                        64
                       + 8
      0 1 0 0 1 0 0 0  <-- 72
```

If we subtract 72 from 76, the difference is 4, which is 2^2. Therefore, bit 2 is also set. The final binary number is 01001100b. Therefore, we were able to convert 76 to binary by dividing successively smaller powers of 2 into the decimal number. The steps may be listed as follows:

```
72 / 64  =  1,  remainder  12
12 / 8   =  1,  remainder   4
 4 / 4   =  1,  remainder   0
```

As soon as the remainder equals 0, we stop. This method involves some trial and error, yet it works well when conversions are done by hand.

Method 2: Repeatedly Divide by 2. Another way to convert a decimal number to binary is to divide the number by 2; then, using the quotient, divide it by 2. Using this quotient, divide it by 2, and so on. The remainders from the division steps comprise the binary digits we want to produce. Let's use this method to find the binary equivalent of 76:

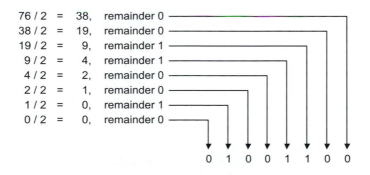

As we see, the division was carried out eight times. The first remainder is placed in bit position 0. This method is ideally suited to a looping algorithm, but is time-consuming when performed by hand.

A.2   HEXADECIMAL NUMBERS

Hexadecimal numbers are base 16 numbers, containing digits from 0 to 9 and letters from A to F. Each digit value is shown here:

```
hexadecimal:     0 1 2 3 4 5 6 7 8 9  A  B  C  D  E  F
decimal:         0 1 2 3 4 5 6 7 8 9 10 11 12 13 14 15
```

Hexadecimal numbers are used almost exclusively when representing computer storage and addresses. Large values may be stored in just a few digits, and the digits correspond closely to binary numbers. We will use the same notation recognized by MASM and TASM: hexadecimal numbers are followed by a lowercase **h.** For example, 45h is a hexadecimal number, while 45 is a decimal number.

A.2.1   Binary to Hexadecimal Conversion

Table 2 shows how each sequence of four binary bits can be translated into a single hexadecimal digit. Large binary numbers may easily be converted to hexadecimal if you convert four binary bits at a time. With a little practice, the conversion can be performed mentally. For example, the binary number 1010101110010111100001101110001 is represented by the hexadecimal number AB9786E5:

```
 A    B    9    7    8    6    E    5
1010 1011 1001 0111 1000 0110 1110 0101
```

Converting a large hexadecimal number to binary is also easy because each hexadecimal digit corresponds to four binary bits. For example:

Table 2. Binary to Hexadecimal Conversion.

Binary	Hex	Binary	Hex
0000	0	1000	8
0001	1	1001	9
0010	2	1010	A
0011	3	1011	B
0100	4	1100	C
0101	5	1101	D
0110	6	1110	E
0111	7	1111	F

```
8A2640 = 1000 1010 0010 0110 0100 0000
           8    A    2    6    4    0
```

More examples are listed here:

```
0AF6h = 0000101011110110
D58Ch = 1101010110001100
F13Bh = 1111000100111011
```

A.2.2 Hexadecimal to Decimal Conversion

Each digit position in a hexadecimal number corresponds to a power of 16, shown in Table 3. For example, using this table, we can calculate the decimal equivalent of 2412h using the following steps:

1. The highest digit in the number 2,412 is 2, located in digit position 3. Add the value 8,192 to the total.

2. The next digit is 4, in digit position 2. Add the value 1,024 to the total.

3. The next digit is 1, in digit position 1. Add the value 16 to the total.

4. The next digit is 2, in digit position 0. Add the value 2 to the total.

5. The total (8,192 + 1,024 + 16 + 2) is 9,234, the decimal equivalent of 2412h.

Table 3. Hexadecimal to Decimal Conversion Table.

Digit	3	2	1	0
1	4,096	256	16	1
2	8,192	512	32	2
3	12,288	768	48	3
4	16,384	1,024	64	4
5	20,480	1,280	80	5
6	24,576	1,536	96	6
7	28,672	1,792	112	7
8	32,768	2,048	128	8
9	36,864	2,304	144	9
A	40,960	2,560	160	10
B	45,056	2,816	176	11
C	49,152	3,072	192	12
D	53,348	3,328	208	13
E	57,344	3,584	224	14
F	61,440	3,840	240	15

A.2.3   Hexadecimal Digit Position Values

Converting numbers from hexadecimal to decimal is similar to converting from binary to decimal. One method involves knowing the values of each hexadecimal digit position. To do this, multiply each digit by its digit position value. Using Table 3 as a guide, we can see that 42h is the sum of decimal 64 and 2:

```
    64       (4 * 16)
  + 2        (2 * 1)
  ------------------
    66       decimal
```

Example: Convert 146h to Decimal. We multiply 1 by 256, 4 by 16, and 6 by 1. The sum of these operations is 326:

```
  256        (1 * 256)
   64        (4 * 16)
  + 6        (6 * 1)
  -----------------
  326        decimal
```

Example: Convert 3BA4h to Decimal. Before multiplying each digit by its position value, remember that the hexadecimal digit "B" is equal to 11 and the digit "A" is equal to 10:

```
  12,288     (3  * 4,096)
   2,816     (11 * 256)
     160     (10 * 16)
  +    4     (4  * 1)
  ---------------------
  15,268     decimal
```

A.2.4   Decimal to Hexadecimal Conversion

Successive Division by 16. A good way to convert from decimal to hexadecimal is to divide the number by 16; take the quotient of this and divide it by 16; take the next quotient and divide by 16, and so on. The remainder from each division operation is converted to a hexadecimal digit. Let's use this method to find the hexadecimal equivalent of decimal 48:

```
  48 / 16 =  3, remainder 0
   3 / 16 =  0, remainder 3
  --------------
  Hexadecimal:          30
```

Example: Convert 326 to Hexadecimal. Divide 326 by 16; then divide each subsequent quotient by 16. Each remainder becomes a digit in the hexadecimal result:

```
326 / 16 =  20, remainder 6
 20 / 16 =   1, remainder 4
  1 / 16 =   0, remainder 1
--------------
Hexadecimal:            1 4 6
```

Example: Convert 15,268 to Hexadecimal. This is the inverse of a conversion we performed earlier when 3BA4h was converted to 15,268 decimal:

```
15,268 / 16 = 954, remainder 4
   954 / 16 = 59,  remainder 10 (A)
    59 / 16 = 3,   remainder 11 (B)
     3 / 16 = 0,   remainder 3
-----------------
Hexadecimal:            3 B A 4
```

A.3   ARITHMETIC

The CPU performs all arithmetic in binary, so it is particularly important to be able to check calculations manually when debugging programs. In this section we focus on binary and hexadecimal arithmetic.

A.3.1   Signed and Unsigned Numbers

Binary numbers may be either signed or unsigned. The CPU performs arithmetic and comparison operations for both types. Let's use an 8-bit number as an example. If unsigned, all 8 bits contribute to the number's value, as with binary 11111111:

```
1 1 1 1 1 1 1 1   =   255
```

Therefore, 255 (hexadecimal FF, binary 11111111) is the largest value that may be stored in a single byte. The largest 16-bit value that may be stored in a word (2 bytes) is 65,535:

```
1111111111111111   =   65,535
```

A signed number is used when an arithmetic operation might involve a negative number. A signed number may be either negative or positive, as indicated by the number's highest bit. If the bit = 1, the number is negative:

The positive number in this example is +10 decimal. What about the negative number: Is it − 10? Negative values are not as easy to recognize. Instead, they are stored in *twos complement* format for machine efficiency reasons.

A.3.2   Twos Complement Notation

When a signed number has its highest bit set, the number must be converted back into unsigned binary before we can determine its magnitude its value. To find the *twos complement* of a number, do two things: Reverse all bits, and then add 1 to the result. Using the signed binary number 11111010 as an example, we can determine that its value is –6:

```
  1 1 1 1 1 0 1 0    <-- signed binary value
  0 0 0 0 0 1 0 1    <-- reverse all bits
+               1    <-- add 1
-----------------
  0 0 0 0 0 1 1 0    <-- unsigned value =  6
```

We add the negative sign to the result, which becomes –6.

Maximum and minimum signed values. A signed byte uses only 7 bits to represent the number's magnitude, so the largest possible value is equal to +127, or 7Fh. A 16-bit signed number has a maximum value of +32,767, or 7FFFh:

```
Byte:     0 1 1 1 1 1 1 1              = +127
Word:     0 1 1 1 1 1 1 1 1 1 1 1 1 1 1 1    = +32,767
```

The smallest negative value an 8-bit byte may have is –128, and the smallest negative value a 16-bit word may have is –32,768:

```
Byte:     1 0 0 0 0 0 0 0              = -128
Word:     1 0 0 0 0 0 0 0 0 0 0 0 0 0 0 0    = -32,768
```

Example: Convert Signed Binary 11111111 to Decimal. To convert binary 11111111 to decimal, find the twos complement and then convert it to decimal. Binary 11111111 is actually the same as decimal –1:

```
11111111
00000000    <--  reverse all bits
+       1    <--  add 1
--------
00000001    <--  unsigned value = 1
```

Example: Convert Signed Binary 11101100 to Decimal. To convert binary 11101100 (-20) to decimal, find the twos complement (00010100) and then convert it to decimal (20):

```
11101100
00010011    <-- reverse all bits
```

```
+       1       <-- add 1
--------
00010100        <-- unsigned value =  20
```

Example: Convert Signed 9Bh to Decimal. We assume that the hexadecimal number 9Bh is negative because its sign bit is set:

10011011

To convert it to decimal, find its twos complement. The decimal value is −101:

```
10011011 = 9Bh
01100100 = 64h
+        1
----------
01100101 = 65h   (101)
```

Hexadecimal Twos Complement. The ones complement of a hexadecimal number may be found by subtracting each digit from 15. Try this using 9Bh:

```
15 - 9 = 6
15 - B = 4
```

This yields 64h. To find the twos complement of the original number, add 1 to 64h, giving 65h. Thus, the twos complement of 9Bh is 65h.

What is the twos complement of 6A295CD4h? The ones complement is 95D6A32Bh, which is found by subtracting each original digit from 15. Adding 1 to this produces 95D6A32Ch. This shows that larger numbers present no special difficulty.

A.3.3   Binary Subtraction

Before subtracting one binary number from another, it must be converted to its twos complement. Then the two operands may be added together. Suppose you want to subtract 00010000b from 00011100b. Intuitively, we understand that this is the same as 28 − 16 = 12. The twos complement of 16 is 11110000b. We add this to 28:

```
  00011100        +28
+ 11110000        + -16
------------------
  00001100         12
```

A.3.4   Hexadecimal Addition and Subtraction

When we add two hexadecimal numbers, each digit of the first number is added to the corresponding digit of the second. As long as no carry is generated, the addition is simple. Each value in the following example is in hexadecimal:

```
  0 4 A 0
+ 3 6 7 5
----------
  3 B 1 5
```

When two digits generate a value larger than 15, a carry is generated. For example, 0Ah plus 7 equals 17: Divide 17 by the hexadecimal number base (16) and carry the quotient (1) to the next highest digit position. The remainder is placed in the lowest digit position of the result, which is 11h:

```
    A
+   7
----
  1 1
```

Example: Add 3BA8h and 02B5h. First, 8 + 5 = 13 (D); then A + B = 21, which requires a carry; then 21 / 16 = 1, remainder 5. Carry the 1, and place the 5 in the current digit position. Next, 1 + B + 2 = Eh. Finally, 3 + 0 = 3:

```
  3 B A 8
+ 0 2 B 5
----------
  3 E 5 D
```

Example: Subtract 0009h from 3E62h. Fortunately, unsigned hexadecimal numbers may be subtracted directly without having to use twos complement notation. In the following example, a borrow was generated in the first digit position, because 9 is greater than 2. In a base-16 numbering system, a borrow returns a value of 16. We can interpret the subtraction in the first digit position as 18 − 9 = 9:

```
      -1
  3 E 6 2
- 0 0 0 9
----------
  3 E 5 9
```

A.4 REVIEW QUESTIONS

1. What is the largest unsigned decimal value that may be stored in (a) a single byte? (b) a single word?

2. Convert the following decimal numbers to hexadecimal:

   a. 26   b. 435

3. Convert the following decimal numbers to 16-bit binary:

   a. 4,096   d. 514
   b. −128   e. −1
   c. 256   f. −32,768

4. Convert the following hexadecimal numbers to binary:

   a. 6AFCh   b. 204Eh   c. BDCAh

5. Convert the following unsigned hexadecimal numbers to decimal:

   a. 100h   b. 06BCh

6. What is the hexadecimal representation of the following sequence of binary bits?

   1011 1000 1010 1111

7. Convert the following unsigned binary numbers to decimal:

   a. 00010110   b. 11010101   c. 10001000   d. 01111100

8. Convert each signed 16-bit binary number to decimal:

   a. 1111111111111110   b. 1111111111111000

9. Convert each signed binary number to its twos complement, and write the decimal value of the latter:

   a. 11110101   b. 00011010   c. 10000000   d. 11111111

10. Convert the following signed hexadecimal values to decimal:

    a. EFFFh   b. 0200h   c. B6DCh   d. FFFFh

11. Assemble and execute the following instructions, using Debug. Assuming both numbers are signed, state the contents of AL after the second instruction, and explain what has happened. Use decimal values in your explanation:

```
mov    al,51
add    al,FE
```

A.5   ANSWERS TO REVIEW QUESTIONS

1. a. 255   b. 65,535

2. a. 1Ah   b. 01B3h

3.   a. 00010000 00000000b   d. 00000010 00000010b

      b. 11111111 10000000b   e. 11111111 11111111b

      c. 00000001 00000000b   f. 10000000 00000000b

4.   a. 01101010 11111100b   c. 10111101 11001010b

      b. 00100000 01001110b

5.   a. 256   b. 1724

6.   B8AFh

7.   a. 22   b. 213   c. 136   d. 124

8.   a. FFFEh = –2   b. FFF8h = –8

9.   a. 00001011 = 11

      b. 11100110 = –26

      c. 10000000 = 128

      d. 00000001 = 1

10.   Convert hexadecimal values to decimal:

      a.   The twos complement of EFFFh is 1001h, which, when converted to decimal, is
           4,097. The sign bit was set, so the value is –4,097.

      b.   The number 0200h is positive, so we don't need to find its twos complement. Its
           decimal value is 512.

      c.   The twos complement of B6DCh is 4924h, which, when converted to decimal, is
           18,724. The sign bit was set, so the value is –18,724.

      d.   The twos complement of FFFFh is 0001h, which translates to a decimal value of –
           1.

11.   First, 51h = decimal 81, and 0FEh = decimal –2. Therefore the sum of these should be 79,
      or 4Fh. When you run the program, the answer in AL is 4Fh, and the Carry flag is set
      because the sum of 51h and FEh is greater than 8 bits. The Carry flag value is irrelevant,
      because the numbers are signed.

Appendix B: Using Debug

B.1   INTRODUCING DEBUG

As you begin to learn assembly language programming, the importance of using a program called a *debugger* cannot be stressed too much. A debugger displays the contents of memory and lets you view registers and variables as they change. You can step through a program one line at a time (called *tracing*), making it easier to find logic errors. In this appendix, we offer a tutorial on using the debug.exe program that is supplied with both DOS and Windows (located in the \Windows\Command directory). From now on, we will just call this program *Debug*. Later, you will probably want to switch to a more sophisticated debugger such as Microsoft CodeView or Borland Turbo Debugger. But for now, Debug is the perfect tool for writing short programs and getting acquainted with the Intel microprocessor.

You can use Debug to test assembler instructions, try out new programming ideas, or to carefully step through your programs. It takes supreme overconfidence to write an assembly language program and run it directly from DOS the first time! If you forget to match pushes and pops, for example, a return from a subroutine will branch to an unexpected location. Any call or jump to a location outside your program will almost surely cause the program to crash. For this reason, you would be wise to run any new program you've written in Debug. Trace the program one line at a time, and watch the stack pointer (SP) very closely as you step through the program, and note any unusual changes to the CS and IP registers. Particularly when CS takes on a new value, you should be suspicious that your program has branched into the *Twilight Zone*®.

Debugging functions. Some of the most rudimentary functions that any debugger can perform are the following:

- Assemble short programs

- View a program's source code along with its machine code

- View the CPU registers and flags

- Trace or execute a program, watching variables for changes

- Enter new values into memory

- Search for binary or ASCII values in memory

- Move a block of memory from one location to another

- Fill a block of memory

- Load and write disk files and sectors

Many commercial debuggers are available for Intel microprocessors, ranging widely in sophistication and cost: CodeView, Periscope, Atron, Turbo Debugger, SYMDEB, Codesmith-86, and Advanced-Trace-86, to mention just a few. Of these, Debug is the simplest. The basic principles learned using Debug may then be applied to nearly any other debugger.

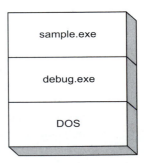

Debug is called an *assembly level* debugger because it displays only assembly mnemonics and machine instructions. Even if you use it to debug a compiled C++ program, for example, you will not see the program's source code. Instead, you will see a disassembly of the program's machine instructions.

To trace or execute a machine language program with Debug, type the name of the program as a command line parameter. For example, to debug the program sample.exe, you would type the following command line at the DOS prompt:

```
debug sample.exe
```

If we could picture DOS memory after typing this command, we would see DOS loaded in the lowest area, debug.exe loaded above DOS, and the program sample.exe loaded above Debug. In this way, several programs are resident in memory at the same time. DOS retains control over the execution of Debug, and Debug controls the execution of sample.exe.

Printing a Debugging Session (local printer only). If you have a printer attached directly to your computer, you can get a printed copy of everything you're doing during a debugging session by pressing the Ctrl-PrtScrn keys. This command is a toggle, so it can be typed a second time to turn the printer output off.

Printing a Debugging Session (network printer). If your computer is attached to a network and there is a printer on the network, printing a debugging session is a bit challenging. The best way we've found is to prepare a script file containing all the debug commands you plan to type. Run Debug, telling it to read its input from the script file, and have Debug send the output to another file. Then, print the output file in the same way you usually print on the network. In Windows, for example, the output file can be loaded into *Notepad* and printed from there. See the section later in this appendix entitled *Using Script Files with Debug.*

Using the Mark and Copy Operations in a DOS Window. Under Windows, when you run Debug in a window, a toolbar has commands that you can use to mark a section of the window, copy it to the clipboard, and paste it into some other application (such as Notepad or Word):

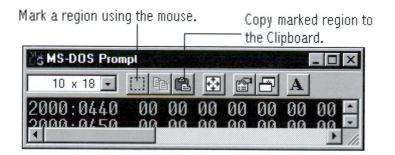

B.2   DEBUG COMMAND SUMMARY

Debug commands may be divided into four categories: program creation/debugging, memory manipulation, miscellaneous, and input-output:

Program Creation and Debugging

A   Assemble a program using instruction mnemonics

G   Execute the program currently in memory

R   Display the contents of registers and flags

P   Proceed past an instruction, procedure, or loop

T   Trace a single instruction

U   Disassemble memory into assembler mnemonics

Memory Manipulation

C   Compare one memory range with another

D   Dump (display) the contents of memory

E   Enter bytes into memory

F   Fill a memory range with a single value

M   Move bytes from one memory range to another

S   Search a memory range for specific value(s)

Miscellaneous

H   Perform hexadecimal addition and subtraction

Q   Quit Debug and return to DOS

Input-Output

I   Input a byte from a port

L   Load data from disk

O   Send a byte to a port

N   Create a filename for use by the L and W commands

W   Write data from memory to disk

Default Values. When Debug is first loaded, the following defaults are in effect:

1. All segment registers are set to the bottom of free memory, just above the debug.exe program.

2. IP is set to 0100h.

3. Debug reserves 256 bytes of stack space at the end of the current segment.

4. All of available memory is allocated (reserved).

5. BX:CX are set to the length of the current program or file.

6. The flags are set to the following values: NV (Overflow flag clear), UP (Direction flag = up), EI (interrupts enabled), PL (Sign flag = positive), NZ (Zero flag clear), NA (Auxiliary Carry flag clear), PO (odd parity), NC (Carry flag clear).

B.2.1 Command Parameters

Debug's command prompt is a hyphen (–). Commands may be typed in either uppercase or lowercase letters, in any column. A command may be followed by one or more parameters. A comma or space may be used to separate any two parameters. The standard command parameters are explained here.

Address. A complete segment-offset address may be given, or just an offset. The segment portion may be a hexadecimal number or register name. For example:

```
F000:100        Segment, offset
DS:200          Segment register, offset
0AF5            Offset
```

Filespec. A file specification, made up of a drive designation, filename, and extension. At a minimum, a filename must be supplied. Examples are:

```
b:prog1.com
c:\asm\progs\test.com
file1
```

List. One or more byte or string values:

```
10,20,30,40
'A','B',50
```

Range. A *range* refers to a span of memory, identified by addresses in one of two formats. In Format 1, if the second address is omitted, it defaults to a standard value. In Format 2, the value following the letter L is the number of bytes to be processed by the command. A range cannot be greater than 10000h (65,536):

Syntax	**Examples**
Format 1: address [,address]	100,500 CS:200,300 200
Format 2: address L [value]	100 L 20 *(Refers to the 20h bytes starting at location 100.)*

Sector. A sector consists of a starting sector number and the number of sectors to be loaded or written. You can access logical disk sectors Using the L (load) and W (write) commands.

String. A string is a sequence of characters enclosed in single or double quotes. For example:

```
'COMMAND'
"File cannot be opened."
```

Value. A value consists of a 1- to 4-character hexadecimal number. For example:

```
3A
3A6F
```

B.3   INDIVIDUAL COMMANDS

This section describes the most common Debug commands. A good way to learn them is to sit at the computer while reading this tutorial and experiment with each command.

B.3.1   ? (Help)

Press ? at the Debug prompt to see a list of all commands. For example:

Figure 1. Debug's List of Commands.

```
assemble              A [address]
compare               C range address
dump                  D [range]
enter                 E address [list]
fill                  F range list
go                    G [=address] [addresses]
hex                   H value1 value2
input                 I port
load                  L [address] [drive] [firstsector] [number]
move                  M range address
name                  N [pathname] [arglist]
output                O port byte
proceed               P [=address] [number]
quit                  Q
register              R [register]
search                S range list
trace                 T [=address] [value]
unassemble            U [range]
write                 W [address] [drive] [firstsector] [number]
```

B.3.2   A (Assemble)

Assemble a program into machine language. Command formats:

```
A
A address
```

If only the offset portion of *address* is supplied, it is assumed to be an offset from CS. Here are examples:

Example	Description
A 100	Assemble at CS:100h.
A	Assemble from the current location.
A DS:2000	Assemble at DS:2000h.

When you press Enter at the end of each line, Debug prompts you for the next line of input. Each input line starts with a segment-offset address. To terminate input, press the Enter key on a blank line. For example:

```
-a 100
5514:0100 mov ah,2
5514:0102 mov dl,41
5514:0104 int 21
5514:0106
```

(bold text is typed by the programmer)

B.3.3   C (Compare)

The C command compares bytes between a specified range with the same number of bytes at a target address. Command format:

```
C range address
```

For example, the bytes between DS:0100 and DS:0105 are compared to the bytes at DS:0200:

```
C 100 105 200
```

The following is displayed by Debug:

```
1F6E:0100  74  00  1F6E:0200
1F6E:0101  15  C3  1F6E:0201
1F6E:0102  F6  0E  1F6E:0202
1F6E:0103  C7  1F  1F6E:0203
1F6E:0104  20  E8  1F6E:0204
1F6E:0105  75  D2  1F6E:0205
```

B.3.4 D (Dump)

The D command displays memory on the screen as single bytes in both hexadecimal and ASCII. Command formats:

```
D
D address
D range
```

If no address or range is given, the location begins where the last D command left off, or at location DS:0 if the command is being typed for the first time. If *address* is specified, it consists of either a segment-offset address or just a 16-bit offset. *Range* consists of the beginning and ending addresses to dump.

Example	Description
D F000:0	Segment-offset
D ES:100	Segment register-offset
D 100	Sffset

The default segment is DS, so the segment value may be left out unless you want to dump an offset from another segment location. A range may be given, telling Debug to dump all bytes within the range:

D 150 15A   **(Dump DS:0150 through 015A)**

Other segment registers or absolute addresses may be used, as the following examples show:

Example	Description
D	Dump 128 bytes from the last referenced location.
D SS:0 5	Dump the bytes at offsets 0-5 from SS.
D 915:0	Dump 128 bytes at offset zero from segment 0915h.
D 0 200	Dump offsets 0-200 from DS.
D 100 L 20	Dump 20h bytes, starting at offset 100h from DS.

Memory Dump Example. The following figure shows an example of a memory dump. The numbers at the left are the segment and offset address of the first byte in each line. The next 16 pairs of digits are the hexadecimal contents of each byte. The characters to the right are the ASCII representation of each byte. This dump appears to be machine language instructions, rather than displayable characters.

Dump of offsets 0100h through 017Fh in COMMAND.COM:

```
-D 100
1CC0:0100   83 7E A4 01 72 64 C7 46-F8 01 00 8B 76 F8 80 7A   .~$.rdGFx...vx.z
1CC0:0110   A5 20 73 49 80 7A A5 0E-75 06 C6 42 A5 0A EB 3D   % sI.z%.u.FB%.k=
1CC0:0120   8B 76 F8 80 7A A5 08 74-0C 80 7A A5 07 74 06 80   .vx.z%.t..z%.t..
1CC0:0130   7A A5 0F 75 28 FF 46 FA-8B 76 FA 8B 84 06 F6 8B   z%.u(.Fz.vz...v.
1CC0:0140   7E F8 3A 43 A5 75 0C 03-36 A8 F4 8B 44 FF 88 43   ~x:C%u..6(t.D..C
1CC0:0150   A5 EB 0A A1 06 F6 32 E4-3B 46 FA 77 D8 8B 46 F8   %k.!.v2d;FzwX.Fx
1CC0:0160   40 89 46 F8 48 3B 46 A4-75 A1 A1 06 F6 32 E4 3B   @.FxH;F$u!!.v2d;
1CC0:0170   46 FC B9 00 00 75 01 41-A1 A8 F4 03 46 FC 8B 16   F|9..u.A!(t.F|..
```

The following dump shows a different part of COMMAND.COM. Because memory at this point contains a list of command names, the ASCII dump is more interesting:

```
-D 3AC0
1CD6:3AC0   05 45 58 49 53 54 EA 15-00 04 44 49 52 01 FA 09   .EXISTj...DIR.z.
1CD6:3AD0   07 52 45 4E 41 4D 45 01-B2 0C 04 52 45 4E 01 B2   .RENAME.2..REN.2
1CD6:3AE0   0C 06 45 52 41 53 45 01-3D 0C 04 44 45 4C 01 3D   ..ERASE.=..DEL.=
1CD6:3AF0   0C 05 54 59 50 45 01 EF-0C 04 52 45 4D 00 04 01   ..TYPE.o..REM...
1CD6:3B00   05 43 4F 50 59 01 CC 1A-06 50 41 55 53 45 00 1F   .COPY.L..PAUSE..
1CD6:3B10   13 05 44 41 54 45 00 38-18 05 54 49 4D 45 00 CE   ..DATE.8..TIME.N
1CD6:3B20   18 04 56 45 52 00 57 0E-04 56 4F 4C 01 C8 0D 03   ..VER.W..VOL.H..
1CD6:3B30   43 44 01 A6 12 06 43 48-44 49 52 01 A6 12 03 4D   CD.&..CHDIR.&..M
1CD6:3B40   44 01 D9 12 06 4D 4B 44-49 52 01 D9 12 03 52 44   D.Y..MKDIR.Y..RD
1CD6:3B50   01 0E 13 06 52 4D 44 49-52 01 0E 13 06 42 52 45   ....RMDIR....BRE
1CD6:3B60   41 4B 00 92 17 07 56 45-52 49 46 59 00 C7 17 04   AK....VERIFY.G..
1CD6:3B70   53 45 54 00 0F 10 07 50-52 4F 4D 50 54 00 FA 0F   SET....PROMPT.z.
1CD6:3B80   05 50 41 54 48 00 A0 0F-05 45 58 49 54 00 C9 11   .PATH. .EXIT.I.
1CD6:3B90   05 43 54 54 59 01 F7 11-05 45 43 48 4F 00 59 17   .CTTY.w..ECHO.Y.
1CD6:3BA0   05 47 4F 54 4F 00 96 16-06 53 48 49 46 54 00 56   .GOTO....SHIFT.V
1CD6:3BB0   16 03 49 46 00 50 15 04-46 4F 52 00 68 14 04 43   ..IF.P..FOR.h..C
1CD6:3BC0   4C 53 00 53 12 00 00 00-00 00 00 00 00 00 00 00   LS.S...........
```

B.3.5   E (Enter)

The E command places individual bytes in memory. You must supply a starting memory location where the values will be stored. If only an offset value is entered, the offset is assumed to be from DS. Otherwise, a 32-bit address may be entered or another segment register may be used. Command formats are:

```
E address
```
                    Enter new byte value at *address*.

E *address list*   Replace the contents of one or more bytes starting at the specified *address*, with the values contained in the *list*.

To begin entering hexadecimal or character data at DS:100, type:

    E 100

Press the space bar to advance to the next byte, and press the Enter key to stop. To enter a string into memory starting at location CS:100, type:

    E CS:100 "This is a string."

B.3.6   F (Fill)

The F command fills a range of memory with a single value or list of values. The range must be specified as two offset addresses or segment-offset addresses. Command format:

    F *range list*

Here are some examples. The commas are optional:

Example	Description
F 100 500,' '	Fill locations 100 through 500 with spaces.
F CS:300 CS:1000,FF	Fill locations CS:300 through 1000 with hex FFh.
F 100 L 20 'A'	Fill 20h bytes with the letter 'A', starting at location 100.

B.3.7   G (Go)

Execute the program in memory. You can also specify a breakpoint, causing the program to stop at a given address. Command formats:

    G
    G *breakpoint*
    G = *startAddr breakpoint*
    G = startAddr *breakpoint1 breakpoint2 ...*

Breakpoint is a 16- or 32-bit address at which the processor should stop, and *startAddr* is an optional starting address for the processor. If no breakpoints are specified, the program runs until it stops by itself and returns to Debug. Up to 10 breakpoints may be specified on the same command line. Examples:

Example	Description
G	Execute from the current location to the end of the program.
G 50	Execute from the current location and stop before the instruction at offset CS:50.
G=10 50	Begin execution at CS:10 and stop before the instruction at offset CS:50.

B.3.8 H (Hexarithmetic)

The H command performs addition and subtraction on two hexadecimal numbers. The command format is:

```
H value1 value2
```

For example, the hexadecimal values 1A and 10 are added and subtracted:

```
H 1A 10
2A 0A                    (displayed by Debug)
```

B.3.9 I (Input)

The I command inputs a byte from a specified input/output port and displays the value in hexadecimal. The command format is:

```
I port
```

Where *port* is a port number between 0 and FFFF. For example, we input a byte from port 3F8 (one of the COM1 ports), and Debug returns a value of 00:

```
-I 3F8
00
```

B.3.10 L (Load)

The L command loads a file (or logical disk sectors) into memory at a given address. To read a file, you must first initialize its name with the N (Name) command. If *address* is omitted, the file is loaded at CS:100. Debug sets BX and CX to the number of bytes read. Command format:

```
L
L address
L address drive firstsector number
```

The first format, with no parameters, implies that you want to read from a file into memory at CS:0100. (Use the N command to name the file.) The second format also reads from a named file, but lets you specify the target address. The third format loads sectors from a disk drive,

Table 1. Examples of the Load Instruction.

Example	Description
L	Load named file into memory at CS:0100
L DS:0200	Load named file into memory at DS:0200
L 100 2 A 5	Load five sectors from drive C, starting at logical sector number 0Ah.
L 100 0 0 2	Load two sectors into memory at CS:100, from the disk in drive A, starting at logical sector number 0.

where you specify the drive number (0 = A, 1 = B, etc.), the first logical sector number, and the number of sectors to read. Examples are shown in Table 1.

Each sector is 512 bytes, so a sector loaded at offset 100 would fill memory through offset 2FF. Logical sectors are numbered from 0 to the highest sector number on the drive. These numbers are different from *physical* sector numbers, which are hardware-dependent. To calculate the number of logical sectors, take the drive size and divide by 512. For example, a 1.44 MB diskette has 2,880 sectors, calculated as 1,474,560 / 512.

Here is a disassembly of sector 0 read from a floppy disk, using Debug. This is commonly called the *boot record*. The boot record contains information about the disk, along with a short program that is responsible for loading the rest of the operating system when the computer starts up:

```
1F6E:0100 EB34            JMP       0136
...
1F6E:0136 FA              CLI
1F6E:0137 33C0            XOR       AX,AX
1F6E:0139 8ED0            MOV       SS,AX
1F6E:013B BC007C          MOV       SP,7C00
```

B.3.11 M (Move)

The M command copies a block of data from one memory location to another. The command format is:

M *range address*

Range consists of the starting and ending locations of the bytes to be copied. *Address* is the target location to which the data will be copied. All offsets are assumed to be from DS unless specified otherwise. Examples:

Example	Description
M 100 105 110	Move bytes in the range DS:100-105 to location DS:110.
M CS:100 105 CS:110	Same as above, except that all offsets are relative to the segment value in CS.

Sample String Move. The following example uses the M command to copy the string 'ABCDEF' from offset 100h to 106h. First, the string is stored at location 100h; then memory is dumped, showing the string. Next, we move (copy) the string to offset 106h and dump offsets 100h-10Bh:

```
-E 100 "ABCDEF"
-D 100 105
19EB:0100   41 42 43 44 45 46                          ABCDEF
-M 100 105 106
-D 100 10B
19EB:0100   41 42 43 44 45 46 41 42-43 44 45 46        ABCDEFABCDEF
```

B.3.12 N (Name)

The N command initializes a filename (and file control block) in memory before using the Load or Write commands. Comand format:

```
N [d:][filename][.ext]
```

Example:

```
N b:myfile.dta
```

B.3.13 P (Proceed)

The P command executes one or more instructions or subroutines. Whereas the T (trace) command traces into subroutine calls, the P command simply executes subroutines. Also, LOOP instruction and string primitive instructions (SCAS, LODS, etc.) are executed completely up to the instruction that follows them. Command format:

```
P
P =address
P =address number
```

Examples are:

Example	Description
P =200	Execute a single instruction at CS:0200.

P =150 6   Execute 6 instructions starting at CS:0150.
P 5   Execute the next 5 instructions.

Example: Debugging a Loop. Let's look at an example where the P command steps through MOV and ADD instructions one at a time. When the P command reaches the LOOP instruction, however, the complete loop is executed five times:

```
-A 100
4A66:0100 mov cx,5      ; loop counter = 5
4A66:0103 mov ax,0
4A66:0106 add ax,cx
4A66:0108 loop 106      ; loop to location 0106h

-R
AX=000F  BX=0000  CX=0000  DX=0000  SP=FFEE  BP=0000  SI=0000  DI=0000
DS=4A66  ES=4A66  SS=4A66  CS=4A66  IP=0100    NV UP EI PL NZ NA PE NC
4A66:0100 B90500        MOV     CX,0005
-P
AX=000F  BX=0000  CX=0005  DX=0000  SP=FFEE  BP=0000  SI=0000  DI=0000
DS=4A66  ES=4A66  SS=4A66  CS=4A66  IP=0103    NV UP EI PL NZ NA PE NC
4A66:0103 B80000        MOV     AX,0000
-P
AX=0000  BX=0000  CX=0005  DX=0000  SP=FFEE  BP=0000  SI=0000  DI=0000
DS=4A66  ES=4A66  SS=4A66  CS=4A66  IP=0106    NV UP EI PL NZ NA PE NC
4A66:0106 01C8          ADD     AX,CX
-P
AX=0005  BX=0000  CX=0005  DX=0000  SP=FFEE  BP=0000  SI=0000  DI=0000
DS=4A66  ES=4A66  SS=4A66  CS=4A66  IP=0108    NV UP EI PL NZ NA PE NC
4A66:0108 E2FC          LOOP    0106
-P
AX=000F  BX=0000  CX=0000  DX=0000  SP=FFEE  BP=0000  SI=0000  DI=0000
DS=4A66  ES=4A66  SS=4A66  CS=4A66  IP=010A    NV UP EI PL NZ NA PE NC
```

B.3.14   Q (Quit)

The Q command quits Debug and returns to DOS.

B.3.15   R (Register)

The R command may be used to do any of the following: display the contents of one register, allowing it to be changed; display registers, flags, and the next instruction about to be executed; display all eight flag settings, allowing any or all of them to be changed. There are two command formats:

```
R
R register
```

Here are some examples:

Example	Description
R	Display the contents of all registers.
R IP	Display the contents of IP and prompt for a new value.
R CX	Same (for the CX register).
R F	Display all flags and prompt for a new flag value.

Once the **R F** command has displayed the flags, you can change any single flag by typing its new state. For example, we set the Zero flag by typing the following two commands:

```
R F    [Press Enter]    ZR
```

The following is a sample register display (all values are in hexadecimal):

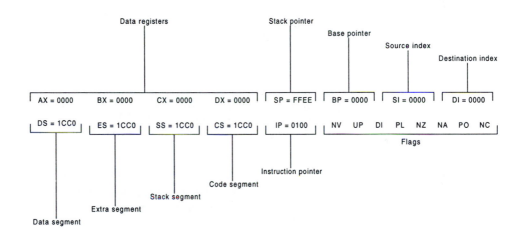

The complete set of possible flag mnemonics in Debug (ordered from left to right) are as follows:

Set	Clear
OV = Overflow	NV = No Overflow
DN = Direction Down	UP = Direction Up
EI = Interrupts Enabled	DI = Interrupts Disabled
NG = Sign Flag negative	PL = Sign Flag positive
ZR = Zero	NZ = Not Zero
AC = Auxiliary Carry	NA = No Auxiliary Carry
PO = Odd Parity	PE = Even Parity
CY = Carry	NC = No Carry

The **R** command also displays the next instruction to be executed:

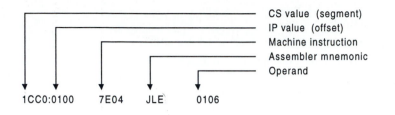

B.3.16 S (Search)

The S command searches a range of addresses for a sequence of one or more bytes. The command format is:

S *range list*

Here are some examples:

Example	Comment
S 100 1000 0D	Search DS:100 to DS:1000 for the value 0Dh.
S 100 1000 CD,20	Search for the sequence CD 20.
S 100 9FFF "COPY"	Search for the word "COPY".

B.3.17 T (Trace)

The T command executes one or more instructions starting at either the current CS:IP location or at an optional address. The contents of the registers are shown after each instruction is executed. The command formats are:

T
T *count*
T =*address count*

Where *count* is the number of instructions to trace, and *address* is the starting address for the trace. Examples:

Example	Description
T	Trace the next instruction.
T 5	Trace the next five instructions.
T =105 10	Trace 16 instructions starting at CS:105.

This command traces individual loop iterations, so you may want to use it to debug statements within a loop. The T command traces into procedure calls, whereas the P (*proceed*) command executes a called procedure in its entirety.

B.3.18 U (Unassemble)

The U command translates memory into assembly language mnemonics. This is also called *disassembling* memory. If you don't supply an address, Debug disassembles from the location where the last U command left off. If the command is used for the first time after loading Debug, memory is unassembled from location CS:100. Command formats are:

```
U
U startaddr
U startaddr endaddr
```

Where *startaddr* is the starting point and *endaddr* is the ending address. Examples are:

Example	Description
U	Disassemble the next 32 bytes.
U 0	Disassemble 32 bytes at CS:0.
U 100 108	Disassemble the bytes from CS:100 to CS:108.

B.3.19 W (Write)

The W command writes a block of memory to a file or to individual disk sectors. To write to a file, its name must first be initialized with the N command. (If the file was just loaded either on the DOS command line or with the Load command, you do not need to repeat the Name command.) The command format is identical to the L (load) command:

```
W
W address
W address drive firstsector number
```

Place the number of bytes to be written in BX:CX. If a file is 12345h bytes long, for example, BX and CX will contain the following values:

```
BX = 0001   CX = 2345
```

Here are a few examples:

Example	Description
N EXAMPLE.COM	Initialize the filename EXAMPLE.COM on the default drive.
R BX 0 R CX 20	Set the BX and CX registers to 00000020h, the length of the file.
W	Write 20h bytes to the file, starting at CS:100.
W 0	Write from location CS:0 to the file.
W	Write named file from location CS:0100.
W DS:0200	Write named file from location DS:0200.

The following commands are extremely dangerous to the data on your disk drive, because writing sectors can wipe out the disk's existing file system. Use them with extreme caution!

```
W 100 2 A 5
```
Write five sectors to drive C from location CS:100, starting at logical sector 0Ah.

```
W 100 0 0 2
```
Write two sectors to drive A from location CS:100, starting at logical sector number 0.

B.4   SEGMENT DEFAULTS

Debug recognizes the CS and DS registers as default segment registers when processing commands. Therefore, the value in CS or DS acts as a base location to which an offset value is added. Table 2 lists the default segment register for selected Debug commands.

The Assemble command, for example, assumes that CS is the default segment. If CS contains 1B00h, Debug begins assembling instructions at location 1B00:0100h when the following command is typed:

```
-A 100
```

The Dump command, on the other hand, assumes that DS is the default segment. If DS contains 1C20h, the following command dumps memory starting at 1C20:0300h:

```
-D 300
```

B.5   USING SCRIPT FILES WITH DEBUG

A major disadvantage of using Debug to assemble and run programs shows up when the programs must be edited. Inserting a new instruction often means retyping all subsequent instructions and recalculating the addresses of memory variables. There is an easier way: All

Table 2. Default Segments for Debug Commands.

Command	Description	Default Segment
A	Assemble	CS
D	Dump	DS
E	Enter	DS
F	Fill	DS
G	Go (execute)	CS
L	Load	CS
M	Move	DS
P	Procedure trace	CS
S	Search	DS
T	Trace	CS
U	Unassemble	CS
W	Write	CS

of the commands and instructions may first be placed a text file, which we will call a script file. When Debug is run from DOS, you can use a redirection symbol (<) to tell it to read input from the *script file* instead of the console. For example, assume that a script file called input.txt contains the following lines:

```
a 100
mov ax,5
mov bx,10
add ax,bx
int 20
```

Debug can be executed, using the script file as input:

```
debug < input.txt
```

If you are running in a task-switching environment such as Windows, you can edit and save the script file with the Notepad editor or DOS Edit (in a separate window). Then switch back to a window in which you are running Debug. In this way, a program may be modified, saved, assembled, and traced within a few seconds. If you would like the output to be sent to a disk file or the printer, use redirection operators on the DOS command line:

```
debug < input.txt > prn          (printer)
debug < input.txt > output.txt   (disk file)
```

Appendix C: Microsoft CodeView

C.1   INTRODUCTION

Suggested Level of Programming Proficiency. I recommend that you at least read through Chapter 3 before reading this guide to CodeView. If possible, compile and debug your programs on the computer's hard drive.

Preparing Programs for Debugging. Before a program may be debugged, it must be assembled and linked with the debugging options turned on. They are **/zi** (for MASM) and **/co** (for LINK). Assuming that no errors were found, run CodeView and tell it to load TEST.EXE. You will have begun what programmers call a *debugging session*. The three commands are

```
masm/zi test;
link/co test;
cv test
```

If you are linking to the irvine.lib link library (introduced in Chapter 4), change the link command to

```
link/co test,,,irvine;
```

There are two types of windows in CodeView: dialog windows (containing commands) and display windows (containing source code).

C.2   EXPRESSIONS

CodeView has a built-in expression evaluator that has unique properties for each of the following source languages: C, C++, FORTRAN, BASIC, or Pascal. By default, CodeView uses the C expression evaluator:

C-Expression Operators (in order of precedence)

```
(), [], ->, .
!, ~, unary -, (type), ++, unary *, &, sizeof
*, /, %, :
+, -
```

```
<,  >,  <=,  >=
==,  !=
&&
||
=  +=  -=  *=  /=  %=
BY  WO  DW
```

An *expression* may be a label, variable, symbol or constant, or some arithmetic combination of these. For example:

`var1`	The address of a variable
`percent * 100`	A symbol multiplied by 100
`es:var2`	Segment-offset memory reference

When debugging an assembly language program, the C expression evaluator changes in the following ways: Numbers are assumed to be hexadecimal unless specified otherwise, the register window is on by default, and case sensitivity is off by default.

Memory Operators. The CodeView expression evaluator does not accept assembly expressions with brackets, such as [bx] or list[si]; instead, one must use a *memory operator*. The latter returns the contents of memory, using a specific size attribute. Examples:

`BY bx`	Byte pointed to by BX (same as byte ptr [bx])
`WO si`	Word value pointed to by SI (same as word ptr [si])
`DW di+4`	Doubleword (same as dword ptr [di+4])

Format Specifiers. Use a format specifier to force an operand to be displayed in a particular format. The following options are available and are case-insensitive:

d   signed decimal integer (or i)
u   unsigned decimal integer
x   hexadecimal integer
f   floating-point decimal
c   single character
s   string, terminated by null (zero) byte

Range. A *range* refers to a group of contiguous memory locations. It may be used to control program execution (when tracing a program, for example), or it may be used when displaying the contents of variables. Two formats are available:

```
Format 1:    startaddress  endaddress
Format 2:    startaddress L count
```

Format 1 is a pair of memory addresses that specify the beginning and ending of a block of memory. Format 2 uses *count* to specify the number of objects to be displayed. Examples:

`var1`	128 bytes starting at a variable called **var1**
`buffer L 5`	The first 5 words of an array called **buffer**
`array L 10`	The first 16 bytes of **array**
`word1 word2`	All bytes between (and including) **word1** and **word2**

C.3   KEYBOARD COMMANDS

The cursor arrow keys, PgUp, and PgDn keys move the cursor only in the current (highlighted) window. The following special keys are active throughout a CodeView session:

Function Keys:

F1	Display help.
F2	Toggle the register window.
F3	Switch between source, mixed, and assembly modes.
F4	Switch to program output screen.
F5	Execute to next breakpoint or the end of the program.
F6	Move cursor between the dialog and display windows.
F7	Execute program up to the current line.
F8	Execute a single statement (trace into calls).
F9	Set/clear breakpoint on the cursor line.
F10	Execute a single statement (step over calls).

Other Keys:

^G	Make current window grow in size.
^T	Make current window smaller.
Home	Top of file or command buffer.
End	Bottom of file or command buffer.
^Break	Halt program execution (unless /D was used on the CodeView command line when the program was started).

Alt-   Pull down a menu choice beginning with the same letter. For example: **Alt-V** pulls down the **View** menu choice.

C.4   CONTROLLING PROGRAM EXECUTION

The following general commands are used for running programs. You can single-step through instructions with **T** and **P**, and you can run the program with **G** and **E**:

T   Trace single step.

P   Procedure trace.

G   Go – run program at full speed.

E   Execute – run program in slow motion.

L   Restart program at beginning.

Q   Quit (return to DOS).

Setting Breakpoints

Breakpoints are locations in your program at which you can choose to pause execution. Once CodeView stops at a breakpoint, you can execute a command and resume execution when ready. Breakpoints are a powerful tool when debugging large programs, because you usually don't want to trace through all instructions one at a time. The easiest way to set a breakpoint is to move the cursor to the desired source line and press F7. To set a permanent breakpoint, move the cursor to the desired line and press F9. To remove it, press F9 again. The following breakpoint commands may be typed in the command window. You may set as many as 20 breakpoints:

BC *   Clear all breakpoints.

BC 0   Clear breakpoint 0 (the first one that was set).

BL   List all breakpoints.

BP   Set breakpoint at current line.

BP sub1   Set a breakpoint at label **sub1**.

BD 1   Disable breakpoint #1.

BE 1   Enable breakpoint #1.

All breakpoints are automatically enabled when you restart a program from the RUN menu (or use the L dialog command).

C.5   EXAMINING AND MODIFYING DATA

C.5.1   Examining and Modifying Data and Expressions

?	Display an expression or identifier.
D	Dump variable or memory contents.
U	Disassemble machine instructions.
V .*n*	View source code starting at line *n*.
A	Assemble new instructions.
E	Enter values into memory.
R	Display/modify register.

Dump Memory (D). If you follow D with a type specifier, the memory bytes will be formatted as one of the following:

B	Hexadecimal byte
A	ASCII string
I	Signed integer
U	Unsigned integer
W	Hexadecimal word
D	Doubleword

The following examples include format specifiers:

DB list	Dump **list** as hexadecimal bytes.
DA string	Dump ASCII characters.
DI val1	Dump **val1** as a singed decimal integer.
DU val1	Dump **val1** as an unsigned decimal integer.
DW val1	Dump **val1** as 16-bit hexadecimal.
DD longVal	Dump **longVal** as 32-bit hexadecimal.
? var1,x	Display **var1** as hexadecimal (the default is decimal).
d var1,i	Display **var1** as signed decimal (the default is hexadecimal).
? var1,u	Display **var1** as unsigned decimal.
da msg	Display ASCII string **msg**.

db 100	Dump memory bytes at offset 100h.
dw var1	Dump the contents of **var1**.
dw es:200	Dump words beginning at offset 200 in the segment pointed to by ES.
db array L 20	Dump 20 bytes beginning at location **array**.
db 200 300	Dump memory bytes, offsets 200 to 300.
dw ds:100	Enter new word value into memory at DS:0100.
eb count	Enter new hexadecimal byte value into **count**.
ei var1	Enter new signed decimal value into **var1**.
r cx=20	Assign 20h to the CX register.
rf zr	Set the Zero flag.
? count=5	Change the value of **count** to 5.

C.5.2   Watching Variables During Program Execution

The **Watch** command opens a window at the top of the screen called a *watch window,* where the contents of variables can be displayed. As you trace and execute a program, any variables in a watch window are automatically updated. There are two basic formats for this command:

```
W? expression
W? expression,format
```

Examples.

`W? var1`	Watch **var1** in hexadecimal.
`W? percent * 100`	Watch **percent** multiplied by 100.
`W? es:var2`	Watch **var1**, located in segment pointed to by ES.

C.5.3   Direct Dialog Output to File/Printer

The **T>** and **T>>** commands allow you to echo debugging output to a file or printer. The changing contents of *watch* and *register* windows will not be written, but you can use the **T**race and **D**ump commands to direct output from the command window at the bottom of the screen to the file or printer. Here are some examples:

`T>  PRN`	Echo CodeView output on the printer.
`T>  outfile`	Echo CodeView output to a file named outfile.
`T>> outfile`	Append CodeView output to a file named outfile.

When tracing a program, press **T** rather than **F8**; the latter will not output to a file.

C.6   HANDS-ON TUTORIAL

Assemble and link the following program and load it into CodeView:

```
Title CodeView Tutorial Example    (cview1.asm)
.model small
.stack 100h
.data
byte1  db  1
byte2  db  0
word1  dw  1234h
word2  dw  0
string db  "This is a string",0

.code
  main proc
  mov  ax,@data
  mov  ds,ax

  mov  ax,0        ; AX = 0000
  mov  al,byte1    ; AX = 0001
  mov  byte2,al
  mov  cx,word1    ; CX = 1234
  mov  word2,cx

  mov  ax,4C00h
  int  21h
main endp
end main
```

The Debugging Screen. After running CodeView, you should see the source code for the CVIEW.ASM program, the registers at the right side, and a small window at the bottom for commands. If the source code does not appear, check the command line options you used for compiling and linking and try again.

Change the View Options. With the program on the screen in CodeView, select **Source** from the **Options** menu and select **Assembly**. You should be able to see the segment:offset address of each statement at the left side of the screen. This is followed by the machine code for each statement. Notice that variable names have been converted to numbers (as is done in Debug).

Next, select **Source** from the **Options** menu and select **Mixed**. Now you see alternating lines of source code and machine instructions. Because this is somewhat hard to read, return the display to Source mode. This is usually best for debugging unless you need to see actual machine addresses.

Using the Mouse. Debugging is easier in CodeView with a mouse. Move it to the horizontal bar under the source code window and hold the left button down. Drag the bar up and down to change the size of the window. You can also use the mouse to choose menu options and to scroll windows horizontally and vertically.

Examining Data. Scroll the code window up so the program variables appear. If nothing happens, press F6 until the cursor moves to the code window and try again.

Now move the cursor to the command window at the bottom of the screen by pressing F6. Type the following commands to display the values of variables:

```
? byte1
? word1
? word1,x
? string
da string
```

Notice that the *x* option (the third command) displays the hexadecimal value of **word1**. Also, the first display command for **string** displays 0x0054, the ASCII code of the string's first byte. The **DA** command correctly displays the string in ASCII format.

Trace the Program. Now we're ready to trace the program one instruction at a time. Press F8 to begin tracing the program. A highlight bar appears over each instruction about to be executed. As you trace the program, keep an eye on the register window to see the changes to AX, CX, DS, and IP. Continue until the **Program Terminated Normally** message appears.

Restart the Program. Choose Restart from the Run menu so CodeView can reload the program and reset IP to the beginning. This time we will create *watch variables,* which allow us to monitor changes to variables as the program is traced.

Create a Watch Window. Choose Add Watch from the Data menu. A dialog box appears, prompting for a *watch expression.* Type **byte2** and press Enter. Notice that the watch window appears at the top of the screen, showing the current value of **byte2**. Do the same for **word2**. Trace the program repeatedly by pressing F8, and notice how the watch window shows the current values of the two variables. (This is immensely useful for checking on programs that accidentally overwrite variables.)

Displaying String Variables. This program has a variable called **string**, whose value we would like to display. We can use either **D**ump or **W**atch:

```
da string
w? &string
w? &string,s
```

The first command, **da**, displays **string** at the bottom of the screen. The second one displays both the address and contents of **string** in the watch window. The third command displays just the contents of **string** in the Watch window.

Final Note. Needless to say, there is much more to CodeView than we have time to show here. Microsoft includes a tutorial with sample files on the CodeView distribution disk. The assembler also includes an extensive CodeView manual.

Appendix D: Borland Turbo Debugger

D.1   PREPARING A PROGRAM TO BE DEBUGGED

If you want to debug a program with Borland Turbo Debugger, it must be assembled and linked with debugging options turned on. Debugging information is stored in the OBJ and EXE files, making them slightly larger. After debugging a program for the last time, you can assemble and link one more time without the debugging options, resulting in the smallest possible EXE program.

Using a program name of SAMPLE.ASM, the following commands would be used to assemble, link, and debug:

```
tasm/zi sample
tlink/v sample
td sample
```

The source file (sample.asm) must be in the same directory as sample.exe when running the debugger, unless you use the **-sd** option (explained in section D.2).

D.2   SELECTED COMMAND-LINE OPTIONS

Run Turbo Debugger with SAMPLE.EXE:

```
td sample
```

Optionally, you can pass command-line arguments to SAMPLE.EXE:

```
td sample one two three
```

Other options:

-do   Run the debugger on secondary display.

-dp   Run the debugger on separate display pages (minimizes screen flipping).

-h   Display a help screen.

-k   Activate the keystroke recording mode.

-vg   Save a complete graphics image on the program screen. Use this if your graphics screen becomes corrupted.

D.3   TRACING PROGRAMS

D.3.1   Stack Window (View / Stack)

Lists all active procedures (the most recently called routine is listed first).

Local Menu. The following options are available from the Stack Window's local menu:

- Inspect: Show the source code of any procedure on the stack.

- Locals: Display symbols local to the current module.

D.3.2   Execution History Window (View / Execution)

The Execution History Window keeps a record of the last 400-3000 instructions executed. There are two panes, the instructions pane and the keystroke recording pane:

Instructions Pane. Display a list of the most recently executed instructions.

Keystroke recording pane. All keys pressed while tracing a program can be replayed, allowing you to return to the current point in the debugging session.

D.3.3   The Run Menu

The Run menu has the following commands:

Command	Description
Run [F9]	Run the program at full speed to the end, to a breakpoint, or until Ctrl-Break is pressed.
Go to Cursor [F4]	Run the program and stop before the current line is executed.
Trace into [F7]	Execute either a single line of source code or a single machine instruction, depending on the type of current module window. This command traces into subroutines.
Step over [F8]	Execute a single source line or machine instruction, skipping over any procedure calls (the procedure is executed). This command fully executes LOOP and INT instructions.
Execute to	Run the program up to a specified address.
Until return	Run the program until the current procedure returns to its caller.
Animate	Perform a continuous series of *Trace Into* commands. Run in slow motion until any key is pressed.
Back trace	Reverse the last traced instruction.
Instruction trace	Use this command to trace into interrupts.

Arguments   Set the MS-DOS command-line arguments for the program being
                             debugged.

Program reset   Reload the program from disk.

D.4   SETTING BREAKPOINTS

A *breakpoint* is a marker that tells the debugger to pause in one of the following ways:

- Unconditionally on a particular statement.

- When a pre-set condition becomes *true*.

- When a memory location changes.

After a program has paused, you can inspect or change variables, reset the instruction pointer,
or resume execution.

You can gain a great deal of control over programs by setting breakpoints, particularly in
programs with loops and conditional jumps. Tracing a program line by line can be tedious to
say the least. It's a good idea to set no more than one or two simultaneous breakpoints until
you have had more practice with the debugger.

Breakpoints / Toggle. To set an unconditional breakpoint on the current cursor line, press F2.
To remove it, press F2 again.

Breakpoints / Changed Memory Global. The Changed Memory Global command sets up a
breakpoint that stops the program whenever a particular variable is modified. Type in a
variable name, press Enter, and then run the program (press F9). The program will stop and
display a message stating which breakpoint was reached, followed by the module name and
source line number. For example, if the debugger stopped in sample.asm on line 30, it would
display this message:

```
"Global breakpoint at #sample#30"
```

The program stops at the statement immediately following the one that caused the breakpoint.
It is a good idea to set up a watch window showing the variable that is being used for the
breakpoint. Then you can see each new value as the variable changes. Continue to run the
program in this manner by pressing F9.

Breakpoints / Expression True Global. You can type in a valid assembler expression (see the
discussion of expressions in another part of this tutorial). When using an *Expression True
Global* breakpoint, the program stops when the expression is true. For example, we could
choose to stop when AX equals 0. The expression is AX EQ 0. You can use any of the following relational operators in expressions: EQ, GT, LT, GE, LE, or NE.

Breakpoints / Delete All. After a number of breakpoints have been set, you can run the
complete program. Use the *Delete All* option to remove all breakpoints, and then execute the
Run command.

D.5   ASSEMBLER EXPRESSIONS

We tend to use assembler expressions most often for both conditional breakpoints and for inspecting variables. In the latter case, you would use the *Evaluate/Modify* window. Expressions can contain the following items:

Symbols: Symbols can be user-defined names for data items, procedures, and labels. A special character is **$**, which identifies the current program location (CS:IP).

Constants: You can use either floating-point or integer constants. Integers are assumed to be in hexadecimal unless overridden with a radix specifier, such as 10d,10o,10q,10b.

Operators: The following operators can be used in expressions: PTR (byte ptr, word ptr, etc.), OR, XOR, AND, NOT, EQ, NE, LT, LE, GT, GE, +, -, *, /, MOD, SHR, SHL, OFFSET, SEG, (), and []. Variables can be modified by the = operator. For example,

```
val1 = 20
val2 = ds:[bx+1]
```

Format Control. Turbo Debugger uses a default format for operands based on their type. You can override the format by following the expression with a comma or an optional repeat count, and one of the following format letters:

Code	Purpose
c	Display a string as raw characters, using all 255 extended ASCII codes.
d	Display an integer in decimal.
f[#]	Display as floating-point with the specified number of digits.
m	Display an expression that references memory in hexadecimal.
md	Display an expression that references memory in decimal.
p	Display a raw pointer value. This is the default format when none is specified.
s	Display an array (or pointer to one) as a quoted string.
h	Display an integer in hexadecimal.

D.6   EXAMINING AND MODIFYING DATA

D.6.1   Variables Window (View / Variables)

A *Variables* window can be created by choosing the *View / Variables* option from the menu. It displays a list of variables and their addresses. The window is divided into an upper pane and a lower pane.

The upper pane contains all global program symbols. It has a local menu attached to it, seen by pressing Alt-F10. Depending on which variable is currently selected in the variables window, you can choose from a list of options:

- Inspect: Display the variable's contents.

- Change: Modify the variable.

- Watch: Add the variable to the watch window.

The lower pane contains all nonglobal symbols in the current program module. Its local menu contains the following options:

- Inspect: Display the variable's contents.

- Change: Modify the variable.

- Watch: Add the variable to the watch window.

- Show: Change the scope of the variable (static, local, or both). You can choose the module from which the variable is to be displayed.

D.6.2   Watch Window (View / Watches)

When you place variables in a *watch* window, the debugger updates them constantly as the program is run or traced. (This does not happen when you simply show a dump of a variable with the *View / Dump* command.) Watch variables drastically slow down the debugger's execution of your program, so they should be used sparingly.

Watch Window Local Menu. A local menu appears above the watch window when you press Alt-F10. The options are:

- **Watch:**   Add a new variable to the window.

- **Edit:**   Edit an expression in the window.

- **Remove:**   Remove the highlighted variable from the window.

- **Delete all:**   Remove all variables from the window.

- **Inspect:**   Inspect individual elements of a compound variable, such as an array.

- **Change:**   Modify a highlighted variable in the watch window.

D.6.3   Viewing a Memory Dump

The (View / Dump) menu command displays a hexadecimal dump of memory pointed to by DS. It's best to trace past the first two instructions that reset DS to the data segment before bringing up this window.

D.6.4   Inspector Windows

An *inspector* window lets you inspect the contents of a variable. The first value displayed in the window is the variable's segment:offset address. Next, the value of the variable is displayed. The item might be a scalar variable such as a single byte, word, or doubleword. It might be a 16-bit or 32-bit pointer, or it might be an array. In the latter case, a separate line in the windows displays each element in the array.

Try the following: Move the cursor to a variable name either in the code or data part of the program listing. Select Data / Inspect from the menu; the variable name appears in a window. Press Enter to display the variable's contents. To assign the variable a new value while it is in an inspector window, just begin typing the new value. The following are samples of acceptable entries:

32	Assumed to be hexadecimal.
32h	Hexadecimal.
32d	Decimal.
'A'	Stores the ASCII code for A in memory.
AX	Copies 16-bit register contents into a variable.
BL	Copies 8-bit register contents into a variable.

Local Menu: Range / Change / Inspect. You can also use the *range local* command to examine a portion of an array or string. To do this, bring up the local menu with Alt-F10. From there, you can modify the range of memory bytes to be displayed.

D.6.5   Evaluate/Modify Dialog Box

The *Data / Evaluate/Modify* menu command displays a box with three windows:

- Expression: Type in a valid expression to be evaluated. See the rules for assembler expressions in this reference.

- Result: When you press Enter after entering an expression, its value displays in the middle box.

- New Value: If the operand can be changed, use this box to type in a new value.

D.7   CONFIGURING TURBO DEBUGGER

You may find it useful to configure Turbo Debugger with certain default options so the options will be in effect when the debugger starts up. You need to run the TDINST.EXE program to do this. A quick survey of the available options is:

1. **Screen colors:** You can customize the colors of windows, menus, and dialog boxes.

2. **Display mode:** If you use an LCD projector or notebook computer, you may want to change the display mode for greatest visibility.

3. **Display parameters:** You can control whether or not the video display is swapped each time the program writes to the console. You can control the number of lines displayed on the screen.

4. **Directories:** You can decide where source and EXE files are kept.

5. **Memory:** You can tell the debugger to use expanded memory if available. You can specify the amount of memory used by the MS-DOS shell.

Appendix E: Guide to the Sample Programs

This book is supplied with a CD-ROM containing a full working copy of the latest version of the Microsoft Macro Assembler. In addition, one of the folders on the disk contains a list of all sample programs from this book, a link library, and a useful DOS-based editor for creating assembly language source programs.

E.1   INFORMATION ABOUT THE SAMPLE PROGRAM FILES

irvine.lib	Compiled link library
ae.exe	Integrated editor for writing assembly language programs. Runs in an MS-DOS window.
ae.cfg	Configuration file for ae.exe
ae.doc	Help file for ae.exe
console.inc	Macro include file for console-oriented routines the link library
disks.inc	Macro include file for disk-based routines in the link library
macros.inc	General-Purpose Macro library
readme.txt	Instructions on using the sample program disk

No doubt, a few errors will be found in the programs on this disk, and updates will be posted on the book's Web page. Be sure to check it from time to time. Either or both of the following URLs should be valid:

www.nuvisionmiami.com/kip/asm
www.pobox.com/~irvinek/asm

If for some reason you can't get through, send me an email message:

kip.irvine@pobox.com

About The Files. All the files in the sample programs directory are sample programs from this book, *Assembly Language for Intel-Based Computers, Third Edition*. I recommend that you create a directory on your computer's hard drive and copy all files and folders from this directory to your hard drive. You will need to install the Microsoft Assembler, of course.

Using The Assembly Language Editor (AE.EXE). The assembly language editor included in the current directory is called AE.EXE. My students and I have been using it for years as a simple way to assemble, link, and debug programs. It runs quickly, supports multiple source code windows with clipboard-type functions, and can be used with multiple assemblers. I distributed it as shareware around 1990, and have had no complaints about it since then.

AE.EXE is a DOS-based editor, and I always run it from Windows using a batch file. For example, I have a file called TASM.BAT located in the C:\TASM directory. This runs the editor and sets the current path to the directory containing the Borland Assembler:

```
path c:\tasm\bin
c:\tasm\ae.exe
```

Similarly, I have another batch file that sets the path to the Microsoft Assembler directories, called MASM.BAT:

```
path c:\masm611\bin;c:\masm611\binr
c:\masm611\ae.exe
```

I created shortcuts to both batch files and placed them on the Windows desktop. Using this method, you can easily switch between assemblers.

The Editor Configuration File (AE.CFG). The configuration file for the AE.EXE program is called AE.CFG. It is a text file containing path names for the assembler, linker, debugger, and link library. Here is the one I use when assembling with MASM:

```
c:\masm611\bin\masm.exe
/z/zi
c:\masm611\bin\link.exe
/co
c:\masm611\bin\cv.exe
c:\masm611\irvine
```

You don't have to edit this file yourself—all this information is set from within the editor, by selecting Run / Set Pathnames from the menu, and automatically saved in AE.CFG when you exit the program. The following is the AE.CFG file I use for Borland TASM:

```
c:\tasm\bin\tasm.exe
/z/zi
c:\tasm\bin\tlink.exe
/v
c:\tasm\bin\td.exe
c:\tasm\irvine
```

Essential Editor Tips. The following tips may be useful when using this editor:

1) Always save the current source file before assembling the program. Otherwise, the assembler will simply use the last saved version of your source code to create the OBJ file.

2) Set the editor's current directory to the location of your source program before assembling and linking. Otherwise, the editor will save the OBJ and EXE files in the current directory, and you will not be able to execute or debug the program.

3) On startup, the editor looks for a configuration file in the current directory. Failing to find one, it looks in the AE.EXE program's home directory. When it exits, it saves all configuration infomration in AE.CFG in the current directory. If you want to switch assemblers, just delete the AE.CFG from your source code directory, and run one of the shortcuts mentioned earlier. The editor will automatically create a new configuration file in your source code directory.

E.2   CONTENTS OF THE MACROS.INC FILE

General-Purpose Macros:

```
mCondCall macro cond,procname
mCompJmp macro dest,flag,source,label
mDisplaystr macro string
mDisplaystr_at macro row,col,string
mExitdos macro ecode
mGetyesno macro prompt
mGotoXY macro row, column
jx&cond macro dest
mLongloop macro dest
mMove macro dest,source
mMult16 macro dest,source
mPrompt_Readint macro row,col,prompt,dest
mPrompt_Readstring macro row,col,prompt,dest,max
mPutchar macro char
mRepeatchar macro char,count
mStartup macro
m&styp macro dest,count (<shl,shr,sal,sar,rol,
   ror,rcl,rcr>)
mWriteint macro value, radix
mWriteliteral macro text
```

Simulations of 80286 Instructions:

```
mENTER
mLEAVE
mPUSHA
mPOPA
mSET&cond
```

E.3   LINK LIBRARY PROCEDURES

Procedure	Description
Close_file	Closes a file handle. *Input:* BX = file handle.
Clrscr	Clears the screen and locates the cursor at the upper left corner. No input. Works only on video page 0, and only in text mode.
Create_file	Creates a new file and returns its handle. *Input:* DX = offset of filename. *Output:* AX = file handle.
Crlf	Writes a carriage return and line feed to standard output.
Delay_seconds	Delays the current program a specified number of seconds. *Input:* EAX = number of seconds.
DOS_Error	Writes a message on the standard error output device that matches a particular MS-DOS error code. *Input:* AX contains the error code.
Get_Commandtail	Retrieves the MS-DOS command tail containing any parameters typed on the command line by the user. *Input:* BX = the PSP segment and DS:SI points to a buffer to hold a copy of the Command Tail.
Get_Deviceparms	Retrieves information about an input/output device from MS-DOS. *Input:* BL = drive number (0 = default drive, 1 = A, 2 = B, etc.). *Output:* AX points to a ParameterStruc (see page 427) where DOS stores the device information.
Get_Diskfreespace	Returns the amount of free space available on a disk drive. *Input:* AL = drive (0=A, 1=B, 2=C). *Output:* DX:AX = free space.
Get_Disksize	Finds out how much total space is available on a disk drive. *Input:* AL = drive number (0=A, 1=B, 2=C, etc.). Output: DX:AX = disk space.
Get_time	Gets the current time of day. *Input:* DS:SI points to a TimeRecord structure. *Output:* The TimeRecord structure is filled.
Gotoxy	Locates the cursor at a specified row and column on the screen. *Input:* DH = row (0-79), DL = column (0-24).
Open_infile	Opens a file for input and returns its handle. *Input:* DX = offset of ASCIIZ file name. *Output:* AX = file handle.
Open_outfile	Opens a file for output and returns its handle. *Input:* DX = offset of ASCIIZ file name. *Output:* AX = file handle.
PackedToBin	Converts a packed decimal (BCD) byte to binary. *Input:* AL = BCD value. *Output:* AL = equivalent binary value.
Randomize	Re-seeds the random number generator. No input or output required.
Random_range	Returns a pseudo-random 32-bit integer between 0 and *n*. *Input:* EAX = *n*.
Random32	Returns a pseudo-random 32-bit integer in the range 0 to FFFFFFFFh.
Readchar	Reads a single character from standard input without waiting or echoing the character. *Input:* none. *Output:* If a character is available, ZF = 0 and AL contains the character. If no character is found, ZF = 1.

Read_record	Reads a record from a file that has been opened for input. *Input:* DX points to input buffer, BX = file handle, CX = number of bytes to read.
Readint	Reads a signed ASCII decimal string from standard input and stores it as a 16-bit binary integer. *Input:* none. *Output:* AX contains the value.
Readkey	Waits for a single key input directly from the keyboard. Cannot be redirected. *Input:* none. *Output:* AH = scan code, AL = ASCII code.
Readlong	Reads a signed ASCII decimal string from standard input and stores it as a 32-bit binary integer. *Input:* none. *Output:* EAX contains the value.
Readstring	Reads a string of characters from standard input and stores them in a null-terminated string. *Input:* DX points to the string, CX = maximum character count. *Output:* AX = number of characters typed.
Scroll	Scrolls a window on the screen with a chosen color. *Input:* CH, CL = upper left corner row and column; DH, DL = lower right row and column; BH = attribute (color) of the scrolled lines.
Seconds_today	Returns the number of seconds that have elapsed since midnight of the current day. *Output:* EAX contains the return value.
Seek_eof	Moves the file pointer to the end of a currently open file. *Input:* BX = file handle of an open file *Output:* DX:AX = new file pointer offset.
Seek_record	Moves the file pointer to a specific record in a currently open file. *Input:* AX = record number, BX = file handle, CX = record length. *Output:* DX:AX = new file pointer offset.
Set_videoseg	Sets the base address of the video segment, for subsequent output to video memory (VRAM). *Input:* AX contains the segment address value.
Show_time	Shows the current time of day. *Input:* DS:SI points to an initialized TimeRecord structure.
Str_compare	Compares two strings according to their collating sequence. *Input:* DS:SI points to the first string, and ES:DI points to the second string. *Output:* CF = 1 if the first string is lesser, ZF = 1 if both strings are equal, and (CF = 0, ZF = 0) if the first string is greater than the second.
Str_copy	Copies a source string to a destination string. *Input:* DS:SI points to the source and ES:DI points to the destination. No range checking is performed on the destination.
Str_length	Finds the length of a string. *Input:* ES:DI points to the string. *Output:* AX is assigned the string length.
Str_ucase	Converts a string to uppercase. *Input:* DS:SI points to the string.
TimeRecord	A structure containing the following data definitions:

```
TimeRecord struc
  hours      db ?
  minutes    db ?
  seconds    db ?
  hhss       db ?  'hundredths of seconds
TimeRecord ends
```

Waitchar	Waits for a character to be read from standard input, with no echo. *Output:* AL contains the character.
Writebcd	Writes an 8-bit binary coded decimal byte to standard output. *Input:* AL contains the byte.
Writechar	Write a single character to standard output. *Input:* AL contains the byte.
Writechar_direct	Writes a single ASCII character to video memory (VRAM). *Input:* AL = character, AH = attribute, DH/DL = row, column on screen (0-24, 0-79).
Write_errorstr	Writes a null-terminated string to the standard error output device. *Input*: DS:DX points to the string.
Writeint	Writes an unsigned 16-bit integer to standard output in ASCII binary, decimal, octal, or hexadecimal format. *Input:* AX = the integer to display, and BX = radix value (2, 8, 10, or 16).
Writeint_signed	Writes a 16-bit integer to standard output in signed decimal ASCII format. *Input:* AX = the integer to display.
Writelong	Writes an unsigned 32-bit binary integer to standard output in binary, decimal, octal, or hexadecimal format. *Input:* EAX = the integer to display, and BX = radix value (2, 8, 10, or 16).
Writestring	Writes a null-terminated string to standard output. *Input:* DX points to the string.
Writestring_direct	Writes a null-terminated string directly to video memory. *Input:* DS:SI points to a null-terminated string, AH = attribute, DH/DL = row/column on the screen (0-24, 0-79).

E.4   SAMPLE PROGRAMS FROM THE CHAPTERS

Chapter 1	hello.asm	Hello World program.
Chapter 2	(none)	
Chapter 3	hello.asm	Hello world program, revisited.
Chapter 4		

delay.asm	Demonstration of the Delay_seconds procedure.
enum.asm	Borland enumerated types.
lnkdemo.asm	Link library demo program.

Chapter 5

largem.asm	Large memory model program example.
subs.asm	Calling near and far subroutines.
videomem.asm	Writing data directly to video memory.

Chapter 6

encrypt.asm	Encrypting a data file with XOR.
fsm.asm	Implementing a finite state machine (FSM).
isalpha.asm	Checking for alphabetic characters.
lgsmal.asm	Finding largest and smallest values in a list.

Chapter 7

bin.asm	Displaying binary bits in a byte.
divide.asm	32-bit division example.
mwadd.asm	Multiword addition example.
qwadd.asm	Quadword addition example.

Chapter 8

list.asm	Creating a linked list using the STRUC and REPT directives.
struc.asm	Entering data into a Student structure and redisplaying the data.

Chapter 9

addsome.asm	Adding a list of integers using a variable number of parameters.
arrayfill.asm	Filling an array using a 32-bit pointer passed on the stack.
display.asm	Demonstrating the DisplayStr procedure.
encode.asm	Reading and encoding an input file.
proc_br.asm	Using Borland's PROC directive.
proc_ms.asm	Using Microsoft's PROC directive.
readint.asm	Reading an integer from standard input.
writeint.asm	Writing an integer to standard output.
xlat.asm	Using a XLAT table to filter input characters.

Chapter 10

strcmp.asm	Str_compare procedure.
strcopy.asm	Str_copy procedure.
strgetl.asm	Str_getline procedure.
strlen.asm	Str_length procedure.

strread.asm	Str_read procedure.
strtest.asm	String library test program.
strucase.asm	Str_ucase procedure.
strwrite.asm	Str_write procedure.
writestr.asm	Writestring procedure.

Chapter 11

cluster.asm	Cluster display program.
device.asm	Get_deviceparms procedure.
sector.asm	Sector display program.
writesec.asm	Writing disk sectors.
disks.inc	Include file for the Disks library module.

Chapter 12

dat.asm	Date stamp program.

Chapter 13

\VisualCPP\InlineTest	Testing inline ASM code
\VisualCPP\FindArray	FindArray procedure
\VisualCPP\Encode	Encoding a string
\VisualCPP\Addem	Adding two integers
\BorlandCPP\ReadSec	Readsector procedure
\BorlandCPP\LongRand	LongRandom procedure

Chapter 14

bitmap.asm	Loading and displaying a bitmap (*Chapter 12 example*).
hellocom.asm	Hello Program, COM structure.
seg1.asm	Multiple segment example.
seg2.asm	Combining segments, Main.
seg2a.asm	Combining segments, Sub.
spkr.asm	Speaker demo program.

Chapter 15

clock.asm	Reading the real-time clock.
ctrlbrk.asm	Control-break handler.
expr.asm	Expression evaluation.
no_reset.asm	Reset-disabling program.
payroll.asm	Payroll calculation program.

Appendix F: The Intel Instruction Set

This appendix is a quick guide to all real-mode instructions in the Intel 80x86 processor family.

F.1   INTRODUCTION

F.1.1   Flags

Each instruction description contains a series of boxes that describe how the instruction will affect the CPU status flags. Each flag is identified by a single letter:

O   Overflow   S   Sign   P   Parity

D   Direction   Z   Zero   C   Carry

I   Interrupt   A   Auxiliary Carry

Inside the boxes, the following notation shows how each instruction will affect the flags:

1	Sets the flag.
0	Clears the flag.
?	May change the flag to an undetermined value.
(blank)	The flag is not changed.
*	Changes the flag according to specific rules associated with the flag.

For example, the following diagram of the Flags register shows the following about an instruction: the Overflow, Sign, Zero, and Parity flags will be changed to unknown values. The Auxiliary Carry and Carry flags will be modified according to rules associated with the flags. The Direction and Interrupt flags will not be changed:

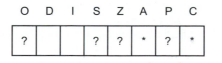

F.1.2   Instruction Descriptions and Formats

When a reference to source and destination operands is made, we use the natural order of operands in all Intel 80x86 instructions, in which the first operand is the destination and the second is the source. In the MOV instruction, for example, the destination will be assigned a copy of the data in the source operand:

```
MOV destination, source
```

There may be several formats available for a single instruction. Table 1 contains a list of symbols that are used in the format descriptions. In the descriptions of individual instructions, we use the notation (80386) to indicate that an instruction or one of its variants is only avail-

Table 1. Symbols Used in Instruction Formats.

Symbol	Description
reg	An 8-, 16-, or 32-bit general register from the following list: AH, AL, BH, BL, CH, CL, AX, BX, CX, DX, SI, DI, BP, SP, EAX, EBX, ECX, EDX, ESI, EDI, EBP, and ESP.
reg8, reg16, reg32	A general register, identified by its number of bits.
segreg	A 16-bit segment register (CS, DS, ES, SS, FS, GS).
accum	AL, AX, or EAX.
mem	A memory operand, using any of the standard memory addressing modes.
mem8, mem16, mem32	A memory operand, identified by its number of bits.
shortlabel	A location in the code segment within −128 to +127 bytes of the current location.
nearlabel	A location in the current code segment, identified by a label.
farlabel	location in an external code segment, identified by a label.
immed	An immediate operand.
immed8, immed16, immed32	An immediate operand, identified by its number of bits.
instruction	An 80x86 assembly language instruction.

able on the 80386 processor and higher. Similarly, the notation (80286) indicates that at least an 80286 processor must be used.

F.2   THE INSTRUCTION SET

O	D	I	S	Z	A	P	C
?			?	?	*	?	*

AAA

ASCII adjust after addition: Adjusts the result in AL after two ASCII digits have been added together. If AL > 9, the high digit of the result is placed in AH, and the Carry and Auxiliary Carry flags are set.

Instruction Format:

    AAA

O	D	I	S	Z	A	P	C
?			*	*	?	*	?

AAD

ASCII adjust before division: Converts unpacked BCD digits in AH and AL to a single binary value in preparation for the DIV instruction.

Instruction Format:

    AAD

O	D	I	S	Z	A	P	C
?			*	*	?	*	?

AAM

ASCII adjust after multiply: Adjusts the result in AX after two unpacked BCD digits have been multiplied together.

Instruction Format:

    AAM

	O	D	I	S	Z	A	P	C
AAS	?			?	?	*	?	*

ASCII adjust after subtraction: Adjusts the result in AX after a subtraction operation. If AL > 9, AAS decrements AH and sets the Carry and Auxiliary Carry flags.

Instruction Format:

```
AAS
```

	O	D	I	S	Z	A	P	C
ADC	*			*	*	*	*	*

Add carry: Adds the source and destination operands, and adds the contents of the Carry flag to the sum, which is stored in the destination.

Instruction Formats:

```
ADC   reg,reg          ADC   reg,immed
ADC   mem,reg          ADC   mem,immed
ADC   reg,mem          ADC   accum,immed
```

	O	D	I	S	Z	A	P	C
ADD	*			*	*	*	*	*

Add: A source operand is added to a destination operand, and the sum is stored in the destination.

Instruction Formats:

```
ADD   reg,reg          ADD   reg,immed
ADD   mem,reg          ADD   mem,immed
ADD   reg,mem          ADD   accum,immed
```

	O	D	I	S	Z	A	P	C
AND	0			*	*	?	*	0

Logical AND: Each bit in the destination operand is ANDed with the corresponding bit in the source operand.

Instruction Formats:

AND	reg,reg	ADD	reg,immed
AND	mem,reg	ADD	mem,immed
AND	reg,mem	ADD	accum,immed

BOUND

O	D	I	S	Z	A	P	C

Check array bounds: (80286) Verifies that a signed index value is within the bounds of an array. On the 80286 processor, the destination operand can be any 16-bit register containing the index to be checked. The source operand must be a 32-bit memory operand in which the high and low words contain the upper and lower bounds of the index value. On the 80386, the destination can be a 32-bit register and the source can be a 64-bit memory operand.

Instruction Formats:

        BOUND   reg16,mem32   BOUND   reg32,mem64

BSF,BSR

O	D	I	S	Z	A	P	C
				*			

Bit scan: (80386) Scans an operand to find the first set bit. If the bit is found, the Zero flag is cleared and the destination operand is assigned the bit number (index) of the first set bit encountered. If no set bit is found, ZF = 1. BSF scans from bit 0 to the highest bit, and BSR starts at the highest bit and scans toward bit 0.

Formats (apply to both BSF and BSR):

        BSF   reg16,reg16   BSF   reg32,reg32
        BSF   reg16,mem16   BSF   reg32,mem32

BSWAP

O	D	I	S	Z	A	P	C

Check array bounds: (80486) Exchanges the first byte with the fourth byte in a 32-bit register.

Instruction Format:

        BSWAP   reg32

BT,BTC,BTR,BTS

O	D	I	S	Z	A	P	C
							1

Bit tests: (80386) Copies a specified bit into the Carry flag. The *destination* operand contains the value in which the bit is located, and the *source* operand indicates the bit's position within the destination. BT just copies the bit to the Carry flag. BTC copies the bit and complements it (in the destination), BTR copies the bit and resets it to 0, and BTS copies the bit and sets it to 1.

Instruction Formats (identical for BT, BTC, BTR, and BTS):

```
BT  reg16,immed8        BT  mem16,immed8
BT  reg16,reg16         BT  mem16,reg16
```

CALL

O	D	I	S	Z	A	P	C

Call a procedure: Pushes the location of the next instruction on the stack and transfers to the destination location. If the procedure is near (in the same segment), only the offset of the next instruction is pushed; otherwise, both the segment and the offset are pushed.

Instruction Formats:

```
CALL  nearlabel        CALL  mem16
CALL  farlabel         CALL  mem32
CALL  reg
```

CBW

O	D	I	S	Z	A	P	C

Convert byte to word: Extends the sign bit in AL throughout the AH register.

Instruction Format:

```
CBW
```

CDQ

O D I S Z A P C

Convert doubleword to quadword: (80386) Extends the sign bit in EAX throughout the EDX register.

Instruction Format:

    CDQ

CLC

O D I S Z A P C

(C column: 0)

Clear carry flag: Clears the Carry flag to zero.

Instruction Format:

    CLC

CLD

O D I S Z A P C

(D column: 0)

Clear direction flag: Clears the Direction flag to zero. String primitive instructions will automatically increment SI and DI.

Instruction Format:

    CLD

CLI

O D I S Z A P C

(I column: 0)

Clear interrupt flag: Clears the Interrupt flag to zero.This disables maskable hardware interrupts until an STI instruction is executed.

Instruction Format:

    CLI

O	D	I	S	Z	A	P	C
							*

CMC

Complement Carry flag: Toggles the current value of the Carry flag.

Instruction Format:

```
CMC
```

O	D	I	S	Z	A	P	C
*			*	*	*	*	*

CMP

Compare: Compares the destination to the source by performing an implied subtraction of the source from the destination.

Instruction Formats:

```
CMP  reg,reg          CMP  reg,immed
CMP  mem,reg          CMP  mem,immed
CMP  reg,mem          CMP  accum,immed
```

O	D	I	S	Z	A	P	C
*			*	*	*	*	*

CMPS, CMPSB, CMPSW, CMPSD

Compare strings: Compares strings in memory addressed by DS:SI and ES:DI. Carries out an implied subtraction of the destination from the source. CMPSB compares bytes, CMPSW compares words, and CMPSD compares doublewords (on the 80386). SI and DI are increased or decreased according to the operand size and the status of the direction flag. If DF = 1, SI and DI are decreased; if DF = 0, SI and DI are increased.

Instruction Formats:

```
CMPS  source,dest          CMPSB
CMPS  segreg:source,ES:dest
CMPSW      CMPSD
```

O	D	I	S	Z	A	P	C
*			*	*	*	*	*

CMPXCHG

Compare and exchange: (80486) Compares the destination to the accumulator (AL, AX, or EAX). If they are equal, the source is copied to the destination. Otherwise, the destination is copied to the accumulator.

Instruction Formats:

    CMPXCHG *reg,reg*   CMPXCHG *mem,reg*

O	D	I	S	Z	A	P	C

CWD

Convert word to doubleword: Extends the sign bit in AX into the DX register. This is usually done in preparation for a signed division (IDIV) operation.

Instruction Format:

    CWD

O	D	I	S	Z	A	P	C

CWDE

Convert word to extended double: (80386) Extends the sign bit in AX into the upper word of the EAX register.

Instruction Format:

    CWDE

O	D	I	S	Z	A	P	C
?			*	*	*	*	*

DAA

Decimal adjust after addition: Adjusts the binary sum in AL after two packed BCD values have been added. Converts the sum to two BCD digits in AL.

Instruction Format:

    DAA

DAS

O	D	I	S	Z	A	P	C
?			*	*	*	*	*

Decimal adjust after subtraction: Converts the binary result of a subtraction operation to two packed BCD digits in AL.

Instruction Format:

```
DAS
```

DEC

O	D	I	S	Z	A	P	C
*			*	*	*	*	

Decrement: Subtracts 1 from an operand. Does not affect the Carry flag.

Instruction Formats:

```
DEC reg    DEC mem
```

DIV

O	D	I	S	Z	A	P	C
?			?	?	?	?	?

Divide, unsigned:Performs either 8-, 16-, or 32-bit unsigned integer division. If the divisor is 8 bits, the dividend is AX, the quotient is AL, and the remainder is AH. If the divisor is 16 bits, the dividend is DX:AX, the quotient is AX, and the remainder is DX. If the divisor is 32 bits, the dividend is EDX:EAX, the quotient is EAX, and the remainder is EDX.

Instruction Formats:

```
DIV reg    DIV mem
```

ENTER

O	D	I	S	Z	A	P	C

Make stack frame: (80286) Creates a stack frame for a procedure that receives stack parameters and uses local stack variables. The first operand indicates the number of bytes to reserve for local stack variables. The second operand indicates the procedure nesting level (must be set to 0 for C, Basic, and FORTRAN).

Instruction Formats:

    ENTER *immed16, immed8*

HLT

O	D	I	S	Z	A	P	C

Halt: Stops the CPU until a hardware interrupt occurs. (*Note:* The Interrupt flag must be set with the STI instruction before hardware interrupts can occur.)

Instruction Format:

    HLT

IDIV

O	D	I	S	Z	A	P	C
?			?	?	?	?	?

Signed Integer Division: Performs a signed integer division operation on EDX:EAX, DX:AX, or AX. If the divisor is 8 bits, the dividend is AX, the quotient is AL, and the remainder is AH. If the divisor is 16 bits, the dividend is DX:AX, the quotient is AX, and the remainder is DX. If the divisor is 32 bits, the dividend is EDX:EAX, the quotient is EAX, and the remainder is EDX. Usually the IDIV operation is prefaced by either CBW CWD to sign-extend the dividend.

Instruction Formats:

    IDIV *reg* IDIV *mem*

IMUL

O	D	I	S	Z	A	P	C
*				?	?	?	?	*

Signed integer multiply: Performs a signed integer multiplication on either AL or AX. If the multiplier is 8 bits, the multiplicand is AL and the product is AX. If the multiplier is 16 bits, the multiplicand is AX and the product is DX:AX. If the multiplier is 32 bits, the mutiplicand is EAX and the product is EDX:EAX. The Carry and Overflow flags are set if a 16-bit product extends into AH, or a 32-bit product extends into DX, or a 64-bit product extends into EDX.

Instruction Formats:

    IMUL *reg* IMUL *mem*

IN

O	D	I	S	Z	A	P	C

Input from port: Inputs a byte or word from a port into AL or AX. The source operand is a port address, expressed as either an 8-bit constant or a 16-bit address in DX. On the 80386, a doubleword can be input from a port.

Instruction Formats:

```
IN accum,immed          IN accum,DX
```

INC

O	D	I	S	Z	A	P	C
*			*	*	*	*	

Increment: Adds 1 to a register or memory operand, but does not affect the Carry flag.

Instruction Formats:

```
INC reg   INC mem
```

INS,INSB,INSW,INSD

O	D	I	S	Z	A	P	C

Input from port to string: (80286) Inputs a string pointed to by ES:DI from a port. The port number is specified in DX. For each value received, DI is adjusted in the same way as LODSB and similar string primitive instructions. The REP prefix may be used with this instruction.

Instruction Formats:

```
INS dest,DX              REP INSB dest,DX
REP INSW dest,DX         REP INSD dest,DX
```

INT

O	D	I	S	Z	A	P	C
		0					

Interrupt: Generates a software interrupt, which in turn calls an operating system subroutine. Clears the Interrupt flag and pushes the flags, CS, and IP on the stack before branching to the interrupt routine.

Instruction Formats:

```
INT immed INT 3
```

INTO

O	D	I	S	Z	A	P	C
		*	*				

Interrupt on overflow: Generates internal CPU Interrupt 4 if the Overflow flag is set. No action is taken by DOS if INT 4 is called, but a user-written routine may be substituted instead.

Instruction Format:

```
INTO
```

IRET

O	D	I	S	Z	A	P	C
*	*	*	*	*	*	*	*

Interrupt return: Returns from an interrupt handling routine. Pops the stack into IP, CS, and the flags.

Instruction Format:

```
IRET
```

Jcondition

O	D	I	S	Z	A	P	C

Conditional jump: Jumps to a label if a specified flag condition is true. Prior to the 80386 processor, the label must be in the range of −128 to +127 bytes from the current location. From the 80386 onward, the label must be in the range of −32,768 to +32,767 bytes from the current location. See Table 2 for a list of mnemonics.

Instruction Format:

```
Jcondition label
```

JCXZ,JECXZ

O	D	I	S	Z	A	P	C

Jump if CX is zero: Jump to a short label if the CX register is equal to zero. The short label must be in the range −128 to +127 bytes from the next instruction. On the 80386 processor, JECXZ jumps if ECX equals zero.

Instruction Formats:

```
JCXZ  label              JECXZ label
```

Table 2. Mnemonics for Conditional Jumps.

Mnemonic	Comment	Mnemonic	Comment
JA	jump if above	JE	jump if equal
JNA	jump if not above	JNE	jump if not equal
JAE	jump if above or equal	JZ	jump if zero
JNAE	jump if not above or equal	JNZ	jump if not zero
JB	jump if below	JS	jump if sign
JNB	jump if not below	JNS	jump if not sign
JBE	jump if below or equal	JC	jump if carry
JNBE	jump if not below or equal	JNC	jump if no carry
JG	jump if greater	JO	jump if overflow
JNG	jump if not greater	JNO	jump if no overflow
JGE	jump if greater or equal	JP	jump if parity
JNGE	jump if not greater or equal	JPE	jump if parity equal
JL	jump if less	JNP	jump if no parity
JNL	jump if not less	JPO	jump if parity odd
JLE	jump if less or equal	JNLE	jump if not less than or equal

JMP

Jump unconditionally to a label: The label may be short (−128 to +128 bytes), near (current segment), or far (different segment).

Instruction Formats:

```
JMP  shortlabel        JMP  reg16
JMP  nearlabel         JMP  mem16
```

JMP *farlabel*   JMP *mem32*

LAHF

	O	D	I	S	Z	A	P	C

Load flags into AH: The lowest 8 bits of the flags are transferred, but not the Trap, Interrupt, Overflow, Direction, or Sign flags.

Instruction Format:

    LAHF

LDS,LES,LFS,LGS,LSS

	O	D	I	S	Z	A	P	C

Load far pointer: Loads the contents of a doubleword memory operand into a segment register and the specified destination register. Prior to the 80386 processor, LDS loads into DS, LES loads into ES. On the 80386 processor, LFS loads into FS, LGS loads into GS, and LSS loads into SS.

Instruction Format (same for LDS, LES, LFS, LGS, LSS):

    LDS *reg,mem*

LEA

	O	D	I	S	Z	A	P	C

Load effective address: Calculates and loads the 16-bit effective address of a memory operand.

Instruction Format:

    LEA *reg,mem*

LEAVE

	O	D	I	S	Z	A	P	C

High level procedure exit: Terminates the stack frame of a procedure. This reverses the action of the ENTER instruction at the beginning of a procedure, by restoring SP and BP to their original values.

Instruction Format:

    LEAVE

O   D   I   S   Z   A   P   C

LOCK

Lock the system bus: Prevents other processors from executing during the next instruction. This instruction is used when another processor might modify a memory operand that is currently being accessed by the CPU.

Instruction Format:

```
LOCK instruction
```

O   D   I   S   Z   A   P   C

LODS, LODSB, LODSW, LODSD

Load accumulator from string: Loads a memory byte or word addressed by DS:SI into the accumulator (AL, AX, or EAX). If LODS is used, the memory operand must be specified. LODSB loads a byte into AL, LODSW loads a word into AX, and LODSD on the 80386 loads a doubleword into EAX. SI is increased or decreased according to the operand size and the status of the direction flag. If DF = 1, SI is decreased; if DF = 0, SI is increased.

Instruction Formats:

```
LODS   mem   LODSB
LODS   segreg:mem          LODSW
LODSD
```

O   D   I   S   Z   A   P   C

LOOP,LOOPW

Loop: Decrements CX and jumps to a short label if CX is greater than zero. The destination must be −128 to +127 bytes from the current location.

Instruction Format:

```
LOOP   shortlabel          LOOPW   shortlabel
```

LOOP

O	D	I	S	Z	A	P	C

Loop: (80386) Decrements ECX and jumps to a short label if ECX is greater than zero. The destination must be −128 to +127 bytes from the current location.

Instruction Format:

```
LOOPD  shortlabel
```

LOOPE, LOOPZ

O	D	I	S	Z	A	P	C

Loop if equal (zero): Decrements CX and jumps to a short label if CX > 0 and the Zero flag is set.

Instruction Formats:

```
LOOPE  shortlabel        LOOPZ  shortlabel
```

LOOPNE, LOOPNZ

O	D	I	S	Z	A	P	C

Loop if not equal (not zero):Decrements CX and jumps to a short label if CX > 0 and the Zero flag is clear.
Instruction Formats:

```
LOOPNE  shortlabel        LOOPNZ  shortlabel
```

MOV

O	D	I	S	Z	A	P	C

Move: Copies a byte or word from a source operand to a destination operand.

Instruction Formats:

```
MOV  reg,reg          MOV  reg,immed
MOV  mem,reg          MOV  mem,immed
MOV  reg,mem          MOV  mem16,segreg
MOV  reg16,segreg     MOV  segreg,mem16
MOV  segreg,reg16
```

MOVS, MOVSB, MOVSW, MOVSD

O	D	I	S	Z	A	P	C

Move string: Copies a byte or word from memory addressed by DS:SI to memory addressed by ES:DI. MOVS requires both operands to be specified. MOVSB copies a byte, MOVSW copies a word, and on the 80386, MOVSD copies a doubleword. SI and DI are increased or decreased according to the operand size and the status of the direction flag. If DF = 1, SI and DI are decreased; if DF = 0, SI and DI are increased.

Instruction Formats:

```
MOVS  dest,source            MOVSB
MOVS  ES:dest,segreg:source  MOVSW
MOVSD
```

MOVZX

O	D	I	S	Z	A	P	C

Move with zero-extend: Copies a byte or word from a source operand to a destination register and zero-extends into the upper half of the destination. This instruction is used to copy an 8-bit or 16-bit operand into a larger destination.

Instruction Formats:

```
MOVZX  reg32,reg16     MOV  reg32,mem16
MOVZX  reg16,reg8      MOV  reg16,mem8
```

MUL

O	D	I	S	Z	A	P	C
*				?	?	?	?	*

Unsigned integer multiply: Multiplies AL or AX by a source operand. If the source is 8 bits, it is multiplied by AL and the product is stored in AX. If the source is 16 bits, it is multiplied by AX and the product is stored in DX:AX. If the source is 32 bits, it is multiplied by EAX and the product is stored in EDX.

Instruction Formats:

```
MUL  reg MUL  mem
```

NEG

O	D	I	S	Z	A	P	C
*			*	*	*	*	*

Negate: Calculates the twos complement of the destination operand, and stores the result in the destination.

Instruction Formats:

```
NEG  reg NEG  mem
```

NOP

O	D	I	S	Z	A	P	C

No operation: This instruction does nothing, but it may be used inside a timing loop or to align a subsequent instruction on a word boundary.

Instruction Format:

```
NOP
```

NOT

O	D	I	S	Z	A	P	C

Not: Performs a logical NOT on an operand by reversing each of its bits.

Instruction Formats:

```
NOT  reg NOT  mem
```

OR

O	D	I	S	Z	A	P	C
0			*	*	?	*	0

Inclusive OR: Performs a logical OR between each bit in the destination operand and each bit in the source operand. If either bit is a 1 in each position, the result bit is a 1.

Instruction Formats:

```
OR  reg,reg          OR  reg,immed
OR  mem,reg          OR  mem,immed
OR  reg,mem          OR  accum,immed
```

OUT

Output to port: Prior to the 80386, this instruction outputs a byte or word from the accumulator to a port. The port address may be a constant if in the range 0-FFh, or DX may contain a port address between 0 and FFFFh. From the 80386 onward, a doubleword can be output to a port.

Instruction Formats:

```
OUT  immed8,accum        OUT DX,accum
```

OUTS,OUTSB,OUTSW,OUTSD

Output string to port: 80286. Outputs a string pointed to by ES:DI to a port. The port number is specified in DX. For each value output, DI is adjusted in the same way as LODSB and similar string primitive instructions. The REP prefix may be used with this instruction.

Instruction Formats:

```
OUTS dest,DX             REP OUTSB dest,DX
REP OUTSW dest,DX        REP OUTSD dest,DX
```

POP

Pop from stack: Copies a word or doubleword at the current stack pointer location into the destination operand, and adds 2 (or 4) to SP.

Instruction Formats:

```
POP  reg16/reg32         POP  segreg
POP  mem16/mem32
```

POPA,POPAD

O	D	I	S	Z	A	P	C

Pop all: Pops 16 bytes from the top of the stack into the eight general-purpose registers, in the following order: DI, SI, BP, SP, BX, DX, CX, AX. The value for SP is discarded, so SP is not reassigned. POPA pops into 16-bit registers, and POPAD on the 80386 pops into 32-bit registers.

Instruction Formats:

    POPA   POPAD

POPF,POPFD

O	D	I	S	Z	A	P	C
*	*	*	*	*	*	*	*

Pop flags from stack: POPF pops the top of the stack into the 16-bit Flags register. POPFD on the 80386 pops the top of the stack into the 32-bit Flags register.

Instruction Formats:

    POPF   POPFD

PUSH

O	D	I	S	Z	A	P	C

Push on stack: Subtracts 2 from SP and copies the source operand into the stack location pointed to by SP. From the 80186 onward, an immediate value can be pushed on the stack.

Instruction Formats:

PUSH	*reg16/reg32*	PUSH	*segreg*
PUSH	*mem16/mem32*	PUSH	*immed16/immed32*

PUSHA,PUSHAD

O	D	I	S	Z	A	P	C

Push all: The PUSHA instruction for the 80186 pushes the following 16-bit registers on the stack, in order: AX, CX, DX, BX, SP, BP, SI, and DI. The PUSHAD instruction for the 80386 pushes EAX, ECX, EDX, EBX, ESP, EBP, ESI, and EDI.
Instruction Formats:

    PUSHA   PUSHAD

PUSHF,PUSHFD

O D I S Z A P C

Push flags: PUSHF pushes the 16-bit Flags register onto the stack. PUSHFD pushes the 32-bit Flags onto the stack (80386).
Instruction Formats:

    PUSHF   PUSHFD

PUSHW,PUSHD

O D I S Z A P C

Push on stack: PUSHW pushes a 16-bit word on the stack, and on the 80386, PUSHD pushes a 32-bit doubleword on the stack.

Instruction Formats:

    PUSH   reg16/reg32   PUSH   segreg
    PUSH   mem16/mem32   PUSH   immed16/immed32

RCL

O D I S Z A P C
*   *

Rotate carry left: Rotates the destination operand left, using the source operand to determine the number of rotations. The Carry flag is copied into the lowest bit, and the highest bit is copied into the Carry flag. The *immed8* operand must be a 1 when using the 8086/8088 processor.

Instruction Formats:

    RCL   reg,immed8   RCL   mem,immed8
    RCL   reg,CL   RCL   mem,CL

RCR

O D I S Z A P C
*   *

Rotate carry right: Rotates the destination operand right, using the source operand to determine the number of rotations. The Carry flag is copied into the highest bit, and the lowest bit is copied into the Carry flag. The *immed8* operand must be a 1 when using the 8086/8088 processor.

Instruction Formats:

```
RCR  reg,immed8          RCR  mem,immed8
RCR  reg,CL              RCR  mem,CL
```

REP

O	D	I	S	Z	A	P	C

Repeat string: Repeats a string primitive instruction, using CX as a counter. CX is decremented each time the instruction is repeated, until CX = 0.

Format (shown with MOVS):

```
REP MOVS  dest,source
```

REP*condition*

O	D	I	S	Z	A	P	C
					*		

Repeat string conditionally: Repeats a string primitive instruction until CX = 0 and while a flag condition is true. REPZ (REPE) repeats while the Zero flag is set, and REPZ (REPNE) repeats while the Zero flag is clear. Only SCAS and CMPS should be used with REP*condition*, because they are the only string primitives that modify the Zero flag.

Formats used with SCAS:

```
REPZ  SCAS  dest         REPNE  SCAS  dest
REPZ  SCASB              REPNE  SCASB
REPE  SCASW              REPNZ  SCASW
```

RET, RETN, RETF

O	D	I	S	Z	A	P	C

Return from procedure: Pops a return address from the stack. RETN (return near) pops only the top of the stack into IP. RETF (return far) pops the stack first into IP, and then into CS. RET may be either near or far, depending on the attribute specified or implied by the PROC directive. An optional 8-bit immediate operand tells the CPU to add a value to SP after popping the return address.

Instruction Formats:

```
RET          RET   immed8
RETN         RETN  immed8
RETF         RETF  immed8
```

ROL

O	D	I	S	Z	A	P	C
*							*

Rotate left: Rotates the destination operand left, using the source operand to determine the number of rotations. The highest bit is copied into the Carry flag and moved into the lowest bit position. The *immed8* operand must be a 1 when using the 8086/8088 processor.

Instruction Formats:

```
ROL  reg,immed8        ROL  mem,immed8
ROL  reg,CL            ROL  mem,CL
```

ROR

O	D	I	S	Z	A	P	C
*							*

Rotate right: Rotates the destination operand right, using the source operand to determine the number of rotations. The lowest bit is copied into both the Carry flag and the highest bit position. The *immed8* operand must be a 1 when using the 8086/8088 processor.

Instruction Formats:

```
ROR  reg,immed8        ROR  mem,immed8
ROR  reg,CL            ROR  mem,CL
```

SAHF

O	D	I	S	Z	A	P	C
				*	*	*	*	*

Store AH into flags: Copies AH into bits 0 through 7 of the Flags register. The Trap, Interrupt, Direction, and Overflow flags are not affected.

Instruction Format:

```
SAHF
```

SAL

O	D	I	S	Z	A	P	C
*			*	*	?	*	*

Shift arithmetic left: Shifts each bit in the destination operand to the left, using the source operand to determine the number of shifts. The highest bit is copied into the Carry flag, and the lowest bit is filled with a zero. The *immed8* operand must be a 1 when using the 8086/8088 processor.

Instruction Formats:

SAL	*reg,immed8*	SAL	*mem,immed8*
SAL	*reg*,CL	SAL	*mem*,CL

SAR

O	D	I	S	Z	A	P	C
*			*	*	?	*	*

Shift arithmetic right: Shifts each bit in the destination operand to the right, using the source operand to determine the number of shifts. The lowest bit is copied into the Carry flag, and the highest bit retains its previous value. This shift is often used with signed operands, because it preserves the number's sign. The *immed8* operand must be a 1 when using the 8086/8088 processor.

Instruction Formats:

SAR	*reg,immed8*	SAR	*mem,immed8*
SAR	*reg*,CL	SAR	*mem*,CL

SBB

O	D	I	S	Z	A	P	C
*			*	*	*	*	*

Subtract with borrow: Subtracts the source operand from the destination operand and then subtracts the Carry flag from the destination.

Instruction Formats:

SBB	*reg,reg*	SBB	*reg,immed*
SBB	*mem,reg*	SBB	*mem,immed* SBB *reg,mem*

SCAS, SCASB, SCASW, SCASD

O	D	I	S	Z	A	P	C
*			*	*	*	*	*

Scan string: Scans a string in memory pointed to by ES:DI for a value that matches the accumulator. SCAS requires the operands to be specified. SCASB scans for an 8-bit value matching AL, SCASW scans for a 16-bit value matching AX, and SCASD scans for a 32-bit value matching EAX. DI is increased or decreased according to the operand size and the status of the direction flag. If DF = 1, DI is decreased; if DF = 0, DI is increased.

Instruction Formats:

```
SCAS   dest              SCASB
SCAS   ES:dest           SCASW
```

O	D	I	S	Z	A	P	C

SETcondition

Set conditionally: If the given flag condition is true, the byte specified by the destination operand is assigned the value 1. If the flag condition is false, the destination is assigned a value of 0. The possible values for *condition* are listed in Table 2, listed earlier in this appendix.

Instruction Formats:

```
SETcond reg8              SETcond mem8
```

O	D	I	S	Z	A	P	C
*			*	*	?	*	*

SHL

Shift left: Shifts each bit in the destination operand to the left, using the source operand to determine the number of shifts. The highest bit is copied into the Carry flag, and the lowest bit is filled with a zero (identical to SAL). The *immed8* operand must be a 1 when using the 8086/8088 processor.

Instruction Formats:

```
SHL   reg,immed8          SHL   mem,immed8
SHL   reg,CL              SHL   mem,CL
```

O	D	I	S	Z	A	P	C
?			*	*	?	*	*

SHLD

Double-precision shift left: 80386. Shifts the bits of the second operand into the first operand. The third operand indicates the number of bits to be shifted. The positions opened by the shift are filled by the most significant bits of the second operand. The second operand must always be a register, and the third operand may be either an immediate value or the CL register.

Instruction Formats:

```
SHLD reg16,reg16,immed8    SHLD mem16,reg16,immed8
SHLD reg32,reg32,immed8    SHLD mem32,reg32,immed8
SHLD reg16,reg16,CL        SHLD mem16,reg16,CL
SHLD reg32,reg32,CL        SHLD mem32,reg32,CL
```

SHR

O	D	I	S	Z	A	P	C
*			*	*	?	*	*

Shift right: Shifts each bit in the destination operand to the right, using the source operand to determine the number of shifts. The highest bit is filled with a zero, and the lowest bit is copied into the Carry flag. The *immed8* operand must be a 1 when using the 8086/8088 processor.

Instruction Formats:

```
SHR  reg,immed8          SHR  mem,immed8
SHR  reg,CL              SHR  mem,CL
```

SHRD

O	D	I	S	Z	A	P	C
?			*	*	?	*	*

Double-precision shift right: 80386. Shifts the bits of the second operand into the first operand. The third operand indicates the number of bits to be shifted. The positions opened by the shift are filled by the least significant bits of the second operand. The second operand must always be a register, and the third operand may be either an immediate value or the CL register.

Instruction Formats:

```
SHRD reg16,reg16,immed8   SHRD mem16,reg16,immed8
SHRD reg32,reg32,immed8   SHRD mem32,reg32,immed8
SHRD reg16,reg16,CL       SHRD mem16,reg16,CL
SHRD reg32,reg32,CL       SHRD mem32,reg32,CL
```

STC

O	D	I	S	Z	A	P	C
							1

Set Carry flag: Sets the Carry flag. This may be done by a procedure that wants to signal an error condition to a calling program.

Instruction Format:

```
STC
```

O	D	I	S	Z	A	P	C
	1						

STD

Set Direction flag: Sets the Direction flag, causing SI and/or DI to be decremented by string primitive instructions. Thus, string processing will be from high addresses to low addresses.

Instruction Format:

```
STD
```

O	D	I	S	Z	A	P	C
		1					

STI

Set Interrupt flag:Sets the Interrupt flag, which enables maskable interrupts. Interrupts are automatically disabled when an interrupt occurs, so an interrupt handler procedure immediately reenables them, using STI.

Instruction Format:

```
STI
```

O	D	I	S	Z	A	P	C

STOS, STOSB, STOSW, STOSD

Store string data: Stores the accumulator in the memory location addressed by ES:DI. If STOS is used, a destination operand must be specified. STOSB copies AL to memory, STOSW copies AX to memory, and STOSD for the 80386 copies EAX to memory. DI is increased or decreased according to the operand size and the status of the direction flag. If DF = 1, DI is decreased; if DF = 0, DI is increased.

Instruction Formats:

```
STOS   mem  STOSB
STOS   ES:mem                STOSW
```

O	D	I	S	Z	A	P	C
*			*	*	*	*	*

SUB

Subtract: Subtracts the source operand from the destination operand.

Instruction Formats:

```
SUB   reg,reg              SUB   reg,immed
SUB   mem,reg              SUB   mem,immed
SUB   reg,mem              SUB   accum,immed
```

TEST

O	D	I	S	Z	A	P	C
0			*	*	?	*	0

Test: Tests individual bits in the destination operand against those in the source operand. Performs a logical AND operation that affects the flags but not the destination operand.

Instruction Formats:

```
TEST   reg,reg             TEST   reg,immed
TEST   mem,reg             TEST   mem,immed
TEST   reg,mem             TEST   accum,immed
```

WAIT

O	D	I	S	Z	A	P	C

Wait for coprocessor: Suspends CPU execution until the coprocessor finishes its current instruction.

Instruction Format:

```
WAIT
```

XADD

O	D	I	S	Z	A	P	C
*			*	*	*	*	*

Exchange and Add: (80486) Adds the source operand to the destination operand. At the same time, the original destination value is moved to the source operand.

Instruction Formats:

```
XADD   reg,reg             XADD   mem,reg
```

XCHG

O	D	I	S	Z	A	P	C

Exchange: Exchanges the contents of the source and destination operands.

Instruction Formats:

```
XCH  reg,reg          XCH  mem,reg
XCH  reg,mem
```

XLAT, XLATB

O	D	I	S	Z	A	P	C

Translate byte: Uses the value in AL to index into a table pointed to by DS:BX. The byte pointed to by the index is moved to AL. An operand may be specified in order to provide a segment override. XLATB may be substituted for XLAT.

Instruction Formats:

```
XLAT       XLAT segreg:mem
XLAT mem   XLATB
```

XOR

O	D	I	S	Z	A	P	C
0			*	*	?	*	0

Exclusive OR: Each bit in the source operand is exclusive ORed with its corresponding bit in the destination. The destination bit is a 1 only when the original source and destination bits are different.

Instruction Formats:

```
XOR  reg,reg          XOR  reg,immed
XOR  mem,reg          XOR  mem,immed
XOR  reg,mem          XOR  accum,immed
```

Appendix G: BIOS and DOS Interrupts

G.1   OVERALL INTERRUPT LIST

Number	Description
0	*Divide by Zero*. Internal: activated when attempting to divide by zero.
1	*Single Step*. Internal: active when the CPU Trap flag is set.
2	*Nonmaskable*. Internal: activated when a memory error occurs.
3	*Breakpoint*. Internal: activated when the 0CCh (INT 3) instruction is executed.
4	*Overflow*. Activated when the INTO instruction is executed and the Overflow flag is set.
5	*Print Screen*. Activated either by the INT 5 instruction or typing SHIFT-PRTSC.
6	*(Reserved)*
7	*(Reserved)*
8	*Timer Interrupt*. Updates the BIOS clock 18.2 times per second. For your own programming, see INT 1Ch.
9	*Keyboard Hardware Interrupt*. Activated when a key is pressed. Reads the key from the keyboard port and stores it in the keyboard typeahead buffer.
0A-0D	*(Reserved)*
0E	*Diskette Interrupt*. Activated when a disk seek is in progress.
0F	*(Reserved)*
10	*Video Services*. Routines for manipulating the video display (see the complete list in a subsequent table).
11	*Equipment Check*. Return a word showing all the peripherals attached to the system.
12	*Memory Size*. Return the amount of memory (in 1,024-byte blocks) in AX.
13	*Floppy Disk Services*. Reset the disk controller, get the status of the most recent disk access, read and write physical sectors, and format a disk.
14	*Asynchronous (Serial) Port Services*. Initialize and read or write the asynchronous communications port, and return the port's status.
16	*Keyboard Services*. Read and inspect keyboard input (see the complete list in a subsequent table).
17	*Printer Services*. Initialize, print, and return the status of the printer.
18	*ROM BASIC*. Execute cassette BASIC in ROM.

19	*Boot Strap* Reboot DOS.
1A	*Time of Day.* Get the number of timer ticks since the machine was turned on, or set the counter to a new value. Ticks occur 18.2 times per second.
1B	*Keyboard Break.* This interrupt handler is executed by INT 9h when CTRL-BREAK is pressed.
1C	*User Timer Interrupt.* Empty routine, executed 18.2 times per second. May be used by your own program.
1D	*Video Parameters.* Point to a table containing initialization and information for the Video Controller chip.
1E	*Diskette Parameters.* Point to a table containing initialization information for the diskette controller.
1F	*Graphics Table.* Table kept in memory of all extended graphics characters with ASCII codes greater than 127.
20	*Terminate Program.* Terminate a COM program (INT 21h, function 4Ch should be used instead).
21	*DOS Services* (see the complete list in the next table).
22	*DOS Terminate Address.* Point to the address of the parent program or process. When the current program ends, this will be the return address.
23	*DOS Break Address.* DOS jumps here when CTRL-BREAK is pressed.
24	*DOS Error Address.* DOS jumps to this address when there is a critical error in the current program, such as a disk media error.
25	*DOS Disk Read.* Used for reading logical sectors from the disk.
26	*DOS Disk Write.* Used for writing logical sectors on the disk.
27	*Terminate and Stay Resident.* Exit to DOS or the calling program, but leave the current program in memory.
28-FF	(Reserved)
40-41	Fixed Disk Services. Fixed disk controller.
4B-7F	Available for application programs to use.
80-F0	Reserved: used by ROM BASIC.
F1-FF	Available for application programs to use.

G.2   INTERRUPT 21H FUNCTIONS (DOS SERVICES)

Function	Description
1	*Keyboard Input.* Wait for a character from the standard input device; echoed on the console. Output: AL = character.
2	*Display Output.* Display the character in DL on the standard output device (console).
5	*Printer Output.* Send the character in DL to the standard printer device.

6   *Direct Console I/O*. If DL = FFh, read a waiting character from standard input. If DL is any other value, write the character in DL to standard output.

7   *Direct Console Input Without Echo*. Wait for a character from the standard input device. The character is returned in AL but not echoed.

8   *Console Input Without Echo*. Wait for a character from the standard input device. The character is returned in AL but not echoed. May be terminated by Ctrl-Break.

9   *Print String*. Output a string of characters to the standard output device. Input: DS:DX = address of string.

0A   *Buffered Keyboard Input*. Read a string of characters from the standard input device.

0B   *Check Standard Input Status*. Check to see if an input character is waiting. Output: AL = 0FFh if the character is ready; otherwise, AL = 0.

0C   *Clear Keyboard Buffer*, Invoke Input Function. Clear the console input buffer, and then execute an input function. Input: AL = desired function (1, 6, 7, 8, or 0Ah).

0E   *Select Disk*. Set the default drive. Input: DL = drive number (0 = A, 1 = B, ect.).

19   *Current Disk*. Return the current default drive. Output: AL = drive number (0 = A, 1 = B, ect.).

1A   *Set Disk Transfer Address*. Set the DTA to the location pointed to by DS:DX.

25   *Set Interrupt Vector*. Set an entry in the Interrupt Vector Table to a new address. Input: DS:DX points to the interrupt-handling routine that is inserted in the table; AL = the interrupt number.

2A   *Get Date*. Get the system date. Output: AL = Day of the week (0-6, where Sunday = 0), CX = year, DH = month, and DL = day.

2B   *Set Date*. Set the system date. Input: CX = year, DH = month, and DL = day. Output: AL = 0 if the date is valid.

2C   *Get Time*. Return the system time. Output: CH = hour, CL = minutes, DH = seconds, and DL = hundredths of seconds.

2D   *Set Time*. Set the system time. Input: CH = hour, CL = minutes, DH = seconds, and DL = hundredths of seconds. Output: AL = 0 if the time is valid.

2F   *Get Disk Transfer Address (DTA)*. Return the current DTA in ES:BX.

31   *Terminate Process and Remain Resident*. Terminate the current program or process, and attempt to set the current memory allocation to the number of paragraphs specified in DX. Input: AL = return code, and DX = requested number of paragraphs.

35   *Get Interrupt Vector*. Get the segment-offset value of an interrupt vector. Input: AL = interrupt number. Output: ES:BX = address of the interrupt handler.

36   *Get Disk Free Space*. (FAT16 only) Return the amount of disk free space. Input: DL = drive number (0 = default, 1 = A, ect.). Output: AX = sectors per cluster, or FFFFh if the drive number is invalid; BX = number of available clusters, CX = bytes per sector, and DX = clusters per drive.

39   *Create Subdirectory*. Create a new subdirectory based on a given path name. Input: DS:DX points to an ASCIIZ string with the path and directory name. Output: AX = error code if the Carry flag is set.

3A	*Remove Subdirectory.* Remove a subdirectory. Input: DS:DX points to an ASCIIZ string with the path and directory name. Output: AX = error code if the Carry flag is set.
3B	*Change Current Directory.* Change to a different directory. Input: DS:DX points to an ASCIIZ string with the new directory path. Output: AX = error code if the Carry flag is set.
3C	*Create File.* Create a new file or truncate an old file to zero bytes. Open the file for output. Input: DS:DX points to an ASCIIZ string with the file name, and CX = file attribute. Output: AX = error code if the Carry flag is set; otherwise AX = the new file handle.
3D	*Open File.* Open a file for input, output, or input-output. Input: DS:DX points to an ASCIIZ string with the filename, and AL = the access code (0 = read, 1 = write, 2 = read/write). Output: AX = error code if the Carry flag is set, otherwise AX = the new file handle.
3E	*Close File.* Close the file or devicespecified by a file handle. Input: BX = file handle from previous open or create. Output: If the Carry Flag is set, AX = error code.
3F	*Read from File or Device.* Read a specified number of bytes from a file or device. Input: BX = file handle, DS:DX points to an input buffer, and CX = number of bytes to read. Output: If the Carry flag is set, AX = error code; otherwise, AX = number of bytes read.
40	*Write to File or Device.* Write a specified number of bytes to a file or device. Input: BX = file handle, DS:DX points to an output buffer, and CX = the number of bytes to write. Output: If the Carry flag is set, AX = error code; otherwise, AX = number of bytes written.
41	*Delete File.* Remove a file from a specified directory. Input: DS:DX points to an ASCIIZ string with the filename. Output: AX = error code if the Carry flag is set.
42	*Move File Pointer.* Move the file read/write pointer according to a specified method. Input: CX:DX = distance (bytes) to move the file pointer, AL = method code, BX = file handle. The method codes are as follows: 0 = move from beginning of file, 1 = move to the current location plus an offset, and 2 = move to the end of file plus an offset. Output: AX = error code if the Carry flag is set.
43	*Get/Set File Attribute.* Get or set the attribute of a file. Input: DS:DX = pointer to an ASCIIZ path and filename, CX = attribute, and AL = function code (1 = set attribute, 0 = get attribute). Output: AX = error code if the Carry flag is set.
44	*I/O Control for Devices.* Get or set device information associated with an open device handle, or send a control string to the device handle, or receive a control string from the device handle.
45	*Duplicate File Handle.* Return a new file handle for a file that is currently open. Input: BX = file handle. Output: AX = error code if the Carry flag is set.
46	*Force Duplicate file Handle.* Force the handle in CX to refer to the same file at the same position as the handle in BX. Input: BX = existing file handle, and CX = second file handle. Output: AX = error code if the Carry flag is set.

47   *Get Current Directory.* Get the full path name of the current directory. Input: DS:SI points to a 64-byte area to hold the directory path, and DL = drive number. Output: a buffer at DS:SI is filled with the path, and AX = error code if the Carry flag is set.

48   *Allocate Memory.* Allocate a requested number of paragraphs of memory, measured in 16-byte blocks. Input: BX = number of paragraphs requested. Output: AX = segment of the allocated block, and BX = size of the largest block availible(in paragraphs), and AX = error code if the Carry flag is set.

49   *Free Allocated Memory.* Free memory that was previously allocated by function call 48h. Input: ES = segment of the block to be freed. Output: AX = error code if the Carry flag is set.

4A   *Modify Memory Blocks.* Modify allocated memory blocks to contain a new block size. The block will shrink or grow. Input: ES = segment of the block, and BX = requested number of paragraphs. Output: AX = error code if the Carry flag is set, and BX = maximum number of available blocks.

4B   *Load or Execute Program.* Create a PSP for another program, load it into memory, and execute it. Input: DS:DX points to an ASCIIZ string with the drive, path, and filename of the program; ES:BX points to a parameter block, and AL = function value. Function values in AL:0 = load and execute the program; 3 = load but do not execute (overlay program). Output: AX = error code if the Carry flag is set.

4C   *Terminate Process.* Usual way to terminate a program and return to either DOS or a calling program. Input: AL = 8-bit return code, which can be queried by DOS function 4Dh or by the ERRORLEVEL command ina batch file.

4D   *Get Return Code of Process.* Get the return code of a process or program, generated by either function call 31h or function call 4Ch. Output: AL = 8-bit code returned by the program, AH = type of exit generated: 0 = normal termination, 1 = terminated by CTRLBREAK, 2 = terminated by a critical device error, and 3 = terminated by a call to function call 31h.

4E   *Find First Matching File.* Find the first filename that matches a given file specification. Input: DS:DX points to an ASCIIZ drive, path, and file specification; CX = File attribute to be used when searching. Output: AX = error code if the Carry flag is set; otherwise, the current DTA is filled with the filename, attribute, time, date, and size. DOS function call 1Ah (set DTA) is ususally called before this function.

4F   *Find Next Matching File.* Find the next filename that matches a given file specification. This is always called after DOS function 4Eh. Output: AX = error code if the Carry flag is set; otherwise, the current DTA is filled with the file's information.

56   *Rename/Move File.* Rename a file or move it to another directory. Input: DS:DX points to an ASCIIZ string that specifies the current drive, path, and filename; ES:DI points to the new path and filename. Output: AX = error code if the Carry flag is set.

57	*Get/Set File Date/Time.* Get or set the date and time stamp for a file. Input: AL = 0 to get the date/time, or AL = 1 to set the date/time; BX = file handle, CX = new file time, and DX = new file date. Output: AX = error code if the Carry flag is set; otherwise, CX = current file time, and DX = current file date.
59	*Get Extended Error Information.* Return additional information about a DOS error, including the error class, locus, and reccommended action. Input: BX = DOS version number (zero for version 3.xx). Output: AX = extended error code, BH = error class, BL = suggested action, and CH = locus.
5A	*Create Unique File.* Generate a unique filename in a specified directory. Input: DS:DX points to an ASCIIZ pathname, ending with a backslash (\); CX = desired file attribute. Output: AX = error code if the Carry flag is set; otherwise, DS:DX points to the path with the new filename appended.
5B	*Create New File.* Try to create a new file, but fail if the filename already exists. This prevents you from overwriting an existing file. Input: DS:DX points to an ASCIIZ string with the path and filename. Output: AX = error code if the Carry flag is set.
62	*Get Program Segment Prefix (PSP) Address.* Return the PSP address of the current program in BX.

G.3   INTERRUPT 10H FUNCTIONS (VIDEO BIOS)

Function	Description
0	*Set Video Mode.* Set the video display to monochrome, text, graphics, or color mode. Input: AL = display mode. 1 *Set Cursor Lines.* Identify the starting and ending scan lines for the cursor. Input: CH = cursor starting line, and CL = cursor ending line.
2	*Set Cursor Position.* Position the cursor on the screen. Input: BH = video page, DH = row, and DL = column.
3	*Get Cursor Position.* Get the cursor's screen position and its size. Input: BH = video page. Output: CH = cursor starting line, CL = cursor ending line, DH = cursor row, and DL = cursor column.
4	*Read Light Pen.* Read the position and status of the light pen. Output: CH = pixel row, BX = pixel column, DH = character row, and DL = character column.
5	*Set Display Page.* Select the video page to be displayed. Input: AL = desired page number.
6	*Scroll Window Up.* Scroll a window on the current video page upward, replacing scrolled lines with blanks. Input: AL = number of lines to scroll, BH = attribute for scrolled lines, CX = upper left corner row and column, and DX = lower right row and column.
7	*Scroll Window Down.* Scroll a window on the current video page downward, replacing scrolled lines with blanks. Input: AL = number of lies to scroll, BH = attribute for scrolled lines, CX = upper left corner row and column, and DX = lower right row and column.

8   *Read Character and Attribute*. Read the character and its attribute at the current cursor position. Input: BH = display page. Output: AH = attribute byte, and AL = ASCII character code.

9   *Write Character and Attribute*. Write a character and its attribute at the current cursor position. Input: AL = ASCII character, BH = video page, BL = attribute or color, and CX = repetition factor.

0A   *Write Character*. Write a character only (no attribute) at the current cursor position. Input: AL = ASCII character, BH = video page, BL = attribute, and CX = replication factor.

0B   *Set Color Palette*. Select a group of available colors for the color or EGA adapter. Input: AL = display mode, and BH = active display page.

0C   *Write Graphics Pixel*. Write a graphics pixel when in color graphics mode. Input: Al = pixel value, CX = *x* coordinate, and DX = *y* coordinate.

0D   *Read Graphics Pixel*. Read the color of a single graphics pixel at a given location. Input: CX = *x* coordinate, and DX = *y* coordinate.

0E   *Write Character*. Write a character to the screen, and advance the cursor. Input: AL = ASCII character code, BH = video page, BL = attribute or color.

0F   *Get Current Video Mode*. Get the current video mode. Output: AL = video mode, and BH = active video page.

10   *Set Video Palette*. (EGA and PCjr only) Set the video palette register, border color, or blink/intensity bit. Input: AL = function code (00 set palette register, 01 = set border color, 02 = set palette and border color, 03 = set/reset blink/intensity bit), BH = color, BL = palette register to set, If AL = 2, ES:DX points to a color list.

11   *Character Generator*. Select the character size for the EGA display. For example, an 8 by 8 font is used for the 43- line display, and an 8 by 14 font is used for the 25-line display.

12   *Alternate Select Function*. Return technical information about the EGA display.

13   *Write String*. (PC/AT only) Write a string of text to the video display. Input: AL = mode, BH = page, BL = attribute, CX = length of string, DH = row, DL = column, and ES:BP points to the string (will not work on the IBM- PC or PC/XT).

G.3   INTERRUPT 16H FUNCTIONS (KEYBOARD)

Function	Explanation
03h	*Set Typematic Repeat Rate*. Call with AH = 3, AL = 5, BH = repeat delay, BL = repeat rate. The delay values in BH are: (0 = 250 ms; 1 = 500 ms; 2 = 750 ms; 3 = 1000ms). The repeat rate in BL varies from 0 (fastest) to 1Fh (slowest).
05h	*Push Key into Buffer*. Pushes a keyboard character and corresponding scan code into the keyboard typeahead buffer. Call with AH = 5, CH = scan code, and CL = character code. If the typeahead buffer is already full, the Carry flag will be set, and AL = 1.

00/10   *Wait for Key.* Wait for an input character and keyboard scan code. Output: AH = scan code, AL = ASCII character.

01/11   *Check Keyboard Buffer.* Find out if a character is waiting in the keyboard typeahead buffer. If one is, return the scan code in AH and the ASCII code in AL, and clear the Zero flag. If no key is waiting, set the Zero flag. (*Note*: the same character will remain in the keyboard buffer.)

02/12   *Get Keyboard Flags.* Return the keyboard flag byte stored in low RAM into AL.

Index

Microsoft License Agreement

```
Microsoft MASM Version 6.11

Licenses: 1
```

IMPORTANT—READ CAREFULLY BEFORE OPENING SOFTWARE PACKETS(S). Unless a separate multilingual license booklet is included in your product package, the following License Agreement applies to you. By opening the sealed packet(s) containing the software, you indicate your acceptance of the following Microsoft License Agreement.

Single-User Products This is a legal agreement between you (either an individual or an entity) and Microsoft Corporation. By opening the sealed software packages and / or by using the software you agree to be bound by the terms of this Agreement. If you do not agree to the terms of this Agreement, promptly return the unopened software packet(s) and the accompanying items (including printed materials and binders or other containers) to the place from which you obtained them for a full refund.

Microsoft Software License

1. Grant of License. This License Agreement ("License") permits you to use one copy of the specified version of the Microsoft software product identified above, which may include "online" or electronic documentation (the "Software") on a single computer. If this package is a License Pak, you may make and use additional copies of the Software up to the number of Licensed Copies authorized above. The Software is in "use" on a computer when it is loaded into temporary memory (i.e., RAM) or installed into permanent memory (e.g., hard disk, CD-ROM, or other storage device) of that computer except that a copy installed on a network server for the sole purpose of distribution to other computers is not "in use."

2. Upgrades. If the Software is an upgrade you may use or transfer the Software only in conjunction with the prior version(s) of the Software.

3. Copyright The Software (including any images, "applets," photographs, animations, video, audio, music, and text incorporated into the Software is owned by Microsoft or its suppliers and is protected by United States copyright laws and international treaty provisions. Therefore, you must treat the Software like any other copyrighted material (e.g., a book or musical recording) except that you may either (a) make one copy of the Software solely for backup or archival purposes, or (b) transfer the Software to a single hard disk provided you keep the original solely for backup or archival purposes. You may not copy the printed materials accompanying the Software.

4. Other Restrictions. You may not rent or lease the Software, but you may transfer the Software and accompanying written materials on a permanent basis provided you retain no copies and the recipient agrees to the terms of this Agreement. If the Software is an upgrade, any transfer must included the most recent upgrade and all prior versions. You may not reverse engineer, decompile, or disassemble the Software, except to the extent such foregoing restriction is expressly prohibited by applicable law.

5. Dual Media Software. You may receive the Software on more than one medium. Regardless of the type or size of medium you receive, you may use only the medium appropriate for your single use computer. You may not use the other medium on another computer or load, rent, lease, or transfer the disks to another user except as part of the permanent transfer as provided above of all Software and printed materials, nor print copies of any user documentation provided in "online" or electronic form.

6. Language Software. If the Software is a Microsoft language product, then you have a royalty-free right to reproduce and distribute executable files created using the Software. If the language product is a Basic or COBOL product, then Microsoft grants you a royalty-free right to reproduce and distribute the run-time modules of the Software *provided* that you (a) distribute the run-time modules only in conjunction with and as a part of your software product; (b) do not use Microsoft's name, logo, or trademark to market your software product; (c) include a valid copyright notice on your software product; and (d) agree to indemnify, hold harmless, and defend Microsoft and its suppliers from any against any claims or lawsuits, including attorney's fees, that arise or result from the use or distribution of your software product. The "run-time modules" are those files in the Software that are identified in the accompanying printed materials as required during execution of your software program. The run-time modules are limited to run-time files and ISAM and REMOLD files. If required in the Software documentation, you agree to display the designated patent notices on the packaging and in the README file in your software product.

Miscellaneous

If you acquired the product in the United States, this EULA is governed by the laws of the State of Washington.

If you acquired this product in Canada, this EULA is governed by the laws of the Province of Ontario, Canada. Each of the parties hereto irrevocably attorns to the jurisdiction of the courts of the Province of Ontario and further agrees to commence any litigation which may arise hereunder in the courts located in the Judicial District of York, Province of Ontario.

If this product was acquired outside the United States, then local laws may apply.

Should you have any questions concerning the EULA, or if you desire to contact Microsoft for any reason, please contract the Microsoft subsidiary serving your country, or write: Microsoft Sales Information Center / One Microsoft Way / Redmond, WA 98052-6399.

Limited Warranty

No Warranties. Microsoft expressly disclaims any warranty for the Software Product. The Software Product and any related documentation is provided "as is" without warranty of any kind, either express or implied, including, without limitation, the implied warranties or merchantability, fitness for a particular purpose, or noninfringement. The entire risk arising out of use or performance of the Software Product remains with you.

No Liability For Damages. In no event shall Microsoft or its suppliers be liable for any damages whatsoever (including, without limitation, damages for loss of business profits, business interruption, loss of business information, or any other pecuniary loss) arising out of the use of or inability to use this Microsoft product, even if Microsoft has been advised of the possibility of such damages. Because some states/jurisdictions do not allow the exclusion or limitation of liability for consequential or incidental damages, the above limitations may not apply to you.